Microsoft®

W9-BFY-719

Microsoft® SQL Server™ 2005 Administrator's Pocket Consultant

William R. Stanek

PUBLISHED BY
Microsoft Press
A Division of Microsoft Corporation
One Microsoft Way
Redmond, Washington 98052-6399

Library of Congress Control Number 2005933933

Printed and bound in the United States of America.

3 4 5 6 7 8 9   QWE   9 8 7 6

Distributed in Canada by H.B. Fenn and Company Ltd.

A CIP catalogue record for this book is available from the British Library.

Microsoft Press books are available through booksellers and distributors worldwide. For further information about international editions, contact your local Microsoft Corporation office or contact Microsoft Press International directly at fax (425) 936-7329. Visit our Web site at www.microsoft.com/learning/. Send comments to *mspinput@microsoft.com*.

Microsoft, Active Directory, ActiveX, Excel, JScript, Microsoft Press, MSDN, MS-DOS, Outlook, SharePoint, Visual Basic, Windows, Windows NT, and Windows Server are either registered trademarks or trademarks of Microsoft Corporation in the United States and/or other countries.

The example companies, organizations, products, domain names, e-mail addresses, logos, people, places, and events depicted herein are fictitious. No association with any real company, organization, product, domain name, e-mail address, logo, person, place, or event is intended or should be inferred.

This book expresses the author's views and opinions. The information contained in this book is provided without any express, statutory, or implied warranties. Neither the authors, Microsoft Corporation, nor its resellers, or distributors will be held liable for any damages caused or alleged to be caused either directly or indirectly by this book.

Acquisitions Editor: Martin DelRe
Project Editor: Denise Bankaitis
Technical Editor: Robert Brunner
Editorial and Production: Custom Editorial Productions, Inc.

Body Part No. X11-50517

Contents at a Glance

Table of Contents

**What do you think
of this book?
We want to hear from you!**   Microsoft is interested in hearing your feedback about this
publication so we can continually improve our books and learning
resources for you. To participate in a brief online survey, please visit:
www.microsoft.com/learning/booksurvey/

Acknowledgments

You know you've been at this thing called writing a long time when people ask how many books you've written and you just have no idea. (This is number 61 for those who may be wondering.) For me, it's always been about the craft of writing. I love writing, and I love challenging projects most of all. Two of the most challenging books I ever wrote were *SQL Server 7.0 Administrator's Pocket Consultant*, published in 1999, and *SQL Server 2000 Administrator's Pocket Consultant*, published in 2000. Writing *SQL Server 2005 Administrator's Pocket Consultant* was no less challenging.

The challenge in writing a day-to-day administrator's guide to SQL Server is that there's so much to cover. When all was said and done, I ended up with a book that was over 750 pages in length and that just isn't what a pocket consultant is meant to be. Pocket consultants are meant to be portable and readable—the kind of book you use to solve problems and get the job done wherever you might be. With that in mind, I had to go back in and carefully review the text, making sure I focused on the core of SQL Server 2005 administration. The result is the book you hold in your hand, which I hope you'll agree is one of the best practical, portable guides to SQL Server 2005.

As I've stated in *Microsoft Windows Server 2003 Administrator's Pocket Consultant* and in *Microsoft IIS 6.0 Administrator's Pocket Consultant*, the team at Microsoft Press is top-notch. Denise Bankaitis was instrumental throughout the writing process. She helped me stay on track and coordinated the materials after I submitted chapters. Martin DelRe was the acquisitions editor for the project. He believed in the book from the beginning and was really great to work with. Completing and publishing the book wouldn't have been possible without their help! Julie Hotchkiss managed the editorial process. This was a new series for her and our first time working together, so it was a challenge, but a good one I think. Thank you so much!

Unfortunately for the writer (but fortunately for readers), writing is only one part of the publishing process. Next came editing and author review. I must say, Microsoft Press has the most thorough editorial and technical review process I've seen anywhere—and I've written a lot of books for many different publishers. Robert Brunner was the technical editor for the book. I believe this was the first time we worked together and it turned out to be a wonderful experience. He was very thorough and helped with testing to ensure things worked as expected on both Windows XP Professional and Windows Server 2003.

I would also like to thank Lucinda Rowley and everyone else at Microsoft who has helped at many points of my writing career and been there when I needed them the most. Thank you also for shepherding my many projects through the publishing process!

Thanks also to Studio B literary agency and my agents, David Rogelberg and Neil Salkind. David and Neil are great to work with.

Hopefully, I haven't forgotten anyone but if I have, it was an oversight. *Honest.*

Introduction

Microsoft SQL Server 2005 Administrator's Pocket Consultant is designed to be a concise and compulsively usable resource for SQL Server 2005 administrators. It covers everything you need to know to perform the core administrative tasks for SQL Server and is the readable resource guide that you'll want on your desk at all times. Because the book focuses on giving you maximum value in a pocket-sized guide, you won't have to wade through hundreds of pages of extraneous information to find what you're looking for. Instead, you'll find exactly what you need to get the job done.

This book is designed to be the one resource you turn to whenever you have questions about SQL Server administration. To this end, the book zeroes in on daily administration procedures, frequently used tasks, documented examples, and options that are representative while not necessarily inclusive. One of its key goals is to keep the content concise so that the book is compact and easy to navigate while also ensuring that it contains as much information as possible. Instead of a 1000-page tome or a 100-page quick reference, you get a valuable resource guide that can help you quickly and easily perform common tasks, solve problems, and implement advanced SQL Server technologies such as replication, distributed queries, and multiserver administration.

Who Is This Book For?

Microsoft SQL Server 2005 Administrator's Pocket Consultant covers the Workgroup, Standard, Enterprise, and Developer editions of SQL Server. The book is designed for

- Current SQL Server 2005 database administrators.
- Accomplished users who have some administrator responsibilities.
- Administrators migrating to SQL Server 2005 from previous versions.
- Administrators transitioning from other database architectures.

To include as much information as possible, I had to assume that you have fundamental networking skills and a basic understanding of SQL Server. With this in mind, I don't devote entire chapters to understanding SQL Server architecture or running simple SQL queries. I do cover SQL Server installation, configuration, enterprise-wide server management, performance tuning, optimization, maintenance, and much more.

I also assumed that you are familiar with SQL commands and stored procedures as well as the standard Microsoft Windows user interface. If you need help learning SQL basics, you should read other resources (many of which are available from Microsoft Press).

How Is This Book Organized?

Microsoft SQL Server 2005 Administrator's Pocket Consultant is designed to be used in the daily administration of SQL Server and, as such, the book is organized according to job-related tasks rather than SQL Server features. Before you use this book, you should be aware of the difference between Administrator's Pocket Consultants and Administrator's Companions. Although both books are designed to be a part of an overall administrator's library, Administrator's Pocket Consultants are the down-and-dirty, in-the-trenches books and Administrator's Companions are the comprehensive tutorials and references that cover every aspect of deploying a product or technology in the enterprise.

Speed and ease of reference are essential parts of this hands-on guide. The book has an expanded table of contents and an extensive index for finding answers to problems quickly. Many other quick reference features have been added to the book as well. These features include quick step-by-steps, lists, tables with fast facts, and cross-references. The book is broken down into both parts and chapters, with the parts containing a part-opener paragraph or two about the chapters grouped in that part.

Part I, "Microsoft SQL Server 2005 Administration Fundamentals," covers the fundamental tasks you need for SQL Server administration. Chapter 1 provides an overview of SQL Server administration tools, techniques, and concepts. Chapter 2 discusses deploying SQL Server. Chapter 3 shows you how to configure SQL Server's services, components, and networking capabilities. Chapter 4 examines the structures available for configuring and tuning SQL Server. This chapter looks at SQL Server 2005's system catalog and then continues with a discussion of catalog queries and stored procedures.

In Part II, "Microsoft SQL Server 2005 Administration," you'll find the essential tasks for administering SQL Server. Chapter 5 details management techniques for server groups and servers. Chapter 6 explores configuring and tuning SQL Server using SQL Server Management Studio. You'll learn about optimizing memory usage, parallel processing, authentication, auditing, and more. The core administration tasks for creating and managing databases are covered in Chapter 7, with a logical follow-up in Chapter 8 on SQL Server security. To manage server security, you'll create user logins, configure login permissions, and assign roles. The permissions and roles you assign determine the actions that users can perform as well as what types of data they can access.

SQL Server data administration is the subject of Part III. Chapter 9 covers techniques for creating, managing, and optimizing schemas, tables, indexes, and views. In Chapter 10, you'll find tasks for importing and exporting data as well as the old standby bulk copy program (BCP). Chapter 11 focuses on integrating SQL Server databases with other SQL Server databases as well as other data sources. You'll find detailed discussions on distributed queries, distributed transactions, Microsoft Distributed Transaction Coordinator (MS DTC), and linked servers. Chapter 12 explores data replication. You'll learn about the latest replication techniques, including merge replication and immediate-updating subscribers.

Part IV, "Microsoft SQL Server 2005 Optimization and Maintenance," covers administration tasks you'll use to enhance and maintain SQL Server. Chapter 13 provides the essentials for working with server logs, monitoring SQL Server performance, and solving performance problems. Chapter 14 starts by explaining how to create a backup and recovery plan. Afterward, the chapter dives into common tasks for creating and restoring backups. Chapter 15 explores database automation and maintenance, describing how to create alerts, schedule jobs, handle operator notifications, and more. You'll also learn how to create maintenance plans and resolve database consistency problems.

Conventions Used in This Book

I've used a variety of elements to help keep the text clear and easy to follow. You'll find code terms and listings in monospace type, except when I tell you to actually type a command. In that case, the command appears in **bold** type. When I introduce and define a new term, I put it in *italics*.

Other conventions include

Note   To provide additional details on a particular point that needs emphasis.

Tip   To offer helpful hints or additional information.

Caution   To warn when there are potential problems to watch for.

Real World   To provide real-world advice when discussing advanced topics.

Best Practice   To explain the best technique to use when working with advanced configuration and administration concepts.

I truly hope you find that *Microsoft SQL Server 2005 Administrator's Pocket Consultant* provides everything you need to perform essential administrative tasks on SQL Server as quickly and efficiently as possible. Your thoughts are welcome at williamstanek@aol.com, or visit *http://www.williamstanek.com/*. Thank you.

Support

Every effort has been made to ensure the accuracy of this book. Microsoft Press provides corrections for books through the World Wide Web at *http://mspress.microsoft.com/support/*.

If you have comments, questions, or ideas regarding this book, please send them to Microsoft Press using either of the following methods:

Postal Mail:

Microsoft Press
Attn: Microsoft SQL Server 2005
Administrator's Pocket Consultant Editor
One Microsoft Way
Redmond, WA 98052-6399

E-mail:

MSPINPUT@MICROSOFT.COM

Please note that product support is not offered through the above mail addresses. For support information, visit Microsoft's Web site at *http://support.microsoft.com/ directory/*.

Part I

Microsoft SQL Server 2005 Administration Fundamentals

Part I of this book examines the fundamental tasks you perform to administer Microsoft SQL Server 2005. Chapter 1 provides an overview of SQL Server administration concepts, techniques, and tools. Chapter 2 provides planning, installation, and deployment details to help you rollout SQL Server 2005. Chapter 3 shows you how to manage surface security, access, and networking. Chapter 4 examines the structures available for configuring and tuning SQL Server. This chapter provides the essential background for understanding how to configure and tune SQL Server 2005.

Chapter 1

Microsoft SQL Server 2005 Administration Overview

Microsoft SQL Server 2005 completely redefines the SQL Server database platform and provides the bedrock foundation on which small, medium, and large organizations can build their next generation IT infrastructure. At the core of SQL Server 2005, you will find:

- **SQL Server Database Services**   Includes the core database, replication, and full-text search components. The core database, the Database Engine, is the heart of SQL Server. Replication increases data availability by distributing data across multiple databases, allowing you to scale out the read workload across designated database servers. Full-text search allows plain-language queries on data stored in SQL Server tables.

- **Analysis Services**   Delivers Online Analytical Processing (OLAP) and data mining functionality for business intelligence applications. Analysis Services allows your organization to aggregate data from multiple data sources, such as relational databases, and work with this data in a wide variety of ways.

- **Data Integration Services**   Provides an enterprise data transformation and integration solution for extracting and transforming data from multiple data sources and moving it to one or more destination sources. This allows you to merge data from heterogeneous data sources, load data into data warehouses and data marts, and more.

- **Notification Services**   Includes a notification engine and client components for generating and sending personalized, timely messages to users when a triggering event occurs. Notifications can be sent to wireless devices, such as mobile phones and PDAs, Windows Messenger accounts, and e-mail accounts.

- **Reporting Services**   Includes Report Manager and Report Server to provide a complete, server-based platform for creating, managing, and distributing reports. The Report Server is built on standard IIS and .NET framework technology, allowing you to combine the benefits of SQL Server and IIS to host and process reports.

■ **Service Broker**   Provides reliable queuing and messaging as a core part of the database. Queues can be used to stack work, such as queries and other requests, and perform them as resources allow. Messaging allows database applications to communicate with each other.

As you get started with Microsoft SQL Server 2005, you should concentrate on these areas:

■ How SQL Server 2005 works with your hardware

■ What versions and editions of SQL Server 2005 are available and how they meet your needs

■ How SQL Server 2005 works with Microsoft Windows-based operating systems

■ What administration tools are available

SQL Server 2005 and Your Hardware

Successful database server administration depends on three things:

■ Good database administrators
■ Strong database architecture
■ Appropriate hardware

The first two ingredients are covered: you're the administrator, you're smart enough to buy this book to help you through the rough spots, and you've enlisted SQL Server 2005 to provide your high-performance database needs. This brings us to the issue of hardware. SQL Server 2005 should run on a system with adequate memory, processing speed, and disk space. You also need an appropriate data and system protection plan at the hardware level.

 Note   Having well written database applications and proper database design makes a database administrator's job much easier. Poor performance is more often due to poor application and data structure design than to anything a database administrator can do. So in a way, this makes the overall design a fourth ingredient for success—but it's an ingredient that's largely beyond your control as a database administrator.

Key guidelines for choosing hardware for SQL Server are as follows:

■ **Memory**   SQL Server 2005 requires a minimum of 512 MB of RAM for Standard Edition or Enterprise Edition, and 1 GB of RAM for 64-bit editions. In most cases, you will want to have at least twice the recommended minimum amount of memory. The primary reason for this extra memory is performance. SQL Server 2005 and standard Windows services together use about 256 MB of memory as a baseline.

Additional database features, such as Analysis Services, Reporting Services, and Notification Services, increase the baseline memory requirements (by about 30 MB of RAM each). Installation of IIS 5.0 or later and related components is required for Reporting Services, which also increases the baseline memory requirements. Running either management studio on the SQL Server uses 50 MB to 60 MB of RAM as a baseline. Also consider the number of user connections. User connections consume about 24 KB each. Data requests and other SQL Server processes use memory as well, and this memory usage is in addition to all other processes and applications running on the server.

- **CPU** 32-bit versions of SQL Server 2005 run on Intel *x*86 or compatible hardware. 64-bit versions run on Intel Itanium (IA-64) and X64 family of processors from AMD and Intel, including AMD64 and Intel Extended Memory 64 Technology (Intel EM64T). SQL Server provides solid benchmark performance with Intel Xeon 3.66 GHz, Intel Itanium 2 1.6 GHz, AMD Opteron 2.6 GHz, and AMD Athlon 2.6 GHz. Any of these CPUs provide good starting points for the average SQL Server system. You can achieve significant performance improvements with a high level on processor cache. Look closely at the L1, L2, and L3 cache options available—a higher cache can yield much better performance overall.

The primary advantages of 64-bit processors over 32-bit processors have to do with memory limitations and data access. Because 64-bit processors can exceed the 4-GB memory limit of 32-bit processors, they can store greater amounts of data in main memory, providing direct access to and faster processing of data. In addition, 64-bit processors can process data and execute instruction sets that are twice as large as 32-bit processors. Accessing 64 bits of data (versus 32 bits) offers a significant advantage when processing complex calculations that require a high level of precision. However, not all applications are optimized for 64-bit processors, which can present an implementation and maintenance challenge.

- **SMP** SQL Server 2005 supports symmetric multiprocessors and can process complex parallel queries. Parallel queries are valuable only when relatively few users are on a system and you're processing large queries. On a dedicated system that runs only SQL Server and supports fewer than 100 simultaneous users who aren't doing complex queries, a single CPU should suffice. If the server supports more than 100 users or doesn't run on a dedicated system, you may want to consider adding processors (or using a system that can support additional processors as your needs grow). Keep in mind that the size of the queries and data sets being processed affects how well SQL Server scales. As the size of jobs being processed increases, you will have increasing memory and CPU needs.

- **Disk drives** The amount of data storage capacity you need depends entirely on the number and size of the databases that the server supports. You need enough disk space to store all your data plus work space, indices, system files, virtual memory, transaction logs, and, in the case of a cluster, the quorum disk. I/O throughput is just as important as drive capacity. For the best I/O performance, FC (Fiber Channel) is the recommended choice for high-end storage solutions. Instead of using a single large drive, you should use several smaller drives, which allows you to configure fault tolerance with RAID (redundant array of independent disks). I recommend separating data and logs and placing them on separate drives. This includes the quorum disk for clustering.

- **Data protection**   You should add protection against unexpected drive failure by using RAID. For data, use RAID 0 or RAID 5. For logs, use RAID 1. RAID 0 (disk striping without parity) offers good read/write performance, but any failed drive means that SQL Server can't continue operation on an affected database until the drive is replaced and data is restored from backup. RAID 1 (disk mirroring) creates duplicate copies of data on separate drives, and you can rebuild the RAID unit to restore full operations. RAID 5 (disk striping with parity) offers good protection against single drive failure but has poor write performance. For best performance and fault tolerance, RAID 0 + 1 is recommended, which consists of disk mirroring and disk striping without parity.

- **Uninterruptible Power Supply (UPS)**   SQL Server is designed to maintain database integrity at all times and can recover information using transaction logs. This does not protect the server hardware, however, from sudden power loss or power spikes. Both of these events can seriously damage hardware. To prevent this, get an uninterruptible power supply. A UPS system gives you time to shut down the system properly in the event of a power outage, and it is also important in maintaining database integrity when the server uses write-back caching controllers.

If you follow these hardware guidelines, you will be well on your way to success with SQL Server 2005.

Microsoft SQL Server 2005 Editions

SQL Server 2005 is distributed in four main editions: Workgroup, Standard, Enterprise, and Developer. In all of these editions, you will find a server installation and a workstation installation. The server installation includes the full version of SQL Server and support services. The workstation installation includes the client components, tools, and documentation.

Workgroup Edition is designed as an entry-level database solution. This edition is ideal for small departments in large enterprises and for small businesses that need a robust database solution, but do not need the extended business intelligence features of the Standard and Enterprise editions. The Workgroup Edition:

- Runs on multiple versions of the Microsoft Windows operating system, including Windows 2000, Windows XP Professional, and Windows Server 2003.

Note   For all editions of SQL Server 2005 running on Microsoft Windows 2000, Service Pack 4 (SP4) or later must be installed. With Windows XP Professional, Service Pack 1 (SP1) or later must be installed. For additional requirements pertaining to the operation of SQL Server 2005 on Windows 2000 and Windows XP Professional, refer to the SQL Server 2005 Books Online.

- Supports an unlimited database size, up to 3 GB of RAM, two CPUs for symmetric multiprocessing, limited replication publishing, and full-text search.
- Enables log shipping, which allows SQL Server to send transaction logs from one server to another. Use this feature to create a standby server.

The most widely deployed edition is the Standard Edition, which is designed for the average-sized organization. The Standard Edition:

- Runs on multiple versions of the Microsoft Windows operating system, including Windows 2000, Windows XP Professional, and Windows Server 2003.
- Supports an unlimited database size, an unlimited amount of RAM, four CPUs for symmetric multiprocessing, full replication publishing, and full-text search.
- Provides business intelligence services, including Analysis Services, Reporting Services, Notification Services, and Data Transformation Services.
- Includes database mirroring, data mining, and data integration services.

While the Standard Edition is a strong database server solution, large organizations will want to consider the Enterprise Edition. The Enterprise Edition adds:

- Unlimited scaling and partitioning, which provides for exceptional performance and the ability to scale SQL Server to support very large database installations. By horizontally partitioning tables across multiple servers, you can configure a group of servers to work together to support a large Web site or enterprise data processing.
- Advanced database mirroring for complete online parallel operations and advanced analysis tools for data mining and full-featured OLAP.
- Failover clustering, which allows you to create four-node clusters on Windows 2000 Datacenter Server and two-node clusters on Windows 2000 Advanced Server. Use this feature to provide failover and failback support.

As you might expect, the SQL Server 2005 Enterprise Edition runs on Windows 2000 Advanced Server, Windows 2000 Datacenter, Windows Server 2003 Enterprise, and Windows Server 2003 Datacenter. The Developer Edition supports all the features of the Enterprise Edition but is licensed for development/test use only.

Other editions of SQL Server 2005 are available. These editions include the Mobile Edition and the Express Edition (which replaces the Personal Edition in previous versions of SQL Server and includes the redistributable Database Engine). The Mobile Edition allows you to use SQL Server as the data store on smart devices. The Express Edition is the version you run when you want an easy-to-use, low-end database solution. The Express Edition is free and can be distributed with third-party applications. It supports up to a 4-GB database size, up to 1 GB of RAM, and a single CPU.

Note With the exception of the Express and Mobile Editions, most of the differences between various editions of SQL Server are below the surface and don't affect the interface. Therefore, this text refers to specific editions and differentiates between the server and the desktop installation only when necessary. As you would expect, the Express and Mobile Editions have simple management interfaces.

All editions of SQL Server 2005 automatically and dynamically configure user connections. This is different from SQL Server 7.0 and earlier versions, in which specific limitations were placed on the number of simultaneous user connections. Therefore, you don't have to worry about managing user connections as much as in previous versions. Just keep in mind that as the number of user connections increases, so does the amount of resource usage on the server. The server has to balance the workload among the many user connections, which can result in decreased throughput for user connections and the server as a whole.

Unlike previous versions of SQL Server, SQL Server 2005 uses the Windows Installer and has a fully integrated installation process. This means you can configure SQL Server 2005 components using Add/Remove Programs much like you can any other application you install on the operating system. The installation can be performed remotely from a command shell as well as locally.

Chapter 2 provides detailed instructions for installing SQL Server 2005. For an initial installation, the installer will first check the system configuration to determine the status of required services and components, which includes checking the configuration and availability of components such as WMI, MSXML, IIS, Internet Explorer, and COM+ as well as the operating system, operating system service packs, installation permissions for the default install path, memory, and hardware.

After checking the system configuration, the installer offers a choice of components to install. Whether you use the Developer, Workgroup, Standard, or Enterprise Edition, you have similar options. You can:

- **Work with the full server installation**   This option will perform a complete installation of the SQL Server Database Services, which includes data files, replication objects, and the full-text search engine. Choose SQL Server on the Components To Install page.

- **Work with the full server and select business intelligence services**   This option will perform a complete installation of the SQL Server Database Services. You can choose to install Analysis Services, Reporting Services, Notification Services, and Data Transformation Services as necessary. If you choose to install Reporting Services, IIS and related components will also be installed and the server will be configured as a Report Server (Standard and Enterprise Editions only).

- **Create a workstation installation**   This option allows you to start a normal installation but choose the Workstation Components, Books Online, And Development Tools option on the Components To Install page. This gives you the connectivity components, management tools, documentation, programming models, and samples. Do not select the server components. (If you use per-server licensing, this is the best option for management and development.)

- **Work with the full server and tool installation**   This option will perform a complete installation of the SQL Server Database Services and the workstation components. You can install Analysis Services, Reporting Services, Notification Services, and Data Transformation Services as necessary if you are using the

Standard or Enterprise Edition. To customize the installation, you can click Advanced on the Components To Install page.

Real World   If you only want to work with the data access components and network libraries, you can use the SQL Native Client Installation process rather than the SQL Server Installation process. The SQL Native Client Installation Wizard is accessible on the Autorun page when you are working with the SQL Server 2005 distribution media. The SQL Server Installation Wizard has this option as well. Click Advanced on the Components To Install page to display the Feature Selection page. Expand Client Components, and then select only the Connectivity Components for installation.

SQL Server and Windows

When you install SQL Server on server operating systems, SQL Server makes several modifications to the environment. These modifications include new system services, integrated authentication, new domain/workgroup accounts, and registry updates.

Services for SQL Server

When you install SQL Server on Windows, several services are installed on the server. These services include:

- **Active Directory Helper**   MSSQLServerADHelper adds and removes objects used to register SQL Server and Analysis Server instances. It also updates object permissions related to SQL Server service accounts.

- **Analysis Services**   The Microsoft SQL Server Analysis Services are used for OLAP and data mining. For the default database instance, this service is named Analysis Services (MSSQLSERVER). When multiple instances of SQL Server are installed, you will also see MSSQLSERVER$*instancename,* where *instancename* is the name of the SQL Server instance.

- **Distributed Transaction Coordinator**   The Distributed Transaction Coordinator service coordinates distributed transactions between two or more database servers.

- **Microsoft Search**   The Full-Text Engine for SQL (MSFTESQL) creates full-text indexes and is used with full-text searches on databases. This feature is only available when full-text search is installed as a custom component.

- **Report Server**   The Microsoft Reporting Services create, manage, and deliver reports. For the default database instance, this service is named Report Server (MSSQLSERVER). When multiple instances of SQL Server are installed, you will also see MSSQLSERVER$*instancename,* where *instancename* is the name of the SQL Server instance.

- **SQL Browser**   The SQL browser provides connection details and information to clients.

- **SQL Server Agent**   The SQL Server Agent service is used with scheduling and alerting. For the default database instance, this service is named SQL Server

Agent (MSSQLServer). When multiple instances of SQL Server are installed, you will also see SQLAgent$*instancename*, where *instancename* is the name of the SQL Server instance.

- **SQL Server**   The SQL Server service is the primary database service. For the default database instance, this service is named SQL Server (MSSQLServer). When multiple instances of SQL Server are installed, you will also see MSSQL$*instancename*, where *instancename* is the name of the SQL Server instance.

 Note   You will learn more about managing services and configuring service-related options in Chapter 5, "Managing the Enterprise."

SQL Server Authentication

SQL Server security is completely integrated with Windows domain security, allowing for authentication based on user and group memberships as well as standard SQL Server user accounts. These authentication techniques make it much easier to manage access and security. You can:

- Combine Windows and SQL Server authentication so users in Windows domains can access the server using a single account and other users can be logged on using a SQL Server login ID.
- Use authentication based on Windows domain accounts only, so only users with a domain account can access the server.

Service Accounts for SQL Server

When using Windows 2000 and Windows Server 2003, SQL Server services can be configured to log on as Local System or to use Windows logon accounts. There are advantages and disadvantages to each of these techniques:

- **Local system accounts**   This option provides administrative privileges to SQL Server on the local system but no privileges on the network. If the server requires resources on the local server only, use the local system account. Use local system accounts when you want to isolate SQL Server and restrict it from interacting with other servers.
- **Domain accounts**   This option sets the service to use a standard domain account with privileges you configure. Use domain accounts when the server requires resources across the network, when you need to forward events to the application logs of other systems, and when you want to configure e-mail or pager notification.

Any domain user accounts used with SQL Server services must have permission to perform the following tasks:

- Read and change the SQL Server installation folder. By default, this folder is located in the %ProgramFiles%\Microsoft SQL Server\MSSQL folder.
- Read and change database files, including the .mdf, .ndf, and .ldf files.

- Read and write SQL Server-related registry keys.
- Log on as a service.

Additional requirements for the SQL Server (MSSQLSERVER) and SQL Server Agent (MSSQLSERVER) services are as follows:

- For SQL Server (MSSQLSERVER) to add and delete SQL Server objects in Active Directory, the service must be a member of the local Power Users or local Administrators group.

- For SQL Server (MSSQLSERVER) to run xp_cmdshell for a user other than a SQL Server administrator, the service needs the Act As Part Of Operating System and Replace A Process Level Token privileges.

- For SQL Server (MSSQLSERVER) to write to a mail slot using xp_sendmail, the service needs the appropriate network write privileges.

- For SQL Server Agent (MSSQLSERVER) to use the autorestart feature or create CmdExec and ActiveScript jobs belonging to someone other than a SQL Server administrator, the service must be a member of the Administrators local group.

Note Security in SQL Server is managed through logins, server roles, database access permissions, and object permissions. Windows domain accounts can be used for user authentication and log in to SQL Server. You can, for example, specify a Windows account to use for authentication and to log on to SQL Server. You will learn more about SQL Server logins, server roles, and security in Chapter 8, "Managing SQL Server 2005 Security."

Using the Graphical Administration Tools

SQL Server 2005 provides several types of tools for administration. The graphical administration tools are the ones you will use most often. You can access these tools by selecting Start, choosing Programs or All Programs, and then using the Microsoft SQL Server 2005 menu.

SQL Server 2005 has several new graphical tools that replace or combine the features of the graphical tools in previous SQL Server editions. SQL Server Management Studio replaces SQL Server Enterprises Manager, Query Analyzer, and Analysis Manager. This means that you can use SQL Server Management Studio to perform most of your core SQL Server administration tasks.

SQL Server Management Studio provides several different views. When you first start working with this tool, you will see the Registered Servers view, the Object Explorer view, and the Summary view shown in Figure 1-1. If they are not displayed, these and others views can be accessed from the View menu, and the following descriptions explain how to use each view:

- **Object Explorer** Allows you to view and connect to SQL Server, Analysis Server, Integration Services Server, Report Server, and SQL Mobile. Once connected to a particular server, you view its components as an object tree and can expand nodes to work your way to lower levels of the tree.

- **Registered Servers** Shows the currently registered servers. The top bar of the view allows you to quickly switch between servers of a particular type (SQL Server, Analysis Server, Integration Services Server, Report Server, SQL Mobile).

- **Template Explorer** Provides quick access to the default Query Editor templates and any custom templates you have created. Templates can be created in any script language supported by SQL Server Management Studio.

- **Solutions Explorer** Provides quick access to existing SQL Server, Analysis Server, and SQL Mobile projects. Projects detail connections, queries, and other functions to perform when the project is executed.

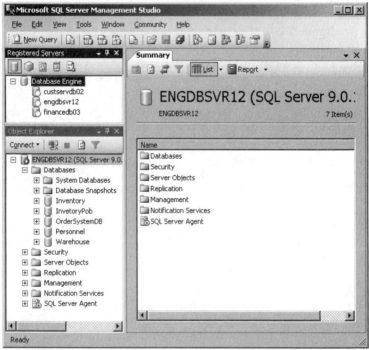

Figure 1-1 Use SQL Server Management Studio to perform core administration tasks.

If you have worked with previous versions of SQL Server, you will find that SQL Server Management Studio is very different from the tools it replaces. Most of the friendly wizards are gone and have been replaced with nonmodal dialog boxes that provide quick access to configuration elements. As shown in Figure 1-2, Script and Help options are provided on the top bar of these dialog boxes to make it easy to generate a script based on your configuration choices and get help when you need it.

Another important tool is SQL Server Configuration Manager, shown in Figure 1-3. SQL Server Configuration Manager replaces Server Network Utility, Client Network Utility, and Services Manager. This means you can use SQL Server Configuration Manager to perform many essential service setup and network configuration tasks.

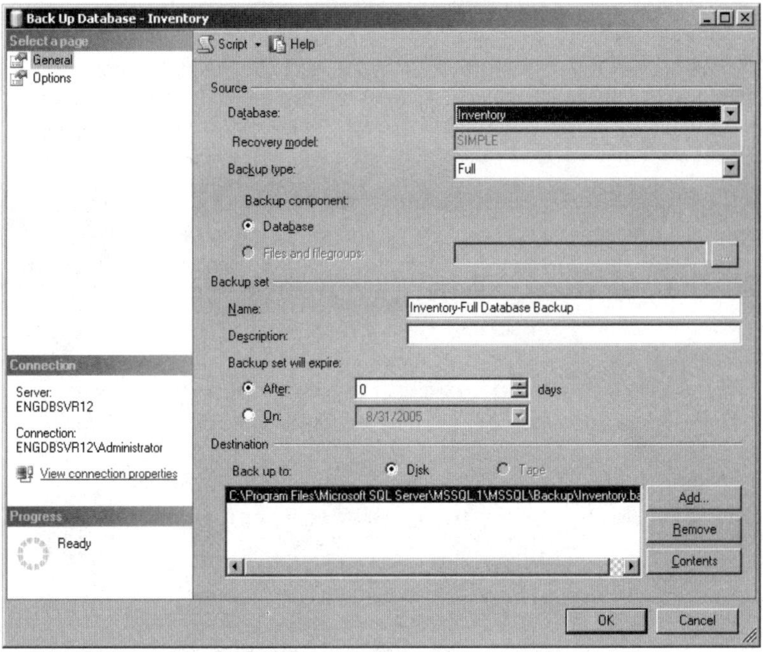

Figure 1-2 Use the top bar options to quickly perform key tasks.

When you select a service under the Services node, you can manage the service in the details pane by right-clicking it and then choosing an appropriate option, such as Start, Stop, or Restart. You can also choose Properties to configure the related settings, such as startup mode, login account, and login account password.

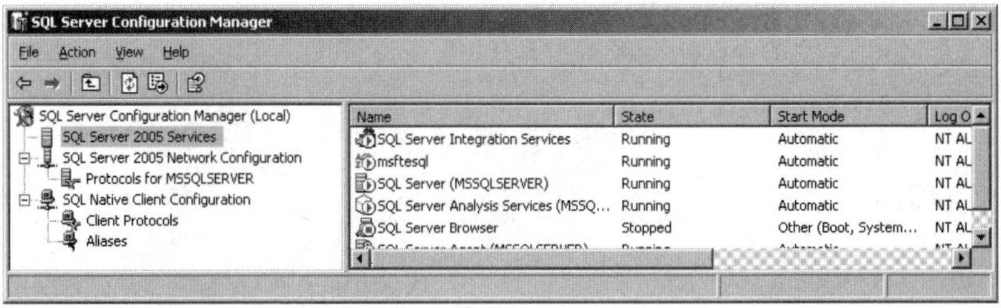

Figure 1-3 Use SQL Server Configuration Manager to manage services and network configurations.

SQL Server 2005 is designed for local and remote management. You can use most of the tools to manage local resources as well as remote resources. For example, in SQL Server Management Studio, you can register a new server and then connect to it. Afterward, you can remotely manage the server and all its databases from your system. Table 1-1 provides a summary of the graphical administration tools discussed as well as other useful graphical tools

Table 1-1   Quick Reference for Key SQL Server 2005 Administration Tools

Administration Tool	Purpose
Business Intelligence Development Studio	Allows you to develop and manage Business Intelligence objects. Includes SSIS Designer, which you can use to create and maintain SSIS packages.
Database Tuning Adviser	Helps you tune the performance of SQL Server databases.
SQL Server Import/Export Wizard	Allows you to define SSIS Services packages for importing and exporting data.
Report Manager	Allows you to manage reports generated by Reporting Services.
SQL Server Configuration Manager	Allows you to configure the client and server network libraries and manage SQL Server services. Replaces Server Network Utility, Client Network Utility, and Services Manager. Covered in Chapter 2., "Deploying Microsoft SQL Server 2005."
SQL Profiler	Allows you to analyze user activity and generate audit trails. SQL Profiler is a graphical interface to SQL Trace. Covered in Chapter 13, "Profiling and Monitoring Microsoft SQL Server 2005."
SQL Server Management Studio	The main administration tool for SQL Server 2005. Manages SQL servers, databases, security, and more. Key aspects are discussed in Chapter 4, "Configuring and Tuning Microsoft SQL Server." Replaces SQL Server Enterprises Manager, Query Analyzer, and Analysis Manager.

Using the Command-line Tools

The graphical administration tools provide just about everything you need to work with SQL Server. Still, there are times when you may want to work from the command line, especially if you want to automate installation, administration, or maintenance with scripts. The primary command-line tool is SQLCMD.EXE, which replaces OSQL.EXE and ISQL.EXE. Another command-line tool you'll use is BCP.EXE.

SQLCMD

SQLCMD is a SQL query tool that you can run from the command line. Unlike OSQL and ISQL, which SQLCMD replaces, SQLCMD communicates with SQL Server only through the OLE DB API. Like OSQL and ISQL, SQLCMD has very little overhead, making it a good choice when system resources are a concern. Sample 1-1 shows the syntax for SQLCMD.

Sample 1-1 SQLCMD Syntax

```
sqlcmd [-U login id] [-P password]
  [-S servername[\instancename]] [-H hostname] [-E trusted connection]
  [-d use database name] [-l login timeout] [-t query timeout]
  [-h headers] [-s colseparator] [-w screen width]
  [-a packetsize] [-e echo input] [-I Enable Quoted Identifier]
  [-c cmdend] [-L[c] list servers[clean output]]
  [-q "cmdline query"] [-Q "cmdline query" and exit]
  [-m errorlevel] [-V severitylevel] [-W remove trailing spaces]
  [-u unicode output] [-r[0|1] msgs to stderr]
  [-i inputfile] [-o outputfile] [-z new password]
  [-f <codepage> | i:<codepage>[,o:<codepage>]] [-Z new password and exit]
  [-k [1|2] remove[replace] control characters]
  [-y variable length type display width]
  [-Y fixed length type display width]
  [-p [1] print statistics[colon format]]
  [-R use client regional setting]
  [-b On error batch abort]
  [-v var = "value"...] [-A dedicated admin connection]
  [-X [1] disable commands[and exit with warning]]
  [-x disable variable substitution]
  [? show syntax summary]
```

Note   Unlike ISQL, SQLCMD does support connecting to named
instances of SQL Server 2005. By default, SQLCMD connects to the default
instance of SQL Server. If you specify the instance name as well as the server
name, SQLCMD will connect to the specified instance name on the designated server.

When you start SQLCMD, you can issue Transact-SQL statements to run queries,
execute stored procedures, and perform additional tasks. Because you're working at
the command line, these commands are not executed automatically, and you need
to use additional commands to tell SQLCMD when to execute statements, when to
ignore statements, and so on. These additional statements must be entered on separate lines and are summarized in Table 1-2.

In previous editions of SQL Server, you used ODBCPING to verify an ODBC connection between a client and server. In SQL Server 2005, OLE DB is the preferred
technique for establishing database connections. You can establish a connection to

a server for the purposes of testing and troubleshooting using SQLCMD –A. See Chapter 15 for an example of using SQLCMD–A.

Table 1-2   SQLCMD Commands

Command	Description
GO [count]	Executes all statements entered up to the previous GO or RESET. If count is used, the cached statements are executed the number of times specified in count as a single batch.
RESET	Clears statements you've entered so they aren't executed.
ED	Calls the text editor, which is defined by the SQLCMDEDITOR environment variable, such as **SET SQLCMDEDITOR=notepad**.
!! *command*	Executes the specified system command or script.
QUIT	Exits SQLCMD.
EXIT *statement*	Sets the exit statement. The batch or query is executed, and then SQLCMD quits.
CTRL+C	Ends a query without exiting from SQLCMD.
r *filename*	Sets the name of a file containing Transact-SQL statements to execute, which can include the GO command.
:ServerList	Lists the locally configured servers and any network servers.
:List	Prints the contents of the statement cache.
:ListVar	Lists currently set variables.
:Setvar	Sets variables.
:Error *filename*	Redirects all error output to the specified file.
:Out *filename*	Redirects all query results to the specified file.
:Perftrace *filename*	Redirects all performance trace information to the specified file.
:Connect	Connects to an instance of SQL Server or closes current connection. The syntax is :Connect [timeout] [ServerName\InstanceName] [Username] [Password]
:Help	Displays SQLCMD help and command syntax.
:On Error [exit|ignore]	Specifies how SQLCMD should handle errors when executing batch of SQL commands. SQLCMD can either quit executing the command or ignore the error and continue execution.

BCP

BCP is the bulk copy program. You can use BCP to import and export data or copy data between instances of SQL Server 2005. The major advantage of BCP is its speed. It is much faster than standard database import/export procedures. Unfortunately, its command-line syntax makes it much harder to use.

The syntax for BCP is shown in Sample 1-2.

Sample 1-2   BCP Syntax

```
bcp {dbtable | query} {in | out | queryout | format} datafile
  [-m maxerrors] [-f formatfile] [-e errfile]
  [-F firstrow] [-L lastrow] [-b batchsize]
  [-n native type] [-c character type] [-w Unicode characters]
  [-N keep non-text native] [-V file format version] [-q quoted id]
```

```
[-C code page specifier] [-t field terminator] [-r row terminator]

[-i inputfile] [-o outfile] [-a packetsize]

[-S server name] [-U username] [-P password]

[-T trusted connection] [-v version] [-R regional enable]

[-k keep null values] [-E keep identity values]

[-h "load hints"] [-x generate xml format file]
```

Other Command-Line Tools

Table 1-3 provides a summary of key command prompt utilities included in SQL Server 2005. As the table shows, most command-line executables are stored in the %ProgramFiles%\Microsoft SQL Server\90\Tools\Binn directory or in the directory for the SQL Server component to which they relate.

Table 1-3   Key Command-Line Tools for SQL Server 2005

Name	Description	Location
bcp	Used to import and export data or to copy data between instances of SQL Server.	%ProgramFiles%\Microsoft SQL Server\90\Tools\Binn
dta	Used to analyze workloads and recommend optimization changes for that workload.	%ProgramFiles%\Microsoft SQL Server\90\Tools\Binn
dtexec	Used to configure and execute a SQL Server Integration Services (SSIS) package. The corresponding GUI tool is DTExecUI.	%ProgramFiles%\Microsoft SQL Server\90\DTS\Binn
dtutil	Used to manage SQL Server Integration Services (SSIS) packages.	%ProgramFiles%\Microsoft SQL Server\90\DTS\Binn
nscontrol	Used to create and manage instances of Notification Services.	%ProgramFiles%\Microsoft SQL Server\90\NotificationServices\9.0.242\bin
profiler90	Used to start SQL Server Profiler from a command prompt.	%ProgramFiles%\Microsoft SQL Server\90\Tools\Binn
rs	Used to run Reporting Services scripts.	%ProgramFiles%\Microsoft SQL Server\90\Tools\Binn
rsconfig	Used to configure a report server connection.	%ProgramFiles%\Microsoft SQL Server\90\Tools\Binn
rskeymgmt	Used to manage encryption keys on a Report Server.	%ProgramFiles%\Microsoft SQL Server\90\Tools\Binn
sac	Used to import or export surface area configuration settings between instances of SQL Server 2005.	%ProgramFiles%\Microsoft SQL Server\90\Shared
sqlagent90	Used to start SQL Server Agent from a command prompt.	%ProgramFiles%\Microsoft SQL Server\<InstanceName>\MSSQL\Binn Default Instance: %ProgramFiles%\Microsoft SQL Server\MSSQL.1\MSSQL\Binn

Table 1-3   Key Command-Line Tools for SQL Server 2005   *(continued)*

Name	Description	Location
sqlcmd	Used to perform administration and enter T-SQL statements at the command prompt.	%ProgramFiles%\Microsoft SQL Server\90\Tools\Binn
sqlmaint	Used to execute database maintenance plans created in previous versions of SQL Server.	%ProgramFiles%\Microsoft SQL Server\MSSQL.1\MSSQL\Binn
sqlservr	Used to start and stop an instance of the SQL Server Database Engine.	%ProgramFiles%\Microsoft SQL Server\MSSQL.1\MSSQL\Binn
tablediff	Used to compare the data in two tables and display differences.	%ProgramFiles%\Microsoft SQL Server\90\COM

Chapter 2

Deploying Microsoft SQL Server 2005

With SQL Server Setup, you can create new instances of SQL Server, add components, rebuild the SQL Server registry, uninstall SQL Server, and perform other common setup tasks. Prior to setup and configuration, you need to decide how SQL Server 2005 will be used in your environment. When you have decided on the role SQL Server 2005 will have, you can plan for your deployment and then roll out SQL Server.

SQL Server Integration Roles

SQL Server 2005 is designed as a comprehensive Business Intelligence platform that can be used for:

- Extraction, Transformation, and Loading (ETL)
- Relational Data warehouses
- Multidimensional databases and data mining
- SQL Server 2005 Analysis Services
- Managed reporting

Using SQL Server Integration Services

In SQL Server 2005, Data Transformation Services (DTS) have been renamed SQL Server Integration Services (SSIS) and redesigned to provide a complete enterprise ETL platform that is fully programmable and extensible. Although basic SSIS packages can be created using SQL Server Management Studio, true ETL packages can only be created with the Business Intelligence Development Studio. With the redesigned services, you no longer have to write self-modifying packages. Instead, you should use package variables and the package configuration framework to customize the way the package runs in different circumstances.

This book will use the terms DTS 2000 and SSIS to differentiate between DTS packages designed for SQL Server 2000 and SSIS packages designed for SQL Server

2005. You can use the DTS 2000 Package Migration Wizard to migrate DTS packages designed for SQL Server 2000 to SSIS packages for SQL Server 2005. A DTS 2000 runtime is also provided so that you can run DTS 2000 packages without upgrading them.

 Note   You will find complete details for working with SSIS in Chapter 10, "Importing, Exporting, and Transforming Data."

Using SQL Server 2005 for Relational Data Warehousing

SQL Server 2005 continues to provide a best-of-class relational database platform in the tradition of SQL Server 2000. Many new features of SQL Server 2005 fundamentally change the way you perform administration, however. Integration with the .NET Framework enables you to build a new class of database application—one that uses managed code rather than Transact-SQL.

Your managed code can be organized into classes and namespaces for ease of management and maintenance. In many cases, you will find that managed code is better than Transact-SQL at processing numbers, managing complicated execution logic, and manipulating data strings with regular expressions. Transact-SQL remains a good choice to perform data access with little or no procedural logic.

As with Transact-SQL, managed code runs on your SQL Server. This keeps the server functionality and the data close together without requiring an additional layer in your infrastructure. It also allows you to take advantage of the server's processing power while reducing network traffic between the database servers and the middle tier.

Using SQL Server 2005 for Multidimensional Databases and Data Mining

In SQL Server 2005, Analysis Services have been enhanced to provide better support for multidimensional databases and data mining. Analysis Services have two key components: an Online Analytical Processing (OLAP) engine and a data mining engine. You can build an analytic database from any data source, including a relational database. You would then define the analytic structure, the data mining models, and the views into this structure.

SQL Server 2005 Analysis Services uses the Unified Dimension Model (UDM). UDM combines the best features of the relational and OLAP data models, serving to blur the lines between traditional relational databases and multidimensional OLAP databases. A set of cubes and dimensions defined in SQL Server 2005 is referred to as a Unified Dimension Model. This model improves query performance and flexibility.

The Data Definition Language for SQL Server 2005 Analysis Services is XML. Because of this, the metadata repository is removed and replaced by XML files that are stored and managed on the SQL Server 2005 Analysis Services server. Additionally, unlike SQL Server 2000 Analysis Services, SQL Server 2005 Analysis Services performs all calculations on the server rather than on the client. This eliminates the need for client-side caching and can improve query performance for complex calculations. To reduce latency and improve performance, proactive caching is used. The way proactive caching works can be customized so that you can configure how often the cache is rebuilt, how queries are answered while the cache is being rebuilt, whether the cache is automatically refreshed when transactions occur, and control other characteristics of the cache as well.

Using SQL Server 2005 for Managed Reporting

SQL Server 2005 Reporting Services are designed to help you create a complete solution for creating, distributing, and managing reports. Reporting Services include a set of tools for working with and viewing reports, an engine for hosting and processing reports, and an extensible architecture for integration with existing IT infrastructure. For example, Reporting Services can be integrated easily with Microsoft SharePoint Portal Server so that a SQL Server 2005 Report Server can deliver automatically generated reports to a SharePoint portal.

As an administrator, you can use the Report Server Web Application to:

- Define role-based security for reports.
- Schedule report generation and delivery.
- Track reporting history.

Reports can be delivered in a variety of ways and formats. You can configure Reporting Services to deliver reports to a portal on a SharePoint Portal Server, send reports by e-mail to users, or allow users to access reports on the Web-based report server. Reports can be created in HTML, PDF, TIFF, Excel, XML, and CSV, as well as other formats. HTML reports are ideal for viewing on the Web. Adobe PDF and TIFF are good formats to use for reports that will be printed. Excel, XML, or CSV reports work well if the data in a report needs to be stored in a database or if the user needs to manipulate the report data.

Planning for Your SQL Server 2005 Deployment

As a SQL Server 2005 administrator or developer, you'll fill several different roles, including database designer and database architect. The organization where you work may have dedicated database designers and database architects, but so much has changed in SQL Server that it is critical that you understand the new configuration and setup options before deploying SQL servers.

Building the Server System for Performance

As with SQL Server 2000, you have many basic options for deploying SQL Server 2005. You need to choose an edition of SQL Server and the version of Windows on which SQL Server will run. After you make this decision, you should spend some time thinking about the system configuration. In Chapter 1, "Microsoft SQL Server 2005 Administration Overview," you learned some key guidelines, but do not overlook the importance of the I/O subsystem.

The I/O subsystem is one of the most fundamental components of the server system and you should give considerable thought to its configuration. Start by choosing drives or storage systems that provide the appropriate level of performance. There really is a substantial difference in speed and performance between various drive specifications. When given a choice for a SQL server's internal drives, look closely at both SATA II or higher and Ultra SCSI (preferable Ultra320 SCSI or higher).

Consider not only the capacity of the drive but also its rotational speed and average seek time. The rotational speed is a measurement of how fast the disk spins. The average seek time is a measurement of how long it takes to seek between disk tracks during sequential I/O operations. Generally speaking, when comparing drives that conform to the same specification, such as SATA II or Ultra320 SCSI, the higher the rotational speed (measured in thousands of rotations per minute) and the lower the average seek time (measured in milliseconds) the better. As an example, a drive with a rotational speed of 15,000 RPM will give you 45 percent to 50 percent more I/O per second than the average 10,000-RPM drive, all other things being equal. A drive with a seek time of 3.5 msec will give you a 25 percent to 30 percent response time improvement over a drive with a seek time of 4.7 msec.

Other factors to consider include the maximum sustained data transfer rate and the mean time to failure (MTTF). Most drives of comparable quality will have similar transfer rates and MTTF. For example, if you compare Ultra320 SCSI drives with a 15,000-RPM rotational speed, you will probably find similar transfer rates and MTTF. As an example, the Maxtor Atlas 15K II has a maximum sustained data transfer rate of up to 98 MBps. The Seagate Cheetah 15K.4 has a maximum sustained data transfer rate of up to 96 MBps. Both have an MTTF of 1.4 million hours.

Transfer rates can also be expressed in gigabits per second. 1.5 gigabits per second is equivalent to a data rate of 187 MBps. 3.0 gigabits per second is equivalent to 374 MBps. Sometimes you'll see a maximum external transfer rate (per the specification to which the drive complies) and an average sustained transfer rate. The average sustained transfer rate is the most important factor. The Seagate Barracuda 7200 SATA II drive has a rotational speed of 7,200 RPM and an average sustained transfer rate of 58 MBps. With an average seek time of 8.5 msec and an MTTF of 1 million hours, the drive performs comparably to other 7,200-RPM SATA II drives. However, most Ultra320 SCSI drives perform better.

 Real World   Temperature is another important factor to consider when you are selecting a drive—but it is a factor few administrators take into account. Typically, the faster a drive rotates, the hotter it will run. This is not always the case, but it is certainly something you should consider when making your choice. For example, 15K drives tend to run hot, and you must be sure to carefully regulate temperature. Both the Maxtor Atlas 15K II and the Seagate Cheetah 15K.4 can become nonoperational at temperatures of 70 °C or higher (as would most other drives).

Configuring the I/O Subsystem

When configuring your server system, you will typically have to make a choice between hardware RAID and software RAID for the server's internal disk drives.

You must make this choice, in most cases, even if your server will use external storage. Cost and performance are the two key issues to consider for internal RAID.

Hardware RAID is more expensive than software RAID because it requires RAID controller cards. The expense of hardware RAID, however, is offset by the performance boost it offers. With software RAID, the server's operating system manages the RAID implementation, which requires system resources: CPU processing power, memory, and so on. With hardware RAID, the server's RAID controllers manage the RAID implementation.

Hardware RAID may also give you additional fault tolerance options. For example, Windows Server 2003 supports software RAID levels 0 (disk striping), 1 (disk mirroring), and 5 (disk striping with parity). With hardware RAID, you may have additional options, such as RAID 0 + 1 (which is also referred to as RAID 10, and combines disk striping and mirroring).

The operating system drive of a SQL Server system is often configured with RAID 1, as are drives used for SQL Server's transaction logs. RAID 1 provides a full duplicate (or mirror) of a drive that can be used in case of failure of a primary drive. Because all data writes must go to two drives, disk mirroring doesn't have the best write performance. Read performance is improved over that of a single disk because seeks typically can be split over both disks in the set. This means you could essentially get twice as many reads as with a single disk.

Note   RAID can be configured in many ways. Sometimes it is more efficient to use both hardware and software RAID. For example, you could use hardware RAID controllers to do parity calculations and software RAID to stripe across the disks. Sometimes, you'll want to use two drive controllers with mirroring (a technique referred to as disk duplexing). Disk duplexing has the same write performance as a single disk.

With RAID 1, failure recovery is easier and quicker than with other RAID options because you have a full duplicate disk. This is also why RAID 1 is recommended for the operating system drive. RAID 1 is recommended for drives containing transaction logs because transaction logs are sequentially written and only read in the case of a rollback operation. Thus, when you put a transaction log on its own mirrored drive, you can achieve good performance and have fault tolerance.

Drives containing SQL Server's data files are often configured with RAID 5 or RAID 0 + 1. RAID 5 provides fault tolerance by striping data across multiple disks and storing parity information as data is written. Sections of data and parity information are written to each disk in the set in turn. In the case of disk failure, the parity information can be used to re-create the data on any lost disk. It is important to point out that this parity information can only be used to recover from the loss of a single drive in the array. If multiple drives fail simultaneously, the entire array will fail.

RAID 5 has advantages and disadvantages. With RAID 1, you can mirror a 150-GB drive onto another 150-GB drive. When you do this, there is a 50 percent overhead requirement, meaning that you use double the number of disks and gain no additional storage space. With a three-disk RAID 5 array, the amount of overhead required is about one-third (33 percent) of the total disk space. As you add volumes to a RAID 5 array, the overhead requirement decreases. Because reads are performed across multiple drives, RAID 5 offers better read performance than RAID 1. Essentially, you can perform as many reads as with a single disk times the number of disks in the array, meaning an array with five disks would have a read capacity of five times that of a single disk.

RAID 5 has poorer write performance than RAID 1 because whenever data is written to a RAID 5 array, four I/O operations are required: two reads and two writes. The target disk stripe and the parity stripe must be read first. The parity is then calculated. Then the target stripe and the parity stripe are written to disk.

RAID 0 + 1 is a combination of disk striping and mirroring. With RAID 0 + 1, you mirror a disk stripe, ensuring that there is a duplicate for each striped disk while gaining the performance of pure disk striping. As with RAID 1, each RAID 0 + 1 write operation requires two I/O operations: a write to each disk in the mirror (as with RAID 1). Read operations typically are spread across multiple disks, offering high performance (as with RAID 0 or RAID 5).

RAID 0 + 1 offers very high fault tolerance. Unlike RAID 1 and 5 the array can continue to operate in many cases even if more than one disk fails. In fact, all the disks on one side of the mirror could fail and the array would continue to operate. Failure of both sides of the mirror would result in a complete failure of the set, however.

 Note   A disadvantage of RAID 0 + 1 is the number of disks required. You need twice as many disks as you would need with a striped set. To mirror a 450-GB stripe set, you need another 450-GB stripe set, but the total capacity of the mirror does not change. It remains 450 GB.

When choosing between RAID 5 and RAID 0 + 1, and without considering the comparative cost, the key factor should be the way the disks will be used. RAID 5 works well when there is a high percentage of reads and few writes. RAID 0 + 1 offers better performance compared to RAID 5 as the amount of write operations increase. Specifically, with 90 percent reads and 10 percent writes, RAID 5 is the better choice. As the ratio of writes to reads increases, you will see improved performance if you select RAID 0 + 1.

 Tip   When using RAID 1, 5, and 0 + 1, be sure that the disks have a battery-backed write cache. A battery-backed write cache can help protect data because it still can be written to disk even in the event of power interruption or failure. This is important when the same data must be written to multiple disks, as with RAID 1 and 0 + 1, and when parity information must be written accurately to ensure fault tolerance.

Ensuring Availability and Scalability

Not long ago, your options for ensuring availability and scalability were limited. This is no longer the case. You have many options—and most of these options do not require expensive storage subsystems or storage area networks (SANs).

To ensure availability, you can use log shipping to establish a standby server that you have to manually bring online if the primary server fails. You can use Microsoft Cluster service to create a failover server—one that could automatically come online if the primary server fails. For scalability, you can use distributed partition views to horizontally distribute tables across multiple servers. To improve read-ahead performance, you can use indexed views.

The key drawback to server clustering is that it is expensive, both in terms of required equipment and in resources required for setup. SQL Server 2005 introduces an extended form of log shipping called *database mirroring*, which works on standard server hardware and requires no special storage or controllers. Database mirroring allows you to continuously stream the transaction log from a source server to a destination server. If the source server fails, applications can reconnect to the database on the secondary server within a matter of seconds. Unlike server clustering, transaction logs can be fully synchronized between the servers. This allows changes to be synchronized in both directions.

Database mirroring requires three servers running SQL Server 2005:

- A source server, also referred to as the principal. The *principal server* is the one to which applications connect and where transactions are processed.

- A destination server, also referred to as the mirror. The *mirroring server* is the target of the shipped transaction logs and it operates in a standby state that does not allow read operations.

- A tracking server, also referred to as the witness. The *witness server* tracks which server currently is acting as the principal and which is acting as the mirror. It is used when automatic failover is needed. Whenever there is contention between which server has which role, the witness makes a decision.

As transaction log records are generated on the principal, they are replayed either synchronously (at the same time) or asynchronously (at different times, such as after a short delay) on the mirror. This ensures that the mirror server is exactly in sync or very close to being in sync with the principal server. For example, there may be no write lag between the two servers, or there may be one or more transaction write lags between the two.

From the client's point of view, failover from the principal to the mirror is automatic and nearly instantaneous. If the principal goes offline, the application fails over to the mirror. The mirror then becomes the principal. When the failed server comes back online, it becomes the mirror and receives transaction log records.

Note SQL Server replication can also be used to create copies of a database. You can use replication to distribute data across multiple databases. SQL Server supports several types of replication including snapshot replication, transactional replication, and merge replication. For more information on replication, see Chapter 12, "Implementing Snapshot, Merge, and Transactional Replication."

Ensuring Connectivity and Data Access

SQL Server 2005 introduces two features that can help ensure consistent connectivity and data access:

- **Dedicated administrator connection**   Designed to ensure that administrators can get consistent access to SQL Server.
- **Multiple active result sets**   Designed to ensure that users accessing the database have consistent access to SQL Server.

Unlike previous editions of SQL Server, in which administrators could be locked out if SQL Server became unresponsive, SQL Server 2005 uses dedicated administrator connections to provide a way for administrators to access a server that is not responding or is otherwise unavailable. With this feature, administrators are able to establish a connection that can be used to troubleshoot and resolve problems.

Any administrator who is a member of the sysadmin fixed server role can establish a dedicated server connection using the SQLCMD command prompt utility with the -A parameter. Consider the following example:

```
sqlcmd –U wrstanek –P moreFunPlease –S corpdbsvr05 –A
```

Here, the user wrstanek, who is a member of the sysadmin fixed server role, is connecting to the default instance on CorpDBSvr05. You could also connect to a named instance, such as:

```
sqlcmd –U wrstanek –P moreFunPlease –S corpdbsvr05\webapp05 –A
```

where webapp05 is the name of the SQL Server instance.

Multiple active results sets (MARS) have improved SQL Server connectivity markedly for users as well. With SQL Server 2000, you could have at most one pending request in a given situation. Although server-side cursors and other techniques can be used to work around this limitation, you still do not have a direct way to handle multiple result sets in a single session. MARS corrects this problem by providing the programming interfaces necessary to represent a connection and a request executed under that connection separately. As an example, with Open Database Connectivity (ODBC) you represent connections and executed requests within connections using handles:

- The SQL_HANDLE_DBC type represents connection handles.
- The SQL_HANDLE_STMT type represents executed statements within connections.

The SQLODBC and SQLOLEDB drivers included in the SQL Native Client Installation for SQL Server 2005 are MARS-enabled, as is the SqlClient .NET Data Provider including in the Microsoft .NET Framework, version 2.0 or later. By default, these drivers establish connections and handle requests using MARS. Technically, execution requests can be a single T-SQL statement, a batch of T-SQL statements, or the name of a stored procedure or function to run along with any appropriate parameter values. Regardless, SQL Server sequentially executes the statements as it iterates through them, and the statements may or may not produce results. Thus, you can have more than one pending request under a given connection and more than one default result set.

Tip Native drivers for SQL Server 2000 or earlier do not support MARS. MARS works by interleaving execution of multiple requests and not by parallel execution. MARS allows a statement, batch, or procedure to run and within the execution allows other requests to run. Interleaving works with SELECT, FETCH, READTEXT, RECEIVE, and BULK INSERT. It also works with asynchronous cursor population.

In contrast to SQL Server 2000, in which implicit spawning of connections under OLEDB and additional requests under ODBC are not allowed, SQL Server 2005 allows both to occur. This means that if a session has an active transaction, all new requests run under the transaction. When there is no active transaction, batches run in autocommit mode, in which each statement is executed under its own transaction.

The SqlClient .NET Provider has separate SqlConnection, SqlCommand, and Sql-Transaction objects. SqlConnection objects represent connections established to a server. SqlCommand objects represent commands (requests) executed under the connection. SqlTransaction objects represent active transactions. When you begin a transaction within the context of a specific connection, a SqlTransaction object is returned to represent this transaction.

Running and Modifying SQL Server Setup

SQL Server Setup is the utility you use to perform key installation tasks for SQL Server. You use SQL Server Setup to create new instances of SQL Server. When you want to manage SQL Server components, you use Add Or Remove Programs. Tasks you can perform with these utilities include the following:

- Creating new instances of SQL Server
- Installing additional client components
- Maintaining existing components
- Rebuilding the SQL Server registry
- Uninstalling SQL Server

Creating New Instances of SQL Server

You can install multiple instances of the SQL Server 2005 database engine on a single computer. Running multiple instances of the database engine is ideal when:

- You need to support multiple test and development environments on a single large server.
- You need to run multiple applications on a desktop and each application installs its own instance of the SQL Server 2005 engine.
- You need to securely isolate the databases that are available on a single server.

In most other situations, however, you should not run multiple instances of the SQL Server 2005 database engine. Each instance of the SQL Server 2005 database engine has its own set of system and user databases. Each instance has separate SQL Server and SQL Server Agent services, and as applicable, separate Analysis Services and Report Server services as well. All other components and services are shared, and this adds to the overhead on the server due to management of the shared resources.

Understanding SQL Server Instances

When you install SQL Server 2005, you have the option of installing a default instance of the SQL Server 2005 database engine or a named instance of the SQL Server 2005 database engine. In most cases, you will want to install the default instance first and then install additional named instances of the SQL Server database engine as necessary. There is no limit to the number of named instances that you can run on a single computer.

A default instance is identified by the name of the computer on which the SQL Server 2005 database engine is running; it does not have a separate instance name. Applications connect to the default instance by using the computer name in their requests. Only one default instance can run on any computer, and this default instance can be any version of SQL Server.

All instances of SQL Server other than the default instance are identified by the instance name that you set during installation. Applications connect to a named instance by specifying the computer name and the instance name in the format computer_name\instance_name. Only the SQL Server 2000 and SQL Server 2005 database engines can run as named instances. Previous versions of SQL Server do not support named instances.

 Note   When you run SQL Server 2005 Enterprise Edition, you can create multinode server clusters. Applications connect to the default instance on a SQL Server cluster by specifying the virtual server name. Applications connect to a named instance on a SQL Server cluster by specifying the virtual server name and the named instance in the format virtual_server_name\instance_name.

Installing a SQL Server Instance

The SQL Server 2005 installation process has changed considerably since SQL Server 2000. The installation process now requires Windows Installer 3.0 or later, which is included in Windows Server 2003 Service Pack 1 or later, as well as in Windows XP Professional Service Pack 2 or later. If you are installing SQL Server 2005 on a different operating system, you should download Windows Installer 3.0 from the Microsoft Download Center at www.microsoft.com/download.

Not only does using Windows Installer help streamline and stabilize the installation process, it also makes modification of installed components easier. You can:

- Perform upgrades directly using the Installation Wizard.

- Install additional components or instances by rerunning the Installation Wizard.

- Maintain installed components using Add Or Remove Programs in Control Panel.
- Resume a failed upgrade or installation using Add Or Remove Programs in Control Panel.

To install an instance of the SQL Server 2005 database engine, complete the following steps:

1. Log on to the server using an account with administrator privileges. Then insert the SQL Server 2005 CD-ROM into the CD-ROM drive.

Tip Be sure to keep a detailed record of the actions you perform. These actions should explicitly state the server, server instance, and installation options you are using. You may need this information later.

2. If Autorun is enabled, the SQL Server 2005 Setup program should start automatically. Otherwise, double-click Splash.hta in the Servers folder of the CD-ROM.

3. Under Install, click Server Components, Tools, Books Online, And Samples. The End User License Agreement is displayed. Select I Accept The Licensing Terms And Conditions, and then click Next.

4. The first time you run the Installation Wizard, the SQL Server Component Update Wizard is started next to determine the status of required services and components. If there are required components as shown in Figure 2-1, click Install to begin the component installation, and then click Next when the installation process is completed.

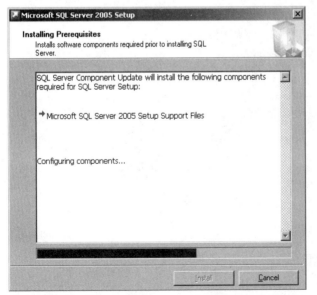

Figure 2-1 Installing required components for Microsoft SQL Server 2005

Note   SQL Server Component Update Wizard checks the configuration and availability of components such as WMI, MSXML, IIS, Internet Explorer, and COM+. It also checks the configuration of the operating system, operating system service packs, installation permissions for the default install path, memory, and hardware.

5. When the SQL Server Installation Wizard starts, click Next. The wizard will then perform a system configuration check. Note any errors and take the necessary corrective actions before continuing. If there are no required corrective actions, click Next to proceed with the installation.

 Real World   Occasionally you may need to reboot prior to continuing the installation process (see Figure 2-2). If you do so, the Installation Wizard will not restart automatically and you will need to repeat the installation process, starting with Step 1.

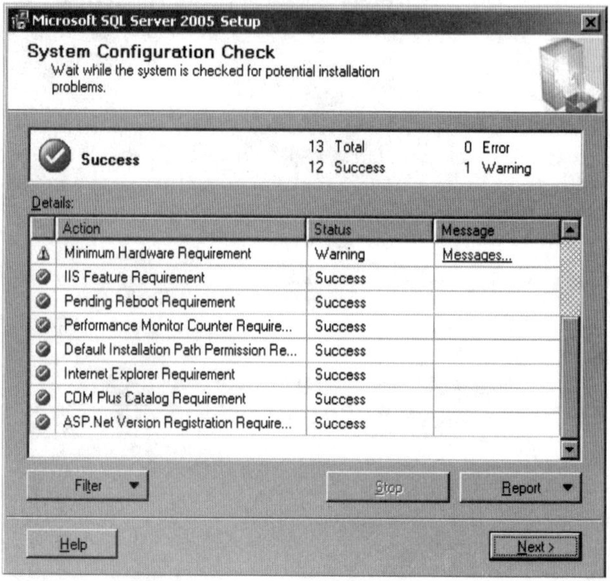

Microsoft SQL Server 2005 Setup

System Configuration Check
Wait while the system is checked for potential installation problems.

✔ **Success**   13 Total   0 Error
                  12 Success   1 Warning

Details:

	Action	Status	Message
⚠	Minimum Hardware Requirement	Warning	Messages...
✓	IIS Feature Requirement	Success	
✓	Pending Reboot Requirement	Success	
✓	Performance Monitor Counter Require...	Success	
✓	Default Installation Path Permission Re...	Success	
✓	Internet Explorer Requirement	Success	
✓	COM Plus Catalog Requirement	Success	
✓	ASP.Net Version Registration Require...	Success	

Filter ▼   Stop   Report ▼

Help   Next >

Figure 2-2   Pending Reboot Requirement indicated on the System Configuration Check page

6. On the Registration Information page, enter your name, the company name, and the 25-character CD key. Click Next to continue.

7. On the Components To Install page, select the components to install. Select one or more of the following options and then click Next:

■ **SQL Server**   Allows you to install a SQL Server instance. You can also install SQL Server 2005 as part of a cluster. If a cluster is detected, the Virtual Server option is selected by default.

- **Analysis Server**   Allows you to install an Analysis Server instance. You can also install Analysis Server as part of a cluster. If a cluster is detected, the Virtual Server option is selected by default.

- **Reporting Services**   Allows you to configure the server as a Report Server. Report Servers require IIS and the .NET Framework 2.0 or later. You will also need to install a Simple Mail Transfer Protocol (SMTP) server for sending reports or know the name of your organization's Exchange gateway.

- **Notification Services**   Allows you to install the notification engine and components for generating and sending notifications.

- **Integration Services**   Allows you to install SSIS for the purposes of ETL.

- **Workstation Components, Books Online and Development Tools**   Allows you to install SQL Native Client components, documentation, and tools.

Note   If you click Advanced instead of selecting individual options, you can customize the set of components to include in the installation. As an example, you could choose to install only the data files for the SQL Server Database Services and not the replication or full-text search components. In this way, you could create a SQL Server database installation with only the core engine.

8. As shown in Figure 2-3, you must now determine the instance type to install. To install a default instance of SQL Server, select Default, and then click Next. Otherwise, select Named Instance, type the instance name in the field provided, and then click Next.

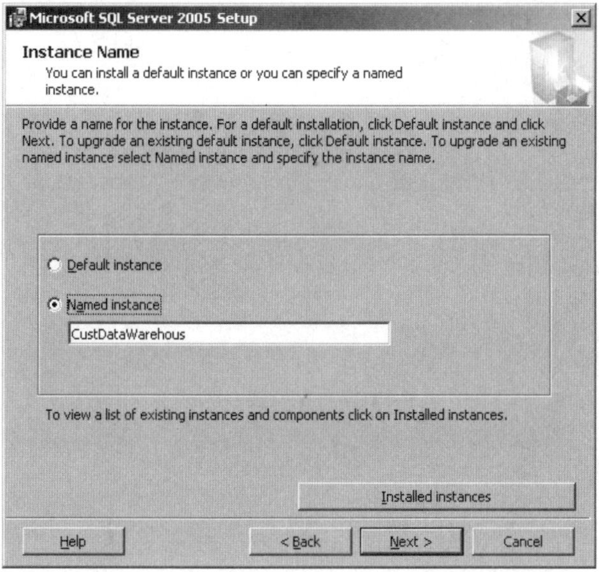

Figure 2-3   Use the options to select the instance type as either default or named

Note You can install only one default instance on a computer. If a default instance already exists, you select Default Instance only if you want to upgrade the existing default instance. The instance name can be up to 16 characters in length and must follow the naming rules for nondelimited identifiers. If you type an invalid instance name, you will see an error message and you will have to change the instance name before you can continue.

9. On the Service Account page, determine how the SQL Server and SQL Server Agent services (and if appropriate, the Analysis Services and Report Server services) will run, as shown in Figure 2-4, and then click Next. You have the following options:

- **Customize the service accounts** If you select Customize For Each Service Account, you can configure each service account individually. Use the drop-down list to configure the settings for each service before continuing.

- **No customization of service accounts** You assign a built-in system account or a specific domain user account to all SQL Server services. If the server requires resources on the local server only, use the Local System account. Otherwise, use a Domain User account.

- **Configure services startup** By selecting a service, you can specify that the service should be started at the end of setup. SQL Server is selected by default. You can also select SQL Server Agent and SQL Browser.

Figure 2-4 Service Account page with login options for SQL Server services

Real World   Use a local system account when you are configuring a SQL Server database instance that will be isolated from other servers, one that will operate independently and not connect to other servers over the network. The permissible actions, of course, depend on the permissions granted to the Local System account. If interaction with other servers is required, rather than granting additional permissions to the Local System account, you should use Domain User accounts and grant the appropriate level of permissions to these accounts.

Although the SQL Server service does not require administrator account privileges, the SQL Server Agent service does require them in some cases. Specifically, if you create CmdExec and ActiveScript jobs that belong to someone other than a SQL Server administrator or if you use the AutoRestart feature, the SQL Server Agent service does require administrator privileges. Additionally, if you are configuring Reporting Services and the report server database is on a remote server, you should use a Domain User account.

10. Use the Authentication Mode page to configure the authentication settings. The SQL Server instance can run under Microsoft Windows authentication or Mixed Mode authentication. With Windows authentication, you use only Domain User accounts to authenticate connections to the SQL Server instance. With Mixed Mode authentication, users can access the SQL Server instance using Domain User accounts or SQL Server IDs. If you've selected mixed-mode authentication, enter a strong password for the sa account. Strong passwords use a mix of numbers, letters, and special characters to make them difficult to crack. Click Next.

11. On the Collation Settings page, define the sorting behavior for the server (see Figure 2-5). If you select Customize For Each Service Account, you can specify separate collation settings for SQL Server and Analysis Services. You would then use the drop-down list options to configure separate settings for SQL Server and Analysis Services before continuing.

Note   The default Collation Designator is the Microsoft Windows locale setting for the server, such as Latin1_General. Typically, you want to use the default locale setting. Binary and Case-Sensitive are the fastest sorting orders. If the sort order is set to Binary, the other options are not available. SQL Collations are used for compatibility with earlier versions of SQL Server and are not used for Analysis Services.

Caution   While you can change the collation settings on individual databases, you cannot change the collation settings on an existing SQL Server installation without rebuilding the master database. Rebuilding the master database detaches all other databases on the server, making them unusable. For more information about this process, see the section "Changing Collation and Rebuilding the Master Database" in Chapter 6.

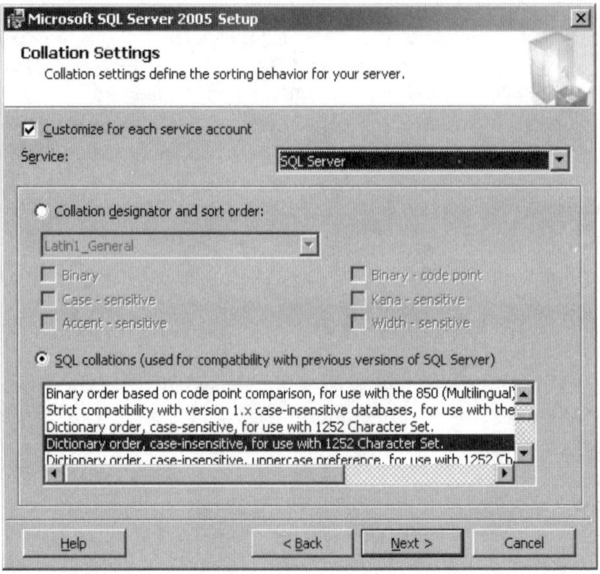

Figure 2-5 Collation Settings page options

12. If you are configuring Report Services, specify the virtual directories to use for Report Server and Report Manager, and then click Next. These directories can be accessed in a Web browser as follow:

   ❑ For the default SQL Server instance, use http://ServerName/DirectoryName, where ServerName is the host name or Domain Name System (DNS) name of the server computer and DirectoryName is the name of the virtual directory for either the Report Server or the Report Manager, such as http://corprs17/reports.

   ❑ For the default SQL Server instance, use http://ServerName/DirectoryName$InstanceName, where ServerName is the host name or DNS name of the server computer, DirectoryName is the name of the virtual directory for either the Report Server or the Report Manager, and InstanceName is the SQL Server instance to which you are connecting, such as http://corprs17/reports$webapp05.

13. If you are configuring Report Services, specify whether the report server instance should use the default configuration or not be configured at this time. Click Details to determine the default configuration values for the report server name, virtual directories and SSL settings. With the default configuration, the report server is installed on the SQL Server instance you are configuring and the names of various components reflect that instance name. So if you are installing a named SQL Server instance called CustData on EngDbSrv12, the default report server name would be ReportServer$CustData and the default

virtual directories would be http://engdbsvr12/ReportServer$CustData and
http://engdbsvr12/Reports$CustData respectively. If you don't want to use the
default configuration, you can install report server at this time and then later
use the Reporting Services Configuration tool to configure the report server.
Click Next to continue.

14. On the Error And Usage Report Settings page, choose whether to automatically report fatal error messages and feature usage data, and then click Next.
Error information is sent over Secure HTTP (HTTPS) to Microsoft by default or
to a designated corporate error reporting server if you have configured one in
Active Directory Group Policy. When Feature Usage Reporting is configured,
reports about component usage are generated and reported to Microsoft. The
intent of these reports is to help Microsoft better understand how components
and features are being used. This feature is also referred to as Customer Feedback Reporting.

15. Click Install to begin the installation process. The Setup Progress page tracks
the components that are being installed and the progress of the installation.
When Setup finishes, note the status of each installed component and check
the setup log file if there are any problems. Click Next, and then click Finish to
complete the installation process.

Real World   Notification Services are integrated with the Microsoft
.NET Framework. This allows you to use managed code with Notification
Services without having to register the Notification Services assembly.
However, if you are using unmanaged code with Notification Services, you
must register the Notification Services assembly.

At a command prompt, use the CD command to change to the .NET Framework directory for the current .NET Framework version. Then use the
Assembly Registration tool (Regasm.exe) to register the Notification Services assembly (Microsoft.SqlServer.NotificationServices.dll). Type the following command:

```
regasm /codebase /tlb
"SQLDir\microsoft.sqlserver.notificationservices.dll"
```

where SQLDir is the full directory path to the SQL Server installation,
such as:

```
regasm /codebase /tlb "%ProgramFiles%\Microsoft SQL
Server\90\NotificationServices\9.0.242\bin\microsoft.sqlserver.no
tificationservices.dll"
```

Adding Components and Instances

SQL Server keeps track of those components you have installed and those you have
not installed. If you ever want to add components and instances, you can do so by
completing the following steps:

1. Log on to the server using an account with administrator privileges. Then
insert the SQL Server 2005 CD-ROM into the CD-ROM drive.

2. If Autorun is enabled, the SQL Server 2005 Setup program should start automatically. Otherwise, double-click Splash.hta in the Servers folder of the CD-ROM.

3. Under Install, click Server Components, Tools, Books Online, And Samples. The End User License Agreement is displayed. Select I Accept The Licensing Terms And Conditions, and then click Next.

4. When the SQL Server Installation Wizard starts, click Next. The wizard will then perform a system configuration check. Note any errors and take the necessary corrective actions before continuing. If there are no required corrective actions, you can click Continue to proceed with the installation.

5. Setup will then search for installed components. On the Registration Information page, enter your name, the company name, and the 25-character CD key. Click Next to continue.

6. On the Components To Install page, select the additional components to install. Keep the following guidelines in mind:

   ❑ If you already installed the SQL Server Database Services and have an existing instance of SQL Server, the Instance Name page will have an Installed Instances button. If you click this button, you can view the component configuration details for installed instances of SQL Server, Analysis Services, and Reporting Services.

   ❑ If there is an existing default instance and you select Default Instance, Setup will assume that you want to upgrade the existing default instance. When you click Next, you will then have options to determine which related components are to be upgraded.

   ❑ If there is an existing named instance and you select Named Instance and specify the instance name, Setup will assume that you want to upgrade that instance. When you click Next, you will then have options to determine which related components are to be upgraded.

Maintaining Installed Components

You cannot use the Setup process to maintain existing components. If you want to maintain existing components, use Add Or Remove Programs in Control Panel.

In Add Or Remove Programs, each component of SQL Server 2005 is listed individually, as shown in Figure 2-6. The basic options are Change and Remove. Click Change to start the SQL Server 2005 Installation Wizard, which allows you to use Setup to modify installed subcomponents or remove the selected component entirely. Click Remove to bypass Setup and remove the selected component completely. If you want to maintain multiple components, you must select and work with each in turn.

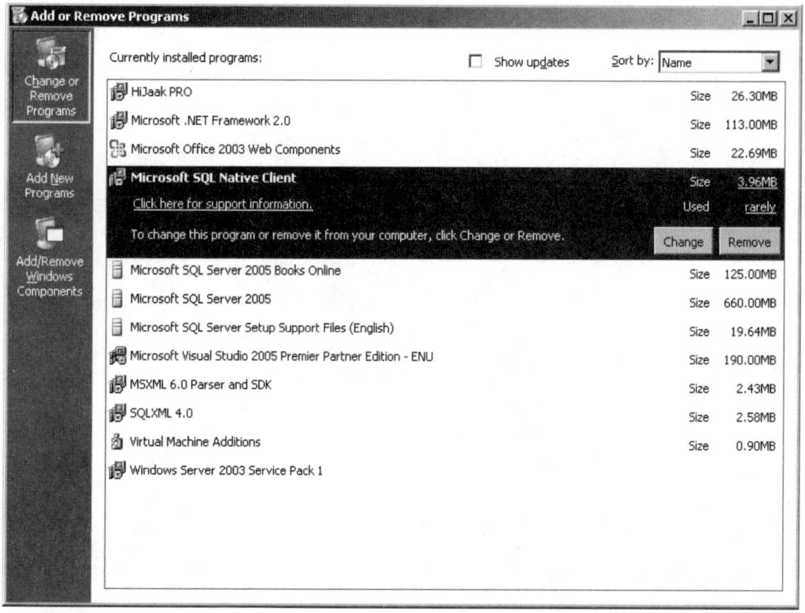

Figure 2-6 Add or Remove Programs in the Control Panel

To modify the configuration of a SQL Server component, follow these steps:

1. Select Microsoft SQL Server 2005 in Add or Remove Programs, and then click Change. When the SQL Server 2005 Maintenance Wizard starts, select the SQL Server instance to change or maintain and then click Next.

2. On the Feature Maintenance page, select the component you want to work with, such as Analysis Services or Database Engine and then click Next. This starts a system configuration check.

3. The SQL Server Installation wizard is started. Click Next to allow setup to perform a system configuration check. When the system configuration check is completed, note any issues and correct problems as necessary. Click Next.

4. Setup will then review the installed components. On the Change Or Remove Instance page, click Change.

5. On the Feature Selection page, double-click the entry for the component. This will expand the component details so you can see subcomponents. Click the icon for the subcomponent to specify its availability.

6. When you are finished modifying the component configuration, click Next, and then click Install.

Uninstalling SQL Server

Use Add Or Remove Programs in Control Panel to uninstall SQL Server or any of its components. You must uninstall each instance of the SQL Server database engine separately.

To uninstall an instance of SQL Server, complete these steps:

1. Select the SQL Server instance in Add Or Remove Programs, and then click Remove. This starts the SQL Server 2005 Uninstall wizard.

2. On the Component Selection page, select the instance and/or components to remove.

3. Click Next and then click Finish. The SQL Server 2005 Uninstall Wizard will remove the selected instances and/or components. If Setup requires access to the SQL Server CD-ROM, you will be prompted to insert the CD into the CD drive.

If you want to completely uninstall SQL Server 2005, use Add Or Remove Programs to uninstall all instances of SQL Server. Then uninstall the following components in this order:

1. Microsoft SQL Native Client

2. Microsoft SQL Server Setup Support Files

Chapter 3

Managing the Surface Security, Access, and Network Configuration

To control access to your server, few things are more important than the configuration of the SQL Server's services, components, and networking capabilities. Every SQL Server installation has a specific configuration for the services, components, and network, and the configuration determines security levels that control access in the surface area of the server such as:

- Who can access the server and by what means
- What SQL Server services run automatically at startup or manually as needed
- Where and by what means SQL Server components can connect to (or be connected from) remote resources

By limiting these who, what, and where aspects of the server's configuration, you reduce the server surface area, which improves the server security and can also enhance overall performance because you are running only necessary services and components.

Client access to SQL Server is managed through SQL Native Client Configuration parameters. SQL Server access to local and remote resources is managed through the SQL Server 2005 services and the SQL Server 2005 network configuration. You can manage client access, SQL Server services, and the network configuration using either SQL Server 2005 Surface Area Configuration or SQL Server Configuration Manager. These two tools are best used together, so you will learn how to use both tools in this chapter.

Getting Started with the Configuration Tools

SQL Server 2005 Surface Area Configuration and SQL Server Configuration Manager are found under Programs or All Programs\Microsoft SQL Server 2005\

Configuration Tools. You can also start either tool from the command line by typing sqlsac or sqlservermanager.msc at a command prompt. By default, SQL Server 2005 Surface Area Configuration and SQL Server Configuration Manager connect to the local computer. You can start SQL Server 2005 Surface Area Configuration with the focus set on a remote computer using the following syntax:

```
sqlsac RemoteComputer
```

where *RemoteComputer* is the name or IP address of the remote computer you want to work with, such as:

```
sqlsac CorpSvr04
```

 Real World   By default, SQL Server 2005 Surface Area Configuration is stored in the %ProgramFiles%\Microsoft SQL Server\90\Shared folder. By default, this folder is not added to the operating system command path. If you plan to use this tool, you can add the folder to the command path by following these steps:

1. Open a command prompt. Change to the base folder of the C drive by typing:

    ```
    cd c:\
    ```

2. Save the current path to a file by typing:

    ```
    path > origpath.txt
    ```

3. Update the path for the current command prompt by typing:

    ```
    set path=%path%;%ProgramFiles%\Microsoft SQL Server\90\Shared
    ```

4. Verify the path is set correctly by typing:

    ```
    path
    ```

5. Update the Registry to reflect the current command prompt's path by typing:

    ```
    setx PATH "%PATH%"
    ```

Be sure to type the commands with the exact case and syntax shown in these steps.

Using SQL Server 2005 Surface Area Configuration

When you start SQL Server 2005 Surface Area Configuration, you will see the main window shown in Figure 3-1. SQL Server 2005 Surface Area Configuration can be used to perform several main tasks:

■ Connect to a specific SQL Server installation

■ Manage the services configuration of a specified server

■ Manage the connections configuration of a specified server

■ Manage features of various SQL Server components

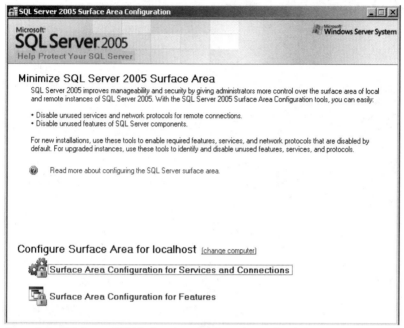

Figure 3-1 SQL Server 2005 Surface Area Configuration main window

Connecting to a Remote SQL Server Implementation

When you start SQL Server 2005 Surface Area Configuration, you are connected to the local computer by default. Once you have accessed the tool and are working with it, you can change the computer you are working with by clicking the Change Computer link provided in the interface to display the Select Computer dialog box, as shown in Figure 3-2. If you want to manage the configuration of the computer the tool is running on, select Local Computer and then click OK. If you want to manage the configuration of a remote computer, select Remote Computer, type the name of the remote computer, such as DBSvr05, and then click OK.

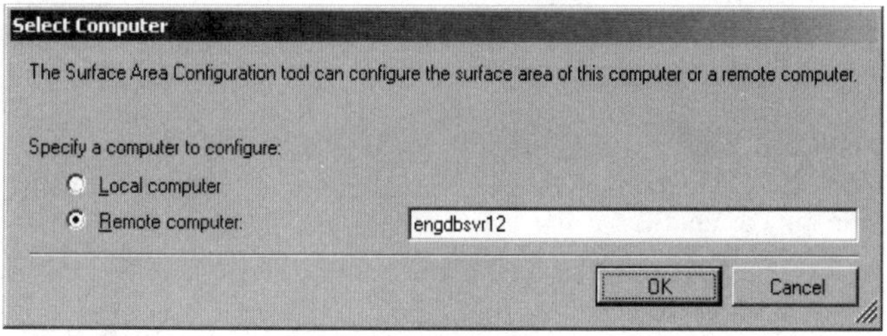

Figure 3-2 The Select Computer dialog box

Managing the Services Configuration

You can use SQL Server 2005 Surface Area Configuration to view and manage the startup state of SQL Server services. Start SQL Server 2005 Surface Area Configuration, and then click the Surface Area Configuration For Services And Connections link provided in the main interface. The tool will examine the configuration of services and connections for all running instances of SQL Server 2005 on the host to which you are currently connected. When the examination is complete, you can use the tabs provided to manage services and connections by instance or by component (see Figure 3-3). The components available depend on what you have installed and include:

- **Database Engine**   Runs as the SQL Server (*InstanceName*) service. The executable file for this service is Sqlservr.exe, and the service runs under a specific instance specified in the startup command line, such as (for the default instance, MSSQLSERVER):

```
"C:\Program Files\Microsoft SQL
    Server\MSSQL.1\MSSQL\Binn\sqlservr.exe" –sMSSQLSERVER
```

Note   Although some components, like the database engine, can be started directly from the command-line, services typically are started with the appropriate tool or with NET START. If you manually start up the database engine, you can set specific startup parameters as discussed in Chapter 4. You can also set startup parameters using the Services utility. In Services, double-click the SQL Server service for the instance with which you want to work. In the Properties dialog box, click Stop to stop the service. Enter the startup parameters in the Start Parameters field, and then click Start to start the service.

- **Analysis Services**   Runs as the Analysis Services (*InstanceName*) service. The executable file for this service is Msmdsrv.exe, and the service runs a specific initialization file specified in the startup command line, such as:

```
"C:\Program Files\Microsoft SQL Server\MSSQL.2\OLAP\bin\msmdsrv.exe"
    -s "C:\Program Files\Microsoft SQL
    Server\MSSQL.2\OLAP\Config\msmdsrv.ini"
```

The initialization file (Msmdsrv.ini) is defined using XML and should not be edited directly.

- **Reporting Services**   Runs as the Report Server (*InstanceName*) service. The executable file for this service is ReportingServicesService.exe, specified with the service startup command line, such as:

```
"C:\Program Files\Microsoft SQL Server\MSSQL.3\Reporting
    Services\ReportServer\bin\ReportingServicesService.exe"
```

- **SQL Server Agent** Runs as the SQL Server Agent (*InstanceName*) service. The executable file for this service is Sqlagent90.exe, and the service runs under a specific instance specified in the startup command line, such as:

```
"C:\Program Files\Microsoft SQL
    Server\MSSQL.1\MSSQL\Binn\SQLAGENT90.EXE" -i MSSQLSERVER
```

- **Full-Text Search** Runs as the Msftesql service. The executable file for this service is Msftesql.exe, and the service runs from a specified startup folder under a specific instance specified in the startup command line, such as:

```
"C:\Program Files\Microsoft SQL
    Server\MSSQL.1\MSSQL\Binn\msftesql.exe" -s:MSSQL.1 -f:MSSQLSERVER
```

- **Integration Services** Runs as the DTS Server service. The executable file for this service is Msdtssrvr.exe, specified with the service startup command line, such as:

```
"C:\Program Files\Microsoft SQL Server\90\DTS\Binn\MsDtsSrvr.exe"
```

- **SQL Server Browser** Runs as the SQL Browser service. The executable file for this service is Sqlbrowser.exe, specified with the service startup command line, such as:

```
"C:\Program Files\Microsoft SQL Server\90\Shared\sqlbrowser.exe"
```

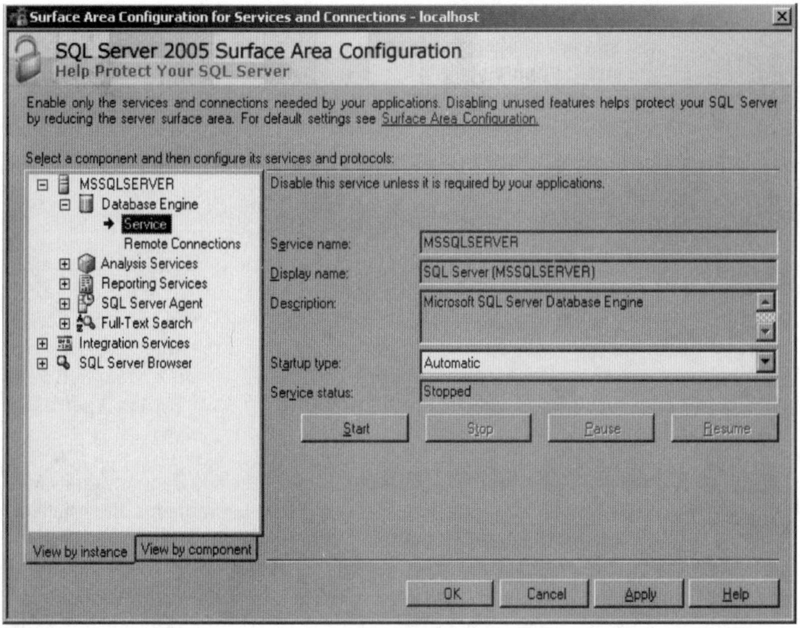

Figure 3-3 Surface Area Configuration options

To view the startup state of a service, expand the appropriate component node(s) for the SQL Server instance you want to work with. Once you have selected a component entry or a service entry, you will see a detailed entry for the service that includes the following information:

- **Service Name**   The internal name for the service used by the operating system
- **Display Name**   The common name for the service shown in the user interface
- **Description**   The related SQL Server 2005 component
- **Startup Type**   The startup state of the service—Automatic, Manual, or Disabled
- **Service Status**   The status of the service as of the last refresh, such as Running or Stopped

Any SQL Server services not being used or not required for your installation should be set to manual startup and stopped if they are running. To change the startup type or the service, select the startup type to use, and then click Apply. To stop a running service, click Stop. If you want to prevent a service from running, select Disabled as the Startup Type. Keep in mind that the SQL Server Browser service provides connection information to client computers. If clients connect to SQL Server remotely, this service is required (in most instances).

 Note   You can also use the Services utility and SQL Server Configuration Manager to manage SQL Server services. With the Services utility, you manage SQL Server services as you would any other service. With SQL Server Configuration Manager, you can manage the service logon account, the startup type, and status. If applicable, you can also manage advanced features such as dump directory, error reporting, and startup parameters. The advantage of SQL Server 2005 Surface Area Configuration and SQL Server Configuration Manager over the Services utility is that they streamline the information and only provide access to SQL Server services rather than all system services.

Managing the Connections Configuration

SQL Server installations can be configured to provide local, remote, and dedicated connections. Local connections are used by applications running on the computer that is also running SQL Server. Remote connections are used by clients connecting to the server, by applications running on other servers, and by other SQL servers. Dedicated connections are a special feature used by administrators to maintain SQL Server installations (and managed as a configurable feature rather than a permissible connection type).

 Note   The default configuration for connections depends on how you have configured service accounts, what components are installed, and other installation options, such as whether you performed an upgrade or new installation. Typically, a new installation will be configured for local connections only. However, if you have installed additional components, such as Report Services or Notification Services, the configuration will usually permit local and remote connections.

Although a configuration for only local connections provides obvious security advantages, you cannot always run SQL Servers in this configuration. Often, and more typically, you will need to allow incoming connections from remote clients and servers, and in this case, the permitted connection protocols can affect the amount of resources used and the relative security of the server. For remote connections, SQL Server 2005 can use TCP/IP, Named Pipes, or both. Because TCP/IP and Named Pipes require specific and different ports to be open across a firewall, you can limit the server to one protocol or the other to reduce the potential attack surface. Before you change the permissible connection types, however, you should make sure that all clients and applications are configured to use the appropriate network library.

Tip   With TCP/IP, SQL Server can communicate using standard IP and the TCP/IP Sockets Net-Library. The default listen port for the default instance is TCP port 1433. The default listen port for named instances is set dynamically, unless otherwise assigned. TCP port 1434 is used for client connections. When you use named pipes, SQL Server 2005 uses the Named Pipes Net-Library to communicate over a standard network address: \\.\pipe\sql\query for the default instance and \\.\pipe\MSSQL$*instancename*\sql\query for a named instance. Named pipes require a range of ports to be open for communication across a firewall. With named pipes, the server will listen on TCP port 445; NetBIOS name lookups are done on UDP port 139. With b-node broadcasts, NetBIOS name resolution requires UDP ports 137 and 138, or you can use a WINS server or LMHOSTS files.

SQL Server 2005 also supports Shared Memory protocol for local connections and Virtual Interface Architecture (VIA) for both local and remote connections. NWLink IPX/SPX and AppleTalk are no longer supported.

You can check and change the connection configuration using the following steps:

1. Start SQL Server 2005 Surface Area Configuration and then click the Surface Area Configuration For Services And Connections link provided in the main interface.

Note   SQL Server 2005 Surface Area Configuration examines the configuration of all running instances of SQL Server 2005 on the host to which you are currently connected. If you have stopped a SQL Server instance, you must start the instance to be able to manage it using this tool. You may need to close the current window and reopen it as well.

2. Expand the node for the SQL Server instance you want to work with, such as the default instance MSSQLSERVER.

3. Expand the Database Engine node and then select Remote Connections from the View By Instance tab, as shown in Figure 3-4.

4. If remote clients, applications, and servers do not need to connect to the server, select Local Connections Only in the main interface. Otherwise, select the

Local And Remote Connections option and then specify the permitted types of connections. The options are:

❑ Using TCP/IP Only

❑ Using Named Pipes Only

❑ Using both TCP/IP and Named Pipes

5. Click Apply.

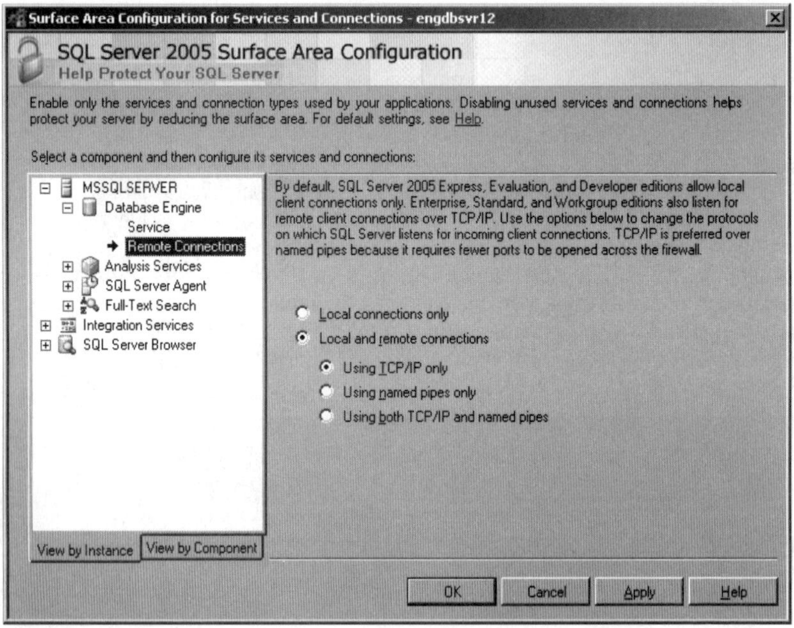

Figure 3-4   Options for configuring local and remote connections

Managing SQL Server Component Feature Access

To reduce the server surface area and improve server security, you should enable only the features needed by your clients and applications. This will limit the ways the server can be exploited by malicious users and close avenues of potential attack. Although you can manage surface area features through configuration parameters in SQL Server Management Studio and through stored procedures, the easiest way to manage surface area features is to use SQL Server 2005 Surface Area Configuration. This tool lets you manage all running instances of the SQL Server Database Engine, Analysis Services, and Reporting Services.

Tip   In a standard installation, most surface area features are disabled by default to enhance security.

You can check and manage surface area features using the following steps:

1. Start SQL Server 2005 Surface Area Configuration and then click the Surface Area Configuration For Features link provided in the main interface.

Note   SQL Server 2005 Surface Area Configuration examines the configuration of all running instances of SQL Server 2005 on the host to which you are currently connected. If you have stopped a SQL Server instance, you must start the instance to be able to manage it using this tool. You may need to close the current window and reopen it as well.

2. Expand the node for the component instance you want to work with, such as the default instance MSSQLSERVER.

3. Table 3-1 details the surface area features you can manage for the SQL Server Database Engine, Analysis Services, and Reporting Services. Select the feature you want to manage, as shown in Figure 3-5.

4. Enable the feature by selecting the check box provided. Alternately, you can disable the feature by clearing the check box if it has been selected.

5. Click Apply.

Table 3-1   Component Features for Managing Surface Area Access

Component/Feature	Description/Usage
Database Engine	
Ad Hoc Remote Queries	The OPENROWSET and OPENDATASOURCE functions can use ad hoc connections to work with remote data sources without an administrator specifically configuring linked or remote servers. If your applications or scripts use these functions, you should enable OPENROWSET and OPEN-DATASOURCE support. Otherwise, this feature should be disabled.
CLR Integration	With Common Language Runtime (CLR) Integration, you can write stored procedures, triggers, user-defined types, and user-defined functions using VB.NET, C#, and any other .NET framework language. If your applications or scripts use .NET framework languages, enable this feature. Otherwise, this feature should be disabled.
Database Mail	Database Mail replaces SQL Mail as the preferred technique for sending e-mail messages from SQL Server using Simple Mail Transfer Protocol (SMTP). Enable this feature if you have created a mail host database (by running the %ProgramFiles%\Microsoft SQL Server\MSSQL.1\MSSQL\Install\Install_DBMail_Upgrade.sql script on the server) and the necessary database mail profiles, and you want applications and scripts to be able to use the *sp_send_dbmail* stored procedure to send e-mail messages from SQL Server. Otherwise, this feature should be disabled.
DAC	Using the SQLCMD command-line utility with the –A parameter, administrators can maintain SQL Server installations using a dedicated connection from the command line, either locally or remotely. By default, only local dedicated connections are permitted. If you want to authorize remote dedicated connections, enable this feature. Otherwise, this feature should be disabled.

Table 3-1   **Component Features for Managing Surface Area Access**   *(continued)*

Component/Feature	Description/Usage
Database Engine	
Native Web Services	With Native Web Services, you can access SQL Server over HTTP using Simple Object Access Protocol (SOAP) messaging. SOAP messages contain text-based commands that are formatted with XML. If you plan to use SOAP for data exchange and have configured the necessary HTTP endpoints, you can configure the state of each endpoint as Started, Stopped, or Disabled. If no HTTP endpoints have been defined, you will not be able to configure or manage this feature. It is important to note that the Report Server Web service, SQL Server Service Broker, and Database Mirroring components make use of the Native Web Services, but they have separate configurations.
OLE Automation	OLE Automation provides the ability to use Transact-SQL batches, stored procedures, and triggers to reference SQL DMO and custom OLE Automation objects. Enable this feature if you want to be able to use OLE Automation, including the extended stored procedures *sp_OACreate, sp_OADestroy, sp_OAGetErrorInfo, sp_OAGetProperty, sp_OAMethod, sp_OASetProperty*, and *sp_OAStop*. Otherwise, this feature should be disabled.
Service Broker	Service Broker provides queuing and messaging for the database engine. Applications can use the Service Broker to communicate across instances of SQL Server. If your applications use Service Broker and you have configured the necessary HTTP endpoints, you can configure the state of each endpoint as Started, Stopped, or Disabled. If no HTTP endpoints have been defined, you will not be able to configure or manage this feature.
SQL Mail	SQL Mail can be used with legacy applications for sending e-mail messages from SQL Server using SMTP. Enable this feature if you want legacy applications and scripts to be able to use the xp_send stored procedure to send e-mail messages from SQL Server. Otherwise, this feature should be disabled.
Web Assistant	In previous versions of SQL Server, Web Assistant stored procedures could be used to generate HTML files from SQL Server data. In SQL Server 2005, Reporting Services takes the place of these stored procedures because this feature is more robust and has more configuration options. If you have legacy applications or scripts that use Web Assistant, enable this feature. Otherwise, this feature should be disabled.
xp_cmdshell	The *xp_cmdshell* executes command strings using the operating system command shell and returns the results as rows of text. If you want applications and scripts to run operating system commands, you must enable this feature. By default, only members of the sysadmin fixed server role can execute *xp_cmdshell*. You can grant execution permission to other users. For sysadmin users, *xp_cmdshell* is executed under the security context in which the SQL Server service is running. For other users, *xp_cmdshell* will impersonate the SQL Server Agent proxy account (as specified using *xp_sqlagent_proxy_account*). If the proxy account is not available, *xp_cmdshell* will fail.

Table 3-1   Component Features for Managing Surface Area Access   *(continued)*

Component/Feature	Description/Usage
Analysis Services	
Ad Hoc Data Mining Queries	The Data Mining Extensions OPENROWSET function establishes a connection to a data source object by using a provider name and connection string. This permits ad hoc connections to remote data sources without an administrator specifically configuring linked or remote servers. Enable this feature if your applications or scripts use OPENROWSET with Data Mining. Otherwise, this feature should be disabled to prevent applications and scripts from passing a provider name and connection string when using the OPENROWSET function.
Anonymous Connections	With anonymous connections, unauthenticated users can establish connections with Analysis Services. Enable this feature if your applications and scripts require unauthenticated user access. Otherwise, disable this feature.
Linked Objects	With Analysis Services, you can use linked objects to link dimensions and measure groups between servers. If you want Analysis Server to link to other servers, select Enable Links To Other Instances. If you want Analysis Server to be linked from other servers, select Enable Links From Other Instances. If dimension and measure group linking are not used, clear both check boxes to disable this feature.
User-Defined Functions	Analysis services is integrated with the .NET framework and can load assemblies containing user-defined functions. These functions can be written using the CLR or component object model (COM) objects. CLR objects and functions have an integrated security model. COM objects do not use this model, and they are therefore less secure inherently. Enable this feature if your applications and scripts require user-defined COM functions. Otherwise, disable this feature to permit only CLR functions.
Reporting Services	
Scheduled Events and Report Delivery	With Report Services, you can use ad hoc, on-demand reports and scheduled reports. Typically, when you have installed Report Services, both types of reports are enabled. If you do not use scheduled reports, you can disable this aspect of report generation and delivery by clearing the Enable Scheduled Events And Report Delivery check box.
HTTP and Web Service Requests	Report Services components use SOAP messaging over HTTP for communications and HTTP for URL access requests. These features are handled by the Report Server Web Service and permit you to work with Report Services through Report Manager, Report Builder, and SQL Server Management Studio. Typically, if Report Services are installed, the server will handle HTTP and Web Service requests. If you do not use Reporting Services, disable this feature by clearing the Enable Web Service And URL Access check box.

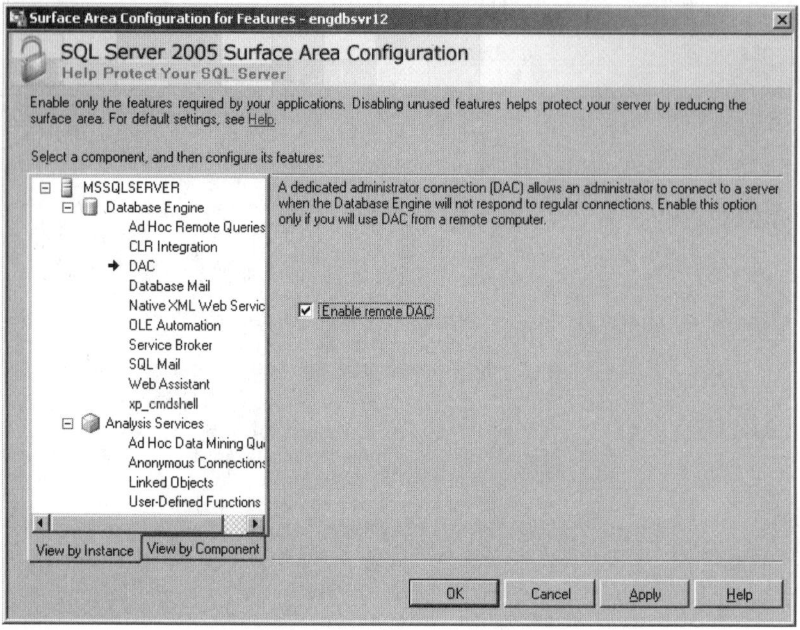

Figure 3-5   Sample check box to enable or disable surface area features

Configuring SQL Server Services

SQL Server Configuration Manager is found under Programs or
All Programs\Microsoft SQL Server 2005\Configuration Tools. It can also be
started from the command line by typing sqlservermanager.msc at a command
prompt (assuming you've modified your path appropriately). This tool provides
quick access for managing and maintaining SQL Server services.

Managing Service State and Start Mode

SQL Server Surface Area Configuration provides basic facilities for managing service startup and startup type. You can use the Services utility or SQL Server Configuration Manager to manage more advanced features. With the Services utility, you
manage SQL Server services as you would any other service. With SQL Server Configuration Manager, you can manage the service login account, the startup type,
and status. If applicable, you can also manage advanced features such as dump
directory, error reporting, and startup parameters. The advantage of SQL Server
Configuration Manager over the Services utility is that it streamlines the information available so you only see SQL Server services rather than all system services.
Additionally, some advanced options, such as the dump directory, can only be configured using SQL Server Configuration Manager.

Using SQL Server Configuration Manager, you can stop, start, pause, or restart a server service by completing the following steps:

1. Start SQL Server Configuration Manager, and then select the SQL Server 2005 Services node.

2. In the right pane, you will see a list of services used by SQL Server and its configured components (see Figure 3-6). You can work with services in several ways:

   ❑ Click the name of the service to select it. Use the Start, Pause, Stop, and Restart buttons on the menu bar to manage the service run state, or click the Properties button to view the service properties.

   ❑ Right-click or double-click the service, and then use the shortcut menu to manage the service run state, or click Properties to view the service properties.

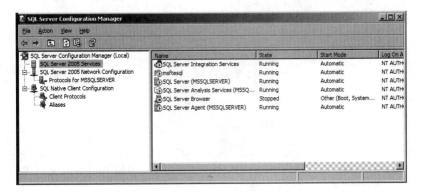

Figure 3-6   SQL Server Configuration Manager

You can set a service's start mode by following these steps:

1. Start SQL Server Configuration Manager, and then select the SQL Server 2005 Services node.

2. In the right pane, right-click the name of a service, and then select Properties from the shortcut menu.

3. On the Service tab of the Properties dialog box, use the Start Mode drop-down menu to select the desired start mode, as shown in Figure 3-7. Options include Automatic, Disabled, and Manual.

4. Click OK.

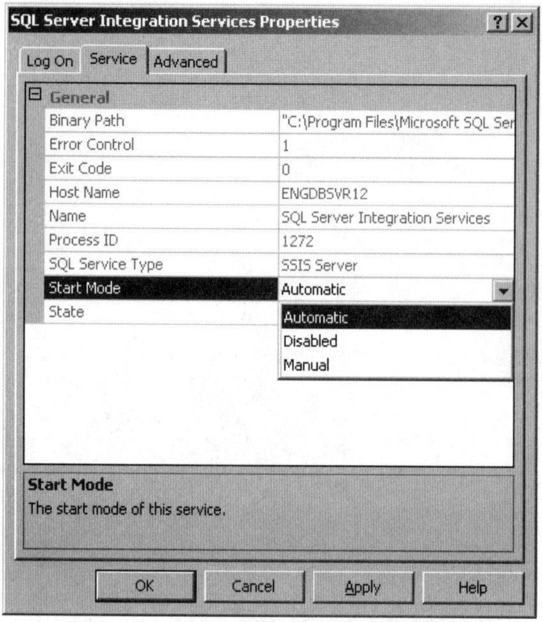

Figure 3-7   Service tab options for start mode

Setting the Startup Service Account

SQL Server and its components have specific rights and permissions from the startup service account. These permissions are used whenever the database engine or another SQL Server component performs tasks on the local system or across the network. As you learned in the section "Service Accounts for SQL Server" in Chapter 1, you can use two types of accounts: local system accounts and domain accounts. If SQL Server performs only local operations, use the local system account. Otherwise, use a properly configured domain account. That said, SQL Server does allow you to use three different built-in accounts:

- Local Service Allows SQL Server to perform operations as a system service and use local resources only.

- Local System Allows SQL Server to perform operations as part of the operating system (with Act As Part Of The Operating System rights) and use local resources only.

- Network Service Allows SQL Server to perform operations as a network service and use both local and remote resources.

You can specify a local system account for a SQL Server service by completing the following steps:

1. Start SQL Server Configuration Manager, and then select the SQL Server 2005 Services node.

2. In the right pane, right-click a service to select it, and then select Properties.

3. On the Log On tab of the Properties dialog box, select Built-In Account and then use the drop-down list to choose the service to use.

4. If the service is running, you must restart the service to stop it and start it again using the new credentials.

5. Click OK.

You can specify a domain account for a SQL Server service by completing the following steps:

1. Start SQL Server Configuration Manager, and then select the SQL Server 2005 Services node.

2. In the right pane, right-click a service to select it, and then select Properties.

3. On the Log On tab of the Properties dialog box, choose the This Account option button, as shown in Figure 3-8. Then type the designated account name and password. If necessary, specify the domain as part of the account name, such as CPANDL\sqlprimary, where CPANDL is the domain name and sqlprimary is the account name.

4. If the service is running, you must restart the service by clicking Restart to stop it and start it again using the new credentials.

5. Click OK.

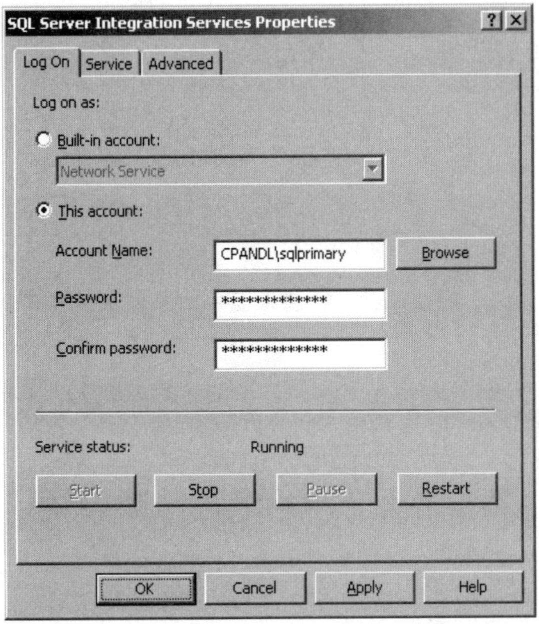

Figure 3-8 Setting the startup account for a selected service

Configuring Service Dump Directories, Error Reporting, and Customer Feedback Reporting

You can use advanced service configuration options to configure reporting and error logging features. When you install SQL Server, you are asked whether you want to enable two types of reports:

- Error reports
- Feature reports (also called Customer Feedback Reporting)

When error reporting is enabled, error reports are generated and sent to Microsoft or a designated corporate error-reporting server whenever fatal errors cause a service to terminate. Error reports help determine the cause of the fatal error so that it can be corrected, and they contain details to identify what caused the error, including the version of SQL Server being used, the operating system and hardware configuration, and data from the memory or files of the process that caused the error.

Error information is also logged in a designated dump directory. The dump directory used depends on the component and its related instance. For example, the dump directory for the default SQL Server instance might be located under %ProgramFiles%\Microsoft SQL Server\MSSQL.1\MSSQL\LOG, and the Reporting Services dump directory might be located under %ProgramFiles%\Microsoft SQL Server\MSSQL.3\Reporting Services\LogFiles.

Customer Feedback Reporting generates reports about component usage that are sent to Microsoft when this feature is configured. These reports help Microsoft understand how components and features are being used.

You can manage reporting and error dumps for each service individually. To do so, complete the following steps:

1. Start SQL Server Configuration Manager, and then select the SQL Server 2005 Services node.

2. In the right pane, right-click a service to select it, and then select Properties.

3. Select the Advanced tab in the Properties dialog box. You can now:

   ❑ Use the Dump Directory to view the current dump directory. To change the dump directory, simply enter the new directory to use. Be sure that the logon account for the selected service has appropriate read and write access to this directory.

   ❑ Use the Error Reporting and Customer Feedback Reporting drop-down menus to enable or disable reporting as appropriate. Select Yes to enable reporting. Select No to disable reporting.

4. If you have made changes and the service is running, you must restart the service by clicking Restart on the Log On tab to stop it and start it again using the new settings.

5. Click OK.

Managing the Network and SQL Native Client Configuration

In the section "Managing the Connections Configuration" earlier in this chapter, you learned that SQL Server installations can be configured to allow local and remote connections. SQL Server can use several protocols, including Shared Memory, Named Pipes, TCP/IP, and VIA. These protocols all have separate server and client configurations.

The network configuration is set separately for each server instance through the SQL Server Network Configuration. The client configuration is set on a per client basis through the SQL Native Client Configuration.

Note   Any system on which you have installed the SQL Native Client is a SQL Server client. This can include systems running Windows 2000, Windows XP Professional, and Windows Server 2003.

Configuring the Shared Memory Network Configuration

The Shared Memory protocol is used for local connections only. If the protocol is enabled, any local client can connect to the server using this protocol. If you do not want local clients to use the Shared Memory protocol, you can disable it.

You can enable or disable the Shared Memory protocol by completing the following steps:

1. Start SQL Server Configuration Manager. Expand the SQL Server 2005 Network Configuration node, and then select the Protocols For ... entry for the SQL Server instance you want to work with.

2. Right-click Shared Memory and select Properties.

3. You can now use the Enabled drop-down menu to enable or disable the protocol. Select Yes to allow the protocol to be used; select No to prevent the protocol from being used.

Configuring the Named Pipes Network Configuration

The Named Pipes protocol is used primarily for local or remote connections by applications written for Windows NT, Windows 98 and earlier versions of the Windows operating system. When you enable Named Pipes, SQL Server 2005 uses the Named Pipes Net-Library to communicate over a standard network address: \\.\pipe\sql\query for the default instance and \\.\pipe\MSSQL$*instancename*\sql\query for a named instance. In addition to enabling or disabling the use of Named Pipes, you can configure properties of this protocol to change the named pipe to use.

You can manage the Named Pipes network configuration by completing the following steps:

1. Start SQL Server Configuration Manager. Expand the SQL Server 2005 Network Configuration node, and then select the Protocols For ... entry for a SQL Server instance.

2. Right-click Named Pipes and select Properties.

3. You can now:

   ❑ Use the Enabled drop-down menu to enable or disable the protocol. Select Yes to allow the protocol to be used; select No to prevent the protocol from being used.

   ❑ Change the name of the default pipe by typing a new value in the Pipe Name field. (Don't forget to update the client configuration.)

4. Click OK.

Configuring the TCP/IP Network Configuration

The TCP/IP protocol is the preferred protocol for local or remote connections to SQL Server. When you use TCP/IP, SQL Server listens on a specific TCP port and IP address for requests. By default, SQL Server listens on TCP port 1433 on all IP addresses. Each IP address on the server can be configured separately, or you can configure all IP addresses for listening.

You can disable TCP/IP by completing the following steps:

1. Start SQL Server Configuration Manager. Expand the SQL Server 2005 Network Configuration node, and then select the Protocols For ... entry for a SQL Server instance.

2. Right-click TCP/IP and select Disable.

You can manage the TCP/IP network configuration by completing the following steps:

1. Start SQL Server Configuration Manager. Expand the SQL Server 2005 Network Configuration node, and then select the Protocols For ... entry for a SQL Server instance.

2. Right-click TCP/IP and select Properties. On the IP Addresses tab of the TCP/IP Properties dialog box, you should see entries representing the IP addresses configured on the server. Individual IP address entries, in numerical order, such as IP1, IP2, IP3, and so on, are for listening on a specific IP address. The IPAll entry configures SQL Server to listen on all IP addresses on the server.

 Note The IP address 127.0.0.1 is the local loopback address. This address is used to listen for connections from local clients.

3. If you want SQL Server to listen on all IP addresses on the server, you should set all individual IP address entries to Active Yes and Enabled No. Then set a specific TCP listen port for IPAll. The default is 1433. To change the TCP listen port, right-click IPAll and select Properties. In the Properties dialog box, type the TCP listen port in the field provided, and then click OK.

4. If you want to enable listening on a specific IP address and TCP port, right-click the individual IP entry, and then select Properties. Set Active to Yes, and then set Enabled to Yes. Type the TCP listen port in the field provided and click OK.

Configuring the Native Client Protocol Order

When multiple client protocols are available and configured for use, clients use the protocols in a specified priority order. The default order is:

1. Shared Memory
2. TCP/IP
3. Named Pipes

Shared Memory is always the preferred local connection protocol. You can disable Shared Memory protocol to preclude its use and change the order of the other protocols by completing the following steps:

1. Start SQL Server Configuration Manager. Expand SQL Native Client Configuration, and then click Client Protocols.

2. Right-click any of the protocols listed, and then select Order. The Client Protocols Properties dialog box displays, as shown in Figure 3-9.

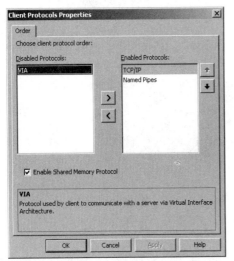

Figure 3-9   Client Protocols Properties dialog box

3. In the Client Protocols Properties dialog box, you can:

    ❑ Change the order of an enabled protocol. First click the name of the protocol you want to move, and then use the arrow buttons to the right of the Enabled Protocols list as appropriate until the protocol is positioned where you want it in the list.

    ❑ Disable or enable protocols. To disable an enabled protocol, select it, and then click the shift left button to move the name of the protocol to the Disabled Protocols list. To enable a disabled protocol, select it, and then click the shift right button to move the name of the protocol to the Enabled Protocols list.

    ❑ Enable or disable Shared Memory protocol. To enable Shared Memory protocol for local client connections, select Enable Shared Memory Protocol. To disable Shared Memory protocol for local client connections, clear Enable Shared Memory Protocol.

4. Click OK.

Configuring the Shared Memory Native Client Configuration

The Shared Memory protocol is used for local client connections only. You can enable or disable the Shared Memory protocol for clients by completing the following steps:

1. Start SQL Server Configuration Manager. Expand SQL Server 2005 Network Configuration, SQL Native Client Configuration, and then click Client Protocols.

2. Right-click Shared Memory and then select Properties.

3. You can now use the Enabled drop-down menu to enable or disable the protocol. Select Yes to allow the protocol to be used; select No to prevent the protocol from being used.

Configuring the TCP/IP Native Client Configuration

The TCP/IP protocol is the preferred protocol for local or remote connections to SQL Server. When connecting to a default instance of the Database Engine using TCP/IP, the client must know the TCP port value. Thus, if a default instance has been configured to listen on a different port, you must change the client TCP/IP configuration to that port number. When connecting to a named instance of Database Engine, the client will attempt to obtain the port number from the SQL Browser Service on the server to which it is connecting. If the SQL Browser Service is not running, the TCP port number must be provided in the client configuration or as part of the connection string.

You can configure the TCP/IP client configuration by completing the following steps:

1. Start SQL Server Configuration Manager. Expand SQL Native Client Configuration, and then click Client Protocols.

2. If you want to enable or disable TCP/IP, right-click TCP/IP, and then select Enable or Disable as appropriate.

3. To view TCP/IP connection properties, right-click TCP/IP, and then select Properties.

4. To set the default port, select Properties. In the TCP/IP Properties dialog box, enter the default port for the client in the field provided.

5. You can also configure parameters that control whether and how the client tries to maintain idle TCP/IP connections. Two parameters are used:

   ■ **Keep Alive** Controls when a client first tries to verify that an idle connection is still valid and attempts to maintain the connection. By default, the client checks a connection after it has been idle for 30,000 milliseconds (30 seconds). In most cases, a value between 30 and 60 seconds will suffice. Depending on how busy the server is and the importance of client activity, you might want to verify and maintain idle connections more quickly, which can ensure that idle connections are not terminated. For example, you could use a smaller value, such as 15,000 or 20,000 milliseconds, to ensure idle connections are validated faster.

   ■ **Keep Alive Interval** Controls how frequently a client rechecks an idle connection when there is no initial response to the KEEPALIVE transmission. By default, the client retransmits the KEEPALIVE request every 1,000 milliseconds (1 second). If many clients are connecting to a busy server, you might want to lengthen the Keep Alive interval to decrease the number of KEEPALIVE retransmissions.

6. Click OK.

Configuring the Named Pipes Native Client Configuration

The Named Pipes protocol is used primarily for local or remote connections by applications written for Windows NT, Windows 98 or earlier versions of the Windows operating system. The default Named Pipes are \\.\pipe\sql\query for the default instance and \\.\pipe\MSSQL$*instancename*\sql\query for a named instance. The default pipe for clients is set using an alias. The standard alias for clients is sql\query, which refers to the default pipe, such as \\.\pipe\sql\query or \\.\pipe\MSSQL$*instancename*\sql\query. If you changed the default pipe in the server's network configuration, you will need to change the default pipe in the client configuration (and for all clients that will connect to SQL Server in this way). For example, if SQL Server is using \\.\pipe\sqlserver\app1 as the default pipe, then the client must use \sqlserver\app1 as the Pipe Name.

You can manage the Named Pipes client configuration by completing the following steps:

1. Start SQL Server Configuration Manager. Expand SQL Native Client Configuration, and then click Client Protocols.

2. Right-click Named Pipes and select Properties. You can now:

   ❑ Use the Enabled drop-down menu to enable or disable the protocol. Select Yes to allow the protocol to be used; select No to prevent the protocol from being used.

   ❑ Set the default pipe. In the Named Pipes Properties dialog box, enter the default pipe for the client in the field provided, and then click OK.

Chapter 4

Configuring and Tuning Microsoft SQL Server

As with SQL Server 2000, SQL Server 2005 is designed to balance the workload dynamically and to self-tune configuration settings. For example, SQL Server can increase or decrease memory usage dynamically based on overall system memory requirements. SQL Server also manages memory efficiently, especially when it comes to queries and user connections—and memory is just one of dozens of areas in which the configuration is automatically adjusted.

Although the SQL Server self-tuning feature works well, there are times when you will need to configure SQL Server settings manually. For example, if you are running a large database with special constraints and the database is not working the way you expect it to perform, you may want to customize the configuration. You may also need to modify configuration settings for SQL Server accounts, authentication, and auditing. Key tools you will use to configure and tune SQL Server include the following:

- **System Catalog Queries** Provide a direct way to determine database configuration characteristics and their related settings.

- **Stored Procedures** Lets you view and manage configuration settings through stored procedures, such as *sp_configure* and *sp_dboption*. Note that you can change some options of *sp_configure* only when Show Advanced Options is set to 1, as in the following example:

```
exec sp_configure "show advanced options", 1
```

- **SQL Server Management Studio** Provides an easy-to-use interface that updates the database and registry settings for you.

- **SQLServr.exe** Starts SQL Server from the command line, and you can use it to set configuration parameters at startup.

In this chapter, we will examine the structures available for configuring and tuning SQL Server. We start with a look at the SQL Server 2005 system catalog, and then continue with a discussion of catalog queries and stored procedures. This discussion provides the essential background for understanding how to configure and tune SQL Server 2005. The next chapter, Chapter 5, "Managing the Enterprise," provides details about using SQL Server Management Studio and SQLServr.exe.

Accessing SQL Server Configuration Data

SQL Server 2005 uses an object-based approach to representing servers, databases, and all of their configuration characteristics and data contents. At the heart of this object-based structure is the system catalog, which describes the objects in a particular instance of SQL Server along with their attributes. For example, attributes of a database describe:

- The number and names of the tables and views.
- The number and names of columns in a table or view.
- The column data type, scale, and precision.
- The triggers and constraints that are defined on a table.
- The indexes and keys that are defined for a table.
- The statistics used by query optimizer for generating query plans.

In queries, you can access this and other system catalog information using:

- **Catalog views**   Provide access to metadata stored in a database, which includes database attributes and their values. Catalog views can be used to access all user-available metadata, except for replication, backup, database maintenance plan, and SQL Agent metadata.
- **Compatibility views**   Provide access to many of the system tables from earlier releases of SQL Server using SQL Server 2005 views. These views are meant for backward compatibility only, and they expose the same metadata that was available in the SQL Server 2000. They do not expose metadata for new SQL Server 2005 features, such as database partitioning and mirroring.
- **Information Schema views**   Provide access to a subset of metadata stored in a database, which includes database attributes and their values. Information Schema views are based on catalog view definitions in the SQL-92 standard and do not contain metadata specific to SQL Server 2005. Applications that use these views are portable between heterogeneous SQL-92-compliant database systems.
- **ODBC catalog functions**   Provide an interface that open database connectivity (ODBC) drivers can use to return result sets containing system catalog information. The result sets present catalog information in a way that is independent of the structure of the underlying catalog tables.
- **OLE DB schema rowsets**   Provide an IDBSchemaRowset interface that OLE DB providers can use to access system catalog information. The rowsets present catalog information independently from the structure of the underlying catalog tables.
- **System stored procedures and functions**   Provide Transact-SQL stored procedures and functions that return catalog information.

Catalog views and stored procedures are the methods recommended to access a database's metadata. This is primarily because catalog views present metadata in a format that is independent of any catalog table implementation, which means that the views are not affected by changes in the underlying catalog tables. When you want to configure or manage a server, you will typically use stored procedures to help you perform the necessary tasks. Stored procedures provide the necessary functionality to view and manage the configuration of SQL Server and related databases with ease.

Working with the System Catalog and Catalog Views

Catalog views contain information used by the SQL Server 2005 Database Engine. They provide the most general interface to the catalog metadata and are the most direct way to access and work with this information. All user-available metadata in the system catalog is exposed through catalog views. Catalog views do not contain information about replication, backup, database maintenance plan, or SQL Agent.

Like all structures in SQL Server 2005 databases, catalog views follow an object-based hierarchy in which lower-level objects inherit attributes of higher-level objects. Some catalog views inherit rows from other catalog views. For example, the Tables catalog view inherits all the columns of the Objects catalog view. Thus, in addition to columns that are specific to the Tables catalog view itself, the Tables catalog view has all the columns from the Objects catalog view. Table 4-1 summarizes the SQL Server 2005 catalog views and their uses.

Table 4-1   SQL Server 2005 Catalog Views

View Type	Description	Key Catalog Views
CLR Assembly Catalog views	Describe Common Language Runtime (CLR) assemblies.	sys.assemblies sys.assembly_files sys.assembly_references
Databases and Files Catalog views	Describe databases, database files, and backup devices associated with a SQL Server instance.	sys.backup_devices sys.database_files sys.databases sys.master_files
Database Mirroring Catalog views	Describe witness roles that a server plays as a database mirroring partner.	sys.database_mirroring_witnesses
Data Spaces and Full-Text Catalog views	Describe filegroups, partition schemes, and full-text catalogs.	sys.data_spaces sys.destination_data_spaces sys.filegroups sys.fulltext_catalogs sys.partition_schemes
Endpoints Catalog views	Describe endpoints used for mirroring, service broker messaging, and Web services.	sys.database_mirroring_endpoints sys.endpoint_webmethods sys.endpoints sys.http_endpoints sys.service_broker_endpoints sys.soap_endpoints sys.tcp_endpoints sys.via_endpoints
Extended Properties Catalog views	Describe extended properties and the class of objects from which they originate.	sys.extended_properties

Table 4-1   SQL Server 2005 Catalog Views   *(continued)*

View Type	Description	Key Catalog Views
Linked Servers Catalog views	Describe linked or remote servers and their related logins.	sys.linked_logins sys.remote_logins sys.servers
Messages (for Errors) Catalog views	Describe system-defined and user-defined error messages.	sys.messages
Objects Catalog views	Describe top-level database objects.	sys.allocation_units sys.assembly_modules sys.check_constraints sys.columns sys.computed_columns sys.default_constraints sys.event_notifications sys.events sys.extended_procedures sys.stats sys.foreign_key_columns sys.foreign_keys sys.fulltext_index_columns sys.fulltext_indexes sys.identity_columns sys.index_columns sys.indexes sys.key_constraints sys.numbered_procedures sys.numbered_procedure_parameters sys.objects sys.parameters sys.partitions sys.procedures sys.service_queues sys.sql_dependencies sys.sql_modules sys.stats_columns sys.synonyms sys.tables sys.traces sys.trigger_events sys.triggers sys.views
Partition Function Catalog views	Describe partition functions, parameters, and range values.	sys.partition_functions sys.partition_parameters sys.partition_range_values
Scalar Types Catalog views	Describe user-defined scalar types for CLR assemblies as well as other system- and user-defined scalar types.	sys.assembly_types sys.types
Schemas Catalog views	Describe database schemas.	sys.schemas
Security Catalog views	Describe server-level, database-level, and encryption security attributes and values.	Database-level views (sys.database_permissions, sys.database_principals, sys.database_role_members) Server-level views (sys.server_permissions, sys.server_principals, sys.server_role_members, sys.sql_logins) Encryption views (sys.asymmetric_keys, sys.certificates, sys.credentials, sys.crypt_properties, sys.key_encryptions, sys.symmetric_keys)

Table 4-1   SQL Server 2005 Catalog Views   *(continued)*

View Type	Description	Key Catalog Views
Service Broker Catalog views	Describe Service Broker endpoints and messaging components.	sys.conversation_endpoints sys.conversation_groups sys.remote_service_bindings sys.service_contract_message_usages sys.service_contract_usages sys.routes sys.service_contracts sys.service_message_types sys.services sys.transmission_queue
Server-Wide Configuration Catalog views	Describe server-wide configuration option values.	sys.configurations sys.fulltext_languages sys.trace_categories sys.trace_columns sys.trace_event_bindings sys.trace_events sys.traces sys.trace_subclass_values
XML Schemas (XML Type System) Catalog views	Describe XML Schema components and values.	sys.xml_indexes sys.xml_schema_attributes sys.xml_schema_collections sys.xml_schema_component_placements sys.xml_schema_components sys.xml_schema_elements sys.xml_schema_facets sys.xml_schema_model_groups sys.xml_schema_namespaces sys.xml_schema_types sys.xml_schema_wildcard_namespaces sys.xml_schema_wildcards

Table 4-2 provides mapping between SQL Server 2000 system tables and SQL Server 2005 system views. The entries are organized by database and view type. Mappings for the *master* database are followed by mappings for all databases.

Table 4-2   Mapping SQL Server 2000 System Tables to SQL Server 2005 System Views

SQL Server 2000 System Table	SQL Server 2005 System View	SQL Server 2005 View Type
Master Database		
sysaltfiles	sys.master_files	Catalog view
syscacheobjects	sys.dm_exec_cached_plans	Dynamic management view
syscharsets	sys.syscharsets	Compatibility view
sysconfigures	sys.configurations	Catalog view
syscurconfigs	sys.configurations	Catalog view
sysdatabases	sys.databases	Catalog view
sysdevices	sys.backup_devices	Catalog view
syslanguages	sys.languages	Compatibility view
syslockinfo	sys.dm_tran_locks	Dynamic management view
syslocks	sys.dm_tran_locks	Dynamic management view
syslogins	sys.server_principals	Catalog view
sysmessages	sys.messages	Catalog view

Table 4-2   Mapping SQL Server 2000 System Tables to SQL Server 2005 System Views *(continued)*

SQL Server 2000 System Table	SQL Server 2005 System View	SQL Server 2005 View Type
Master Database		
sysoledbusers	sys.linked_logins	Catalog view
sysopentapes	sys.dm_io_backup_tapes	Dynamic management view
sysperfinfo	sys.dm_os_performance_counters	Dynamic management view
sysprocesses	sys.dm_exec_connections sys.dm_evec_sessions sys.dm_exec_requests	Dynamic management views
sysremotelogins	sys.remote_logins	Catalog view
sysservers	sys.servers	Catalog view
All Databases		
syscolumns	sys.columns	Catalog view
syscomments	sys.sql_modules	Catalog view
sysconstraints	sys.check_constraints sys.default_constraints sys.key_constraints sys.foreign_keys	Catalog views
sysdepends	sys.sql_dependencies	Catalog view
sysfilegroups	sys.filegroups	Catalog view
sysfiles	sys.database_files	Catalog view
sysforeignkeys	sys.foreign_keys	Catalog view
sysfulltextcatalogs	sys.fulltext_catalogs	Catalog view
sysindexes	sys.indexes	Catalog view
sysindexkeys	sys.index_columns	Catalog view
sysmembers	sys.databases_role_members	Catalog view
sysobjects	sys.objects	Catalog view
syspermissions	sys.database_permissions, sys.server_permissions	Catalog views
sysprotects	sys.database_permissions, sys.server_permissions	Catalog views
sysreferences	sys.foreign_keys	Catalog view
systypes	sys.types	Catalog view
sysusers	sys.database_principals	Catalog view

Working with System Stored Procedures

You can use system stored procedures to view SQL Server configuration details and to perform general administration. SQL Server 2005 has two main categories of system stored procedures:

- Those meant for administrators
- Those used to implement functionality for database application programming interfaces (APIs)

Naturally, you will want to work with system stored procedures meant for administration and not those that implement database API functions. System stored procedures are written using Transact-SQL (T-SQL). Most return a value of 0 to indicate success and a nonzero value to indicate failure. As an example, *sp_dboption* is a stored procedure for managing the configuration options of SQL Server databases (except for the *master* and *tempdb* databases). When you use *sp_dboption* to set a database configuration value, a return code of 0 indicates that the option was set as expected. A return code of 1 indicates that the stored procedure failed and the option was not set as expected.

The following example takes the *Personnel* database offline if there are no current users:

```
USE master;

GO

EXEC sp_dboption "Personnel", "offline", "TRUE";

GO
```

If the stored procedure returns 0, then the database was successfully taken offline. A return value of 1 indicates that there was a problem taking the database offline, which means that the database is still online. For more information on using stored procedures, see the section titled "Configuring SQL Server Stored Procedures" later in this chapter.

Table 4-3 provides a summary of stored procedures for administration. The table entries are organized by the type of administration activity for which the stored procedure is designed.

Table 4-3   Key System Stored Procedures by Type

Stored Procedure Type	Description	Related System Stored Procedures
Active Directory Stored Procedures	Register instances of SQL Server and SQL Server databases in Active Directory.	*sp_ActiveDirectory_Obj, sp_ActiveDirectory_SCP*
Catalog Stored Procedures	Implement ODBC data dictionary functions.	*sp_column_privileges, sp_columns, sp_databases, sp_fkeys, sp_pkeys, sp_server_info, sp_special_columns, sp_sproc_columns, sp_statistics, sp_stored_procedures, sp_table_privileges, sp_tables*
Cursor Stored Procedures	Implement cursor variable functionality.	*sp_cursor_list, sp_describe_cursor, sp_describe_cursor_columns, sp_describe_cursor_tables*
Database Engine Stored Procedures	Maintain SQL Server instances and perform general administration activities.	*sp_add_data_file_recover_suspect_db, sp_add_log_file_recover_suspect_db, sp_addextendedproc, sp_addextendedproperty, sp_addmessage, sp_addtype, sp_addumpdevice, sp_altermessage, sp_attach_db, sp_attach_single_file_db,*

Table 4-3 **Key System Stored Procedures by Type** *(continued)*

Stored Procedure Type	Description	Related System Stored Procedures
		sp_autostats, sp_bindefault, sp_bindrule, sp_bindsession, sp_certify_removable, sp_configure, sp_create_removable, sp_createstats, sp_cycle_errorlog, sp_datatype_info, sp_dbcmptlevel, sp_dboption, sp_dbremove, sp_delete_backuphistory, sp_depends, sp_detach_db, sp_dropdevice, sp_dropextendedproc, sp_dropextendedproperty, sp_dropmessage, sp_droptype, sp_executesql, sp_getapplock, sp_getbindtoken, sp_help, sp_helpconstraint, sp_helpdb, sp_helpdevice, sp_helpextendedproc, sp_helpfile, sp_helpfilegroup, sp_helpindex, sp_helplanguage, sp_helpserver, sp_helpsort, sp_helpstats, sp_helptext, sp_helptrigger, sp_indexoption, sp_invalidate_textptr, sp_lock, sp_monitor, sp_procoption, sp_recompile, sp_refreshview, sp_releaseapplock, sp_rename, sp_renamedb, sp_resetstatus, sp_serveroption, sp_setnetname, sp_settriggerorder, sp_spaceused, sp_tableoption, sp_unbindefault, sp_unbindrule, sp_updateextendedproperty, sp_updatestats, sp_validname, sp_who
Database Mail Stored Procedures	Perform e-mail operations from within SQL Server.	*sp_send_dbmail,* sysmail_add_account_sp, sysmail_add_principalprofile_sp, sysmail_add_profile_sp, sysmail_add_profileaccount_sp, sysmail_configure_sp, sysmail_delete_account_sp, sysmail_delete_principalprofile_sp, sysmail_delete_profile_sp, sysmail_delete_profileaccount_sp, sysmail_help_account_sp, sysmail_help_configure_sp, sysmail_help_principalprofile_sp, sysmail_help_profile_sp, sysmail_help_profileaccount_sp, sysmail_start_sp, sysmail_stop_sp, sysmail_update_account_sp, sysmail_update_principalprofile_sp, sysmail_update_profile_sp, sysmail_update_profileaccount_sp
Database Maintenance Plan Stored Procedures	Configure and manage database maintenance plans and related tasks.	*sp_add_maintenance_plan, sp_add_maintenance_plan_db, sp_add_maintenance_plan_job, sp_delete_maintenance_plan, sp_delete_maintenance_plan_db, sp_delete_maintenance_plan_job, sp_help_maintenance_plan*

Table 4-3   Key System Stored Procedures by Type   *(continued)*

Stored Procedure Type	Description	Related System Stored Procedures
Distributed Queries Stored Procedures	Implement and manage Distributed Queries.	*sp_addlinkedserver, sp_addlinkedsrvlogin, sp_catalogs, sp_column_privileges_ex, sp_columns_ex, sp_droplinkedsrvlogin, sp_foreignkeys, sp_indexes, sp_linkedservers, sp_primarykeys, sp_serveroption, sp_table_privileges_ex, sp_tables_ex, sp_testlinkedserver*
Full-Text Search Stored Procedures	Implement and query full-text indexes.	*sp_fulltext_catalog, sp_fulltext_column, sp_fulltext_database, sp_fulltext_service, sp_fulltext_table, sp_help_fulltext_catalogs, sp_help_fulltext_catalogs_cursor, sp_help_fulltext_columns, sp_help_fulltext_columns_cursor, sp_help_fulltext_tables, sp_help_fulltext_tables_cursor*
General Extended Stored Procedures	Provide an interface from SQL Server to external programs, primarily for server maintenance.	*xp_cmdshell, xp_enumgroups, xp_findnextmsg, xp_grantlogin, xp_logevent, xp_loginconfig, xp_logininfo, xp_msver, xp_revokelogin, xp_sprintf, xp_sqlmaint, xp_sscanf*
Log Shipping Stored Procedures	Implement, manage, and monitor log ship-ping configurations.	*sp_add_log_shipping_alert_job, sp_add_log_shipping_primary_database, sp_add_log_shipping_primary_secondary, sp_add_log_shipping_secondary_database, sp_add_log_shipping_secondary_primary, sp_change_log_shipping_primary_database, sp_change_log_shipping_secondary_database, sp_change_log_shipping_secondary_primary, sp_cleanup_log_shipping_history, sp_delete_log_shipping_alert_job, sp_delete_log_shipping_primary_database, sp_delete_log_shipping_primary_secondary, sp_delete_log_shipping_secondary_database, sp_delete_log_shipping_secondary_primary, sp_help_log_shipping_alert_job, sp_help_log_shipping_monitor_primary, sp_help_log_shipping_monitor_secondary, sp_help_log_shipping_primary_database, sp_help_log_shipping_primary_secondary, sp_help_log_shipping_secondary_database, sp_help_log_shipping_secondary_primary, sp_refresh_log_shipping_monitor, sp_resolve_logins*
Notification Services Stored Procedures	Manage, debug, and troubleshoot Microsoft SQL Server 2005 Notification Services.	NSAdministrationHistory, NSDiagnosticDeliveryChannel, NSDiagnosticEventClass, NSDiagnosticEventProvider, NSDiagnosticFailedNotifications, NSDiagnosticNotificationClass, NSDiagnosticSubscriptionClass,

Table 4-3 Key System Stored Procedures by Type *(continued)*

Stored Procedure Type	Description	Related System Stored Procedures
		NSEventBatchDetails, NSEventBeginBatch<EventClassName>, NSEventFlushBatch<EventClassName>, NSEventSubmitBatch<EventClassName>, NSEventWrite<EventClassName>, NSExecuteRuleFiring, NSNotificationBatchDetails, NSNotificationBatchDetails, NSNotificationBatchList, NSPrepareRuleFiring, NSQuantumDetails, NSQuantumExecutionTime, NSQuantumFailures, NSQuantumList, NSQuantumPerformance, NSQuantumsSkipped, NSScheduledSubscriptionDetails, NSScheduledSubscriptionList, NSSetQuantumClock, NSSetQuantumClockDate, NSSnapshotApplications, NSSnapshotDeliveryChannels, NSSnapshotEvents, NSSnapshotProviders, NSSnapshotSubscriptions, NSSubscriptionConditionInformation, NSVacuum
OLE Automation Stored Procedures	Create and manage OLE automation objects.	*sp_OACreate, sp_OADestroy, sp_OAGetErrorInfo, sp_OAGetProperty, sp_OAMethod, sp_OASetProperty, sp_OAStop*
Security Stored Procedures	Manage server and database security.	*sp_addalias, sp_addapprole, sp_addgroup, sp_addlinkedsrvlogin, sp_addlogin, sp_addremotelogin, sp_addrole, sp_addrolemember, sp_addserver, sp_addsrvrolemember, sp_adduser, sp_approlepassword, sp_change_users_login, sp_changedbowner, sp_changegroup, sp_changeobjectowner, sp_dbfixedrolepermission, sp_defaultdb, sp_defaultlanguage, sp_denylogin, sp_dropalias, sp_dropapprole, sp_dropgroup, sp_droplinkedsrvlogin, sp_droplogin, sp_dropremotelogin, sp_droprolemember, sp_dropserver, sp_dropsrvrolemember, sp_dropuser, sp_grantdbaccess, sp_grantlogin, sp_helpdbfixedrole, sp_helpgroup, sp_helplinkedsrvlogin, sp_helplogins, sp_helpntgroup, sp_helpremotelogin, sp_helprole, sp_helprolemember, sp_helpprotect, sp_helpsrvrole, sp_helpsrvrolemember, sp_helpuser, sp_MShasdbaccess, sp_password, sp_remoteoption, sp_revokedbaccess, sp_revokelogin, sp_setapprole, sp_srvrolepermission, sp_validatelogins*

Table 4-3   Key System Stored Procedures by Type   (continued)

Stored Procedure Type	Description	Related System Stored Procedures
SQL Mail Stored Procedures	Perform e-mail operations from within SQL Server. (In SQL Server 2005, Database Mail is preferred over SQL Mail.)	sp_processmail, xp_deletemail, xp_findnextmsg, xp_readmail, xp_sendmail, xp_startmail, xp_stopmail
SQL Server Profiler Stored Procedures	Used by SQL Profiler to monitor performance and activity.	sp_trace_create, sp_trace_generateevent, sp_trace_setevent, sp_trace_setfilter, sp_trace_setstatus
SQL Server Agent Stored Procedures	Manage scheduled alerts and other SQL Server Agent activities.	sp_add_alert, sp_add_category, sp_add_job, sp_add_jobschedule, sp_add_jobserver, sp_add_jobstep, sp_add_notification, sp_add_operator, sp_add_proxy, sp_add_schedule, sp_add_targetservergroup, sp_add_targetsvrgrp_member, sp_apply_job_to_targets, sp_attach_schedule, sp_cycle_agent_errorlog, sp_cycle_errorlog, sp_delete_alert, sp_delete_category, sp_delete_job, sp_delete_jobschedule, sp_delete_jobserver, sp_delete_jobstep, sp_delete_jobsteplog, sp_delete_notification, sp_delete_operator, sp_delete_proxy, sp_delete_schedule, sp_delete_targetserver, sp_delete_targetservergroup, sp_delete_targetsvrgrp_member, sp_detach_schedule, sp_enum_login_for_proxy, sp_enum_proxy_for_subsystem, sp_enum_sqlagent_subsystems, sp_grant_login_to_proxy, sp_grant_proxy_to_subsystem, sp_help_alert, sp_help_category, sp_help_downloadlist, sp_help_job, sp_help_jobactivity, sp_help_jobcount, sp_help_jobhistory, sp_help_jobs_in_schedule, sp_help_jobschedule, sp_help_jobserver, sp_help_jobstep, sp_help_jobsteplog, sp_help_notification, sp_help_operator, sp_help_proxy, sp_help_schedule, sp_help_targetserver, sp_help_targetservergroup, sp_manage_jobs_by_login, sp_msx_defect, sp_msx_enlist, sp_msx_get_account, sp_msx_set_account, sp_notify_operator, sp_post_msx_operation, sp_purge_jobhistory, sp_remove_job_from_targets, sp_resync_targetserver, sp_revoke_login_from_proxy, sp_revoke_proxy_from_subsystem, sp_start_job, sp_stop_job, sp_update_alert, sp_update_category, sp_update_job, sp_update_jobschedule, sp_update_jobstep, sp_update_notification, sp_update_operator, sp_update_proxy, sp_update_schedule, sp_update_targetservergroup

Table 4-3   Key System Stored Procedures by Type   (continued)

Stored Procedure Type	Description	Related System Stored Procedures
XML Stored Procedures	Manage Extensible Markup Language (XML) text.	*sp_xml_preparedocument, sp_xml_removedocument*

Techniques for Managing SQL Server Configuration Options

You can think of configuration options as a set of rules that define how SQL Server is configured and used. Individual server instances can have different configurations, as can the databases they support, the connections made by applications, and any statements or batch programs that are executed.

Setting Configuration Options

Configuration options can be set for:

- **A specific server instance** Server options are also referred to as instance-wide options and are set by executing the *sp_configure* stored procedure.

- **A specific database** Database options are also referred to as database-level options and are set by executing the ALTER DATABASE statement. The database compatibility level can be set by executing the *sp_dbcmptlevel* stored procedure.

- **A specific connection** Connection options are set by the Microsoft OLE DB Provider for SQL Server or the SQL Server ODBC driver properties and by ANSI SET options when a connection is established.

- **A specific statement or batch** Batch-level options are specified with SET statements. Statement-level options are specified in individual Transact-SQL statements.

Each of these configuration areas can be thought of as a level in the SQL Server configuration hierarchy. When an option is supported at more than one level, the applicable option setting is determined according to the following precedence order:

1. A server option
2. A database option
3. A connection (ANSI SET) or batch (SET) option
4. A specific statement (HINT) option

Note The stored procedure *sp_configure* provides the option user options, which allows you to change the default values of several SET options. Although user options appears to be an instance option, it is a SET option. In previous releases of SQL Server, batch-level options are called *connection-level options*. When you disable Multiple Active Result Sets (MARS), batch-level options are considered connection-level options as well.

You use ALTER DATABASE to change settings for a database, *sp_configure* to change server-level settings, and the SET statement to change settings that affect only the current session. If there are conflicts among configuration options, the options applied later have precedence over previously set options. For example, connection options have precedence over database and server options.

Working with SET Options

Typically, SET options are configured by users within a batch or script and they apply until they are reset or the user's session with the server is terminated. SET options can also be configured within a stored procedure or trigger. In that case, the SET options apply until they are reset inside that stored procedure or trigger, or until control returns to the code that invoked the stored procedure or trigger.

SET options are applied at either parse time or execute time. The parse-time options are QUOTED_IDENTIFIER, PARSEONLY, OFFSETS, and FIPS_FLAGGER. All other SET options are execute-time options. Parse-time options are applied during parsing as they are encountered. Execute-time options are applied during the execution of the code in which they are specified.

Batch statements are parsed in their entirety prior to execution. This means that control flow statements do not affect parse-time settings. In contrast, both control flow and execution affect whether execute-time options are set. Execute-time options are only set if control is changed to a section of the batch containing execute-time options and the related statements are executed without error. If execution fails before an execute-time option is set or during the processing or the statement that sets the option, the option is not set.

When a user connects to a database, some options may be set ON automatically. These options can be set through user options, server options, or the ODBC and OLE DB connection properties. If the user changes the SET options within a dynamic SQL batch or script, those changes apply only for the duration of that batch or script.

Note   MARS-enabled connections maintain a list of default SET option values. When a batch or script executes under that connection, the default SET option values are copied to the current request's environment. These values remain in effect unless they are reset within the connection. Once the batch or script ends, the execution environment is copied back to the session's default. This ensures that multiple batches executing simultaneously under the same connection run in an isolated SET options environment. However, because the execution environment is copied back to the session default when batch or script execution completes, the current default environment for a connection depends on the last batch or script that completes execution.

Table 4-4 lists the batch/connection SET options available, providing the corresponding database and server options supported in SQL Server 2005 as well as the default setting (as applicable). The SET ANSI_DEFAULTS statement is provided as a shortcut for setting SQL-92 standard options to their default values. The options that reset when this statement is used are as follows: SET ANSI_NULLS, SET CURSOR_CLOSE_ON_COMMIT, SET ANSI_NULL_DFLT_ON, SET IMPLICIT_TRANSACTIONS, SET ANSI_PADDING, SET QUOTED_IDENTIFIER, and SET ANSI_WARNINGS.

Table 4-4   SET Options

SET Option	Database Option	Server Option	Default Setting
ANSI_DEFAULTS	None	None	N/A
ANSI_NULL_DFLT_OFF ANSI_NULL_DFLT_ON	ANSI_NULL_DEFAULT	user options default	OFF
ANSI_NULLS	ANSI_NULLS	user options default	OFF
ANSI_PADDING	ANSI_PADDING	user options default	ON
ANSI_WARNINGS	ANSI_WARNINGS	user options default	OFF
ARITHABORT	ARITHABORT	user options default	OFF
ARITHIGNORE	None	user options default	OFF
CONCAT_NULL_YIELDS_NULL	CONCAT_NULL_YIELDS_NULL	None	OFF
CURSOR_CLOSE_ON_COMMIT	CURSOR_CLOSE_ON_COMMIT	user options default	OFF
DATEFIRST	None	None	7
DATEFORMAT	None	None	mdy
DEADLOCK_PRIORITY	None	None	NORMAL
FIPS_FLAGGER	None	None	OFF
FMTONLY	None	None	OFF
FORCEPLAN	None	None	OFF
IDENTITY_INSERT	None	None	OFF
IMPLICIT_TRANSACTIONS	None	user options default	OFF
LANGUAGE	None	None	us_english
LOCK_TIMEOUT	None	None	No limit
NOCOUNT	None	user options default	OFF
NOEXEC	None	None	OFF
NUMERIC_ROUNDABORT	NUMERIC_ROUNDABORT	None	OFF
OFFSETS	None	None	OFF
PARSEONLY	None	None	OFF
QUERY_GOVERNOR_COST_LIMIT	None	query governor cost limit	OFF

Table 4-4 SET Options *(continued)*

SET Option	Database Option	Server Option	Default Setting
QUOTED_IDENTIFIER	quoted identifier	user options default	OFF
REMOTE_PROC_TRANSACTIONS	None	None	OFF
ROWCOUNT	None	None	OFF
SHOWPLAN_ALL	None	None	OFF
SHOWPLAN_TEXT	None	None	OFF
SHOWPLAN_XML	None	None	OFF
STATISTICS IO	None	None	OFF
STATISTICS PROFILE	None	None	OFF
STATISTICS TIME	None	None	OFF
STATISTICS XML	None	None	OFF
TEXTSIZE	None	None	OFF
TRANSACTION ISOLATION LEVEL	None	None	N/A
XACT_ABORT	None	None	OFF

Working with Server Options

Server options can be set using the properties dialog boxes in SQL Server Management Studio or the *sp_configure* stored procedure. The difference between the two methods is which options are available to set. Only the most commonly used server configuration options are available through SQL Server Management Studio, but all configuration options are accessible through *sp_configure*. Table 4-5 lists the server options available and provides the corresponding SET options and database options that are supported in SQL Server 2005, as well as the default setting (as applicable).

Table 4-5 Server Options

Server Option	SET Option	Database Option	Default Setting
affinity mask	None	None	0
allow updates	None	None	0
awe enabled	None	None	0
c2 audit mode	None	None	0
cost threshold for parallelism	None	None	5
cursor threshold	None	None	−1
default full-text language	None	None	1033
default language	None	None	0
fill factor	None	None	0
index create memory	None	None	0
lightweight pooling	None	None	0
locks	None	None	0
max degree of parallelism	None	None	0

Table 4-5   Server Options   (continued)

Server Option	SET Option	Database Option	Default Setting
max server memory	None	None	2147483647
max text repl size	None	None	65536
max worker threads	None	None	255; varies based on number of processors
media retention	None	None	0
min memory per query	None	None	1024
min server memory	None	None	8
nested triggers	None	None	1
network packet size	None	None	4096
priority boost	None	None	0
query governor cost limit	QUERY_GOVERNOR_COST_LIMIT	None	0
query wait	None	None	−1
recovery interval	None	None	0
remote access	None	None	1
remote login timeout	None	None	20
remote proc trans	None	None	0
remote query timeout	None	None	600
scan for startup procs	None	None	0
show advanced options	None	None	0
two digit year cutoff	None	None	2049
user connections	None	None	0
user options	ANSI_NULL_DFLT_ON ANSI_NULL_DFLT_OFF	ANSI_NULL_DEFAULT	OFF
	ANSI_NULLS	ANSI_NULLS	OFF
	ANSI_PADDING	ANSI_PADDING	ON
	ANSI_WARNINGS	ANSI_WARNINGS	OFF
	CURSOR_CLOSE_ON_COMMIT	CURSOR_CLOSE_ON_COMMIT	OFF
	IMPLICIT_TRANSACTIONS	None	OFF
	QUOTED_IDENTIFIER	QUOTED_IDENTIFIER	OFF
	ARITHABORT	ARITHABORT	OFF
	ARITHIGNORE	None	OFF
	DISABLE_DEF_CNST_CHK	None	OFF
	NOCOUNT	None	OFF

Working with Database Options

Database options are set by executing the ALTER DATABASE statement. In new SQL Server installations, the settings in the *model* and *master* databases are the same. When you create new databases, the default database options for those databases are taken from the model database. Whenever you change a database option, the Database Engine recompiles everything in the database cache. Table 4-6 lists the database options available and provides the corresponding SET and server options supported in SQL Server 2005, as well as the default setting (as applicable).

Table 4-6   Database Options

Database Option	SET Option	Server Option	Default Setting
ANSI_NULL_DEFAULT	ANSI_NULL_DFLT_ON ANSI_NULL_DFLT_OFF	user options default	OFF
ANSI_NULLS	ANSI_NULLS	user options default	OFF
ANSI_PADDING	ANSI_PADDING	user options default	OFF
ANSI_WARNINGS	ANSI_WARNINGS	user options default	OFF
AUTO_CLOSE	None	None	OFF
AUTO_CREATE_STATISTICS	None	None	ON
AUTO_SHRINK	None	None	OFF
AUTO_UPDATE_STATISTICS	None	None	ON
AUTO_UPDATE_STATISTICS_ASYNC	None	None	OFF
CONCAT_NULL_YIELDS_NULL	CONCAT_NULL_YIELDS_NULL	None	OFF
CURSOR_CLOSE_ON_COMMIT	CURSOR_CLOSE_ON_COMMIT	user options default	OFF
CURSOR_DEFAULT	None	None	GLOBAL
MERGE PUBLISH	None	None	FALSE
DB_STATE	None	None	ONLINE
PUBLISHED	None	None	FALSE
QUOTED_IDENTIFIER	QUOTED_IDENTIFIER	user options default	ON
READ_ONLY	None	None	FALSE
RECOVERY BULK_LOGGED	None	None	FALSE
RECOVERY SIMPLE	None	None	TRUE
RECURSIVE_TRIGGERS	None	None	FALSE
RESTRICTED_USER	None	None	FALSE
SINGLE_USER	None	None	FALSE
SUBSCRIBED	None	None	TRUE
TORN_PAGE_DETECTION	None	None	TRUE

Managing Database Compatibility

By default, when you create a new database in SQL Server 2005 database, the default compatibility level is 90. When a database is upgraded to SQL Server 2005, the database retains its existing compatibility level:

- 80 for SQL Server 2000 compatibility level
- 70 for SQL Server 7.0 compatibility level
- 65 for SQL Server 6.5 compatibility level

Although the compatibility level of the *master* database cannot be modified, the compatibility level setting of the *model* database can be changed. This allows you to create new databases with a nondefault compatibility level. To change the compatibility level, you can use the *sp_dbcmptlevel* stored procedure.

The *sp_dbcmptlevel* stored procedure allows you to set the database compatibility level to use for a specific database. The *sp_dbcmptlevel* stored procedure sets certain database behaviors to be compatible with the specified earlier version of SQL Server. The following example changes the compatibility level of the *Personnel* database to SQL Server 7.0:

```
EXEC sp_dbcmptlevel "Personnel", "80";

GO
```

When there are possible conflicts between compatibility (and other) settings, it is important to know which database context is being used. Generally speaking, the current database context is the database defined by the USE statement if it is in a batch/script, or it is the database that contains the stored procedure if it is in a stored procedure applied to that statement. When a stored procedure is executed from a batch or another stored procedure, it is executed under the option settings of the database in which it is stored. For example, when a stored procedure in the *Support* database calls a stored procedure in the *Personnel* database, the *Support* procedure is executed under the compatibility level setting of the *Support* database and the *Personnel* procedure is executed under the compatibility level setting of the *Personnel* database.

Note   Databases with indexed views cannot be changed to a compatibility level lower than 80. CONCAT_NULL_YIELDS_NULL database option and CONCAT_NULL_YIELDS_NULL SET option settings are ignored when the compatibility level is set lower than 70.

Configuring SQL Server with Stored Procedures

You can configure many areas of SQL Server using the SQL Server Properties dialog box, which will be discussed in Chapter 5, "Managing the Enterprise." As you have learned in this chapter, you can also configure SQL Server with stored procedures, such as *sp_configure* and *sp_dboption*. You execute stored procedures and other queries in SQL Server Management Studio. SQL Server Management Studio has a built-in client tool that sends commands to a SQL Server instance, which in turn parses, compiles, and executes the commands.

The following sections explain how to configure SQL Server using SQL Server Management Studio and stored procedures. You will find more detailed coverage of SQL Server Management Studio in other chapters.

Using SQL Server Management Studio for Queries

You can start SQL Server Management Studio and access the built-in query client by completing the following steps:

1. Select Start, Programs or All Programs, Microsoft SQL Server 2005, SQL Server Management Studio. Or type **sqlwb** at a command prompt.

2. In the Connect To Server dialog box, use the Server Type drop-down list to select the database component to which you want to connect, such as Database Engine.

3. In the Server Name field, type the name of the server on which SQL Server is running, such as CorpSvr04.

Note   You can only connect to registered servers. If the SQL Server you want to work with is not registered, you will need to register the server before you can work with it. See the section titled "Managing Servers" in Chapter 5 for details.

4. Use the Authentication selection menu to choose the authentication type as Windows Authentication or SQL Server Authentication (based on the allowed authentication types when you installed the server). Provide a Windows user name or SQL Server login ID and password as necessary.

   - **Windows Authentication**   Uses your current domain account and password to establish the database connection. This works only if Windows authentication is enabled and you have appropriate privileges.

   - **SQL Server Authentication**   Allows you to specify a SQL Server login ID and password.

5. Click Connect. You connect to the default instance (unless you have configured another default previously). To change the instance to which you connect, click Option, select the Connection Properties tab, and then use the Connect To Database drop-down list to select the instance to which you want to connect.

6. In SQL Server Management Studio, select New Query on the tool bar, and then select the query type, such as Database Engine Query.

7. In the Connect To... dialog box shown in Figure 4-1, specify the server name, or select Browse For More in the drop-down list to search for all SQL servers within an entire Active Directory Forest.

8. Specify the authentication technique to use. Click Connect. As before, you connect to the default instance (unless you have configured another default previously). To change the instance to which you connect, click Option, select the Connection Properties tab, and then use the Connect To Database drop-down list to select the instance to which you want to connect.

If you are working with an active database in SQL Server Management Studio and have already authenticated the connection, you can automatically connect to the currently selected database server instance and use your current authentication information to log on. To do this, right-click the database in the Object Explorer view in SQL Server Management Studio, and then select New Query.

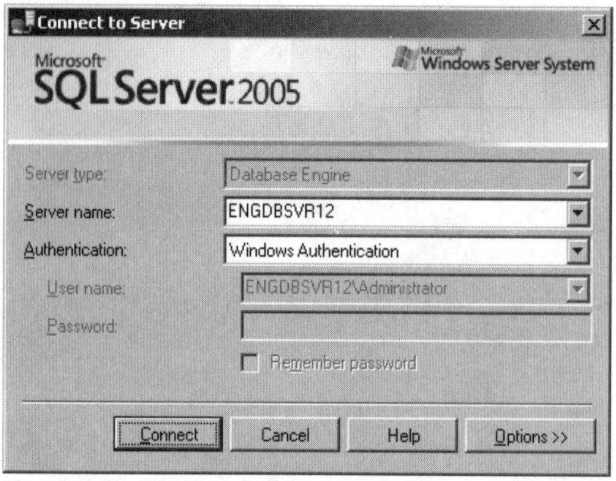

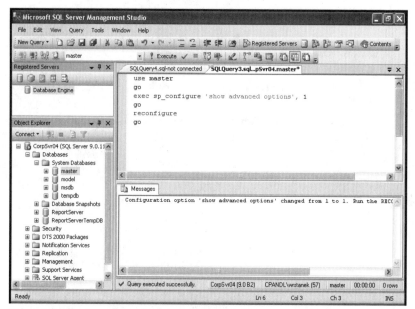

Figure 4-1   The Connect To ... dialog box

Executing Queries and Changing Settings

The query window in SQL Server Management Studio is normally divided into three panes (see Figure 4-2). The left pane allows you to browse objects that are available on the currently selected database server instance. Use the upper-right pane to enter queries. The lower-right pane displays results.

Figure 4-2   The four panes of the query window in SQL Server Management Studio

If you do not see a separate pane at the lower right of the window, don't worry. It displays automatically when you type a query. You can also set the pane to display by default. Select the Show Results Pane option on the Window menu.

As you know, you can use *sp_configure* to view and change SQL Server configuration settings. Two types of configuration settings are available: those that are dynamic and those that are not. In this instance, a dynamic setting is one that you can change without having to stop and restart SQL Server. To execute *sp_configure* or other types of queries, type a command in the top pane and then click the Execute Query button on the toolbar (the red exclamation point). You can also execute commands using these key sequences:

- F5
- Ctrl+E
- Alt+X

Note   By default, all users have execute permissions on *sp_configure* so that they can view settings. However, only users with the Alter Settings server-level permission can use *sp_configure* to change configuration options. By default, only members of the sysadmin and serveradmin fixed server roles have this permission. As with *sp_configure*, only users with Alter Settings server-level permission can execute the RECONFIGURE or RECON-FIGURE WITH OVERRIDE command.

Whenever you use *sp_configure* to modify settings, the changes do not actually take place until you also execute the RECONFIGURE command. You can change some highly risky settings only with the RECONFIGURE WITH OVERRIDE command. Additionally, *sp_configure* settings are divided into two categories: standard and advanced. You can execute standard commands at any time, but you can execute advanced commands only when Show Advanced Options is set to 1. With this setting in effect, you can modify both standard and advanced settings. Follow this procedure to allow modification of advanced settings:

1. In SQL Server Management Studio, type:

```
exec sp_configure "show advanced options", 1
go
reconfigure
go
```

Tip   You can disable advanced options later by setting the value to 0.

2. Execute the commands by pressing **Ctrl+E**.
3. Clear the query window.
4. Now type one *sp_configure* command for each option you want to change.

5. Type **reconfigure** (or **reconfigure with override**).

6. Type **go**.

7. Execute the commands by pressing **Ctrl+E**.

8. If you changed any nondynamic settings, stop and start the server. (See Table 4-7 and Table 4-8 for details.)

Checking and Setting Configuration Parameters

Table 4-7 provides a summary of the standard configuration parameters. The parameters are listed in alphabetical order, with the minimum, maximum, and default values shown. The dynamic parameter column tells you if the setting is dynamic. If you see an "N" in this column, you will need to stop and restart the server to enforce changes.

Table 4-7   Quick Reference Summary for Standard Configuration Parameters

Configuration Option	Minimum Value	Maximum Value	Default Value	Dynamic Yes/No
allow updates	0	1	0	Y
clr enabled	0	1	0	Y
cross db ownership chaining	0	1	0	Y
cursor threshold	−1	2147483647	−1	Y
default language	0	9999	0	Y
nested triggers	0	1	1	Y
remote access	0	1	1	N
remote admin connections	0	1	0	Y
remote login timeout	0	2147483647	20	Y
remote proc trans	0	1	0	Y
remote query timeout	0	2147483647	600	Y
server trigger recursion	0	1	1	Y
show advanced options	0	1	0	Y
user options	0	32767	0	Y

Table 4-8 provides a summary of the advanced configuration parameters. To view or change these parameters, you have to set the parameter Show Advanced Options to 1. Self-configuring options have an asterisk (*) after the name. With max worker threads, 1024 is max recommended for 32-bit operating systems. The default value zero (0) autoconfigures using the formula: 256 + (number of processors − 4) * 8. Note also that you cannot change some advanced options (you can only view them).

Table 4-8   Quick Reference Summary for Advanced Configuration
Parameters

Configuration Option	Minimum Value	Maximum Value	Default Value	Dynamic Yes/No
Ad Hoc Distributed Queries	0	1	0	Y
affinity I/O mask	–2147483648	2147483647	0	N
affinity mask	–2147483648	2147483647	0	N
Agent XPs	0	1	0	Y
awe enabled	0	1	0	N
blocked process threshold	0	86400	0	Y
c2 audit mode	0	1	0	N
cost threshold for parallelism	0	32767	5	Y
Database Mail XPs	0	1	0	Y
default full-text language	0	2147483647	1033	Y
default trace enabled	0	1	1	Y
disallow results from triggers	0	1	0	Y
fill factor	0	100	0	N
ft crawl bandwidth max	0	32767	100	Y
ft crawl bandwidth min	0	32767	0	Y
ft notify bandwidth max	0	32767	100	Y
ft notify bandwidth min	0	32767	0	Y
index create memory*	704	2147483647	0	N
in-doubt xact resolution	0	2	0	Y
lightweight pooling	0	1	0	N
locks*	5000	2147483647	0	N
max degree of parallelism	0	64	0	Y
max full-text crawl range	0	256	4	Y
max server memory*	16	2147483647	2147483647	N
max text repl size	0	2147483647	65536	Y
max worker threads	128	32767	0	N
media retention	0	365	0	N
min memory per query	512	2147483647	1024	Y
min server memory*	0	2147483647	0	N
network packet size	512	32767	4096	Y
OLE Automation Procedures	0	1	0	Y
open objects	0	2147483647	0	N
ph_timeout	1	3600	60	Y
precompute rank	0	1	0	Y
priority boost	0	1	0	N
query governor cost limit	0	2147483647	0	Y
query wait	–1	2147483647	–1	Y
recovery interval*	0	32767	0	N

Table 4-8   Quick Reference Summary for Advanced Configuration Parameters   *(continued)*

Configuration Option	Minimum Value	Maximum Value	Default Value	Dynamic Yes/No
Replication XPs	0	1	0	Y
scan for startup procs	0	1	0	N
set working set size	0	1	0	N
SMO and DMO XPs	0	1	1	Y
SQL Mail XPs	0	1	0	Y
transform noise words	0	1	0	Y
two digit year cutoff	1753	9999	2049	Y
user connections*	0	32767	0	N
Web Assistant Procedures	0	1	0	Y
xp_cmdshell	0	1	0	Y

You can view the current settings of all configuration options by executing the following query:

```
exec sp_configure
go
```

 Note   Show Advanced Options must be set to 1 to see advanced options.

To view the current setting of a configuration option, execute the following query:

```
exec sp_configure "optionName"
go
```

where optionName is the name of the option you want to examine, such as:

```
exec sp_configure "allow updates"
go
```

To change the value of a setting, execute the following query:

```
exec sp_configure "optionName" newValue
go
reconfigure with override
go
```

where optionName is the name of the option you want to examine, and newValue is the new value for this option, such as:

```
exec sp_configure "allow updates" 1
go
reconfigure with override
go
```

Note   You do not always have to use RECONFIGURE WITH OVERRIDE. This value is required only when making ad hoc updates and setting an option to a value that is not generally recommended. Keep in mind that some setting changes are only applied when you restart the SQL Server instance.

Changing Settings with *sp_dboption*

By default, all users have execute permissions on *sp_dboption* so that they can view settings. However, only members of the sysadmin and dbcreator fixed server roles and the db_owner fixed database role can use *sp_dboption* to change database settings. When you execute *sp_dboption*, a checkpoint occurs in the database for which the option was changed and this causes the change to take effect immediately.

Table 4-9 provides an overview of the options you can use with *sp_dboption*. All of the listed options accept a TRUE (1) or FALSE (0) value, which is used to set the state of the option. For example, if there were no current users connected to the *CustomerSupport* database, you could set it to read-only using the following command:

```
USE master;

GO

EXEC sp_dboption "CustomerSupport", "read only", "TRUE";
```

Table 4-9   Quick Reference Summary for Database Options

Option	When TRUE...
ANSI null default	CREATE TABLE uses SQL-92 rules to determine if a column allows null values.
ANSI nulls	All comparisons to a null value evaluate to UNKNOWN. (When FALSE, non-UNICODE values evaluate to TRUE if both values are NULL.)
ANSI padding	Trailing blanks are inserted into character values and trailing zeroes are inserted into binary values to pad to the length of the column.
ANSI warnings	Errors or warnings are issued when conditions such as "divide by zero" occur.
Arithabort	An overflow or divide-by-zero error causes the query or batch to terminate. If the error occurs in a transaction, the transaction is rolled back. (When FALSE, a warning message is displayed, but execution continues as if no error occurred.)
auto create statistics	Any missing statistics needed for query optimization are automatically generated.
auto update statistic	Any out-of-date statistics needed for query optimization are automatically generated.
Autoclose	After the last user logs off, the database is shut down cleanly and its resources are freed.
Autoshrink	Automatic periodic shrinking is enabled for the database.
concat null yields null	If either operand in a concatenation operation is NULL, the result is NULL.

Table 4-9   Quick Reference Summary for Database Options   *(continued)*

Option	When TRUE...
cursor close on commit	Any cursors that are open when a transaction is committed or rolled back are closed. (When FALSE, cursors remain open when a transaction is committed. Rolling back a transaction closes any cursors except those defined as INSENSITIVE or STATIC.)
db_chaining	The database can be the source or target of a cross-database ownership chain.
dbo use only	Only the database owner can use the database.
default to local cursor	Cursor declarations default to LOCAL.
merge publish	The database can be published for a merge replication.
numeric roundabort	An error is generated when loss of precision occurs in an expression. (When FALSE, losses of precision do not generate error messages and the result is rounded to the precision of the column or variable storing the result.)
Offline	The database is offline. (When FALSE, the database is online.)
Published	The database can be published for replication.
quoted identifier	Double quotation marks can be used to enclose delimited identifiers.
read only	The database is set to read-only (but can be deleted using the DROP DATABASE statement). The database cannot be in use when this option is set (except for master).
recursive triggers	Enables recursive firing of triggers. (When FALSE, prevents direct recursion but not indirect recursion. To disable indirect recursion, set the nested triggers server option to 0 using *sp_configure*.)
select into/bulkcopy	Causes the recovery model to be reset to BULK_LOGGED.
single user	Only one user at a time can access the database.
Subscribed	The database can be subscribed for publication.
torn page detection	Incomplete pages can be detected.
trunc. log on chkpt.	Sets the recovery model of the database to SIMPLE and allows a checkpoint to truncate the inactive part of the log. (When FALSE, sets the recovery model to FULL.) The *master* database must allow checkpoints.

Part II

Microsoft SQL Server 2005 Administration

In Part II, you will learn about essential tasks for administering Microsoft SQL Server 2005. Chapter 5 introduces general management techniques for servers. In this chapter, you will also learn how to control processes and manage related server components. Chapter 6 presents information about how to use SQL Server Management Studio to configure SQL Server. Chapter 7 covers the core administration tasks for creating and managing databases.

Managing the Enterprise

SQL Server Management Studio is the primary tool you will use to manage database servers. Other tools that are available to manage local and remote servers include SQL Server 2005 Surface Area Configuration, SQL Server Configuration Manager, Performance Monitor, and Event Viewer. You will use Configuration Manager to manage SQL Server services, networking, and client configurations. Performance Monitor is available to track SQL Server activity and performance, and Event Viewer provides a way to examine events generated by SQL Server, which can provide helpful details for troubleshooting. In this chapter, you will learn how to use SQL Server Management Studio. SQL Server 2005 Surface Area Configuration and SQL Server Configuration Manager are discussed in Chapter 3, "Managing the Surface Security, Access, and Network Configuration." For details on Performance Monitor and Event Viewer, see Chapter 13, "Profiling and Monitoring Microsoft SQL Server 2005."

Managing SQL Server Startup

The SQL Server Database Engine has two modes of operation. It can run as a command-line application (SQLServr.exe) or as a service. Use the command-line application when you need to troubleshoot problems or modify configuration settings in single-user mode. Other than that, you will normally run SQL Server as a service.

Enabling or Preventing Automatic SQL Server Startup

In Chapter 3, you learned that you can use SQL Server Configuration Manager to manage the SQL Server (MSSQLSERVER) service, related services for other

Database Engine instances, and other SQL Server-related services. Any of these services can be configured for automatic startup or can be prevented from starting automatically. To enable or prevent automatic startup of a service, follow these steps:

1. Start SQL Server Management Studio by clicking the Start button, pointing to Programs or All Programs, Microsoft SQL Server 2005 and then selecting SQL Server Management Studio. Or type **sqlwb** at a command prompt.

2. In the Connect To Server dialog box, use the Server Type drop-down list to select the type of server to which you want to connect, such as Database Engine, and then, in the Server Name box, type the fully qualified domain name or host name of the server on which SQL Server is running, such as **corpsvr04.cpandl.com** or **CorpSvr04** (see Figure 5-1).

Note You can only connect to registered servers. If the SQL Server you want to work with is not registered, you will need to register the server before you can work with it. See the section titled "Managing Servers" later in this chapter for details.

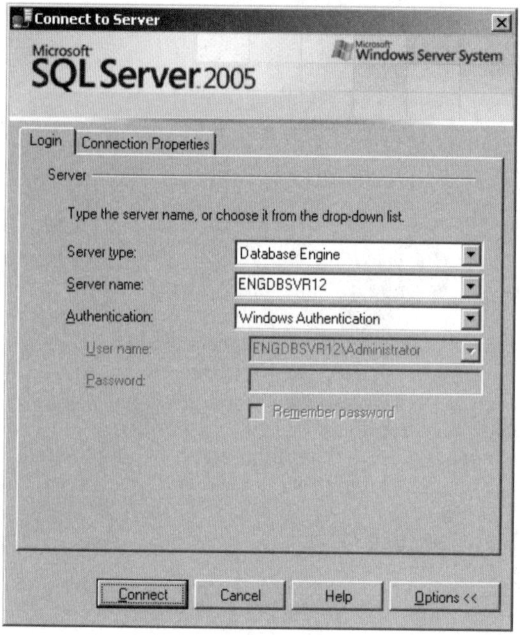

Connect to Server

Microsoft
SQL Server 2005

Windows Server System

| Login | Connection Properties |

Server

Type the server name, or choose it from the drop-down list.

Server type: Database Engine

Server name: ENGDBSVR12

Authentication: Windows Authentication

User name: ENGDBSVR12\Administrator

Password:

☐ Remember password

[Connect]   [Cancel]   [Help]   [Options <<]

Figure 5-1 The Connect To Server dialog box

3. Use the Authentication selection menu to choose the authentication type, either Windows Authentication or SQL Server Authentication (based on the allowed authentication types when you installed the server). Provide a Windows user name or SQL Server login ID and password as necessary.

- **Windows Authentication**   Uses your current domain account and password to establish the database connection. This authentication type works only if Windows authentication is enabled and you have appropriate privileges.

- **SQL Server Authentication**   Allows you to specify a SQL Server login ID and password. To save the password so that you do not have to re-enter it each time you connect, select Remember Password.

4. Click Connect. You connect to the default instance (unless you have configured another default previously). To change the instance to which you connect, click Options, select the Connection Properties tab, and then use the Connect To Database drop-down list to select the instance to which you want to connect.

5. Right-click the server you want to configure in the SQL Server Management Studio Object Explorer view, and then choose SQL Server Configuration Manager. This starts SQL Server Configuration Manager with the target computer set to the computer where the server you want to configure is located.

6. Select the SQL Server 2005 Services node. Right-click the SQL Server service that you want to start automatically, and then select Properties. You can now:

- **Enable automatic startup**   On the Service tab, set the Start Mode to Automatic. If the server state is Stopped, click Start on the Log On tab to start the service.

- **Prevent automatic startup**   On the Service tab, set the Start Mode to Manual.

7. Click OK.

You can also use Computer Management to configure services. To configure automatic startup of a service using Computer Management, follow these steps:

1. Click the Start button, point to Programs or All Programs, and then select Administrative Tools | Computer Management.

2. By default, you are connected to the local computer. To connect to a remote computer, right-click the Computer Management node and select Connect To Another Computer. In the Select Computer dialog box, select Another Computer, and then type the name of the computer. The name can be specified as a host name, such as **CorpSvr04**, or a fully qualified domain name, such as **corpsvr04.cpandl.com**.

3. Expand Services And Application, and then select Services.

4. Right-click the SQL Server service that you want to start automatically, and then select Properties.

5. You can now:

- **Enable automatic startup**   On the General tab, set the Startup Type to Automatic. If the Service Status reads Stopped, click Start.

- **Prevent automatic startup**   On the General tab, set the Startup Type to Manual.

6. Click OK.

Setting Database Engine Startup Parameters

Startup parameters control how the SQL Server Database Engine starts and which options are set when it does. You can configure startup options using SQL Server Configuration Manager or Computer Management. SQL Server Configuration Manager is the recommended tool for this task because it provides the current default settings and allows you to easily make modifications.

 Tip   Startup parameters can be passed to the command-line utility SQLServr.exe as well. Passing the –c option to this utility starts SQL Server without using a service. You must run SQLServr.exe from the Binn directory that corresponds to the instance of the SQL Server database engine that you want to start. For the default instance, the utility is located in MSSQL.1\mssql\Binn. For named instances, the utility is located in mssql$instancename\Binn.

Adding Startup Parameters

You can add startup parameters by completing the following steps:

1. In SQL Server Management Studio, right-click the server you want to configure in the SQL Server Management Studio Object Explorer view and choose choose SQL Server Configuration Manager. This starts SQL Server Configuration Manager with the target computer set to the computer where the server you want to modify is located.

2. Select the SQL Server 2005 Services node. Right-click the SQL Server service that you want to modify, and then select Properties.

3. On the Advanced tab, click in the Startup Parameters box, and then press End to go to the end of the currently entered parameters. The –d, –e and –l parameters are set by default. Be careful not to modify these or other existing parameters accidentally.

4. Each parameter is separated by a semicolon. Type a semicolon and then a dash followed by the letter of the parameter you are adding, such as ;–g512.

5. Type the value for the parameter.

6. Repeat step 3 through step 5 as necessary to specify additional parameters and values.

7. Click Apply to save the changes. The parameters are applied the next time the SQL Server instance is started. To apply the parameters right away, you must stop and then start the service by clicking Restart on the Log On tab.

Removing Startup Parameters

You can remove startup parameters by completing the following steps:

1. In SQL Server Management Studio, right-click the server you want to configure in the SQL Server Management Studio Object Explorer view and choose Manage Service.

2. Select the SQL Server 2005 Services node. Right-click the SQL Server service that you want to modify, and then select Properties.

3. On the Advanced tab, click in the Startup Parameters box. Each parameter is specified with a dash, parameter letter, and parameter value. A semicolon is used to separate parameter values, as shown in the following example:

   -g512;

4. Remove the parameter by deleting its related parameter entry.

5. The change is applied the next time the SQL Server instance is started. To apply the parameters right away, you must stop and then start the service by clicking Restart.

Common Startup Parameters

Table 5-1 shows startup parameters and how they are used. The first three parameters (−d, −e, and −l) are the defaults for SQL Server. The remaining parameters allow you to configure additional settings.

Table 5-1   Startup Parameters for SQL Server

Parameter	Description	Example
−d<path>	Sets the full path for the *master* database. If omitted, the registry values are used.	−dC:\Program Files\Microsoft SQL Server\MSSQL.1\MSSQL\DATA\master.mdf
−e<path>	Sets the full path for the error log. If omitted, the registry values are used.	−eC:\Program Files\Microsoft SQL Server\MSSQL.1\MSSQL\LOG\ERRORLOG
−l<path>	Sets the full path for the *master* database transaction log. If omitted, the registry values are used.	−lC:\Program Files\Microsoft SQL Server\MSSQL.1\MSSQL\DATA\mastlog.ldf
−B	Sets a breakpoint on error; used with the −y option when debugging.	
−c	Prevents SQL Server from running as a service. This makes startup faster when you are running SQL Server from the command line.	
−f	Starts SQL Server with minimal configuration. Enables the *sp_configure* Allow Updates option, which is disabled by default.	
−g number	Specifies the amount of virtual address space memory in megabytes to reserve for SQL Server. This memory is outside the memory pool and is used by the extended procedure .dlls, OLE DB providers referenced in distributed queries, and the automation object referenced in Transact-SQL (T-SQL).	−g256
−m	Starts SQL Server in single-user mode. Only a single user can connect, and the checkpoint process is not started.	
−n	Tells SQL Server not to log errors in the application event log. Use with −e.	
−p<level>	Sets the precision level for numeric and decimal data types. Default is 38 digits, but the range is 1 to 38. Maximum precision (38) is assumed if you use the switch without setting a level.	−p38

Table 5-1   Startup Parameters for SQL Server   *(continued)*

Parameter	Description	Example
—s instance	Starts the named instance of SQL Server. You must be in the relevant Binn directory for the instance.	—sdevapps
—T<tnum>	Sets a trace flag. Trace flags set nonstandard behavior and are often used in debugging or diagnosing performance issues.	—T237
—t<tnum>	Sets an internal trace flag for SQL Server. Used only by SQL Server support engineers.	—t8837
—x	Disables statistics tracking for CPU time and cache-hit ratio. Allows maximum performance.	
—y number	Sets an error number that causes SQL Server to dump the stack.	—y1803

Managing Services from the Command Line

You can start, stop, and pause SQL Server as you would any other service. On a local system, you can type the necessary command at a standard command prompt. On a remote system, you can connect to the system using Telnet, and then issue the necessary command. With Windows Server 2003, you can also establish a remote Terminal Server session to the server and access the command console remotely. To manage the Default database server instance, use these commands:

- **NET START MSSQLSERVER**   Starts SQL Server as a service.
- **NET STOP MSSQLSERVER**   Stops SQL Server when running as a service.
- **NET PAUSE MSSQLSERVER**   Pauses SQL Server when running as a service.
- **NET CONTINUE MSSQLSERVER**   Resumes SQL Server when running as a service.

To manage named instances of SQL Server, use the following commands:

- **NET START MSSQL$***instancename*   Starts SQL Server as a service, where *instancename* is the actual name of the database server instance.
- **NET STOP MSSQL$***instancename*   Stops SQL Server when running as a service, where *instancename* is the actual name of the database server instance.
- **NET PAUSE MSSQL$***instancename*   Pauses SQL Server when running as a service, where *instancename* is the actual name of the database server instance.
- **NET CONTINUE MSSQL$***instancename*   Resumes SQL Server when running as a service, where *instancename* is the actual name of the database server instance.

Note   If you choose not to install the default instance of SQL Server during the initial setup and instead create a new named instance as the initial SQL Server instance, you will not be able to use the NET command to manage services from the command line.

Managing the SQL Server Command-Line Executable File

The SQL Server command-line executable file (SQLServr.exe) provides an alternative to the SQL Server service. You must run SQLServr.exe from the Binn directory that corresponds to the instance of the SQL Server Database Engine that you want to start. For the default instance, the utility is located in MSSQL.1\mssql\Binn. For named instances, the utility is located in MSSQL.1\mssql$*instancename*\Binn.

When SQL Server is installed on a local system, start SQL Server by changing to the directory where the instance of SQL Server you want to start is located, and then type **sqlservr** at the command line. On a remote system, connect to the system by using Telnet, change to the appropriate directory, and then issue the startup command. In Windows Server 2003 Editions, you can also establish a remote Terminal Server session and access the command line remotely. Either way, SQL Server reads the default startup parameters from the registry and starts execution.

You can also enter startup parameters and switches that override the default settings. (The available parameters were summarized in Table 5-1.) You can still connect SQL Server Management Studio to the server (although when you do, it may incorrectly report that it is starting the SQL Server service).

To stop an instance of SQL Server started from the command line, complete the following steps:

1. Press Ctrl+C to break into the execution stream.

2. When prompted, press Y to stop SQL Server.

Using SQL Server Management Studio

The SQL Server Management Studio graphical point-and-click interface makes server, database, and resource management easy to do. Using SQL Server Management Studio, you can manage both local and remote server instances by establishing a connection to SQL Server and then administering its resources. If you have disabled remote server connections to a particular server, however, you can only work with the server locally (by logging on to the system at the keyboard or by establishing a remote Terminal Server session in Windows and then running the local management tools) or through a Telnet session.

Getting Started with SQL Server Management Studio

To run SQL Server Management Studio, click the Start button, point to Programs or All Programs, and then select Microsoft SQL Server 2005 | SQL Server Management Studio, or type **sqlwb** at a command prompt. Then you must connect to the server with which you want to work. There are several ways to do this:

- Connect using a standard login to a server instance.
- Connect using a login to a specific database.
- Connect using server groups and registered servers.

Connecting to a server instance allows you to work with that particular server and its related components. Typically, you will want to connect to a server's Database Engine. As you can see in Figure 5-2, the Database Engine gives you access to:

- **Databases**   Manage system databases including *master* and *model*, as well as user databases and database snapshots. You can also access the *ReportServer* and *Report ServerTempDB* databases under this node.

- **Security**   Manage SQL logins, server roles, linked servers, and stored credentials.

- **Notification Services**   Register, list, and unregister Notification Services instances.

- **Replication**   Configure distribution, update replication passwords, and launch Replication Monitor.

- **Management**   Configure SQL Server logs, maintenance plans, Full-Text Search, Distributed Transaction Coordinator, and Database Mail. You can also configure legacy features, such as SQL Server 2000 database maintenance plans, SQL Mail, and DTS 2000 packages.

- **Server Objects**   Configure backup devices, HTTP endpoints, linked servers, and server triggers.

- **SQL Server Agent**   Configure SQL Server Agent jobs, alerts, operators, proxies, and error logs.

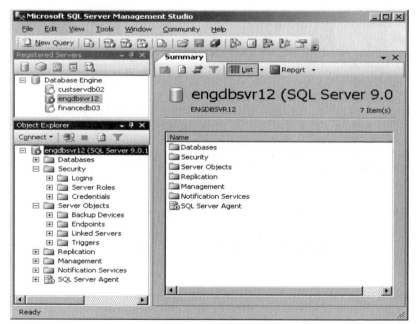

Figure 5-2   The Database Engine with access to core SQL Server components and features

If you are not automatically connected or you exited the Connection dialog box, you can connect to a server instance by clicking Connect in Object Explorer view. You store server and login information using the registration feature. Registered servers can be organized using server groups and then can be accessed quickly in Registered Servers view. Methods to manage server groups and register servers are discussed in sections later in this chapter titled "Managing SQL Server Groups" and "Managing Servers," respectively.

Connecting to a Specific Server Instance

To connect to a specific server instance using a standard login, follow these steps:

1. Start SQL Server Management Studio by clicking the Start button, pointing to Programs or All Programs, Microsoft SQL Server 2005 and then selecting SQL Server Management Studio. Or type **sqlwb** at a command prompt.

2. In the Connect To Server dialog box, use the Server Type drop-down list to select the database component to which you want to connect, such as Database Engine.

3. In the Server Name box, type the fully qualified or host name of the server on which SQL Server is running, such as **corpsvr04.cpandl.com** or **CorpSvr04**. Or select Browse For More on the related drop-down list. In the Browse For Server dialog box, select the Local Servers or Network Servers tab as appropriate.

4. After the instance data has been retrieved, expand the nodes provided, select the server instance, and then click OK.

5. Use the Authentication selection menu to choose the authentication type, either Windows Authentication or SQL Server Authentication (based on the authentication types selected when you installed the server). Provide a Windows user name or SQL Server login ID and password as necessary.

   - **Windows Authentication**   Uses your current domain account and password to establish the database connection. This authentication type works only if Windows authentication is enabled and you have appropriate privileges.

   - **SQL Server Authentication**   Allows you to specify a SQL Server login ID and password. To save the password so that you do not have to re-enter it each time you connect, select Remember Password.

6. Click Connect. You can now use Object Explorer view to work with this server.

Connecting to a Specific Database

To connect to a specific database using a standard login, follow these steps:

1. Start SQL Server Management Studio by clicking the Start button, pointing to Programs or All Programs, Microsoft SQL Server 2005 and then selecting SQL Server Management Studio. Or type **sqlwb** at a command prompt.

2. In the Connect To Server dialog box, use the Server Type drop-down list to select the database component to which you want to connect, such as

Database Engine, and then, in the Server Name box, type the fully qualified or host name of the server on which SQL Server is running, such as **coprsvr04.cpandl.com** or **CorpSvr04**.

3. Use the Authentication selection menu to choose the authentication type, either Windows Authentication or SQL Server Authentication (based on the authentication types selected when you installed the server). Provide a Windows user name or SQL Server login ID and password as necessary.

4. Click Options to display the advanced view of the Connect To Server dialog box. Select the Connection Properties tab, as shown in Figure 5-3.

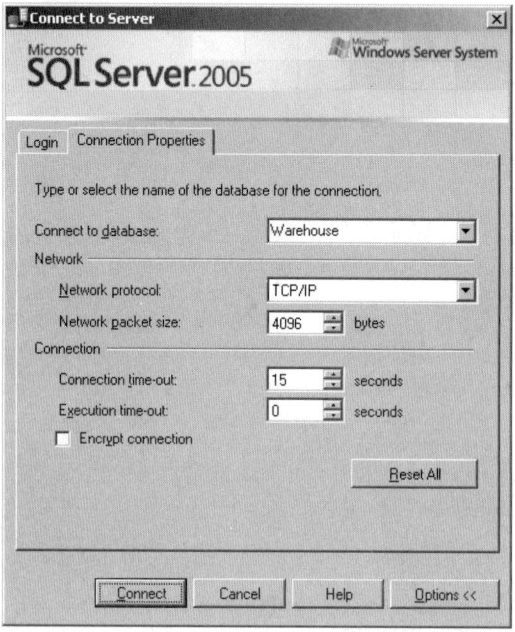

Figure 5-3   The Connection Properties tab in the Connect to Server dialog box

5. Type the name of the database to which you want to connect, such as **Personnel**. Or select Browse Server on the related drop-down list. When prompted, click Yes to establish a connection to a previously designated server.

6. In the Browse Server For Database dialog box, select the database you want to use, and then click OK.

7. Select the network protocol and any other connection properties if you are prompted to do so. Shared Memory is the default network protocol for local connections. TCP/IP is the default for remote connections.

8. Click Connect. You will then be able to work with the specified database in Object Explorer view.

Managing SQL Server Groups

You use SQL Server groups to organize sets of SQL servers. You define these server groups, and you can organize them by function, department, or any other criteria. Creating a server group is easy. You can even create subgroups within a group, and if you make a mistake, you can delete groups as well.

Introducing SQL Server Groups

In SQL Server Management Studio, you use Registered Servers view to work with server groups. To use this view or to display it if it is hidden, press Ctrl+Alt+G.

The top-level groups are already created for you, based on the SQL Server instances. Use the Registered Servers toolbar to switch between the various top-level groups. These top-level groups are organized by SQL Server instance:

- Database Engine
- Analysis Services
- Reporting Services
- SQL Server Mobile Edition Database
- Integration Services

Although you can add registered servers directly to the top-level groups (as explained in the section titled "Managing Servers" later in this chapter), in a large enterprise with many SQL Server instances, you will probably want to create additional levels in the server group hierarchy. These additional levels make it easier to access and work with your SQL servers. You can use the following types of organizational models:

- **Division or business unit model**   In this model, group names reflect the divisions or business units to which the SQL servers belong or in which they are located. For example, you could have Engineering, IS, Operations, and Support server groups.

- **Geographic location model**   In this model, group names reflect the geographic location of SQL servers, such as North America and Europe. You could have additional levels under North America for USA, Canada, and Mexico, for example, and levels under Europe could include UK, Germany, and Spain.

Subgroups are organized under their primary group. Under Database Engine, you might have Engineering and Operations groups. Within Engineering, you might have Dev, Test, and Core subgroups.

Creating a Server Group

You can create a server group or a subgroup by completing the following steps:

1. In the Console Root pane (the left pane of the SQL Server Management Studio window), select Registered Servers view by pressing Ctrl+Alt+G. If the view was previously hidden, this also displays the view.

2. Use the Registered Servers toolbar to select the top-level group in which you will create the new group. For example, if you want to create a second-level or third-level group for Database Engine instances, select Database Engine.

3. Right-click in Registered Servers view. Point to New, and then choose Server Group to display the New Server Group dialog box shown in Figure 5-4.

4. In the New Server Group dialog box, type a name and description for the new group in the boxes provided.

5. In the Select A Location For The New Server Group area, you will see the names of the top-level server group and any second-level server groups that you created. You can now:

   ❑ Add the server group to one of the top-level or second-level groups by clicking the group name.

   ❑ Add the server group to a lower-level group by expanding the server group entries until the group you want to use is displayed. Then select the name of the group.

6. Click Save.

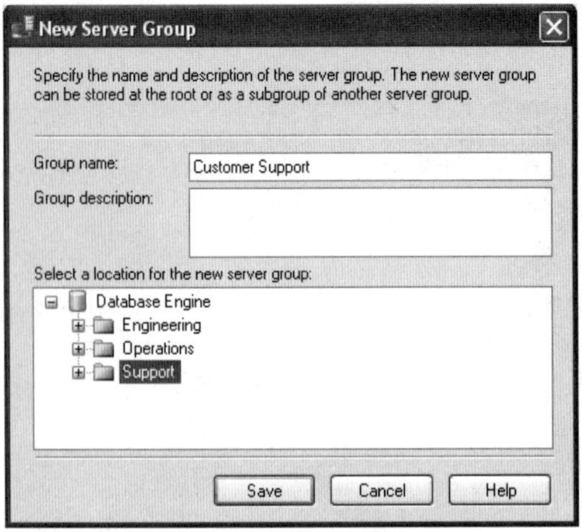

Figure 5-4   The New Server Group dialog box

Deleting a Server Group

You can delete a group or subgroup by completing the following steps:

1. In Console Root pane of the SQL Server Management Studio window, select Registered Servers view by pressing Ctrl+Alt+G. If the view was previously hidden, this also displays the view.

2. Use the Registered Servers toolbar to select the top-level group in which the group you want to delete is located. For example, if you want to delete a second-level or third-level group for Database Engine instances, select Database Engine.

3. Click the plus sign (+) next to the group or subgroup you want to delete. If the group has servers registered in it, move them to a different group. (The steps involved in moving servers to a new group are explained in the section later in this chapter titled "Moving a Server to a New Group.")

4. Select the group or subgroup entry.

5. Press Delete. When prompted to confirm the action, click Yes.

Editing and Moving Server Groups

Server groups have several key properties you can edit: the name, the description, and the location in the Registered Server hierarchy. To edit a group's name or description, follow these steps:

1. Right-click the group in Registered Servers view, point to Edit, and then select Server Group Properties.

2. In the Edit Server Group Properties dialog box, enter the new group name and description.

3. Click Save.

To move a group (and all its associated subgroups and servers) to a new level in the server group hierarchy, follow these steps:

1. Right-click the group in Registered Servers view and select Move To.

2. In the Move Server Registration dialog box, expand the top-level group to see a list of subgroups. Expand subgroups as necessary. You can now:
   - ❑ Move the group to the top-level group by selecting the top-level group. This will make the group a second-level group.
   - ❑ Move the group to a different level by selecting a subgroup into which you want to place the group.

3. Click OK.

Adding SQL Servers to a Group

When you register a SQL Server for use with SQL Server Management Studio, you can choose the group in which you want the server. You can even create a new group specifically for the server. The next section, "Managing Servers," covers the topic of server registration.

Managing Servers

Servers and databases are the primary resources you manage in SQL Server Management Studio. When you select a top-level group in Registered Servers view, you can see the available server groups. If you expand the view of these groups by double-clicking the group name, you can see the subgroups or servers assigned to a particular group. Local servers are registered automatically (in most cases). If the remote server you want to manage is not shown, you will need to register it. If a local server is not shown, you will need to update the local registration information. Once you do that, you can connect to the server to work with it and then disconnect when you are finished simply by double-clicking the server entry in Registered Servers view. If you are not automatically connected, you can force a connection by right-clicking the server entry, pointing to Connect, and then selecting New Query (if you want to make a SQL query) or Object Explorer (if you want to view and manage the server).

You can start the registration process by using either of the following techniques:

- Register a server to which you are connected in Object Explorer.
- Register a new server in Registered Servers view.

You can manage previous registrations in a variety of ways. You can:

- Import registration information on previously registered SQL Server 2000 servers.
- Update registration information for local servers.
- Copy registration information from one computer to another using import and export.

Registering a Connected Server

Any server to which you have connected in the Object Explorer can be registered easily. Registration saves the current connection information and assigns the server to a group for easy future access using Registered Servers view. To register a connected server, follow these steps:

1. Right-click any server to which you are currently connected in Object Explorer view, and then choose Register to display the Register Server dialog box shown in Figure 5-5.

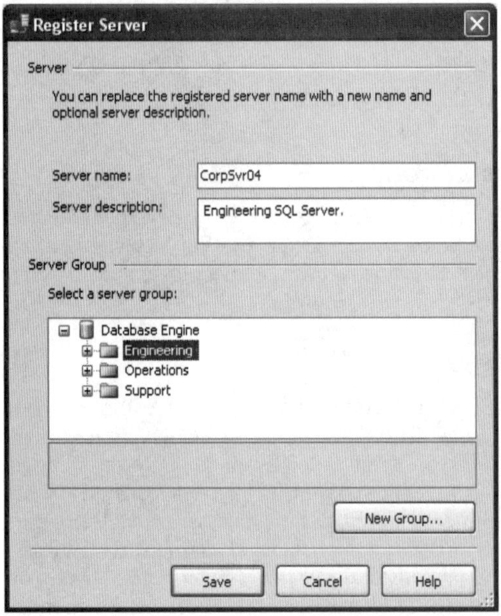

Figure 5-5   The Register Server dialog box

2. The server name defaults to the current name. You can modify this name and add a description if desired.

3. Under Server Group, you will see the top-level server group and any second-level server groups you created. You can now:

   ❑ Add the server to one of the top-level or second-level groups by clicking the group name.

   ❑ Add the server to a lower-level group by expanding the server group entries until the group you want to use is displayed. Select this group.

4. Add the server to a new group by clicking New Group. Create the new group using the New Server Group dialog box.

5. Click Save.

Registering a New Server in Registered Servers View

You do not have to connect to a server in Object Explorer to register it. You can register new servers directly in Registered Servers view by following these steps:

1. In Registered Servers view, use the toolbar to select the type of server to which you want to connect, such as Database Engine.

2. Expand the available groups as necessary, and then right-click the group into which you want to place the server in Registered Servers view.

3. Point to New, and then select Server Registration to display the New Server Registration dialog box shown in Figure 5-6.

4. In the Server Name box, type the fully qualified domain name or host name of the server on which SQL Server is running, such as **corpsvr04.cpandl.com** or **CorpSvr04**.

5. Use the Authentication selection menu to choose the authentication type, either Windows Authentication or SQL Server Authentication (based on the authentication types selected when you installed the server). Provide a Windows user name or SQL Server login ID and password as necessary.

   ■ **Windows Authentication** Uses your current domain account and password to establish the database connection. This authentication type works only if Windows authentication is enabled and you have appropriate privileges.

   ■ **SQL Server Authentication** Allows you to specify a SQL Server login ID and password. To save the password so that you do not have to re-enter it each time you connect, select Remember Password.

6. You can also set connection settings using the options on the Connection Properties tab. These options allow you to connect to a specific database instance and to set the network configuration.

7. The registered server name is filled in for you based on the previously entered server name. Change the default name only if you want SQL Server Management Studio to use an alternate display name for the server.

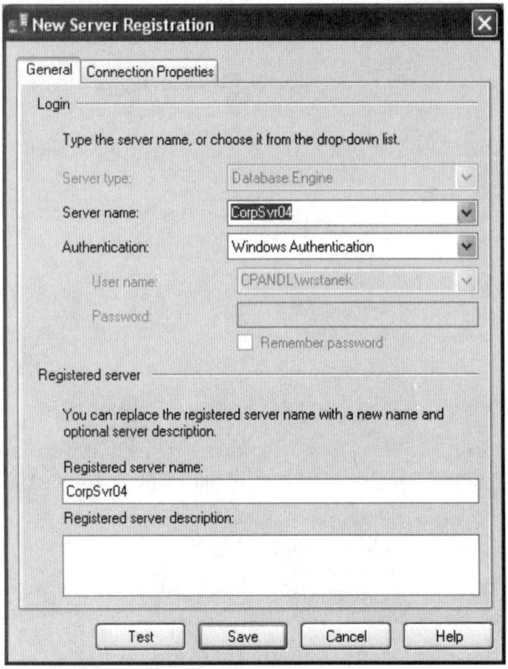

Figure 5-6   The New Server Registration dialog box

8. To test the settings, click Test. If you successfully connect to the server, you will see a prompt confirming this. If the test fails, verify the information you provided, make changes as necessary, and then test the settings again.

9. Click Save.

Registering Previously Registered SQL Server 2000 Servers

Registration details for servers registered by SQL Server 2000 can be imported into SQL Server Management Studio. This makes it easier to work with existing SQL Server 2000 installations. If the SQL Server 2000 installations were previously registered on the computer, you can import the registration details into a specific server group by completing the following steps:

1. In Registered Servers view, use the toolbar to select the type of servers you are registering, such as Database Engine.

2. Expand the available groups as necessary, and then right-click the group into which you want to place the SQL Server 2000 servers. Select Previously Registered Servers.

3. Available registration information for SQL Server 2000 servers will be imported. If an error prompt is displayed, you might not be logged on locally to the computer on which the servers were registered previously.

Updating Registration for Local Servers

Local servers are registered automatically (in most cases). If you have added or removed SQL Server instances to the local computer and those instances are not displayed, you will need to update the local server registration. Updating the registration information ensures that all currently configured local server instances are shown in SQL Server Management Studio.

To update registration details for local servers, follow these steps:

1. In Registered Servers view, use the toolbar to select the type of servers you are registering, such as Database Engine.

2. Right-click the top-level group entry, and then select Update Local Server Registration.

Copying Server Groups and Registration Details from One Computer to Another

Once you have registered servers in SQL Server Management Studio and placed the servers into a specific group hierarchy, you may find that you want to use the same registration information and server group structure on another computer. SQL Server Management Studio allows you to copy registration information from one computer to another using an import/export process. You can copy the registration details with or without the user names and passwords.

To export the registration and group information to a file on one computer and then import it onto another computer, complete the following steps:

1. Start SQL Server Management Studio on the computer with the registration and group structure details that you want to copy.

2. Select Registered Servers view by pressing Ctrl+Alt+G.

3. In Registered Servers view, use the toolbar to select the type of servers you want to work with, such as Database Engine.

4. Right-click the top-level group, and then select Export to display the Export Registered Servers dialog box shown in Figure 5-7.

5. Under Server Group, select the point from which the export process will begin. You can start copying registration information at any level in the group structure:

   ❑ To copy the structure for a top-level group, all its subgroups, and all registration details for all related servers, select the top-level group.

   ❑ To copy the structure for a subgroup, its subgroups (if any), and all registration details for all related servers, select a subgroup.

   ❑ To copy the registration details for a single server, select the server.

   ❑ To copy the structure for a subgroup and all registered servers, right-click the subgroup, and then select Export.

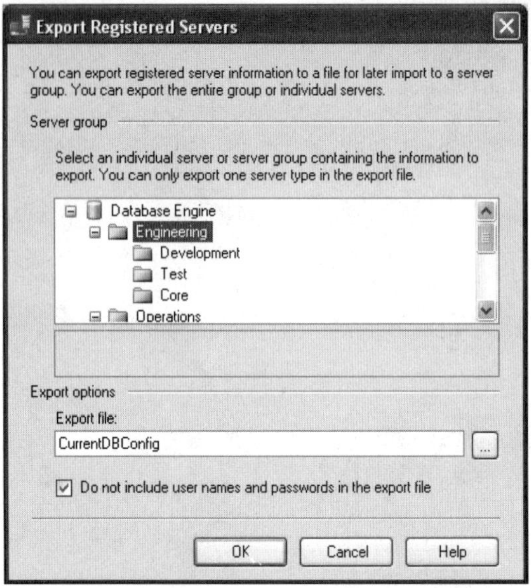

Export Registered Servers ⊠

You can export registered server information to a file for later import to a server group. You can export the entire group or individual servers.

Server group

Select an individual server or server group containing the information to export. You can only export one server type in the export file.

- Database Engine
  - Engineering
    - Development
    - Test
    - Core
  - Operations

Export options

Export file:

CurrentDBConfig   [...]

☑ Do not include user names and passwords in the export file

[OK]   [Cancel]   [Help]

Figure 5-7   The Export Registered Servers dialog box

6. The server group structure and registration details are exported to a Registration Server File with the .regsrvr extension. By default, this file is created in your My Documents folder. Under Export Options, type a name for the Registration Server File, such as **CurrentDBConfig**.

 Tip   If you place the registration server file on a secure network share, you can access it on the computer to which you want to copy the registration information. Otherwise, you will need to copy this file to this computer later.

7. By default, the current authentication details for server connections are not exported into the save file. If you want to export user names and passwords, clear the Do Not Include User Names And Passwords In The Export File check box.

8. Click OK. If the export was successful, you will see a dialog box confirming this. Click OK in the dialog box. If there was a problem, note and correct the problem.

9. Start SQL Server Management Studio on the computer to which you want to copy the server group and registration details. If you did not place the registration server file on a secure network share, you will need to copy the file to this computer now.

10. Select Registered Servers view by pressing Ctrl+Alt+G.

11. In Registered Servers view, use the toolbar to select the type of servers you want to work with, such as Database Engine.

12. Right-click the top-level group, and then select Import to display the Import Registered Servers dialog box shown in Figure 5-8.

13. Click the button to the right of the Import File text box in the dialog box, and then use the Open dialog box that displays to select the Registration Server File you want to import.

14. Under Server Group, select the server group under which you want the imported groups and servers to be created.

15. Click OK. If the import was successful, you will see a dialog box confirming this. Click OK in the dialog box. If there was a problem, note and correct the problem.

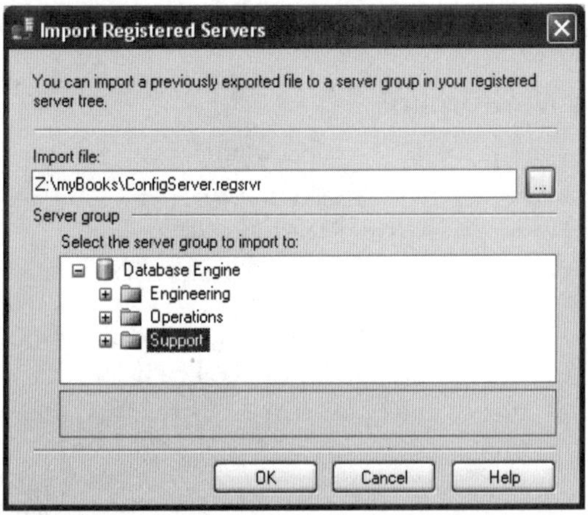

Figure 5-8 The Import Registered Servers dialog box

Editing Registration Properties

You can change a server's registration properties at any time by right-clicking the server entry in Registered Servers view in SQL Server Management Studio, pointing to Edit, and then selecting SQL Server Registration Properties. Use the Edit Server Registration Properties dialog box to make necessary changes. The only property you cannot change is the server type. Be sure to test the settings before saving them.

Connecting to a Server

Once you have registered a server, connecting to it is easy. Right-click the server entry in the Registered Servers view in SQL Server Management Studio, point to Connect, and then select New Query (if you want to make a SQL query) or Object Explorer (if you want to view and manage the server). Or you can double-click the server entry to establish a connection and display the server's Properties dialog box.

Note   SQL Server Management Studio connects to other SQL servers using the network protocol set in the registration properties. If you have disabled the network protocol or remote access entirely, however, you will not be able to connect to that server in SQL Server Management Studio. You will need to make the appropriate changes in the registration properties or in the surface area configuration. Chapter 3 discusses surface area configuration.

Disconnecting from a Server

When you are finished working with a server, you may want to disconnect from it. This cuts down on the back-and-forth communications to the server. To disconnect, right-click the server's entry in Object Explorer view in SQL Server Management Studio, and then select Disconnect from the shortcut menu.

Moving a Server to a New Group

To move the server to a new group, complete the following steps:

1. Right-click the server in Registered Servers view and select Move To from the shortcut menu to display the Move Server Registration dialog box.
2. In the Move Server Registration dialog box, expand the top-level group to see a list of subgroups. Expand subgroups as necessary. You can now:
   - ❑ Move the server to the top-level group by selecting the top-level group. This will make the server a member of the top-level group.
   - ❑ Move the server to a different level by selecting a subgroup into which you want to place the server.
3. Click OK.

Deleting a Server Registration

If you change a server name or remove a server, you may want to delete the server registration in SQL Server Management Studio so that SQL Server Management Studio no longer tries to connect to a server that cannot be accessed. Right-click the server entry in the Console Root pane, and then select Delete. When prompted to confirm the action, click Yes to delete the server registration details.

Starting, Stopping, and Configuring SQL Server Agent

SQL Server Agent runs as a service, and it is used to schedule jobs, alerts, and other automated tasks. After you have scheduled automated tasks, you will usually want SQL Server Agent to start automatically when the system starts. This ensures that the scheduled tasks are performed as expected. Using SQL Server Configuration Manager, you can control the related service (SQLServerAgent or SQLAgent$*instancename*) just as you do the SQL Server service. For details, see the section titled "Configuring SQL Server Services" in Chapter 3.

You use SQL Server Management Studio to configure SQL Server Agent. Chapter 15, "Database Automation and Maintenance," covers the agent configuration in detail, but the basic steps are as follows:

1. Connect to the Database Engine on the server you want to configure. You can do this in Registered Servers view by double-clicking the server entry, or you can use Object Explorer view. In Object Explorer view, click Connect, and then select Database Engine to display the Connect To Server dialog box, which you can use to connect to the server.

2. Right-click the SQL Server Agent node, and then select Properties from the shortcut menu. You can now configure SQL Server Agent. Keep in mind that if the service is not running, you will need to start it before you can manage its properties.

3. The SQL Server Agent shortcut menu also lets you manage the SQL Server Agent service. Select Start, Stop, or Restart as appropriate.

Starting, Stopping, and Configuring the Microsoft Distributed Transaction Coordinator

Microsoft Distributed Transaction Coordinator (MS DTC) is a transaction manager that makes it possible for client applications to work with multiple sources of data in one transaction.

When a distributed transaction spans two or more servers, the servers coordinate the management of the transaction using MS DTC. When a distributed transaction spans multiple databases on a single server, SQL Server manages the transaction internally.

SQL Server applications can call MS DTC directly to start an explicit distributed transaction. Distributed transactions can also be started implicitly by using one of the following methods:

- Calling stored procedures on remote servers running SQL Server
- Updating data on multiple OLE DB data sources
- Enlisting remote servers in a transaction

If you work with transactions under any of these scenarios, you will want to have DTC running on the server, and you will probably also want DTC to start automatically when the server starts. As with SQL Server itself, DTC runs as a service. This service is named Distributed Transaction Coordinator. Unlike the SQL Server service, only one instance of the MS DTC service runs on a computer, regardless of how many database server instances are available. This means that all instances of SQL Server running on a computer use the same transaction coordinator.

You can view the current state of the Distributed Transaction Coordinator in SQL Server Management Studio by connecting to the server's Database Engine. In

Object Explorer, expand the server and Management nodes. If the service is running, you will see a green circle with a right-facing triangle in it (similar to a play button). If the service is stopped, you will see a red circle with a square in it (similar to a stop button). You can control the DTC service with Computer Management. Follow these steps:

1. Start SQL Server Management Studio by clicking the Start button, pointing to Programs or All Programs, Microsoft SQL Server 2005 and then selecting SQL Server Management Studio.

2. By default, you are connected to the local computer. To connect to a remote computer, right-click the Computer Management node, and then select Connect To Another Computer. In the Select Computer dialog box, choose Another Computer, and then type the name of the computer. The name can be specified as a host name, such as **CorpSvr04**, or a fully qualified domain name, such as **corpsvr04.cpandl.com**.

3. Expand Services And Application, and then select Services. Right-click Distributed Transaction Coordinator, and then choose Properties. You can now manage MS DTC.

Starting, Stopping, and Configuring the Microsoft Search Service

Microsoft Search is a service that performs the necessary management and search tasks for full-text indexes and their related catalogs. These indexes and catalogs are created automatically when you start and stop the search service. You can view the current state of Full-Text Search in SQL Server Management Studio by connecting to the server's Database Engine. In Object Explorer, expand the server and Management nodes. If the service is running, you will see a green circle with a right-facing triangle in it (similar to a play button). If the service is stopped, you will see a red circle with a square in it (similar to a stop button).

Using SQL Server Configuration Manager, you can control the related service (msftesql) just as you do the SQL Server service. For details, see the section titled "Configuring SQL Server Services" in Chapter 3. You can manage the service by completing the following steps:

1. Connect to the Database Engine on the server you want to manage. You can do this in Registered Servers view by double-clicking the server entry, or you can use Object Explorer view. In Object Explorer view, click Connect, and then select Database Engine to display the Connect To Server dialog box, which you can use to connect to the server.

2. In Object Explorer view, expand the server and Management nodes so that you can see the support services options.

3. Right-click the Full-Text Search node, and then choose Start, Stop or Restart as appropriate.

Working with Full-Text Search

Full-text search allows extensive word searches of textual data, and it is an additional component that you can add to the SQL Server installation. (For details, see the section titled "Adding Components and Instances" in Chapter 2, "Deploying Microsoft SQL Server 2005.") After you install the full-text search component, you can manage full-text searches by using the methods described in the following sections.

Several administration tasks are required to utilize full-text search. You must:

- Install the Full-Text Search component using SQL Server 2005 Setup.
- Start the related service, which is called the Microsoft Search service, shown in the interface as msftesql.
- Enable full-text search of the database using *sp_fulltext_database* enable.
- Create a full-text catalog for the database.
- Have a unique index.
- Create a full-text index on a specific table or view.

Real World   You can use CREATE FULLTEXT CATALOG to create full-text catalogs. Be sure to use the IN PATH clause to set the file location. Because the file may be searched frequently, you probably will want to have the catalog file on its own drive, and the IN PATH clause lets you specify the file location.

Before you create a searchable full-text index from a catalog, you must ensure the table or view has a unique, single-column, non-nullable index. The full-text search engine uses this unique index to map rows in the tables to unique keys. You can create a unique index using CREATE UNIQUE INDEX. The syntax is:

```
CREATE UNIQUE INDEX indexname on table(uniquecolumn)
```

The following example creates an index called *ui_per* on *Employee* table in the *Personnel* database using the EmpID column:

```
use Personnel

go

CREATE UNIQUE INDEX ui_per on dbo.Employee(EmpID)

go
```

Once you have a unique key, you can create a full-text index on the database table using CREATE FULLTEXT INDEX or Object Explorer view.

When you create a full-text catalog, the search service (msftesql) creates full-text indexes of textual data contained in the database. Then the service manages the indexes and provides the primary mechanism for examining the data they contain. Unlike previous versions of the search service, the search service is managed separately for each instance of SQL Server. There is, however, only one search service per server. The search service runs under the same service account as the related SQL Server service. Thus, if you change the service account for the SQL Server service, you must change the service account for the search service as well.

Note   In the Support Services folder in SQL Server Management Studio, the Microsoft Search service is referred to as Full-Text Search. Don't let the terminology confuse you. Both references are to the same service, and the correct name is Microsoft Search service.

The concept of a full-text index in SQL Server may be a bit different than you have encountered elsewhere. In SQL Server, a full-text index stores information about keywords and their location within a specific column. These text indexes are created for each table in the database, and groups of indexes are contained in catalogs. Each full-text catalog is treated as a file, and it is included in the database file set to facilitate backup and restore utilities so that you can back up and restore full-text catalogs like other SQL Server data, eliminating the need to repopulate catalogs completely after a database restore. The BACKUP and RESTORE statements in Transact-SQL can be used to back up and restore full-text catalogs with a database automatically. For backup and recovery options, see Chapter 14, "Backing Up and Recovering SQL Server 2005."

Note   Full-text catalogs are also attached and detached with the database, so full-text catalogs are preserved when you move databases to new locations. You no longer have to delete and rebuild the full-text catalog. You simply detach the database, copy it to a new location, and then reattach it. The full-text catalog is preserved.

The all-table column text is indexed, including the columns containing the new XML data type. This allows you to perform full-text searches on column values that contain XML data as well as any other type of textual data. In earlier versions of SQL Server, you could query linked servers, but you could not perform full-text queries against linked servers. When searching tables in previous versions, you were limited to searching one column or all columns, but now you can search any number of columns. New features in SQL Server 2005 allow you to issue full-text queries referencing a remote linked server and to search across multiple columns.

Full-text indexes are defined on base tables and views that have one or more full-text indexed base tables. They are not defined on views, system tables, or temporary tables. The ability to search on views is an important new change for SQL Server 2005. Indexes are populated with key values that have information about the significant words in a table, such as the column they are in and their location in the column. You can create, modify, and implement full-text catalogs and indexes using both stored procedures and data definition language (DDL) statements. In Transact-SQL, you can test rows against a full-text search condition using the functions *contains* and *freetext*. You can also return the set of rows that match a full-text search condition using the functions *containstable* and *freetexttable*.

Managing Full-Text Catalogs

Each database that you want to search must have its own full-text catalog. When you create a catalog, you can set a schedule for populating the catalog on a regular basis, or you elect to manually populate the catalog as necessary. Populating the catalog updates the full-text indexes for the catalog and ensures that the search results are accurate. SQL Server supports several methods for populating catalogs including:

- **Full population** The search service builds index entries for all rows in all the tables or views covered by the full-text catalog. In most cases, you perform a full population only when you create a catalog or need to refresh the entire contents of a catalog.

- **Incremental population** The search service only changes index entries for rows that have been added, deleted, or modified since the last population. You can perform incremental population only on tables or views that have a time-stamp column. If a table or view does not have a time-stamp column, full populations are always performed.

- **Update population** The search service uses update population in conjunction with change tracking. Change tracking of tables and views allows full-text search to track changes in the catalog or views and update the catalog either automatically or manually. If you disable change tracking, you can perform incremental population only on tables or views that have a time-stamp column (and if a table or view does not have a time-stamp column, full populations are always performed).

Creating a catalog is only one part of the indexing process. After you create the catalog, you must select individual tables or views for indexing and associate these with the catalog. You also need to specify the individual table or view columns that should be indexed. Periodically, you may also need to clean up old catalogs.

Viewing Catalog Properties

Catalogs are stored separately from the databases themselves. You can set the catalog file location when you create the catalog. You cannot change or view the file location after the catalog is created. To examine other catalog configuration properties on a database for which you have configured full-text search, complete the following steps:

1. Start SQL Server Management Studio, and then connect to a server of your choice.
2. Use Object Explorer view to access a database. Expand the server node and the Databases node.
3. Under the Databases node, expand Storage and Full Text Catalogs nodes to display the catalog(s) for the selected database (see Figure 5-9).

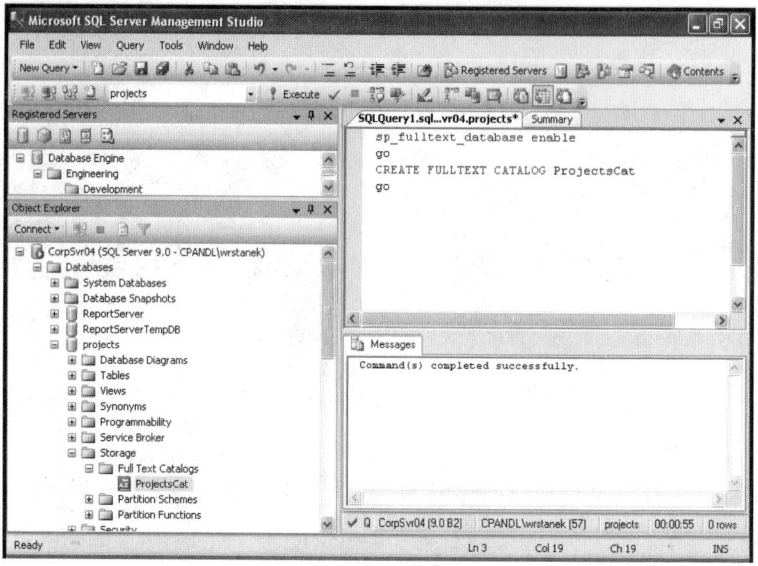

Figure 5-9   List of catalogs associated with a database

4. Right-click the catalog, and then choose Properties to open the Full-Text Catalog Properties dialog box shown in Figure 5-10.

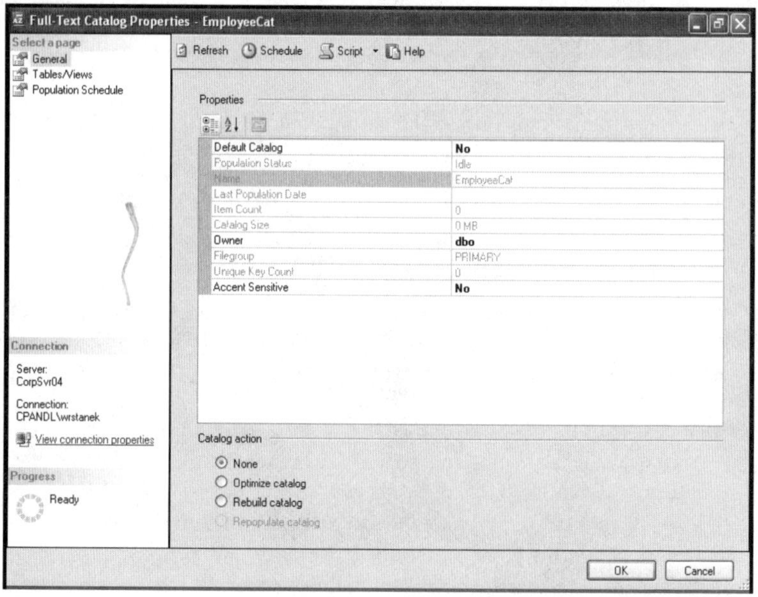

Figure 5-10   The General page of the Full-Text Catalog Properties dialog box

5. The General tab provides the following information:

   - **Default Catalog** Indicates if the catalog is the default for the database.
   - **Population Status** Indicates whether the catalog is being built or updated (referred to as populating).
   - **Name** Specifies the name of the catalog.
   - **Last Populate Date** Specifies the date the catalog was last populated. For new catalogs, this will be blank.
   - **Item Count** Specifies the number of items cataloged.
   - **Catalog Size** Specifies the total size of the catalog on disk.
   - **Owner** Specifies the catalog owner. If no owner was set when the catalog was created, the owner is set as dbo.
   - **Filegroup** Specifies the filegroup with which the catalog is associated. Whenever the associated filegroup is backed up or restored, the catalog will be backed up or restored as well.
   - **Unique Key Count** Specifies the number of unique keys cataloged.
   - **Accent Sensitive** Indicates if the catalog is accent sensitive. The default sensitivity is set the same as the database.

Creating Catalogs

You need catalogs to perform full-text searches of databases. A single database can have multiple catalogs associated with it, and you can use these catalogs to perform different types of searches. For example, in a customer database, you could create one catalog for searching company contact information and another for searching account history.

You cannot create full-text catalogs in the *master*, *model*, or *tempdb* databases. Although a full-text catalog can have several full-text indexes, a full-text index can only be part of one full-text catalog. To create a catalog for a database, complete the following steps:

1. Start SQL Server Management Studio, and then connect to a server.

2. Use Object Explorer view to access a database. Expand the server node and the Databases node.

3. Under the Databases node, expand Storage and Full Text Catalogs nodes to display the catalog(s) for the selected database.

4. Right-click Full-Text Catalogs, and then select New Full-Text Catalog to display the New Full-Text Catalog dialog box shown in Figure 5-11.

5. Type a descriptive name for the catalog in the Full-Text Catalog Name text box.

6. Use the Catalog Location box to set the physical file location of the catalog. You can type the folder path or click the location button (. . .) to choose a folder path.

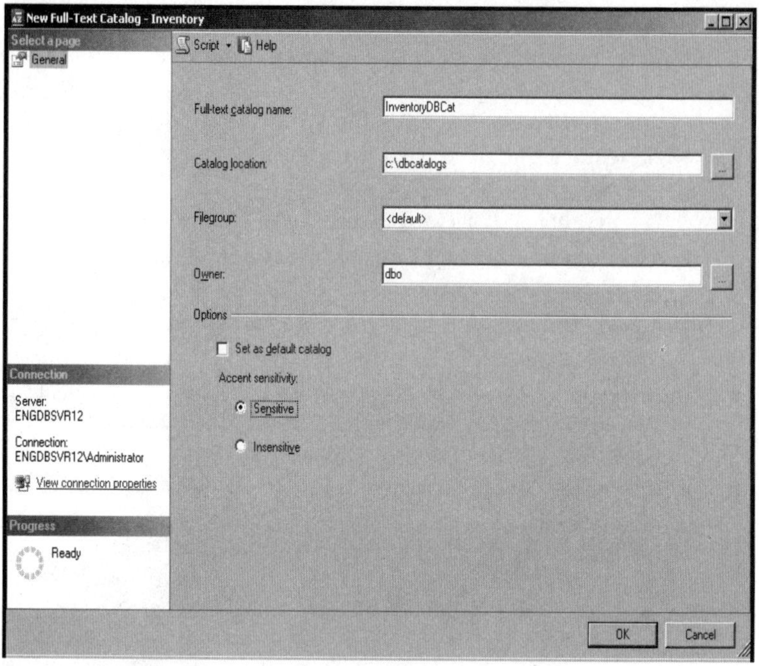

Figure 5-11 New Full-Text Catalog dialog box

 Note Catalogs are considered to be a type of database file, and they are associated with a specific filegroup. You can set the location of the catalog only when you create the catalog. After the location is set, the value cannot be changed without re-creating the catalog. If catalogs will be searched frequently, you should plan where they will be located carefully. Catalog searches are read intensive. Data is written to catalogs when catalogs are updated. Also, note that a catalog's location is no longer listed in the standard properties, so you should document the location of each catalog.

7. The catalog is backed up and restored as part of a designated filegroup. Use the Filegroup box to associate the catalog with a specific database filegroup.

8. Use the Owner box to set the catalog owner. The default catalog owner is dbo. If you do not want to use the default, type a new user or database role name in the text box provided or click the object button (. . .) to browse for a user or database role to use.

9. If you want to make the catalog the default for the selected database, select Set As Default Catalog.

10. By default, catalog accent sensitivity is set the same as the selected database. If you want to allow accent-sensitive searches, select the Sensitive option.

Otherwise, select Insensitive to allow searches to match characters without regard to accents.

11. Click OK to create the catalog.

Next, you will need to enable indexing and populate the catalog.

Enabling Indexing of Tables and Views

You can enable indexing of a table or view by completing the following steps:

1. Start SQL Server Management Studio, and then connect to a server.

2. Use Object Explorer view to access a database. Expand the server node and the Databases node.

3. Under the Databases node, expand Tables or Views as appropriate. Right-click the table or view, point to Full-Text Index, and then select Define Full-Text Index to start the Full-Text Indexing Wizard. Click Next.

4. Select a unique index for the table or view, and then click Next. The index is used as a unique constraint on a single column in the table and can be used in joins. If the table or view does not have a unique index, you must exit the wizard, create an index (as discussed in the section titled "Working with Full-Text Search" earlier in this chapter), and then restart this process.

5. As shown in Figure 5-12, select the character or image-based columns that you want to index. Each column can be set with a language constraint that identifies the natural language of the column. With text and binary data, you can also specify a document type. Click Next.

Figure 5-12   The Full-Text Indexing Wizard

6. Specify if you want the changes to the tables and views to be tracked for the purpose of updating the full-text catalog. When you make a decision about automatically tracking changes, keep the following information in mind:

   ❑ If you elect to automatically track changes, the wizard will fully populate the catalog with the index for this table before exiting. The catalog will also be configured so that changes are tracked as they occur, and the changes will be applied automatically to keep the catalog up to date with regard to the current table or view.

   ❑ If you elect to manually track changes, the wizard will fully populate the catalog with the index for this table before exiting. Then you can apply tracked changes manually to keep the catalog up to date with regard to the current table or view.

   ❑ If you do not want to track changes and do not want the catalog to be populated at this time, select Do Not Track Changes and clear Start Full Population When Index Is Created.

7. Click Next. Use the Select Full-Text Catalog drop-down list to choose an existing catalog, or select Create A New Catalog, and then configure the new catalog options.

8. Click Next. You can now select or create population schedules for the catalog. You can also select or create a population schedule for the currently selected table.

 Real World In most cases, you will want to create schedules for populating an entire catalog rather than an individual table. However, in some cases, populating individual tables makes sense, especially if the contents of a particular table change frequently and contents of other tables change rarely.

9. Click Next, and then click Finish. SQL Server Management Studio defines the full-text index for the table. If you selected the Do Not Track Changes option and cleared Start Full Population When Index Is Created, you must populate the index manually or create a schedule for performing this task. Otherwise, the index is populated in the catalog.

Editing Indexing of Tables and Views

To change the indexing settings of a table, complete the following steps:

1. Start SQL Server Management Studio, and then connect to a server.

2. Use Object Explorer view to access a database. Expand the server node and the Databases node.

3. Under the Databases node, expand Tables or Views as appropriate. Right-click the table or view, point to Full-Text Index, and then select Properties to display the Full-Text Indexing Properties dialog box for the table or view. Then use the dialog box options to edit the settings you want to change.

The Full-Text Indexing Properties dialog box has three pages:

- **General**   Shows the current configuration. Properties in bold can be changed, and properties that are dimmed cannot be changed. Select or clear the Full-Text Indexing Enabled option to enable or disable indexing. Use the Change Tracking option to configure manual or automatic change tracking, or to turn change tracking off.

- **Columns**   Shows the unique index and index columns. You can change the unique index and the index column settings using the options provided.

- **Schedule**   Shows currently defined schedules for populating the full-text index. You can add and modify schedules using the options provided.

Disabling and Removing Full-Text Indexing from Tables and Views

If you want to stop full-text indexing of a table or view temporarily, you can disable the related full-text index. It is useful to disable full-text indexing if you are making a lot of updates to a table or view, to avoid triggering an update, or to prevent a scheduled incremental or full population of the database.

If you decide that you do not want to index a table or view any more, you can remove full-text indexing completely. Removing full-text indexing removes all references to the table or view in the related catalog. This data must be recreated if you later decide to restore full-text indexing.

To disable or remove full-text indexing from a table or view, complete the following steps:

1. Start SQL Server Management Studio, and then connect to a server.
2. Use Object Explorer view to access a database. Expand the server node and the Databases node.
3. Under the Databases node, expand Tables or Views as appropriate. You can now:
   - ❑ Disable the full-text index. To do so, right-click the table or view, point to Full-Text Index, and then select Disable Full-Text Index.
   - ❑ Remove the full-text index. To do so, right-click the table or view, point to Full-Text Index, and then select Remove Full-Text Index. When prompted to confirm the action, click OK.

Populating Full-Text Catalogs

After you select the tables and views you want to index, you can fully populate the catalog so that the table or view can be searched in connection with the related catalog. After the catalog is populated with this data, you can maintain the catalog related to a table or view manually, according to a schedule, or through change tracking. With scheduled jobs, you set a schedule that instructs SQL Server Agent to run a one-time or recurring job that populates the catalog. You can populate catalogs at the database level or at the table level. In most cases, you will want to create schedules for populating an entire catalog rather than an individual table.

However, there are times when populating individual tables makes sense, especially if the contents of a particular table change frequently and the contents of other tables change rarely.

Populating Catalogs Manually for All Selected Tables and Views

To populate a catalog manually with text for all tables and views selected for indexing, complete the following steps:

1. Start SQL Server Management Studio, and then connect to a server.
2. Use Object Explorer view to access a database. Expand the server node and the Databases node.
3. Under the Databases node, expand Storage and Full Text Catalogs nodes to display the catalog(s) for the selected database.
4. Right-click Full Text Catalogs, and then select Rebuild All to rebuild the entire full-text index. To rebuild only a catalog of interest, right-click the catalog and select Rebuild.

Using Scheduled Jobs to Populate Catalogs for All Selected Tables and Views

To set a schedule for populating a catalog with text for all tables and views selected for indexing, complete the following steps:

1. Start SQL Server Management Studio, and then connect to a server.
2. Use Object Explorer view to access a database. Expand the server node and the Databases node.
3. Under the Databases node, expand Storage and Full Text Catalogs nodes to display the catalog(s) for the selected database.
4. Right-click the catalog you want to work with, and then select Properties to display the Full-Text Catalog Properties dialog box.
5. Select the Population Schedule page under Select A Page. Any currently scheduled jobs are listed by name and population type. You can edit or delete existing jobs, or click New to create a new schedule for populating the catalog.
6. In the New Full-Text Indexing Catalog Schedule dialog box, type a descriptive name for the job used to schedule the catalog population.
7. Set the schedule type. Typically, you will want to select either One Time or Recurring.
8. Use the remaining options to determine when the job runs. One-time jobs run at a specific date and time. Recurring jobs run daily, weekly, or monthly at a specific date and time.

Tip In most cases, you will want to create a recurring job. The first time the job is run, it will perform a full population of the catalog if this task has not been performed previously. On successive runs, the job will perform the population according to the population type. SQL Server Agent runs scheduled tasks. The agent identifies scheduled tasks by the unique job name you specify. You will learn more about SQL Server Agent in Chapter 15.

9. Click OK to close the New Full-Text Indexing Catalog Schedule dialog box.

10. In the Full-Text Catalog Properties dialog box, click in the Population Type column for the scheduled job you just created. The options depend on the state of the catalog and include:

   ■ **Catalog – Full**   Performs a full population of the catalog, which essentially rebuilds the catalog. This is a task that you will select only occasionally. For example, you might rebuild a catalog once a quarter.

   ■ **Catalog – Incremental**   Performs an incremental population of the catalog based on time-stamp changes. With change tracking, an incremental build updates the catalog for tracked changes as well. You can also apply tracked changes manually.

   ■ **Catalog – Optimize**   Performs an optimize build of the catalog to improve performance. This is a task you might want to schedule periodically to enhance search performance. However, optimization, like a rebuild, can be a time-consuming and resource-intensive process, so you will want to schedule this task when activity levels are low.

11. Click OK.

Populating Catalogs Manually for a Specific Table or View

To manually populate a catalog with text for a single table or view, complete the following steps:

1. Start SQL Server Management Studio, and then connect to a server.

2. Use Object Explorer view to access a database. Expand the server node and the Databases node.

3. Under the Databases node, expand Tables or Views as appropriate. Right-click the table or view, point to Full-Text Index, and then select Start Full Population or Start Incremental Population. If you want to stop the population, right-click the table or view, select to Full-Text Index, and then select Stop Population.

Using Scheduled Jobs to Populate Catalogs for a Specific Table or View

To set a schedule for populating a catalog with text for a single table, complete the following steps:

1. Start SQL Server Management Studio, and then connect to a server.

2. Use Object Explorer view to access a database. Expand the server node and the Databases node.

3. Under the Databases node, expand Tables or Views as appropriate. Right-click the table or view, point to Full-Text Index, and then select Properties.

4. Select the Schedules page under Select A Page. Any current scheduled jobs are listed by name and population type. You can edit or delete existing jobs, or click New to create a new schedule for populating the catalog with text for the table or index.

5. In the New Full-Text Indexing Table Schedule dialog box, type a descriptive name for the job used to schedule the catalog population.

6. Set the schedule type. Typically, you will want to use One Time or Recurring.

7. Use the remaining options to determine when the job runs. One-time jobs run at a specific date and time. Recurring jobs run daily, weekly, or monthly at a specific date and time.

Note   In most cases, you will want to create a recurring job. The first time the job is run, it will perform a full population of the catalog if this task has not been performed previously. On successive runs, the job will perform the population according to the population type. SQL Server Agent runs scheduled tasks. The agent identifies scheduled tasks by the unique job name you specify. You will learn more about SQL Server Agent in Chapter 15.

8. Click OK to close the New Full-Text Indexing Table Schedule dialog box.

9. In the Full-Text Index Properties dialog box, click in the Population Type column for the scheduled job you just created. The options are:

   ■ **Table – Full**   Performs a full population of the catalog, which essentially rebuilds the index for the table in the catalog. This is a task that you will select only occasionally.

   ■ **Table – Incremental**   Performs an incremental population of the catalog based on time-stamp changes to the table or index.

   ■ **Table – Update**   Performs an update population of the catalog based on tracked changes. You can also apply tracked changes manually.

10. Click OK.

Rebuilding Current Catalogs

When you make frequent changes to a database, catalogs can sometimes become inconsistent with the contents of a database. Over an extended period of time, catalogs also can become quite large. To resynchronize the catalog with the contents of the database or to compress a large catalog so that it does not waste space, you must rebuild the catalog.

You can rebuild catalogs individually or you can rebuild all the catalogs used by a database. To rebuild a single catalog, complete the following steps:

1. Start SQL Server Management Studio, and then connect to a server.

2. Use Object Explorer view to access a database. Expand the server node and the Databases node.

3. Under the Databases node, expand Storage and Full Text Catalogs nodes to display the catalog(s) for the selected database.

4. Right-click the catalog, and then select Rebuild. When prompted to confirm the action, click OK.

5. Use the Rebuild Full-Text Catalog dialog box to track the rebuild status, stop the rebuild, and display a rebuild report. Note any errors or warnings and read the related details in the report carefully. Click Close.

To rebuild all catalogs associated with a database, complete the following steps:

1. Start SQL Server Management Studio, and then connect to a server.

2. Use Object Explorer view to access a database. Expand the server node and the Databases node.

3. Under the Databases node, expand Storage and Full Text Catalogs nodes to display the catalog(s) for the selected database.

4. Right-click Full Text Catalogs, and then select Rebuild All. When prompted to confirm the action, click OK.

5. Use the Rebuild All Full-Text Catalog dialog box to track the rebuild status, stop the rebuild, and display a rebuild report. Note any errors or warnings and read the related details in the report carefully. Click Close.

Caution   Rebuilding catalogs can be a time-consuming and resource-intensive process. In a production environment, you should rebuild catalogs only during off-peak hours.

Cleaning Up Old Catalogs

Although the full-text search components do a good job of maintaining indexes and cleaning up after themselves, you will want to monitor the number and size of catalog files. You should also regularly clean up old catalogs to eliminate wasted storage space. You do this by completing the following steps:

1. Start SQL Server Management Studio, and then connect to a server.

2. Use Object Explorer view to access a database. Expand the server node and the Databases node.

3. Under the Databases node, expand Storage and Full Text Catalogs nodes to display the catalog(s) for the selected database.

4. Right-click the catalog, and then select Properties to display the Full-Text Catalog Properties dialog box.

5. On the General page, select Optimize Catalog, and then click OK.

Removing Catalogs

To remove a catalog, complete the following steps:

1. Start SQL Server Management Studio, and then connect to a server.

2. Use Object Explorer view to access a database. Expand the server node and the Databases node.

3. Under the Databases node, expand Storage and Full Text Catalogs nodes to display the catalog(s) for the selected database.

4. Right-click the catalog, and then select Delete. Click OK in the Delete Object dialog box.

To remove all catalogs associated with a database, complete the following steps:

1. Start SQL Server Management Studio, and then connect to a server.

2. Use Object Explorer view to access a database. Expand the server node and the Databases node.

3. Under the Databases node, expand Storage. Right-click Full Text Catalogs, and then select Delete All. When prompted to confirm the action, click OK.

Managing Server Activity

As a database administrator, it is your job to make sure that SQL Server runs smoothly. To ensure that SQL Server is running optimally, you can actively monitor the server to:

- Keep track of user connections and locks.
- View processes and commands that active users are running.
- Check the status of locks on processes and objects.
- See blocked or blocking transactions.
- Ensure that processes complete successfully and detect errors if they do not.

When problems arise, you can terminate a process, if necessary.

 Note For more coverage of monitoring SQL Server, see Chapter 13, "Profiling and Monitoring Microsoft SQL Server 2005." In that chapter, you will learn how to use Performance Monitor and SQL Server Profiler to keep track of SQL Server activity, performance, and errors.

Examining Process Information

Process information provides detailed information about the status of processes, current user connections, and other server activity. You can view process information by completing the following steps:

1. Start SQL Server Management Studio, and then connect to a server.

2. Use Object Explorer view to access a database. Expand the server node and the Management node.

3. Under the Management node, double-click Activity Monitor. You should see a summary of process activity similar to the report shown in Figure 5-13.

 Tip By default, process information is not updated automatically. To refresh the information, click Refresh on the toolbar. To configure automatic refresh, click the View Refresh Settings link under Status. In the Refresh Settings dialog box, select Auto-Refresh Every. After you set the refresh interval, click OK.

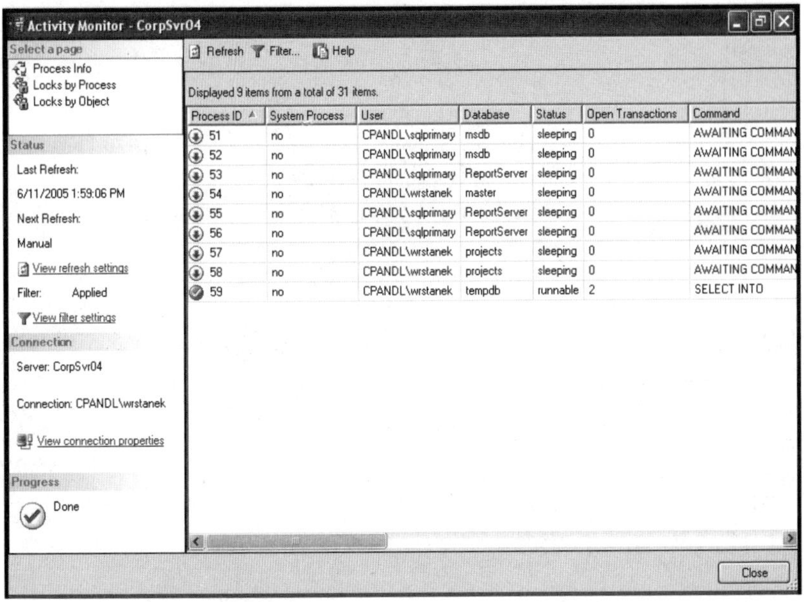

Figure 5-13   An Activity Monitor report

Initially, processes are sorted by process ID, but you can arrange them by any of the available information categories summarized in Table 5-2. Click a category header to sort processes based on that category. Click the same category header again to perform a reverse sort on the category.

Table 5-2   Process Information Used in Database Administration

Category	Description
Process ID	Provides the server process ID of the current user process.
System Process	Indicates if the process is a system process.
User	Shows which user is running the process by SQL Server ID or domain account, depending on the authentication technique used.
Database	Indicates the database with which the process is associated.
Status	Shows the status of the process, which is usually runnable, sleeping, or background. A runnable process is active. A sleeping process is waiting for input or a lock. A background process is running in the background and periodically performing tasks.
Open Transactions	Shows the number of open transactions.
Command	Displays the command being executed or the last command executed.
Application	Shows the application or SQL Server component connecting to the server and running the process, such as Report Server.
Wait Time	Indicates the elapsed wait time in milliseconds.

Table 5-2   Process Information Used in Database Administration   *(continued)*

Category	Description
Wait Type	Specifies whether the process is waiting or not waiting.
Resource	Displays the resource that the process is waiting for (if any).
CPU	Shows the amount of processor time (in milliseconds) used by the process.
Physical I/O	Indicates the physical input/output used by the process.
Memory Usage	Displays the amount of memory the process is using (in KB).
Login Time	Indicates when the connection was established.
Last Batch	Indicates when the last command was executed using the connection.
Host	Displays the host from which the connection originated.
Net Library	Shows the network library used to establish the connection.
Net Address	Shows the network address for the connection.
Blocked By	Displays the Process ID blocking this process.
Blocking	Displays the Process ID waiting for this process to finish.
Execution Context	Indicates the execution context of the process.

Tracking Locks by Process ID and Object

Locks can be tracked by process ID and object. Either technique provides the same information, but each method presents the information in a different way. You can view locks by process ID or object by completing the following steps:

1. Start SQL Server Management Studio, and then connect to a server.

2. Use Object Explorer view to access a database. Expand the server node and the Management node.

3. Under the Management node, double-click Activity Monitor to start the Activity Monitor.

4. With processes, you can view a summary of all objects the process is locking. Under Select A Page, click Locks By Process, and then in the right pane, select the process ID you want to examine, such as 51.

5. With objects, you can see a list of all processes with locks on the object. Under Select A Page, click Locks By Object, and then select the database object you want to examine, such as (internal).

6. Lock statistics are not updated automatically, and you will occasionally have to refresh the view. To do this, click Refresh on the toolbar.

Although locks by process ID and locks by object are presented in a slightly different manner, the information is almost identical. With process ID, you see a list of objects that the process has a lock on. With objects, you see a list of processes that have locks on the object. You will also see information on the type, status, and mode of the lock, as well as information about the lock owner, the resource being locked, and the index being locked (if applicable). The available lock-related information is summarized in Table 5-3.

Table 5-3   **Lock-Related Information Used in Database Administration**

Category	Type	Description
Process ID		The server process ID of the related user process.
Context		The ID of the thread associated with the process ID.
Batch ID		The batch ID associated with the process ID.
Type	RID	Row identifier; used to lock a single row within a table.
	KEY	A row lock within an index; used to protect key ranges.
	PAGE	A lock on a data or index page.
	EXTENT	A lock on a contiguous group of eight data or index pages.
	TABLE	A lock on an entire table, including all data and indexes.
	DATABASE	A lock on an entire database.
	METADATA	A lock on descriptive information about the object.
Subtype		The lock subtype, frequently used with METADATA locks to identify metadata lock activity.
Description		Optional descriptive information.
Request Mode	S	Shared; used for read-only operations, such as a *select* statement.
	U	Update; used when reading/locking an updateable resource. Prevents some deadlock situations.
	X	Exclusive; allows only one session to update the data. Used with the modification operations, such as INSERT, DELETE, and UPDATE.
	I	Intent; used to establish a lock hierarchy.
	Sch-S	Schema stability; used when checking a table's schema.
	Sch-M	Schema modification; used when modifying a table's schema.
	BU	Bulk update; used when bulk copying data into a table and the TABLOCK hint is specified.
	RangeS_S	Serializable range scan; used with shared resource locks on shared ranges.
	RangeS_U	Serializable update; used updating resource locks on shared ranges.
	RangeI_N	Insert range with a null resource lock; used to test ranges before inserting a new key into an index.
	RangeX_X	Exclusive range with an exclusive lock; used when updating a key in a range.
Request Type		The type of object requested.
Request Status	GRANT	The lock was obtained.
	WAIT	The lock is blocked by another process.
	CNVT	The lock is being converted; that is, it is held in one mode but waiting to acquire a stronger lock mode.

Table 5-3   Lock-Related Information Used in Database Administration   *(continued)*

Category	Type	Description
Owner Type	CURSOR	The lock owner is a cursor.
	SESSION	The lock owner is a user session.
	TRANSACTION	The lock owner is a transaction.
	SHARED_TRANSACTION _WORKSPACE	The lock owner is the shared portion of the transaction workspace.
	EXCLUSIVE_TRANSACTION _WORKSPACE	The lock owner is the exclusive portion of the transaction workspace.
Owner ID		The owner ID associated with the lock.
Owner GUID		The GUID of the owner associated with the lock.
Database		The database containing the lock.
Object		The name of the object being locked.

Troubleshooting Deadlocks and Blocking Connections

Two common problems you may encounter are deadlocks and blocking connections. Deadlocks and blocking connections can occur in almost any database environment, especially when many users are making connections to databases.

- Deadlocks occur when two users have locks on separate objects and each wants a lock on the other's object. Each user waits for the other user to release the lock, but this does not happen.

- Blocking connections occur when one connection holds a lock and a second connection wants a conflicting lock type. This forces the second connection either to wait or to block the first.

Both deadlocks and blocking connections can degrade server performance.

Although SQL Server can detect and correct deadlock and blocking situations, you can help speed up this process by identifying potential problems and taking action, if necessary. Process information can tell you when deadlocks or blocking occur. Examine these process information columns: Wait Time, Wait Type, Resource, Blocking, and Blocked By. When you have a deadlock or blocking situation, take a closer look at the locks on the objects that are causing problems. Refer to the section titled "Tracking Locks by Process ID and Object" earlier in this chapter for details. You may also want to stop the offending processes, and you can do this by following the steps described in the section titled "Killing Server Processes" later in this chapter.

Tracking Command Execution in SQL Server

Sometimes you will want to track the commands that users are executing. You can do this by using the Current Activity resource viewer:

1. Start SQL Server Management Studio, and then connect to a server.
2. Use Object Explorer view to access a database. Expand the server node and the Management node.

3. Under the Management node, double-click Activity Monitor to start the Activity Monitor. The Last Refresh entry under Status shows a date and time when the activity snapshot was taken.

Tip If the snapshot is old, you can refresh the snapshot by clicking Refresh on the toolbar.

4. Select Process Info. The entries in the User column can help you track user sessions and the processes they are using.

5. Double-click a process to display the dialog box shown in Figure 5-14. This dialog box shows the last command batch executed by the user.

6. To track current commands being executed by the user, click Refresh periodically.

7. To kill the process, click Kill Process. Then, when prompted, choose Yes.

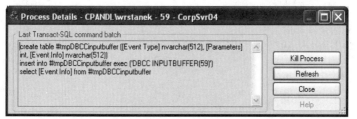

Figure 5-14   The Process Details dialog box

Killing Server Processes

You may need to stop processes that are blocking connections or are using too much CPU time. To do this, complete the following steps:

1. Start SQL Server Management Studio, and then connect to a server.

2. Use Object Explorer view to access a database. Expand the server node and the Management node.

3. Under the Management node, double-click Activity Monitor to start the Activity Monitor. The Last Refresh entry shows a date and time when the activity snapshot was taken.

4. Select Process Info, and then right-click the process you want to stop.

Note Usually, you will not want to kill processes that SQL Server is running. If you are concerned about a process, stop it, and then restart the related service instead of trying to kill the process.

5. From the shortcut menu, choose Kill Process. Then, when prompted, click Yes.

Chapter 6

Configuring SQL Server with SQL Server Management Studio

SQL Server 2005 replaces Enterprise Manager with SQL Server Management Studio to compliment the expanding role of SQL Server administrators and developers. SQL Server Management Studio provides the easiest way to configure SQL Server. In SQL Server Management Studio, you can access the properties of a registered server easily, and then use the pages and options provided to configure the server.

Managing the Configuration with SQL Server Management Studio

After you connect to a registered server in SQL Server Management Studio, you can view and manage its configuration properties using the Server Properties dialog box. To access this dialog box, complete the following steps:

1. Click the Start button, point to Programs or All Programs, and then select Microsoft SQL Server 2005 | SQL Server Management Studio. Or type **sqlwb** at a command prompt.

2. In the Connect To Server dialog box, use the Server Type drop-down list to select the server instance to which you want to connect, such as Database Engine.

3. Select or type the name of the server on which SQL Server is running in the Server Name box, such as **DBSvr18**.

Note   You can only connect to registered servers. If you want to work with a SQL Server that is not registered, you must register the server before you can use SQL Server Management Studio to configure it. See the section titled "Managing Servers" in Chapter 5, "Managing the Enterprise," for details.

4. Use the Authentication selection menu to choose the authentication type, either Windows Authentication or SQL Server Authentication (based on the authentication types selected when you installed the server). Provide a Windows user name or SQL Server login ID and password as necessary.

- **Windows Authentication**   Uses your current domain account and password to establish the database connection. This authentication type works only if Windows authentication is enabled and you have appropriate privileges.

- **SQL Server Authentication**   Allows you to specify a SQL Server login ID and password.

5. Click Connect. You connect to the default instance (unless you have configured another default previously). To change the instance to which you connect, click Option, select the Connection Properties tab, and then use the Connect To Database drop-down list to select the instance to which you want to connect.

6. Right-click the server name in the SQL Server Management Studio Object Explorer view and choose Properties from the shortcut menu to open the dialog box shown in Figure 6-1.

7. You can now manage common SQL Server configuration settings. For more advanced settings, you need to use a stored procedure, such as *sp_configure*, as discussed in Chapter 4, "Configuring and Tuning Microsoft SQL Server."

The Server Properties dialog box has many pages, which are listed at the top of the left pane in Figure 6-1. The rest of the sections in this chapter explain how to use the configuration options provided on these Server Properties pages. Permissions are discussed in Chapter 8, "Managing SQL Server 2005 Security."

If you want to view a summary of current settings, run the following query in query view:

```
use master
```

```
go
```

```
exec sp_configure
```

```
go
```

Note   Show Advanced Options must be set to 1 to see advanced options, as discussed in Chapter 4.

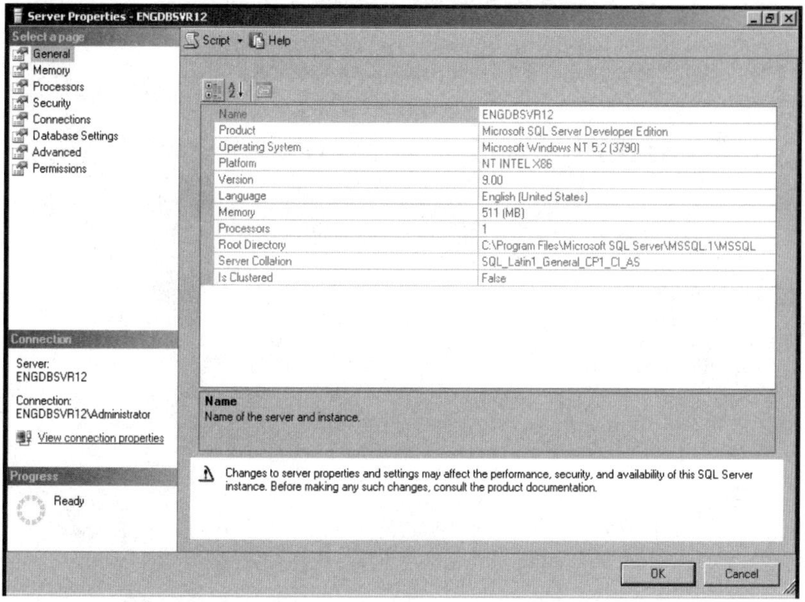

Figure 6-1   The General page of the Server Properties dialog box

Determining System and Server Information

General system and server information is available on the General page of the
Server Properties dialog box (see Figure 6-1). The information on the General page
helps you determine the following:

- SQL Server edition
- Operating system version
- SQL Server version
- Platform and chip architecture
- Default language
- Amount of RAM installed on the system
- Number of CPUs
- Root directory location for the selected instance
- Default server collation

You also can obtain similar information using the extended stored procedure
xp_msver. Execute the following command:

```
exec xp_msver "ProductName", "ProductVersion", "Language", "Platform",
"WindowsVersion", "PhysicalMemory", "ProcessorCount"
```

Tip You can use Query view to execute the command shown. Basic techniques for using this utility are covered in the section titled "Configuring SQL Server with Stored Procedures" in Chapter 4.

Configuring Authentication and Auditing

You configure authentication and auditing options with the Security page of the Server Properties dialog box. This page is shown in Figure 6-2.

Setting Authentication Mode

SQL Server security is completely integrated with Windows domain security, allowing for authentication based on user and group memberships as well as standard SQL Server user accounts. To use combined authentication, select the SQL Server and Windows Authentication mode option button. Now users in Windows domains can access the server using a domain account, and other users can be logged on using a SQL Server logon ID.

Note Windows authentication is not available in SQL Server Express Edition running on Windows 95 or Windows 98.

To use domain authentication only, select the Windows Authentication Mode option button. Now only users with a domain account can access the server.

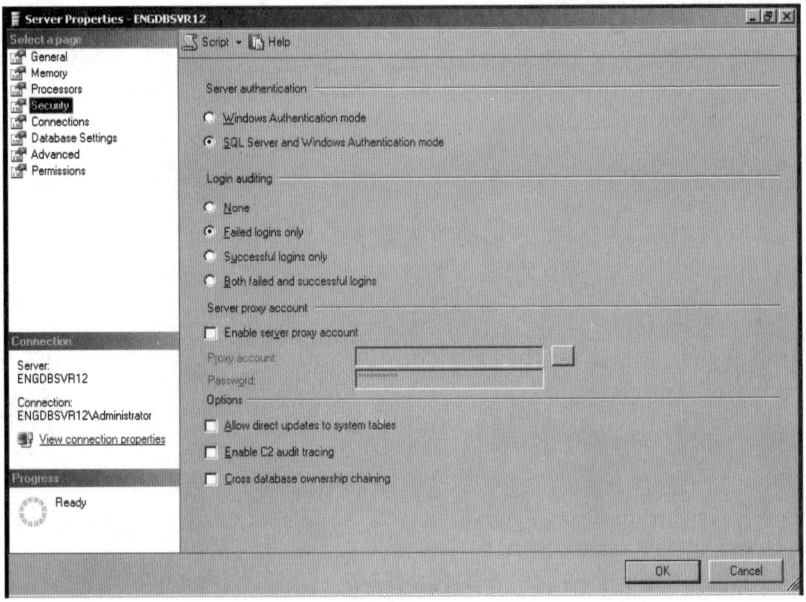

Figure 6-2 The Security page options

Tip With combined authentication, SQL Server first checks to see if a new login is a SQL Server login. If the login exists, SQL Server then uses the password provided to authenticate the user. If the login does not exist, it uses Windows authentication.

Setting Auditing Level

Auditing allows you to track user access to SQL Server. You can use auditing with both authentication modes as well as with trusted and untrusted connections.

When auditing is enabled, user logins are recorded in the Windows application log, the SQL Server error log, or both, depending on how you configure logging for SQL Server. The available auditing options include:

- **None** Disables auditing.
- **Failed Logins Only** Audits only failed login attempts (the default setting).
- **Successful Logins Only** Audits only successful login attempts.
- **Both Failed And Successful Logins** Audits both successful and failed login attempts.

Tuning Memory Usage

SQL Server is designed to manage memory needs dynamically, and it does an excellent job in most cases. Using dynamic memory allocation, SQL Server can add memory to handle incoming queries, release memory for another application you are starting, or reserve memory for possible needs. The default memory settings are the following:

- Dynamically configure SQL Server memory
- Minimum memory allocation set at 0 MB
- Maximum memory allocation set to allow SQL Server to use virtual memory on disk as well as physical RAM
- No memory reserved specifically for SQL Server
- Address Windowing Extensions (AWE) not enabled
- Minimum memory for query execution set at 1024 KB

You can change these settings, but you need to be careful about allocating too little or too much memory to SQL Server. Too little memory may prevent SQL Server from handling tasks in a timely manner. Too much memory may cause SQL Server to take essential resources from other applications such as the operating system, which may result in excessive paging and a drain on overall system performance.

Tip Some statistics can help you allocate memory correctly, such as the number of page faults per second and the cache-hit ratio. Page faults per second can track paging to and from virtual memory. The cache-hit ratio can determine if data being retrieved is in memory. You will learn more about using these types of statistics in Chapter 13, "Profiling and Monitoring Microsoft SQL Server 2005."

This section examines important areas of memory management. The primary method to configure memory usage is by selecting options on the Memory page of the Server Properties dialog box, shown in Figure 6-3. You will also learn a better way to configure Windows memory usage for SQL Server.

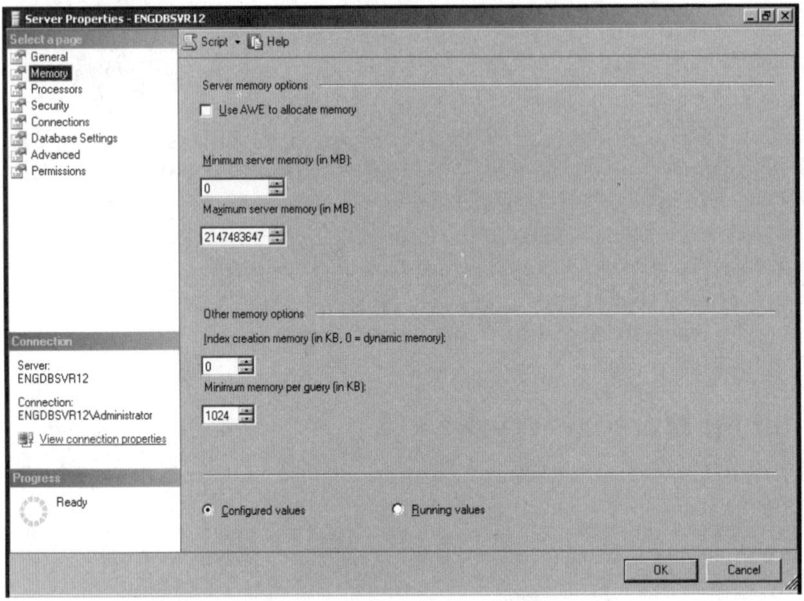

Figure 6-3   The Memory page of the Server Properties dialog box

Real World   Do not use the Maximize Data Throughput For Network Applications setting with SQL Server 2005. This setting gives priority to applications that perform buffered I/O by caching their I/O pages in file system cache. Using this option may limit memory available to SQL Server 2005. To view and change this setting, complete the following steps:

1. Access Network Connections in Control Panel.

2. Right-click Local Area Connection, and then select Properties.

3. Select File And Printer Sharing For Microsoft Networks, and then choose Properties.

4. On the Server Optimization tab, choose an appropriate setting other than Maximize Data Throughput For Network Applications.

5. Restart the server to apply the setting change.

Working with Dynamically Configured Memory

With dynamically configured memory, SQL Server configures memory usage automatically based on workload and available resources. Total memory usage varies between the minimum and maximum values that you set. The minimum server memory sets the baseline usage for SQL Server, but this memory is not allocated at startup. Memory is allocated as needed based on the database workload. When the minimum server memory threshold is reached, this threshold becomes the baseline, and memory is not released if it would leave SQL Server with less than the minimum server memory threshold.

To use dynamically configured memory, complete the following steps:

1. From the Server Properties dialog box, go to the Memory page.
2. Set minimum and maximum memory usage values to different values with the Minimum and Maximum boxes, respectively. The recommended Maximum value for standalone servers is at or near total RAM (physical + virtual memory). However, if multiple instances of SQL Server are running on a computer, you should consider setting the maximum server memory so that the instances are not competing for memory.
3. Click OK.

You can use the stored procedure *sp_configure* to change the minimum and maximum settings. Use the following Transact-SQL commands:

```
exec sp_configure "min server memory", <number of megabytes>
exec sp_configure "max server memory", <number of megabytes>
```

Best Practices   With dynamically configured memory, you usually do not need to set minimum and maximum memory usage values. On a dedicated system running only SQL Server, however, you may achieve smoother operation by setting minimum memory to 8 MB † (24 KB * *NumUsers*), where *NumUsers* is the average number of users simultaneously connected to the server. You may also want to reserve physical memory for SQL Server. SQL Server uses about 8 MB for its code and internal structures. Additional memory is used as follows: 96 bytes for locks, 2880 bytes for open databases, and 276 bytes for open objects, which include all tables, views, stored procedures, extended stored procedures, triggers, rules, constraints, and defaults. You can check the baseline memory usage using the SQLServer:Memory Manager performance object. Select all counters for monitoring and use the Report view to examine the memory usage. Pay particular attention to the Total Server Memory counter. See Chapter 13 for more details on monitoring SQL Server performance.

Using Fixed Memory

If you want to override the dynamic memory management features, you can do this by reserving memory specifically for SQL Server. When you reserve physical memory for SQL Server, the operating system does not swap out SQL Server memory pages even if that memory could be allocated to other processes when SQL Server is idle. This means SQL Server has a fixed memory set. On a dedicated system, reserving memory can improve SQL Server performance by cutting down on paging and cache hits.

To reserve physical memory for SQL Server, complete the following steps:

1. From the Server Properties dialog box, go to the Memory page.
2. Set the Minimum Server Memory and Maximum Server Memory fields to the desired working set memory size. Use the same value for both fields.
3. Click OK.

You can also use the stored procedure *sp_configure* to reserve physical memory. The Transact-SQL command to do this is:

```
exec sp_configure "set working set size", 1
go
exec sp_configure "min server memory", <number of megabytes>
go
exec sp_configure "max server memory", <number of megabytes>
go
reconfigure with override
go
```

Caution   Setting fixed working set memory incorrectly can cause serious performance problems on SQL Server. Use fixed working set memory only in circumstances in which you need to ensure that an exact amount of memory is available for SQL Server.

Enabling AWE Memory Support

SQL Server 2005 Enterprise and Developer Editions support Address Windowing Extensions (AWE) memory. When AWE memory support is enabled, SQL Server 2005 dynamically allocates AWE memory at startup and allocates or deallocates AWE-mapped memory as required within the constraints of the minimum server memory and maximum server memory options. The goal is to balance SQL Server memory use with the overall system requirements. SQL Server always attempts to use AWE-mapped memory, even on computers configured to provide applications with less than 3 GB of user mode address space.

Note   When SQL Server 2005 runs on Windows Server 2003, Microsoft recommends enabling AWE memory support. The Hot-Add Memory feature requires AWE to be enabled during SQL Server startup. Additionally, it is important to note that SQL Server can dynamically release AWE-mapped memory, but the current amount of allocated AWE-mapped memory cannot be swapped out to the page file.

Tip If you enable AWE support, the user or system account under which the instance runs must have the Lock Pages In Memory user privilege. This privilege can be assigned to the account using Group Policy. See Chapters 8 and 9 of the Windows Server 2003 Administrator's Pocket Consultant for details.

To enable AWE support, complete the following steps:

1. From the Server Properties dialog box, go to the Memory page and select the Use AWE To Allocate Memory option.

2. Consider setting a specific maximum server memory for SQL Server to ensure other applications have additional memory. For example, you might want to set minimum server memory to 2 GB (2048 MB) and maximum server memory to 4 GB (4096 MB) to limit the amount of memory SQL Server 2005 can use.

3. Click OK.

You can also use the stored procedure *sp_configure* to enable AWE support. The Transact-SQL command you would use is:

```
exec sp_configure "awe enabled", 1

reconfigure

go
```

Optimizing Memory for Indexing

By default, SQL Server 2005 dynamically manages the amount of memory allocated for index creation operations. If additional memory is needed for creating indexes, and the memory is available based on the server memory configuration settings, the server will allocate additional memory for index creation operations. If additional memory is needed but not available, the index creation will use the memory already allocated to perform index creation.

Normally, the self-tuning works very well with this feature. The main exception is in cases in which you use partitioned tables and indexes, and have nonaligned partitioned indexes. In these cases, if there is a high degree of parallelism (lots of simultaneous index creation operations), you might encounter problems creating indexes. If this happens, you can allocate a specific amount of index creation memory.

To use a specific index creation memory allocation, complete the following steps:

1. From the Server Properties dialog box, go to the Memory page and set a value in the Index Creation Memory box. This value is set in kilobytes.

2. Click OK.

You can also use the stored procedure *sp_configure* to set the index creation memory size. The related command is:

```
exec sp_configure "index create memory", <number of kilobytes>
```

Note   The amount of memory allocated to index creation operations should be at least as large as the minimum memory per query. If it is not, SQL Server will use the amount of memory specified as the minimum memory per query and display a warning about this.

Allocating Memory for Queries

By default, SQL Server allocates a minimum of 1024 KB of memory for query execution. This memory allocation is guaranteed per user, and you can set it anywhere from 512 KB to 2 GB. If you increase the minimum query size, you can improve the performance of queries that perform processor-intensive operations, such as sorting or hashing. If you set the value too high, however, you can degrade the overall system performance. Because of this, adjust the minimum query size only when you are having trouble executing queries quickly.

 Best Practices   The default setting of 1024 KB of RAM works in most cases. However, you may want to consider changing this value if the server operates in an extremely busy environment, with lots of simultaneous queries running in separate user connections, or in a relatively slow environment, with few (but large or complex) queries. In this case, four factors should determine your decision to adjust the minimum query size:

■ The total amount of free memory (when the system is idle and SQL Server is running)

■ The average number of simultaneous queries running in separate user connections

■ The average query size

■ The query response time you hope to achieve

 Best Practices   Often a compromise is necessary with these values. You cannot always get an instant response, but you can optimize performance based on available resources.

Use the following equation to get a starting point for the optimization:

FreeMemory / (AvgQuerySize * AvgNumSimulQueries)

For example, if the system has 200 MB of free memory, the average query size is 2 MB, and the average number of simultaneous queries is five, then the optimal value for query size is 200 MB / (2 * 5) or 20 MB. Generally, this value represents the maximum you should assign given the current environment, and you will want to lower this value if possible.

To allocate memory for queries, complete the following steps:

1. From the Server Properties dialog box, go to the Memory page and set a value for the Minimum Memory Per Query box. This value is set in kilobytes.

2. Click OK.

You can also use the stored procedure *sp_configure* to set the minimum query size. The related command is:

```
exec sp_configure "min memory per query", <number of kilobytes>
```

Configuring Processors and Parallel Processing

Systems that use multiprocessors can take advantage of the enhancements provided by SQL Server for parallel and symmetric multiprocessing. You can control how and when processors are used by SQL Server as well as when queries are processed in parallel.

Optimizing CPU Usage

Multitasking is an important part of the operating system. Often the operating system will need to move threads of execution among different processors. On a system with a light load, this allows the server to improve performance by balancing the workload. On a system with a heavy load, however, this shuffling of threads can reduce performance because processor cache has to be reloaded repeatedly.

SQL Server 2005 supports processor affinity and I/O affinity to optimize how processors are used. Processor affinity assigns processors to specific threads of execution to eliminate processor reloads and reduce thread migration across processors. I/O affinity specifies which processors are eligible to process SQL Server–related disk I/O operations. If you decide to manage affinity manually, you will want some processors to have priority for threading and some processors to have priority for disk I/O, with no overlap between the two. For example, on a 32-processor system running SQL Server 2005 Enterprise Edition, you might want processors 0 to 15 to have processor affinity (which means they will manage threads of execution) and processors 16 to 31 to have I/O affinity (which means they will manage disk I/O operations).

> **Note** There is no specific formula for allocation. You do not need to allocate half of the CPUs to processor affinity and half to I/O affinity. The actual configuration will depend on server usage and load.

Affinity settings are automatically configured and optimized when you install SQL Server. If you are trying to optimize performance for a server under a heavy load, you might want to try to optimize the affinity settings. Keep the following guidelines in mind before reconfiguring affinity settings:

- Do not change these settings without careful forethought. You can reduce performance by incorrectly managing affinity settings.
- Do not configure CPU affinity in both the operating system and in SQL Server. Both techniques have the same goal. Use one technique or the other.

- Do not enable the same CPU for both processor and I/O affinity. Each processor can have only one affinity. This means that there are three possible affinity states: processor affinity enabled, I/O affinity enabled, or no affinity enabled.

You can manually configure processor usage by completing the following steps:

1. Start SQL Server Management Studio, and then connect to the server you want to configure.

2. Right-click the server name in the SQL Server Management Studio Object Explorer view, and then choose Properties from the shortcut menu.

3. From the Server Properties dialog box, go to the Processors page, as shown in Figure 6-4.

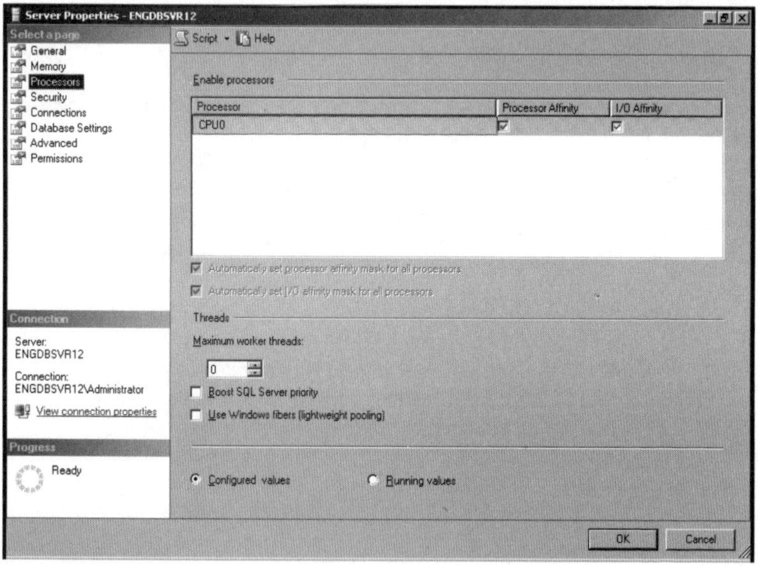

Figure 6-4   The Processors page of the Server Properties dialog box

4. Use the Processor list to determine which processors SQL Server uses. Select the check box for processors you want to use, and clear the check box for processors you do not want to use. The first CPU on the system is identified as CPU 0, the second as CPU 1, and so on.

Best Practices   If the system has more processors than SQL Server supports, SQL Server does not use all of them. For example, on an eight-way symmetric multiprocessing (SMP) system, SQL Server Standard can use only four processors. This leaves four processors for other applications and system-level tasks.

Best Practices   You may want to assign SQL Server to the higher numbered processors (5, 6, 7, and 8), but this is not a good idea. Windows assigns deferred process calls associated with network interface cards (NICs) to the highest numbered processors. So, if the system described in the example had two NICs, these calls would be directed to CPU 8 and CPU 7. Be sure to consult the equipment documentation before changing these values.

5. Click OK. The new settings will apply when the server has been stopped and restarted.

You can also use the stored procedure *sp_configure* to set the affinity mask. The related command is:

```
exec sp_configure "affinity mask", <integer value>

exec sp_configure "affinity i/o mask", <integer value>
```

SQL Server interprets the integer value as a bit mask representing the processors you want to use. In this bit mask, CPU 0 is represented by bit 0, CPU 1 with bit 1, and so on. A bit value of 1 tells SQL Server to use the CPU. A bit value of 0 tells SQL Server not to use the CPU. For example, if you wanted to turn on support for processors 1, 2, and 5, you would have a binary value of

000100110

The corresponding integer value is 38:

32 + 4 + 2 = 38

Setting Parallel Processing

A lot of calculations are required to determine if parallel processing should be used or not. Generally, SQL Server processes queries in parallel in these cases:

- When the number of CPUs is greater than the number of active connections
- When the estimated cost for the serial execution of a query is higher than the query plan threshold (The estimated cost refers to the elapsed time in seconds required to execute the query serially.)

Certain types of statements cannot be processed in parallel unless they contain clauses, however. For example, UPDATE, INSERT, and DELETE are not normally processed in parallel even if the related query meets the criteria. But if the UPDATE or DELETE statements contain a WHERE clause, or an INSERT statement contains a SELECT clause, the WHERE and SELECT can be executed in parallel. Changes are applied serially to the database in these cases.

You can configure parallel processing by completing the following steps:

1. From the Server Properties dialog box, go to the Advanced page.
2. By default, the Max Degree Of Parallelism setting has a value of 0, which means that the maximum number of processors used for parallel processing is controlled automatically. Essentially, SQL Server uses the actual number of available

processors, depending on the workload. To limit the number of processors used for parallel processing to a set amount (up to the maximum supported by SQL Server), change the Max Degree Of Parallelism setting to a value greater than 1. A value of 1 tells SQL Server not to use parallel processing.

3. Large, complex queries usually can benefit from parallel execution. However, SQL Server performs parallel processing only when the estimated number of seconds required to run a serial plan for the same query is higher than the value set in the cost threshold for parallelism. Set the cost estimate threshold using the Cost Threshold For Parallelism box on the Advanced page of the Server Properties dialog box. You can use any value from 0 to 32,767. On a single CPU, the cost threshold is ignored.

4. Click OK. These changes are applied immediately. You do not need to restart the server.

You can use the stored procedure *sp_configure* to configure parallel processing. The Transact-SQL commands are:

```
exec sp_configure "max degree of parallelism", <integer value>
exec sp_configure "cost threshold for parallelism", <integer value>
```

Configuring Threading, Priority, and Fibers

Threads are an important part of a multitasking operating system, and they enable SQL Server to do many things at once. Threads are not processes, however. They are concurrent execution paths that allow applications to use the CPU more effectively.

SQL Server tries to match threads to user connections. When the number of threads that are available is greater than the number of user connections, at least a one-to-one ratio of threads to user connections exists, which allows each user connection to be handled uniquely. When the number of threads available is less than the number of user connections, SQL Server must pool threads; as a result, the same thread may serve multiple user connections, which can reduce performance and response time if additional resources are available and are not being used.

Normally, the operating system handles threads in kernel mode, but it handles applications and user-related tasks in user mode. Switching between modes, such as when the kernel needs to handle a new thread, requires CPU cycles and resources. To allow the application to handle threading directly, you can use fibers. Switching fibers does not require changing modes and therefore can sometimes improve performance.

Another way to improve performance is by increasing the priority of SQL Server threads. Normally, threads have a priority of 1 to 31, and higher priority threads get more CPU time than lower priority threads. Higher priority threads can also preempt lower priority threads, forcing threads to wait until higher priority threads finish executing. By increasing thread priority, you can give the threads a higher preference for CPU time and ensure that other threads do not preempt them.

Note   The complete range for thread priority is 0 to 31. Thread priority 0 is reserved for operating system use.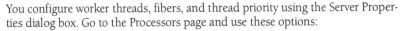

You configure worker threads, fibers, and thread priority using the Server Properties dialog box. Go to the Processors page and use these options:

- **Maximum Worker Threads**   Sets the maximum number of threads. By default, the value is set to 0, which allows SQL Server to configure the number of worker threads. However, you can use any value from 10 to 32,767. On a busy server with many user connections, you may want to increase this value. On a slow server with few connections, you may want to decrease this value. Computers with multiple processors can concurrently execute one thread per CPU. Microsoft recommends a maximum setting on 32-bit systems of 1024.

- **Boost SQL Server Priority**   Increases the priority of SQL Server threads. Without boosting, SQL Server threads have a priority of 7 (normal priority). With boosting, SQL Server threads have a priority of 13 (high priority). On a dedicated system running only SQL Server, this option can improve performance. However, if the server runs other applications, the performance of those applications may be degraded.

- **Use Windows Fibers (Lightweight Pooling)**   Configures SQL Server to use fibers, which it can handle directly. SQL Server still needs threads to carry out tasks. SQL Server allocates one thread per CPU, and then allocates one fiber per concurrent user connection up to the Maximum worker threads value. You must restart the server to apply this option.

Tip   Fibers work best when the server has multiple CPUs and a relatively low user-to-CPU ratio. For example, on an Enterprise installation with 32 CPUs and 250 users, you may see a noticeable performance boost with fibers. But if you have a system with eight CPUs and 5000 users, you may see performance decrease with fibers.

You can use *sp_configure* to set fibers, maximum worker threads, and priority boost. The commands are:

```
exec sp_configure "lightweight pooling", <0 or 1>
exec sp_configure "max worker threads", <integer value>
exec sp_configure "priority boost", <0 or 1>
```

When setting lightweight pooling (fibers) and priority boost, you use 0 to disable and 1 to enable.

Configuring User and Remote Connections

Requests for data are handled through user connections to client systems. The client opens a connection to SQL Server, makes a request, and waits for a response from SQL Server. When the client is finished with its request, it closes the connection. Other servers and applications can also connect to SQL Server remotely. To configure client connections and remote server connections, you can use the Connections page in the Server Properties dialog box.

Many settings are associated with client and server connections, as you can see in Figure 6-5, which shows the default configuration. This section examines connection settings and cases in which you might want to change these settings.

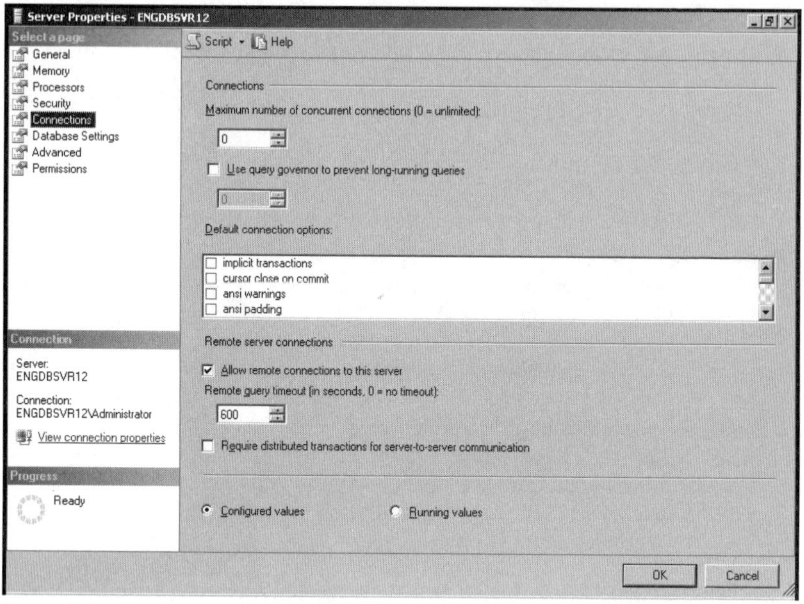

Figure 6-5   The default connection settings on the Connections page of the Server Properties dialog box

Setting Maximum User Connections

On the Connections page, the Maximum Number Of Concurrent User Connections box provides you with the ability to set the maximum number of connections to SQL Server at any one time. You can set this value from 0 to 32,767. By default, the value is set to 0, which means that an unlimited number of connections can be made to SQL Server. However, the actual number of possible user connections really depends on hardware, application, and other server limitations. You can determine the number of user connections your system can handle by executing the following command in query view:

```
select @@max_connections
```

To set the maximum number of user connections, complete the following steps:

1. From the Server Properties dialog box, go to the Connections page.
2. Type a new value in the Maximum Number Of Concurrent Connections box, and then click OK.
3. Stop and restart the server to apply the change.

You can also set the maximum number of concurrent connections by using the following command:

```
exec sp_configure "user connections", <integer value>
```

Note You should not need to change the maximum connections value. If you do change the setting, be careful. When the server reaches the maximum number of connections, users receive an error message and are not able to connect to the server until another user disconnects and a connection becomes available. The only time you would need to set this option is in a situation with a large number of users in which you need to limit the number of active connections to ensure that requests for connected users are handled in a timely manner. A better alternative is to add sufficient memory to the system or configure a cluster to balance the workload, or both. If you administer a system with a large numbers of users, you should also ensure that SQL applications connect and then disconnect promptly when finished to reallocate resources quickly to other users.

Setting Default Connection Options

On the Connections page, you will see a list box labeled Default Connection Options (see Figure 6-5). Use the list box options to set default query-processing options for user connections. Select an option by selecting its check box. Cancel an option by clearing the check box. Any changes you make will affect new logins only; current logins are not affected. Furthermore, users can override the defaults by using set statements, if necessary.

Table 6-1 provides a summary of the connection options, as well as the default state for ODBC (open database connectivity) and OLE DB (object linking and embedding database, which may be different from the SQL Server default). The table also includes a list of commands you can use with *sp_configure*, the corresponding value for the configuration bit mask, and the SET commands that can override the default settings in a user session.

Table 6-1 Configuring Connection Options

Connection Option	When On...	Default State	Bit Mask Value	SET Command
Implicit transactions *(continued)*	Uses transactions implicitly whenever statements are executed.	OFF	2	IMPLICIT_TRANSACTIONS
Cursor close on COMMIT	Automatically closes a cursor at the end of a transaction.	OFF	4	CURSOR_CLOSE_ON _COMMIT
ANSI warnings	SQL Server displays null, overflow, and divide-by-zero warnings. Otherwise, no error or NULL may be returned.	OFF	8	ANSI_WARNINGS

Table 6-1 Configuring Connection Options

Connection Option	When On...	Default State	Bit Mask Value	SET Command
ANSI padding	Data in fixed-length fields are padded with trailing spaces to fill out the width of the column.	OFF	16	ANSI_PADDING
ANSI nulls	Comparing anything with NULL gives an unknown result.	OFF	32	ANSI_NULLS
Arithmetic abort	Causes a query to terminate when an overflow or divide-by-zero error occurs.	OFF	64	ARITHABORT
Arithmetic ignore	Returns NULL when an overflow or divide-by-zero error occurs during a query.	OFF	128	ARITHIGNORE
Quoted identifier	SQL Server interprets double quotation marks as indicating an identifier rather than as delimiting a string.	OFF	256	QUOTED_IDENTIFIER
No count	Turns off the display of the number of rows returned in a query.	OFF	512	NOCOUNT
ANSI null default ON	New columns are defined to allow nulls (if you do not explicitly allow or disallow nulls).	OFF	1024	ANSI_NULL_DFLT_ON
ANSI null default OFF	New columns are defined not to allow nulls (if you don't explicitly allow or disallow nulls).	OFF	2048	ANSI_NULL_DFLT_OFF
concat null yields null	Returns NULL when concatenating a NULL value within a string.	OFF	4096	CONCAT_NULL_YIELDS _NULL
numeric round abort	Generates an error when a loss of precision occurs.	OFF	8192	NUMERIC_ROUNDABORT
xact abort	Rolls back a transaction if a T-SQL statement raises a runtime error.	OFF	16384	XACT_ABORT

For *sp_configure*, the default options are set with the following user options parameter:

```
exec sp_configure "user options", <integer bit mask value>
```

In this case, the bit mask value is the sum of the numeric values for all the options you want to use. Each option has a corresponding SET command as well. When you make a connection, you can use the SET command to override the default setting for the session. For example, if you want to turn on ANSI padding, ANSI nulls, and ANSI warnings, use the bit mask value 56, such as:

```
exec sp_configure "user options", 56
```

In a user session, you could later turn these options on or off by using:

```
set ansi_padding on set ansi_nulls off
```

Configuring Remote Server Connections

Connections from other servers are handled differently than user connections. You can determine whether or not servers can connect to this server, how long it takes for remote queries to time out, and if distributed transactions are used. To configure remote connections, complete these steps:

1. From the Server Properties dialog box, go to the Connections page.

2. To allow servers to connect to this server, select the option Allow Remote Connections To This Server. Remote servers can then log on to the server to execute stored procedures remotely. You must stop and restart the server to apply the change if you select this option.

> **Caution**   Remote Procedure Call (RPC) connections are allowed by default. If you change this behavior, remote servers cannot log on to SQL Server. This secures SQL Server from remote server access.

3. By default, queries executed by remote servers time out in 600 seconds. To change this behavior, type a time-out value in the Remote Query Timeout box on the Connections page. Time-out values are set in seconds, and the acceptable range of values is from 0 to 2,147,483,647. A value of 0 means that there is no query time-out for remote server connections.

4. Stored procedures and queries executed on the server can be handled as distributed transactions by using MS DTC. If you want to execute procedures this way, select the Require Distributed Transactions For Server-To-Server Communication check box. If you change this option, you must stop and restart the server.

5. Click OK.

These options can also be set with *sp_configure*. The related Transact-SQL statements are:

```
exec sp_configure "remote access", <0 or 1>
exec sp_configure "remote query timeout", <number of seconds>
exec sp_configure "remote proc trans", <0 or 1>
```

> **Note**   A value of 0 turns a remote server connection option off and a value of 1 turns an option on.

Managing Server Settings

You use the Advanced page of the Server Properties dialog box to configure most general server settings. As shown in Figure 6-6, you can set the default language, general server behavior, and other options on this page.

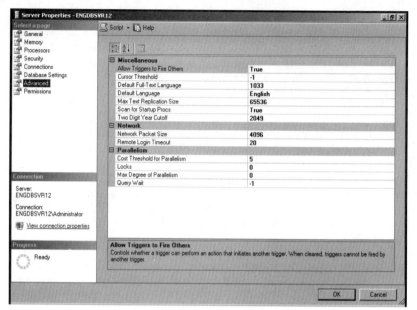

Figure 6-6   General server setting options on the Misc Server Settings page

Setting Default Language for SQL Server

The default language determines default display formats for dates as well as the names of months and days. All output is in U.S. English unless you are running a localized version of SQL Server. Localized versions of SQL Server are available for French, German, Japanese, Spanish, and other languages. On a localized server, two sets of system messages are available, one in U.S. English and one in the local language. If the default language is set to the local language, SQL Server messages are displayed in the local language. Otherwise, they are displayed in U.S. English.

On the Advanced page of the Server Properties dialog box, use the Default Language drop-down list box to select the default language, and then click OK. You must stop and restart the server to apply a new default language setting. With *sp_configure*, the related Transact-SQL statement is:

```
exec sp_configure "default language", <language id number>
```

The language ID number for U.S. English is always 0. The sys.languages system view contains one row for each language present on a server.

Allowing and Disallowing System Updates

By default, users can only update the systems table with system stored procedures, even if they have proper permissions. This is a valuable feature because it prevents users from executing statements that may corrupt the database or could prevent SQL Server from starting. However, you may want to change this behavior to allow direct updates to system tables. Once you allow modifications, anyone with proper permissions can update systems tables by executing statements or stored procedures.

It is risky to give this control to other users. To minimize the risk involved, follow this procedure to update systems tables:

1. From the Server Properties dialog box, go to the Security page.
2. Enable system table modifications by selecting Allow Direct Updates To System Tables.
3. Click OK, and then stop SQL Server.
4. Start SQL Server in single-user mode at the command line by typing **sqlservr -m**.

Note   If multiple instances are installed, you must use the –s *instancename* option to start the instance.

5. Make the necessary changes to the system tables.
6. From the Server Properties dialog box, go to the Security page.
7. Disable system table modifications by clearing the Allow Direct Updates To System Tables checkbox.
8. From the command line in the window running SQL Server, press **Ctrl+C**.
9. When prompted, type **Y** for Yes. This stops SQL Server.
10. Restart the SQL Server service.

With *sp_configure*, the related Transact-SQL statement to allow updates to systems tables is:

```
exec sp_configure "allow updates", <0 or 1>
```

Note   You use 0 to disable and 1 to enable. If you use *sp_configure* to allow updates, you must use the RECONFIGURE WITH OVERRIDE statement as well. Then stop and restart the server.

Allowing and Disallowing Nested Triggers

By default, SQL Server allows you to nest up to 32 levels of triggers. Nested triggers are useful for executing a series of tasks within a single transaction. For example, an action can initiate a trigger that starts another trigger, which in turn can start another trigger, and so on. Because the trigger is handled within a transaction, a failure at any level causes the entire transaction to roll back, which reverses all changes to the database. As a fail-safe measure, triggers are terminated when the maximum nesting level is exceeded. This protects against an infinite loop.

An option on the Misc Server Settings page allows you to configure SQL Server to use nested triggers. To do so, complete the following steps:

1. From the Server Properties dialog box, go to the Advanced page.
2. Set Allow Triggers to True or False as appropriate.
3. Click OK.

With *sp_configure*, the related Transact-SQL statement is:

```
exec sp_configure "nested triggers", <0 or 1>
```

You use 0 to disable and 1 to enable.

Controlling Query Execution

The query governor does not allow the execution of any query that has a running time that exceeds a specified query cost. The query cost is the estimated time, in seconds, required to execute a query, and it is estimated prior to execution based on an analysis by the query engine. By default, the query governor is turned off, meaning there is no maximum cost. To activate the query governor, complete the following steps:

1. From the Server Properties dialog box, go to the Connections page.
2. Select the option Use Query Governor To Prevent Long-Running Queries.
3. In the box below the option, type a maximum query cost limit. The valid range is 0 to 2,147,483,647. A value of 0 disables the query governor; any other value sets a maximum query cost limit.
4. Click OK.

With *sp_configure*, the following Transact-SQL statement will activate the query governor:

```
exec sp_configure "query governor cost limit", <limit>
```

You can also set a per-connection query cost limit in Transact-SQL using the following statement:

```
set query_governor_cost_limit <limit>
```

 Note   Before you activate the query governor, you should use Query view to estimate the cost of current queries you are running on the server. This will give you a good idea of a value to use for the maximum query cost. You can also use Query view to optimize queries.

Configuring Year 2000 Support

SQL Server allows you to insert or modify dates without specifying the century part of the date. However, to be Year 2000 compliant, SQL Server interprets two-digit dates within a certain time span. By default, this time span includes the years 1950 to 2049. Using this default setting, all two-digit dates from 50 to 99 are read as years beginning with 19, and all two-digit dates from 00 to 49 are read as years beginning with 20. Thus, SQL Server would interpret a two-digit year of 99 as 1999 and a two-digit year of 02 as 2002.

To maintain backward compatibility, Microsoft recommends that you leave the setting at the default value. You can, however, change this value by completing the following steps:

1. From the Server Properties dialog box, go to the Advanced page.

2. Set Two Digit Year Cutoff to a value that is the ending year of the time span you want to use. The valid range for the ending year is 1753 to 9999.

3. Click OK.

> **Note**   The time span you select will affect all databases on the current server. Also, some older OLE clients only support dates in a range of years from 1931 to 2030. To maintain compatibility with these clients, you may want to use 2030 as the ending year for the time span.

With *sp_configure*, the related Transact-SQL statement is:

```
exec sp_configure "two digit year cutoff", <ending year>
```

Managing Database Settings

You use the Database Settings page of the Server Properties dialog box to configure server-wide database settings. As shown in Figure 6-7, you can use this page to set index fill, backup and restore options, and recovery intervals for checkpoint execution.

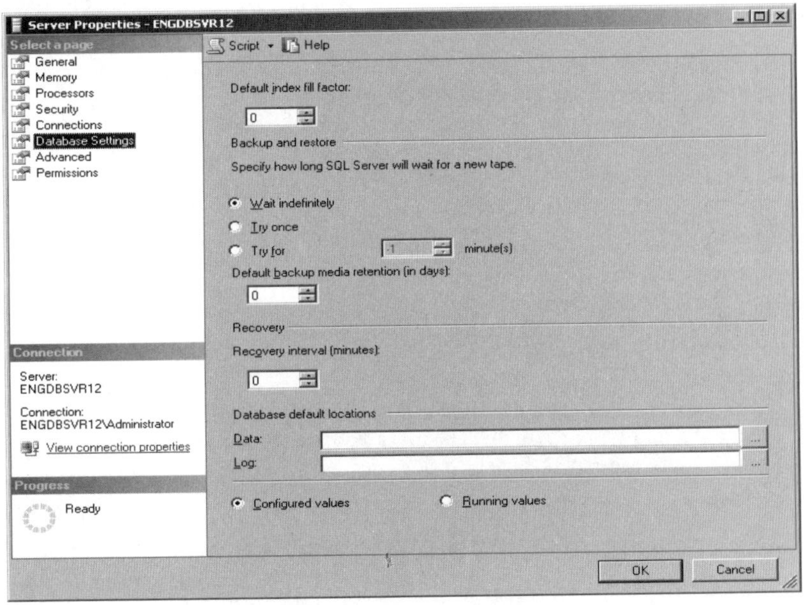

Figure 6-7   The Database Settings page of the Server Properties dialog box

Setting the Index Fill

The default index fill determines how much space SQL Server should reserve when it creates a new index using existing data. Setting the fill factor involves a tradeoff—if you set the fill factor too high, SQL Server will slow down when you add data to a table. However, if you set the fill factor too low, this can affect read performance by an amount inversely proportional to the fill factor. For example, a fill factor of 25 percent can degrade read performance by a factor of 4 (or 4 times normal), but the setting makes it possible to perform large updates faster initially. Ideally, you should balance the need to make updates quickly with the need to have good read performance, and then select a fill factor that makes sense for your situation.

 Best Practices   The fill factor is used only when an index is created; it is not maintained afterward. This allows you to add, delete, or update data in a table without worrying about maintaining a specific fill factor.

 Best Practices   Therefore, the empty space in the data pages can fill up if you make extensive additions or modifications to the data. To redistribute the data, re-create the index and specify a fill factor when you do so. Indexes are discussed more completely in Chapter 9, "Manipulating Schemas, Tables, Indexes, and Views."

By default, the index fill is set at 0, but the valid range is 0 to 100. The setting of 0 is the optimized index fill setting; any other value is an actual fill percentage.

SQL Server handles the optimized setting in much the same way as a fill percentage of 100—SQL Server creates clustered indexes with full data pages and nonclustered indexes with full leaf pages. But the optimized setting of 0 leaves space for growth in the upper level of the index tree, which an index fill setting of 100 does not do. This is the reason why you should use this value only with read-only tables in which you never plan to add data.

If necessary, you can override the default setting when you create indexes, but you have to remember to do this. You can also set a fixed index fill as the default by completing the following steps:

1. From the Server Properties dialog box, go to the Database Settings page.
2. Use the Default Index Fill Factor box to set a fill percentage. A low fill factor provides more room for insertions without requiring page splits, but the index takes up more space. A high fill factor provides less room for insertions that do not require page splits, but the index uses less space.
3. Click OK.

With *sp_configure*, the related Transact-SQL statement is:

```
exec sp_configure "fill factor (%)", <integer percentage>
```

Configuring Backup and Restore Time-Out Options

You often make SQL Server backups on tape devices. When working with tape devices and the DB-Library, you may want to control whether or not you want to enforce a read/write time-out to wait for a new tape. The options you can use include:

- **Wait Indefinitely**   DB-Library waits until a new tape is found. If you select this option, however, you will not necessarily receive an error message to let you know that you are having backup problems.

- **Try Once**   The DB-Library tries once for a response from SQL Server. If there is no response or no tape is available, it quits and typically generates an error.

- **Try For...**   The DB-Library tries to get a response from SQL Server for a specified number of minutes. If there is no response or no tape is available within the wait time, DB-Library quits and typically generates an error.

You set the time-out period by completing the following steps:

1. From the Server Properties dialog box, go to the Database Settings page.
2. To set an indefinite time-out, select the Wait Indefinitely option.
3. To set the backup process to try once and then quit, select the Try Once option button.
4. To set the backup process to try for a specified amount of time, select the Try For *n* Minute(s) option, and then enter the time-out period in the box provided.
5. Click OK.

Configuring Backup and Restore Retention Options

As you will learn in Chapter 14, "Backing Up and Recovering SQL Server 2005," SQL Server has many features to help you back up and restore data. When you write data to tapes using DB-Library, you can specify the number of days to maintain old files. This value is called the *retention period*, and you set it by completing the following steps:

1. From the Server Properties dialog box, go to the Database Settings page.
2. Enter the number of days you want to maintain old files in the Default Backup Media Retention (In Days) box. The minimum value is 0, which specifies that old files are always overwritten. The valid range is 0 to 365.
3. Click OK.

With *sp_configure*, the related Transact-SQL statement to set the retention period for backup files is:

```
exec sp_configure "media retention", <number of days>
```

Flushing Cache with Checkpoints

Database checkpoints flush all cached data pages to the disk, and these checkpoints are done on a per-database basis. In SQL Server, you control how often checkpoints occur using the recovery interval setting. By default, the recovery interval is set to 0, which allows SQL Server to control when checkpoints occur dynamically. This usually means that checkpoints occur about once a minute on active databases. Unless you are experiencing performance problems that are related to checkpoints, you should not change this option.

If you need to set the checkpoint interval manually, you must complete the following steps:

1. From the Server Properties dialog box, go to the Database Settings page.

2. Enter the checkpoint time in minutes in the Recovery Interval (Minutes) box. The valid range is 0 to 32,767, and this is a server-wide setting.

3. Click OK.

With *sp_configure*, the related Transact-SQL statement is:

```
exec sp_configure "recovery interval", <number of minutes>
```

Adding and Removing Active Directory Information

For servers that are part of an Active Directory domain, you use the Active Directory page of the Server Properties dialog box to manage SQL Server information published in Active Directory services. The page has three buttons:

- **Add**   Publishes information about a SQL Server instance in Active Directory.

- **Refresh**   Updates information related to a SQL Server instance in Active Directory. This option is useful when you create databases, server cubes, or data mining models and you want the updates reflected throughout the directory before normal replication.

- **Remove**   Removes information about a SQL Server instance from Active Directory.

Troubleshooting Configuration Problems

There are two specific techniques that you can use to resolve SQL Server configuration problems. In this section, you will learn how to recover from a bad configuration and how to rebuild the *master* database.

Recovering from a Bad Configuration

Although SQL Server 2005 has many safeguards that help you avoid configuration settings that keep SQL Server from starting, you may occasionally find that a configuration change prevents SQL Server from starting. If you encounter this situation, you can recover the server instance by completing the following steps:

1. Log on to the affected server locally, or log on remotely through Telnet or Terminal Server. You must log on using a local administrator account or the account used by the database server instance.

2. Make sure that the MSSQLServer or MSSQL$*instancename* service is stopped. If it is not, stop the service using one of the following methods:
   - ❑ SQL Server Configuration Manager
   - ❑ Computer Management
   - ❑ Services

3. If the instance of SQL Server was installed as a default installation, you can stop the service by using the following command:

   `net stop MSSQLSERVER`

4. From the command prompt, switch to the directory of the associated SQL Server instance (either MSSQL.1\mssql\binn or MSSQL.1\mssql$*instancename*\Binn). You must be in this directory to use the sqlservr utility.

5. Start SQL Server from the command line with the following option:

   `sqlservr -s(instancename) -f`

6. You must use the –s option to specify the instance of SQL Server if multiple instances of SQL Server are installed. The –f option starts SQL Server in single-user mode with a minimum configuration. This ensures that the bad configuration is not loaded.

7. Wait for the server to start up. SQL Server should write a few pages of output to the screen. Leave the server running.

8. In another command prompt window or Telnet session, start SQLCMD with the user name of a SQL account with administrator privileges and password:

   `sqlcmd -U username -P password`

   Note You must specify the instance to which you are connecting (sqlcmd –U username –P password –Scomputername\instancename) if multiple instances of SQL Server 2005 are installed.

9. If you have accessed SQLCMD properly, you should see the prompt change to >.

10. Reverse the changes made to the configuration by entering commands as you would in SQL Server Management Studio. The main difference is that you follow the commands with GO, as shown in the following example:

    ```
    exec sp_configure "max server memory", 128
    go
    reconfigure
    go
    ```

11. When you are finished, exit SQLCMD by typing **exit**.

12. From the command line in the window running SQL Server, press **Ctrl+C**.

13. When prompted, type **Y** for Yes. This stops SQL Server.

14. Restart SQL Server as you normally would. If you have made the appropriate changes, the server should start normally. Otherwise, repeat this procedure.

Changing Collation and Rebuilding the Master Database

Rebuilding the *master* database restores all system databases to their original contents and attributes. The main reasons for rebuilding the *master* database are as follows:

- To set a new default collation for a database server instance

 Tip   In SQL Server 2000 and later, collation can be set separately for each database, as well as for tables, parameters, and literal strings, without having to rebuild the *master* database.

- To repair a corrupted *master* database when no backup of the master is available
- To repair a corrupted *master* database when the SQL Server instance cannot be started

The Rebuildm utility is no longer used for rebuilding the *master* database. Instead, run the SQL Server 2005 Setup program again to rebuild the *master* database. If you choose to rebuild the *master* database, keep the following guidelines in mind:

- After you rebuild the *master* database, you should restore the most recent *master*, *model*, and *msdb* databases. If the server was configured for replication, you must restore the most recent distribution database. Any data that cannot be restored must be manually created.
- After you rebuild the *master* database, all user databases are detached and unreadable. To recover them, you must re-create all your user databases. You cannot restore the user databases from backup—the restore maintains the information that was set when you created the backup, and you may instead want to move the databases to another server by means of import and export, covered in Chapter 10, "Importing, Exporting, and Transforming Data."
- You must reapply any SQL Server updates to bring the *Resource* database up to date. The *Resource* database is updated whenever patches, hot fixes, or service packs are applied to SQL Server.

To rebuild the *master* database, follow these steps:

1. Log on to the server using an account with administrator privileges. In Control Panel, double-click Add Or Remove Programs.
2. Select Microsoft SQL Server 2005 in Add or Remove Programs, and then click Change. When the SQL Server 2005 Maintenance Wizard starts, select the SQL Server instance to maintain and then click Next
3. On the Feature Maintenance page, select the component you want to work with, such as Analysis Services or Database Engine and then click Next.
4. The SQL Server Installation wizard is started. Click Next to allow setup to perform a system configuration check. When the system configuration check is completed, note any issues and correct problems as necessary. Click Next.
5. Setup will then review the installed components. On the Change Or Remove Instance page, click Change.

6. On the Feature Selection page, double-click the entry for the component. This will expand the component details so you can see subcomponents. Click the icon for the subcomponent to specify its availability.

7. Click Next and then click Install. SQL Server will then verify the installation and rebuild a damaged installation as necessary. When this process completes, click Next and then click Finish.

Chapter 7
Core Database Administration

Core database administration tasks involve creating, manipulating, and supporting databases. In Microsoft SQL Server 2005, a database is a collection of data and the objects that represent and interact with that data. Tables, views, stored procedures, triggers, and constraints are typical database objects.

A single database server instance can have up to 32,767 databases, and each database can have more than 2 billion objects. These are theoretical limits, of course, but they demonstrate that SQL Server can handle just about any job. To perform most administration tasks, you must log on to the database using an account that has the Sysadmin fixed server role, such as the local sysadmin account (sa). Detailed information on roles and SQL Server security is found in Chapter 8, "Managing SQL Server 2005 Security."

Database Files and Logs

Each SQL Server database has a transaction log associated with it. A *transaction log* is a history of modifications to the database, and SQL Server uses it to ensure database integrity. All changes to the database are first written to the transaction log and then applied to the database. If the database update is successful, the transaction is completed and recorded as successful. If the database update fails, SQL Server uses the transaction log to restore the database to its original state (which is called *rolling back* the transaction). This two-phase commit process makes it possible for SQL Server to restore a database automatically in case of power failure, server outage, or other problems that occur when you enter a transaction.

SQL Server databases and transaction logs are contained in separate database files. This means that each database always has at least two files associated with it—a data file and a log file. Databases also can have secondary data files. SQL Server uses three types of database files:

- **Primary data files**   Every database has one primary data file. These files store data and maintain records of other files used in a database. By default, these files end with the .mdf extension.
- **Secondary data files**   These files store additional data for a database. By default, these files end with the .ndf extension.
- **Transaction log files**   Every database has at least one transaction log file. This file contains information necessary to restore the database. By default, log files end with the .ldf extension.

 Note   SQL Server also uses backup devices. Backup devices can be physical devices, such as tape drives, or files that are stored on a local drive or a network share. SQL Server data and log files can be stored on either File Allocation Table (FAT) or NT File System (NTFS) partitions, but they cannot be stored on any compressed file system.

 Tip   In SQL Server 2005, full-text catalogs are treated as files and are included in the database file set for the purposes of backup and restore. See the section titled "Working with Full-Text Search" in Chapter 5, "Managing the Enterprise," for more information.

Database files are set when you create or modify the database. Because multiple database files are allowed, SQL Server can create databases that span multiple disk drives and that can grow in size as needed. Although the size of a SQL Server database is often measured in gigabytes, with all editions of SQL Server except the Express Edition, databases can range in size from 1 MB to a theoretical limit of 1,048,516 terabytes. With the Express Edition, databases have a maximum size limit of 4 GB.

As you work with databases, keep in mind that SQL Server is designed to expand databases automatically as necessary. This means that *master, tempdb, msdb,* and other critical databases will not run out of space under normal conditions—provided, of course, that there is file space on the configured drives and that you have not set a maximum database size manually.

System databases are the most important databases on the server. You should never directly update tables in system databases. Instead, use the appropriate management tools or stored procedures to modify the system databases if necessary. The only exception is the *model* database, which you can update with settings for new databases.

Database Administration Basics

You perform most database administration work through SQL Server Management Studio. Use SQL Server Management Studio to carry out many common database administration tasks, including:

- Viewing database information

- Checking user and system databases
- Examining database objects

This section examines each of these tasks.

Viewing Database Information in SQL Server Management Studio

SQL Server organizes information using a top-down hierarchy that starts with server groups at the highest level and then moves down to servers, and then to databases, and then to objects. Therefore, you must work your way down to the database level to view the databases installed on a particular server instance. If you have registered a server instance and have connected to it previously, you can view its databases by completing the following steps:

1. In SQL Server Management Studio, use Registered Servers view to select a type of server, such as Database Engine. If you need to expand a server group to see the servers listed in the group, click the plus sign (+) next to the name of the group.

2. In Registered Servers view, select a server by double-clicking its name in the list. This connects you to the server in Object Explorer view.

> **Note**   If the SQL Server service is stopped, you must restart it before accessing the server. Additionally, if you have not authenticated the server connection, you may need to provide a SQL login account and password. You may also need to reestablish a connection with the server. In either case, enter any necessary information and then click OK/Yes to continue.

3. In Object Explorer view, click the plus sign (+) next to the server's Databases folder to see a list of the databases available on the server.

4. Right-click the database you want to work with, and then select Properties. This displays the Database Properties dialog box shown in Figure 7-1.

5. The Database Properties dialog box includes several different properties pages:
   - **General**   Provides general database information, such as status, owner, date created, size, and space available. Also details the last backup date and collation setting.
   - **Files**   Provides details on the data and log files associated with the database. If the database has been configured for full-text search, the Use Full-Text Indexing check box is selected. However, catalog files associated with the database are not listed.
   - **Filegroups**   Lists the filegroups associated with the database and allows you to add or remove filegroups.
   - **Options**   Provides boxes for viewing and managing standard database options and settings.
   - **Permissions**   Lists users or roles that have specific permissions allowed or denied in the database and allows you to set database permissions for users or roles.

- **Extended Properties** Provides boxes for viewing and managing extended database properties.

- **Mirroring** Provides boxes for viewing and managing database mirroring settings.

- **Transaction Log Shipping** Details the current log shipping configuration (if any) and allows you to manage log shipping.

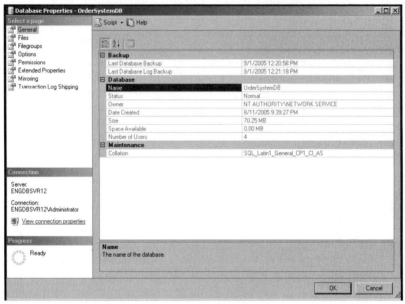

Figure 7-1 The General page of the Database Properties dialog box

Viewing Database Information Using T-SQL

You can also use Transact-SQL (SQL) to examine database information. Transact-SQL is an enhanced version of the standard structured query language that SQL Server uses. In SQL Server Management Studio, access the Query view. You can do this by right-clicking the name of a server to which you have already connected in Object Explorer view, and then selecting New Query. Alternately, click New Query on the main toolbar, select Database Engine Query, and then establish a connection to the database engine on a specific server.

Once you have accessed the Query view, use the following command to view database information:

```
sp_helpdb <dbname>

go
```

where *dbname* is the name of the database you want to examine.

When you view database information in this way, you get an overview of the database as well as a listing of current data and log files. Table 7-1 summarizes the information available when you view database properties using T-SQL. This data is returned in two different result sets; you will need to scroll down in the Results pane to see the additional result set.

Table 7-1   Database Properties Viewable Using T-SQL

Column Name	Description
compatibility_level	The current compatibility level of the database. The level 90 indicates SQL Server 2005 compatibility.
created	The date the database was created.
db_size	The total size of the database including all data and log files.
dbid	The unique identifier for the database on the current server.
filegroup	The filegroup associated with the database file. Filegroups allow you to group sets of database files together.
fileid	The unique identifier for the file in the current database.
filename	The full file name and path.
growth	The number of megabytes or percent by which the file grows.
maxsize	The maximum file size. *Unlimited* means there is no limit.
name	The name of the database or file (without a file extension).
owner	The database owner.
size	The current size of a file.
status	The database status.
usage	The way the file is used, such as data only or log only.

Checking System and Sample Databases

A new SQL Server installation includes the system databases listed in Table 7-2. System databases are critical to the proper operation of SQL Server, and an important aspect of the administration process is backing up and maintaining these databases. Sample databases can also be installed, but they are meant only to provide examples and do not need regular maintenance.

Table 7-2   Summary of System Databases

Database Name	Database Type	Description
master	System	Maintains information on all databases installed on the server. This database is modified anytime you create databases, manage accounts, or change configuration settings. Back up the *master* database regularly.
model	System	Provides a template for all new databases. If you want new databases to have certain properties or permissions, put these changes in the *model* database, and then all new databases will inherit the changes.
tempdb	System	Provides a temporary workspace for processing queries and handling other tasks. This database is recreated each time SQL Server is started, and it is based on the *model* database.

Table 7-2 Summary of System Databases   *(continued)*

Database Name	Database Type	Description
msdb	System	Used by the SQL Server Agent service when performing handling alerts, notifications, and scheduled tasks. You can access all the information in this database using SQL Server Management Studio options.
distribution	System/ Replication	Used by Replication Services when you configure a server as a publisher, distributor, or both. This database is created when you configure replication, and it is not created automatically with a new installation.

 Real World You can install the sample databases during or after setup. To install sample databases during setup, select Workstation Components | Books Online And Development Tools on the Components To Install page, and then click Advanced, expand Books Online And Samples, expand Databases, expand Samples, and then select the sample databases and samples to install. To install sample databases after setup, use Add Or Remove Programs. In the Add Or Remove Programs dialog box, select Microsoft SQL Server 2005 and click Change. Setup will then inspect your system. On the Change Or Remove Instance page, select Workstation Components as the existing component to change and click Change Installed Components. From Feature Selection, expand the Books Online And Samples node, expand Databases, expand Samples, and then select the sample databases or samples to be installed. To install and attach the sample database, select Attach Sample Databases during the setup process.

Examining Database Objects

The main elements of a SQL Server database are referred to as *objects*. The objects you can associate with a database are:

- Constraints
- Defaults
- Indexes
- Keys
- Stored procedures
- Extended stored procedures
- Tables
- Triggers
- User-defined data types
- User-defined functions
- Views

You can also associate users, roles, rules, and full-text catalogs with databases.

To examine objects within a database, complete the following steps:

1. In SQL Server Management Studio, use Registered Servers view to select a type of server, such as Database Engine. If you need to expand a server group to see the servers available in the group, click the plus sign (+) next to the name of a group.

2. In Registered Servers view, select a server by double-clicking its name in the list. This connects you to the server in Object Explorer view.

Note   If you have not authenticated the server connection, you may need to provide a SQL login account and password. You may also need to reestablish a connection with the server. In either case, enter any necessary information, and then click Connect to continue.

3. In Object Explorer view, work your way down to the database level. Expand the Databases folder, and then expand the entry for a specific database to see a list of nodes for database objects, including:

- **Database Diagrams**   Contains database diagrams, which are visual diagrams of a database and the information it contains. Use Database Designer to create and manage diagrams.

- **Tables**   Contains system and user tables. System tables are used for many purposes including database mail, database maintenance plans, replication, backup and restore, and log shipping. System tables should not be modified directly.

- **Views**   Contains system and user views. Standard views combine data from one or more tables to make it easier to work with the data. Indexed views have unique clusters to improve query performance. Partitioned views join horizontally partitioned data from tables on one or more servers.

- **Synonyms**   Contains synonyms, which are alternate names for schema scoped objects. Applications can use synonyms to refer to objects in the database abstractly. You could then change the underlying name of the object without having to modify the application programming.

- **Programmability**   Contains nodes used to represent most programmable object types and subtypes, including stored procedures, functions, triggers, assemblies, data types, rules, and defaults.

- **Service Broker**   Contains Service Broker–related objects, including message types, contracts, queues, services, routes, and remote service bindings.

- **Storage**   Contains storage-related objects, including full-text catalogs, partition schemes, and partition functions.

- **Security**   Contains security-related objects, including users, roles, schemas, and keys.

Note   Database objects are covered in detail in chapters in Part III. For example, you will find more information on tables, indexes, and views in Chapter 9, "Manipulating Schemas, Tables, Indexes, and Views."

Creating Databases

SQL Server uses the *model* database as the prototype for new databases. If you want new databases to have a particular setup, first modify the *model* database, and then create the new databases. Otherwise, you will have to modify the settings of each new database manually.

The easiest way to create a new database is by using SQL Server Management Studio. You can also create databases using Transact-SQL.

Creating Databases in SQL Server Management Studio

In SQL Server Management Studio, you set database properties with buttons and input boxes and let SQL Server do all the SQL detail work. Create a database with the default options by completing these steps:

1. In SQL Server Management Studio, use Registered Servers view to select a type of server, such as Database Engine. If you need to expand a server group to see the servers available in a group, click the plus sign (+) next to the name of a group.

2. In Registered Servers view, select a server by double-clicking its name in the list. This connects you to the server in Object Explorer view.

3. Right-click the Databases folder, and then from the shortcut menu, choose New Database to display the dialog box shown in Figure 7-2.

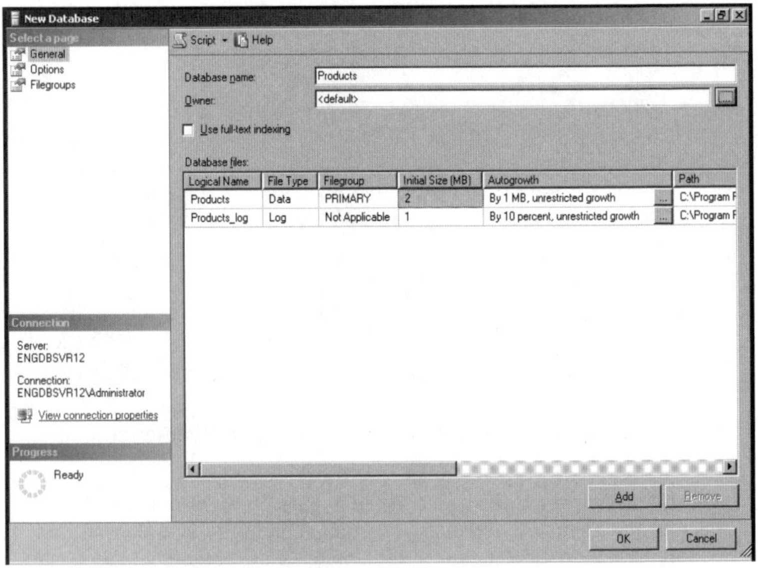

Figure 7-2   The New Database dialog box

4. On the General page, type a name for the database in the Database Name box. Although database names can have up to 128 characters, it is a good idea to give a new database a short but descriptive name to make it easier to track.

> **Note** The names of database objects are referred to as *identifiers*. Identifiers can contain from 1 to 128 characters (except for local temporary tables, which can have from 1 to 116 characters), and they must follow the specific naming conventions for the identifier class to which they belong. Generally, if the identifier name uses spaces or if it begins with a number, you must use brackets ([]) or double quotation marks (" ") to delimit the name when referencing it in Transact-SQL commands.

5. Click OK. SQL Server creates the database.

To customize the creation process, follow steps 1 through 4 (but not 5) in the previous example, and then continue with these steps:

1. On the General page, set the database owner by clicking the button to the right of the Owner box to display the Select Database Owner dialog box.

2. In the Select Owner dialog box, click Browse, and then in the Browse For Objects dialog box that opens, select the login that will be the owner of the database.

3. Click OK twice.

4. If the database will be used with full-text indexing, select Use Full-Text Indexing. You will then need to configure full-text indexing. (Refer to the section titled "Working with Full-Text Search" in Chapter 5.)

5. By default, SQL Server bases the data file name on the database name. For example, if you type **Projects** as the database name, the data file is named Projects. You can change the default name by typing a new value.

6. The File Group box shows which filegroup the data file belongs to. By default, all files are placed in the primary group. Although the primary data file must be in the primary group, you can create other data files and place them in different filegroups. Filegroups provide additional options for determining where data is stored and how it is used, as well as how data is backed up and restored.

> **Tip** Filegroups are designed primarily for large databases and advanced administration. If your database might grow to 1 GB or larger, consider using multiple filegroups. Otherwise, you really do not need to use multiple filegroups. The primary reason to use filegroups is to improve database response time. You do this by allowing database files to be created across multiple disks or to be accessed by multiple disk controllers, or both.

7. In the Initial Size box, type an initial size for the database in megabytes. Use a size that makes sense for the amount of data that the database will store. By default, new databases have the same size as the *model* database. The size range for databases is 1 MB to many terabytes.

Tip   Setting the initial database size to a reasonable value cuts down on the overhead that may be associated with growing the database. Whether you grow the database manually or SQL Server grows it automatically, the database is locked until the growth is complete. This can cause delays in processing queries and handling transactions.

Note   Keep in mind that you cannot shrink a database to make it smaller than it was when you created it. However, you can shrink individual data and log files to make them smaller than their original sizes by using the DBCC SHRINKFILE statement. With DBCC SHRINKFILE, you must shrink each file individually; you cannot shrink the entire database.

8. By default, new databases are set to auto grow each time a data file needs to be expanded. Click the button to the right of the Autogrowth box to adjust the settings. As Figure 7-3 shows, the Autogrowth feature can be set to grow using a percentage or an amount in megabytes, and you can either restrict the maximum file growth to a specific size or allow unrestricted file growth.

Real World   The Autogrowth feature is a good tool to use to ensure that databases do not run out of space. Be careful when configuring the database to enable growth by a certain percentage, however. Setting a 10 percent growth rate, for example, will cause a database that is 5 GB in size to grow by a whopping 500 MB each time a data file needs to be expanded, and a server with multiple databases may run out of space as a result of the growth factor. If you set the growth in megabytes, with 1 MB as a minimum growth size, you will know exactly how much the database will grow each time the data file expands. You may also want to configure an alert to notify you when the database grows to a certain size. You will learn how to configure an alert in Chapter 15, "Database Automation and Maintenance."

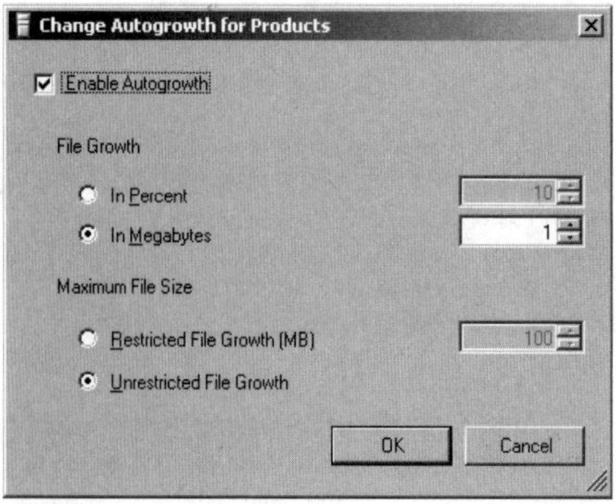

Figure 7-3   Configuring the Autogrowth feature

9. In the Path box, type the full path to the data file. The primary data file name should end with the .mdf file extension. By default, SQL Server uses the default data location you selected when you installed the server. Click the button to the right of the Path box to find a new path, or you can enter a new path directly.

10. Secondary data files provide an additional location for data. If you want to configure secondary data files, click Add to start on a new line, and then repeat steps 5 through 9. Secondary data file names should end with the .ndf file extension.

11. Transaction logs are listed with the Log file type. After you configure data files, you can configure one or more transaction log files in much the same way that you configured the data files. Type the file name, filegroup, initial size, and path information. Configure Autogrowth as necessary. Be sure to name the log files with the .ldf file extension.

Note Setting a size for the transaction log can be tricky. You do not want to rob the system of needed space for data, but you do want to avoid a situation in which the transaction logs are resized again and again because a file is locked when it is being expanded. I recommend 2 MB to 3 MB as a minimum for most databases and 25 percent of total data file size on a moderately active database. Note also that placing transaction logs on separate drives from data files can usually improve database performance.

12. On the Options page, use the Collation selection menu to choose a collation for the database. Microsoft Windows collation names have two components: a collation designator and a comparison style. The collation designator specifies the alphabet or language whose sorting rules are applied with dictionary sorting and the code page to use when storing non-Unicode character data. The comparison style specifies additional collation style as identified by the following abbreviations:

- **90** Code-point sorting (updated collation to include code-point sorting)
- **CI** Case insensitive
- **CS** Case sensitive
- **AI** Accent insensitive
- **AS** Accent sensitive
- **KS** Kanatype sensitive
- **WS** Width sensitive
- **BIN** Binary sort order
- **BIN2** Code-point binary sort (for pure code-point comparison collations)

13. Click OK to complete the creation process.

After you finish creating a new database, you should set options and permissions for that database. You will learn about setting options in the section titled "Setting Database Options in SQL Server Management Studio" later in this chapter. Setting permissions is covered in Chapter 8, "Managing SQL Server 2005 Security."

Creating Databases Using T-SQL

You can also create a database by using the CREATE DATABASE command. This command has options that are similar to those in the Database Properties tab, and the best way to learn how the command works is by creating databases in SQL Server Management Studio first and then trying the CREATE DATABASE command.

The syntax and usage for CREATE DATABASE are shown in Sample 7-1.

Sample 7-1   CREATE DATABASE Command Syntax and Usage

```
Syntax

CREATE DATABASE database_name
    [ ON
        [ <filespec> [ ,...n ] ]
        [ , <filegroup> [ ,...n ] ]
    ]
[
    [ LOG ON { <filespec> [ ,...n ] } ]
    [ COLLATE collation_name ]
    [ WITH <external_access_option> ]
]
[;]

<filespec> ::=
{
[ PRIMARY ]
(     NAME = logical_file_name ,
    FILENAME = "os_file_name"
        [ , SIZE = size [ KB | MB | GB | TB ] ]
        [ , MAXSIZE = { max_size [ KB | MB | GB | TB ] | UNLIMITED } ]
        [ , FILEGROWTH = growth_increment [ KB | MB | % ] ]
) [ ,...n ] }


<filegroup> ::=
{ FILEGROUP filegroup_name [ DEFAULT ] <filespec> [ ,...n ]  }


<external_access_option> ::=
{ DB_CHAINING { ON | OFF }
  | TRUSTWORTHY { ON | OFF } }


Usage

USE MASTER
GO
CREATE DATABASE Sample
ON
```

```
PRIMARY
( NAME = Sample1,
FILENAME = "c:\data\sampledat1.mdf",
SIZE = 100MB,
MAXSIZE = UNLIMITED,
FILEGROWTH = 10%),
( NAME = Sample2,
FILENAME = "c:\data\sampledat2.ndf",
SIZE = 100MB,
MAXSIZE = UNLIMITED,
FILEGROWTH = 10%)
LOG ON
( NAME = SampleLog1,
FILENAME = "c:\data\samplelog1.ldf",
SIZE = 3MB,
MAXSIZE = UNLIMITED,
FILEGROWTH = 5MB)
GO
```

Altering Databases and Their Options

New databases inherit options from the *model* database. After you create a database, you can modify these settings at any time by using SQL Server Management Studio, the ALTER DATABASE statement, and other SQL commands. In most SQL Server editions, many standard options can be set to TRUE (ON) or FALSE (OFF) states. Other options accept specific values that specify their configured state, such as GLOBAL or LOCAL.

Setting Database Options in SQL Server Management Studio

To set database options in SQL Server Management Studio, complete the following steps:

1. In SQL Server Management Studio, use Registered Servers view to select a type of server, such as Database Engine. If you need to expand a server group to see the servers listed in the group, click the plus sign (+) next to the name of a group.

2. In Registered Servers view, select a server by double-clicking its name in the list. This connects you to the server in Object Explorer view.

3. Click the plus sign (+) next to the Databases folder. Right-click the name of a database, and then choose Properties from the shortcut menu to display the Database Properties dialog box.

4. In the Database Properties dialog box, select Options from the Select A Page list as shown in Figure 7-4. You can now configure options for the database by selecting or clearing the appropriate check boxes.

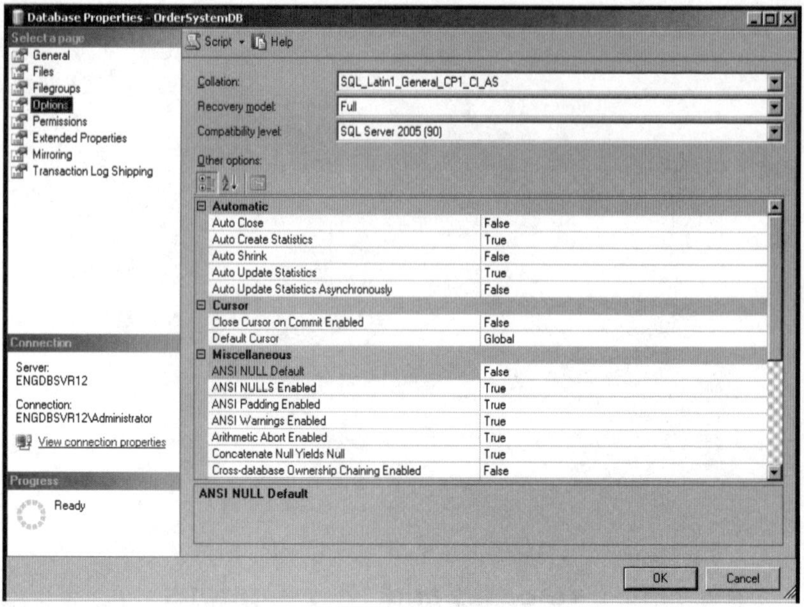

Figure 7-4   The Options page of the Database Properties dialog box

5. Click OK when you are finished selecting options. Your changes take effect immediately, and you do not need to restart the server.

Modifying Databases Using ALTER DATABASE

SQL Server Management Studio gives you one easy way to modify the configuration of a database. Another way to modify a database is to use ALTER DATABASE. You can use the ALTER DATABASE command to perform the following tasks:

- Set database options. You can use it instead of the *sp_dboption* stored procedure.

- Add new data and log files to a database. All the files must be placed in the same filegroup.

- Modify properties of data and log files, such as increasing file size, changing the maximum size, or setting file growth rules.

- Add a new filegroup to a database.

- Modify the properties of an existing filegroup, such as designating whether the filegroup is read-only or read-write, and which filegroup is the default.

- Remove files and filegroups from a database. These elements can be removed only when they do not contain data.

The ALTER DATABASE command is designed to make one database change at a time, and it uses the syntax shown in Sample 7-2. The examples in the listing show how you could use ALTER DATABASE to perform important administrative tasks. You can use the Query view in SQL Server Management Studio or SQLCMD. Execute commands with either the Execute Command button or the GO statement, respectively.

Sample 7-2   ALTER DATABASE Syntax and Usage

Syntax

```
ALTER DATABASE database_name
{ <add_or_modify_files>
  | <add_or_modify_filegroups>
  | <set_database_options>
  | MODIFY NAME = new_database_name
  | COLLATE collation_name }
[;]
<add_or_modify_files>::=
{ ADD FILE <filespec> [ ,...n ]
      [ TO FILEGROUP { filegroup_name | DEFAULT } ]
  | ADD LOG FILE <filespec> [ ,...n ]
  | REMOVE FILE logical_file_name
  | MODIFY FILE <filespec>
}
<filespec>::=
(   NAME = logical_file_name
    [ , NEWNAME = new_logical_name ]
    [ , FILENAME = 'os_file_name' ]
    [ , SIZE = size [ KB | MB | GB | TB ] ]
    [ , MAXSIZE = { max_size [ KB | MB | GB | TB ] | UNLIMITED } ]
    [ , FILEGROWTH = growth_increment [ KB | MB | % ] ]
    [ , OFFLINE ]
)
<add_or_modify_filegroups>::=
{   | ADD FILEGROUP filegroup_name
    | REMOVE FILEGROUP filegroup_name
    | MODIFY FILEGROUP filegroup_name
        { <filegroup_updatability_option>
        | DEFAULT
        | NAME = new_filegroup_name
        }
}
<filegroup_updatability_option>::=
{ { READONLY | READWRITE }
    | { READ_ONLY | READ_WRITE }
}
<set_database_options>::=
SET {
    { <optionspec> [ ,...n ] [ WITH <termination> ] }
    | ALLOW_SNAPSHOT_ISOLATION {ON | OFF }
    | READ_COMMITTED_SNAPSHOT {ON | OFF } [ WITH <termination> ]
}
```

```
<optionspec>::=
{ <db_state_option>
  | <db_user_access_option>
  | <db_update_option>
  | <external_access_option>
  | <cursor_option>
  | <auto_option>
  | <sql_option>
  | <recovery_option>
  | <database_mirroring_option>
  | <supplemental_logging_option>
  | <service_broker_option>
  | <date_correlation_optimization_option>
  | <parameterization_option>
}
<db_state_option> ::=
    { ONLINE | OFFLINE | EMERGENCY }
<db_user_access_option> ::=
    { SINGLE_USER | RESTRICTED_USER | MULTI_USER }
<db_update_option> ::=
    { READ_ONLY | READ_WRITE }
<external_access_option> ::=
    { DB_CHAINING { ON | OFF }
  | TRUSTWORTHY { ON | OFF } }
<cursor_option> ::=
{   CURSOR_CLOSE_ON_COMMIT { ON | OFF }
  | CURSOR_DEFAULT { LOCAL | GLOBAL }
}
<auto_option> ::=
{   AUTO_CLOSE { ON | OFF }
  | AUTO_CREATE_STATISTICS { ON | OFF }
  | AUTO_SHRINK { ON | OFF }
  | AUTO_UPDATE_STATISTICS { ON | OFF }
  | AUTO_UPDATE_STATISTICS_ASYNC { ON | OFF }
}
<sql_option> ::=
{   ANSI_NULL_DEFAULT { ON | OFF }
  | ANSI_NULLS { ON | OFF }
  | ANSI_PADDING { ON | OFF }
  | ANSI_WARNINGS { ON | OFF }
  | ARITHABORT { ON | OFF }
  | CONCAT_NULL_YIELDS_NULL { ON | OFF }
  | NUMERIC_ROUNDABORT { ON | OFF }
  | QUOTED_IDENTIFIER { ON | OFF }
  | RECURSIVE_TRIGGERS { ON | OFF }
}
<recovery_option> ::=
{   RECOVERY { FULL | BULK_LOGGED | SIMPLE }
  | TORN_PAGE_DETECTION { ON | OFF }
```

```
    | PAGE_VERIFY { CHECKSUM | TORN_PAGE_DETECTION | NONE }
}
<database_mirroring_option> ::=
{ <partner_option> | <witness_option> }

<partner_option> ::=
    PARTNER { = 'partner_server'
            | FAILOVER
            | FORCE_SERVICE_ALLOW_DATA_LOSS
            | OFF
            | RESUME
            | SAFETY { FULL | OFF }
            | SUSPEND
            | REDO_QUEUE ( integer { KB | MB | GB } | OFF )
            | TIMEOUT integer
            }
<witness_option> ::=
    WITNESS { = 'witness_server'
            | OFF }

<supplemental_logging_option> ::=
    SUPPLEMENTAL_LOGGING { ON | OFF }

<service_broker_option> ::=
{   ENABLE_BROKER
  | DISABLE_BROKER
  | NEW_BROKER
  | ERROR_BROKER_CONVERSATIONS
}
<date_correlation_optimization_option> ::=
{   DATE_CORRELATION_OPTIMIZATION { ON | OFF }
}
<parameterization_option> ::=
{   PARAMETERIZATION { SIMPLE | FORCED }
}
<termination> ::=
{   ROLLBACK AFTER integer [ SECONDS ]
  | ROLLBACK IMMEDIATE
  | NO_WAIT
}
```

Usage: Adding a File to a Database

```
ALTER DATABASE Customer
ADD FILE
( NAME = Customerdata2,
FILENAME = "c:\data\customerdat2.ndf",
SIZE = 10MB,
MAXSIZE = 500MB,
FILEGROWTH = 5MB )
```

Usage: Adding a Filegroup

```
ALTER DATABASE Customer
ADD FILEGROUP Secondary
```

Usage: Adding Files and Placing Them in a Filegroup

```
ALTER DATABASE Customer
ADD FILE
( NAME = Customerdata3,
FILENAME = "c:\data\customerdat3.ndf",
SIZE = 10MB,
MAXSIZE = UNLIMITED,
FILEGROWTH = 5MB),
( NAME = Customerdata4,
FILENAME = "c:\data\customerdat4.ndf",
SIZE = 10MB,
MAXSIZE = UNLIMITED,
FILEGROWTH = 5MB)
TO FILEGROUP Secondary
```

Usage: Setting the Default Filegroup

```
ALTER DATABASE Customer
MODIFY FILEGROUP Secondary DEFAULT
```

Usage: Modifying a File

```
ALTER DATABASE Customer
MODIFY FILE
(NAME = Customerdata3,
SIZE = 20MB)
```

Usage: Removing a File from a Database

```
USE Customer
DBCC SHRINKFILE (Customerdata3, EMPTYFILE)
ALTER DATABASE Customer
REMOVE FILE Customerdata3
```

Usage: Setting the Recovery Model Option

```
ALTER DATABASE Customer
SET RECOVERY FULL
GO
```

Usage: Setting Single User with Rollback of Incomplete Transactions

```
ALTER DATABASE Customer
SET SINGLE_USER
WITH ROLLBACK IMMEDIATE
GO
```

Note   The EMPTYFILE option of DBCC SHRINKFILE empties a file by moving its data to other files in the same filegroup. Then you can use the REMOVE FILE option of the ALTER DATABASE command to delete the file.

Configuring Automatic Options

SQL Server 2005 has several important features that can be managed automatically. You will find the automatic options on the Options page of the Database Properties dialog box (shown in Figure 7-4). These options are shown as TRUE when they are set to ON and FALSE when they are set to OFF. In the following list, Database Properties dialog box options are listed first, with the related ALTER DATABASE keyword following in parentheses. (Note that some options can only be managed in T-SQL as there is no comparable Database Properties dialog box option.) Automatic options include:

■ **Auto Close (auto_close)**   When this option is set to TRUE, the database closes and resources become available again when the last user connection ends and all database processes are completed. The database reopens automatically when a user connects to the database again. In the SQL Server 2005 Express Edition, this option is set to TRUE by default. All other editions set this option to FALSE by default, which can improve database performance as the overhead of opening and closing databases is eliminated. When FALSE, the database remains open even if no users are currently using it.

Tip   In the Express Edition, Auto Close is a useful feature that allows databases to be treated like any other files. When the database is closed, you can move, copy, or change it.

■ **Auto Create Statistics (auto_create_statistics)**   When this option is set to TRUE (the default), statistics are automatically created by SQL Server for columns used in a WHERE clause and as otherwise needed. These statistics are used to determine the best way to evaluate a query, which in turn can improve query performance.

■ **Auto Shrink (auto_shrink)**   When this option is set to TRUE, data and log files are reduced in size and compacted automatically. When records are deleted or purged, SQL Server automatically reduces the size of data or log files, or both. However, log files are reduced in size only when you back up the transaction log or set the Recovery Model to Simple.

Note   Several caveats apply to Auto Shrink. The Auto Shrink option is applied only when more than 25 percent of a file contains unused space. This causes SQL Server to reduce the file size so that only 25 percent of file space is free or to set the file size to its original size setting, whichever is greater. The process that shrinks the database checks the database size at 30-minute intervals. As with the Auto-growth feature discussed earlier, the database is locked when SQL Server shrinks files, which can reduce query response time. Because of this, it is usually a better choice to run the DBCC SHRINKDATABASE command periodically or to schedule this task on a recurring basis, as explained in the subsection titled "Compressing" later in this chapter.

- **Auto Update Statistics (auto_update_statistics)**   When this option is set to TRUE (the default), existing statistics are updated automatically if data in the related tables changes. Otherwise, existing statistics are not updated automatically; you can only update them manually. The UPDATE STATISTICS statement reenables automatic statistical updating unless the NORECOMPUTE clause is specified.

- **auto_update_statistics_async**   When TRUE, queries that initiate an automatic update of out-of-date statistics will not wait for the statistics to be updated before compiling. Otherwise, queries that initiate an automatic update of out-of-date statistics wait for the statistics to be updated before compiling. This option is new for SQL Server 2005 and can only be managed in T-SQL.

To manage the automatic features using SQL Server Management Studio, follow these steps:

1. In Object Explorer view in SQL Server Management Studio, right-click the database you want to configure, and then select Properties from the shortcut menu.

2. In the Database Properties dialog box, select Options from the Select A Page list.

3. Set the individual Automatic options to True or False as necessary. Click OK when you are finished setting options. Your changes take effect immediately without restarting the server.

To manage the automatic features using T-SQL, follow these steps:

1. In Object Explorer view in SQL Server Management Studio, right-click the database you want to configure, and then select New Query from the shortcut menu.

2. In the Query view, type **ALTER DATABASE <dbname> SET <option> <option_value> GO**, where *dbname* is the name of the database you want to examine, *option* is the name of the option to set, and *option_value* is the value for the specified option. The following example shows the commands required to turn on the Auto Shrink option for the *Personnel* database:

```
ALTER DATABASE Personnel
SET auto_shrink ON
GO
```

3. Execute the query by clicking Execute or by pressing F5. If the option is set properly, the command should complete successfully.

Controlling ANSI Compliance at the Database Level

ANSI compliance can be controlled at the database level using database options. You will find these options listed under the Miscellaneous heading on the Options page of the Database Properties dialog box. The settings for these options are shown as TRUE when they are set to ON and FALSE when they are set to OFF. In the following list, Database Properties dialog box options are listed first, followed by the related ALTER DATABASE keyword in parentheses:

- **ANSI NULL Default (ansi_null_default)** When TRUE, changes the database default to NULL when no value is specified. You can override this setting by explicitly stating NULL or NOT NULL when you create user-defined data types or column definitions.

- **ANSI Nulls Enabled (ansi_nulls)** When this option is set to TRUE, any comparison to a null value evaluates to NULL. Otherwise, comparisons of non-Unicode values evaluate to TRUE only when both values are NULL.

- **ANSI Padding Enabled (ansi_padding)** When this option is set to TRUE, non-null values shorter than the defined column size are padded to fill the length of the column. Values are padded as appropriate for the relevant data type; for example, char columns are padded with trailing blanks, and binary columns are padded with trailing zeroes. When FALSE, trailing blanks are trimmed.

- **ANSI Warnings Enabled (ansi_warnings)** When this option is set to TRUE, SQL Server issues certain warnings that would otherwise not display. For example, if TRUE, divide-by-zero errors are displayed; if FALSE, these errors do not display.

- **Arithmetic Abort Enabled (arithabort)** When this option is set to TRUE, it terminates a query when an overflow or divide-by-zero error occurs. If the error occurs in a transaction, the transaction is rolled back. When the option is set to FALSE, a warning message may display, but queries and transactions continue as if no error occurred.

- **Concat Null Yields Null (concat_null_yields_null)** When this option is set to TRUE, concatenating a string containing NULL with other strings results in NULL. If FALSE, the null value is treated as an empty string.

- **Numeric Round-Abort (numeric_roundabort)** When this option is set to TRUE, an error is generated when a loss of precision occurs in an expression. When it is set to FALSE, losses of precision do not generate error messages, and the result is rounded to the precision of the column or variable storing the result.

- **Quoted Identifiers Enabled (quoted_identifier)** When this option is set to TRUE, identifiers must be delimited by double quotation marks ("...") and literals must be delimited by single quotation marks ('...'). All strings that are delimited by double quotation marks are interpreted as object identifiers and do not have to follow the Transact-SQL rules for identifiers. When FALSE, you only need to use quoted identifiers if names contain spaces.

- **Recursive Triggers Enabled (recursive_triggers)** When this option is set to TRUE, a trigger can execute recursively. Triggers can be executed directly or indirectly. If a trigger is direct, a trigger in Table A1 modifies Table A1, which in turn causes the trigger to fire again. If a trigger is indirect, a trigger in Table A1 could modify data in Table A2, which in turn has a trigger that modifies data in Table A1, and this causes the original trigger to fire again. When FALSE, only indirect triggers are allowed.

To manage the ANSI compliance features using SQL Server Management Studio, follow these steps:

1. In Object Explorer view in SQL Server Management Studio, right-click the database you want to configure, and then select Properties from the shortcut menu.

2. In the Database Properties dialog box, select Options from the Select A Page list.

3. Set the ANSI compliance options to True or False as necessary. Click OK when you have finished setting these options. Your changes take effect immediately without restarting the server.

To manage the ANSI compliance features using T-SQL, follow these steps:

1. In Object Explorer view in SQL Server Management Studio, right-click the database you want to configure, and then select New Query from the shortcut menu.

2. In the Query view, type **ALTER DATABASE <dbname> SET <option> <option_value> GO**, where *dbname* is the name of the database you want to examine, *option* is the name of the option to set, and *option_value* is the value for the specified option. The following example shows the commands required to turn on the numeric_roundabort option for the *Personnel* database:

```
ALTER DATABASE Personnel
SET numeric_roundabort ON
GO
```

3. Execute the query by clicking Execute or by pressing F5. If the option is set properly, the command should complete successfully.

Configuring Cursor Options

Cursors are used with stored procedures, triggers, and in batch scripts to make the contents of a result set available to other statements. You have limited control over cursor behavior using the options listed under the Cursor heading on the Options page of the Database Properties dialog box. These options are shown as TRUE when they are set to ON and FALSE when they are set to OFF. In the following list, Database Properties dialog box options are listed first, with the related ALTER DATABASE keyword following in parentheses:

- **Cursor Close on Commit Enabled (cursor_close_on_commit)**   When this option is set to TRUE, open cursors are closed automatically when a transaction is committed or rolled back. This behavior is in compliance with SQL-92, but the option is not set to TRUE by default. As a result, cursors remain open across transaction boundaries, and they close only when the related connection is closed or when the cursor is explicitly closed.

Note SQL-92 is the most widely used version of the SQL standard and is sometimes referred to as ANSI SQL.

■ **Default Cursor (cursor_default)** When this option is set to LOCAL, cursors are created with local scope unless otherwise specified, and as a result, the cursor name is valid only within this scope. When the option is set to GLOBAL, cursors not explicitly set to LOCAL are created with a global scope and can be referenced in any stored procedure, batch, or trigger that the connection executes.

To manage the cursor settings using SQL Server Management Studio, follow these steps:

1. In Object Explorer view in SQL Server Management Studio, right-click the database you want to configure, and then select Properties from the shortcut menu.

2. In the Database Properties dialog box, select Options from the Select A Page list.

3. Set the Cursor options as necessary. Click OK when you have finished setting options. Your changes take effect immediately without restarting the server.

To manage the cursor settings using T-SQL, follow these steps:

1. In Object Explorer view in SQL Server Management Studio, right-click the database you want to configure, and then select New Query from the shortcut menu.

2. In the Query view, type **ALTER DATABASE <dbname> SET <option> <option_value> GO**, where *dbname* is the name of the database you want to examine, *option* is the name of the option to set, and *option_value* is the value for the specified option. The following example shows the commands required to set cursor_default to GLOBAL for the *Personnel* database:

```
ALTER DATABASE Personnel
SET cursor_default GLOBAL
GO
```

3. Execute the query by clicking Execute or by pressing F5. If the option is set properly, the command should complete successfully.

Controlling User Access and Database State

As you might expect, managing user access and database state is a complex process. In SQL Management Studio, you can control the general state of the database, including whether the database is read-only or read-write, and who has access to the database.

When a database is set to READ_ONLY, you can read data but not modify it. You use this option to prevent users from changing data and modifying database configuration settings. Several caveats apply when a database is read-only: automatic recovery is skipped at system startup, locking does not take place, and the database will not shrink. The normal mode is READ_WRITE, which allows the database to be read and modified.

When a database is set to SINGLE_USER, only the database owner can access the database. You use this option when you are modifying a database and temporarily want to block access to it. When set to RESTRICTED_USER, only members of the db_owner, dbcreator, or sysadmin roles can use the database. When set to MULTI_USER, all users with the appropriate permissions to connect to the database are permitted to use it.

To manage the database state using SQL Server Management Studio, follow these steps:

1. In Object Explorer view in SQL Server Management Studio, right-click the database you want to configure, and then select Properties from the shortcut menu.

2. In the Database Properties dialog box, select Options from the Select A Page list. You can now manage the database state:

   ❑ To set the database to the READ_WRITE state, set the Database Read-Only option to False.

   ❑ To set the database to the READ_ONLY state, set the Database Read-Only option to True.

   ❑ To allow access only to the database owner, set the Restrict Access option to Single.

   ❑ To allow access to the members of the db_owner, dbcreator, or sysadmin roles, set the Restrict Access option to Restricted.

   ❑ To allow access to all users with the appropriate permissions to connect to the database, set the Restrict Access option to Multiple.

3. Click OK when you have finished setting the options. Your changes take effect immediately without restarting the server.

To manage the state settings using T-SQL, follow these steps:

1. In Object Explorer view in SQL Server Management Studio, right-click the database you want to configure, and then select New Query from the shortcut menu.

2. In the Query view, type **ALTER DATABASE <dbname> SET <keyword> GO**, where *dbname* is the name of the database you want to examine, and *keyword* is one of these states: READ_ONLY, READ_WRITE, SINGLE_USER, RESTRICTED_USER, or MULTI_USER. The following example shows the commands required to set the *Personnel* database for multiple-user access:

```
ALTER DATABASE Personnel

SET MULTI_USER

GO
```

3. Execute the query by clicking Execute or by pressing F5. If the option is set properly, the command should complete successfully.

Setting Online, Offline, or Emergency Mode

In SQL Server 2005, you can put an individual database online or offline, or you can set an emergency state that allows you to troubleshoot for database problems. When the option is set to ONLINE, the database is open and available for use. When it is set to OFFLINE, the database is offline, and you can mount or dismount it as necessary. When it is set to EMERGENCY, the database is marked READ_ONLY, logging is disabled, and access is limited to members of the sysadmin fixed server role.

> **Note** In SQL Server 2005, the offline or online state of a database file is maintained independently from the state of the database. For a filegroup to be available, all files in the filegroup must be online. If a filegroup is offline, you cannot query the related data using SQL statements. The query optimizer does not consider the filegroup state when selecting a query plan.

To put a database in the online, offline, or emergency state, follow these steps:

1. In Object Explorer view in SQL Server Management Studio, right-click the database you want to configure, and then select New Query from the shortcut menu.

2. In the Query view, type **ALTER DATABASE** <dbname> SET <keyword> GO, where *dbname* is the name of the database you want to examine, and *keyword* is one of these states: ONLINE, OFFLINE, EMERGENCY. The following example shows the commands required to put the *Personnel* database in the emergency state for troubleshooting:

   ```
   ALTER DATABASE Personnel

   SET EMERGENCY

   GO
   ```

3. Execute the query by clicking Execute or by pressing F5. If the option is set properly, the command should complete successfully.

Managing Cross-Database Chaining and External Access Options

Ownership chaining is used to determine how multiple objects access each other sequentially. When chaining is allowed, SQL Server compares ownership of a calling object to the owner of the object being called. If both objects have the same owner, the object being called is considered to have the same object permissions as the calling object. In this case, you can achieve a cascade effect if the initial permissions on a view are used when the view needs access to other objects and the owners of these objects are the same.

In some limited circumstances, you might need to configure cross-database ownership chaining between specific databases and across all databases in a single instance. Although this feature is disabled by default, you can enable it using

ALTER DATABASE SET DB_CHAINING ON. When DB_CHAINING is TRUE (ON), the database can be the source or target of a cross-database ownership chain. You cannot set DB_CHAINING on *master*, *model*, or *tempdb*, and you must log on as a member of the sysadmin fixed server role to set this option.

A related option is TRUSTWORTHY. When TRUSTWORTHY is TRUE (ON), database modules that use an impersonation context can access resources outside of the database. For example, user-defined functions and stored procedures could access resources outside of the database. By default, the *master* database has TRUSTWORTHY set to ON. The *model* and *tempdb* databases always have TRUST-WORTHY set to OFF, however, and the value cannot be changed for these databases. If you want to permit another database to access outside resources, you must set TRUSTWORTHY to TRUE (ON). You must be logged on as a member of the sysadmin fixed server role to set this option.

To configure chaining or trustworthiness, follow these steps:

1. In Object Explorer view in SQL Server Management Studio, right-click the database you want to configure, and then select New Query from the shortcut menu.

2. In the Query view, type **ALTER DATABASE <dbname> SET <option> <option_value> GO**, where *dbname* is the name of the database you want to examine, *option* is the name of the option to set, and *option_value* is the value for the specified option. The following example shows the commands required to turn on cross-database chaining for the *Personnel* database:

```
ALTER DATABASE Personnel
SET db_chaining ON
GO
```

3. Execute the query by clicking Execute or by pressing F5. If the option is set properly, the command should complete successfully.

Configuring Recovery, Logging, and Disk I/O Error-Checking Options

SQL Server 2005 has several options for managing recovery, logging, and I/O error checking. In SQL Management Studio, you manage recovery settings using the Recovery Model and Page Verify settings on the Options page. In T-SQL, you manage these options using the ALTER DATABASET SET RECOVERY and ALTER DATABASE SET PAGE_VERIFY commands.

Three recovery options are available:

- **FULL**   When recovery is set to FULL, transactions are fully logged, and the database can be recovered to the point of failure or to a specific point in time using the transaction logs.
- **BULK_LOGGED**   When recovery is set to BULK_LOGGED (previously managed using select into/bulk copy), certain SQL commands are not logged in the transaction log. These commands include using SELECT INTO and BULK INSERT with a permanent table, running fast bulk copy, using UPDATETEXT

or WRITETEXT without logging, and using a table load. If you set this option and execute any command that bypasses the transaction log, you cannot recover the database from transaction logs, and BACKUP LOG commands are prohibited. Instead, use BACKUP DATABASE to back up the entire database, and then later you can back up from the log (provided that you do not run any more commands that bypass the transaction log).

- **SIMPLE**   When set to SIMPLE (previously managed using trunc. log on chkpt), the transaction log can be automatically truncated. This setting allows the log to be cleared out after transactions have been committed. After the transaction log has been cleared out, you can perform BACKUP/RESTORE only at the database level (and not with the transaction log).

Note   Checkpoints occur at various times. A checkpoint is issued for each database when the SQL Server service shuts down normally. Checkpoints do not occur when the SHUTDOWN WITH NOWAIT statement is used. A checkpoint is executed in a single database when a database is changed with *sp_dboption*. SQL Server also automatically issues a checkpoint on a database as necessary to ensure that the designated recovery interval can be achieved and when the log becomes 70 percent full.

Note   The transaction log must be large enough to store all active transactions. Otherwise, you cannot roll back transactions. In a deployment environment, you should use this option only when you can rely solely on database backups and do not supplement with transaction log backups. Note also that the *tempdb* database is always truncated on checkpoint, regardless of the setting of this option.

Disk I/O errors can cause database corruption problems and are usually the result of power failures or disk hardware failures that occur at the time a page is written to disk. There are three page verification options to help identify incomplete I/O transactions caused by disk I/O errors:

- **CHECKSUM**   When PAGE_VERIFY is set to CHECKSUM, checksums are used to find incomplete I/O transactions caused by disk I/O errors. The checksum is computed over the contents of the entire page and stored in the page header when a page is written to disk. When the page is read from disk, the checksum is recomputed and compared to the checksum value stored in the page header. When there are mismatches, error message 824 is reported to both the SQL Server error log and the Windows Event Viewer. Any I/O errors detected by the operating system are logged with error message 823.

- **TORN_PAGE_DETECTION**   When PAGE_VERIFY is set to TORN_PAGE_DETECTION, a bit is reversed for each 512-byte sector in an 8-KB database page when the page is written to disk. If a bit is in the wrong state when the page is later read, the page was written incorrectly and a torn page is detected. If SQL Server detects a torn page during a user connection, it sends an I/O error message 824 indicating a torn page error and terminates the user connection. If it detects a torn page during recovery, it marks the database as suspect.

In either case, you may want to restore the database from backup and apply any backup transaction logs.

 Tip   You can use battery-backed disk caches to ensure that data is successfully written to disk or not written at all. But in this case, do not set torn page detection to TRUE.

■ **NONE**   When PAGE_VERIFY is set to NONE (OFF), future data page writes will not contain a checksum or torn page bit, and pages will not be verified at read time, even for previously written pages that contain a checksum or torn page bit.

 Note   Previous versions of SQL Server used the TORN_PAGE_DETECTION option to help detect I/O errors. This option is still supported, but its use is usually rejected in favor of PAGE_VERIFY. When TORN_PAGE_DETECTION is set to TRUE (ON), SQL Server automatically detects incomplete I/O operations known as torn pages.

SQL Server 2005 also supports supplemental logging, which adds information to the logs for third-party products. You can enable logging of additional information by setting the SUPPLEMENTAL_LOGGING option to TRUE (ON). Using this option adds a lot of information to the logs, however, and can impact overall performance.

Viewing, Changing, and Overriding Database Options

Although SQL Server Management Studio makes it easy to set database options, you will often want to view or change options using SQL commands. To do this, you can use the *sp_dboption* stored procedure, individual SET commands, or the ALTER DATABASE command. Tasks you can perform with the *sp_dboption* and SET commands include:

■ **Displaying an options list**   To display a list of available options, type **EXEC sp_dboption**.

■ **Viewing database option settings**   To view the current option settings for a database, type **EXEC sp_dboption <dbname>**, where *dbname* is the name of the database you want to examine, such as **EXEC sp_dboption Subs**.

■ **Enabling database options**   To turn on a database option, type **ALTER DATABASE <dbname> SET <option>**, where *dbname* is the name of the database you want to examine and *option* is the name of the option flag to set to the TRUE (ON) state.

■ **Setting specific database option values**   To set a specific database option value, type **ALTER DATABASE <dbname> SET <option> <option_value>**, where *dbname* is the name of the database you want to examine, *option* is the name of the option to set, and *option_value* is the value for the specified option.

■ **Overriding database options**   Use SET options for individual sessions or database drivers to override default settings. You can also check options using properties of the *Databaseproperty* function. See the section titled "Working with SET Options" in Chapter 4, "Configuring and Tuning Microsoft SQL Server," for more information.

Note   The *sp_dboption* stored procedure should not be used to modify the *master* or *tempdb* databases. It is only supported for backward compatibility, and it should be used primarily to display database options. Whenever possible, use the ALTER DATABASE command to modify database options instead.

Managing Database and Log Size

With SQL Server 2005, you can manage database and log size either automatically or manually. You can use SQL Server Management Studio or Transact-SQL to configure database or log size. This section looks primarily at configuration through SQL Server Management Studio.

Configuring SQL Server to Automatically Manage File Size

To configure automatic management of database and log size in SQL Server Management Studio, complete the following steps:

1. Start SQL Server Management Studio. In Object Explorer view, connect to the appropriate server, and then work your way down to the Databases folder.

2. Right-click the database you want to configure, and then select Properties from the shortcut menu.

3. Select Files from the Select A Page list in the Database Properties dialog box. Each data and log file associated with the database is listed under Database Files. For each data and log file, do the following:

   a. Click the button to the right of the file's Autogrowth box to adjust the related settings. This will display the Change Autogrowth For ... dialog box.

   b. Set the file to grow using a percentage or an amount in megabytes, and then either restrict the maximum file growth to a specific size or allow unrestricted file growth.

   c. Click OK.

4. Optionally, access the Options page and select the Auto Shrink check box. Auto Shrink compacts and shrinks the database periodically.

5. Click OK when you have finished. Your changes take effect immediately without restarting the server.

Note   See the section titled "Creating Databases in SQL Server Management Studio" earlier in this chapter for tips and advice on sizing databases and transaction logs.

Expanding Databases and Logs Manually

Sometimes you may want to increase the size of a database or log file manually. You can do this by completing the following steps:

1. Start SQL Server Management Studio. In Object Explorer view, connect to the appropriate server, and then work your way down to the Databases folder.

2. Right-click the database you want to configure, and then select Properties from the shortcut menu.

3. Select Files from the Select A Page list in the Database Properties dialog box. Each data and log file associated with the database is listed under Database Files.

4. To expand a data file, click in the related Initial Size box, and then enter a larger file size. (You can also create and size a new secondary file for the database. The advantage provided by using a new file rather than an existing file is that SQL Server does not need to lock what may be an active database file in order to expand the database.)

5. To expand a log file, click in the appropriate Initial Size box, and then enter a larger file size in the text box that becomes available. (You can also create and size a new transaction log file.)

Tip   With data and log files, the new file size must be larger than the current size. If it is not, you will get an error. The reason for this is that shrinking the database is handled in a different way. See the following subsection, "Compressing and Shrinking a Database Manually," for details.

6. Click OK to make the changes. SQL Server locks the database while expanding it, which blocks access.

Tip   You can add files using Transact-SQL as well. The command you use is ALTER DATABASE. For more information about using this command, see the section titled "Altering Databases and Their Options" earlier in this chapter.

Compressing and Shrinking a Database Manually

Compressing and shrinking a database is a bit different from expanding it, and in many cases, you will want finer control over the process than you get with the Auto Shrink option. Fortunately, you can manage this process manually, and you can also schedule this process on a recurring basis.

To compress or shrink all database files (both data and log files) manually in SQL Server Management Studio, complete the following steps:

1. Start SQL Server Management Studio. In Object Explorer view, connect to the appropriate server, and then work your way down to the Databases folder.

2. Right-click the database you want to configure. Select Tasks from the shortcut menu, then choose Shrink, and then choose Database to display the Shrink Database dialog box shown in Figure 7-5.

3. The Database Size area in the dialog box shows the total amount of space allocated to all database files and the amount of free space. Use this information to decide if you really want to shrink the database.

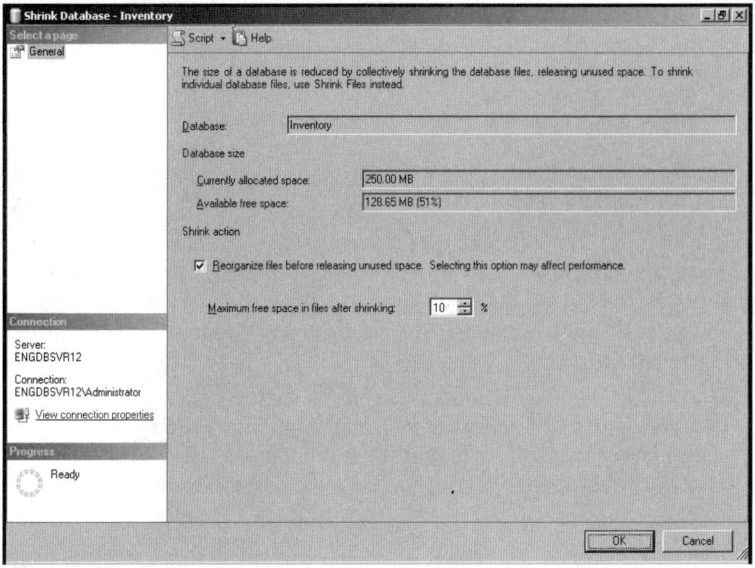

![Shrink Database - Inventory dialog box. Select a page: General. The size of a database is reduced by collectively shrinking the database files, releasing unused space. To shrink individual database files, use Shrink Files instead. Database: Inventory. Database size. Currently allocated space: 250.00 MB. Available free space: 128.65 MB (51%). Shrink action. Reorganize files before releasing unused space. Selecting this option may affect performance. Maximum free space in files after shrinking: 10 %. Connection: Server: ENGDBSVR12. Connection: ENGDBSVR12\Administrator. View connection properties. Progress: Ready. OK Cancel.]

Figure 7-5   The Shrink Database dialog box

4. To reorganize data pages and move them to the beginning of the data files, select Reorganize Files Before Releasing Unused Space. This compresses the data pages but does not remove empty data pages.

Note   Selecting the option Reorganize Files Before Releasing Unused Space performs the same task accomplished by using DBCC SHRINKDATA-BASE and specifying the amount of free space that you want left in the database after shrinking. If you clear the check box for this option, the database files are compressed in the same way as when you use DBCC SHRINK-DATABASE with TRUNCATEONLY, which means that the file size is reduced without moving any data or reallocating rows to unallocated pages.

Log files are not reduced in size immediately. Instead, the size is reduced when the transaction log is backed up or the log is truncated, whichever occurs first. Also, you normally cannot shrink a database smaller than the *model* database (which is the database template).

5. Set the percentage of free space in the database in the Maximum Free Space In Files After Shrinking box. To squeeze all the extra space out of the database, use a value of 0 percent, but be aware that the next write operation may cause the database to grow automatically.

6. Click OK to begin or continue on to step 7 to schedule shrinking the database on a recurring basis. SQL Server locks the database while shrinking it, which blocks access.

7. The property settings you make in this dialog box are saved and are unique to the current database. If you want to use these properties to shrink the database on a recurring basis, click Schedule on the toolbar in the dialog box. You can now schedule this task as explained in Chapter 15, "Database Automation and Maintenance."

To compress or shrink individual database files manually in SQL Server Management Studio, complete the following steps:

1. Start SQL Server Management Studio. In Object Explorer view, connect to the appropriate server, and then work your way down to the Databases folder.

2. Right-click the database you want to configure. Select Tasks from the shortcut menu, then choose Shrink, and then choose Files to display the Shrink File dialog box shown in Figure 7-6.

3. Use the File Type, Filegroup, and File Name selection menus to choose the data or log file that you want to shrink. When you select a specific file, the total amount of space allocated and the amount of free space are shown. Use this information to decide if you really want to shrink the file.

4. Choose a shrink action:

   ■ **Release Unused Space** Truncates free space from the end of the file. Unused space is released and the file is reduced in size to the last allocated extent. The file size is reduced without moving any data or reallocating rows to unallocated pages. You can accomplish the same task by using DBCC SHRINKDATABASE with TRUNCATEONLY and specifying the target file.

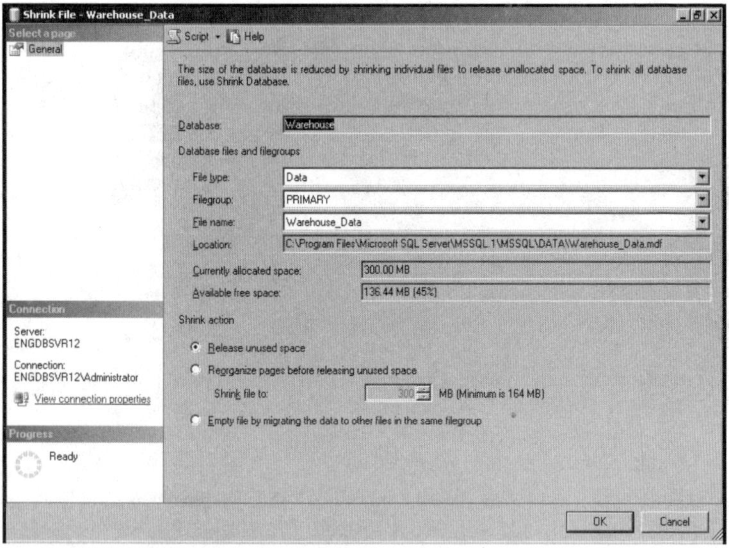

Figure 7-6 The Shrink File dialog box

- **Reorganize Pages Before Releasing Unused Space**   Reorganizes data pages and moves them to the beginning of the data files. This compresses the data pages but does not remove empty data pages. You can accomplish the same task by using DBCC SHRINKDATABASE and specifying the amount of free space that you want left in a target file after shrinking. After you select this option, set the file size by selecting a value in the Shrink To File box. The size cannot be less than the current allocated space or more than the total extents allocated.

- **Empty File by Migrating the Data...**   Migrates the data in this file to other files in the same filegroup. This option is equivalent to executing DBCC SHRINKFILE with the EMPTYFILE option, and it allows the file to be dropped later using the ALTER DATABASE command.

5. If you want to use these properties to shrink the data or log file later, select Shrink The File Later, and then select a date and time.

6. Click OK.

Another way to shrink a database is to use Transact-SQL. Two commands are provided, as shown in Sample 7-3.

Sample 7-3   DBCC SHRINKDATABASE and DBCC SHRINKFILE Syntax

```
DBCC SHRINKDATABASE Syntax

( "database_name" | database_id | 0
    [ ,target_percent ]
    [ , { NOTRUNCATE | TRUNCATEONLY } ] ] )
[ WITH NO_INFOMSGS ]


DBCC SHRINKFILE Syntax

(   { " file_name " | file_id }
    { [ , EMPTYFILE]
    | [ [ , target_size ] [ , { NOTRUNCATE | TRUNCATEONLY } ] ] ]
    } )
[ WITH NO_INFOMSGS ]
```

You use DBCC SHRINKDATABASE to shrink all data files in the database and DBCC SHRINKFILE to shrink a specific data file. By default, these commands also compress the database. You can override this option with TRUNCATEONLY or specify that you only want to compress the database with NOTRUNCATE. To suppress informational messages, use WITH NO_INFOMSGS.

The following command compresses and then shrinks the *Customer* database to 30 percent free space:

```
DBCC SHRINKDATABASE ( Customer, 30 )
```

The following commands compress and then shrink an individual file in the *Customer* database to 5 MB free space:

```
USE Customer
DBCC SHRINKFILE ( Customer_Data, 5 )
```

Note The DBCC SHRINKFILE command is the only method you can use to shrink individual data and log files to make them smaller than their original size. With DBCC SHRINKFILE, you must shrink each file individually, rather than trying to shrink the entire database. Additionally, the truncation options for DBCC SHRINKDATABASE and DBCC SHRINKFILE only apply to data files; they are ignored for log files. You cannot truncate transaction logs with these commands.

Manipulating Databases

Other core administration tasks include renaming, dropping, detaching, copying, and moving databases. These tasks are examined in this section.

Renaming a Database

You can rename user databases in SQL Server Management Studio and with the ALTER DATABASE MODIFY NAME statement. With the database in single-user or offline mode, right-click the database name in SQL Server Management Studio and select Rename from the shortcut menu. Then type the database name and press Tab.

To use T-SQL to put the database in single-user mode and change the name, complete the following steps:

1. Ask all users to disconnect from the database. Make sure that all SQL Server Management Studio connections to the database are closed. If necessary, kill the user processes, as explained in Chapter 5.

2. Access the Query view in SQL Server Management Studio, and then put the database in single-user mode. The following example puts a database called *Customer* in single-user mode:

```
use master
ALTER DATABASE Customer
SET single_user
GO
```

Tip You execute commands in the Query view by clicking Execute Query or by pressing F5. With SQLCMD, you can execute commands by entering the GO statement.

3. Rename the database using the ALTER DATABASE statement. In the following example, the *Customer* database is renamed *cust*:

```
ALTER DATABASE Customer

MODIFY NAME = cust

GO
```

4. After you run the SQL commands, set the renamed database back to multiuser mode. The following example sets the *cust* database to multiuser mode:

```
ALTER DATABASE cust

SET multi_user

GO
```

5. Be sure that all commands, applications, and processes that use the old database name are pointed to the new database name. If you do not do this, you will have problems using the database.

Dropping and Deleting a Database

In SQL Server 2005, dropping and deleting a database are the same thing. When you drop a database, you remove the database and its associated files from the server. After you drop a database, it is permanently deleted, and you cannot restore it without using a backup. To delete references to a database without removing the database files, use *sp_detach_db*, as described later in this section.

You cannot drop system databases, and you cannot drop databases that are currently in use by SQL Server or other users. A database can be dropped regardless of its state. However, any replication or database snapshots on a database must be stopped or dropped before the database can be deleted. Furthermore, if the database is configured for log shipping, you should remove log shipping before dropping the database. Also note that a dropped database can be re-created only by restoring a backup. After you drop a database, you should back up the *master* database.

You can drop a database by completing the following steps:

1. In SQL Server Management Studio, right-click the database you want to drop, and then select Delete from the shortcut menu to display the Delete Object dialog box.

2. To delete backup and history information from the *msdb* database, select Delete Backup And Restore History Information For Databases.

3. To close existing connections to the database before deleting it, select Close Existing Connections.

Note You cannot drop a database that is being used by SQL Server or by other users. For example, if you are restoring the database or the database is published for replication, you cannot delete it. You also cannot delete the database if there are any active user sessions.

4. Click OK. Optionally, back up the *master* database as explained in Chapter 14, "Backing Up and Recovering SQL Server 2005." You back up the *master* database to ensure that the most current system information is stored and that information for the old database will not be restored accidentally with the *master* database.

You can also delete a database with the DROP DATABASE command. The syntax and usage for this command are shown in Sample 7-4.

Sample 7-4 DROP DATABASE Syntax and Usage

Syntax

```
DROP DATABASE { database_name | database_snapshot_name} [,..n]
```

Usage

```
use master
ALTER DATABASE Customer
SET single_user
GO
DROP DATABASE "Customer"
GO
```

Attaching and Detaching Databases

The attach and detach operations are designed primarily to move database files or disable databases without deleting their files. When you detach a database, you remove references to the server in the *master* database, but you do not delete the related database files. Detached databases are not displayed in SQL Server Management Studio, and they are not accessible to users. If you want to use the database again, you can reattach it. Attaching a database creates a new database that references data stored in existing data and log files.

Before you can detach a database, you must ensure that none of the following conditions are true:

- A database snapshot exists on the database. You must drop all of the database's snapshots before you can detach it. Snapshots can be deleted, but they cannot be detached or attached.

- The database is being mirrored. You must stop database mirroring and end the mirror session.

- The database is replicated and published. If it is replicated, the database must be unpublished. Before you can detach it, you need to disable publishing by running *sp_replicationdboption* or *sp_removedbreplication*.

- The database is suspect. You must put the database into EMERGENCY mode and then detach it.

Usually, attaching a database places it in the same state that it was in when it was detached. However, SQL Server 2005 disables cross-database ownership chaining and sets the TRUSTWORTHY option to OFF when a database is attached. You can re-enable these features if necessary as discussed in the section titled "Managing Cross-Database Chaining and External Access Options" earlier in this chapter.

When you attach a database, all primary and secondary data files must be available. If any data file has a different path than it had when the database was first created or last attached, you must specify the file's current path.

Detaching a Database

When you detach a database, you can specify if you want to update the statistics before the database is detached. Updating statistics makes the database easier to use with read-only media; otherwise, you really do not need the update. To update statistics, set the *skipchecks* flag to TRUE.

Because full-text catalogs are associated with databases in SQL Server 2005, you can also control whether they are maintained or dropped during the detach operation. By default, full-text catalogs are maintained as part of the database. To drop catalogs, set the *keepfulltextindexfile* flag to FALSE.

You detach a database using *sp_detach_db*, as shown in Sample 7-5.

Listing 7-5   *sp_detach_db* Syntax and Usage

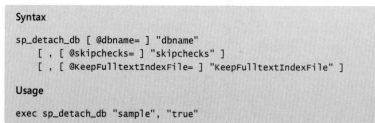

```
Syntax

sp_detach_db [ @dbname= ] "dbname"
    [ , [ @skipchecks= ] "skipchecks" ]
    [ , [ @KeepFulltextIndexFile= ] "KeepFulltextIndexFile" ]

Usage

exec sp_detach_db "sample", "true"
```

Tip   You cannot detach system databases, and you can only detach user databases when they are not in use. Furthermore, before detaching a user database, you may want to close all current connections, put the database in single-user mode, and then run the detach operation.

Attaching a Database with Multiple Files

When you reattach a database, use the CREATE DATABASE statement with FOR ATTACH. For this statement to work, all primary and secondary data files must be available. If the database has multiple log files, all the log files must be available. The only exception is for a read-write database with a single log file that is currently unavailable. If the database was shut down with no users or open transactions before it was detached, FOR ATTACH automatically rebuilds the log file and updates the primary data file as appropriate. The log file for a read-only database cannot be rebuilt because the primary data file cannot be updated; you must provide the log files or files in the FOR ATTACH clause.

Any full-text catalogs that are part of the database being attached will be attached with the database. To specify a new path to the full-text catalog, you can specify the catalog file by supplying a directory name without a file name.

When you use the CREATE DATABASE statement with FOR ATTACH, you can specify only the primary file name. This file contains pointers to the original locations of all other database files. If the other files have not changed location, you can specify only the primary file name, and then let the database engine use the primary file to find the rest of the files.

Sample 7-6 shows the code required to attach the database using the CREATE DATABASE statement with FOR ATTACH.

Sample 7-6   The CREATE DATABASE Statement with FOR ATTACH Syntax and Usage

Syntax

```
CREATE DATABASE database_name
    ON <filespec> [ ,...n ]
    FOR { ATTACH [ WITH <service_broker_option> ]
        | ATTACH_REBUILD_LOG }
[;]


<filespec> ::=
{
[ PRIMARY ]
(
    [ NAME = logical_file_name , ]
    FILENAME = "os_file_name"
        [ , SIZE = size [ KB | MB | GB | TB ] ]
        [ , MAXSIZE = { max_size [ KB | MB | GB | TB ] | UNLIMITED } ]
        [ , FILEGROWTH = growth_increment [ KB | MB | % ] ]
) [ ,...n ]
}
```

Usage

```
CREATE DATABASE Customer
ON (FILENAME = "c:\data\customer_data.mdf")
FOR ATTACH
GO
```

Attaching a Database with Only Data Files

You may not need old transaction logs in a new database. If this is the case, you may want only to restore data files and let SQL Server create new log files for you. To do this, use the CREATE DATABASE statement with FOR ATTACH_REBUILD_LOG, as shown in Sample 7-7.

Sample 7-7   The CREATE DATABASE Statement with FOR ATTACH_REBUILD_LOG Syntax and Usage

Syntax

```
CREATE DATABASE database_name
    ON <filespec> [ ,...n ]
    FOR ATTACH_REBUILD_LOG }
[;]

<filespec> ::=
{
[ PRIMARY ]
(
    [ NAME = logical_file_name , ]
    FILENAME = "os_file_name"
        [ , SIZE = size [ KB | MB | GB | TB ] ]
        [ , MAXSIZE = { max_size [ KB | MB | GB | TB ] | UNLIMITED } ]
        [ , FILEGROWTH = growth_increment [ KB | MB | % ] ]
) [ ,...n ]
}
```

Usage

```
CREATE DATABASE Customer
ON (FILENAME = "c:\data\customer_data.mdf")
FOR ATTACH_REBUILD_LOG
GO
```

Tips and Techniques

All great administrators know a few tricks to help manage databases more efficiently and to keep things running smoothly. Here are a few tips to help you with database administration.

Copying and Moving Databases

All databases except *model*, *msdb*, and *master* can be copied or moved using the Copy Database Wizard. You can also use this wizard to create a copy of a database, to copy or move databases between different instances of Microsoft SQL Server, and to upgrade databases from SQL Server 2000 to SQL Server 2005. The Copy Database Wizard uses one of two techniques for copy and move operations:

- **Detach and Attach**   This method is the fastest way to copy a database, but it requires the source database to be offline so it can be detached and copied/moved. The database is then reattached when the copy/move operation is complete. To use this technique, you must be a member of the sysadmin fixed server role on both the source and destination servers. Also, you should place the database in single-user mode before starting the copy operation to ensure that there are no active sessions. If there are active sessions, the Copy Database Wizard will not execute the move or copy operation.

- **SQL Management Object**   This method is slower, but it does not require the source database to be offline. To use this technique, you must be a database owner for the source database and you must have the CREATE DATABASE permission or be a member of the dbcreator fixed server role on the destination database. You do not have to place the database in single-user mode prior to starting the copy/move operation. Active connections are allowed during the operation because the database is never taken offline.

 Note   The copy/move operation preserves full-text catalogs if both the source and destination servers are SQL Server 2005 servers. However, if the source server is a SQL Server 2000 server, the full-text catalogs must be rebuilt and fully populated again after the copy/move is completed.

When you move databases between different servers or disk drives, the Copy Database Wizard copies the database to the destination server and verifies that it is online. When you move databases between two instances on the same server, a file system move operation is performed. If you elect to move a database, the Copy Database Wizard deletes the source database automatically after the move is completed. However, the Copy Database Wizard does not delete the source database when you perform a copy operation.

You can copy or move a database by completing the following steps:

1. In SQL Server Management Studio, right-click a database in Object Explorer view, point to Tasks, and then select Copy Database.

2. When the Copy Database Wizard starts, click Next.

3. On the Select A Source Server page, specify the server that has the database you want to copy or move. Type the DNS or host name of the source server, such as **CORPSVR09** (see Figure 7-7). Alternately, you can click the button to the right of the Source Server box to browse for available source servers.

4. Windows Authentication is used by default, which means that your current login credentials are used to determine if you have appropriate permissions. If you want to use SQL Server Authentication, select SQL Server Authentication, and then enter your SQL Server login and password in the text boxes provided. Click Next.

5. On the Select A Destination Server page, specify the server to which you are copying or moving the selected database, and then specify the authentication technique to use. Click Next.

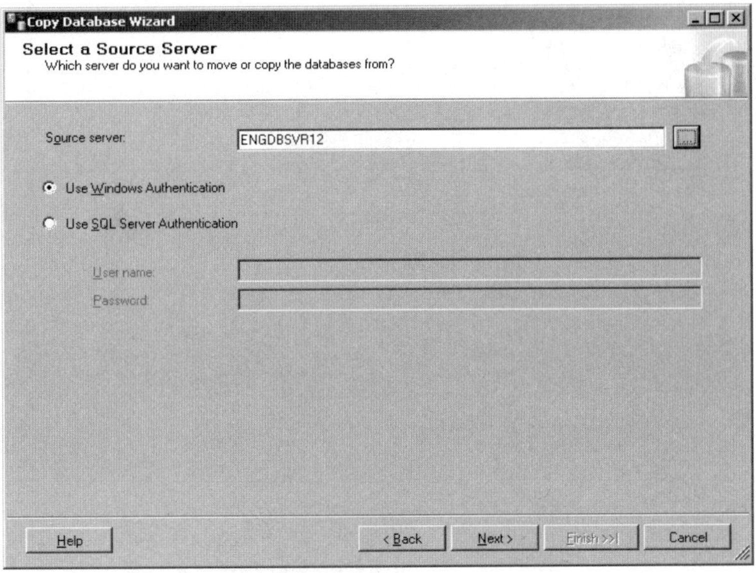

Figure showing the Copy Database Wizard — Select a Source Server page:

Copy Database Wizard

Select a Source Server
Which server do you want to move or copy the databases from?

Source server: ENGDBSVR12

(•) Use Windows Authentication

( ) Use SQL Server Authentication

    User name:
    Password:

Help   < Back   Next >   Finish >>| Cancel

Figure 7-7   The Select A Source Server page of the Copy Database Wizard

Note   SQL Server Agent must be running on the destination server.

6. Select the transfer method—either Use The Detach And Attach Method or Use The SQL Management Object method. If you choose to detach and attach the database, the source database is reattached automatically by default if failure occurs. To prevent this, clear the check box for the option If A Failure Occurs, Reattach The Database. Click Next.

7. As shown in Figure 7-8, you can now select the database you want to copy or move. Click Next.

8. Use the Configure Destination Database page shown in Figure 7-9 to define the destination configuration of each database you are copying or moving, one at a time. Pay particular attention to the Source Database and Destination Database boxes. The Source Database box shows the current name of the database on the source. Use the Destination Database box to set the name that will be used on the destination server.

9. Any data and log files associated with the database are shown with their destination file name and folder. You can change the default locations by typing new values. If you are creating a copy of a database on the same source and destination instance, be sure to change the database name and file names.

10. If the destination database already exists, the default option is to stop the transfer. You can drop the existing database and force the transfer by selecting the Drop Any Database... option.

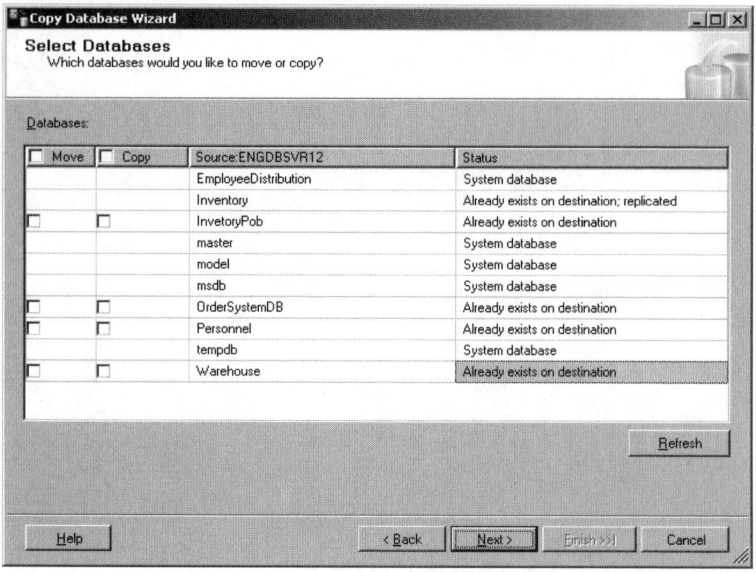

Figure 7-8   The Select Databases page of the Copy Database Wizard

11. Click Next. If you are copying or moving multiple databases, you will see a Configure Destination Database page for each database.

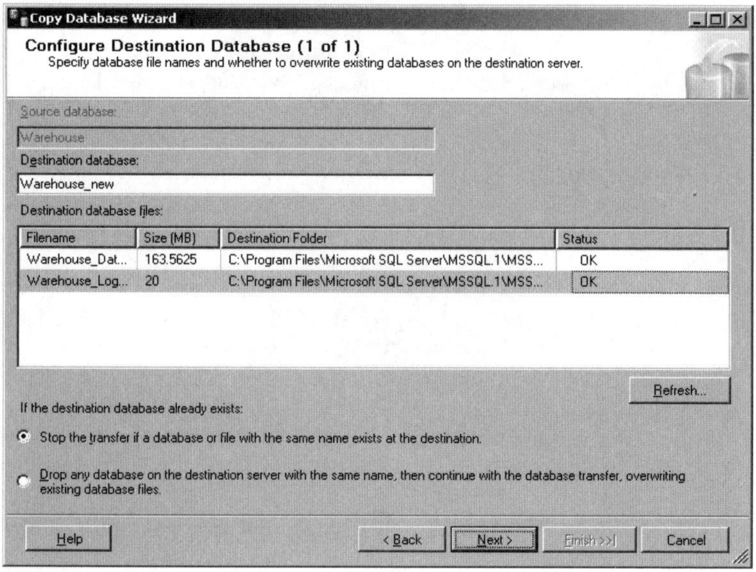

Figure 7-9   The Configure Destination page of the Copy Database Wizard

12. When you have configured all destination databases, the next page you will see is the Configure The Package page. Set the package name and logging options you prefer, and then click Next.

13. You can run the wizard now or schedule the wizard to run at a later time. To run the wizard immediately and perform the copy/move operations, select Run Immediately. To schedule the wizard to run at a later time, select Schedule, and then click Change. You will then be able to schedule this task as a new job. See Chapter 15, "Database Automation and Maintenance" for details on scheduling.

14. Click Next. Review your choices, and then click Finish. The wizard will perform the necessary tasks to prepare and create the copy/move package. If a critical error occurs during these tasks, the operation will fail, and you should view the report to determine what error occurred and then resolve it.

Moving Databases

You can move any system or user-defined database files except for *Resource* database files using the ALTER DATABASE statement. To move files, you specify the current logical name of the file and the new file path, which includes the new file name. You can move only one file at a time in this manner.

To move data or log files to a new location, follow these steps:

1. Get the logical name of the data and log files associated with the database by typing:

```
USE master
SELECT name, physical_name
FROM sys.master_files
WHERE database_id = DB_ID("Personnel");
```

2. Take the database you want to work with offline by typing:

```
ALTER DATABASE Personnel
SET offline
GO
```

3. Move one file at a time to the new location by typing:

```
ALTER DATABASE Personnel
MODIFY FILE ( NAME = Personnel_Data, FILENAME =
"C:\Data\Personnel_Data.mdf")
GO
```

4. Repeat the previous step to move other data and log files.

5. Put the database online by typing:

```
ALTER DATABASE Personnel
SET online
GO
```

You can verify the change(s) by typing:

```
USE master
SELECT name, physical_name
FROM sys.master_files
WHERE database_id = DB_ID("Personnel");
```

You can move full-text catalogs by their logical name as well. However, when specifying the new catalog location, you only specify the new_path rather than new_path/file_name. To move a full-text catalog file to a new location, follow these steps:

1. Take the database you want to work with offline by typing:
   ```
   ALTER DATABASE database_name
   SET offline
   GO
   ```

2. Move one file at a time to the new location by typing:
   ```
   ALTER DATABASE database_name
   MODIFY FILE ( NAME = logical_name, FILENAME = "new_path".
   GO
   ```

3. Repeat the previous step to move other full-text catalog files as necessary.

4. Put the database online by typing:
   ```
   ALTER DATABASE database_name
   SET online
   GO
   ```

Moving and Resizing *tempdb*

The *tempdb* database contains temporary tables created by users or by SQL Server, or both. SQL Server 2005 does not store complete transactions for temporary tables in *tempdb*. With temporary tables, SQL Server 2005 stores only enough information to roll back a transaction and not enough to redo a transaction.

The *tempdb* database is created each time you start the SQL Server service, which ensures that the database starts clean. As with other databases, the default structure of *tempdb* is based on the *model* database. This means that each time you start SQL Server, a snapshot is taken of the current *model* database and applied to *tempdb*.

By default, the *tempdb* primary data file has a size of 8 MB and is set to automatically grow the database by 10 percent when necessary. On a busy server, this 8 MB can fill up quickly, and as a result the server may need to frequently expand *tempdb*. Unfortunately, while *tempdb* expands, SQL Server locks the database. This can slow down queries and make the server seem unresponsive. Following are some ways you can improve the performance of *tempdb*:

- Permanently expand *tempdb* to accommodate space needs during busy periods. To do this, follow the steps described in the earlier section of this chapter titled "Expanding Databases and Logs Manually." Even if the *model* database is smaller, *tempdb* will retain this new size.

■ By default, *tempdb* is stored in the same location as other data. To resolve any performance issues, you can create a secondary data file for *tempdb* and put this file on its own drive. Or you can move *tempdb* and all its associated files to a new location.

You can move individual *tempdb* files or all *tempdb* files by completing the following steps:

1. Get the logical name of the data and log files associated with *tempdb* by typing:

```
Use Master
SELECT name, physical_name
FROM sys.master_files
WHERE database_id = DB_ID("tempdb");
GO
```

2. Move each data and log file to a new location one at a time by typing:

```
USE master
GO
ALTER DATABASE tempdb
MODIFY FILE (NAME = logical_name, FILENAME = "new_path/file_name")
GO
ALTER DATABASE  tempdb
MODIFY FILE ( NAME = logical_name, FILENAME = "new_path/file_name")
GO
```

3. Repeat the previous step to move other data and log files as necessary.

4. Stop and restart SQL Server.

You can verify the change(s) by typing:

```
USE master
SELECT name, physical_name
FROM sys.master_files
WHERE database_id = DB_ID("tempdb");
```

Creating Secondary Data and Log Files

Secondary data and log files can improve the performance of busy databases and can help make large databases easier to manage. You may want to create secondary files to distribute the load over several drives. For example, you could place the primary file on drive D, secondary files on drive E, and transaction logs on drive F. See the section titled "SQL Server 2005 and Your Hardware" in Chapter 1, "Microsoft SQL Server 2005 Administration Overview," for more tips on drives and RAID arrays.

Another reason you may want to create secondary files is to make it easier to restore a large database. For example, if you have a 10-GB database in a single file, you can restore the database only on a 10-GB drive, which you may not have at 3:00 A.M. on a Sunday if a drive fails. Instead, create several smaller files for the database, such as five 2-GB files, and then you can restore these files to several smaller drives if necessary.

You can create secondary data or log files by completing the following steps:

1. Start SQL Server Management Studio. In Object Explorer view, connect to the appropriate server, and then work your way down to the Databases folder.

2. Right-click the database you want to manage, and then select Properties from the shortcut menu to open the Database Properties dialog box.

3. Select the Files page from the Select A Page list in the Database Properties dialog box.

4. On the Files page, click Add to set a secondary data file. Then, in the Database Files area, type a new file name, such as **Personnel_Data2** or **Personnel_Log2**.

5. Set the file type:

   ❑ To create the new file as a data file, select Data under File Type.

   ❑ To create the new file as a log file, select Log under File Type.

6. Set the initial size of the file, and then click the button to the right of the Autogrowth box. Then you can set Autogrowth options for the new data or log file.

7. Click the button to the right of the Path box to find a new path, or you can enter a new path directly. The file name is set based on the logical name and file type.

8. Click OK to make the changes.

Preventing Transaction Log Errors

The transaction log is essential to the smooth running of SQL Server. If the log fills up or otherwise fails, SQL Server cannot process most types of queries. To ensure that the transaction log runs smoothly, you may want to use these techniques:

- To reduce the load on the transaction log, use SQL commands that are not logged. This invalidates the transaction logs, as explained in Chapter 15.

- To ensure that the log is cleaned out periodically, set the database Recovery Model to Simple. This invalidates the transaction logs, as explained in Chapter 15.

- To prevent the log from running out of space, do not set a maximum file size, but do increase the frequency of the log backup and watch the amount of free drive space closely.

■ To make sure you can recover transactions, increase the permanent size of the log and increase the frequency of the log backup.

Preventing a Filegroup Is Full Error

When you encounter a situation in which it is not possible to write to a data file, you will see a Filegroup Is Full error. This error usually occurs when the data file has reached its maximum size or you have run out of file space. To reduce the chances of this error reoccurring, you can use the following techniques:

■ Do not set a maximum file size.

■ Watch the amount of free drive space closely.

■ Schedule data files to be compacted periodically.

■ Remove unused tables, indexes, or objects.

Creating a New Database Template

The *model* database is used as the template for all new databases. If you modify the options and properties of the *model* database, any new databases created on the server will inherit these options and properties.

Managing SQL Server 2005 Security

Microsoft SQL Server 2005 is being used more frequently both within organizations and for external access to information. Whether employees, contractors, or outside users access your databases, your job as an administrator is to manage that database access efficiently. You do this by creating user logins, configuring login permissions, and assigning roles. The permissions and roles you assign determine which actions users can perform as well as what kinds of data they can access.

Your primary goals in managing security should be to:

- Balance the user's need for access to data against your need for protection from unauthorized access to data.

- Restrict database permissions so that users are less likely to execute harmful commands and procedures (maliciously or accidentally).

- Close off other security holes, such as those that may be caused by ordinary users with membership in the Windows Administrators group.

Overview of SQL Server 2005 Security

In SQL Server 2005, all objects in a database are located in *schemas*. Each schema is owned by roles rather than individual users, allowing multiple users to administer database objects. This resolves an issue in earlier versions of SQL Server, in which users could not be dropped from a database without having to reassign the ownership of every object they owned. Now you only need to change ownership for the schema, not for each object.

Working with Security Principals and Securables

SQL Server 2005 makes extensive uses of security principals and securables. An entity that can request a server, database, or schema resource is referred to as a security principal. Each security principal has a unique Security Identifier (SID). Security principals are managed at three levels: Windows, SQL Server, and Database. The level at which the security principal is defined sets its scope of influence. Generally, Windows- and SQL Server–level security principals have an instance-wide scope, and database-level principals have a scope of influence within a specific database.

Table 8-1 lists the security principals at each level. Some security principals, including Windows groups, database roles, and applications roles, can include other security principals. These security principals are also referred to as *collections*. Every database user belongs to the public database role. When a user has not been granted or denied specific permissions on a securable, the user inherits the permissions granted to the public role on that securable.

Table 8-1 SQL Server Principal Levels and the Included Principals

Principal Level	Principals Included
Windows Level	Windows Domain Login
	Windows Local Login
	Windows Group
SQL Server Level	Server Role
	SQL Server Login
	SQL Server Login mapped to an asymmetric key
	SQL Server Login mapped to a certificate
	SQL Server login mapped to a Windows login
Database Level	Database User
	Database user mapped to an asymmetric key
	Database user mapped to a certificate
	Database user mapped to a Windows login
	Application Role
	Database Role
	Public Database Role

Security principals can be assigned specific permissions on hierarchical collections of entities referred to as *securables*. As Table 8-2 shows, the three top-level securables are server, database, and schema. Each of these securables contains other securables, which in turn can contain other securables. These nested hierarchies are referred to as *scopes*. Thus, you can also say that the main securable scopes in SQL Server are server, database, and schema.

Table 8-2   SQL Server Securable Scopes and the Securables They Contain

Securable Scope	Securable Contained
Server	Servers/current instance
	Database
	Endpoint
	Login
	Server role
Database	Application role
	Assembly
	Asymmetric Key
	Certificate
	Contract
	Database Role
	Full-Text Catalog
	Message Type
	Remote Service Binding
	Route
	Schema
	Service
	Symmetric Key
	User
Schema	Aggregate
	Function
	Procedure
	Queue
	Synonym
	Table
	Type
	View
	XML Schema Collection

Understanding Permissions of Securables

Each SQL Server 2005 securable has permissions that can be granted to a security principal. These permissions begin with a keyword or keywords that identify the permission being granted, and these are summarized in Table 8-3.

Table 8-3   Permission Keywords and How They Work

Permission Keyword(s)	Permission Granted	Primarily Applies To...
ALTER ANY <Database>	Grants ability to CREATE, ALTER, or DROP individual securables for the database. For example, granting a principal ALTER ANY SCHEMA for a database gives the principal the ability to CREATE, ALTER, or DROP any schema in the database.	

Table 8-3   Permission Keywords and How They Work   *(continued)*

Permission Keyword(s)	Permission Granted	Primarily Applies To...
ALTER ANY <Server>	Grants ability to CREATE, ALTER, or DROP individual securables for the server. For example, granting a principal ALTER ANY LOGIN for a server gives that principal the ability to CREATE, ALTER, and DROP any login in that server instance.	
ALTER	Grants ability to alter properties of a particular securable except for ownership. When a principal is granted on a scope, the principal has the ability to ALTER, CREATE, or DROP any securable contained within that scope. For example, granting a principal ALTER on a schema gives that principal the ability to CREATE, ALTER, and DROP objects from the schema.	Stored procedures, Service Broker queues, functions, synonyms, tables, and views
BACKUP/DUMP	Grants permission to back up (dump).	
CONTROL	Grants ownership-like capabilities. The principal has all defined permissions on the securable and can grant permissions on the securable as well. When you assign CONTROL permissions, consider the security model's hierarchy. Granting CONTROL at a particular scope implicitly includes CONTROL on all the securables under that scope. For example, CONTROL on a database implies all permissions on the database, including all assemblies and schemas in the database and all objects within all schemas.	Stored procedures, functions, synonyms, Service Broker queues, tables, and views
CREATE <Database Securable>	Grants permission to create the database securable.	
CREATE <Schema contained Securable>	Grants permission to create the schema-contained securable. Remember that ALTER permissions on the schema are needed to create the securable in a particular schema.	
CREATE <Server Securable>	Grants permission to create the server securable.	
DELETE	Grants permission to delete the securable.	Synonyms, tables, and views
EXECUTE	Grants permission to execute the securable.	Stored procedures, functions, and synonyms
IMPERSONATE <Login>	Grants ability to impersonate the login.	
IMPERSONATE <User>	Grants ability to impersonate the user.	
INSERT	Grants permission to insert data into the securable.	Synonyms, tables, and views
RECEIVE	Grants permission to receive Service Broker messages.	Service Broker queues
REFERENCES	Grants permission to reference the securable.	Functions, Service Broker queues, tables, and views

Table 8-3   Permission Keywords and How They Work   *(continued)*

Permission Keyword(s)	Permission Granted	Primarily Applies To...
RESTORE/LOAD	Grants permission to restore (load).	
SELECT	Grants permission to view data stored in the securable.	Synonyms, tables, table-valued functions, and views
TAKE OWNERSHIP	Grants ability to take ownership of the securable.	Stored procedures, functions, synonyms, tables, and views
UPDATE	Grants permission to change data stored in the securable.	Synonyms, tables, and views
VIEW DEFINITION	Grants permission to view the securable definition.	Stored procedures, Service Broker queues, functions, synonyms, tables, and views

Examining Permissions Granted to Securables

SQL Server functions that you will find helpful for examining permissions granted to securables include:

- *sys.fn_builtin_permissions*
- *Has_perms_by_name*

You will learn more about how these functions are used in the sections that follow.

Examining Built-in Permissions

Each object class from the server scope down has a specific set of grantable permissions. The *sys.fn_builtin_permissions* function returns a description of the server's built-in permissions hierarchy:

```
sys.fn_built_permissions( [ DEFAULT | NULL
    | empty_string | < securable_class > } )

< securable_class >::= APPLICATION ROLE | ASSEMBLY | ASYMMETRIC KEY
    | CERTIFICATE | CONTRACT | DATABASE | ENDPOINT | FULLTEXT CATALOG
    | LOGIN | MESSAGE TYPE | OBJECT | REMOTE SERVICE BINDING | ROLE
    | ROUTE | SCHEMA | SERVER | SERVICE | SYMMETRIC KEY | TYPE
    | USER | XML SCHEMA COLLECTION
```

where DEFAULT, NULL, or an empty string return a complete list of built-in permissions, or you can specify the name of a specific securable class to return all permissions that apply to the class.

The *sys.fn_builtin_permissions* function is accessible to the public role. You can view the grantable permissions for all objects by using the following query:

```
USE master
GO
SELECT * FROM sys.fn_builtin_permissions(default)
GO
```

If you want to view the grantable permissions for a specific object class, you can use the following query:

```
USE master
GO
SELECT * FROM sys.fn_builtin_permissions('object_class')
GO
```

where *object_class* is the object class you want to work with. The following example examines the grantable permissions for the *LOGIN* class:

```
SELECT * FROM sys.fn_builtin_permissions('login')
```

You can also list object classes for which a specific permission has been granted. In the following example, you list object classes that have the SELECT permission:

```
USE master
GO
SELECT * FROM sys.fn_builtin_permissions(DEFAULT)
     WHERE permission_name = 'SELECT';
GO
```

Examining Effective Permissions

The *Has_perms_by_name* built-in function returns the effective permission on a securable. Effective permissions include:

- Permissions granted directly to the user, and not denied.
- Permissions implied by a higher-level permission held by the user, and not denied.
- Permissions granted to a role of which the user is a member, and not denied.
- Permissions held by a role of which the user is a member, and not denied.

The *Has_perms_by_name* function is accessible to the public role. However, you cannot use *Has_perms_by_name* to check permissions on a linked server. The basic syntax of the *Has_perms_by_name* function follows:

```
Has_perms_by_name (
                    securable ,
                    securable_class ,
                    permission
                    [, sub-securable ]
                    [, sub-securable_class ]
                    )
```

where *securable* sets the name of the securable or NULL if the securable is the server itself, *securable_class* sets the name of the securable class or NULL if the securable is the server itself, and *permission* is a non-NULL value representing the permission name to be checked. You can use the permission name "ANY" as a wildcard to determine if the securable has any effective permissions. The optional *sub-securable* and *sub-securable_class* values specify the name of the securable subentity and the class of securable subentity against which the permission is tested.

Both of these optional values default to NULL. If the function returns true (1), the securable has the effective permission. If the function returns false (0), the securable does not have the effective permission. A return value of NULL indicates that the query failed.

You can determine if the currently logged-on user has a specific permission on the server by executing the following query:

```
USE master
GO
SELECT has_perms_by_name(null, null, 'permission_name');
GO
```

where *permission_name* is the name of the permission to examine. The following example checks to see if the current user has the VIEW SERVER STATE permissions:

```
select has_perms_by_name(null, null, 'VIEW SERVER STATE');
```

A true (1) or false (0) value is returned to indicate whether or not the user is granted the permission.

To determine if the current user has any permissions in a specific database, you can execute the following query:

```
USE master
GO
SELECT has_perms_by_name('database_name', 'DATABASE', 'ANY')
GO
```

where *database_name* is the name of the database for which you are determining permissions. The following example determines if the current user has any permissions in the *Personnel* database:

```
SELECT has_perms_by_name('Personnel', 'DATABASE', 'ANY')
```

If the query returns 1, the current user has some permissions for the specific database. You can indicate the current database with the *db_name()* function, such as:

```
SELECT has_perms_by_name(db_name(),'DATABASE', 'ANY')
```

You can determine the permissions of a specific user using EXECUTE AS. In the following example, you check to see if EdwardM has any permissions in the *Personnel* database:

```
EXECUTE AS user = 'EdwardM'
GO
SELECT has_perms_by_name('Personnel', 'DATABASE', 'ANY')
GO
REVERT
GO
```

Permissions on schema objects, like *Tables* and *Views*, can be examined as well. To do this, set the securable to name, the securable class to object, and permission to the permission you want to examine. To determine which tables the current user has SELECT permission on, you would use the following query:

```
USE Personnel
GO
SELECT has_perms_by_name(name, 'OBJECT', 'SELECT') as Have_Select,
    * from sys.tables;
go
```

The current user has SELECT permission on tables with a 1 in the Have_Select column. By specifying the two-part or three-part name, you can examine permissions on a specific table as well. For example, to determine if the current user has INSERT permission on the *Address* table in the current database, you would use a two-part name:

```
select has_perms_by_name('Employee.Address', 'OBJECT', 'INSERT')
    as Have_Select, * from sys.tables;
```

or a three-part name:

```
select has_perms_by_name('Personnel.Employee.Address', 'OBJECT', 'INSERT')
    as Have_Select, * from sys.tables;
```

SQL Server 2005 Authentication Modes

The SQL Server security model has two authentication modes:

- **Windows Authentication only**   Works best when the database is accessed within the organization only.
- **Mixed security**   Works best when outside users need to access the database or when you do not use Windows domains.

You configure these security modes at the server level, and they apply to all databases on the server. It is important to note, however, that each database server instance has separate security architecture. This means that different database server instances can have different security modes.

Windows Authentication

If you use the Windows Authentication mode, you can use the user and group accounts available in the Windows domain for authentication. This lets domain users access databases without a separate SQL Server login ID and password. This is beneficial because this means that domain users do not have to keep track of multiple passwords, and if they update their domain password, they will not have to change SQL Server passwords as well. However, users are still subject to all the rules of the Windows security model, and you can use this model to lock accounts, audit logins, and force users to change their passwords periodically.

When you use Windows Authentication, SQL Server automatically authenticates users based on their user account names or their group membership. If you have granted the user or the user's group access to a database, the user is automatically granted access to that database. By default, several local accounts are configured to use SQL Server. These accounts are the local Administrators group account and the local Administrator user account. (Administrator is included because it is a member of the Administrators group by default.) Local accounts are displayed as *BUILTIN\<AccountName>* or *COMPUTERNAME\<AccountName>* in SQL Server Management Studio. For example, Administrators is displayed as *BUILTIN\Administrators*.

Real World   Domain accounts are the best way to manage users who access the database from within the organization. Also, if you assign users to domain groups and then configure access for these groups in SQL Server, you cut down on the amount of administration you have to do. For example, if you assign users in the marketing department to a marketing group and then configure this group in SQL Server, you have only one account to manage instead of 10, 20, 50, or more. When employees leave the organization or change departments, you do not have to delete user accounts. When new employees are hired, you do not have to create new accounts either—you only need to make sure that they are added to the correct group in Windows.

Mixed Security and SQL Server Logins

With mixed security, you use both Windows Authentication and SQL Server logins. SQL Server logins are primarily used by users outside the company, such as those who might access the database from the Internet. You can configure applications that access SQL Server from the Internet to use specific accounts automatically or to prompt the user for a SQL Server login ID and password.

With mixed security, SQL Server first determines if the user is connecting using a valid SQL Server login. If the user has a valid login and has the proper password, the user connection is accepted. If the user has a valid login but has an improper password, the user connection is refused. SQL Server checks the Windows account information only if the user does not have a valid login. In this case, SQL Server determines whether or not the Windows account has permission to connect to the server. If the account has permission, the connection is accepted. Otherwise, the connection is refused.

All SQL Server servers have the built-in sa login and may also have NETWORK SERVICE and SYSTEM logins (depending on the server instance configuration). All databases have built-in SQL Server users known as dbo, guest, INFORMATION_SCHEMA, and sys. These logins and users that are provided for special purposes are discussed in the following section titled "Special Purpose Logins and Users."

Special Purpose Logins and Users

You configure access to SQL Server using server logins. You can configure various levels of access to these logins:

- By the roles to which those logins belong.
- By permitting access to specific databases.
- By allowing or denying object permissions.

Just as there are two authentication modes, there are also two kinds of server logins. You create domain logins using domain accounts, which can be domain or local user accounts, local group accounts, or universal and global domain group accounts. You create SQL Server logins by specifying a unique login ID and password. Several logins are configured by default, and these include local Administrators, local Administrator, sa, NETWORK SERVICE, and SYSTEM.

To narrow the scope of access to a specific database, you use database user accounts. Several database users are configured by default including the dbo user (a special database user), the guest user (a special database user with limited access), the INFORMATION_SCHEMA user, and the sys user.

In this section, you will learn more about these special purpose logins.

Working with the Administrators Group

The Administrators group is a local group on the database server. This group's members normally include the local Administrator user account and any other users set to administer the system locally. In SQL Server, this group is granted the sysadmin server role by default.

Working with the Administrator User Account

Administrator is a local user account on the server. This account provides administrator privileges on the local system, and you use it primarily when you install a system. If the host computer is part of a Windows domain, the Administrator account usually has domain-wide privileges as well. In SQL Server, this account is granted the sysadmin server role by default.

Working with the sa Login

The sa login is the system administrator's account for SQL Server. With the new integrated and expanded security model, sa is no longer needed, and it is primarily provided for backward compatibility with previous SQL Server versions. As with other administrator logins, sa is granted the sysadmin server role by default. When you install SQL Server, the sa login is not assigned a password.

To prevent unauthorized access to the server, you should set a strong password for this account, and you should also change the password periodically as you would the passwords for Windows accounts.

 Best Practices   Because the sa login is widely known to malicious users, you may want to delete or disable this account if possible. Instead of using the sa login, make System Administrators members of the sysadmin server role and have them log on using their own logins. Anyone with the sysadmin server role can then log on and administer the server. If you ever get locked out of the server, you can log on to the server locally using an account with local administrator privileges, and then reset passwords or assign privileges as necessary.

Working with the NETWORK SERVICE and SYSTEM Logins

NETWORK SERVICE and SYSTEM are built-in local accounts on the server. Whether or not server logins are created for these accounts depends on the server configuration. For example, if you have configured the server as a Report Server, you will have a login for the NETWORK SERVICE account, and this login will be a member of the special database role RSExecRole on the *master*, *msdb*, *ReportServer*, and *ReportServerTempDB* databases. RSExecRole is used primarily to manage the Report Server schema, and the service account for the server instance will also be a member of this role.

During setup of the server instance, the NETWORK SERVICE and SYSTEM accounts can be the selected service account for SQL Server, SQL Server Agent, Analysis Services, and Report Server. In this case, the SYSTEM account will typically have the sysadmin server role, giving it full access for administration of the server instance.

Working with the Guest User

The guest user is a special user that you can add to a database to allow anyone with a valid SQL Server login to access the database. Users who access a database with the guest account assume the identity of the guest user and inherit all the privileges and permissions of the guest account. For example, if you configure the domain account GOTEAM to access SQL Server, GOTEAM can access any database with a guest login, and when GOTEAM does so, that person is granted all the permissions of the guest account. If you were to configure the Windows group DEVGROUP with guest access, you could simplify administration since any user that is a member of the group would be able to access any database as a guest.

By default, the guest user exists in the *model* database and is granted guest permissions. Because *model* is the template for all databases you create, this means that all new databases will include the guest account, and this account will be granted guest permissions. You can add or delete guest from all databases except *master* and *tempdb*. Most users access *master* and *tempdb* as guests, and for this reason, you cannot remove the guest account from these databases. This is not a problem, however, because a guest has limited permissions and privileges in *master* and *tempdb*.

Before using the guest user, you should note the following information about the account:

- The guest user is a member of the public server role and inherits the permissions of this role.
- The guest user must exist in a database before anyone can access it as a guest.
- The guest user is used only when a user account has access to SQL Server but does not have access to the database through this user account.

Working with the dbo User

The database owner, or dbo, is a special type of database user and is granted special privileges. Generally speaking, the user who created a database is the database owner. The dbo is implicitly granted all permissions on the database and can grant these permissions to other users. Because members of the sysadmin server role are mapped automatically to the special user dbo, logins with the sysadmin role can perform any tasks that a dbo can perform.

Objects created in SQL Server databases also have owners. These owners are referred to as the *database object owners*. Objects created by a member of the sysadmin server role belong to the dbo user automatically. Objects created by users who are not members of the sysadmin server role belong to the user creating the object and must be qualified with the name of that user when other users reference them. For example, if GOTEAM is a member of the sysadmin server role and creates a table called *Sales*, *Sales* belongs to dbo and is qualified as *dbo.Sales*, or simply *Sales*. However, if GOTEAM is not a member of the sysadmin server role and creates a table called *Sales*, *Sales* belongs to GOTEAM and must be qualified as *GOTEAM.Sales*.

 Note Technically, dbo is a special user account and not a special-purpose login. However, you may see it referred to as a login. You cannot log in to a server or database as dbo, but you may be the person who created the database or a set of objects in it.

Working with the sys and INFORMATION_SCHEMA Users

All system objects are contained in the schemas named sys or INFORMATION_ SCHEMA. These are two special schemas that are created in each database, but they are only visible in the *master* database. The related sys and information schema views provide an internal system view of the metadata for all data objects stored in a database. The sys and INFORMATION_SCHEMA users are used to reference into these views.

Permissions

Permissions determine the actions that users can perform on SQL Server or in a database. Permissions are granted according to the login ID, group memberships, and role memberships. Users must have appropriate permissions before they can perform any action that changes database definitions or accesses data. Three types of permissions are used in SQL Server:

- Object permissions
- Statement permissions
- Implicit permissions

Object Permissions

In SQL Server 2005, all object permissions are grantable. You can manage permissions for specific objects, all objects of particular types, and all objects belonging to a specific schema. The objects for which you can manage permissions depend on the scope. At the server level, you can grant object permissions for servers, endpoints, logins, and server roles. You can also manage permissions for the current server instance.

At the database level, you can manage object permissions for application roles, assemblies, asymmetric keys, certificates, database roles, databases, full-text catalogs, functions, schemas, stored procedures, symmetric keys, synonyms, tables, user-defined data types, users, views, and XML schema collections.

You control access to these objects by granting, denying, or revoking the ability to execute particular statements or stored procedures. For example, you can grant a user the right to SELECT information from a table, but deny the right to INSERT, UPDATE, or DELETE information in the table. Table 8-4 provides a summary of object permissions.

Table 8-4 Object Permissions

Base Securable	Configurable Permissions	Highest Permission	Contained In	Implied Permission from Parent
APPLICATION ROLE	ALTER, CONTROL, VIEW DEFINITION	CONTROL	DATABASE	ALTER ANY APPLICATION ROLE, CONTROL, VIEW DEFINITION
ASSEMBLY	ALTER, CONTROL, EXECUTE, REFERENCES, TAKE OWNERSHIP, VIEW DEFINITION	CONTROL	DATABASE	ALTER ANY ASSEMBLY, CONTROL, EXECUTE, REFERENCES, VIEW DEFINITION
ASYMMETRIC KEY	ALTER, CONTROL, REFERENCES, TAKE OWNERSHIP, VIEW DEFINITION	CONTROL	DATABASE	ALTER ANY ASYMMETRIC KEY, CONTROL, REFERENCES, VIEW DEFINITION
CERTIFICATE	ALTER, CONTROL, REFERENCES, TAKE OWNERSHIP, VIEW DEFINITION	CONTROL	DATABASE	ALTER ANY CERTIFICATE, CONTROL, REFERENCES, VIEW DEFINITION
CONTRACT	ALTER, CONTROL, REFERENCES, TAKE OWNERSHIP, VIEW DEFINITION	CONTROL	DATABASE	ALTER ANY CONTRACT, CONTROL, REFERENCES, VIEW DEFINITION
DATABASE	ALTER, ALTER ANY APPLICATION ROLE, ALTER ANY ASSEMBLY, ALTER ANY ASYMMETRIC KEY, ALTER ANY CERTIFICATE, ALTER ANY CONTRACT, ALTER ANY DATABASE EVENT NOTIFICATION, ALTER ANY DATASPACE, ALTER ANY FULLTEXT CATALOG, ALTER ANY MESSAGE TYPE, ALTER ANY REMOTE SERVICE BINDING, ALTER ANY ROLE, ALTER ANY ROUTE, ALTER	CONTROL, CONNECT REPLICATION, ALTER ANY ASSEMBLY, ALTER ANY CERTIFICATE, ALTER ANY CONTRACT, ALTER ANY DATABASE EVENT NOTIFICATION, ALTER ANY	SERVER	ALTER ANY DATABASE, CONTROL SERVER, EXTERNAL ACCESS, CREATE ANY DATABASE, VIEW ANY DEFINITION

Table 8-4 **Object Permissions** *(continued)*

Base Securable	Configurable Permissions	Highest Permission	Contained In	Implied Permission from Parent
	SERVICE, ALTER ANY SYMMETRIC KEY, ALTER ANY TRIGGER, ALTER ANY USER, ALTER ANY XML SCHEMA COLLECTION, AUTHENTICATE, BACKUP DATABASE, BACKUP LOG, CHECKPOINT, CONNECT, CONNECT REPLICATION, CONTROL, CREATE AGGREGATE, CREATE ASSEMBLY, CREATE CERTIFICATE, CREATE CONTRACT, CREATE DATABASE, CREATE DATABASE EVENT NOTIFICATION, CREATE DEFAULT, CREATE FULLTEXT CATALOG, CREATE FUNCTION, CREATE MESSAGE TYPE, CREATE PROCEDURE, CREATE QUEUE, CREATE REMOTE SERVICE BINDING, CREATE ROLE, CREATE ROUTE, CREATE RULE, CREATE SCHEMA, CREATE SERVICE, CREATE SYMMETRIC KEY, CREATE SYNONYM, CREATE TABLE, CREATE TYPE, CREATE VIEW, CREATE XML SCHEMA COLLECTION, DELETE, EXECUTE, INSERT, REFERENCES, SELECT, SHOWPLAN, SUBSCRIBE QUERY NOTIFICATIONS, TAKE OWNERSHIP, UPDATE, VIEW DEFINITION	FULLTEXT CATALOG, ALTER ANY MESSAGE TYPE, ALTER ANY REMOTE SERVICE BINDING, ALTER ANY ROLE, ALTER ANY ROUTE, ALTER ANY SCHEMA, ALTER ANY SERVICE, ALTER ANY SYMMETRIC KEY, ALTER ANY XML SCHEMA COLLECTION		
ENDPOINT	ALTER, CONNECT, CONTROL, TAKE OWNERSHIP, VIEW DEFINITION	CONTROL	SERVER	ALTER ANY ENDPOINT, CONTROL SERVER
FULLTEXT CATALOG	ALTER, CONTROL, REFERENCES, TAKE OWNERSHIP, VIEW DEFINITION	CONTROL	DATABASE	ALTER ANY FULLTEXT CATALOG, CONTROL, REFERENCES, VIEW DEFINITION
LOGIN	ALTER, CONTROL, IMPERSONATE, VIEW DEFINITION	CONTROL	SERVER	ALTER ANY LOGIN, CONTROL SERVER
MESSAGE TYPE	ALTER, CONTROL, REFERENCES, TAKE OWNERSHIP, VIEW DEFINITION	CONTROL	DATABASE	ALTER ANY MESSAGE TYPE, CONTROL, REFERENCES, VIEW DEFINITION

Table 8-4   Object Permissions   *(continued)*

Base Securable	Configurable Permissions	Highest Permission	Contained In	Implied Permission from Parent
OBJECT	ALTER, CONTROL, DELETE, EXECUTE, INSERT, RECEIVE, REFERENCES, SELECT, TAKE OWNERSHIP, UPDATE, VIEW DEFINITION	CONTROL	SCHEMA	ALTER, CONTROL, DELETE, EXECUTE, INSERT, RECEIVE, REFERENCES, SELECT, UPDATE, VIEW DEFINITION
REMOTE SERVICE BINDING	ALTER, CONTROL, TAKE OWNERSHIP, VIEW DEFINITION	CONTROL	DATABASE	ALTER ANY REMOTE SERVICE BINDING, CONTROL, VIEW DEFINITION
ROLE	ALTER, CONTROL, TAKE OWNERSHIP, VIEW DEFINITION	CONTROL	DATABASE	ALTER ANY ROLE, CONTROL, VIEW DEFINITION
ROUTE	ALTER, CONTROL, TAKE OWNERSHIP, VIEW DEFINITION	CONTROL	DATABASE	ALTER ANY ROUTE, CONTROL, VIEW DEFINITION
SCHEMA	ALTER, CONTROL, DELETE, EXECUTE, INSERT, REFERENCES, SELECT, TAKE OWNERSHIP, UPDATE, VIEW DEFINITION	CONTROL	DATABASE	ALTER ANY SCHEMA, CONTROL, DELETE, EXECUTE, INSERT, REFERENCES, SELECT, UPDATE, VIEW DEFINITION
SERVER	ADMINISTER BULK OPERATIONS, ALTER ANY CONNECTION, ALTER ANY CREDENTIAL, ALTER ANY DATABASE, ALTER ANY ENDPOINT, ALTER ANY EVENT NOTIFICATION, ALTER ANY LINKED SERVER, ALTER ANY LOGIN, ALTER RESOURCES, ALTER SERVER STATE, ALTER SETTINGS, ALTER TRACE, AUTHENTICATE SERVER, CONTROL SERVER, CREATE ANY DATABASE, CREATE DDL EVENT, CREATE ENDPOINT, CREATE EVENT NOTIFICATION, CREATE MANAGEMENT EVENT, CREATE SECURITY EVENT, CREATE USER EVENT, EXTERNAL ACCESS, SHUTDOWN, VIEW ANY DEFINITION, VIEW SERVER STATE	CONTROL SERVER, ALTER ANY DATABASE, ALTER ANY EVENT NOTIFICATION, ALTER ANY ENDPOINT, ALTER SERVER STATE	Not applicable	Not applicable
SERVICE	ALTER, CONTROL, SEND, TAKE OWNERSHIP, VIEW DEFINITION	CONTROL	DATABASE	ALTER ANY SERVICE, CONTROL, VIEW DEFINITION

Table 8-4   Object Permissions   *(continued)*

Base Securable	Configurable Permissions	Highest Permission	Contained In	Implied Permission from Parent
SYMMETRIC KEY	ALTER, CONTROL, REFERENCES, TAKE OWNERSHIP, VIEW DEFINITION	CONTROL	DATABASE	ALTER ANY SYMMETRIC KEY, CONTROL, REFERENCES, VIEW DEFINITION
TYPE	CONTROL, EXECUTE, REFERENCES, TAKE OWNERSHIP, VIEW DEFINITION	CONTROL	SCHEMA	CONTROL, EXECUTE, REFERENCES, VIEW DEFINITION
USER	ALTER, CONTROL, IMPERSONATE, VIEW DEFINITION	CONTROL	DATABASE	ALTER ANY USER, CONTROL, VIEW DEFINITION
XML SCHEMA COLLECTION	ALTER, CONTROL, EXECUTE, REFERENCES, TAKE OWNERSHIP, VIEW DEFINITION	CONTROL	SCHEMA	ALTER, CONTROL, EXECUTE, REFERENCES, VIEW DEFINITION

Statement Permissions

Statement permissions control administration actions, such as creating a database or adding objects to a database. Only members of the sysadmin role and database owners can assign statement permissions. By default, normal logins are not granted statement permissions, and you must specifically grant these permissions to logins that are not administrators. For example, if a user needs to be able to create views in a database, you would assign permission to execute CREATE VIEW. Table 8-5 provides a summary of statement permissions that you can grant, deny, or revoke.

Table 8-5   Statement Permissions

Statement Permission	Description
CREATE DATABASE	Determines if the login can create databases. The user must be in the *master* database or must be a member of the sysadmin server role.
CREATE DEFAULT	Determines if the user can create a default value for a table column.
CREATE FUNCTION	Determines if the user can create a user-defined function in the database.
CREATE PROCEDURE	Determines if the user can create a stored procedure.
CREATE RULE	Determines if the user can create a table column rule.
CREATE TABLE	Determines if the user can create a table.
CREATE VIEW	Determines if the user can create a view.
BACKUP DATABASE	Determines if the user can back up the database.
BACKUP LOG	Determines if the user can back up the transaction log.

Implied Permissions

Only members of predefined system roles or database/database object owners have implied permissions. Implied permissions for a role cannot be changed. You make other accounts members of the role to give the accounts the related implied permissions. For example, members of the sysadmin server role can perform any activity in SQL Server. They can extend databases, kill processes, and so on. Any account you add to the sysadmin role can perform these tasks as well.

Database and database object owners also have implied permissions. These permissions allow them to perform all activities with either the database or the object they own, or with both. For example, a user who owns a table can view, add, change, and delete data. That user can also alter the table's definition and control the table's permissions.

Roles

Roles are a lot like Windows—they allow you to assign permissions to a group of users easily and they can have built-in permissions (implicit permissions) that cannot be changed. Two types of roles are available:

- **Server roles**   Applied at the server level
- **Database roles**   Applied at the database level

Server Roles

You use server roles to grant server administration capabilities. If you make a login a member of a role, users who use this login can perform any tasks permitted by the role. For example, members of the sysadmin role have the highest level of permissions on SQL Server and can perform any type of task.

You set server roles at the server level, and you predefine them. This means that these permissions affect the entire server and you cannot change the permission set. The following list provides a summary of each server role, from the lowest-level role (bulkadmin) to the highest-level role (sysadmin):

- **bulkadmin**   Designed for domain accounts that need to perform bulk inserts into the database. Members of this role can add members to bulkadmin and can execute the BULK INSERT statements.

- **dbcreator**   Designed for users who need to create, modify, drop, and restore databases. Members of this role can add members to dbcreator and perform these tasks: ALTER DATABASE, CREATE DATABASE, DROP DATABASE, EXTEND DATABASE, RESTORE DATABASE, RESTORE LOG, and *sp_renamedb*.

- **diskadmin**   Designed for users who need to manage disk files. Members of this role can add members to diskadmin and can perform these tasks: DISK INIT, *sp_addumpdevice*, *sp_diskdefault*, and *sp_dropdevice*.

- **processadmin**   Designed for users who need to control SQL Server processes. Members of this role can add members to processadmin and can kill processes.

- **securityadmin**   Designed for users who need to manage logins, create database permissions, and read error logs. Members of this role can add members to securityadmin; grant, deny, and revoke server-level and database-level permissions; reset passwords; and read the error logs. In addition, they can also perform these tasks: *sp_addlinkedsrvlogin, sp_addlogin, sp_defaultdb, sp_defaultlanguage, sp_denylogin, sp_droplinkedsrvlogin, sp_droplogin, sp_grantlogin, sp_helplogins, sp_remoteoption,* and *sp_revokelogin*.

- **serveradmin** Designed for users who need to set server-wide configuration options and shut down the server. Members of this role can add members to serveradmin and can perform these other tasks: DBCC FREEPROCCACHE, RECONFIGURE, SHUTDOWN, *sp_configure*, *sp_fulltext_service*, and *sp_tableoption*.

- **setupadmin** Designed for users who need to manage linked servers and control startup procedures. Members of this role can add members to setupadmin; can add, drop, and configure linked servers; and can control startup procedures.

- **sysadmin** Designed for users who need complete control over SQL Server and installed databases. Members of this role can perform any activity in SQL Server.

Fixed server roles can be mapped to the more granular permissions for SQL Server 2005, as shown in Table 8-6.

Table 8-6 Granular Permissions Associated with Fixed Server Roles

Fixed Server Role	Permissions Granted with This Role
bulkadmin	ADMINISTER BULK OPERATIONS
dbcreator	CREATE DATABASE
diskadmin	ALTER RESOURCES
processadmin	ALTER SERVER STATE, ALTER ANY CONNECTION
securityadmin	ALTER ANY LOGIN
serveradmin	ALTER SETTINGS, SHUTDOWN, CREATE ENDPOINT, ALTER SERVER STATE, ALTER ANY ENDPOINT, ALTER RESOURCES
setupadmin	ALTER ANY LINKED SERVER
sysadmin	CONTROL SERVER

Database Roles

When you want to assign permissions at the database level, you can use database roles. You set database roles on a per database basis, which means that each database has its own set of roles. SQL Server 2005 supports three types of database roles:

- User-defined standard roles
- User-defined application roles
- Predefined (or fixed) database roles

Standard roles allow you to create roles with unique permissions and privileges. You can use standard roles to logically group users together and then assign a single permission to the role rather than having to assign permissions to each user separately. For example, you could create a role called Users that allows users to SELECT, INSERT, and UPDATE specific tables in the database but does not allow them to perform any other tasks.

Application roles allow you to create password-protected roles for specific applications. For example, a user could connect through a Web-based application called NetReady; this application would activate the role and the user would then gain the role's permissions and privileges. Standard database roles or other roles cannot be assigned to an application role. Instead, the application role is activated when the application connects to the database.

SQL Server also has predefined database roles. Predefined roles are built in, and they have permissions that cannot be changed. You use predefined roles to assign database administration privileges, and you can assign a single login to multiple roles. These privileges are summarized in the following list:

- **public**   The default role for all database users. Users inherit the permissions and privileges of the public role and this role provides the minimum permissions and privileges. Any roles that you assign to a user beyond the public role may add permissions and privileges. If you want all database users to have specific permissions, assign the permissions to the public role.

- **db_accessadmin**   Designed for users who need to add or remove logins in a database.

- **db_backupoperator**   Designed for users who need to back up a database.

- **db_datareader**   Designed for users who need to view data in a database. Members of this role can select all data from any user table in the database.

- **db_datawriter**   Designed for users who need to add or modify any data in any user table in the database. Members of this role can perform these tasks on any objects in the selected database: DELETE, INSERT, and UPDATE.

- **db_ddladmin**   Designed for users who need to perform tasks related to the data definition language (DDL) for SQL Server. Members of this role can issue any DDL statement except GRANT, REVOKE, or DENY.

- **db_denydatareader**   Designed to restrict access to data in a database by login. Members of this role cannot read any data in user tables within a database.

- **db_denydatawriter**   Designed to restrict modifications permissions in a database by login. Members of this role cannot add, modify, or delete any data in user tables within a database.

- **db_securityadmin**   Designed for users who need to manage permissions, object ownership, and roles.

- **db_owner**   Designed for users who need complete control over all aspects of the database. Members of this role can assign permissions, modify database settings, perform database maintenance, and perform any other administration task on the database, including dropping the database.

Fixed database roles can be mapped to the more granular permissions for SQL Server 2005, as shown in Table 8-7.

Table 8-7 Granular Permissions Associated with Fixed Database Roles

Fixed Database Role	Permissions Denied with This Role
db_denydatareader	SELECT
db_denydatawriter	DELETE, INSERT, UPDATE
db_accessadmin	ALTER ANY USER, CONNECT with GRANT option, CREATE SCHEMA
db_backupoperator	BACKUP DATABASE, BACKUP LOG, CHECKPOINT
db_datareader	SELECT
db_datawriter	DELETE, INSERT, UPDATE
db_ddladmin	ALTER ANY ASSEMBLY, ALTER ANY CERTIFICATE, ALTER ANY CONTRACT, ALTER ANY EVENT NOTIFICATION, ALTER ANY DATASPACE, ALTER ANY FULLTEXT CATALOG, ALTER ANY MESSAGE TYPE, ALTER ANY REMOTE SERVICE BINDING, ALTER ANY ROUTE, ALTER ANY SCHEMA, ALTER ANY SERVICE, ALTER ANY SYMMETRIC KEY, ALTER ANY TRIGGER, ALTER ANY XML SCHEMA COLLECTION, CHECKPOINT, CREATE AGGREGATE, CREATE ASSEMBLY, CREATE CONTRACT, CREATE DEFAULT, CREATE FUNCTION, CREATE MESSAGE TYPE, CREATE PROCEDURE, CREATE QUEUE, CREATE REMOTE SERVICE BINDING, CREATE ROUTE, CREATE RULE, CREATE SCHEMA, CREATE SERVICE, CREATE SYMMETRIC KEY, CREATE SYNONYM, CREATE TABLE, CREATE TYPE, CREATE VIEW, CREATE XML SCHEMA COLLECTION, REFERENCES
db_owner	CONTROL with GRANT option
db_securityadmin	ALTER ANY APPLICATION ROLE, ALTER ANY ROLE, CREATE SCHEMA, VIEW DEFINITION

Managing Server Logins

SQL Server can use Windows logons as well as logins for SQL Server. If you have configured the server for mixed security, you can use both logon types. Otherwise, you can use only Windows logons.

Viewing and Editing Existing Logins

To view or edit an existing login, follow these steps:

1. Start SQL Server Management Studio. In Object Explorer view, connect to the appropriate server, and then work your way down to the Security folder.

2. Expand the Security folder and the Logins folder to list the current logins. Right-click a login, and then select Properties to view the properties of the login.

3. The Login Properties dialog box, shown in Figure 8-1, has four pages:

   ■ **General** Provides an overview of the login configuration, including the authentication mode (which cannot be changed), the default database and language (which can be changed), and any mapped credentials (which can be added or removed).

   ■ **Server Roles** Lists the server roles and allows you to add or remove the login's server roles.

- **Database Access**   Lists databases accessible by the login and allows you to manage, on a per database basis, the default schema, the user identity for the database, and the assigned database roles.
- **Permissions**   Shows current object permissions and allows you to manage object permissions for the login.

Note   In the Connection area of any page, you can click View Connection Properties link to see detailed information about the user's current connection properties. This information is helpful for troubleshooting connection issues.

4. When you are finished working with the account, click OK.

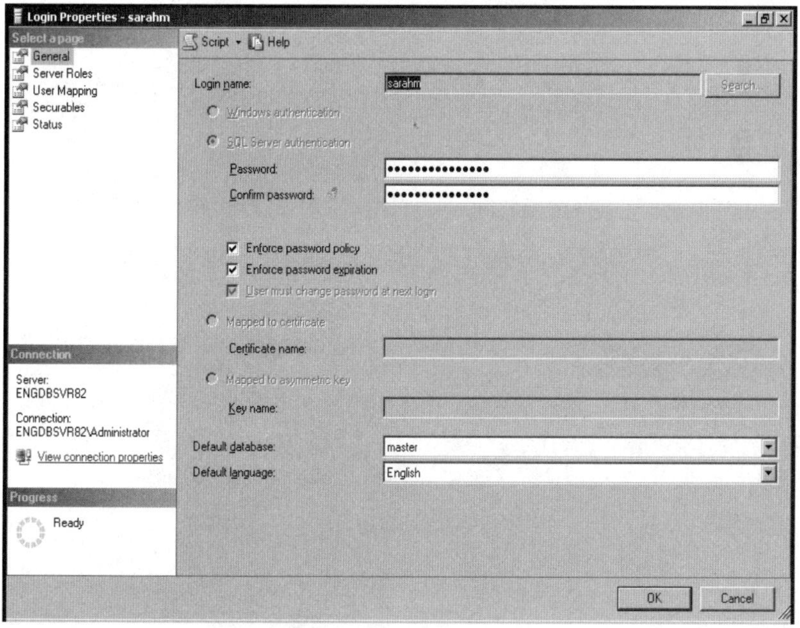

Figure 8-1   Login Properties dialog box

To view information about a login with Transact-SQL, use *sp_helplogins*. Sample 8-1 shows the syntax and usage for this command.

Sample 8-1   *sp_helplogins* Syntax and Usage

Syntax

```
sp_helplogins [[@LoginNamePattern =] 'login']
```

Usage

```
EXEC sp_helplogins 'goteam'
```

The output provided by *sp_helplogins* includes the login name, security identifier, default database, and default language. To determine the server roles and Windows groups to which the currently logged on user belongs either implicitly or expressly, you can execute the following query:

```
USE master
GO
SELECT * FROM sys.login_token;
GO
```

Creating Logins

You create new logins in SQL Server Management Studio by using the Login – New dialog box. If you want to use Windows user or group accounts, you must create these accounts on the local machine or in the Windows domain and then create the related SQL Server logins. Ask a network administrator to set up the necessary accounts.

To create a SQL Server login, follow these steps:

1. Start SQL Server Management Studio. In Object Explorer view, connect to the appropriate server, and then work your way down to the Security folder.

2. Right-click Logins, and then select New Login to display the Login – New dialog box shown in Figure 8-2.

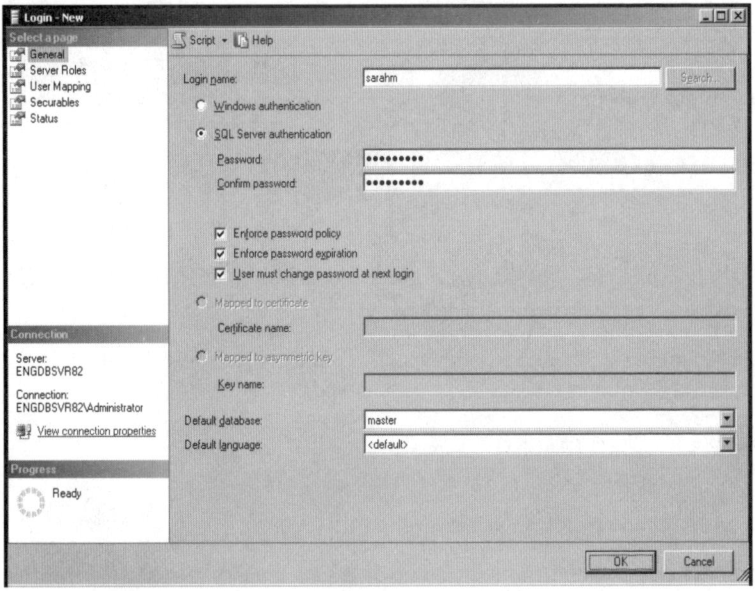

Figure 8-2 The Login – New dialog box

3. If you are creating a logon for a Windows account, select the Windows Authentication option button, and then type the user name in *DOMAIN\username* format, such as **CPANDL\wrstanek**. If you want to search Active Directory for the domain and user information, click Search, and then use the Select User Or Group dialog box to select the user for which you are creating the SQL Server account. Password policy and expiration enforcement are handled by the local Windows password policy automatically.

4. If you want to create a new SQL Server login, select the SQL Server Authentication option button, and then type the name of the account you want to use, such as **Sales** or **WRSTANEK**. Then, enter and confirm the password for the account. To enforce the local Windows password expiration policy on the SQL Server login, select Enforce Password Policy. If you elect to enforce password policy, you can also elect to enforce password expiration. To do this, select Enforce Password Expiration.

5. Specify the default database and default language for the login. Assigning a default database does not give the login permission to access the database. Instead, it merely specifies the database that is used when no database is specified in a command.

6. Click OK to create the login. If you are creating a SQL Server login and an identically named login already exists on the server, you will see an error. Click OK and change the login, or click Cancel if you determine that the new login is not needed.

7. You have not yet assigned any roles or access permissions. Refer to the sections later in this chapter titled "Configuring Server Roles" and "Controlling Database Access and Administration" to learn how to configure these options.

You can also create logins with Transact-SQL. Use CREATE LOGIN as shown in Sample 8-2. To use this statement, you need ALTER ANY LOGIN permission on the server (and if using credentials, you need ALTER ANY CREDENTIAL permission).

Sample 8-2   CREATE LOGIN Syntax and Usage

Syntax

```
CREATE LOGIN login_name { WITH < option_list1 > | FROM < sources > }

< sources >::=
    WINDOWS [ WITH windows_options [,...] ]
    | CERTIFICATE certname
    | ASYMMETRIC KEY asym_key_name

< option_list1 >::=
    PASSWORD = ' password ' [ HASHED ] [ MUST_CHANGE ]
    [ , option_list2 [ ,... ] ]

< option_list2 >::=
    SID = sid
    | DEFAULT_DATABASE = database
    | DEFAULT_LANGUAGE = language
```

```
    | CHECK_EXPIRATION = { ON | OFF}
    | CHECK_POLICY = { ON | OFF}
    [ CREDENTIAL = credential_name ]
< windows_options >::=
    DEFAULT_DATABASE = database
    | DEFAULT_LANGUAGE = language
```

Usage for SQL Logins

```
create login wrstanek WITH PASSWORD = 'MZ82$!408765RTM'
```

Usage for SQL Logins Mapped to Credentials

```
create login wrstanek WITH PASSWORD = 'MZ82$!408765RTM',
    CREDENTIAL = StanekWR
```

Usage for Logins from a Domain Account

```
CREATE LOGIN [CPANDL\wrstanek] FROM WINDOWS;
```

 Note   Although the logins *sp_grantlogin* and *sp_addlogin* allow users to connect to SQL Server, these logins cannot access databases. To configure database access, you need to run *sp_grantdbaccess* for each database to which the login needs access. For details, see the section titled "Controlling Database Access and Administration" later in this chapter.

Editing Logins with T-SQL

You can edit logins in SQL Server Management Studio as explained in the section titled "Viewing and Editing Existing Logins" earlier in this chapter. Editing logins with T-SQL is more work, however, and requires you to use the ALTER LOGIN statement. You need ALTER ANY LOGIN permission to alter logins (and if working with credentials, ALTER ANY CREDENTIAL permission). When a login is a member of the sysadmin server role, only another member of this role can make the following changes:

1. Reset the password without supplying the old password
2. Enable MUST_CHANGE, CHECK_POLICY, or CHECK_EXPIRATION
3. Change the login name
4. Enable or disable the login
5. Change the login credential

Sample 8-3 shows the syntax and usage for ALTER LOGIN.

Sample 8-3   ALTER LOGIN Syntax and Usage

Syntax

```
ALTER LOGIN login_name
    {
    < status_option >
```

```
    | WITH set_option [ ,... ]
    }

< status_option >::=
        ENABLE | DISABLE

< set_option >::=
    PASSWORD = ' password '
    [
            OLD_PASSWORD = ' oldpassword '
        | secadmin_pwd_option [ secadmin_pwd_option ]
    ]
    | DEFAULT_DATABASE = database
    | DEFAULT_LANGUAGE = language
    | NAME = login_name
    | CHECK_POLICY = { ON | OFF }
    | CHECK_EXPIRATION = { ON | OFF }
    | CREDENTIAL = credential_name
    | NO CREDENTIAL

< secadmin_pwd_opt >::=
        MUST_CHANGE | UNLOCK
```

Usage for Changing the Login Name

```
ALTER LOGIN wrstanek WITH NAME = stanekwr
```

Usage for Changing the Login Password

```
ALTER LOGIN wrstanek WITH PASSWORD = '3948wJ698FFF7';
```

Usage for Enabling a Disabled Login

```
ALTER LOGIN wrstanek ENABLE;
```

Granting or Denying Server Access

When you create a new login or modify an existing login based on a Windows account, you can explicitly grant or deny access to the server's database engine. Explicitly denying access to the server is useful when a particular Windows account should be temporarily restricted from accessing the server.

To grant or deny access for an existing login, complete the following steps:

1. Start SQL Server Management Studio. In Object Explorer view, connect to the appropriate server, and then work your way down to the Security folder.

2. Expand the Security folder and the Logins folder to list the current logins. Right-click a login, and then select Properties to view the properties of that login. This opens the SQL Server Login Properties dialog box (shown previously in Figure 8-1).

3. Under Select A Page, select Status to display the Status page.

4. To grant access to the server, select the Grant Access option.

5. To deny access to the server, select the Deny Access option.

Note Denying access to the server does not prevent users from logging on to SQL Server. Instead, it prevents them from using their Windows domain account to log on. Users can still log on if they have a valid SQL Server login ID and password.

6. Click OK.

You can also grant or deny logins with Transact-SQL. To grant a login for a domain account, use *sp_grantlogin*, as shown in Sample 8-4.

Note Only members of the sysadmin or securityadmin fixed server roles can execute *sp_grantlogin* and *sp_denylogin*.

Sample 8-4   *sp_grantlogin* Syntax and Usage

Syntax
```
sp_grantlogin [@loginame =] 'login'
```

Usage
```
EXEC sp_grantlogin 'GALAXY\WRSTANEK'
```

To deny access to the server for the account, use *sp_denylogin* as shown in Sample 8-5.

Sample 8-5   *sp_denylogin* Syntax and Usage

Syntax
```
sp_denylogin [@loginame =] 'login'
```

Usage
```
EXEC sp_denylogin 'GALAXY\WRSTANEK'
```

Enabling, Disabling, and Unlocking Logins

Similar to Windows accounts, SQL Server logins can be enabled and disabled by administrators. Logins can also become locked based on policy settings and may need to be unlocked. For example, if a login's password expires, the login may become locked.

Tip You can determine whether a login is disabled or locked by selecting the server's Logins node in SQL Server Management Studio. The icon for the login is updated to show the status as locked or disabled.

To enable, disable, or unlock a login, complete the following steps:

1. Start SQL Server Management Studio. In Object Explorer view, connect to the appropriate server, and then work your way down to the Security folder.

2. Expand the Security folder and the Logins folder to list the current logins. Right-click a login, and then select Properties to view the properties of that login. This opens the SQL Server Login Properties dialog box.

3. Under Select A Page, select Status to display the Status page.

4. You can now:

   ❑ Enable the login by selecting Enabled under Login.

   ❑ Disable the login by selecting Disabled under Login.

   ❑ Unlock the login by clearing Login Is Locked Out.

5. Click OK.

Removing Logins

When a user leaves the organization or a login is no longer needed for another reason, you should remove the login from SQL Server. To remove a login, complete the following steps:

1. Start SQL Server Management Studio, and then access the appropriate server.

2. In the server's Security folder, expand the Logins folder.

3. Right-click the login you want to remove, and then select Delete from the shortcut menu.

4. The Delete Object dialog box shows you which account you are deleting. Click OK to remove the account. Remember that you may also need to delete users in each database.

Use *sp_revokelogin* to delete Windows user and group accounts, as shown in Sample 8-6.

Listing 8-6   *sp_revokelogin* Syntax and Usage

Syntax

```
sp_revokelogin [@loginame =] 'login'
```

Usage

```
EXEC sp_revokelogin 'GALAXY\WRSTANEK'
```

Use DROP LOGIN to remove a SQL Server login, as shown in Sample 8-7.

Sample 8-7   DROP LOGIN Syntax and Usage

Syntax

```
DROP LOGIN login
```

Usage

```
DROP LOGIN sarahm
```

Changing Passwords

You manage Windows user and group accounts in the Windows domain or on the local machine. Users can change their own passwords or ask the Windows administrator to reset their passwords, if necessary. For SQL Server logins, you change passwords through SQL Server Management Studio using the following steps:

1. Start SQL Server Management Studio, and then access the appropriate server.
2. In the server's Security folder, expand the Logins folder.
3. Right-click the login you want to change, and then select Properties to display the SQL Server Login Properties dialog box.
4. Type and then confirm the new password in the boxes provided.
5. Click OK.

To change passwords with Transact-SQL, you can use ALTER LOGIN as discussed previously, or use *sp_password*, as shown in Sample 8-8.

 Note Because execute permissions for *sp_password* default to the public role, users can change their own passwords. Members of the securityadmin and sysadmin server roles can change passwords of other logins. However, if the user is a member of the sysadmin server role, a securityadmin member must supply the old password. Members of the sysadmin role never need to supply the old password.

Listing 8-8 *sp_password* Syntax and Usage

Syntax

```
sp_password [[@old =] 'old_password',]
    {[@new =] 'new_password'}
    [,[@loginame =] 'login']
```

Usage

```
EXEC sp_password 'changeme', 'h4rt5', 'GOTEAM'
```

Configuring Server Roles

Server roles set server-wide administrator privileges for SQL Server logins. You can manage server roles by role or by individual logins.

Assigning Roles by Login

To assign or change server roles for a login, follow these steps:

1. Start SQL Server Management Studio. In Object Explorer view, connect to the appropriate server, and then work your way down to the Security folder.
2. Expand the Security folder and the Logins folder to list the current logins. Right-click a login, and then select Properties to display the SQL Server Login Properties dialog box and view the properties of the login.

3. Select the Server Roles page, as shown in Figure 8-3.

4. Grant server roles by selecting the check boxes next to the roles you want to use. You learned about server roles in the section titled "Server Roles" earlier in this chapter.

5. When you have finished configuring server roles, click OK.

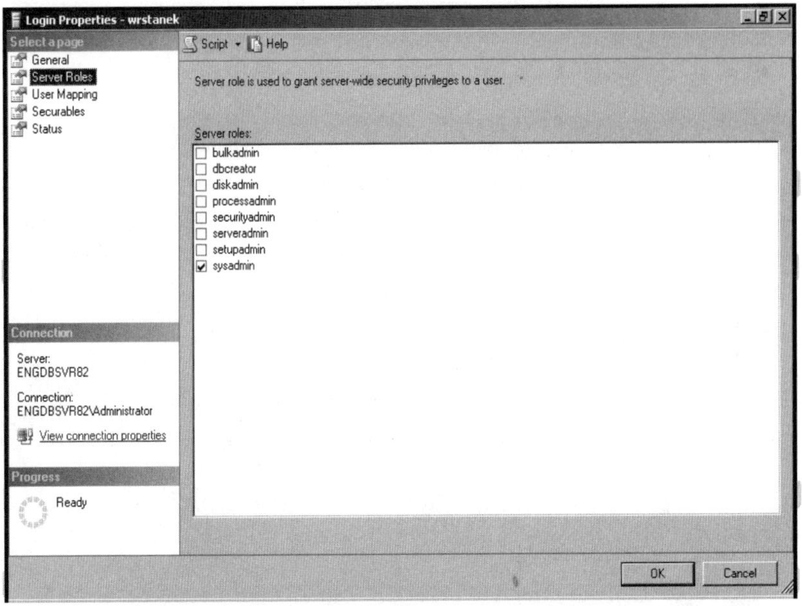

Figure 8-3   The Server Roles page of the Login Properties dialog box

You can also configure server roles with Transact-SQL. The *sp_addsrvrolemember* stored procedure adds a login to a server role, and you can use it as shown in Sample 8-9.

Note   To use *sp_addsrvrolemember* or *sp_dropsrvrolemember*, you must have ALTER ANY LOGIN permission on the server and membership in the role to which you are adding the new member.

Listing 8-9   *sp_addsrvrolemember* Syntax and Usage

Syntax

```
sp_addsrvrolemember [@loginame =] 'login', [@rolename =] 'role'
```

Usage

```
EXEC sp_addsrvrolemember 'GALAXY\WRSTANEK', 'sysadmin'
```

The *sp_dropsrvrolemember* stored procedure removes a login from a role, and you can use it as shown in Sample 8-10.

Sample 8-10   *sp_dropsrvrolemember* Syntax and Usage

Syntax

```
sp_dropsrvrolemember [@loginame =] 'login', [@rolename =] 'role'
```

Usage

```
EXEC sp_dropsrvrolemember 'GALAXY\WRSTANEK', 'sysadmin'
```

Assigning Roles to Multiple Logins

The easiest way to assign roles to multiple logins is to use the Server Roles Properties dialog box. To access this dialog box and configure multiple logins, follow these steps:

1. Start SQL Server Management Studio. In Object Explorer view, connect to the appropriate server, and then work your way down to the Security folder.

2. Expand the Server Roles node, and then right-click the role you want to configure. This opens the Server Role Properties dialog box shown in Figure 8-4.

3. To add logins, click Add, and then use the Select Logins dialog box to select the logins to add. You can enter partial names, and then click Check Names to expand the name. To search for names, click Browse.

4. To remove a login, select it, and then click Remove.

5. When you have finished configuring server roles, click OK.

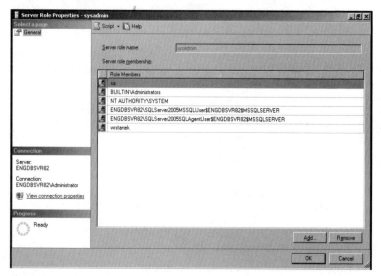

Figure 8-4   The Server Role Properties dialog box

Revoking Access Rights and Roles by Server Login

To revoke access rights or to remove a user from a role in a database, complete the following steps:

1. Start SQL Server Management Studio. In Object Explorer view, connect to the appropriate server.

2. Expand the server's Security folder, and then expand the related Logins folder.

3. Double-click the login that you want to configure to display the Login Properties dialog box.

4. Select the Server Roles page. Clear the check box next to the server roles that you want to remove from this login.

5. Select the Database Access page. Clear the check box next to the databases to which this user should not have access. Alternately, select a database to which access is permitted, and then modify the granted roles by clearing options under Database Roles For...

6. When you have finished, click OK.

Controlling Database Access and Administration

You control database access and administration with database users and roles. Database users are the logins that have the right to access the database. Database access roles set administration privileges and other database permissions.

Assigning Access and Roles by Login

For individual logins, you can grant access to databases and assign roles by completing the following steps:

1. Start SQL Server Management Studio. In Object Explorer view, connect to the appropriate server, and then work your way down to the Security folder.

2. Expand the Security folder and the Logins folder to list the current logins. Right-click the login you want to configure, and then select Properties. This opens the SQL Server Login Properties dialog box.

3. Select the User Mapping page, as shown in Figure 8-5.

4. Select the check box for a database that you want the login to be able to access. Then, in the Database Role Membership For... list box, select the check boxes next to the database roles that this login should have on the currently selected database.

5. Repeat step 5 for other databases that you want the login to be able to access.

6. When you have finished configuring database roles, click OK.

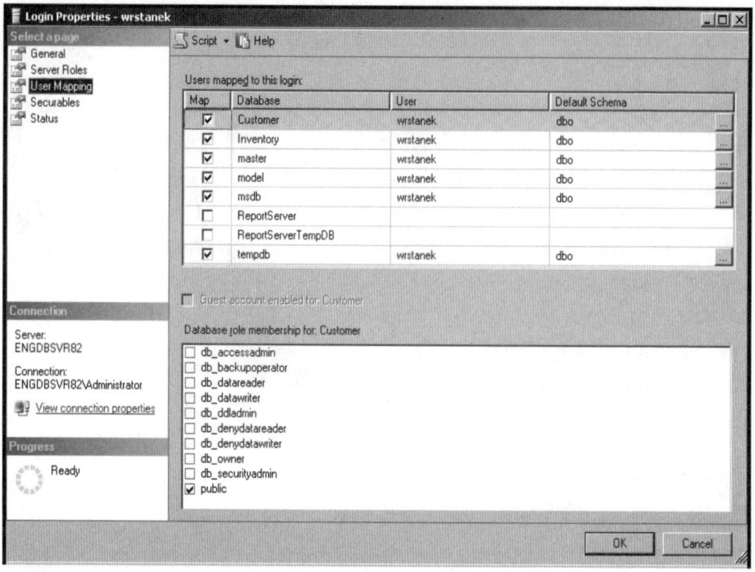

Figure 8-5   The User Mapping page of the Login Properties dialog box

Assigning Roles for Multiple Logins

At the database level, you can assign database roles to multiple logins. To do this, complete the following steps:

1. Start SQL Server Management Studio. In Object Explorer view, connect to the appropriate server.

2. Expand the Databases folder, and then expand the node for the database you want to configure.

3. Expand the database's Security, Roles, and Database Roles folders. Double-click the role you want to configure. This opens the Database Role Properties dialog box shown in Figure 8-6.

4. To add role members, click Add to display the Select Database User Or Role dialog box.

5. In the dialog box, enter the name of the user or role to add. Separate names with semicolons. You can enter partial names, and then click Check Names to expand the names. To search for names, click Browse.

6. To remove a role member, select a database user or other role, and then choose Remove.

7. When you have finished configuring database roles, click OK.

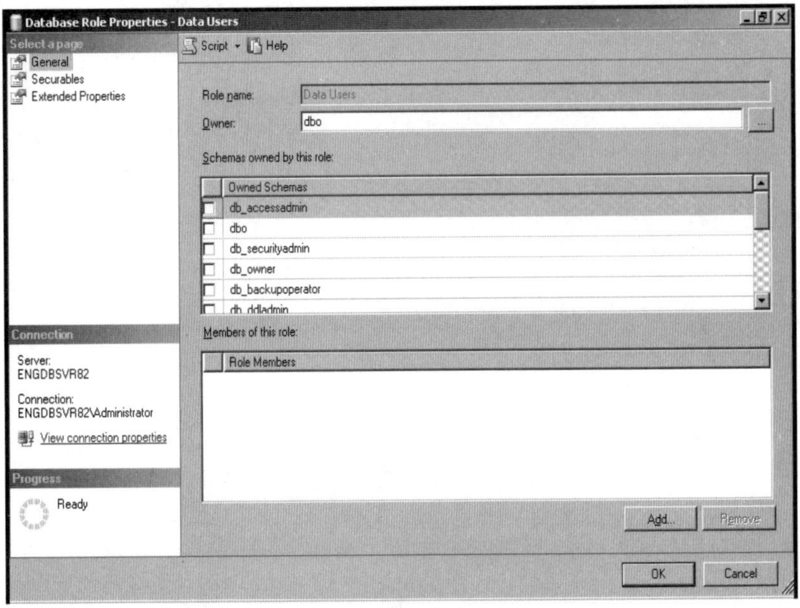

Figure 8-6   The Database Role Properties dialog box

Creating Standard Database Roles

Although predefined roles have a specific set of permissions that you cannot change, you can set permissions for roles you create for a particular database. For example, suppose that a database has three different types of users: normal users who need to view data, managers who need to be able to modify data, and developers who need to be able to modify database objects. In this situation, you can create three roles to handle these user types. Then you need to manage only these roles and not the many different user accounts.

To create a standard database role, complete the following steps:

1. Start SQL Server Management Studio. In Object Explorer view, connect to the appropriate server.

2. Expand the Databases folder, and then select a database and expand the node for it.

3. Expand the database's Security and Roles folders. Right-click Roles, point to New, and then choose New Database Role. This opens the Database Role dialog box shown in Figure 8-7.

4. Type a name for the role in the Role Name box.

> **Tip**   Use a name for the role that is short but descriptive, such as Normal Users, Editors, or Testers And Developers.

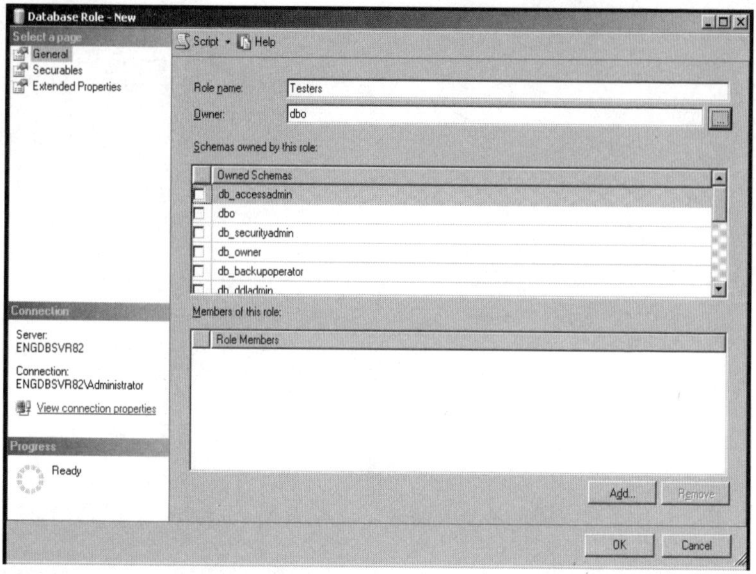

Figure 8-7   The Database Role dialog box

5. The default owner of the role is dbo. To set a different owner, click the button to the right of the Owner box to display the Select Database User Or Role dialog box.

6. In the dialog box, enter the name of the users, the roles, or both that should be the owners of this role. Separate names with semicolons. You can enter partial names, and then click Check Names to expand the names. To search for names, click Browse.

7. To add role members, click Add to display the Select Database User Or Role dialog box.

8. In the dialog box, enter the names of the users or roles to add. Separate names with semicolons. You can enter partial names, and then click Check Names to expand the names. To search for names, click Browse. Click OK.

9. Choose Permissions from the Select A Page list in the dialog box, and then use the Permissions page options to configure database access permissions for this role. For more information about configuring database access permission, see the section titled "Managing Database Permissions" later in this chapter.

10. Click OK.

Creating Application Database Roles

Application roles are designed to be used by applications that access the database and do not have logins associated with them. You can configure an application role by completing the following steps:

1. Start SQL Server Management Studio. In Object Explorer view, connect to the appropriate server.

2. Expand the Databases folder, and then select a database and expand the node for it.

3. Expand the database's Security and Roles folders. Right-click Roles, point to New, and then choose New Application Role. This opens the Application Role – New dialog box shown in Figure 8-8.

4. Type a name for the role in the Role Name box.

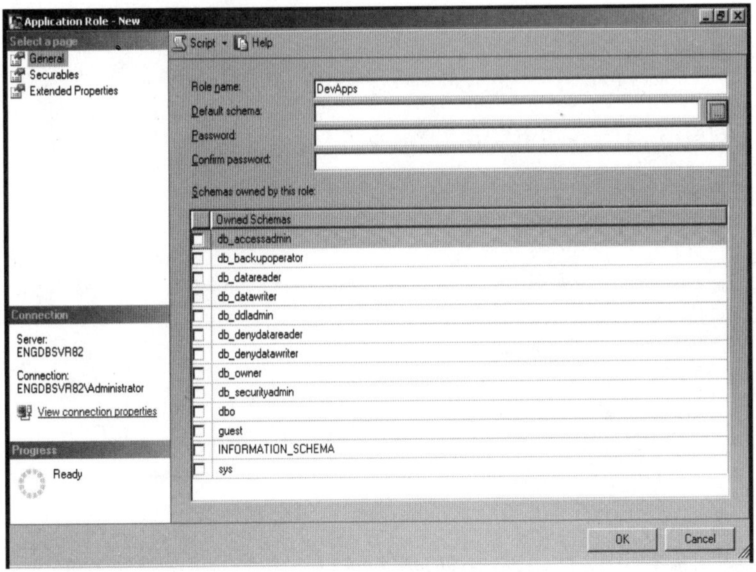

Figure 8-8   The Application Role – New dialog box

5. The default schema for the role is dbo. The default (or base) schema sets the base permissions for the new role. To set a different default schema, click the button to the right of the Default Schema box to display the Locate Schema dialog box.

6. In the dialog box, enter the name of the default schema. You can enter a partial name, and then click Check Names to expand the name. To search for a schema to use, click Browse. Click OK.

7. Choose Permissions from the Select A Page list, and then use the Permissions page options to configure database access permissions for this role. For more information about configuring database access permission, see the section titled "Managing Database Permissions" later in this chapter.

8. Click OK.

Removing Role Memberships for Database Users

To revoke access rights or to remove a user from a role in a database, complete the following steps:

1. Start SQL Server Management Studio. In Object Explorer view, connect to the appropriate server.
2. Expand the Databases folder, and then select a database and expand the node for it.
3. Expand the database's Security and Users folders. Double-click the user name. This opens the Database User dialog box.
4. On the General page, clear the check box next to the database roles that this user should not have on the currently selected database.
5. When you have finished removing roles for the database user, click OK.

Deleting User-Defined Roles

To delete a user-defined role, complete the following steps:

1. Start SQL Server Management Studio. In Object Explorer view, connect to the appropriate server.
2. Expand the Databases folder, and then select a database and expand the node for it.
3. Expand the database's Security and Roles folders.
4. If the role you want to remove is a Database Role, expand Database Roles. If the role you want to remove is an Application Role, expand Application Roles.
5. Select the role you want to delete, and then press the DELETE key.
6. The Delete Object dialog box shows you which role you are deleting. Click OK to remove the role.

 Note   User-defined roles cannot be deleted if they have members. First edit the properties for the role, deleting any currently listed members, and then delete the role.

Transact-SQL Commands for Managing Access and Roles

SQL Server provides different commands for managing database access and roles. These commands are summarized in Sample 8-11.

Sample 8-11   Commands for Managing Database Access and Roles

Adding a User to Current Database

```
CREATE USER user_name
    [ FOR
        { LOGIN login_name
        | CERTIFICATE cert_name
        | ASYMMETRIC KEY asym_key_name
```

```
        }
    ]
    [ WITH DEFAULT_SCHEMA = schema_name ]
```

Renaming a User or Changing Default Schema

```
ALTER USER user_name
    WITH < set_item > [ ,...n ]

< set_item > ::=
    NAME = new_user_name
    | DEFAULT_SCHEMA = schema_name
```

Removing a User from a Database

```
DROP USER user_name
```

Displaying Permissions of Database Roles

```
sp_dbfixedrolepermission [[@rolename =] 'role']
```

Managing Database Standard Roles

```
CREATE ROLE role_name [ AUTHORIZATION owner_name ]
ALTER ROLE role_name WITH NAME = new_name
DROP ROLE role_name
sp_helprole [[@rolename =] 'role']
```

Managing Database Role Members

```
sp_addrolemember [@rolename =] 'role',
    [@membername =] 'security_account'
sp_droprolemember [@rolename =] 'role',
    [@membername =] 'security_account'
sp_helprolemember [[@rolename =] 'role']
```

Managing Application Roles

```
sp_addapprole [@rolename =] 'role', [@password =] 'password'
sp_dropapprole [@rolename =] 'role'
sp_setapprole [@rolename =] 'role' ,
    [@password =] {Encrypt N 'password'} | 'password'
    [,[@encrypt =] 'encrypt_style']
```

Managing Database Permissions

The database owner, members of sysadmin, and members of securityadmin can assign database permissions. The available permissions include the following:

- **GRANT**   Gives permission to perform the related task. With roles, all members of the role inherit the permission.

- **REVOKE** Removes prior GRANT permission but does not explicitly prevent a user or role from performing a task. A user or role could still inherit GRANT permission from another role.

- **DENY** Explicitly denies permission to perform a task and prevents the user or role from inheriting the permission. DENY takes precedence over all other grant permissions.

 Note DENY is a Transact-SQL command and is not part of the ANSI SQL-92 standard.

You can grant, deny, and revoke permissions at the database level or the object level. You can also assign permissions using database roles. For more information, see the section titled "Controlling Database Access and Administration" earlier in this chapter.

Assigning Database Permissions for Statements

At the database level, you can grant, revoke, or deny permission to execute data definition language statements, such as CREATE TABLE or BACKUP DATABASE. These statements were summarized in Table 8-5 earlier in this chapter.

In SQL Server Management Studio, you grant, revoke, or deny database permissions for statements by completing the following steps:

1. Start SQL Server Management Studio. In Object Explorer view, connect to the appropriate server.

2. Work your way down to the Databases folder using the entries in the left pane.

3. Select a database, right-click the database name, and then select Properties from the shortcut menu to display the Database Properties dialog box.

4. Select the Permissions page from the Select A Page list, as shown in Figure 8-9.

5. To assign default permissions for all users, assign permissions to the public role. To add users or roles, click Add and then use the Select Users Or Roles dialog box to select the user or role you want to add. To assign permissions for individual users or roles, select the user or role, and then use the Permissions For ... list box to Allow or Deny permissions as appropriate. Clear both check marks to revoke a previously granted or denied permission.

6. Click OK to assign the permissions.

With Transact-SQL, you use the GRANT, REVOKE, and DENY commands to assign permissions. Sample 8-12 shows the syntax and usage for GRANT, Sample 8-13 shows the syntax and usage for REVOKE, and Sample 8-14 shows the syntax and usage for DENY.

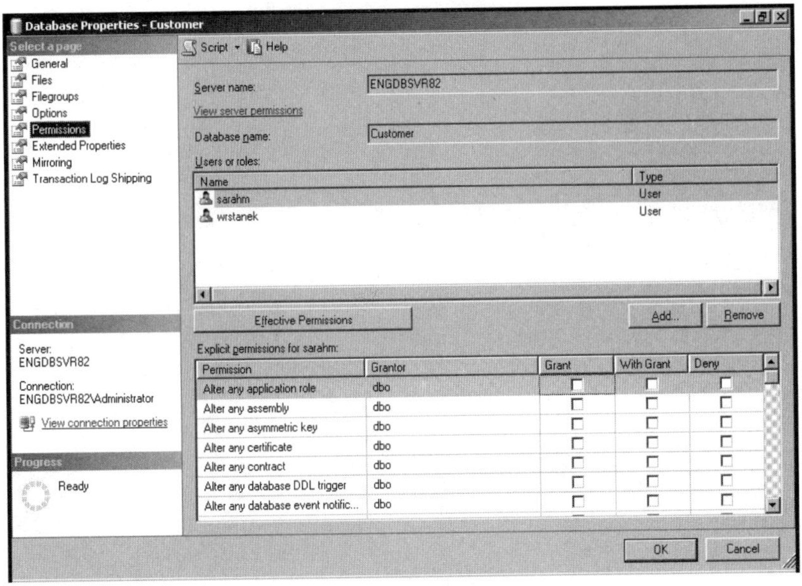

Figure 8-9   The Permissions page of the Database Properties dialog box

Sample 8-12   GRANT Syntax and Usage

Syntax for Permissions on Servers and Databases

```
GRANT < permission > [ ,...n ]
    TO < principal > [ ,...n ] [ WITH GRANT OPTION ]
    [ AS
        {
                windows_group | SQL_Server_login | database_user
            | database_role | application_role
        }
    ]
< permission >::=  ALL [ PRIVILEGES ] | permission_name
        [ ( column [ ,...n ] ) ]
< principal >::= Windows_login | SQL_Server_login
        | SQL_Server_login_mapped_to_certificate
        | SQL_Server_login_mapped_to_asymmetric_key
        | Database_user | Database_role | Application_role
        | Database_user_mapped_to_certificate
        | Database_user_mapped_to_asymmetric_key
```

Syntax for Permissions on Members of the Object Class

```
GRANT < permission > [ ,...n ] ON [ OBJECT ::] < securable_name >
    TO < principal > [ ,...n ] [ WITH GRANT OPTION ]
    [ AS
```

```
        {
                Windows_group | SQL_Server_login | database_user
        | database_role | application_role
        }
    ]
< permission >::= ALL [ PRIVILEGES ] | permission_name
    [ ( column [ ,...n ] ) ]
< principal >::= Windows_login | SQL_Server_login
    | SQL_Server_login_mapped_to_certificate
    | SQL_Server_login_mapped_to_asymmetric_key
    | Database_user | Database_role | Application_role
    | Database_user_mapped_to_certificate
    | Database_user_mapped_to_asymmetric_key
```

Syntax for Permissions on All Other Securables

```
GRANT < permission > [ ,...n ] ON < scope >
    TO < principal > [ ,...n ] [ WITH GRANT OPTION ]
    [ AS
        {
                Windows_group | SQL_Server_login | database_user
        | database_role | application_role
        }
    ]
< permission >::= ALL [ PRIVILEGES ] | permission_name
    [ ( column [ ,...n ] ) ]
< scope >::= [ securable_class :: ] securable_name
< securable_class >::= APPLICATION ROLE | ASSEMBLY | ASYMMETRIC KEY
    | CERTIFICATE | CONTRACT | ENDPOINT | FULLTEXT CATALOG
    | LOGIN | MESSAGE TYPE | REMOTE SERVICE BINDING | ROLE
    | ROUTE | SCHEMA | SERVICE | SYMMETRIC KEY | TYPE
    | USER | XML SCHEMA COLLECTION
< principal >::= Windows_login | SQL_Server_login
    | SQL_Server_login_mapped_to_certificate
    | SQL_Server_login_mapped_to_asymmetric_key
    | Database_user | Database_role | Application_role
    | Database_user_mapped_to_certificate
    | Database_user_mapped_to_asymmetric_key
```

Usage

```
GRANT CREATE DATABASE, CREATE TABLE
TO Users, [GALAXY\Sales]
GRANT SELECT
ON customer..customers
TO public
GRANT INSERT, UPDATE, DELETE
ON customer..customers
TO Devs, Testers
```

Sample 8-13   REVOKE Syntax and Usage

Syntax for Permission on Servers and Databases

```
REVOKE [ GRANT OPTION FOR ] < permission > [ ,...n ]
    { TO | FROM } < principal > [ ,...n ] [ CASCADE ]
    [ AS
        {
                Windows_group | SQL_Server_login
            | database_role | application_role
        }
    ]
< permission >::=  ALL [ PRIVILEGES ] | permission_name
    [ ( column [ ,...n ] ) ]
< principal >::= Windows_login | SQL_Server_login
    | SQL_Server_login_mapped_to_certificate
    | SQL_Server_login_mapped_to_asymmetric_key
    | Database_user | Database_role | Application_role
    | Database_user_mapped_to_certificate
    | Database_user_mapped_to_asymmetric_key
```

Syntax for Permissions on Members of the Object Class

```
REVOKE [ GRANT OPTION FOR ] < permission > [ ,...n ]
    ON [ OBJECT ::] < securable_name >
    { TO | FROM } < principal > [ ,...n ] [ CASCADE ]
    [ AS
        {
                Windows_group | SQL_Server_login
            | database_role | application_role
        }
    ]
< permission >::=  ALL [ PRIVILEGES ] | permission_name
    [ ( column [ ,...n ] ) ]
< principal >::= Windows_login | SQL_Server_login
    | SQL_Server_login_mapped_to_certificate
    | SQL_Server_login_mapped_to_asymmetric_key
    | Database_user | Database_role | Application_role
    | Database_user_mapped_to_certificate
    | Database_user_mapped_to_asymmetric_key
```

Syntax for Permissions on All Other Securables

```
REVOKE [ GRANT OPTION FOR ] < permission > [ ,...n ] [ ON < scope > ]
    { TO | FROM } < principal > [ ,...n ] [ CASCADE ]
    [ AS
        {
                Windows_group | SQL_Server_login
            | database_role | application_role
        }
    ]
```

```
< permission >::=  ALL [ PRIVILEGES ] | permission_name
    [ ( column [ ,...n ] ) ]
< scope >::= [ < securable_class > :: ] securable_name
< securable_class >::= APPLICATION ROLE | ASSEMBLY | ASYMMETRIC KEY
    | CERTIFICATE | CONTRACT | ENDPOINT | FULLTEXT CATALOG
    | LOGIN | MESSAGE TYPE | REMOTE SERVICE BINDING | ROLE
    | ROUTE | SCHEMA | SERVICE | SYMMETRIC KEY | TYPE
    | USER | XML SCHEMA COLLECTION
< principal >::= Windows_login | SQL_Server_login
    | SQL_Server_login_mapped_to_certificate
    | SQL_Server_login_mapped_to_asymmetric_key
    | Database_user | Database_role | Application_role
    | Database_user_mapped_to_certificate
    | Database_user_mapped_to_asymmetric_key
```

Usage

```
REVOKE CREATE TABLE, CREATE DEFAULT
FROM Devs, Testers
REVOKE INSERT, UPDATE, DELETE
FROM Users, [GALAXY\Sales]
```

Sample 8-14   DENY Syntax and Usage

Syntax for Permission on Servers and Databases

```
DENY < permission > [ ,...n ]
    TO < principal > [ ,...n ] [ CASCADE ]
    [ AS
      {
                Windows_group | SQL_Server_login | database_user
        | database_role | application_role
      }
    ]
< permission >::=  ALL [ PRIVILEGES ] | permission_name
    [ ( column [ ,...n ] ) ]
< principal >::= Windows_login | SQL_Server_login
    | SQL_Server_login_mapped_to_certificate
    | SQL_Server_login_mapped_to_asymmetric_key
    | Database_user | Database_role | Application_role
    | Database_user_mapped_to_certificate
    | Database_user_mapped_to_asymmetric_key
```

Syntax for Permissions on Members of the Object Class

```
DENY < permission > [ ,...n ] ON [ OBJECT ::] < securable_name >
        TO < principal > [ ,...n ] [ CASCADE ]
    [ AS
      {
                Windows_group | SQL_Server_login | database_user
```

```
        | database_role | application_role
        }
    ]
< permission >::=  ALL [ PRIVILEGES ] | permission_name
    [ ( column [ ,...n ] ) ]
< principal >::= Windows_login | SQL_Server_login
    | SQL_Server_login_mapped_to_certificate
    | SQL_Server_login_mapped_to_asymmetric_key
    | Database_user | Database_role | Application_role
    | Database_user_mapped_to_certificate
    | Database_user_mapped_to_asymmetric_key
```

Syntax for Permissions on All Other Securables

```
DENY < permission > [ ,...n ] ON < scope >
    TO < principal > [ ,...n ] [ CASCADE ]
        [ AS
        {
                Windows_group | SQL_Server_login | database_user
        | database_role | application_role
        }
    ]
< permission >::=  ALL [ PRIVILEGES ] | permission_name
    [ ( column [ ,...n ] ) ]
< scope >::= [ securable_class :: ] securable_name
< securable_class >::= APPLICATION ROLE | ASSEMBLY | ASYMMETRIC KEY
    | CERTIFICATE | CONTRACT | ENDPOINT | FULLTEXT CATALOG
    | LOGIN | MESSAGE TYPE | REMOTE SERVICE BINDING | ROLE
    | ROUTE | SCHEMA | SERVICE | SYMMETRIC KEY | TYPE
    | USER | XML SCHEMA COLLECTION
< principal >::= Windows_login | SQL_Server_login
    | SQL_Server_login_mapped_to_certificate
    | SQL_Server_login_mapped_to_asymmetric_key
    | Database_user | Database_role | Application_role
    | Database_user_mapped_to_certificate
    | Database_user_mapped_to_asymmetric_key
```

Usage

```
DENY CREATE TABLE
    TO Devs, Testers
DENY INSERT, UPDATE, DELETE
    ON customer..customers
    TO Users, [GALAXY\Sales]
```

Object Permissions by Login

Object permissions apply to tables, views, and stored procedures. Permissions you assign to these objects include SELECT, INSERT, UPDATE, and DELETE. A summary of permitted actions by object was provided in Table 8-4 earlier in the chapter.

In SQL Server Management Studio, you grant, revoke, or deny object permissions by completing the following steps:

1. Start SQL Server Management Studio. In Object Explorer view, connect to the appropriate server.

2. Work your way down to the Databases folder using the entries in the left pane.

3. Expand the Databases folder, and then select a database and expand the node for it.

4. Expand the Security and Users folders.

5. Double-click the user you want to configure to display the Database User dialog box.

6. Select the Securables page from the Select A Page list as shown in Figure 8-10.

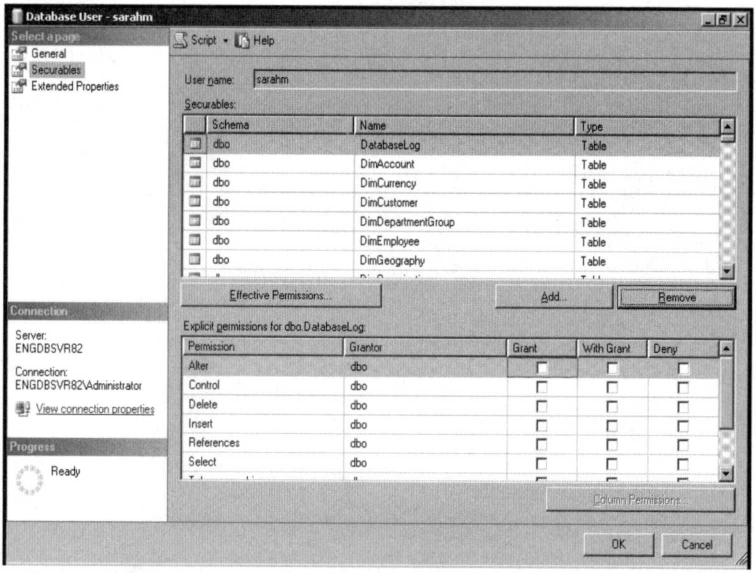

Figure 8-10   The Permissions page of the Database User dialog box

7. To assign object permissions, click Add to display the Add Objects dialog box.

8. In the Add Objects dialog box, select the type of objects for which you want to manage permissions:

   ❑ Select Specific Objects if you know the name of the objects for which you want to manage permissions, and then click OK. In the Select Objects dialog box, click Object Types. Next, in the Select Object Types dialog box, select the type of objects to find, such as Tables And Views, and then click OK. In the Select Objects dialog box, enter the object names. Separate multiple names with a semicolon, and click Check Names to expand any partial name you enter to full names. To browse for objects of the previously selected type, click Browse. When you are finished selecting objects, click OK. The selected objects then will be listed in the Database User dialog box.

❑ Select All Objects Of The Types if you want to manage permissions for all objects of a specific type, such as all tables and views, and then click OK. In the Select Objects dialog box, click Object Types. Next, in the Select Object Types dialog box, select the type of objects to find, such as Tables And Views, and then click OK. In the Select Object Types dialog box, select the object types you want to manage, and then click OK. All objects of the selected types then will be listed in the Database User dialog box.

❑ Select All Objects Belonging To The Schema ... if you want to manage permissions for all objects owned by a particular schema. In the Add Objects dialog box, use the Schema Name selection menu to choose the schema whose objects you want to manage, and then click OK. All objects belonging to the schema will then be listed in the Database User dialog box.

9. To set permissions on an object for the currently selected user, select the object in the Objects list box, and then use the Permissions For... list box to Allow or Deny permissions as appropriate. Clear both check marks to revoke a previously granted or denied permission.

10. When you are finished, click OK to assign the permissions.

Object Permissions for Multiple Logins

You can also assign permission by object, and in this way assign object permissions for multiple logins. To do this, complete the following steps:

1. Work your way down to the Databases folder using the entries in the left pane.

2. Expand the Databases folder, and then select the folder for the type of objects you want to work with, such as Tables, Views, or Stored Procedures.

3. Double-click the object you want to configure to display a Properties dialog box. Or right-click and select Properties.

4. In the Properties dialog box, select the Permissions page from the Select A Page list. This opens the Object Properties dialog box, such as the Table Properties dialog box shown in Figure 8-11.

5. Any user or roles directly assigned permissions on the object are listed in the Users Or Roles list box.

6. To add specific permissions for users, roles, or both, click Add to open the Select Users Or Roles dialog box.

7. Enter the names of the users or roles to add. Separate names with semicolons. You can enter partial names, and then click Check Names to expand the names. To search for names, click Browse.

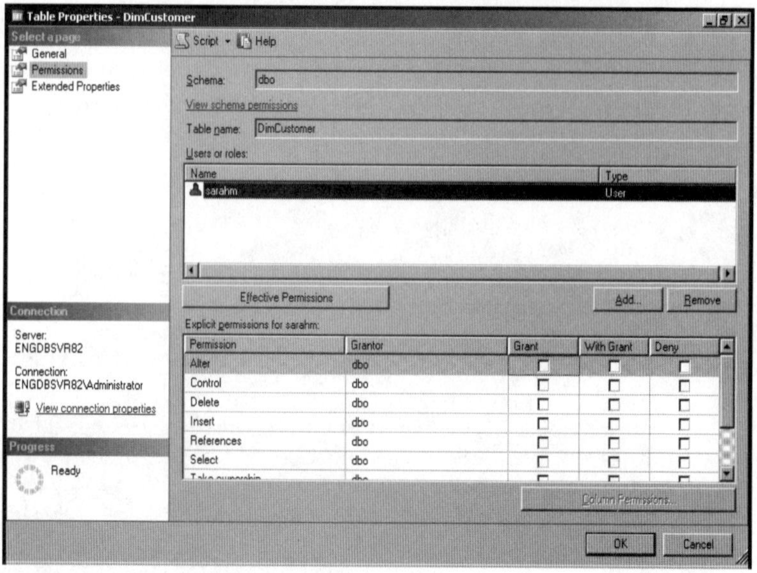

Figure 8-11   The Table Properties dialog box

8. To set permissions for the object, select a user or role in the Users Or Roles list box, and then use the Permissions For list box to Allow or Deny permissions as appropriate. Clear both check marks to revoke a previously granted or denied permission.

9. When you are finished, click OK to assign the permissions.

More information about Transact-SQL commands for assigning permissions can be found in the section titled "Assigning Database Permissions for Statements" earlier in this chapter.

Part III

Microsoft SQL Server 2005
Data Administration

The chapters in Part III guide you through Microsoft SQL Server 2005 data administration. Chapter 9 provides techniques for managing schemas, tables, indexes, and views. You will also find tips for working with constraints and rules. In Chapter 10, you will learn about importing, exporting, and transforming data. Chapter 11 focuses on integrating SQL Server databases with other SQL Server databases and with other data sources. It includes detailed discussions on distributed queries, distributed transactions, Distributed Transaction Coordinator, and linking remote servers. Chapter 12 explores data replication. You will learn about the latest replication techniques, including how to use merge replication and how to immediately update subscribers.

Chapter 9

Manipulating Schemas, Tables, Indexes, and Views

SQL Server 2005 introduces a new model for managing the fundamental units of data within databases. All data within a database is contained within a *Database* object. Each *Database* object contains *Schema* objects and those *Schema* objects contain the tables, indexes, views, and other objects that make up the database. So there are three basic levels of scoping and ownership:

- **Database**   Includes all objects defined within a database and is owned by a specific user.
- **Schema**   Includes all objects defined within a schema and is owned by a database-level security principal
- **Schema-contained object**   Refers to any individual table, view, or so forth that is defined in the database and is "owned" by a specific schema.

When you move databases designed for previous versions of SQL Server to SQL Server 2005, this model still applies. In these databases, the dbo schema is the owner of tables, views, and other related objects, and you can extend the database structure by creating and using other schemas as necessary.

Working with Schemas

Schemas are containers of objects that are used to define the namespaces for objects within databases. They are used to simplify management and create object subsets that can be managed collectively. Schemas are separate from users. Users own schemas and always have a default schema that the server uses when it resolves unqualified objects in queries. This means that the schema name does not need to be specified when accessing objects in the default schema. To access objects in other schemas, a two- or three-part identifier is required. A two-part identifier specifies the schema name and the object name in *schema_name.object_name* format. A three-part identifier specifies the database name, the schema name, and the object name in *database_name.schema_name.object_name* format.

Database synonyms can be used to create alternate names so that a user's default schema contains references to other schema. For example, if you create a synonym for the *Customers.Contact* table as *dbo.Contact*, any user with *dbo* as the default schema could access the table using only the table name. Although synonyms can refer to objects in other databases, including remote instances of SQL Server, synonyms are only valid within the scope of the database in which they are defined. This means that each database can have identically named synonyms, and these synonyms could possibly refer to different objects.

Schemas have many benefits. Because users are no longer the direct owners of objects, removing users from a database is a simpler task; you no longer need to rename objects before dropping the user that created them. Multiple users can own a single schema through membership in a role or Windows group, which makes it easier to manage tables, views, and other database-defined objects. Multiple users can share a single default schema, which makes it easier to grant access to shared objects.

Schemas can be used to scope database access by function, role, or purpose to make it easier to access objects contained in a database. For example, you could have schemas named for each application that accesses the database. In this way, when users of a particular application access the database, their namespace is set appropriately for the objects they routinely access.

Creating Schemas

Before you create a table, you should carefully consider the schema name. Schema names can be up to 128 characters long. Schema names must begin with an alphabetic character, but they can also contain underscores (_), "at" symbols (@), pound signs (#), and numerals. Schema names must be unique within each database. Different databases, however, can contain like-named schemas; for example, two different databases could each have an *Employees* schema.

In SQL Server Management Studio, you create a new schema by completing the following steps:

1. In SQL Server Management Studio, connect to the server instance that contains the database in which you want to work.
2. In Object Explorer, expand the Databases node, and then select a database and expand the view to show its resource nodes.
3. Expand the database's Security node, and then right-click the Schemas node. From the shortcut menu, choose New Schema to display the Schema – New dialog box shown in Figure 9-1.

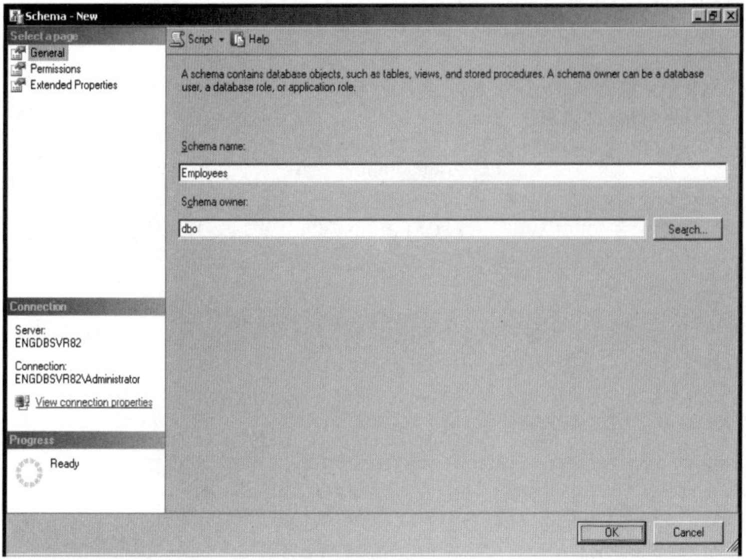

Figure 9-1   The Schema – New dialog box

4. On the General page, specify the name of the schema and set the schema
    owner. To search for an available database-level security principal to use as the
    owner, click Search to display the Search Roles And Users dialog box, and then
    click Browse to open the Browse For Objects dialog box. Select the user or role
    to act as the schema owner, and then click OK twice.

    Note   The schema owner can be any database-level security princi-
    pal (database user, database role, or application role). Although the
    schema owner can own other schemas, the owner cannot use this
    schema as the default schema. If the schema owner is set as a role or
    Windows group, multiple users will own the schema.

5. Click OK to create the schema.

The Transact-SQL command for creating schemas is CREATE SCHEMA. Sample 9-1
shows the syntax and usage for this command. The *schema_element* for the command allows you to use CREATE TABLE, CREATE VIEW, GRANT, REVOKE, and
DENY statements to define tables, views, and permissions that should be created
and contained within the schema you are defining.

Note   To specify another user as the owner of the schema being
created, you must have IMPERSONATE permission on that user. If a
database role is specified as the owner, you must be a member of the
role or have ALTER permission on the role.

Sample 9-1   CREATE SCHEMA Syntax and Usage

Syntax

```
CREATE SCHEMA schema_name_clause [ < schema_element > [ , ...n ] ]
< schema_name_clause >::=
    { schema_name | AUTHORIZATION owner_name
    | schema_name AUTHORIZATION owner_name }
< schema_element >::=
    { table_definition | view_definition | grant_statement
    revoke_statement | deny_statement }
```

Usage

```
CREATE SCHEMA Employees AUTHORIZATION DataTeam
```

Modifying Schemas

You may need to change the schema ownership or modify its permissions. One of the primary reasons for changing the schema owner is because the owner cannot use the schema as the default schema. You may also want to allow or deny specific permissions on a per user or per role basis. After a schema is created, however, you cannot change the schema name. You must drop the schema and create a new schema with the new name.

In SQL Server Management Studio, you can change the schema owner by completing the following steps:

1. In SQL Server Management Studio, connect to the server instance that contains the database in which you want to work.

2. In Object Explorer, expand the Databases node, and then select a database and expand the view to show its resource nodes.

3. Expand the database's Security node, and then Schemas node. Right-click the schema you want to work with. From the shortcut menu, choose Properties to display the Schema Properties dialog box.

4. To change the schema owner, click Search on the General page to display the Search Roles And Users dialog box, and then click Browse to open the Browse For Objects dialog box. Select the user or role to act as the schema owner, and then click OK twice.

You can manage granular permissions for a schema on the Permissions page in the Schema Properties dialog box. Any user or roles that are directly assigned permissions on the object are listed under Users Or Roles. To configure permissions for a user or role:

1. Select the Permissions page from the Select A Page list in the Schema Properties dialog box.

2. Click Add to add specific permissions for users, roles, or both. This opens the Select Users Or Roles dialog box.

3. Enter the names of the users or roles to add. Separate names with semicolons. You can enter partial names, and then click Check Names to expand the names. To search for names, click Browse.

4. Select a user or role in the Users Or Roles list box. Use the Permissions For ... list box to Allow or Deny permissions as appropriate. Clear both check marks to revoke a previously granted or denied permission.

5. When you are finished, click OK to assign the permissions.

Moving Objects to a New Schema

As discussed previously, schemas are containers for objects, and there are times when you will want to move an object from one container to another. Objects can be moved from one schema to another only within the same database. When you do this, you change the namespace associated with the object, which changes the way the object is queried and accessed.

Moving the object to a new schema also affects permissions on the object. All permissions on the object are dropped when it is moved to a new schema. If the object owner is set to a specific user or role, that user or role will continue to be the owner of the object. If the object owner is set to SCHEMA OWNER, the ownership will remain as SCHEMA OWNER, and after the move, the owner will become the owner of the new schema.

To move objects between schemas, you must have CONTROL permissions on the object and ALTER permissions on the schema to which you are moving the object. If the object has an EXECUTE AS OWNER specification on it, and the owner is set to SCHEMA OWNER, you must also have IMPERSONATION permission on the owner of the target schema.

In SQL Server Management Studio, you can move an object to a new schema by completing the following steps:

1. In SQL Server Management Studio, connect to the server instance that contains the database in which you want to work.

2. In Object Explorer, expand the Databases node, and then select a database and expand the view to show its resource nodes.

3. Right-click the table, view, or other object you want to move. From the shortcut menu, choose View Dependencies. The Object Dependencies dialog box shows the database objects that must be present for this object to function properly and the objects that depend on the selected object. Use this dialog box to understand any dependencies that may be affected by moving the selected object. Click OK.

4. Right-click the table, view, or other object, and then select Modify. One of several views displayed in the right pane is the Properties view for the selected object. If this view is not displayed, press F4.

5. Under Identity, click in the Schema drop-down list and select a new schema to contain the selected object.

Caution All permissions on the object are dropped immediately and irreversibly if you have previously selected the option Don't Warn Me Again, Proceed Every Time. If you see the warning prompt, click Yes to continue and move the object to the designated schema, or click No to cancel the move.

The Transact-SQL command for moving objects between schemas is ALTER SCHEMA. Sample 9-2 shows the syntax and usage for this command. When you alter schema, make sure you are using the correct database and are not using the *master* database.

Sample 9-2 ALTER SCHEMA Syntax and Usage

Syntax
```
ALTER SCHEMA target_schema TRANSFER source_schema.object_to_move
```

Usage
```
ALTER SCHEMA Employees TRANSFER Location.Department
```

Dropping Schemas

If you no longer need a schema, you can drop it and, in this way, remove it from the database. To drop a schema, you must have CONTROL permission on the schema. Before dropping a schema, you must first move or drop all the objects that it contains. If you try to delete a schema that contains other objects, the drop operation will fail.

In SQL Server Management Studio, you can drop a schema by completing the following steps:

1. In SQL Server Management Studio, connect to the server instance that contains the database in which you want to work.

2. In Object Explorer, expand the Databases node, and then select a database and expand the view to show its resource nodes.

3. Expand the database's Security and Schema nodes. Right-click the schema you wish to drop. From the shortcut menu, choose Delete. This displays the Delete Object dialog box.

4. Click OK to confirm the deletion.

The Transact-SQL command for deleting schemas is DROP SCHEMA. Sample 9-3 shows the syntax and usage for this command. When you drop a schema, make sure you are using the correct database and are not using the *master* database.

Sample 9-3 DROP SCHEMA Syntax and Usage

Syntax
```
DROP SCHEMA schema_name
```

Usage
```
DROP SCHEMA Employees
```

Getting Started with Tables

In Microsoft SQL Server 2005, the structures of tables and indexes are just as important as the database itself, especially when it comes to performance. Tables are collections of data about a specific entity, such as a customer or an order. To describe the attributes of these entities, you use named columns. For example, to describe the attributes of a customer, you could use these columns: cust_name, cust_address, and cust_phone.

Each instance of data in a table is represented as a single data entry or row. Typically, rows are unique and have unique identifiers called *primary keys* associated with them. However, a primary key is not mandatory in ANSI SQL, and it is not required in SQL Server. The job of the primary key is to set a unique identifier for each row in the table and to allow SQL Server to create a unique index on this key. Indexes are user-defined data structures that provide fast access to data when you search on an indexed column. Indexes are separate from tables, and you can configure them automatically with the Database Tuning Advisor.

Most tables are related to other tables. For example, a *Customers* table may have a cust_account column that contains a customer's account number. The cust_account column may also appear in tables named *Orders* and *Receivables*. If the cust_account column is the primary key of the *Customers* table, a foreign key relationship can be established between *Customers* and *Orders* as well as between *Customers* and *Receivables*. The foreign key creates a link between the tables that you can use to preserve referential integrity in the database.

After you have established the link, you will not be able to delete a row in the *Customers* table if the cust_account identifier is referenced in the *Orders* or *Receivables* tables. This feature prevents you from invalidating references to information used in other tables. You would first need to delete or change the related references in the *Orders* or *Receivables* tables, or both, before deleting a primary key row in the *Customers* table. Foreign key relationships allow you to combine data from related tables in queries by matching the foreign key constraint of one table with the primary or unique key in another table. Combining tables in this manner is called a *table join*, and the keys allow SQL Server to optimize the query and quickly find related data.

Table Essentials

Tables are defined as objects in SQL Server databases. Tables consist of columns and rows of data, and each column has a native or user-defined data type. Tables have two units of data storage: data pages and extents. *Data pages* are the fundamental units of data storage. *Extents* are the basic units in which space is allocated to tables and indexes. Data within tables can be organized using partitions.

Understanding Data Pages

For all data types except large object data types, table data is stored in data pages that have a fixed size of 8 KB (8,192 bytes). Each data page has a page header, data rows, and free space that can contain row offsets. The page header uses the first 96 bytes of each page, leaving 8,096 bytes for data and row offsets. Row offsets indicate the logical order of rows on a page, which means that offset 0 refers to the first row in the index, offset 1 refers to the second row, and so on. If a table contains text and image data, the text or image may not be stored with the rest of the data for a row. Instead, SQL Server can store a 16-byte pointer to the actual data, which is stored in a collection of 8-KB pages that are not necessarily contiguous. This same technique is used with variable-length columns when the row data exceeds 8 KB.

SQL Server 2005 supports six types of data pages:

- **Bulk Changed Map**   Contains information about extents modified by bulk operations since the last log file backup.

- **Data**   Contains data rows with all data except for *nvarchar(max)*, *varchar(max)*, *varbinary(max)*, and *xml* data (as well as *text*, *ntext*, and *image* data when *text in row* is set to ON).

- **Differential Changed Map**   Contains information about extents that have changes since the last database backup.

- **Global Allocation Map, Shared Global Allocation Map**   Contains information about extents that have been allocated by SQL Server.

- **Index Allocation Map**   Contains information about extents used by a table or index.

- **Index**   Contains index entries.

- **Page Free Space**   Contains information about free space available in data pages.

- **Text/Image**   (large object data types)   Contains *text*, *ntext*, *image*, *nvarchar(max)*, *varchar(max)*, *varbinary(max)*, and *xml* data as well as data for variable-length columns when the data row exceeds 8 KB (*varchar*, *nvarchar*, *varbinary*, and *sql_variant*).

Within data pages, SQL Server stores data in rows. Data rows do not normally span more than one page. The maximum size of a single data row is 8,096 bytes (including any necessary overhead). Effectively, this means that the maximum size of a column is 8,000 bytes, not including large object data types, and that a column can store up to 8,000 ASCII characters or up to 4,000 2-byte Unicode characters. Large object data type values can be up to 2 GB in size, which is too large to be stored in a single data row. With large object data types, data is stored in a collection of 8-KB pages, which may or may not be stored contiguously.

Although collections of pages are ideal for large object data that exceeds 8,096 bytes, this storage mechanism is not ideal when the total data size is 8,096 bytes or less. In this case, you will want to store the data in a single row, and to do this, you must set the *text in row* table option. The *text in row* option allows you to place small *text, ntext,* and *image* values directly in a data row instead of in separate pages. This can reduce the amount of space used to store small *text, ntext,* and *image* data and can also reduce the amount of disk input/output (I/O) needed to retrieve the values.

> **Note**   A table that has fixed-length rows always stores the same amount of rows on each page. A table with variable-length rows, however, stores as many rows as possible on each page, based on the length of the data entered. As you might expect, there is a distinct performance advantage to keeping rows compact and allowing more rows to fit on a page. With more rows per page, you will have an improved cache-hit ratio and reduce I/O.

Understanding Extents

An *extent* is a set of eight contiguous data pages, which means extents are allocated in 64-KB blocks and there are 16 extents per megabyte. SQL Server 2005 has two types of extents:

- **Mixed extents**   With mixed extents, different objects can own pages in the extent. This means that up to eight objects can own a page in the extent.
- **Uniform extents**   With uniform extents, a single object owns all the pages in the extent. This means that only the owning object can use all eight pages in the extent.

When you create a new table or index, SQL Server allocates pages from a mixed extent to the new table or index. The table or index continues to use pages in the mixed extent until it grows to the point at which it uses eight data pages. When this happens, SQL Server changes the table or index to uniform extents. As long as the table or index continues to use at least eight data pages, it will use uniform extents.

Understanding Table Partitions

In SQL Server 2005, tables are contained in one or more partitions, and each partition contains data rows in either a heap or clustered index structure. Partitioning large tables allows you to manage subsets of the table data and can improve response times when working with the table data. To improve read/write performance, you can place partitions into multiple filegroups as well.

By default, tables have only one partition. When a table has multiple partitions, the data is partitioned horizontally so that groups of rows are mapped into individual partitions based on a specific column. For example, you might partition a *Customer_Order* table by purchase date. In this example, you would split the partition on date ranges, and each partition could hold yearly, quarterly, or monthly data.

For a *Customer* table, you might partition by customer ID. You would split the partition on name ranges, and each partition would store customer data that starts with a certain character, such as A, B, C, D and so on, or a character sequence such as Aa to Ez, Fa to Jz, Ka to Oz, Pa to Tz, and Ua to Zz.

Working with Tables

SQL Server provides many ways to work with tables. You can create new tables by using the New Table feature in SQL Server Management Studio or the CREATE TABLE command. You can modify existing tables by using the Modify Table feature in SQL Server Management Studio or the ALTER TABLE command. You can also perform other table management functions, including copy, rename, and delete.

Creating Tables

Before you create a table, you should consider the table name carefully. Table names can be up to 128 characters long. Table names must begin with an alphabetic character, but can also contain underscores (_), "at" symbols (@), pound signs (#), and numerals. The exceptions to this rule are temporary tables. Local temporary tables have names that begin with # and are accessible to you only during the current user session. Global temporary tables have names that begin with ## and are accessible to anyone as long as your user session remains connected. Temporary tables are created in *tempdb* and are automatically deleted when your user session ends.

Table names must be unique for each schema within a database. Different schemas, however, can contain like-named tables. This means you could create multiple *contacts* tables as long as they are defined in separate schemas. Thus, the *Customers*, *Employees*, and *Services* schemas all could have a *contacts* table.

Each table can have up to 1,024 columns. Column names follow the same naming rules as tables and must be unique only on a per table basis. That is, a specific table can have only one StreetAddress column, but any number of other tables can have this same column.

In SQL Server Management Studio, you create a new table by completing the following steps:

1. In SQL Server Management Studio, connect to the server instance that contains the database in which you want to work. You must have CREATE TABLE permission in the database and ALTER permission on the schema in which the table is being created.

2. In Object Explorer, expand the Databases node, and then select a database and expand the view to show its resource nodes.

3. To create a new table, right-click the Tables node, and then select New Table from the shortcut menu. Then access the Table Designer in SQL Server Management Studio, and you will see a window similar to Figure 9-2.

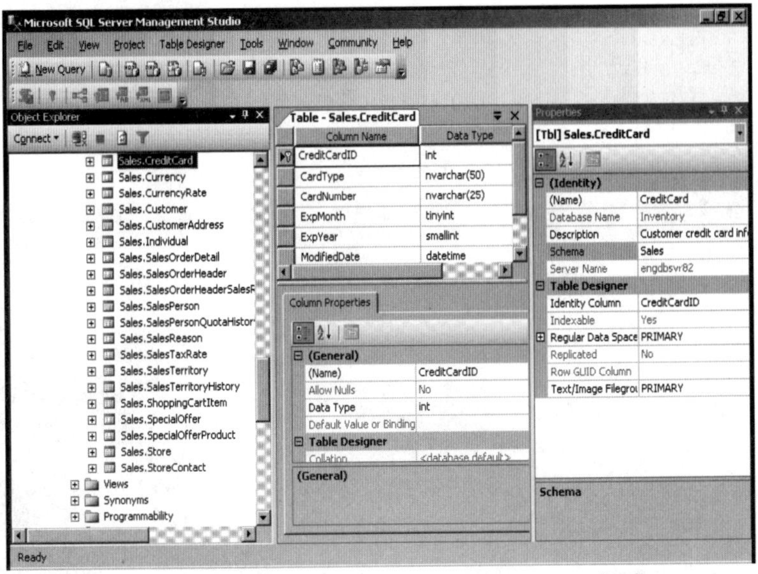

Figure 9-2   Create and modify tables in SQL Server Management Studio

4. You can now design the table using the views provided. These views are:

   ■ **Active File/Table view**   Provides quick access tabs for switching between open files and a summary. If you select the Table view in the Active File view, you will see an overview of the table's columns. Each column is listed by Column Name, Data Type, and Allow Nulls. For fixed or variable-length data types, you follow the data type designator with the field length. If you select the Summary view in the Active File view, you will see all the tables in the current database listed by name, associated schema, and creation date. You can double-click a listed table to see the objects it contains.

   ■ **Column Properties view**   When you select a column in the Table view, you can use the Column Properties view to configure the settings for that column. Column properties that appear dimmed are fixed in value and cannot be changed. The values of these fixed properties typically depend on the column data type and properties inherited from the *Database* object itself.

   ■ **Table Properties view**   Allows you to view and set general table properties, including the table name, description and schema. You can open this view by pressing F4. Any dimmed properties cannot be changed at the table level and must be managed at the database level.

5. The Table Designer menu also provides options for designing the table. Because the options apply to the selected column in the Table view, you can apply them by selecting a column first and then choosing the appropriate option on the Table Designer menu. The same options are displayed when you right-click a column in the Table view.

When you have started the table creation process, you will want to:

- Use the Table Properties view to set the table name, description, and schema. Type the name and description in the boxes provided. Use the drop-down list to select the schema that will contain this table.

- Use the Table Properties view to specify the filegroup (or filegroups) in which the table data will be stored. Regular data and large object data are configured separately.

    ❏ To specify the storage location for regular data, expand the Regular Data Space Specification node, and then use the Filegroup or Partition Schema drop-down list to specify the filegroup.

    ❏ Use the Text/Image Filegroup drop-down list to specify the storage location for large object data.

- Use the Table view to create and manage columns.

    ❏ Rows in the Table view correspond to columns in the table in which you are working. In Figure 9-2, columns listed include CreditCardID, Card-Type, and Card Number.

    ❏ Columns in the Table view correspond to column properties in the table in which you are working. In Figure 9-2, column properties listed include Name, Data Type, and Allow Nulls.

- Use Table Designer menu options to work with a selected column. You can mark the column as the primary key, establish foreign key relationships, check constraints, and more.

- Use the Column Properties view to specify the characteristics for the column you are creating. The characteristics include:

    - **Name** Shows or determines the name of the column.

    - **Allow Nulls**   Shows or determines whether or not null values are allowed in this column.

    - **Default Value or Binding** Shows or determines the default value or binding for the column, which is used whenever a row with a null value for this column is inserted into the database and nulls are not allowed in this column.

    - **Precision** Shows or determines the maximum number of digits for values in the column. This property only applies when the column contains *numeric* or *decimal* data type values.

    - **Scale** Shows or determines the maximum number of digits that can appear to the right of the decimal point for values in the column. This property only applies when the column contains *numeric* or *decimal* data type values.

- **Is Identity**   Shows or determines if the column is used as an identifier column.

- **Identity Seed**   Shows or sets the base value for generating unique identifiers. This property only applies to columns whose Is Identity option is set to Yes.

- **Identity Increment**   Shows or sets the increment for generating unique identifiers. This property only applies to columns whose Is Identity option is set to Yes.

- **Is RowGuid**   Shows or determines if the column contains globally unique identifiers. This property only applies to columns whose Is Identity option is set to Yes or Yes (Not for Replication).

- **Formula**   Shows or sets the formula for a computed column.

- **Collation**   Shows or sets the default collating sequence that SQL Server applies to the column whenever the column values are used to sort rows of a query result.

- When you are finished creating the table, click Save or press Ctrl+S.

You can create tables with Transact-SQL using the CREATE TABLE command. Sample 9-4 shows the syntax and usage for this command. Here you create the *Customers* table under the *Sales* schema. You must have CREATE TABLE permission in the database and ALTER permission on the schema in which the table is being created.

Sample 9-4 CREATE TABLE Syntax and Usage

Syntax

```
CREATE TABLE
    [ database_name . [ schema_name ] . | schema_name . ] table_name
        ( { <column_definition> | <computed_column_definition> }
        [ <table_constraint> ] [ ,...n ] )
    [ ON { partition_scheme_name ( partition_column_name ) | filegroup
        | " DEFAULT " } ]
    [ { TEXTIMAGE_ON { filegroup | " DEFAULT " } ]
[ ; ]

<column_definition> ::=
column_name <data_type>
    [ COLLATE collation_name ]
    [ NULL | NOT NULL ]
    [ [ CONSTRAINT constraint_name ] DEFAULT constant_expression ]
    | [ IDENTITY [ ( seed ,increment ) ] [ NOT FOR REPLICATION ]   ]
    [ ROWGUIDCOL ] [ <column_constraint> [ ...n ] ]

<data type> ::=
[ type_schema_name . ] type_name
    [ ( precision [ , scale ] | max |
        [ { CONTENT | DOCUMENT } ] xml_schema_collection ) ]
```

```
<column_constraint> ::=
[ CONSTRAINT constraint_name ]
{      { PRIMARY KEY | UNIQUE }
          [ CLUSTERED | NONCLUSTERED ]
          [ WITH FILLFACTOR = fillfactor
            | WITH ( < index_option > [ , ...n ] ) ]
          [ ON { partition_scheme_name ( partition_column_name )
              | filegroup | "default" } ]
      | [ FOREIGN KEY ]
          REFERENCES [ schema_name . ] referenced_table_name [ (
ref_column ) ]
          [ ON DELETE { NO ACTION | CASCADE | SET NULL | SET DEFAULT } ]
          [ ON UPDATE { NO ACTION | CASCADE | SET NULL | SET DEFAULT } ]
          [ NOT FOR REPLICATION ]
   | CHECK [ NOT FOR REPLICATION ] ( logical_expression )
}


<computed_column_definition> ::=
column_name AS computed_column_expression
[ PERSISTED [ NOT NULL ] ]
[ [ CONSTRAINT constraint_name ]
    { PRIMARY KEY | UNIQUE }
          [ CLUSTERED | NONCLUSTERED ]
          [ WITH FILLFACTOR = fillfactor
            | WITH ( <index_option> [ , ...n ] ) ]
      | [ FOREIGN KEY ]
          REFERENCES referenced_table_name [ ( ref_column ) ]
          [ ON DELETE { NO ACTION | CASCADE } ]
          [ ON UPDATE { NO ACTION } ]
          [ NOT FOR REPLICATION ]
    | CHECK [ NOT FOR REPLICATION ] ( logical_expression )
    [ ON { partition_scheme_name ( partition_column_name )
       | filegroup | "default" } ] ]
< table_constraint > ::=
[ CONSTRAINT constraint_name ]
{ { PRIMARY KEY | UNIQUE }
          [ CLUSTERED | NONCLUSTERED ]
                    (column [ ASC | DESC ] [ ,...n ] )
          [  WITH FILLFACTOR = fillfactor
             |WITH ( <index_option> [ , ...n ] ) ]
          [ ON { partition_scheme_name (partition_column_name)
             | filegroup | "default" } ]
      | FOREIGN KEY
                    ( column [ ,...n ] )
          REFERENCES referenced_table_name [ ( ref_column [ ,...n ] ) ]
          [ ON DELETE { NO ACTION | CASCADE | SET NULL | SET DEFAULT } ]
          [ ON UPDATE { NO ACTION | CASCADE | SET NULL | SET DEFAULT } ]
```

```
        [ NOT FOR REPLICATION ]
      | CHECK [ NOT FOR REPLICATION ] ( logical_expression )
}


<index_option> ::=
{ PAD_INDEX = { ON | OFF }
  | FILLFACTOR = fillfactor
  | IGNORE_DUP_KEY = { ON | OFF }
  | STATISTICS_NORECOMPUTE = { ON | OFF }
  | ALLOW_ROW_LOCKS = { ON | OFF}
  | ALLOW_PAGE_LOCKS ={ ON | OFF}
}
```

Usage

```
USE OrderSystemDB
CREATE TABLE Sales.Customers
(
    cust_lname varchar(40) NOT NULL,
    cust_fname varchar(20) NOT NULL,
    phone char(12) NOT NULL,
    uid uniqueidentifier NOT NULL
    DEFAULT newid()
)
```

Modifying Existing Tables

In SQL Server Management Studio, you modify an existing table by completing the following steps:

1. In SQL Server Management Studio, connect to the server instance that contains the database in which you want to work.

2. In Object Explorer, expand the Databases node, and then select a database and expand the view to show its resource nodes.

3. Expand the Tables node, and then right-click the table you want to modify. From the shortcut menu, choose Modify. Then you can access the views for designing tables, which were shown previously in Figure 9-2.

4. Make any necessary changes to the table, and then click Save or press Ctrl+S. If the changes you make affect multiple tables, you will see a prompt showing which tables will be updated and saved in the database. Click Yes to continue and complete the operation.

The Transact-SQL command for modifying tables is ALTER TABLE. Sample 9-5 shows the syntax and usage for this command. Here you alter the *Customers* table under the *Sales* schema. You must have ALTER TABLE permission.

Sample 9-5   ALTER TABLE Syntax and Usage

Syntax

```
ALTER TABLE [ database_name . [ schema_name ] . | schema_name . ] table_name
{ALTER COLUMN column_name
    {[ type_schema_name. ] type_name [ ( { precision [ , scale ]
                                | max | xml_schema_collection } ) ]
        [ NULL | NOT NULL ]
        [ COLLATE collation_name ]
    | {ADD | DROP } { ROWGUIDCOL | PERSISTED }
    } }
    | [ WITH { CHECK | NOCHECK } ] ADD
    { <column_definition>
      | <computed_column_definition>
      | <table_constraint> ] } [ ,...n ]
    | DROP
    {   [ CONSTRAINT ] constraint_name
        [ WITH ( <drop_clustered_constraint_option> [ ,...n ] ) ]
        | COLUMN column_name } [ ,...n ]
    | [ WITH { CHECK | NOCHECK } ] { CHECK | NOCHECK } CONSTRAINT
        { ALL | constraint_name [ ,...n ] }
    | { ENABLE | DISABLE } TRIGGER
        { ALL | trigger_name [ ,...n ] }
    | SWITCH [ PARTITION source_partition_number_expression ]
        TO [ schema_name. ] target_table
        [ PARTITION target_partition_number_expression ]
}
[ ; ]

    <drop_clustered_constraint_option> ::=
        { MAXDOP = max_degree_of_parallelism
          | ONLINE = {ON | OFF }
          | MOVE TO { partition_scheme_name ( column_name ) | filegroup
          | "default"} } }
```

Usage

```
USE OrderSystemDB
ALTER TABLE Sales.Customers
ADD uid2 uniqueidentifier NOT NULL DEFAULT newid()
ALTER TABLE Sales.Customers
ALTER COLUMN cust_fname CHAR(10) NOT NULL
ALTER TABLE Sales.Customers
DROP Address2
```

Viewing Table Row and Size Information

In SQL Server Management Studio, you can view table row and size information by
completing the following steps:

1. In SQL Server Management Studio, connect to the server instance that con-
    tains the database in which you want to work.

2. In Object Explorer, expand the Databases node, and then select a database and expand the view to show its resource nodes.

3. Expand the Tables node, right-click the table you want to examine, and then select Properties from the shortcut menu. This displays the Table Properties dialog box shown in Figure 9-3.

4. On the General page, entries under the Storage node provide details about space used:

   ❑ Data Space shows the amount of space the table uses on disk.

   ❑ Index Space shows the size of the table's index space on disk.

   ❑ Row Count shows the number of rows in the table.

You can also view row, size, and space statistics for individual tables using the *sp_spaceused* stored procedure. The following code accesses the *OrderSystemDB* database and then checks the statistics for the *Customers* table under the *Sales* schema:

```
USE OrderSystemDB
EXEC sp_spaceused 'Sales.Customers'
```

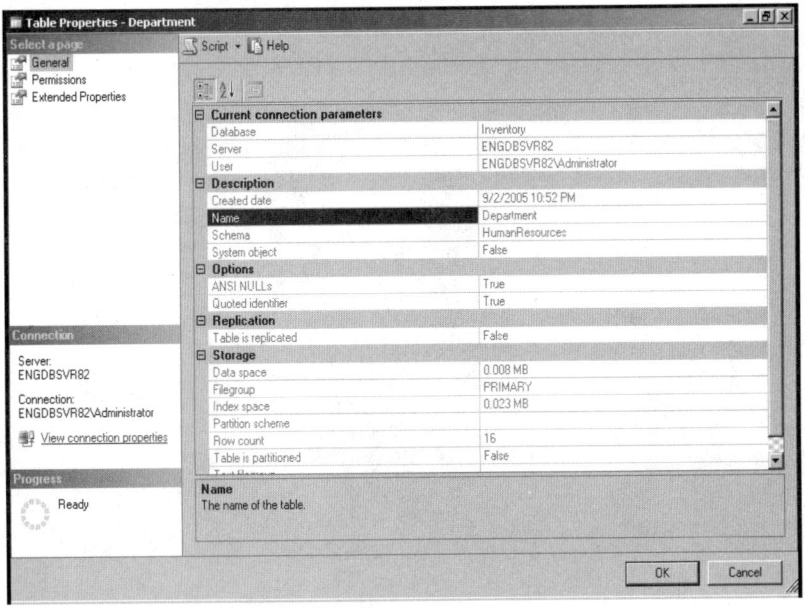

Figure 9-3   The Table Properties dialog box

Displaying Table Properties and Permissions

In SQL Server Management Studio, you can display table properties and permissions by completing the following steps:

1. In SQL Server Management Studio, connect to the server instance that contains the database in which you want to work.

2. In Object Explorer, expand the Databases node, and then select a database and expand the view to show its resource nodes.

3. Expand the Tables node, right-click the table you want to examine, and then select Properties from the shortcut menu to display the Table Properties dialog box shown previously in Figure 9-3.

4. Use the General, Permissions, and Extended Properties pages of the dialog box to view the table's properties and permissions.

Displaying Current Values in Tables

In SQL Server Management Studio, you view a table's current data by completing the following steps:

1. In SQL Server Management Studio, connect to the server instance that contains the database in which you want to work.

2. In Object Explorer, expand the Databases node, and then select a database and expand the view to show its resource nodes.

3. Expand the Tables node, right-click the table you want to examine, and then select Open Table from the shortcut menu to display all the row data contained in the table.

4. The lower portion of the Query Results pane provides buttons for moving between the rows and a status area. If you select a read-only cell, the status area displays "Cell Is Read Only." If you have modified a cell, the status area displays "Cell Is Modified."

You can also list a table's current data using the SELECT FROM statement. In the following example, you are selecting from the *Department* table under the *Human-Resources* schema in the *Personnel* database:

```
SELECT * FROM [Personnel].[HumanResources].[Department]
```

or

```
SELECT DepartmentID,Name,GroupName,ModifiedDate
  FROM [Personnel].[HumanResources].[Department]
```

Copying Tables

The easiest way to create a copy of a table is to use a Transact-SQL command. Use SELECT INTO to extract all the rows from an existing table into the new table. The new table must not exist already. The following example will copy the *Customers* table under the *Sales* schema to a new table called *CurrCustomers* under the *BizDev* schema:

```
SELECT * INTO BizDev.CurrCustomers FROM Sales.Customers
```

You can also create the new table from a specific subset of columns in the original table. In this case, you specify the names of the columns to copy after the SELECT keyword. Any columns not specified are excluded from the new table. The following example copies specific columns to a new table:

```
SELECT CustName, Address, Telephone, Email INTO BizDev.CurrCustomers
FROM Sales.Customers
```

Renaming and Deleting Tables

In SQL Server Management Studio, the easiest way to rename or delete a table is to complete the following steps:

1. In SQL Server Management Studio, access a database, and then expand the Tables node to list the tables in the database.

2. Right-click the table you want to rename or delete. From the shortcut menu, choose View Dependencies. The Object Dependencies dialog box shows the database objects that must be present for this object to function properly and the objects that depend upon the selected object. Use the information in this dialog box to understand any dependencies that may be affected by renaming or deleting the selected table. Click OK to close the View Dependencies dialog box.

3. To rename a table, right-click the table, and then choose Rename from the shortcut menu. You can now type a new name for the table.

4. To delete a table, right-click the table, and then choose Delete from the shortcut menu to display the Delete Object dialog box. Click OK.

You can also rename tables using the *sp_rename* stored procedure. You must have ALTER TABLE permission and be a member of the sysadmin or dbcreator fixed server roles to rename a table with *sp_rename*. In the following example, you rename the *Customers* table under the *Sales* schema *CurrCustomers*:

```
EXEC sp_rename 'Sales.Customers', 'CurrCustomers'
```

As long as you have ALTER permission on the schema to which the table belongs or CONTROL permission on the table, you can remove a table from the database using the DROP TABLE command:

```
DROP TABLE Sales.CurrCustomers
```

If you want to delete the rows in a table but leave its structure intact, you can use DELETE. The following DELETE command deletes all the rows in a table but does not remove the table structure:

```
DELETE Sales.CurrCustomers
```

To use DELETE, you must be a member of the sysadmin fixed server role, the db_owner or db_datawriter fixed database roles, the table owner, or be granted DELETE permission.

Adding and Removing Columns in a Table

You learned how to add or remove columns in a table in SQL Server Management Studio in the section titled "Working with Tables" earlier in this chapter. In

Transact-SQL, you modify table columns using the ALTER TABLE command, which was shown previously in Sample 9-5.

Adding Columns

The following example adds a unique identifier column to the *Customers* table under the *Sales* schema:

```
USE OrderSystemDB
ALTER TABLE Sales.Customers
ADD uid uniqueidentifier NOT NULL DEFAULT newid()
```

Modifying Columns

To change the characteristics of an existing column, use the ALTER COLUMN command, such as in the following example:

```
USE OrderSystemDB
ALTER TABLE Sales.Customers
ALTER COLUMN cust_fname CHAR(10) NOT NULL
```

Removing Columns

The following example removes the Address2 column from the *Customers* table:

```
USE OrderSystemDB
ALTER TABLE Sales.Customers
DROP COLUMN Address2
```

Scripting Tables

You can recreate and store all the SQL commands used to create tables in a database in an .sql file for later use. To do this, complete the following steps:

1. In SQL Server Management Studio, access a database, and then expand the Tables node to list the tables in the database.

2. Select a table, right-click its name, and then select Script Table As from the shortcut menu.

3. Point to CREATE TO and select File to open the Select A File dialog box.

4. In the dialog box, set a folder and file path for the .sql script, and then click Save.

If you open the .sql file, you will find all the Transact-SQL statements required to recreate the table structure. The actual data in the table is not stored with this procedure, however.

Managing Table Values

In this section, you will learn about the techniques and concepts you need to work with table values. Whether you want to create a new table or modify an existing one, the techniques and concepts you need to understand are similar.

Using Native Data Types

Native data types are those built into SQL Server and supported directly. All data types have a length value, which is either fixed or variable. The length for a *numeric* or *binary* data type is the number of bytes used to store the number. The length for a *character* data type is the number of characters. Most *numeric* data types also have precision and scale. *Precision* is the total number of digits in a number. *Scale* is the number of digits to the right of the decimal point in a number. For example, the number 8714.235 has a precision of seven and a scale of three.

Table 9-1 summarizes native data types that work with numbers and money. The first column shows the general data type or data type synonym for SQL-92 compatibility. The second column shows the SQL Server data type. The third column shows the amount of storage space used.

Table 9-1   Native Data Types for Numbers and Money

SQL-92 Name—Type	SQL Server Name	Range—Description	Storage Size
Integers			
Bit	*bit*	0, 1, or NULL	1 byte (for each 1- to 8-bit column)
Big integer	*bigint*	-2^{63} through $2^{63} - 1$.	8 bytes
Integer	*int*	-2^{31} (–2,147,483,648) through $2^{31} - 1$ (2,147,483,647)	4 bytes
small integer	*smallint*	2^{15} (–32,768) through $2^{15} - 1$ (32,767)	2 bytes
tiny integer	*tinyint*	0 through 255	1 byte
Money			
Money	*money*	–922,337,203,685,477.5808 through +922,337,203,685,477.5807	8 bytes
small money	*smallmoney*	–214,748.3648 through +214,748.3647	4 bytes
Decimal			
dec, decimal	*decimal*	$-10^{38} + 1$ through $10^{38} - 1$	5 to 17 bytes
Numeric	*decimal*	$-10^{38} + 1$ through $10^{38} - 1$	5 to 17 bytes
Approximate Numeric			
Double precision	*float*	–1.79E + 308 through 1.79E + 308	4 to 8 bytes
Float	*float*	–1.79E + 308 through 1.79E + 308. float[(n)] for n = 1 – 53	4 to 8 bytes
Float	*real*	–1.18E - 38, 0 and –1.18E – 38 through 3.40E + 38. float[(n)] for n = 1 – 24	4 bytes
Other Numerics			
Cursor	*cursor*	A reference to a cursor	Varies

Table 9-1   Native Data Types for Numbers and Money   *(continued)*

SQL-92 Name—Type	SQL Server Name	Range—Description	Storage Size
Rowversion	rowversion, timestamp	A database-wide unique number that indicates the sequence in which modifications took place in the database (*Rowversion* is a synonym for *timestamp*.)	8 bytes
SQL Variant	sql_variant	A special data type that allows a single column to store multiple data types [except *text, ntext, sql_variant, image, timestamp, xml, varchar(max), varbinary(max), nvarchar(max)* and .NET CLR user-defined types]	Varies
Table	table	A special data type that is used to store a result set temporarily for processing; can be used only to define local variables and as the return type for user-defined functions	Varies
Uniqueidentifier	uniqueidentifier	A globally unique identifier (GUID)	16 bytes
Xml	xml	A special data type that allows you to store XML data; XML markup is defined using standard text characters.	Varies

Table 9-2 summarizes native data types for dates, characters, and binary data. Again, the first column shows the general data type or data type synonym for SQL-92 compatibility. The second column shows the SQL Server data type. The third column shows the amount of storage space used.

Table 9-2   Native Data Types for Dates, Characters, and Binary Values

SQL-92 Name—Type	SQL Server Name	Range—Description	Storage Size
Date			
Datetime	datetime	January 1, 1753, to December 31, 9999; accuracy of three-hundredths of a second	Two 4-byte integers
small datetime	smalldatetime	January 1, 1900, through June 6, 2079; accuracy of one minute	Two 2-byte integers
Character			
Character	char	Fixed-length, non-Unicode character data with a maximum length of 8,000 characters	1 byte per character
character varying	varchar	Variable-length, non-Unicode data with a maximum length of 8,000 characters	1 byte per character
	varchar(max)	Variable-length data to $2^{31} - 1$ (2,147,483,647) characters	1 byte per character + 2-byte pointer
Text	text	Variable-length, non-Unicode data with a maximum length of $2^{31} - 1$ (2,147,483,647) characters	1 byte per character
national character	nchar	Fixed-length, Unicode data with a maximum length of 4,000 characters	2 bytes per character

Table 9-2   Native Data Types for Dates, Characters, and Binary Values   *(continued)*

SQL-92 Name—Type	SQL Server Name	Range—Description	Storage Size
national char varying	nvarchar	Variable-length, Unicode data with a maximum length of 4,000 characters	2 bytes per character
	nvarchar(max)	Variable-length, Unicode data with a maximum length of 2^31 – 1 (1,073,741,823) characters	2 bytes per character plus 2-byte pointer
national text	ntext	Variable-length, Unicode data with a maximum length of 2^30 – 1 (1,073,741,823) characters	2 bytes per character
Binary			
binary	binary	Fixed-length, binary data with a maximum length of 8,000 bytes	Size of data in bytes
binary varying	varbinary	Variable-length, binary data with a maximum length of 8,000 bytes	Size of data in bytes
	varbinary(max)	Variable-length binary data to 2^31 – 1 (2,147,483,647) bytes	Size of data in bytes + 2-byte pointer
Image	image	Variable-length, binary data with a maximum length of 2^31 – 1 (2,147,483,647) bytes	Size of data in bytes

When you create or modify a table in SQL Server Management Studio, you assign a native data type by clicking in the Data Type column and using the selection list to select a data type. In Transact-SQL, you set the data type when you create the table and populate its columns or when you alter a table and add or change columns. Sample 9-6 shows how you could use Transact-SQL commands to create a table and its columns.

Sample 9-6   Creating a Table and Its Columns

```
USE OrderSystemDB
CREATE TABLE Sales.Customers
    (CustomerID nchar(5) NOT NULL,
    CompanyName nvarchar(40) NOT NULL,
    ContactName nvarchar(30) NOT NULL,
    ContactTitle nvarchar(30) NOT NULL,
    Address nvarchar(60) NOT NULL,
    City nvarchar(15) NULL,
    Region nvarchar(15) NULL,
    PostalCode nvarchar(5) NULL,
    Country nvarchar(15) NULL,
    Phone nvarchar(24) NULL,
    Fax nvarchar(24) NULL)
```

Using Fixed-Length, Variable-Length, and Max-Length Fields

You can create binary and character data types as fixed-length, variable-length, or max-length fields. When you use fixed-length data types, the column size you specify is reserved in the database and can be written to without manipulating the data in the column. This makes updates to the database quicker than with variable-length fields. When you use variable-length data types, SQL Server will squeeze more rows into data pages, if possible. When there are more rows per data page, the process of reading data is usually more efficient, which can translate into improved performance for read operations. When you use max-length data types, SQL Server stores a 2-byte pointer to the actual data in the table's regular data space and stores the actual data in the large object data space. Generally speaking, you should:

- Use fixed-length data types when the size of the data is consistent.
- Use variable-length data types when the size of the data varies.
- Use max-length data types when the size of the data exceeds the fixed-length or variable-length limit.

To gain a better understanding of the performance implications, consider the following scenario. With fixed-length columns of 80, 120, 40, and 500 bytes each, rows would always be written using 750 bytes of storage (740 bytes for data plus 10 bytes of overhead for each row). In this example, 10 rows will fit on each data page (8096/750, without the remainder).

If you use variable-length columns, however, the number of bytes used per row and the number of rows stored per page would vary. For example, assume that the average variable-length row uses 400 bytes. This includes 380 bytes of data and 20 bytes of overhead (12 bytes of overhead for rows that use variable-length data plus 2 bytes of overhead per variable-length column, thus 4 * 2 + 12 = 20). In this case, 20 rows will fit on each data page (8096/400, without the remainder), which would make data reads more efficient than the fixed-length example.

Using User-Defined Data Types

User-defined data types are special data types that are based on a native data type. You will want to use user-defined data types when two or more tables store the same type of data in a column and these columns must have exactly the same data type, length, and nullability. You can create user-defined data types yourself, or you can let SQL Server do the job. For example, *sysname* is a user-defined data type that is used to reference database object names. The data type is defined as a variable Unicode character type of 128 characters, which is why object names are limited to 128 characters throughout SQL Server. You can apply this same concept to ensure that specific data is used exactly as you want it to be used.

Creating User-Defined Data Types

You create user-defined data types at the database level rather than at the table level, which is why user-defined data types are static and immutable (unchangeable). This ensures that there is no performance penalty associated with user-defined data types. User-defined data types do have some limitations, however. You cannot declare a default value or check constraint as part of the user-defined data type. You also cannot create a user-defined data type based on a user-defined data type.

Tip   When you create user-defined data types in a user-defined database, they apply only to that database. If you want user-defined data types to apply to multiple databases, define the data type in the *model* database. Then the user-defined data type will exist in all new user-defined databases.

In SQL Server Management Studio, you create a user-defined data type by completing the following steps:

1. In SQL Server Management Studio, connect to the server instance containing the database in which you want to work.

2. In Object Explorer, expand the Databases node, and then select a database and expand the view to show its resource nodes.

3. Expand the Programmability node, right-click Types, point to New, and then select User-Defined Data Type. This opens the New User-Defined Data Type Properties dialog box shown in Figure 9-4.

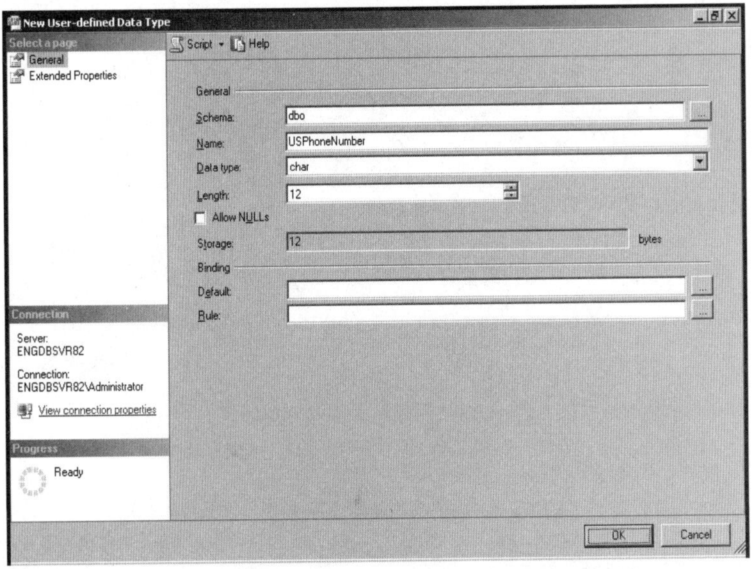

Figure 9-4   The New User-Defined Data Type Properties dialog box

4. The *dbo* schema is the default schema. To place the data type in a different schema, click the button to the right of the Schema box, and then click Browse. Select the schema you want to use, and then click OK twice.

5. Type a name for the new data type.

6. In the Data Type list, select the data type on which you want to base the user-defined data type.

7. If the data type has a variable length, set the number of bytes or characters for the data type. For fixed-length variables, such as *int*, you will not be able to set a length.

8. To allow the data type to accept null values, select Allow Nulls.

9. Optionally, use the Default and Rule lists to select a default or rule to bind to the user-defined data type.

10. Click OK. If you open a new table or edit an existing table, you will see the new data type as one of the last entries in the Data Type selection list.

You can also create user-defined data types with the CREATE TYPE statement. Sample 9-7 shows this procedure's syntax and usage.

Sample 9-7 CREATE TYPE Syntax and Usage

Syntax

```
CREATE TYPE [ schema_name. ] type_name
  {  FROM base_type
  [ ( precision [ , scale ] )  ]
  [ NULL | NOT NULL ]
  | EXTERNAL NAME assembly_name [ .class_name ] } [ ; ]
```

Usage

```
USE master
CREATE TYPE USPhoneNumber
FROM char(12) NOT NULL
```

Managing User-Defined Data Types

After you create user-defined data types, you often will need to manage their properties. To manage user-defined data types, complete the following steps:

1. In SQL Server Management Studio, connect to the server instance that contains the database in which you want to work.

2. In Object Explorer, expand the Databases node, and then select a database and expand the view to show its resource nodes.

3. Expand Programmability, Types, and User-Defined Data Types to list the current user-defined data types.

4. Right-click the user-defined data type you want to manage and then select:
   - ❑ Properties to view the data type's properties and set dependencies.
   - ❑ Delete to delete the data type.
   - ❑ Rename to rename the data type.

5. To see where the data type is used in the database, right-click the user-defined data type, and then select View Dependencies from the shortcut menu.

Allowing and Disallowing Nulls

When you create columns in a table, you can specify whether or not nulls are allowed. A null means there is no entry in the column for that row; it is not the same as zero or an empty string. Columns defined with a primary key constraint or identity property cannot allow null values.

If you add a row but do not set a value for a column that allows null values, SQL Server inserts the value NULL—unless a default value is set for the column. When a default value is set for a column and you insert a null value, SQL Server replaces NULL with the default value. Additionally, if the column allows nulls, you can explicitly set a column to null using the NULL keyword. Do not use quotation marks when setting null explicitly.

In SQL Server Management Studio's Table view, you can:

- Allow nulls in a column by selecting the Allow Nulls column property.
- Disallow nulls in a column by clearing the Allow Nulls column property.

For an example of how to allow and disallow nulls with Transact-SQL, refer to Sample 9-4 earlier in this chapter.

Using Default Values

Null values are useful when you do not know a value or a value is missing. The use of null values is controversial, however, and a better alternative is to set a default value. The default value is used when no value is set for a column you are inserting into a table. For example, you may want a character-based column to have the value N/A rather than NULL, so you would set the default value as N/A.

Table 9-3 summarizes combinations of default values and nullability that are handled in different ways. The main thing to remember is that if you set a default value, the default is used whenever a value is not specified for the column entry. This is true even if you allow nulls.

Table 9-3 Default Values and Nullability

Column Definition	No Entry, No DEFAULT Definition	No Entry, DEFAULT Definition	Enter a Null Value
Allows null values	Sets NULL	Sets default value	Sets NULL
Disallows null values	Error occurs	Sets default value	Error occurs

Using Identities and Globally Unique Identifiers

When you design tables, you will often need to think about unique identifiers that can be used as primary keys or can ensure that merged data does not conflict with existing data. Unique identifiers for primary keys could include customer account numbers or Social Security numbers. However, if a unique identifier is not available, you may want to use the identity property to generate sequential values that are unique for each row in a table. You could also use this unique identifier to generate a customer account number, an order number, or whatever other unique value you need automatically.

Although the identity property provides a local solution for a specific table, it does not guarantee that the value used as an identifier will be unique throughout the database. Other tables in the database may have identity columns with the same values. In most cases, this is not a problem because the identity values usually are used only within the context of a single table and do not relate to other tables.

However, in some situations, you may want to use a value that is unique throughout one or more databases, and then globally unique identifiers provide the solution you need.

Globally unique identifiers are guaranteed to be unique across all networked computers in the world, which is extremely useful in merge replication. When you are merging data from multiple databases, globally unique identifiers ensure that records are not inadvertently associated with each other. For example, a company's New York, Chicago, and San Francisco offices may have customer account numbers that are unique within those local offices but are not unique at the national level. Globally unique identifiers would ensure that account XYZ from New York and account XYZ from Chicago are not merged as the same account.

Identities and globally unique identifiers are not mutually exclusive. Each table can have one identifier column and one globally unique identity property. These values are often used together. For example, all clustered indexes in SQL Server should be unique, but they do not have to be unique.

In SQL Server Management Studio's Table view, you set identity values for a table by completing the following steps:

1. Create or modify other columns in the table as appropriate, and then start a new column for the identity value.

2. Give the identity column a name, and then select a data type. Identifier columns must use one of the following data types: *tinyint, smallint, int, bigint, decimal*, or *numeric*. Globally unique identifier columns must have a data type of *uniqueidentifier*.

Tip   When you set the data type for an identifier column, be sure to consider how many rows are in the table as well as how many rows may be added in the future. A *tinyint* identifier provides only 256 unique values (0 to 255). A *smallint* identifier provides 32,768 unique values (0 to 32,767).

3. Clear the Allow Nulls check box for the identity column.

4. To assign a globally unique identifier, select the identity column in the Table view. In the Column Properties view, set Is RowGuid to Yes. A default value of *newid()* is created automatically for you.

Note   The *newid()* function is used to generate new unique identifier values by combining the identification number of a network card with a unique number from the CPU clock. If a server process generates the identifier, the server's network card identification number is used. If the identifier is returned by application API function calls, the client's network card is used. Network card manufacturers guarantee that no other network card in the next 100 years will have the same number.

5. To assign a unique identifier, select the identity column in the Table view, expand Identity Specification in the Column Properties view, and then set (Is Identity) to Yes.

6. Type a value in the Identity Increment cell. This value is the increment that is added to the Identity Seed for each subsequent row. If you leave this cell blank, the value 1 is assigned by default.

7. Type a value in the Identity Seed cell. This value is assigned to the first row in the table. If you leave this cell blank, the value 1 is assigned by default.

8. If you are replicating a database as discussed in Chapter 12, Implementing Snapshot, Merge, and Transactional Replication," and do not want the column to be replicated, set Is Not For Replication to Yes. Otherwise, you will typically want to set Is Not For Replication to No to allow the column to be replicated.

Note The identity seed and increment values are used to determine the identifier for rows. If you enter a seed value of 100 and an increment of 10, the first row has a value of 100, the second has a value of 110, and so on.

When you create a table in Transact-SQL, globally unique identifiers are not generated automatically. You must reference the *newid()* function as the default value for the identifier column, as shown in this example:

```
USE OrderSystemDB
CREATE TABLE Sales.Customers
    (cust_lname varchar(40) NOT NULL,
    cust_fname varchar(20) NOT NULL,
    phone char(12) NOT NULL,
    uid uniqueidentifier NOT NULL DEFAULT newid())
```

Then when you insert a new row into the table, you call *newid()* to generate the globally unique identifier:

```
INSERT INTO Sales.Customers
Values ('Stanek', 'William', '123-555-1212', newid())
```

Using Views

Views can be thought of as virtual tables because the result sets returned by views have the same general form as a table, with columns and rows, and views can be referenced much like tables in queries. Several types of views can be created. Most views are used to join data from multiple tables so it can be accessed in a single result set. For example, you could create a *CustOrder* view that gets the customer's first name, last name, address, account number, and telephone number from the *Customers* table and the last order details from the *Orders* table, which makes the information more manageable for your company's sales representatives.

Views can be created from other views as well, which allows you to extract subsets of data from views and to create supersets that combine data from multiple views. For example, you could create a subset view of the *CustOrder* view that shows only the customer's first name, last name, and telephone number. You could also create a superset view that combines elements of the *CustOrder* view, the *AllCustOrders* view, and *LastOrder* view.

Working with Views

To create a view, you use a SELECT statement to select the data in one or more tables and display it as a view. Like tables, views can be partitioned and indexed. A partitioned view joins horizontally partitioned data from a set of base tables from one or more servers. A partitioned view in which all base tables reside in the same database is referred to as a local partitioned view. A partitioned view in which one or more base tables reside on one or more different, remote servers is referred to as a distributed partitioned view.

 Tip Typically, you will use distributed partitioned views rather than local partitioned views because the preferred method for partitioning data locally is through partitioned tables (and local partitioned views are supported only for backward compatibility). Distributed partitioned views are used to create a federation of database servers. A *federation* is a group of servers that are managed separately, but which cooperate to share the query processing load of a large application or Web site.

Partitioned views also may be updatable or read-only. Updatable partitioned views are updatable copies of the underlying tables. Read-only partitioned views are read-only copies of the underlying tables. To perform updates on a partitioned view, the partitioning column must be part of the base table's primary key. If this is not possible (or to make read-only partitioned views updatable), you can use INSTEAD OF triggers. INSTEAD OF triggers execute whenever a user attempts to modify data using INSERT, UPDATE, or DELETE. Views comprising multiple base tables must use an INSTEAD OF trigger to support inserts, updates, and deletes that reference data in more than one table.

You index views to improve query performance. The first index created on a view must be a unique clustered index. After the unique clustered index is created, you can create additional nonclustered indexes on the view. A view for which you want to create a unique clustered index must not reference any other views. It can only reference base tables, and those base tables must be in the same database as the view and have the same owner as the view.

The query processor handles indexed and nonindexed views in different ways. The rows of an indexed view are stored in the database in the same format as a table. If the query optimizer uses an indexed view in a query plan, the indexed view is handled the same way as a base table. With nonindexed views, only the view definition is stored in the database, not the rows of the view. If the query optimizer uses a nonindexed view in an execution plan, only the logic from the view definition is used.

When an SQL statement references a nonindexed view, the parser and query optimizer analyze the source of both the SQL statement and the view and resolve them into a single execution plan. This means that there is not one plan for the SQL statement and a separate plan for the view—there is only one execution plan.

As with tables, views are contained in schemas, and you can assign permissions to views. Typically, you want the base tables and the related views to be in the same schema. It is also important to note that permissions assigned to views are separate from the table permissions.

Creating Views

Views can have up to 1,024 columns. If you understand tables, creating views is a fairly straightforward process. However, there are a few rules to follow. Although the SELECT statement used to create a view can use more than one table and other views, you must have appropriate permissions to select from the referenced objects. The view definition cannot include COMPUTE or COMPUTE BY clauses, an ORDER BY clause (unless there is also a TOP clause), the INTO keyword, the OPTION clause, or a reference to a temporary table or a table variable.

You can create a view in SQL Server Management Studio by completing the following steps:

1. In SQL Server Management Studio, select a database, and then expand the Views node to list the current views in the database. Two types of views are available: system and user. System views provide a summarized report of database information, such as table constraints and table privileges. User views are defined by you or by other database users.

2. To create a new view, right-click the Views node. From the shortcut menu, choose New View to display the Add Table dialog box shown in Figure 9-5. The Add Table dialog box has tabs that allow you to work with tables, views, functions, and synonyms. If you select Add Derived Tables from the Query Designer menu and display the dialog box again, you will see a Local Tables tab containing derived tables.

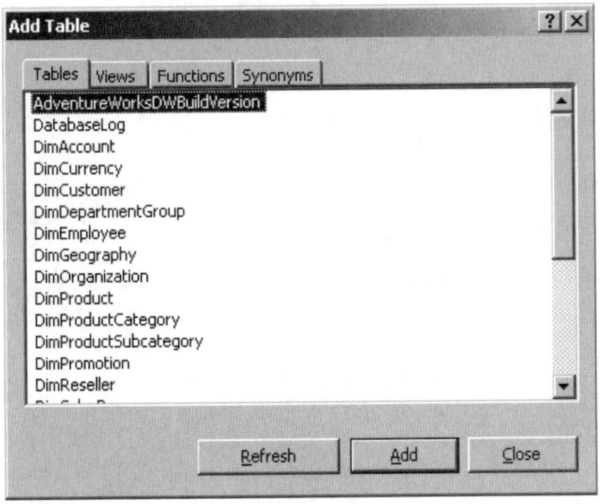

Figure 9-5 The Add Table dialog box

3. In the Add Table dialog box, select a table or other object that contains data you want to add to the view, and then click Add. This displays a view pane for the selected object, which you can use to add columns, fields, and so on to the view you are creating.

4. When you are finished working with the Add Table dialog box, click Close. You can display this dialog box again at any time by selecting Add Table on the Query Designer menu.

5. Use the view panes provided to select the columns and fields to use in the view, as shown in Figure 9-6. Your actions create a SELECT statement that can be used to generate the view.

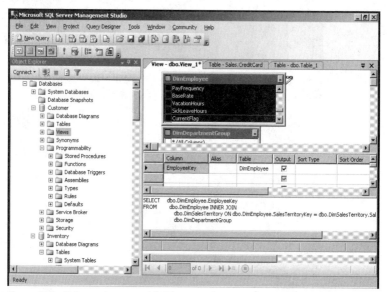

Figure 9-6   Select columns and fields to use for a view

6. The View Properties pane is not displayed by default. In the right pane, click the tab with the name of the view, and then press F4 to display the View Properties pane.

7. Set the view name, description, and schema. Type the name and description in the fields provided. Use the drop-down list to select the schema that will contain this view.

8. You may want to create a dependency within a schema to ensure that any modifications to the underlying structures that comprise the view are not changed without first changing the view. You do this by binding the view to the schema. If you want to bind the view to the schema, set Bind To Schema to Yes.

Note When you bind a view to the schema, views or tables used in the view cannot be dropped unless that view is dropped or changed so that it no longer has schema binding. Furthermore, executing ALTER TABLE statements on tables that participate in views that have schema binding will fail when these statements affect the view definition.

9. If you want to ensure that the view shows only distinct rows and filters out duplicate rows, set Distinct Values to Yes.

10. If you want the view to return a partial result set containing the top matches, set Top to Yes, and then define the number of top matches to return as either a fixed maximum or a percentage of total results.

    ❑ To define a fixed maximum, set Expression to the maximum number of results to return and set Percent to No. For example, set Expression to 50 to return the top 50 results.

    ❑ To define a percentage of the total results to return, set Expression to the percentage of results to return and set Percent to Yes. For example, set Expression to 10 and Percent to Yes to return the top 10 percent of the result set.

11. If you want to create an updatable view, set Update Using View Rules to Yes. Updatable views cannot be created with distinct values or from top result sets. To make sure data remains visible through the view after a modification is committed, set Check Option to Yes. Remember, however, that updates performed directly to a view's base tables are not verified against the view even when you select the Check Option.

12. When you are finished configuring the view, verify the SQL syntax by selecting Verify SQL Syntax from the Query Designer menu. Correct any errors or issues reported during the verification process before continuing.

13. To create the view, press Ctrl+R or select Execute SQL on the Query Designer menu.

14. After you run the view to update it for the latest changes, save the view. Press Ctrl+S or click Save on the toolbar.

You can also create views using the CREATE VIEW statement. You can create a simple view by selecting all the values in a table:

```
CREATE VIEW Sales.CustomView As
SELECT *
FROM Sales.Customers
```

Then you can work directly with the view:

```
SELECT * FROM Sales.CustomView
```

Sample 9-8 shows the full syntax and usage for CREATE VIEW.

Sample 9-8   CREATE VIEW Syntax

Syntax

```
CREATE VIEW [ schema_name . ] view_name [ (column [ ,...n ] ) ]
[ WITH <view_attribute> [ ,...n ] ]
AS select_statement [ ; ]
[ WITH CHECK OPTION ]

<view_attribute> ::=
{    [ ENCRYPTION ]
     [ SCHEMABINDING ]
     [ VIEW_METADATA ]       }
```

Usage

```
CREATE VIEW Sales.CustomView As
SELECT cust_id AS Account, cust_lname AS [Last Name],
   cust_fname AS [First Name], state AS Region
FROM Sales.Customers
WHERE (state = 'WA') OR
   (state = 'HI') OR
   (state = 'CA')
```

Modifying Views

You can modify a view in SQL Server Management Studio by completing the follow-ing steps:

1. In SQL Server Management Studio, select a database, and then expand the Views node to list the current views in the database.
2. To modify an existing view, right-click the view, and then select Modify.
3. If you want to add tables, views, and so on, you can display the Add Table dia-log box by selecting Add Table from the Query Designer menu.
4. If you want to set view properties, click the tab with the name of the view and then press F4 to display the View Properties pane.

To change an existing view without having to reset its permissions and other prop-erties, you use ALTER VIEW. The following example changes the definition of the *Sales Custom* view used in previous examples:

```
ALTER VIEW Sales.CustomView As
   SELECT cust_id AS Account, cust_lname AS [Customer Last Name],
   cust_fname AS [Customer First Name], state AS Region
   FROM Sales.Customers
   WHERE (state = 'WA') OR
         (state = 'CA')
```

Sample 9-9 shows the full syntax for ALTER VIEW.

Sample 9-9   ALTER VIEW Syntax

Syntax

```
ALTER VIEW [ schema_name . ] view_name [ ( column [ ,...n ] ) ]
[ WITH <view_attribute> [ ,...n ] ]
AS select_statement [ ; ]
[ WITH CHECK OPTION ]


<view_attribute> ::=
{    [ ENCRYPTION ]
     [ SCHEMABINDING ]
     [ VIEW_METADATA ]    }
```

Using Updatable Views

SQL Server supports updatable views as well. With an updatable view, you can change the information in the view using INSERT, UPDATE, and DELETE statements. You can create updatable views if the table columns being modified are not affected by GROUP BY, HAVING, or DISTINCT clauses. Furthermore, an updatable view can only be modified when the columns from one base table are being modified and those columns directly reference the underlying data. This means the data cannot be derived from an aggregate function or computed from an expression that uses other columns.

With updatable views, you will usually want to set Check Option to Yes. If you do not set the option, changes to the view may result in rows that are no longer displayed in the view. For example, consider the view created as an example previously. The view included customer information from Washington (WA), Hawaii (HI), and California (CA). If you change a state value to GA, the row would disappear from the view because Georgia-based customers are not displayed in the view.

Managing Views

You can examine view properties, set view permissions, and perform other management tasks, just as you do with tables. To get started managing views, complete the following steps:

1. In SQL Server Management Studio, select a database, and then expand the Views node to list the current views in the database.

2. Select a view, and then right-click it to open a shortcut menu that gives you the following choices to manage the view:

   - **Open View**   View the result set for the view.
   - **Properties**   Examine view properties.
   - **Rename**   Rename the view.
   - **Delete**   Delete the view.

■ **View Dependencies**   View objects that depend on the view or objects on which the view depends.

3. To set permissions for a view, right-click the view, and then select Properties. In the View Properties dialog box, select the Permissions page. You can now manage the permissions for the view.

Creating and Managing Indexes

Indexes provide quick access to data without searching through an entire database. With SQL Server 2005, you can create indexes on tables, views, and columns. By creating indexes on tables, you can search through the data in a table quickly. By creating indexes on views, you can generate a result set of the view that is stored and indexed in the database. By creating indexes on computed columns, you can evaluate expressions and index the results (if certain criteria are met).

Indexes are separate from tables, and you can configure them automatically using the Database Tuning Advisor. This section examines the techniques you will use to work with indexes.

Understanding Indexes

Indexes, like tables, use pages. The structure of index pages is similar to the structure used for table data pages. Index pages are 8 KB (8,192 bytes) in size and have a 96-byte header. But unlike data pages, they do not have row offsets. Each index has a corresponding row in the sys.indexes catalog view with an index ID value (index_id) of 1 for clustered indexes or 2–250 for nonclustered indexes. An index ID value of 255 indicates large object data such as *image, ntext, text, varchar(max),* *nvarchar(max), varbinary(max),* or *xml* data. (Large object data types cannot be index key columns; *varchar(max), nvarchar(max), varbinary(max),* and *xml* data types can be included columns, however.)

SQL Server maintains indexes using a BTree structure, which is a basic tree structure consisting of a root node, intermediate level nodes, and leaf nodes. Because indexes use a tree structure, you can search them quickly and efficiently. Without the tree structure, SQL Server would need to read each table data page in the database in turn, searching for the correct record.

To put this in perspective, consider a simple table in which each data page contains a single row. In this case, if SQL Server searches for data in row 800 and there is no index, SQL Server may have to search 799 other rows before finding the right row. With a tree structure, SQL Server navigates the nodes down the index searching for the row that matches the corresponding index key. In the best-case scenario, in which the index keys have been arranged in a full tree, the number of nodes that need to be searched is proportional to the height of the tree. For example, 27,000 rows may be represented by 30 levels of nodes, and if so, SQL Server would have to navigate a maximum of 15 nodes to find the matching row.

Note   You may have noticed that I simplified this example to demonstrate the power of indexing. Nevertheless, indexing can improve
performance by orders of magnitude, and accessing a database without indexing can seem extremely slow. You must be careful, however;
indexing the wrong information also can make the database perform
slowly, which is why it is so important to select the most referenced/
used column in the table to index.

In SQL Server 2005, indexing performance has been enhanced in many ways:

- Index operations can be performed online, and online indexing depends on the amount of memory allocated for indexing. Online indexing makes it possi- ble for users to access table data and use other indexes on a table while an index is being created, modified, or dropped.

- Columns that are not part of the index key can be included in nonclustered indexes to improve query performance by making all the required data avail- able without the need to access the table data rows. These included columns can exceed the index size limitations of 16 key columns and the maximum key size of 900 bytes.

- Both row-level and page-level index locks are allowed when accessing the index. If you allow row locks, page locks, or both, the Database Engine deter- mines when the locks are used.

- The maximum degree of parallelism can be set using MAXDOP. This controls the number of parallel operations when creating, alerting, or dropping an index.

- Indexes can be partitioned on value ranges using existing partition schemes. When you partition a nonunique, clustered index, the Database Engine adds the partitioning column to the list of clustered index keys if it is not already specified. When you partition a nonunique, nonclustered index, the Database Engine adds the partitioning column as a nonkey (included) column of the index if it is not already specified.

SQL Server 2005 supports two types of indexing:

- Clustered indexes
- Nonclustered indexes

SQL Server 2005 also supports a special type of index for XML data. An XML index can be either a nonclustered index (the default) or a clustered index. A clus- tered index is created for XML data from the clustering key of the user table and an XML node identifier. Each table can have up to 249 XML indexes. You will learn more about XML indexes in the subsection titled "Using XML Indexes" later in this chapter.

You can create clustered and nonclustered indexes on almost any column. Excep- tions include common language runtime (CLR) user-defined types and very large object data types—you cannot create indexes on these data types. If you want to create indexes on computed columns, you must ensure the computed column expression always returns the same result for a specific set of inputs. Although you can create an index on any other type of column, you should always select the index column carefully. Selecting the correct column to index improves response time dramatically. Selecting the wrong column to index actually can degrade response time. For more information about which column to index, use the Database Tuning Advisor.

Using Clustered Indexes

A clustered index stores the actual table data pages at the leaf level, and the table data is physically ordered around the key. A table can have only one clustered index, and when this index is created, the following events also occur:

- Table data is rearranged.
- New index pages are created.
- All nonclustered indexes within the database are rebuilt .

As a result, there are many disk I/O operations and extensive use of system and memory resources. So if you plan to create a clustered index, make sure you have enough free space, equal to at least 1.5 times the amount of data in the table. The extra free space ensures that you have enough space to complete the operation efficiently.

Normally, you create a clustered index on a primary key. You can, however, create a clustered index on any named column, such as cust_lname or cust_id. When you create a clustered index, the values you are indexing should be unique. If the values are not unique, SQL Server creates secondary sort keys on rows that have duplicates of their primary sort keys.

Using Nonclustered Indexes

In a nonclustered index, pages at the leaf level contain a bookmark that tells SQL Server where to find the data row corresponding to the key in the index. If the table has a clustered index, the bookmark indicates the clustered index key. If the table does not have a clustered index, the bookmark is an actual row locator.

When you create a nonclustered index, SQL Server creates the required index pages but does not rearrange table data, and other indexes for the table are not deleted. Each table can have up to 249 nonclustered indexes.

Using XML Indexes

As mentioned earlier, an XML index is a special type of index that can be either clustered or nonclustered. Before you can create an XML index, there must be a clustered index based on the primary key of the user table, and this key is limited to 15 columns. Two types of XML indexes can be created: primary and secondary. Each *xml* column in a table can have one primary XML index and one or more secondary XML indexes. However, there must be a primary XML index before a secondary XML index can be created on a column, and you cannot create a primary XML index on a computed *xml* column.

Also note that an XML index can only be created on a single *xml* column. You cannot create an XML index on a non-*xml* column, nor can you create a relational index on an *xml* column. You cannot create an XML index on an *xml* column in a view, on a table-valued variable with *xml* columns, or on an *xml* type variable. Finally, the SET options must be the same as those required for indexed views and computed-column indexes. This means ARITHABORT must be set to ON when an XML index is created and when inserting, deleting, or updating values in the *xml* column.

Determining Which Columns Should Be Indexed

Now that you know how indexes work, you can focus on which columns you should index. Ideally, you will select columns for indexing based on the types of queries executed on the database. SQL Server Profiler can help you determine the types of queries being run. You use SQL Profiler to create a trace that contains a good snapshot of activities performed by users on the database.

You can examine this trace manually to see what types of queries are executed, or you can use the trace file as a saved workload file in the Database Engine Tuning Advisor. Regardless of which method you use, keep in mind that the maximum length of all key columns that comprise an index is 900 bytes. This means that the total size in bytes of all columns must be 900 or less. (Columns that are not part of the index key can be included, and these included columns can exceed the index size limitations of 16 key columns and maximum key size of 900 bytes.) Table 9-4 offers some guidelines about the kinds of tables and columns that can be successfully indexed and those that do not result in useful indexes.

Table 9-4   Guidelines for Selecting Tables and Columns to Index

Index	Do Not Index
Tables with lots of rows	Tables with few rows
Columns that are often used in queries	Columns that are rarely used in queries
Columns that have a wide range of values and have a high likelihood of rows being selected in a typical query	Columns that have a wide range of values and have a low likelihood of rows being selected in a typical query
Columns used in aggregate functions	Columns that have a large byte size
Columns used in GROUP BY queries	Tables with many modifications but few actual queries
Columns used in ORDER BY queries	
Columns used in table joins	

Table 9-5 provides suggestions for the types of columns that should use clustered or nonclustered indexes.

Table 9-5   Guidelines for Using Clustered and Nonclustered Indexes

Use Clustered Index for	Use Nonclustered Index for
Primary keys that are searched for extensively, such as account numbers	Primary keys that are sequential identifiers, such as identity columns
Queries that return large result sets	Queries that return small result sets
Columns used in many queries	Columns used in aggregate functions

Table 9-5   Guidelines for Using Clustered and Nonclustered Indexes   *(continued)*

Use Clustered Index for	Use Nonclustered Index for
Columns with strong selectivity	Foreign keys
Columns used in ORDER BY or GROUP BY queries	
Columns used in table joins	

Indexing Computed Columns and Views

With SQL Server 2005, you can index computed columns and views as well as tables. Indexes on computed columns and views involve storing results in the database for future reference. With computed columns, the column values are calculated and then used to build the keys stored in the index. With views, the result set is stored by creating a clustered index on the view. In both cases, the stored results are valid only if all connections referring to the results can generate an identical result set, which puts specific restrictions on how you can create indexes on computed columns and views.

You must establish connections referring to the results using specific SET options, and these options must have the same settings. The options you must set are as follows:

- ANSI_NULLS must be set ON.
- ANSI_PADDING must be set ON.
- ANSI_WARNINGS must be set ON.
- ARITHABORT must be set ON.
- CONCAT_NULL_YIELDS_NULL must be set ON.
- QUOTED_IDENTIFIER must be set ON.
- NUMERIC_ROUNDABORT must be set OFF.

Furthermore, all operations referencing the view must use the exact same algorithm to build the view result set, including:

- The CREATE INDEX statement that builds the initial result set or is used to calculate the initial keys.
- Any subsequent INSERT, UPDATE, or DELETE statements that affect the data used to build the view result set or are used to calculate keys.
- All queries for which the query optimizer must determine if the indexed view is useful.

Viewing Index Properties

Both tables and views can have indexes. In SQL Server Management Studio, you can view indexes associated with a table or view by completing the following steps:

1. In SQL Server Management Studio, select a database, and then expand the Tables or Views node as appropriate.

2. Select a table or view and expand its node to list the objects it contains.

3. Expand the Indexes node to list the indexes associated with the selected table or view (if any).

4. Right-click an index, and then select Properties from the shortcut menu to open the Index Properties dialog box shown in Figure 9-7. This dialog box has several pages that you can select to view and manage index properties, including:

- **General** Shows general properties, including the index name and type. You can change the index type and add or remove key columns.

- **Options** Allows you to set options for rebuilding the index, recomputing statistics, using row or page locks, setting the fill factor, and determining maximum degree of parallelism.

- **Included Columns** Allows you to view and manage the included columns (with nonclustered indexes.)

- **Storage** Lists the current storage configuration. Allows you to configure filegroups and partition schemes.

- **Fragmentation** Lists the index fragmentation data, which you can use to determine if you need to reorganize or rebuild the index.

- **Extended Properties** Lists extended properties. Allows you to add or remove extended properties.

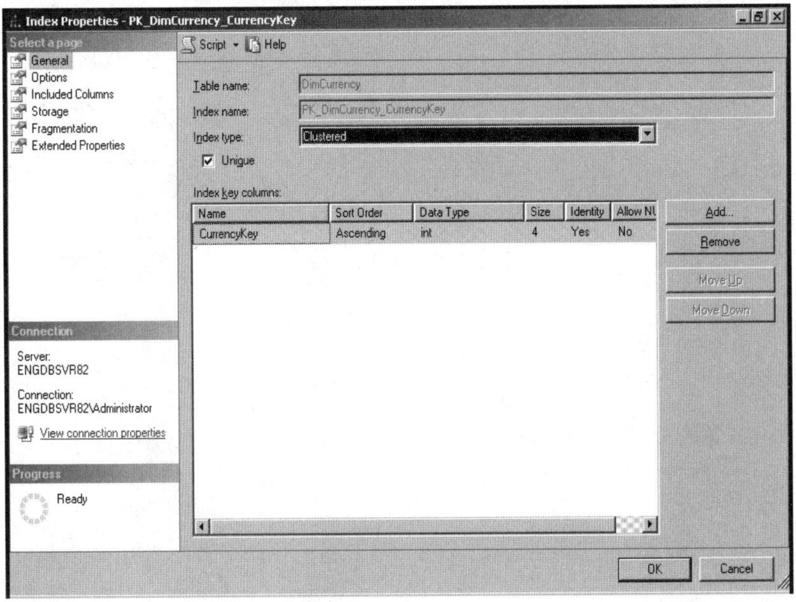

Figure 9-7 Index Properties dialog box

Using the *sp_statistics* stored procedure, you can examine the indexes for a specific table or view. To do this, you simply specify the name of the table or view whose indexes you want to examine, as shown in the following example:

```
USE OrderSystemDB
EXEC sp_statistics Sales.Customers
```

Creating Indexes

Only the owner of a table or view can create indexes on that table or view. You can create indexes with a wizard in the SQL Server Management Studio or with the Transact-SQL CREATE INDEX command. To create indexes with the wizard, complete the following steps:

1. In SQL Server Management Studio, connect to the server instance containing the database in which you want to work.

2. In Object Explorer, expand the Databases node, and then select a database and expand it to show the database's resource nodes.

3. Expand the Tables or Views node as appropriate. Right-click the table or view for which you are creating the index, and then select Modify from the shortcut menu.

4. On the Table Designer menu, select Indexes/Keys to display the Indexes/Keys dialog box shown in Figure 9-8.

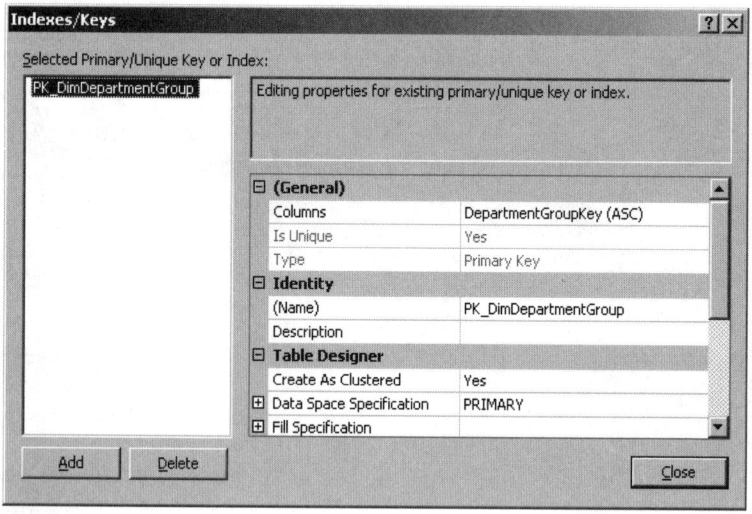

Figure 9-8   The Indexes/Keys dialog box

5. Any current primary/unique keys and indexes are listed in the left pane of the dialog box, and you can manage the properties of any of the keys by selecting it and making the necessary changes. To add an index, click Add.

6. Click in the Columns text box, and then click the button to the right of the Columns box. This displays the Index Columns dialog box shown in Figure 9-9.

7. Under Column Name, select the column(s) you want to include in the index. You can only select columns that have valid data types for indexing.

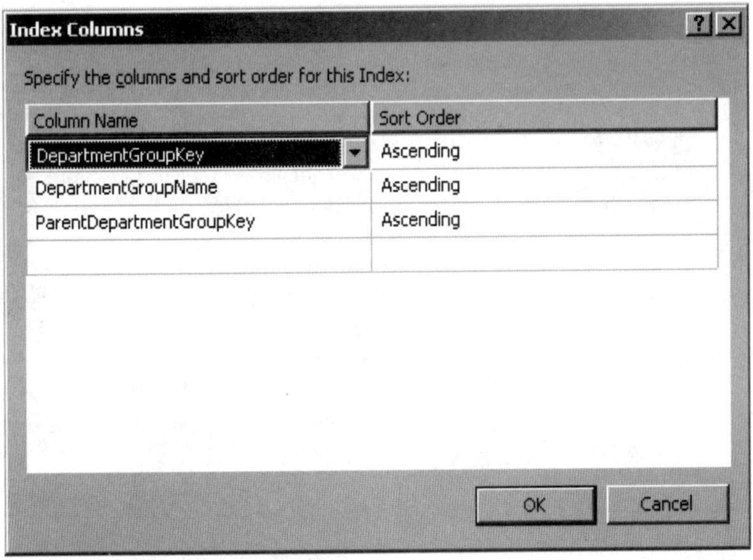

Index Columns   ? ✕

Specify the columns and sort order for this Index:

Column Name	Sort Order
DepartmentGroupKey ▼	Ascending
DepartmentGroupName	Ascending
ParentDepartmentGroupKey	Ascending

OK   Cancel

Figure 9-9   The Index Columns dialog box

8. Each column can have a separate sort order for the index. By default, the sort order is set to Ascending. You can set the sort order to Descending.

9. When you have finished selecting columns to index, click OK to close the Index Columns dialog box.

10. If you want to ensure that data entered into this index is unique, set the option Is Unique to Yes. This ensures the uniqueness of values stored in the index. You cannot set this option for XML indexes.

11. Type should be set to Index by default. Use the text boxes provided to type the index name and description. You can use up to 128 characters for the index name. Ideally, the index name should be short and easy to associate with its purpose, such as [*Index for Cust ID*].

12. Set the option Create As Clustered to Yes to create a clustered index on the columns selected. Otherwise, a nonclustered index is created. Remember that you can have only one clustered index per table, so if the table already has a clustered index, this option is shaded and you cannot select it.

13. To specify the storage location for the index, expand the Data Space Specification node, and then use the Filegroup Or Partition Schema drop-down list to specify the filegroup.

14. To set the fill parameters, expand the Fill Specification node. Set the Fill Factor to 0 (the default value) to let SQL Server use an optimized fill, as described in the section titled "Setting the Index Fill" in Chapter 6, " Configuring SQL Server with SQL Server Management Studio." Refer to this same section for information about setting the Fill Factor to a different value to set a specific index fill.

15. If you want to ignore duplicate keys, set the option Ignore Duplicates Keys to Yes. When this option is on, any attempt to insert rows that violate the unique index fails with a warning, and the rows are not inserted. Whether this option is set on or off, however, SQL Server does not allow you to create a unique index on columns that already have duplicate values. Columns that are used in a unique index should be set so they do not allow nulls. Furthermore, you cannot use the Ignore Duplicates Keys option with XML indexes or indexes created on views.

16. Optionally, turn on automatic statistics updating by setting the option Re-Compute Statistics to Yes. If you set Re-Compute Statistics to No, out-of-date statistics are not automatically recomputed.

17. When you are finished configuring the index, click Close. Select File | Save or press Ctrl+S to save the table, which in turn saves the index you created.

Use the Transact-SQL CREATE INDEX command to create indexes with the syntax shown in Sample 9-10.

Sample 9-10 CREATE INDEX Syntax

Syntax Relational Index

```
CREATE [ UNIQUE ] [ CLUSTERED | NONCLUSTERED ] INDEX index_name
    ON <object> ( column [ ASC | DESC ] [ ,...n ] )
    [ INCLUDE ( column_name [ ,...n ] ) ]
    [ WITH ( <relational_index_option> [ ,...n ] ) ]
    [ ON { partition_scheme_name ( column_name )
        | filegroup_name
        | default
        } ]
[ ; ]
<object> ::=
{ [ database_name. [ schema_name ] . | schema_name. ]
        table_or_view_name }

<relational_index_option> ::=
{ PAD_INDEX = { ON | OFF }
    | FILLFACTOR = fillfactor
    | SORT_IN_TEMPDB = { ON | OFF }
    | IGNORE_DUP_KEY = { ON | OFF }
    | STATISTICS_NORECOMPUTE = { ON | OFF }
    | DROP_EXISTING = { ON | OFF }
    | ONLINE = { ON | OFF }
    | ALLOW_ROW_LOCKS = { ON | OFF }
```

```
  | ALLOW_PAGE_LOCKS = { ON | OFF }
  | MAXDOP = max_degree_of_parallelism }
```

Syntax XML Index

```
CREATE [ PRIMARY ] XML INDEX index_name
    ON <object> ( xml_column_name )
    [ USING XML INDEX xml_index_name
        [ FOR { VALUE | PATH | PROPERTY } ]
    [ WITH ( <xml_index_option> [ ,...n ] ) ]
[ ; ]


<object> ::=
{ [ database_name. [ schema_name ] . | schema_name. ]
        table_name }
<xml_index_option> ::=
{ PAD_INDEX   = { ON | OFF }
  | FILLFACTOR = fillfactor
  | SORT_IN_TEMPDB = { ON | OFF }
  | STATISTICS_NORECOMPUTE = { ON | OFF }
  | DROP_EXISTING = { ON | OFF }
  | ALLOW_ROW_LOCKS = { ON | OFF }
  | ALLOW_PAGE_LOCKS = { ON | OFF }
  | MAXDOP = max_degree_of_parallelism }
```

Managing Indexes

After you create an index, you may need to change its properties, rename it, or delete it. You handle these tasks in SQL Server Management Studio by completing the following steps:

1. In SQL Server Management Studio, select a database, and then expand the Tables or Views node as appropriate.
2. Select a table or view and expand its node to list the objects it contains.
3. Expand the Indexes node to list the indexes associated with the selected table or view.
4. Right-click an index. You can now:
   - Select Properties to view the index properties, including details on space usage and fragmentation.
   - Select Rename to rename an index.
   - Select Rebuild to rebuild the index. In the Rebuild Indexes dialog box, use the Total Fragmentation and Index Status values to help you determine whether or not to proceed. Click OK to proceed with the rebuild. Click Cancel to exit without performing the rebuild. SQL Server 2005 performs online index rebuilds and reorganizations.
   - Select Reorganize to reorganize the index. In the Reorganize Indexes dialog box, check the total fragmentation of the index to determine if the index needs to be reorganized. By default, both regular data and large

object data are reorganized. Clear the Compact Large Object Column Data option if you only want to compact regular index data. Click OK to proceed with the reorganization. Click Cancel to exit without performing the reorganization.

❏ Select Delete to drop the index (as long as it is not a primary key or unique constraint).

You can also manage indexes with the Transact-SQL commands ALTER INDEX and DROP INDEX. Unfortunately, you must use these commands cautiously because there are several limitations to these commands. For example, you cannot drop an index that was created by defining a primary key or unique constraints. You must instead drop the constraint with ALTER TABLE. Sample 9-11 shows the syntax for ALTER INDEX and Sample 9-12 shows the syntax for DROP INDEX.

Sample 9-11 ALTER INDEX Syntax

Syntax

```
ALTER INDEX { index_name | ALL }
    ON <object>
    { REBUILD [ [ WITH ( <rebuild_index_option> [ ,...n ] ) ]
        | [ PARTITION = partition_number
            [ WITH ( <single_partition_rebuild_index_option> [ ,...n ]
) ] ] ]
    | DISABLE
    | REORGANIZE
        [ PARTITION = partition_number ]
        [ WITH ( LOB_COMPACTION = { ON | OFF } ) ]
    | SET ( <set_index_option> [ ,...n ] ) }
[ ; ]

<object> ::=
{ [ database_name. [ schema_name ] . | schema_name. ]
        table_or_view_name }

<rebuild_index_option > ::=
{ PAD_INDEX  = { ON | OFF }
    | FILLFACTOR = fillfactor
    | SORT_IN_TEMPDB = { ON | OFF }
    | IGNORE_DUP_KEY = { ON | OFF }
    | STATISTICS_NORECOMPUTE = { ON | OFF }
    | ONLINE = { ON | OFF }
    | ALLOW_ROW_LOCKS = { ON | OFF }
    | ALLOW_PAGE_LOCKS = { ON | OFF }
    | MAXDOP = max_degree_of_parallelism }

<single_partition_rebuild_index_option> ::=
{ SORT_IN_TEMPDB = { ON | OFF }
    | MAXDOP = max_degree_of_parallelism }

<set_index_option>::=
{ ALLOW_ROW_LOCKS= { ON | OFF }
```

```
| ALLOW_PAGE_LOCKS = { ON | OFF }
| IGNORE_DUP_KEY = { ON | OFF }
| STATISTICS_NORECOMPUTE = { ON | OFF } }
```

Sample 9-12   DROP INDEX Syntax

Syntax
```
DROP INDEX
{ <drop_relational_or_xml_index> [ ,...n ]
| <drop_backward_compatible_index> [ ,...n ] }

<drop_relational_or_xml_index> ::=
    index_name ON <object>
    [ WITH ( <drop_clustered_index_option> [ ,...n ] ) ]

<drop_backward_compatible_index> ::=
    [ owner_name. ] table_or_view_name.index_name

<object> ::=
{ [ database_name. [ schema_name ] . | schema_name. ]
        table_or_view_name }

<drop_clustered_index_option> ::=
{ MAXDOP = max_degree_of_parallelism
    | ONLINE = { ON | OFF }
    | MOVE TO { partition_scheme_name ( column_name )
              | filegroup_name
              | "default"
              } }
```

Using the Database Engine Tuning Advisor

The Database Engine Tuning Advisor is one of the best tools a database administrator can use to facilitate the indexing and optimization process. But before you start this wizard, you should create a trace containing a representative snapshot of database activity. You will use this snapshot as the workload file in the Database Engine Tuning Advisor. For specific pointers on creating a trace file, see the subsection titled "Creating and Managing Performance Monitor Logs" in Chapter 13, "Profiling and Monitoring Microsoft SQL Server 2005." To use the Database Engine Tuning Advisor, complete the following steps:

1. In SQL Server Management Studio, select Database Engine Tuning Advisor on the Tools menu. Use the Connect To Server dialog box to connect to the server you want to use.

2. The Database Engine Tuning Advisor opens to start a new session, as shown in Figure 9-10. On the Workload tab, type a name for the session, such as **Personnel DB Check**. Using the Database For Workload Analysis drop-down list provided, select a database to which Database Tuning Advisor will connect for analyzing the workload.

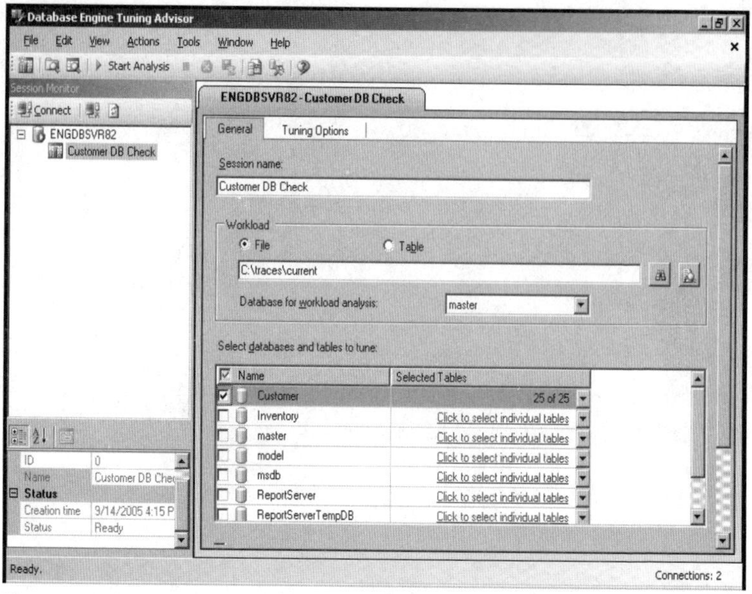

Figure 9-10 The Database Engine Tuning Advisor

- If you saved the trace data to a file, select File on the Workload panel, and then click the Browse For A Workload File button (the binoculars icon). Next, use the Select Workload File dialog box to select the trace file you previously created, and then click Open.
- If you saved the trace data to a table, select Table on the Workload panel, and then click the Browse For A Workload Table button (the binoculars icon). Next, use the Select Workload Table dialog box to specify which SQL Server to connect to and the source table to use.

3. Select the database you want to analyze. You can analyze multiple databases as well as individual tables within specific databases if you want. In most cases, you will want to examine a single database and possibly a subset of tables to reduce the analysis time. Because you are using a trace file, the analysis does not have to be performed on the server where the database(s) you are tuning is located.

4. Select the tables to analyze. If you select a database for tuning, all tables are selected for tuning by default. Click in the appropriate cell under Selected Tables to display a list of tables in the selected database. Select the check box for the associated table you want added or click the Name check box to add all tables.

5. Select the Tuning Options tab, as shown in Figure 9-11. You can limit the tuning time by setting a specific stop time. By default, the stop time is approximately one hour from the time you created the session.

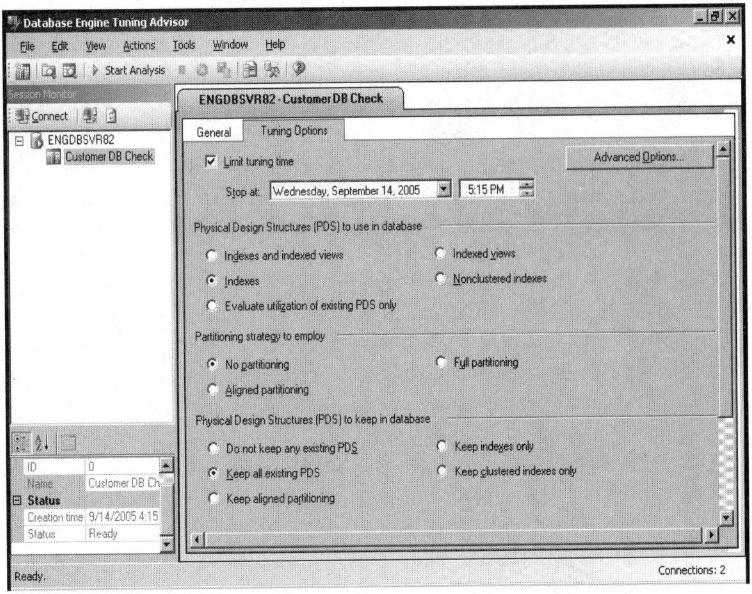

Figure 9-11   The Tuning Options tab of the Database Tuning Advisor

6. From the Physical Design Structures (PDS) To Use In Database options, select the type of structures that you want the tuning wizard to recommend. The options are as follows:

   ■ **Indexes and Indexed Views**   The Database Engine Tuning Advisor will recommend both clustered and nonclustered indexes as well as indexed views to improve performance.

   ■ **Indexes**   The Database Engine Tuning Advisor will recommend clustered and nonclustered indexes to improve performance.

   ■ **Indexed Views**   The Database Engine Tuning Advisor will recommend only indexed views to improve performance.

   ■ **Nonclustered Indexes**   The Database Engine Tuning Advisor will recommend only nonclustered indexes to improve performance.

   ■ **Evaluate Utilization of Existing PDS Only**   The Database Engine Tuning Advisor will not recommend options for improving performance and instead will only analyze the usage of existing structures.

   Note   This option cannot be used with the Keep All Exiting PDS option under Physical Design Structure To Keep In Database.

7. Use the Partitioning Strategy To Employ options to determine if the Database Engine Tuning Advisor should consider partitioning strategies. The options are as follows:

- **No Partitioning**   The Database Engine Tuning Advisor will not consider any partitioning strategies.

- **Aligned Partitioning**   Newly recommended structures will be partition-aligned to make partitions easy to maintain. (This option cannot be used with the Keep Indexes Only option under Physical Design Structure To Keep In Database.)

- **Full Partitioning**   Newly recommended structures will be partitioned to provide the best performance for the workload.

8. Use the Physical Design Structures To Keep In Database options to determine which (if any) existing structures will be considered for removal from the database. The options are as follows:

- **Do Not Keep Any Existing PDS**   The Database Engine Tuning Advisor will consider all existing structures for possible removal from the database.

- **Keep All Existing PDS**   The Database Engine Tuning Advisor will not consider any existing structures for possible removal from the database.

- **Keep Aligned Partitioning**   The Database Engine Tuning Advisor will retain existing partitioned-aligned structures, and any recommended new structures will be aligned with the existing partitioning scheme. (Aligned Partitioning must also be selected as the Partitioning Strategy To Employ option).

- **Keep Indexes Only**   The Database Engine Tuning Advisor will keep existing clustered and nonclustered indexes. All other structures will be considered for possible removal from the database.

- **Keep Clustered Indexes Only**   The Database Engine Tuning Advisor will keep existing clustered indexes. All other structures will be considered for possible removal from the database.

 Note   If you have selected a strong, representative snapshot of database activity in the trace, you will probably want to select an option other than Keep All Existing PDS and let the Database Engine Tuning Advisor make the appropriate suggestions for you to ensure that existing structures do not conflict with the recommendations the wizard may make.

9. Click the Advanced Options button to set advanced options, as shown in Figure 9-12. The advanced options are as follows:

- **Define Max. Space For Recommendations (MB)**   Sets the maximum space that can be used by recommended structures. The default value depends on the database and structures selected.

- **Max. Columns Per Index**   Sets the maximum number of columns that can be used in a single index. The default is 1,024, which allows all the columns in a table to be considered.

- **Online Index Recommendations**   Sets the type of indexing recommendations. By default, the Database Engine Tuning Advisor uses recommendations that require the server to be taken offline. Alternately, you can elect to generate online recommendations when possible or to generate only online recommendations. Online recommendations can be performed when the server is online.

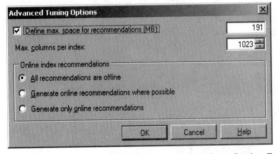

Figure 9-12   Advanced Options for the Database Engine Tuning Advisor

10. Click OK to close the Advanced Options dialog box. When you are ready to proceed, click the Start Analysis button or press F5. The Database Engine Tuning Advisor will begin analyzing your workload file. Progress is shown on the Progress tab. You can click Stop Analysis to stop the analysis at any time.

11. When it has finished the analysis, the wizard displays recommendations on the Recommendations tab, shown in Figure 9-13. The recommendations are listed in two separate panels, Partition Recommendations and Index Recommendations. You can view a tuning summary and tuning reports on the Reports tab of the Database Engine Tuning Advisor. Be sure to note the percentage of estimated improvement by making the recommended changes. In the example shown in the figure, the estimated improvement is 0%, which can be an indicator that the trace file may not accurately reflect the database workload

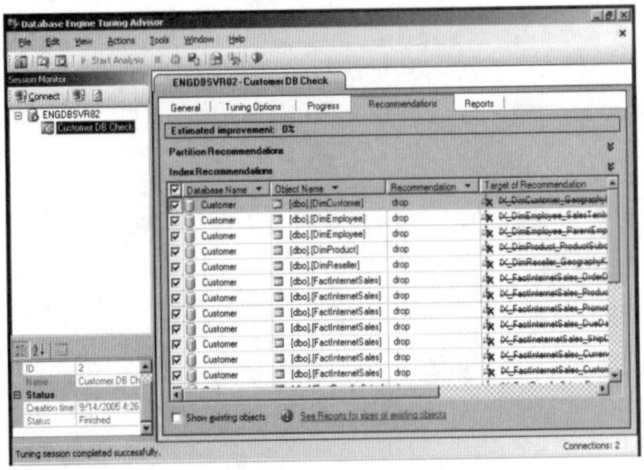

Figure 9-13   The Recommendations tab

12. You can now:

   ❑ Select Save Recommendations on the Actions menu to save the recommended changes as an SQL script file. You can review or edit the script using a text editor and schedule a job to implement the changes later.

   ❑ Select Apply Recommends on the Actions menu to apply the recommendations or schedule the recommendations to be applied later. In the Apply Recommendations, select Apply Now or Schedule For Later as appropriate, and then click OK. If you schedule for later, you can set the run date and time as well.

13. If you choose to apply the changes, the status of each change is displayed in the Applying Recommendations dialog box. The status of each change should be listed as Success. If you see a failure status, read the related error message to determine why the change failed.

Column Constraints and Rules

Column constraints and rules are important aspects of database administration. You use constraints to control the way column values are used, such as whether a value must be unique or whether it must have a specific format. Although you usually apply constraints directly to a specific column, you also can use rules to create constraints that you can apply to multiple tables in a database.

Using Constraints

SQL Server enforces the uniqueness of column values using unique and primary key constraints. You will often use unique constraints to create secondary keys (for nonclustered indexes) that you can use in conjunction with the primary key. Foreign key constraints identify the relationships between tables and ensure that referential integrity is maintained. Other types of constraints that you may want to use are check and not null constraints. Check constraints restrict the format or range of acceptable values for columns. Not null constraints prevent null values in a column.

Constraints can apply to columns or to entire tables. A column constraint is specified as part of a column definition and applies only to that column. A table constraint is declared independently from a column definition and can apply to several columns in the table. You must use table constraints when you want to include more than one column in a constraint. For example, if a table has three columns in the primary key, you must use a table constraint to include all three columns in the primary key.

Setting Unique Constraints

When you set a unique constraint on a column or columns, SQL Server automatically creates a unique index, and then checks for duplicate values. If duplicate key values exist the index creation operation is cancelled and an error message displays. SQL Server also checks the data each time you add data to the table. If the new data contains duplicate keys, the insert or update operation is rolled back and an error message is generated. You can specify that duplicate keys should be ignored by using the IGNORE_DUP_KEY option.

In SQL Server Management Studio, you make a unique index by setting the option Is Unique to Yes when creating the index, as described in the section titled "Creating Indexes" earlier in this chapter, or by selecting the Unique check box on the General page of the Index Properties dialog box. In Transact-SQL, you can set the unique constraint when you create the index, as shown in the following example:

```
USE OrderSystemDB
CREATE UNIQUE INDEX [Cust ID Index]
ON Sales.Customers(cust_id)
```

A nonclustered index is created unless a clustered index is explicitly specified, such as:

```
USE Customer
CREATE UNIQUE CLUSTERED INDEX [Cust ID Index]
ON Sales.Customers(cust_id)
```

Designating Primary Key Constraints

SQL Server also allows you to designate any column or group of columns as a primary key, but primary keys are often defined for identity columns. A table can have only one primary key, and because unique values are required, no primary key column can accept null values. Also, when you use multiple columns, the values of all the columns are combined to determine uniqueness.

As with unique constraints, SQL Server creates a unique index for the primary key columns. With primary key constraints, however, the index is created as a clustered index—unless a clustered index already exists on the table or a nonclustered index is explicitly specified.

In SQL Server Management Studio, you set the primary key when designing a new table or modifying an existing table by completing the following steps:

1. Clear the Allow Nulls option check box for any columns that will be used in the primary key.

2. Select the column or columns that you want to use as the primary key by pressing Ctrl and clicking the shaded box to the left of the column name.

3. Click Set Primary Key on the toolbar or select Set Primary Key on the Table Designer menu.

You can also set the primary key when you create or alter tables using Transact-SQL. Examples are shown in Sample 9-13.

Sample 9-13   Creating a Table and Its Columns with a Primary Key Constraint

```
USE CUSTOMER
CREATE TABLE Sales.Customers
    (cust_id int NOT NULL,
    cust_lname varchar(40) NOT NULL,
    cust_fname varchar(20) NOT NULL,
```

```
    phone char(12) NOT NULL,
    CONSTRAINT PK_Cust PRIMARY KEY (cust_id))

USE CUSTOMER
ALTER TABLE Sales.Customers
    ADD CONSTRAINT PK_Cust PRIMARY KEY (cust_id)
```

Using Foreign Key Constraints

Foreign key constraints identify the relationships between tables and ensure that referential integrity is maintained. A foreign key in one table points to a candidate key in another table. Foreign keys prevent changes that would leave rows with foreign key values when there are no candidate keys with that value in the related table. You cannot insert a row with a foreign key value if there is no candidate key with that value. The exception is when you insert a null foreign key value.

In the following example, the *Orders* table establishes a foreign key referencing the *Customer* table defined earlier:

```
CREATE TABLE Sales.Orders
    (order_nmbr int,
    order_item varchar(20),
    qty_ordered int,
    cust_id int
        FOREIGN KEY REFERENCES Sales.Customers(cust_id)
        ON DELETE NO ACTION
)
```

The ON DELETE clause defines that actions are taken if you try to delete a row to which existing foreign keys point. The ON DELETE clause has several options:

- **NO ACTION**   Specifies that the deletion fails with an error and the delete action on the row is rolled back.
- **CASCADE**   Specifies that all rows with foreign keys pointing to the deleted row are to be deleted as well. (CASCADE cannot be used if there is an INSTEAD OF trigger ON DELETE.)
- **SET NULL**   Specifies that all values that make up the foreign key are set to NULL if the corresponding row in the parent table is deleted. (Foreign key columns must be nullable.)
- **SET DEFAULT**   Specifies that all the values that make up the foreign key are set to their default values if the corresponding row in the parent table is deleted. (Foreign key columns must have default definitions. If a column is nullable and there is no explicit default, the column is set to NULL.)

You can also set an ON UPDATE clause in Transact-SQL, as shown in the following example:

```
CREATE TABLE Sales.Orders
    (order_nmbr int,
    order_item varchar(20),
    qty_ordered int,
    cust_id int
```

```
FOREIGN KEY REFERENCES Sales.Customers(cust_id)
ON UPDATE CASCADE
)
```

The ON UPDATE clause defines the actions that are taken if you try to update a row to which existing foreign keys point. The clause also supports the NO ACTION, CASCADE, SET NULL, and SET DEFAULT options.

Using Check Constraints

Check constraints allow you to control the format or range of values, or both, that are associated with tables and columns. For example, you could use this type of constraint to specify that postal codes must be entered in the format 99999 or that phone numbers must be entered as 9999999999.

In SQL Server Management Studio, you set check constraints when designing a new table or modifying an existing table by completing the following steps:

1. Select Check Constraints from the Table Designer menu. This displays the Check Constraints dialog box shown in Figure 9-14.

2. You can now:

   ❑ Edit an existing constraint. First select it in the Selected Check Constraint selection list, and then modify the existing constraint expression and definition using the boxes provided.

   ❑ Delete a constraint. First select it in the Selected Check Constraint selection list, and then click Delete. In the Delete Object dialog box, confirm the deletion by clicking OK.

   ❑ Create a new constraint. Click Add, and then type a name and description of the constraint in the boxes provided. Click the button to the right of the Expression box, enter the check expression, and then click OK.

3. Click Close when you are finished working with check constraints.

Check constraint expressions specify the permitted characters using regular expressions:

- Use [0-9] to indicate that any numeral from 0 to 9 is permitted in the designated position. As an example, to format a column to accommodate a nine-digit postal code, you would use the following expression:

  ```
  PostalCode LIKE '[0-9][0-9][0-9][0-9][0-9][0-9][0-9][0-9][0-9]'
  ```

- Use [a-z] or [A-Z] to indicate that any lowercase letter from a to z or any uppercase letter from A to Z is permitted in the designated position. As an example, to format a column to accommodate any five-letter word with the first letter capitalized, you would use the following expression:

  ```
  PostalCode LIKE '[A-Z][a-z][a-z][a-z][a-z]'
  ```

- Use [a-zA-Z0-9] to indicate that any letter or numeral is permitted in the designated position. As an example, to format a column to accommodate any five-character value, you would use the following expression:

  ```
  PostalCode LIKE '[a-zA-Z0-9][a-zA-Z0-9][a-zA-Z0-9][a-zA-Z0-9]
  [a-zA-Z0-9]'
  ```

You can also add and remove constraints in Transact-SQL by using the CREATE TABLE or ALTER TABLE command, such as in the following example:

```
USE CUSTOMER
ALTER TABLE Sales.Customers
ADD CONSTRAINT CheckZipFormat
CHECK (([PostalCode] like '[0-9][0-9][0-9][0-9][0-9][0-9][0-9][0-9]
[0-9]'))
```

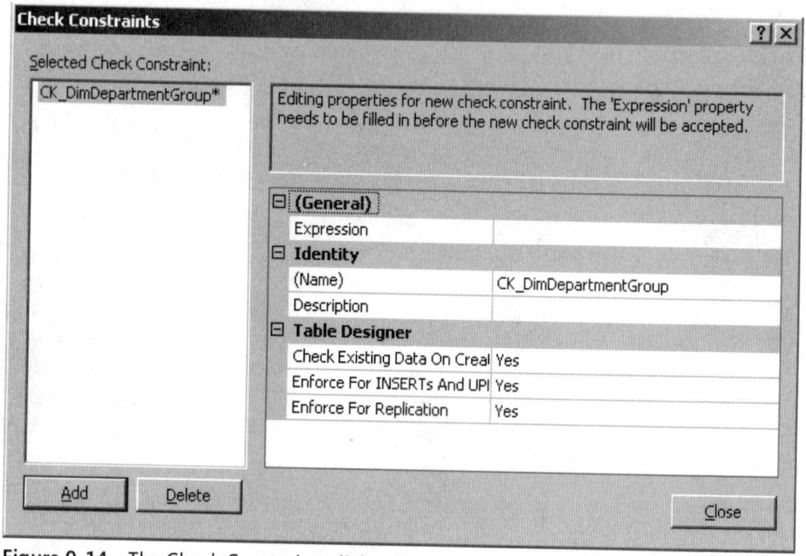

Figure 9-14   The Check Constraints dialog box

Using Not Null Constraints

Not null constraints specify that the column does not accept null values. Normally, you set not null constraints when you create the table. You can also set not null constraints when you alter a table. In SQL Server Management Studio, the Allow Nulls column in the Table view controls the use of this constraint. If the Allow Nulls column is cleared, the related table column does not accept nulls.

Using Rules

A *rule* is a constraint that you can apply to multiple columns or tables. Rules perform the same function as check constraints and are maintained in SQL Server 2005 for backward compatibility with earlier versions of SQL Server. Microsoft recommends that you use check constraints rather than rules. Check constraints are more customizable and more concise than rules. For example, although you can apply only one rule to a column, you can apply multiple check constraints to a column.

Rules can be useful in certain situations, however. Constraints are defined within table definitions, whereas rules are independently defined objects, and therefore, are not limited to only one particular table. Rules are also bound to a table after the table is created, and they are not deleted if the table is deleted. Another advantage of rules is that they can be bound to any user-defined data type.

If you use care when you apply rules, you can still use rules in situations that make them a better choice than constraints. To view existing rules in SQL Server Management Studio, complete the following steps:

1. In SQL Server Management Studio, connect to the server instance that contains the database in which you want to work.

2. In Object Explorer view, expand the Databases node, and then expand the database to show its resource nodes.

3. Expand the Programmability and Rules nodes. You will see any existing rules listed.

The Transact-SQL commands for creating and managing rules are CREATE RULE and DROP RULE. You can use CREATE RULE as follows:

```
CREATE RULE CheckFormatZip
AS @value LIKE '[09][09][09][09][09][09][09][09][09]'
```

After you have created a rule, you must activate the rule in order to use it. You use a special stored procedure called *sp_bindrule* to bind the rule to a particular table column or user-defined data type. You can also use *sp_unbindrule* to remove a rule that is bound to a table column or user-defined data type. Use the following syntax when binding and unbinding rules:

```
sp_bindrule <'rule'>, '<object_name'>, [<'futureonly_flag'>]
sp_unbindrule 'object name'
```

Chapter 10
Importing, Exporting, and Transforming Data

<table>
<tr><td colspan="2">In this chapter:</td></tr>
<tr><td>Working with Integration Services</td><td>315</td></tr>
<tr><td>Creating Packages with the SQL Server Import and Export Wizard</td><td>319</td></tr>
<tr><td>Understanding BCP</td><td>336</td></tr>
<tr><td>BCP Scripts</td><td>341</td></tr>
<tr><td>Using the BULK INSERT Command</td><td>342</td></tr>
</table>

Whether you need to move data from a legacy system to a new system permanently or you want to continually move data back and forth for data warehousing, Microsoft SQL Server 2005 Integration Services (SSIS) should be your first choice. With Integration Services, you have access to an extraction, transformation, and loading (ETL) platform that can be fully customized for your specific application and is optimized for high-performance data movement and transformation. You can use Integration Services to copy and transform data to or from almost any data source, including flat file, OLE DB, and ODBC data sources. In addition, BULK COPY (BCP) remains available in SQL Server 2005 as a basic means of importing and exporting data.

Working with Integration Services

As an administrator, the Integration Services tasks you will most often perform include:

- Installing the Integration Services components using SQL Server 2005 Setup.
- Using the SQL Server Import And Export Wizard to move data.
- Upgrading DTS 2000 to SQL Server 2005 Integration Services.
- Managing or migrating existing DTS 2000 Packages to Integration Services as necessary.
- Creating and managing Integration Services packages using Business Intelligence Development Studio.
- Running Integration Services packages using Business Intelligence Development Studio, SQL Server Management Studio, or the dtexec command-line utility.

Before you try to perform any of these tasks, you should know how the Integration Services feature works and how it is used. Once you are familiar with Integration

Services, its tools, and its structures, you will be better prepared to manage its components.

Getting Started with Integration Services

Integration Services are designed to move data accurately and efficiently as well as to convert or transform data between heterogeneous data sources. You can use Integration Services when you want to perform any of the following tasks:

- Move data between heterogeneous systems, such as from Oracle to SQL Server or from SQL Server to Oracle
- Move data between SQL Servers, including primary and foreign keys
- Move data from Microsoft Access or Microsoft Excel to SQL Server or from SQL Server to Access or Excel
- Extract data; transform the data by performing column mappings, filling in missing values, and so on; and then import the data on the destination system
- Copy views from one database to another

Although SQL Server 2005 supports existing Data Transformation Services (DTS) packages and provides an upgrade/migration path for those packages, Integration Services are the functional replacement for DTS. The architecture of Integration Services is very different from that of DTS. With DTS, the workflow controls and the data movement were all managed through a single component: the DTS engine. The Integration Services process separates workflow controls and data movement using two separate components:

- **Integration Services runtime engine** Stores package layout, executes packages, controls workflow between tasks, and provides other essential runtime services.
- **Integration Services data flow engine** Manages data movement and transformation and supports multiple sources, multiple transformations, and multiple destinations.

Integration Services has an extensible object model that includes a runtime API and data flow API that supports the Microsoft .NET Framework. These APIs allow developers to extend and customize the Integration Services object model. Custom extensions can be developed for tasks, log providers, connection managers, data flow components, and more.

Integration Services Tools

The primary tools for working with Integration Services are the Business Intelligence Development Studio and SQL Server Management Studio. Business Intelligence Development Studio is used to build data transformation solutions, and SQL Server Management Studio is used to manage Integration Services packages. Within Business Intelligence Development Studio, you can access Integration Services Designer, the graphical tool for creating Integration Services packages.

The SQL Server Import And Export Wizard is the new face of the old DTS Import/ Export Wizard. The wizard has been updated to support Integration Services and has been extended to provide better support for data in flat files and for real-time preview of data. Integration Services packages created by using the Import And Export Wizard can be opened in Business Intelligence Development Studio and then can be extended using Integration Services Designer.

Tip   The SQL Server Import And Export Wizard can run the import/ export process between any of the available data sources; you do not have to set SQL Server as either the source or the destination. For example, you can use the DTS Import/Export Wizard to copy data from a text file to an Excel spreadsheet.

As with DTS, Integration Services packages are stored in either the *msdb* database or in the file system. The Integration Services Service is responsible for managing package storage. You can manage packages from the command line using the dtutil command-line utility. You can use dtutil to copy, move, sign, and delete packages. To run packages, you can use Business Intelligence Development Studio or SQL Server Management Studio to access the Execute Package Utility (dtexecui). The command-line counterpart is the dtexec command-line utility.

Integration Services includes the Package Configuration Wizard to assist with configuration management. By running the Integration Services package deployment utility from within Business Intelligence Development Studio, you can install packages to the *msdb* database in an instance of SQL Server 2005 or to the file system. The deployment utility automatically detects and includes all package dependencies, making it easier to deploy packages.

SQL Server 2005 includes tools for managing and migrating DTS packages from previous versions of SQL Server. When you connect to a server in SQL Server Management Studio's Object Explorer, you can expand the DTS 2000 Packages node to list available DTS 2000 packages. You can edit or execute these packages and migrate the packages to the Integration Services format.

Integration Services and Data Providers

Data providers are a key part of Integration Services. Without these data providers, you would not be able to communicate with other systems. SQL Server includes .NET Framework, OLE DB, and ODBC data providers for the following:

- SQL Server
- Oracle
- Microsoft Access and Excel
- Microsoft Analysis Services
- Microsoft Data Mining Services
- Microsoft Internet Publishing
- SQLXML
- Text files

The text file driver is the all-purpose driver for import and export procedures. If you do not have a native provider for your legacy database and you cannot use the generic ODBC providers, you can usually export your data to a text file and then import it into SQL Server. You can go from SQL Server to a legacy system using the same technique.

Integration Services Packages

The SQL Server Import And Export Wizard is the fastest, easiest way to move data between systems. You use the SQL Server Import And Export Wizard to create basic Integration Services packages, which you can later view or modify using Integration Services Designer. Packages are simply sets of tasks for importing, transforming, and exporting data that you can reuse or schedule to run as often as needed. Packages can be:

- Stored in the *msdb* database on a local or remote server.
- Shared through SQL Server Meta Data Services.
- Saved to the filesystem in DTSX files, which is useful when you want to copy, move, and e-mail packages to another location.

 Note Integration Services does not support storage in Visual Basic files. DTS 2000 packages that are stored in Visual Basic files cannot be migrated to SQL Server 2005 Integration Services.

You execute packages directly from SQL Server Management Studio or Business Intelligence Development Studio. You can also execute packages from the command prompt using the dtexec command-line utility. Within Integration Services packages, you will find the following features:

- **Connections** Store information about the source or destination of data. In a connection, you specify the data provider to use (such as the Microsoft OLE DB Data Provider for SQL Server), the server to which you want to connect, the login to use for the connection, and the database to work with for the import/export operation. In Integration Services Designer, you select connections using the Data menu.
- **Tasks** Set the operations that need to be performed within the package. Tasks can consist of ActiveX scripts, SQL scripts, SQL queries, commands to transfer SQL Server objects, data-driven queries, bulk insert commands, and external processes to execute. You can even have Integration Services send e-mail when a package completes.
- **Workflow containers** Set when and how a particular task should be executed, such as on completion, on failure, or on success. For example, you could schedule a task that sends e-mail on failure or on success.
- **Control flow procedures** A control flow consists of one or more tasks and containers that execute sequentially or in parallel when the package runs. Precedence constraints connect the package's tasks and containers and define the conditions for running the next task or container in the package control flow.

Tasks and containers can also be grouped in a loop and run repeatedly as a unit within the package control flow.

■ **Data flow procedures**   Set the step-by-step transformation process for the data. Before you can add a data flow to a package, the package control flow must include a Data Flow task that is responsible for running the data flow. A data flow consists of the source and destination adapters that extract and load data, the transformations that modify and extend data, and the paths that link adapters and transformations.

You can store an Integration Services package on any SQL Server, and you do not need to create or store it on the source or destination server associated with the package. If you are editing, modifying, scheduling, or just viewing an Integration Services package, you need to use the user account of the package owner or an account that operates under the sysadmin role on the SQL Server on which the package is actually stored.

Creating Packages with the SQL Server Import and Export Wizard

Creating an Integration Services package is one of the most complex tasks you will perform as a database administrator. Fortunately, the SQL Server Import And Export Wizard is designed to help you build Integration Services packages with minimal difficulty, but it is still an involved process. To help reduce complexity, we can divide the creation process into stages and then examine each stage individually. The stages you use to create Integration Services packages are as follows:

■ Stage 1: Source and Destination Configuration
■ Stage 2: Copy or Query
■ Stage 3: Formatting and Transformation
■ Stage 4: Save and Execute

To begin using Integration Services, start the SQL Server Import And Export Wizard, and then click Next to advance to the Source selection page. You start the SQL Server Import And Export Wizard in SQL Server Management Studio by completing the following steps:

1. In SQL Server Management Studio, connect to the server instance containing the database with which you want to work.

2. In Object Explorer view, expand the Databases node. Select a database, and then right-click its name, point to Tasks, and select either Import Data or Export Data.

You can also run the SQL Server Import And Export Wizard from the command line by typing **dtswizard**.

Stage 1: Source and Destination Configuration

The first task associated with creating an Integration Services package is to choose the source and destination for the import/export operation. If you started SQL

Server Import And Export Wizard and clicked Next, you will see the Choose A Data Source page. At this point, complete the following steps:

1. Use the Data Source drop-down list box to select the source for the import/ export operation. SQL Server has .NET Framework, OLE DB, and ODBC data providers. These data providers allow you to work with SQL Server, Oracle, Access and Excel, Microsoft Analysis Services, Microsoft Data Mining Services, Microsoft Internet Publishing, SQLXML, and flat files. Select the data source that matches the type of file, application, or database you want to use as the source. For example, if you are copying from an Excel spreadsheet, choose Microsoft Excel as the source for the import/export operation.

2. Fill in any additional information required to establish a connection to the source. (The source you select determines what additional information you need to supply.) Click Next.

3. Use the Destination drop-down list box to select the destination for the import/export operation.

4. Fill in any additional information required to establish a connection to the destination. As with the source, the destination you select determines what additional information you need to supply.

5. Click Next to proceed to the next stage of the operation: Copy or Query.

If choosing a source and destination were as easy as these simple steps appear, this task would require very little effort. But sometimes it is not clear what additional information you need to provide because there are several different kinds of sources and destinations that you can select. These sources include:

- .NET Framework Data Provider connections.
- File-based data connections.
- Server-based connections to databases other than SQL Server.
- Server-based connections to SQL Server.
- Flat files.

We will examine each of these connection categories more closely.

.NET Framework Data Provider Connections

SQL Server 2005 includes .NET Framework Data providers for ODBC, Oracle, and SQL Server. The .NET Framework Data Provider for ODBC is the only ODBC driver supported. You configure the .NET Framework Data Providers through a dialog box similar to the one shown in Figure 10-1. You must provide the following information, depending on the .NET Framework Data Provider you are using:

- If you are using .NET Framework Data Provider for ODBC, you must specify the connection string, the data source name (DSN), and the name of the ODBC driver to use when connecting to the data source.

- If you are using .NET Framework Data Provider for Oracle, you must specify the connection string to use in the ConnectionString box, the User ID and Password to use in establishing the connection, and the name of the database to which you want to connect in the Data Source text box. As necessary, you can configure other initialization, pooling, and security parameters as well.

■ If you are using .NET Framework Data Provider for SQL Server, you must specify the Network Library (options are provided on a drop-down list when you click in the text box), the connection string to use in the ConnectionString box, the User ID and Password to use in establishing the connection, and the name of the database to which you want to connect in the Data Source text box. As necessary, you can configure other initialization, pooling, and security parameters as well.

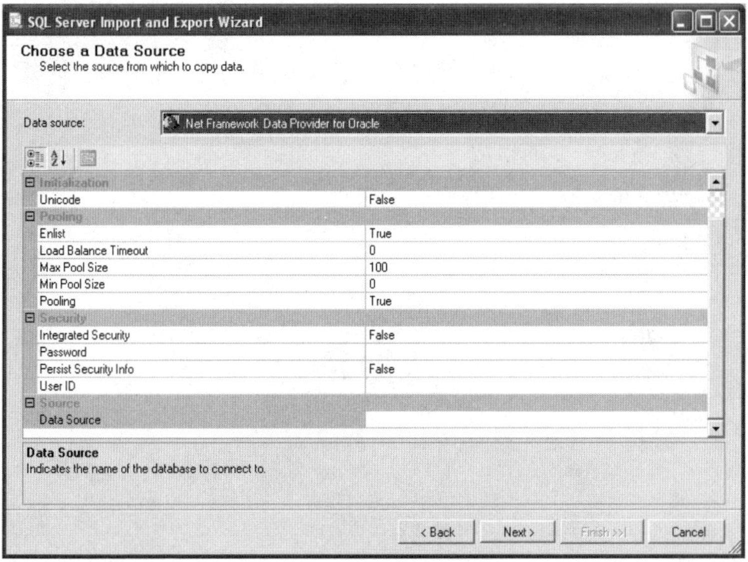

Figure 10-1 SQL Server Import And Export Wizard page for .NET Framework Data provider connections

File-Based Data Connections

You use file-based data connections with applications and databases that are file-based. For example, you would use this type of connection with Access and Excel. You use a dialog box similar to the one shown in Figure 10-2 to configure file-based connections. For Access, you must provide the following information:

■ **File Name** The full file name or Uniform Naming Convention (UNC) path to the source or destination file, such as //omega/data/excel/cust.xls

■ **User Name** A valid user name for accessing the source or destination file

■ **Password** A valid password for accessing the source or destination file

For Excel, you must provide the following information:

- **Excel File Path** The full file name or Uniform Naming Convention (UNC) path to the source or destination file, such as //omega/data/excel/cust.xls
- **Excel Version** The version of Excel from which you are copying data

Note If the first row of the Excel spreadsheet does not have column names, be sure to clear the First Row Has Column Names check box.

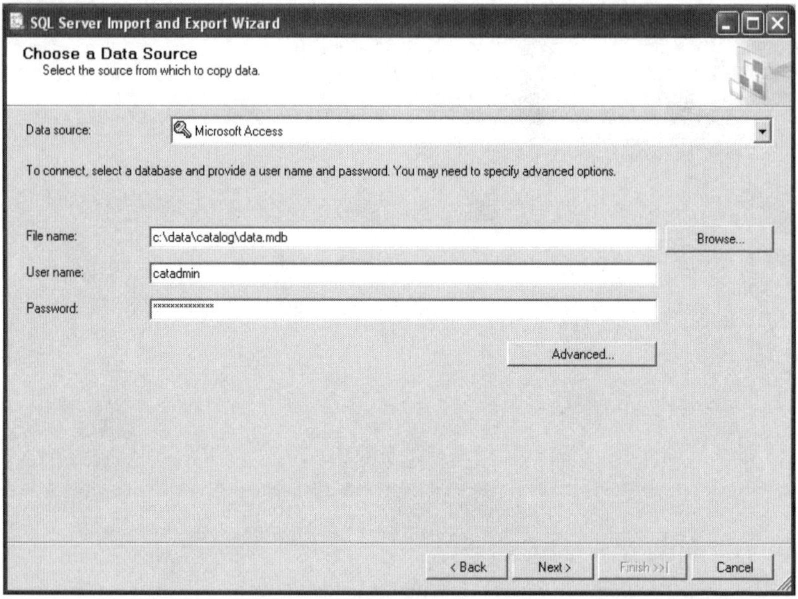

SQL Server Import and Export Wizard

Choose a Data Source
Select the source from which to copy data.

Data source: Microsoft Access

To connect, select a database and provide a user name and password. You may need to specify advanced options.

File name: c:\data\catalog\data.mdb   Browse...

User name: catadmin

Password: ***************

Advanced...

< Back   Next >   Finish >>| Cancel

Figure 10-2 SQL Server Import and Export Wizard page for an Access file-based data connection

Server-Based Connections to Databases Other Than SQL Server

You use server-based data connections to connect to databases other than SQL Server. Use this type of connection with Microsoft OLE DB Provider for Oracle, Microsoft OLE DB Provider for Analysis Services 9.0, Microsoft OLE DB Provider for Data Mining Services, Microsoft OLE DB Provider for OLAP Services 8.0, and SQLXMLOLEDB. You configure server-based connections by setting Data Link properties that connect to a data source. Data Link properties have four components:

- An OLE DB provider, which you select from the Source or Destination selection list in the SQL Server Import And Export Wizard.
- Connection options, which you set using the Connection tab in the Data Link Properties dialog box. Connection options typically include a data source name or connection string accompanied by the user name and password information needed to log on to the database.

- Advanced options, which you set using the Advanced tab in the Data Link Properties dialog box. Advanced options let you configure network settings, time-outs, and access permissions (as long as these options are configurable).

- Initialization properties, which you view using the All tab in the Data Link Properties dialog box. The initialization properties display all the options you have configured for the provider and provide a central location for editing values. Simply double-click a value to edit the associated settings.

If you are using Oracle, the Oracle client and networking components must be installed on the system running SQL Server. If these components are not installed, you will not be able to use the OLE DB provider. Assuming that the Oracle client is installed on your system, you can set the Data Link properties for Oracle by completing the following steps:

1. In the SQL Server Import And Export Wizard, select Microsoft OLE DB Provider for Oracle on the Source or Destination selection list, and then click Properties to display the Connection tab of the Data Link Properties dialog box, as shown in Figure 10-3.

2. Type the name of the Oracle server to which you want to connect in the Enter A Server Name text box.

3. Then type the user name and password needed to log on to the database in the appropriate text boxes.

4. To test the connection to the server, click Test Connection. If the connection fails, you may have improperly configured the Oracle client.

5. You can use the Advanced and All tabs to view additional options. Change these options as necessary.

6. When you have finished setting the Data Link properties for Oracle, click OK.

Figure 10-3 The Connection tab of the Data Link Properties dialog box for Oracle

Server-Based Connections to SQL Server

In addition to using the .NET Framework Provider for SQL Server, you can connect to SQL Server using the SQL Native Client or the Microsoft OLE DB Provider for SQL Server. The options you have available using either of these alternate connections are shown in Figure 10-4, and you can configure the connection by completing the following steps:

1. Use the Server Name drop-down list box to select the SQL Server for the connection. If the server you want to use is not listed, type in the server name.

2. Next, select an authentication method. Type a user name and password, if necessary.

3. Use the Database drop-down list box to select a database. You must provide valid credentials and those credentials must have sufficient privileges.

4. Click Advanced to set advanced options for the driver/provider.

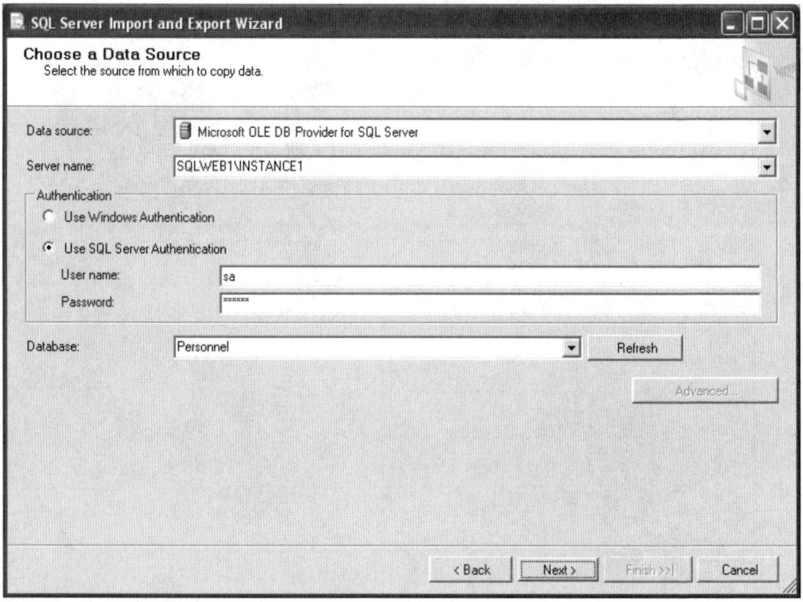

Figure 10-4   SQL Server Import And Export Wizard page for SQL Native Client or Microsoft OLE DB Provider for SQL Server

Importing and Exporting Flat Files

You can use flat files as a data source or destination. When you do, you must provide additional information about the input or output formatting. The steps in the process are similar when using flat files as either the source or the destination. To use text files as a data source, use the process below as an example and complete the following steps:

1. From the SQL Server Import And Export Wizard, choose the Flat File Source option. Then enter the full file name or UNC path to the file with which you want to work.

Tip If the file is in use, you will get an error message. Click OK, and then select the file again. (This forces the SQL Server Import And Export Wizard to try to read the file again. Otherwise, you will not be able to edit the Format specifications for the file.)

2. After you enter the text file information, the wizard page is updated as shown in Figure 10-5.

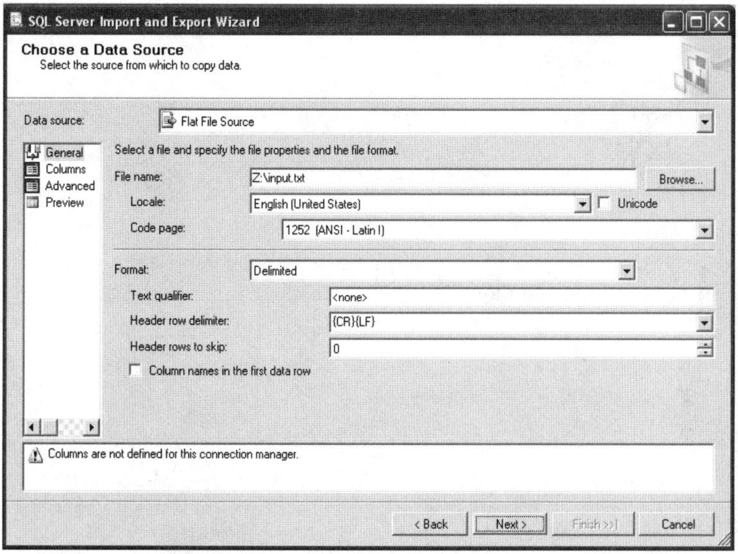

Figure 10-5   SQL Server Import and Export Wizard page for a flat file data source

3. The values in the Locale and Code Page boxes are set based on the file you have selected. If the values are incorrect, select the appropriate values.

4. Select the file type using the Format drop-down list box. The file must be formatted in an acceptable flat file format such as ANSI (ASCII text), IBM EBCDIC, MAC, OEM (original equipment manufacturer), UTF-7, or UTF-8.

Note   When you are importing data, OEM normally refers to the native SQL Server format. If the file contains Unicode characters, select the Unicode check box.

5. Specify how the file is delimited. If the file has fixed-width columns, select the Fixed Width option from the Format selection list. If the columns are delimited with commas, tabs, semicolons, or other unique characters, select the Delimited option from the Format selection list.

6. Use the Text Qualifier box to specify the qualifier for text as Double Quote ("), Single Quote ('), or <None>.

7. Specify the header row delimiter using the Header Row Delimiter drop-down list box. The available options are:

   ❑ {CR} {LF} for carriage return and line feed

   ❑ {CR} for carriage return only

   ❑ {LF} for line feed only

   ❑ Semicolon

   ❑ Colon

   ❑ Comma

   ❑ Tab

   ❑ Vertical bar for the | character

8. To skip rows at the beginning of a file, use the Header Rows To Skip box to set the number of rows to skip.

Note   If you indicated that the first row contains column names, the first row is read and then the specified number of rows is skipped.

9. If the first row contains column headers, select the check box for the option Column Names In The First Data Row.

Note   Column headers make it easier to import data. If the file does not contain column names, you may want to click Cancel, add the column names to the first line, and then restart the import/export procedure.

10. This completes the General page options. For an export, the other pages are not available or applicable, so skip to step 17.

11. Select Columns from the selection list in the left pane of the wizard to proceed. The wizard will attempt to determine the row and column delimiters and then will display a preview of the data.

12. If you selected fixed-width columns, you must indicate to the SQL Server Import And Export Wizard where columns start and end. Vertical lines indicate the start and end of columns. Add column markers by clicking in the Source Data Columns area to create a column marker. Remove column markers by

double-clicking them. Move column markers by clicking them and dragging them to a new position.

13. If necessary, specify the end-of-row delimiter using the Row Delimiter drop-down list box.

14. If necessary, specify the column delimiter within rows.

15. Select the Advanced page from the selection list in the left pane of the wizard to configure the output properties for each column, including the output column name, output column width, and output data type. If there are different delimiters between columns, you can specify the delimiter on a per column basis.

16. Select the Preview page from the Data Source list to see the data format for the options you have chosen. If you notice data elements out of place, you should reconfigure the options before continuing. You may also need to modify the source file. In this case, click Cancel, modify the file, and then restart the SQL Server Import And Export Wizard.

17. Click Next when you are ready to select the destination for the import/export operation. After selecting the destination, you are ready to move on to the second stage of creating an Integration Services package.

Stage 2: Copy or Query

With most import or export procedures, the second stage of the process involves specifying tables and views to copy or building a query to specify the objects to transfer. You first select the operation using the dialog box shown in Figure 10-6, and then depending on the choice you have made, you will proceed as described in the following subsections.

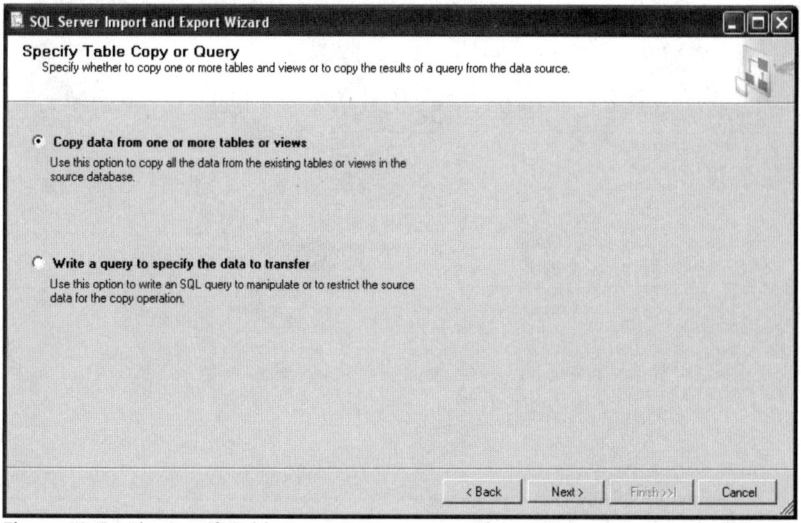

Figure 10-6   The Specify Table Copy Or Query page of the SQL Server Import And Export Wizard

Specifying Tables and Views to Copy

If you want to copy tables and views to the destination, you must select which tables and views you want to copy. When a text file is the data source, making the selection is easy—only one table is available, and you cannot select any views. If you are using any other data sources, however, you must select the tables and views you want to copy. You use the Select Source Tables And Views page of the wizard, shown in Figure 10-7, to make your selections.

To select tables and views, complete the following steps:

1. On the Specify Table Copy Or Query page (shown in Figure 10-6), select Copy Data From One Or More Tables Or Views, and then click Next.

2. On the Select Source Tables And Views Page (shown in Figure 10-7), select a table or view by clicking its entry, and then preview the data the table contains by clicking Preview.

3. When you find a table or view you want to copy, select the check box next to it in the Source column.

4. By default, the destination name of the table is set to be the same as the source table name. If you want to change the table name, edit the corresponding value in the Destination column.

5. If you want to manipulate the row values in a table, select the table, and then click the corresponding Edit button in the Mapping column. Mapping row values is covered in the section titled "Stage 3: Formatting and Transformation" later in this chapter.

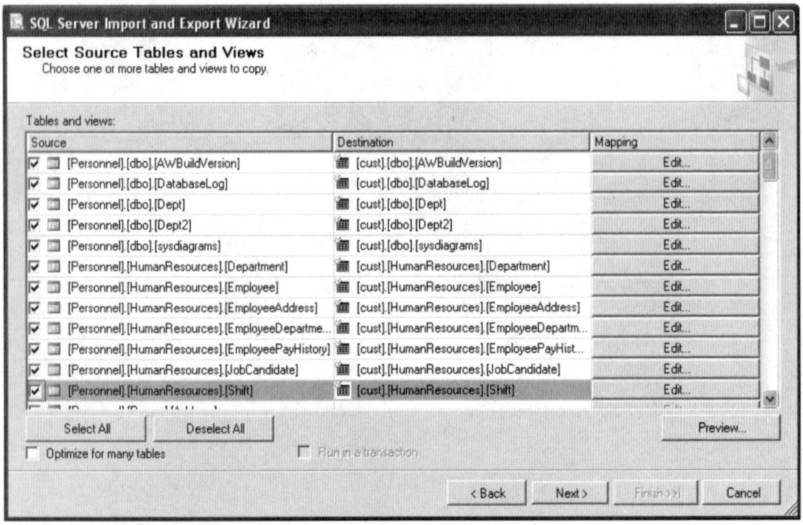

Figure 10-7 The Select Source Tables And Views page of the SQL Server Import And Export Wizard

Building a Query

Another way to select data for exporting is to build a query and execute it against the source file, spreadsheet, or database. Regardless of the type of data source you select, you build the query in the same way by completing the following steps:

1. On the Specify Table Copy Or Query page (shown in Figure 10-6), select Write A Query To Specify The Data To Transfer, and then click Next.

2. On the Provide A Source Query page, you can:

   ❏ Type a query directly in the text box provided, and then parse it to check for accuracy using the Parse button.

   ❏ Click Browse to open a previously saved query.

Tip   You can also create a query in your favorite query designer and then paste the results into the SQL Statement text box. See the discussion that follows for details on using the Query Designer provided in SQL Server Management Studio.

3. Click Next. On the Select Source Tables And Views page, the tables and views selected by the previously defined query are listed and selected.

4. By default, the destination name of the table is set to be the same as the source table name. If you want to change the table name, edit the corresponding value in the Destination column.

5. If you want to manipulate the row values in a table, select the table, and then click the corresponding Edit button in the Mapping column. Mapping row values is covered in the section titled "Stage 3: Formatting and Transformation" later in this chapter.

The Query Designer in SQL Server Management Studio provides the easiest way to design a query to export data. You can start and work with the Query Designer by completing the following steps:

1. In SQL Server Management Studio, connect to the server instance containing the database in which you want to work.

2. In Object Explorer view, expand the Databases node. Select a database, right-click it, and then select New Query to display a query window with its own toolbar. A similar list of options (with more selections) is provided on the Query menu.

3. Access the Query Designer by selecting Design Query In Editor on the Query menu or by pressing Ctrl+Shift+Q.

4. When you first start the Query Designer, the Add Table dialog box shown in Figure 10-8 is displayed. The Add Table dialog box has tabs that allow you to select the tables, views, functions, and synonyms you want to work with.

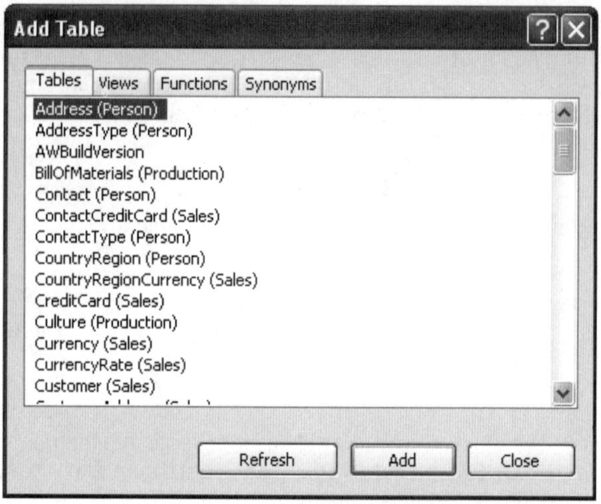

Figure 10-8   The Add Table dialog box

5. In the Add Table dialog box, select a table or other object that contains data you want to add to the query, and then click Add. This displays a view pane for the selected object, which you can use to add columns, fields, and so on to the query you are building. When you are finished working with the Add Table dialog box, click Close. You can display this dialog box again at any time by selecting Add Table on the Query Designer menu.

6. Use the view panes provided to select the columns and fields to use in the view, as shown in Figure 10-9. Your actions create a SELECT statement that can be used to generate the query.

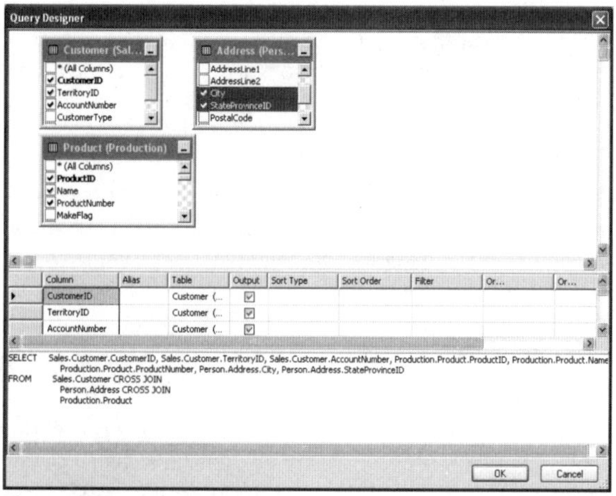

Figure 10-9   Query Designer

7. When you have finished designing the query, click OK to close the Query Designer window. The query you have generated is then added to the Query window.

8. The result of the Query Designer procedure is a complete SQL statement that you can use to select data for exporting. Click Parse to ensure that the query runs properly. If necessary, rebuild the query or remove statements that are causing errors.

9. Copy the query to the SQL Server Import And Export Wizard.

Stage 3: Formatting and Transformation

Transformation is the process of manipulating the source data and formatting it for the chosen destination. The way you transform and format data depends on the destination you chose. With most types of files, databases, and spreadsheets, you are guided through a column mapping and transformation process. But if you have chosen a text file as the destination, you must also specify the format of the output file. Because the formatting options are essentially the same as those used for importing, you can find more information about these options in the section titled "Importing and Exporting Flat Files" earlier in this chapter.

Unless you specify otherwise, the SQL Server Import And Export Wizard sets default mapping for all selected tables. This default mapping:

-   Specifies that every column in the source table is copied.

-   Maps the original column name, data type, nullability, size, precision, and scale to the destination table.

-   Appends the source data to the destination table or creates the destination table if it does not exist.

You can override the default mapping by completing the following steps:

1. The Select Source Tables And Views page lists the results of your query or all of the available tables in the source database, spreadsheet, or file that you have selected. If you have selected a particular table, you will see an Edit button in the Mapping column. Click this button to open the Column Mappings dialog box shown in Figure 10-10.

2. In the Column Mappings dialog box, set the general transfer options:

    -   **Create Destination Table** Creates the destination table before copying source data. If the destination table exists, you must select the check box for the Drop And Re-create Destination Table option or an error will occur.

    -   **Delete Rows In Destination Table** Deletes all rows in the destination table before copying the source data. Indexes and constraints on the destination table remain.

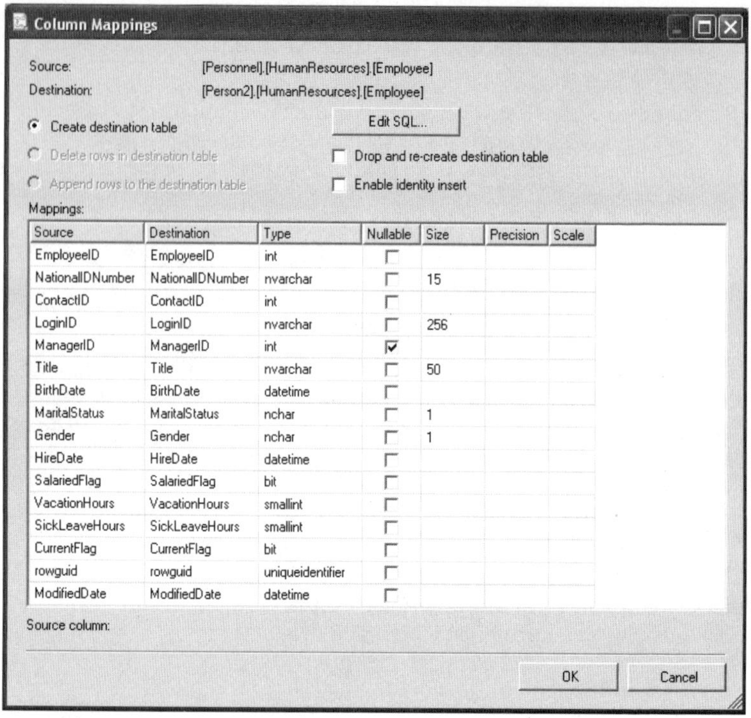

Column Mappings

Source: [Personnel].[HumanResources].[Employee]
Destination: [Person2].[HumanResources].[Employee]

(•) Create destination table   Edit SQL...

( ) Delete rows in destination table   ☐ Drop and re-create destination table

( ) Append rows to the destination table ☐ Enable identity insert

Mappings:

Source	Destination	Type	Nullable	Size	Precision	Scale
EmployeeID	EmployeeID	int	☐			
NationalIDNumber	NationalIDNumber	nvarchar	☐	15		
ContactID	ContactID	int	☐			
LoginID	LoginID	nvarchar	☐	256		
ManagerID	ManagerID	int	☑			
Title	Title	nvarchar	☐	50		
BirthDate	BirthDate	datetime	☐			
MaritalStatus	MaritalStatus	nchar	☐	1		
Gender	Gender	nchar	☐	1		
HireDate	HireDate	datetime	☐			
SalariedFlag	SalariedFlag	bit	☐			
VacationHours	VacationHours	smallint	☐			
SickLeaveHours	SickLeaveHours	smallint	☐			
CurrentFlag	CurrentFlag	bit	☐			
rowguid	rowguid	uniqueidentifier	☐			
ModifiedDate	ModifiedDate	datetime	☐			

Source column:

OK   Cancel

Figure 10-10   The Column Mappings dialog box

- **Append Rows to the Destination Table**   Inserts the source data into the destination table instead of overwriting existing data. This option does not affect existing data, indexes, or constraints in the destination table.

Note   Rows may not necessarily be appended to the end of the destination table. To determine where rows will be inserted, use a clustered index on the destination table.

- **Drop and Re-create Destination Table**   Drops and re-creates the destination table before attempting to copy data into it, which permanently deletes all existing data and indexes.

Tip   If the table exists at the destination, you must drop and re-create it to map new column values to the destination table. Otherwise, you can only map source columns to different destination columns.

- **Enable Identity Insert**   Allows you to insert explicit values into the identity column of a table. This option is available only on SQL Server and only if an identity column is detected.

- **Edit SQL** Displays the Create Table SQL Statement dialog box, which allows you to customize the default CREATE TABLE statement.

3. After you set the general transfer options, use the fields in the Mappings list box to determine how values are mapped from the source to the destination. The fields are all set to default values based on the source column. If you want to override these values for a new table or if you are dropping and recreating an existing table, you can modify these values. The Mappings fields are used as follows:

   - **Source** Sets the source column to map to a Destination column.
   - **Destination** Click in this column, and then select an existing column name or type a new column name for the destination table. Use the <ignore> option if a Destination column should not be created.

Note If a Destination column already exists and you choose <ignore>, the source data will not be copied into this column.

   - **Type** Select a data type for the Destination column. If you select a different data type than the data type of the Source column, the data is converted to the new data type during the transfer.

Note Make sure you select a valid conversion option. The SQL Server Import And Export Wizard will not let you truncate data, and if you try to do so, an error will occur.

   - **Nullable** Select this check box if the destination allows NULL values.
   - **Size** Sets the length of the Destination column. This value is applicable only for the *char, varchar, nchar, nvarchar, binary,* and *varbinary* data types.

Note Setting the size smaller than the length of the source data can result in data truncation. If this happens, the SQL Server Import And Export Wizard will generate an error and will not complete the data transfer.

   - **Precision** Sets the maximum number of decimal digits, including decimal places. For *decimal* and *numeric* data types only.
   - **Scale** Sets the maximum number of digits to the right of the decimal point. This value must be less than or equal to the Precision value, and it applies to *decimal* and *numeric* data types only.

4. Click OK, and then repeat this process for other tables you want to transform.
5. When you are ready to continue, click Next.

Stage 4: Save and Execute

You have nearly completed the process of creating an Integration Services package. At this stage, you specify when to use the package you have created and decide if the package should be saved for future use. After you clicked Next in the Select Source

Tables And Views dialog box, the Save And Execute Package page, shown in Figure 10-11, will display. To use this page, complete the following steps:

1. By default, the Execute Immediately option is selected so you can run the package. If you do not want to run the package immediately, simply clear the check box for this option.

2. Use the options in the Save area to save the package for future use. If you want to save the package to use later, select the Save SSIS Package check box, and then specify where the package should be saved. The available locations are:

    - **SQL Server**   Saves as a local package in the *msdb* database so the package is accessible for use on the designated server.

    - **File System**   Saves as a DTSX file. You can add additional packages to the file as long as they have a different package name. You can then copy, move, or e-mail the file to a different location.

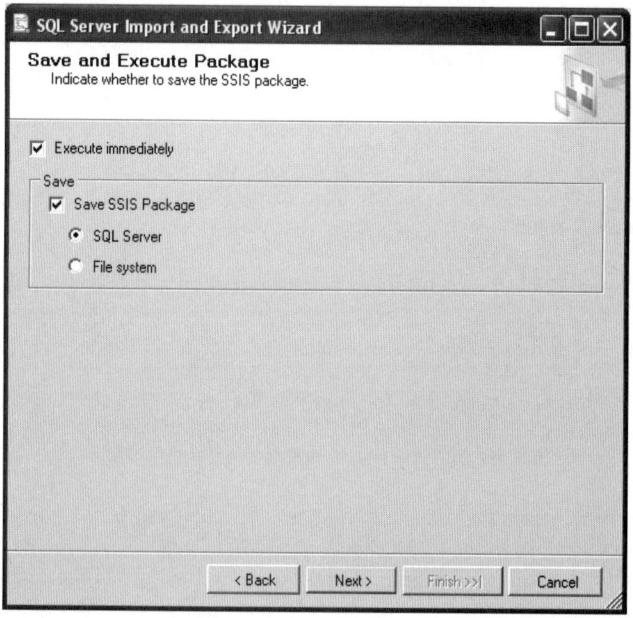

Figure 10-11   The Save and Execute Package page of the SQL Server Import and Export Wizard

3. When you have finished configuring the run and save options, click Next to display the Package Protection Level dialog box.

4. Use the options in this dialog box to set the encryption options for the package. The options are:

    - **Do Not Save Sensitive Data**   Creates the package but does not save sensitive data in the package.

- **Encrypt Sensitive Data With User Key**   Creates the package with sensitive data encrypted. The package can only be opened or executed by the user who created the package (the current login account).

- **Encrypt Sensitive Data With Password**   Creates the package with sensitive data encrypted. The package can be opened or executed with the password you specify. This means that anyone with the password can open or execute the package.

- **Encrypt All Data With User Key**   Creates the package with all data encrypted. The package can only be opened by the user who created the package (the current login account).

- **Encrypt All Data With Password**   Saves the package with all data encrypted. The package can be opened or executed with the password you specify. This means that anyone with the password can open or execute the package.

- **Rely On Server Storage And Roles For Access Control**   Creates a package that uses SQL Server permissions and roles to control access (only available if you save the package to SQL Server).

5. If you have opted to save the package, the next page lets you set the save location (see Figure 10-12). The options may differ slightly from those shown, depending on the save location you previously selected.

6. Type a name and description of the package in the Name and Description boxes. The name should be unique for the target location.

7. If you are saving the package to SQL Server, use the Server Name drop-down list to select the name of the SQL Server to which you want to save the package. The package is saved in the *msdb* database on the designated server.

8. Select the type of authentication to use by selecting one of the option buttons for either Windows Authentication or SQL Server Authentication. Provide an authorized user name and password if you select the Use SQL Server Authentication option.

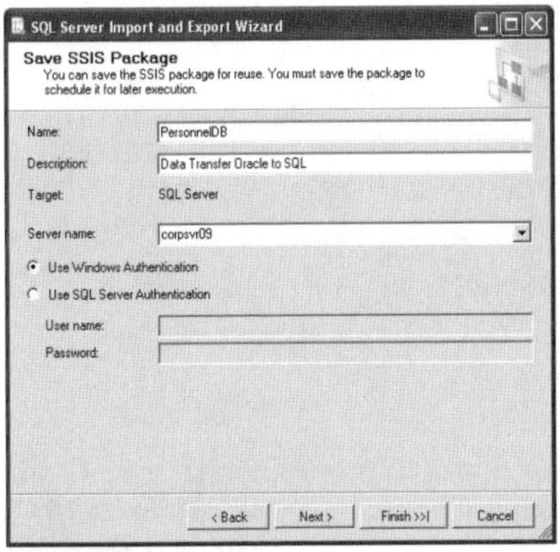

Figure 10-12   The Save SSIS Package page of the SQL Server Import And Export Wizard

9. If you selected to save the package to a file, set the file location using the File Name box.

10. Click Next. Review the actions that will be performed, and then click Finish.

If you have elected to run the package immediately, SQL Server runs the package. As each step is completed (or fails), the status is updated. If an error occurs, you can click its message entry to view a detailed report of the error. Errors may halt execution of the package, and if they do, you will have to redesign the package using Integration Services Designer or re-create the package using the SQL Server Import And Export Wizard.

SQL Server stores Integration Services packages as local packages in a designated server's *msdb* database and as file-based packages. You manage packages by using SQL Server Management Studio, Business Intelligence Development Studio, or the Execute Package Utility (dtexecui). Two command-line utilities are provided as well: dtutil for copying, moving, signing, and deleting packages and dtexec for executing packages.

Understanding BCP

BULK COPY (BCP) offers a command-line alternative to the SQL Server Import And Export Wizard. The Transact-SQL counterpart to BCP import is BULK INSERT. You will find that BULK INSERT has a similar syntax when used for importing data. To learn more about BCP, we will examine its features:

- Basics
- Syntax
- Permissions
- Modes
- Importing data
- Exporting data

BCP Basics

BCP may continue to be a favorite of database administrators because of its great performance and minimal overhead. You will find that import and export processes tend to be very fast and that BCP requires very little memory to operate. BCP does not have a graphical user interface (GUI) and is best used in two situations:

- To import data from a text file to a single SQL Server table or view
- To export data to a text file from a single SQL Server table or view

When transferring data to or from SQL Server, BCP uses ODBC.

 Tip Dates are written in ODBC format. You will find that the *datetime* format is yyyymmdd hh:mm:ss rather than mmm dd yyy hh:mm (A.M./P.M.), and the *money* format has no commas with four digits after the decimal (instead of commas and two digits after the decimal).

Note When you import data using BCP, columns with computed values and time stamps are ignored. SQL Server can automatically assign values. To do this, use a format file to specify that the computed values or time-stamp columns in the table should be skipped; SQL Server then automatically assigns values for the column. During export, computed values and time stamps are handled like other values.

BCP Syntax

Before we examine how to use BCP, let's look at the command syntax, shown in Sample 10-1 and extended in Tables 10-1 and 10-2. As you can see, the syntax is fairly extensive. BCP switches are case sensitive and order sensitive. You must use these switches exactly as indicated, or you will have problems executing the BCP command.

Sample 10-1 BCP Syntax and Usage

Syntax

```
bcp {[[dbname.][owner].]{tablename | viewname } | "query"}
    {in | out | queryout | format} datafile
    [switch1 [parameter1]] [switch2 [parameter2]]
    [switchN [parameterN]]
```

Usage

```
bcp pubs..customer out customers.txt —c —U sa —P"guerilla"
bcp pubs..customer in customers.txt —f customers.fmt —U sa —P"guerilla"
```

Table 10-1 provides a summary of key BCP parameters.

Table 10-1 Key Parameters Used with BCP

Parameter	Description
Dbname	The name of the database. This parameter is optional, and if it is not supplied, the user's default database is used.
Owner	The schema (owner) of the table or view being used. Use the .. syntax for a default schema, such as *pubs..authors* instead of *pubs.dbo.authors*.
Tablename	The name of the table to access. Use the # or ## syntax to copy a temporary table.
Viewname	The name of the destination view when copying data into SQL Server; the source view when copying data from SQL Server.
Query	T-SQL statement that generates a result set. You must use double quotation marks around the query and specify the queryout parameter; these are mandatory with this option.
In	Specifies an import process.
Out	Specifies an export process.
Format	Sets the creation of a format file. You must set the name of the format file with the —f switch and also specify the format for this file with —n, —c, —w, —6, or —N. When creating an XML file, you must also specify —x.
Queryout	Must be used when exporting output from an SQL query or stored procedure.
Datafile	The name of the file for importing or the name of the file to create when exporting. This can include the full file path.

BCP also supports a wide variety of switches. These switches and their associated parameters are summarized in Table 10-2.

Table 10-2   Switches Used with BCP

Switch	Description
−a *packetsize*	Sets the number of bytes in a network packet. Default is 4,096 bytes. The valid range is 512 bytes to 65,535 bytes.
−b *batchsize*	The number of rows to transfer in the batch. Each batch is copied to the server as one transaction. By default, all rows are copied in a single batch. Do not use with the −h ROWS_PER_BATCH option.
−c	Character data mode (ASCII text) for transfers to and from non-SQL Server products.
−C *codepage*	Code page being used by the import file. This is only relevant when the data contains *char*, *varchar*, or *text* columns with character values greater than 127 or less than 32. Use the code page value ACP with ANSI ISO 1252 data, RAW when no conversion should occur, OEM to use the client's default code page, or type a specific code page value, such as 850.
−e *errfile*	Stores error messages in the specified error file.
−E	Uses identity values. Otherwise, identity values are ignored and automatically assigned new values.
−F *firstrow*	Sets the number of the first row to use.
−f *formatfile*	Sets the name and path to a BCP format file. The default file name is BCP.FMT. If you use −n, −c, −w, −6, or −N and do not specify −f, you will be prompted for format information, and your responses will be saved in a format file (named BCP.FMT by default).
−h *loadhints*	Used to set load hints: FIRE_TRIGGERS, ROWS_PER_BATCH, KILOBYTES_PER_BATCH, TABLOCK, CHECK_CONSTRAINTS, and ORDER.
−I *inputfile*	Sets the name of a response file that contains responses to the command prompt questions for each field when performing a bulk copy using interactive mode.
−k	Preserves null values.
−L *lastrow*	Sets the last row to use.
−m *maxerrors*	Sets the maximum number of errors that can occur before terminating BCP. The default is 10.
−N	Sets native export for noncharacter data and Unicode character export for character data.
−n	Sets native data mode, which is SQL Server–specific.
−o *outfile*	File to redirect output of BCP during unattended operation.
−P *password*	Password to use to log on. Do not store passwords in files as this is poor security practice.
−q	Uses quoted identifiers.
−R	Enables regional format copy for currency, date, and time data.
−r *rowterminator*	Sets the row terminator. The default is the new line character (\n).
−S *servername*	Sets the SQL Server name. You can also follow the server name by the instance name: −S *servername\instancename*.
−t *fieldterminator*	Sets the field terminator. The default is the tab character (\t).
−T	Uses a trusted connection, which is a good security practice.
−U *username*	Sets the user name for login.

Table 10-2   **Switches Used with BCP**   *(continued)*

Switch	Description
–V	Sets the data type version for native and character formats to a previous SQL Server version. For SQL Server 6.0 format, use 60; for SQL Server 6.5, use 65; for SQL Server 7.0, use 70; for SQL Server 2000, use 80.
–v	Displays the BCP version number.
–w	Sets wide character (Unicode) mode.
–x	Used with the format and –f options to create an XML format file instead of a standard text-based format file.

BCP Permissions and Modes

Although any user can run BCP, only users with appropriate permissions can access SQL Server and the specified database objects. When you run BCP, you can set login information using the U and P switches, or you can use a trusted connection, which is more secure. For unattended operations, it is essential to use these switches to ensure that permissions are granted appropriately. To import data into a table, the user needs INSERT permission on the target table. To export data from a table, the user needs SELECT permission for the source table.

BCP can use three different modes:

- **Character mode**   Used when you want to import or export data as ASCII text. The switch to set this mode is c.
- **Native mode**   Used when you want to import or export data in native format. The switch to set this mode is n or N.
- **Wide mode**   Used when you want to import or export data as Unicode text. The switch to set this mode is w.

The character and wide modes are the best choices when you are copying to a non-SQL Server product. Use native mode when you are copying data between SQL Server tables. These modes all have their strengths and weaknesses. With character or wide mode files, you can view the contents and make sure that you have the right data set, but for imports, you must also tell SQL Server how this data is formatted. You can do this through interactive prompts or by using a format file containing the responses to these prompts. With native mode, you cannot view the contents of native data files, but you do not have to specify data formatting information when importing files either.

Importing Data with BCP

You can import data with BCP in two ways. You can start an interactive session, or you can set the necessary responses in a format file. The following example shows how to start an interactive session using a trusted connection:

```
bcp pubs..customer in customers.txt –T
```

To specify a format file, use the –f flag, such as in the following example:

```
bcp pubs..customer in customers.txt –w –f customers.fmt –T
```

In an interactive session, BCP prompts you for information needed to complete the import or export process. BCP starts an interactive session when either of the following situations occurs:

- You import without specifying the –c, –n, –w, or –N parameters.
- You export without specifying the –c, –n, –w, or –N parameters.

The interactive session allows you to customize the BCP process, much as you do with a format file. In fact, before you try to create a format file, you should run BCP in interactive mode and then choose to have BCP create the necessary format file for you. This operation will show you the best way to configure the format file.

For each column in a table you are importing, you will see the prompts similar to the following during an interactive session:

```
Enter the file storage type of field [nchar]:
Enter prefix length of field [0]:
Enter length of field [5]:
Enter field terminator [none]:
```

 Note Pressing Enter accepts the default values. To skip a column in an import file, type **0** for the prefix length, **0** for the field length, and **none** for the terminator type. You cannot skip a column when exporting data.

These prompts ask you to type various kinds of information, and in every case the default value for the current column is shown in brackets. At the end of the interactive session, you will be asked if you want to save your responses in a format file. If you answer yes (by typing **Y**), you can type the name of the format file when prompted, such as:

```
Do you want to save this format information in a file? [Y/N]
Host filename [bcp.fmt]: customers.fmt
```

You can then use the format file for other BCP sessions by setting the f switch as explained previously. Because the format file has a rigid syntax that you must follow, I recommend creating a sample file to get started. As Sample 10-2 shows, each line in the file contains information fields that determine how data should be imported.

Sample 10-2 BCP Non-XML Format File

```
9.0
50
1 SQLINT    0 8    ""  1  CUSTOMERID  ""
2 SQLNCHAR 2 25   ""  2  CUSTNAME    SQL_Latin1_General_CP1_CI_AS
3 SQLNCHAR 2 20   ""  3  CUSTORG     SQL_Latin1_General_CP1_CI_AS
..
50 SQLNCHAR 2 9   ""  3  POSTALCODE  SQL_Latin1_General_CP1_CI_AS
```

The lines give you the following information:

- The first line sets the version of BCP used. Here the version is 9.0.
- The second line sets the number of columns in the table you are importing. In the example, the table contains 50 columns.
- Subsequent lines set the formats for each column in the table, from the first column to the last column.

The lines defining table columns are broken down into fields, and each field sets a different input parameter. Normally, these fields are separated by spaces. The number of spaces does not really matter—provided there is at least one space. BCP treats one or more spaces as a field separator. File format fields operate in the following manner:

- Field 1 sets the column number you are describing from the data file.
- Field 2 sets the file storage type, which is simply the data type of the column.
- Field 3 sets the prefix length for compacted data. A value of zero specifies that no prefix is used.
- Field 4 sets the field length, which is the number of bytes required to store the data type. Use the default value provided whenever possible.
- Field 5 sets the field terminator. By default, BCP separates all fields but the last one with tabs (\t) and separates the last field with a carriage return and newline field (\r\n).
- Field 6 sets the table column number in the database. For example, a value of 1 means that the column corresponds to the first column in the database.
- Field 7 sets the table column name.
- Field 8 sets the column collation.

Exporting Data with BCP

When you export data, BCP creates a data file using the name you specify. If you are exporting data from nonnative files (ASCII and Unicode text), the columns in this file are separated with tabs by default, and the last column has a carriage return and newline. You specify a tab as a terminator with \t and a carriage return and newline with \r\n. In a format file, a tab can be an actual tab character or a series of five or more spaces.

As when importing data, you can handle data export interactively. For example, if you start an export session without specifying format information, you are prompted for this information. In the following example, you export a table to a file called customers.txt and use semicolons as the delimiter:

```
bcp pubs..customer out customers.txt -c -t -T;
```

BCP Scripts

A BCP script is simply a batch file or a Windows Script Host file that contains BCP commands. Sample 10-3 shows examples of how to run BCP using various scripting options. If you do not know how to use batch files or Windows Script Host, two great resources are *Windows Command-Line Administrator's Pocket Consultant* (Microsoft Press, 2005) and *Windows 2000 Scripting Guide* (Microsoft Press, 2002).

Sample 10-3   Using BCP in a Script

sched-export.bat
```
@echo off
@if not "%OS%"=="Windows_NT" goto :EXIT
bcp pubs..customer out customers.txt -c -t, -T
:EXIT
```

sched-export.vbs
```
'Nightly Bulk Copy export for the customers table
'Writes output to cust.txt and errors to err.txt
Set ws = WScript.CreateObject("WScript.Shell")
ret = ws.Run("bcp pubs..customers out cust.txt -c -t, -T
-eerr.txt",0,"TRUE")
```

sched-export.js
```
\\Nightly Bulk Copy export for the customers table
\\Writes output to cust.txt and errors to err.txt
var ws = WScript.CreateObject("WScript.Shell");
ret = ws.Run("bcp pubs..customers out cust.txt -c -t, -T -
eerr.txt",0,"TRUE")
```

After you create a script file for the bulk copy command, you can schedule it as a task to run on your system. To schedule these scripts to run every night at midnight, for example, use the following commands:

```
AT 00:00 /every:M,T,W,Th,F,S,Su "sched-export.bat"
AT 00:00 /every:M,T,W,Th,F,S,Su "cscript //B sched-export.js"
AT 00:00 /every:M,T,W,Th,F,S,Su "cscript //B sched-export.vbs"
```

Tip   For more information on scheduling tasks, refer to *Microsoft Windows Server 2003 Administrator's Pocket Consultant*, 2nd ed. (Microsoft Press, 2005) or *Microsoft Windows XP Administrator's Pocket Consultant*, 2nd ed. (Microsoft Press, 2005).

Using the BULK INSERT Command

A Transact-SQL command for importing data into a database is BULK INSERT. You can use BULK INSERT in much the same way that you use BCP. In fact, most of the parameters for BULK INSERT are the same as those used with BCP–they just have a different syntax. This syntax is shown in Sample 10-4.

Sample 10-4 BULK INSERT Syntax and Usage

Syntax

```
BULK INSERT [database_name.[schema_name][table_name|view_name]
   FROM 'data_file'
   [ WITH (
   [ [ , ] BATCHSIZE = batch_size ]
   [ [ , ] CHECK_CONSTRAINTS ]
   [ [ , ] CODEPAGE = { 'ACP' | 'OEM' | 'RAW' | 'code_page' } ]
   [ [ , ] DATAFILETYPE =
      { 'char' | 'native'| 'widechar' | 'widenative' } ]
   [ [ , ] FIELDTERMINATOR = 'field_terminator' ]
   [ [ , ] FIRSTROW =first_row ]
   [ [ , ] FIRE_TRIGGERS ]
   [ [ , ] FORMATFILE = 'format_file_path' ]
   [ [ , ] KEEPIDENTITY ]
   [ [ , ] KEEPNULLS ]
   [ [ , ] KILOBYTES_PER_BATCH =kilobytes_per_batch ]
   [ [ , ] LASTROW = last_row ]
   [ [ , ] MAXERRORS = max_errors ]
   [ [ , ] ORDER ( { column [ ASC | DESC ] } [ ,...n ] ) ]
   [ [ , ] ROWS_PER_BATCH = rows_per_batch ]
   [ [ , ] ROWTERMINATOR = 'row_terminator' ]
   [ [ , ] TABLOCK ]
   [ [ , ] ERRORFILE = 'file_name' ]
   )]
```

Usage

```
BULK INSERT pubs..customers FROM 'c:\data\customer.txt '
BULK INSERT pubs..customers FROM 'c:\cust.txt' with
   (DATAFILETYPE = 'char ',
   FORMATFILE='c:\cust.fmt')
```

In order to use BULK INSERT, you must have INSERT and ADMINISTER BULK OPERATION permissions. You may also need ALTER TABLE permission if any of the following conditions are true:

- Constraints are disabled (the default setting). To keep constraints enabled, use the CHECK_CONSTRAINTS option.

- Triggers are disabled (the default setting). To fire triggers, use the FIRE_TRIGGER option.

- KEEPIDENTITY is used to import identity values from the specified data file.

Additionally, before using BULK INSERT, you may want to set the database recovery model to bulk-logged. This mode minimally logs bulk operations and increases performance when bulk inserting. To set this option, select a database, open its Properties dialog box, choose the Options page, and then select Bulk-Logged under Recovery Model. You may also want to use *sp_tableoption* to set the table lock on bulk load value. When this option is set to FALSE (the default setting), the bulk load process obtains row locks when inserting into user-defined tables. If you set this option to TRUE, the bulk load process obtains a bulk update lock instead. Members of the sysadmin fixed server role, the db_owner and db_ddladmin fixed database roles, and the table owner can modify the table lock on bulk load value.

Sample 10-5 shows how to set the table lock on bulk load value using *sp_tableoption*.

Listing 10-5   *sp_tableoption* Syntax and Usage

Syntax

```
sp_tableoption [ @TableNamePattern = ] 'table' list.ordered
        , [ @OptionName = ] 'option_name' list.ordered
        , [ @OptionValue = ] 'value'
```

Usage

```
EXEC sp_tableoption Sales.Customers 'table lock on bulk load', 'true'
```

Chapter 11
Linked Servers and Distributed Transactions

Networking environments are becoming more and more complex. Organizations that managed with a single Microsoft SQL Server now need additional servers, or they need to integrate their existing server with other heterogeneous data sources. SQL Server 2005 provides several features for integrating SQL Server databases with other SQL Server databases and with other data sources, including distributed data, linked servers, and replication. This chapter focuses on linked servers and distributed data. Distributed data includes support for distributed queries, distributed transactions, and remote stored procedure execution. These distributed data features are handled through linked servers, which can be SQL Servers or non-SQL Servers. You will learn about replication in the next chapter, "Implementing Snapshot, Merge, and Transactional Replication."

Working with Linked Servers and Distributed Data

Before you use distributed data, you must configure the linked servers you want to use. Linked servers depend on OLE DB providers to communicate with one another. Through OLE DB, you can link instances of SQL Server to other instances of SQL Server as well as to other data sources.

You use linked servers to handle distributed queries, distributed transactions, remote stored procedure calls, and replication. Basically, queries and transactions are *distributed* when they make use of two or more database server instances. For example, if a client is connected to one server instance and starts a query that accesses a different server instance, the query is distributed. On the other hand, if the same client queries two different databases on the same server instance, the query is considered a local query and is handled internally.

Using Distributed Queries

When you execute a distributed query, SQL Server interprets the command and then breaks it down for the destination OLE DB provider using rowset requests. A *rowset* is a type of database object that enables OLE DB data providers to support data with a tabular format. As their name implies, rowset objects represent a set of rows and columns of data. After creating the rowset objects, the OLE DB provider calls the data source, opens the necessary files, and returns the requested information as rowsets. SQL Server then formats the rowsets as result sets and adds any applicable output parameters.

> **Note**   With SQL-92, user connections must have the ANSI_NULLS and ANSI_WARNINGS options before they can execute distributed queries. Be sure to configure these options, if necessary. For more information, see the section titled "Configuring User and Remote Connections" in Chapter 6, "Configuring SQL Server with SQL Server Management Studio."

You can create simple distributed queries quickly by making your own rowsets. To do this, you use the *Openrowset* function. When you use this function, you do not need to use linked servers, and you can use the *Openrowset* function in place of a table in a query if you pass parameters that identify the OLE DB data source and provider.

You use the *Openrowset* function in the same way that you use virtual tables; simply replace the virtual table reference with an *Openrowset* reference. Sample 11-1 shows the syntax and usage of *Openrowset*.

Sample 11-1   *Openrowset* Syntax and Usage

Syntax for SELECT with Table Alias

```
SELECT selection FROM OPENROWSET(rowset_options) AS table_alias
```

Syntax for *Openrowset*

```
OPENROWSET
( { 'provider_name' , { 'datasource' ; 'user_id' ; 'password'
  | 'provider_string' }
      , { [ catalog. ] [ schema. ] object
  | 'query' }
  | BULK 'data_file' ,
      { FORMATFILE = 'format_file_path' [ <bulk_options> ]
      | SINGLE_BLOB | SINGLE_CLOB | SINGLE_NCLOB }
} )
<bulk_options> ::=
    [ , CODEPAGE = { 'ACP' | 'OEM' | 'RAW' | 'code_page' }]
    [ , ERRORFILE = 'file_name' ]
    [ , FIRSTROW = first_row ]
    [ , LASTROW = last_row ]
    [ , MAXERRORS = maximum_errors ]
    [ , ROWS_PER_BATCH = rows_per_batch ]
```

Usage

```
USE pubs
GO
SELECT a.*
FROM OPENROWSET('SQLOLEDB','Pluto';'netUser';'totem12',
```

```
'SELECT * FROM pubs.dbo.authors ORDER BY au_lname, au_fname')
AS a
GO
SELECT o.*
FROM OPENROWSET('Microsoft.Jet.OLEDB.4.0','C:\
northwind.mdb';'Admin';", 'Orders')
AS o
```

The BULK rowset provider is similar to the BULK INSERT statement. The data_file parameter is used to specify the data file from which data will be copied into the target table. A format file is required to define the column types in the result set, except when you use SINGLE_BLOB, SINGLE_CLOB, or SINGLE_NCLOB. SINGLE_BLOB returns the contents of the data file as a single-row, single-column rowset of type *varbinary(max)*. SINGLE_CLOB reads the data file as ASCII text and returns the contents of the data file as a single-row, single-column rowset of type *varchar(max)*. SINGLE_NCLOB reads the data file as Unicode text and returns the contents as a single-row, single-column rowset of type *nvarchar(max)*. Both SINGLE_CLOB and SINGLE_NCLOB use the collation of the current database.

When the OPENROWSET BULK option is used with an INSERT statement, you can use standard table hints, such as TABLOCK, as well as the special BULK INSERT table hints: IGNORE_CONSTRAINTS, IGNORE_TRIGGERS, KEEPDE-FAULTS, and KEEPIDENTITY. When you use the BULK rowset provider with OPENROWSET, you must either specify column aliases in the FROM clause or specify column names in the format file. The syntax for the SELECT statement with the table alias then becomes:

```
SELECT selection FROM OPENROWSET(BULK rowset_options) AS
table_alias[(column1_alias, column2_alias,...)]
```

Using Distributed Transactions

Distributed transactions are transactions that use distributed queries or remote procedure calls (RPCs). As you might expect, distributed transactions are more involved than distributed queries, primarily because you need a mechanism that ensures that transactions are committed uniformly or rolled back on all the linked servers. For example, if you start a transaction that updates databases on three different server instances, you want to make certain that the transaction is committed when it has completed successfully or that the transaction is rolled back if an error occurs. In this way, you ensure the integrity of the databases involved in the distributed transaction.

On SQL Server, three components are required for distributed transactions to be handled properly:

- **Resource managers** You must configure resource managers, which are the linked servers used in the distributed transactions. For details about how to configure resource managers, see the section titled "Managing Linked Servers" later in this chapter.

- **Distributed Transaction Coordinator service** The Distributed Transaction Coordinator service must be running on all servers that are handling distributed transactions. If it is not, distributed transactions will not work properly.

- **Transaction manager** The transaction manager coordinates and manages distributed transactions. The transaction manager on SQL Server is the Distributed Transaction Coordinator.

 Note Applications other than SQL Server can use the Distributed Transaction Coordinator. If you try to analyze Distributed Transaction Coordinator performance, you should note which applications besides SQL Server are using Distributed Transaction Coordinator.

Each server instance involved in a distributed transaction is known as a *resource manager*. Resource managers coordinate transactions through a transaction manager, such as the Microsoft Distributed Transaction Coordinator. You can use other transaction managers if they support the X/Open XA specification for distributed transaction processing.

You handle distributed transactions in much the same manner as local transactions. Applications start distributed transactions in several ways:

- Explicitly, by using BEGIN DISTRIBUTED TRANSACTION
- Explicitly, by using OLE DB methods or ODBC functions to join a distributed transaction started by the application
- Implicitly, by executing a distributed query within a local transaction
- Implicitly, by calling a remote stored procedure within a local transaction (provided the REMOTE_PROC_TRANSACTIONS option is set ON)

At the end of the transaction, the application requests that the transaction be either committed or rolled back. To ensure that the transaction is handled properly on all servers, even if problems occur during the transaction, the transaction manager uses a commit process with two phases:

- **Phase 1: The prepare phase** The transaction manager sends a prepare to commit request to all the resource managers involved in the transaction. Each resource manager performs any necessary preparatory tasks and then reports their success or failure to the transaction manager. If all the resource managers are ready to commit, the transaction manager broadcasts a commit message and the transaction enters phase 2, the commit phase.

- **Phase 2: The commit phase** The resource managers attempt to commit the transaction. Each resource manager then sends back a success or failure message. If all the resource managers report success, the transaction manager marks the transaction as completed and reports this to the application. If a resource manager fails in either phase, the transaction is rolled back and the failure is reported.

SQL Server applications manage distributed transactions either through Transact-SQL or through the SQL Server database application programming interface (API). SQL Server itself supports distributed transactions using the ITransactionLocal (local transaction) and ITransactionJoin (distributed transactions) OLE DB interfaces as well as the rowset objects discussed previously. If an OLE DB provider does not support ITransactionJoin, then only read-only procedures are allowed for that provider. Similarly, the types of queries you can execute on a linked server depend on the OLE DB provider you are using.

With distributed queries and transactions, you can use most data manipulation language (DML) commands, such as SELECT, INSERT, UPDATE, and DELETE. You cannot, however, use data definition language (DDL) commands, such as CREATE, DROP, or ALTER. If you need to use DDL commands on linked servers, you may want to create stored procedures and then execute these stored procedures remotely, as necessary.

You can use the EXECUTE statement to execute commands and stored procedures on a linked server. Sample 11-2 shows the syntax for using EXECUTE in this way.

Sample 11-2 EXECUTE at *linked_server*

Syntax
```
EXEC [UTE] ( { @string_variable | [ N ] 'command_string' } [ + ...n ]
    [ {, { value | @variable [ OUTPUT ] } } [...n] ] )
    [ AS { LOGIN | USER } = ' name ' ]
    [ AT linked_server_name ] [;]
```

Usage
```
EXEC ( 'SELECT * FROM william.sales') AT ORADBSVR8;
```

Running the Distributed Transaction Coordinator Service

The Distributed Transaction Coordinator service must run on each server that handles distributed transactions, and you usually will want the service to start automatically when the system starts. This ensures that the distributed transactions are executed as expected. By using SQL Server Configuration Manager, you can control the Distributed Transaction Coordinator service just as you do other SQL Server-related services. For details, see the section titled "Configuring SQL Server Services" in Chapter 3, "Managing the Surface Security, Access, and Network Configuration."

You can view the Distributed Transaction Coordinator service in SQL Server Management Studio by completing the following steps:

1. In SQL Server Management Studio, connect to the server instance you want to use.

2. In Object Explorer view, expand the Management node. You will see the status of the Distributed Transaction Coordinator and Full-Text Search services

displayed. A green circle with a triangle indicates that the service is running. A red circle with a square indicates that the service is stopped.

Managing Linked Servers

To work properly, distributed queries and transactions depend on linked servers. You configure the linked servers you are using by registering their connection and data source information in SQL Server. Then you will be able to reference the linked server by using a single logical name. If you no longer need to link to a server, you can remove the linked server connection.

Adding Linked Servers

If you want a server to be able to use distributed queries, distributed transactions, or remote command execution, you must configure linked server connections to other servers. For example, if clients that access a server named Zeta make distributed queries to Pluto and Omega, you must configure Pluto and Omega as linked servers on Zeta. If clients that connect to Pluto make distributed queries to Zeta and Omega, you must configure Zeta and Omega as linked servers on Pluto. To add a linked server, complete the following steps:

1. In SQL Server Management Studio, connect to the server instance you want to configure.
2. In Object Explorer view, expand the Server Objects node.
3. Right-click the Linked Servers entry, and then choose New Linked Server from the shortcut menu to open the dialog box shown in Figure 11-1.
4. In the Linked Server text box, type the name of the linked server to create.
5. If you are linking to a SQL Server, select the SQL Server option.
6. If you are linking to a different data source, select the Other Data Source option, and then configure the data source using the text boxes provided. If there is no text box available in the dialog box for a specific option, then you cannot configure that option for the selected provider. Provide information in the text boxes as follows:
   - **Provider**   Select the name of the OLE DB provider to use when communicating with the specified linked server from the drop-down list box.
   - **Product Name**   Set the server product name for the OLE DB data source.
   - **Data Source**   Provide the OLE DB data source, which is used to initialize the OLE DB provider.
   - **Provider String**   Type a provider-specific connection string that identifies a unique data source.
   - **Location**   Set the location of the database for the OLE DB provider.
   - **Catalog**   Indicate the catalog to use when connecting to the OLE DB provider.

The most commonly used option combinations are provider name and data source. For example, if you were configuring a linked server for a Microsoft Access database or a Microsoft Excel spreadsheet, you would select Microsoft Jet 4.0 OLE DB Provider and then set the data source name. With Oracle, you would select Microsoft OLE DB Provider For Oracle and then set the data source name.

New Linked Server	_ B x

Select a page
- General
- Security
- Server Options

Script ▾ Help

Linked server: ORACLEDB27

Server type:
- ○ SQL Server
- ● Other data source

Provider: Microsoft OLE DB Provider for Oracle ▾
Product name: oracle8
Data source: oracledb27
Provider string:
Location:
Catalog:

Connection
Server:
ENGDBSVR82

Connection:
ENGDBSVR82\Administrator

View connection properties

Progress
Ready

This is the entire provider string.

OK   Cancel

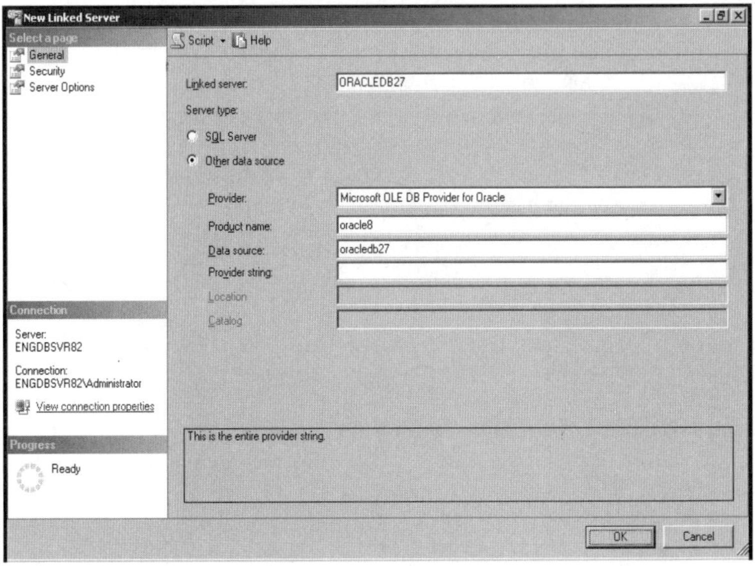

Figure 11-1 The New Linked Server dialog box

7. Select the Server Options page from the list in the left pane of the dialog box to configure server-specific settings as follows:

- **Collation Compatible** Set this option to enable SQL Server to send comparisons on character columns to the provider. Otherwise, SQL Server evaluates comparisons on character columns locally. Set this option only when the linked server has the same collation as the local server.

Note Collation compatible controls sort order settings. If you do not select this option, SQL Server uses the local sort order. This affects the order of result sets, and you should note it when you develop SQL Server applications or configure clients that support distributed transactions.

- **Data Access** Set this option to enable the linked server for distributed query access.
- **RPC** Set this option to enable remote procedure calls from the linked server.

- **RPC Out**   Set this option to enable remote procedure calls to the linked server.

- **Use Remote Collation**   Set this option to have SQL Server use the collation from the linked server's character columns. If you do not set this option, SQL Server interprets data from the linked server using the default collation of the local server instance. Note that only SQL Server databases take advantage of this option.

- **Collation Name**   Set this option to assign a specific collation for queries and transactions. You must set the Collation Compatible option to False before you can set this option.

- **Connection Timeout**   Use this text box to set the time-out value for connections made to the remote server.

- **Query Timeout**   Use this text box to set the time-out value for queries made to the remote server.

8. Click OK to create the linked server. Next, you must configure security settings for the linked server, as discussed in the section titled "Configuring Security for Linked Servers" later in this chapter.

The corresponding Transact-SQL command for adding linked servers is *sp_addlinkedserver*. Use this stored procedure as shown in Sample 11-3.

Sample 11-3   *sp_addlinkedserver* Syntax and Usage

Syntax

```
sp_addlinkedserver [@server =] 'server'
    [, [@srvproduct =] 'product_name']
    [, [@provider =] 'provider_name']
    [, [@datasrc =] 'data_source']
    [, [@location =] 'location']
    [, [@provstr =] 'provider_string']
    [, [@catalog =] 'catalog']
```

Usage

```
EXEC sp_addlinkedserver
        @server='ORADBSVR8',
        @srvproduct='Oracle',
        @provider='OraOLEDB.Oracle',
        @datasrc='ORACLE10';
GO
```

Table 11-1 provides a summary of parameter values you can use when configuring various OLE DB providers. The table also shows the *sp_addlinkedserver* parameter values to use for each OLE DB provider. Because some providers have different configurations, there may be more than one row for a particular data source type.

Table 11-1   Parameter Values for Configuring OLE DB Providers

Remote OLE DB data source	OLE DB provider	product_name	provider_name	data_source	Other
SQL Server	Microsoft SQL Native Client OLE DB Provider	SQL Server (default)	—	—	—
SQL Server	Microsoft SQL Native Client OLE DB Provider	—	SQLNCLI	Network name of SQL Server (for default instance)	Database name optional for catalog field
SQL Server	Microsoft SQL Native Client OLE DB Provider	—	SQLNCLI	*Servername\ instancename* (for specific instance)	Database name optional for catalog field
Oracle	Microsoft OLE DB Provider for Oracle	Any	MSDAORA	SQL*Net alias for Oracle database	—
Oracle 8.0 and later	Oracle Provider for OLE DB	Any	OraOLEDB. Oracle	Alias for the Oracle database	—
Access/Jet	Microsoft OLE DB Provider for Jet	Any	Microsoft.Jet. OLEDB.4.0	Full path name of Jet database file	—
ODBC data source	Microsoft OLE DB Provider for ODBC	Any	MSDASQL	System DSN of ODBC data source	—
ODBC data source	Microsoft OLE DB Provider for ODBC	Any	MSDASQL	—	ODBC connection string for *provider_string*
File system	Microsoft OLE DB Provider for Indexing Service	Any	MSIDXS	Indexing Service catalog name	—
Microsoft Excel Spreadsheet	Microsoft OLE DB Provider for Jet	Any	Microsoft.Jet. OLEDB.4.0	Full path name of Excel file	Excel 5.0 for *provider_string*
IBM DB2 Database	Microsoft OLE DB Provider for DB2	Any	DB2OLEDB	—	Catalog name of DB2 database in catalog field

Configuring Security for Linked Servers

You use linked server security to control access and to determine how local logins are used. By default, new linked servers are set to have no security context when a user login is not defined. This blocks access to all logins not explicitly mapped to the linked server.

To change the security settings for a linked server, complete the following steps:

1. Start SQL Server Management Studio, and then access the local server that contains the linked server definitions you want to change.

2. In Object Explorer view, expand the Server Objects node, and then expand the Linked Servers node. You should now see an entry for each linked server that you created on the currently selected server.

3. Right-click the icon for the linked server you want to configure, and then choose Properties to open the Linked Server Properties dialog box.

4. In the Linked Server Properties dialog box, click the Security page, as shown in Figure 11-2.

5. Map local logins to remote logins by clicking Add.

6. Configure the following options on a per login basis:

   ■ **Local Login**   Sets the ID of a local login that can connect to the linked server.

   ■ **Impersonate**   Select this check box to use the local login ID to connect to the linked server. The local login ID must match a login ID on the linked server exactly.

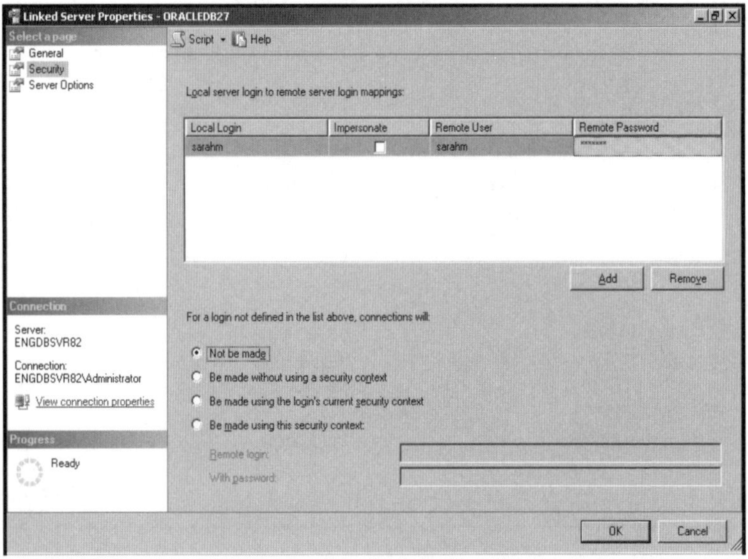

Figure 11-2   The Security page of the Linked Server Properties dialog box

> **Note**   If you select the Impersonate check box, you cannot map the local login to a remote login.

   ■ **Remote User**   Sets the remote user to which the local login ID maps on the linked server.

- **Remote Password** Sets the password for the remote user. If it is not provided, the user may be prompted for a password.

7. Use the option buttons and text boxes in the lower portion of the Security page to set a default security context for all users who do not have a specific login setting for the linked server. These options are used as follows:

   - **Not Be Made** Users without logins are not allowed access to the linked server.

   - **Be Made Without Using A Security Context** Blocks access to all logins not explicitly mapped to the linked server.

   - **Be Made Using The Login's Current Security Context** Logins not explicitly mapped to the linked server use their current login and password to connect to the linked server. Access is denied if the login and password do not exist on the linked server.

   - **Be Made Using This Security Context** Logins not explicitly mapped to the linked server will use the login and password provided in the Remote Login and With Password text boxes.

8. When you have finished configuring logins, click OK.

The related Transact-SQL command for configuring logins is *sp_addlinkedsrvlogin*. Use this stored procedure as shown in Sample 11-4.

Sample 11-4 *sp_addlinkedsrvlogin* Syntax and Usage

Syntax

```
sp_addlinkedsrvlogin [@rmtsrvname =] 'rmtsrvname'
[,[@useself =] 'useself']
[,[@locallogin =] 'locallogin']
[,[@rmtuser =] 'rmtuser']
[,[@rmtpassword =] 'rmtpassword']
```

Usage

```
EXEC sp_addlinkedsrvlogin
    @rmtsrvname='ORADBSVR8',
    @useself='false',
    @locallogin=null,
    @rmtuser='william',
    @rmtpassword='tango98';
GO
```

Setting Server Options for Remote and Linked Servers

You set server options for remote and linked servers using *sp_serveroption*. Use this stored procedure as shown in Sample 11-5. Key options are summarized in Table 11-2.

Sample 11-5   *sp_serveroption* Syntax and Usage

Syntax
```
sp_serveroption [@server =] 'server'
    ,[@optname =] 'option_name'
    ,[@optvalue =] 'option_value' ;
```

Usage
```
EXEC sp_serveroption 'ORADBSVR8', 'rpc out', true;
```

Table 11-2   **Key Options for *sp_serveroption***

Option Name	Option Usage/Description
collation compatible	If TRUE, compatible collation is assumed with regard to character set and collation sequence (or sort order) and SQL Server sends comparisons on character columns to the provider. Otherwise, SQL Server always evaluates comparisons on character columns locally.
collation name	Sets the name of the collation used by the remote data source if use remote collation is TRUE and the data source is not a SQL Server data source. The name must be a specific, single collation supported by SQL Server.
connect timeout	Sets the time-out value for connecting to the linked server. Set to 0 to use the *sp_configure* default.
data access	Set to TRUE to enable a linked server for distributed query access. Set to FALSE to disable.
lazy schema validation	If TRUE, SQL Server skips schema checking of remote tables at the beginning of a query.
query timeout	Sets the time-out value for queries against a linked server. Set to 0 to use the *sp_configure* default.
rpc	Set to TRUE to enable RPC from the linked server.
rpc out	Set to TRUE to enable RPC to the linked server.
use remote collation	If TRUE, the collation of remote columns is used for SQL Server data sources, and the collation specified in collation name is used for non-SQL Server data sources. Otherwise, distributed queries will always use the default collation of the local server, while collation name and the collation of remote columns are ignored.

Deleting Linked Servers

If you do not need a linked server anymore, you can delete it by completing the following steps:

1. Start SQL Server Management Studio, and then access the local server that contains the linked server definitions you want to delete.

2. In Object Explorer view, expand the Server Objects node, and then expand the Linked Servers node. You should now see an entry for each linked server that you created on the currently selected server.

3. Right-click the icon for the linked server you want to remove, and then choose Delete to open the Delete Object dialog box.

4. In the Delete Object dialog box, click OK.

The Transact-SQL command to drop linked servers is *sp_dropserver*. The Transact-SQL command to drop linked server logins is *sp_droplinkedsrvlogin*. Use these stored procedures as shown in Samples 11-6 and 11-7.

Sample 11-6 *sp_dropserver* Syntax and Usage

Syntax
```
sp_dropserver [@server =] 'server'
    [, [@droplogins =]{'droplogins' | NULL}]
```

Usage
```
EXEC sp_dropserver 'ORADBSVR8', 'droplogins'
```

Sample 11-7 *sp_droplinkedsrvlogin* Syntax and Usage

Syntax
```
sp_droplinkedsrvlogin [@rmtsrvname =] 'rmtsrvname',
    [@locallogin =]'locallogin'
```

Usage
```
EXEC sp_droplinkedsrvlogin 'ORADBSVR8', 'william'
```

Chapter 12

Implementing Snapshot, Merge, and Transactional Replication

Data replication allows you to distribute data from a source database to one or more destination databases. The source and destination databases can be on different Microsoft SQL Servers or on other database systems as long as an OLE DB provider is available for each destination database. You have precise control over when replication occurs, what data is replicated, and how other aspects of replication are handled. For example, you can configure replication to happen continuously or periodically. Before we examine how to implement replication, let's look at why you would want to use replication and review the main concepts it involves.

An Overview of Replication

You use replication to copy data on one server and distribute it to other servers. You can also use replication to copy data, transform it, and then distribute the customized data to multiple servers. You generally use replication when you need to manage data on multiple servers on a recurring basis. If you need to create a copy of a database just once, you do not need replication—instead you should copy the database as discussed in the section titled "Tips and Techniques" in Chapter 7, "Core Database Administration," or in the subsection titled "Restoring a Database to a Different Location" in Chapter 14, "Backing Up and Recovering SQL Server 2005." If you need to copy and transform data from one server to another server, you do not need replication either; instead you should use the import and export procedure discussed in Chapter 10, "Importing, Exporting, and Transforming Data." Some reasons to use replication include:

■ To synchronize changes to remote databases with a central database. For example, if the sales team uses remote laptops, you may need to create a copy of data for their sales region on the laptop. Later, a salesperson in the field may add information or make changes when they are disconnected from the network. By using replication, these modifications could be synchronized with the central database.

■ To create multiple instances of a database so that you can distribute the workload. For example, if you have a central database that is updated regularly, you may want to push changes out to departmental databases as they occur. Employees can then access data through these departmental databases instead of trying to connect to the central database.

■ To move specific data sets from a central server and distribute them to several other servers. For example, you would use replication if you had a central database and needed to distribute sales data to all the databases in your company's department stores.

■ To customize data and distribute it to multiple subscribers. For example, if your company sold subscriptions to your consumer credit database, you could replicate the data for subscribers, customizing the data for each subscriber.

Replication is designed to meet the needs of a wide variety of environments. Replication architecture is divided into several different processes, procedures, and components, each of which is used to customize replication for a particular situation. The replication architecture includes:

■ **Replication components**   The server and data components used in replication
■ **Replication agents**   Applications that assist in the replication process
■ **Replication variants**   The types of replication you can configure

Replication Components

Before working with replication, you will need to know the main components of the process and how you use them. Servers in the replication model can have one or more of the following roles:

■ **Publisher**   Publishers are servers that make data available for replication to other servers. Publishers also track changes to data and maintain other information about source databases. Each data grouping has only one publisher.

■ **Distributor**   Distributors are servers that distribute replicated data. Distributors store the distribution database, metadata, historical data, and (for transactional replication) transactions.

■ **Subscriber**   Subscribers are the destination servers for replication. These servers store the replicated data and receive updates. Subscribers can also make changes to data. You can publish data to multiple subscribers.

The data being published for replication are referred to as *articles* and *publications*. Articles are the basic units for replication and can consist of a table, a subset of a table, or other database objects. Publications are collections of articles that subscribers can receive. You should associate articles with a publication and then publish the publication. Articles can contain:

■ An entire table.
■ Only certain columns from a table, obtained by using a vertical filter.

- Only certain rows from a table, obtained by using a horizontal filter.
- A table subset containing certain rows and columns.
- A view, indexed view, or user-defined function.
- A stored procedure.

You can also specify whether schema objects are replicated. Schema objects include constraints, indexes, triggers, collation, and extended properties. When you alter tables, views, procedures, functions, or triggers using DDL statements like ALTER TABLE or ALTER VIEW on a published object, the changes are propagated by default to all SQL Server subscribers. You cannot publish any of the following for replication:

- The *model*, *tempdb*, and *msdb* databases
- System tables in the *master* database

In the publication and subscription model, setting up replication involves the following steps:

1. Selecting a replication type and model
2. Performing any necessary preliminary tasks
3. Configuring a distributor and enabling publishers and publication databases
4. Creating a publication
5. Creating subscriptions to the publication and designating subscribers

Replication Agents and Jobs

SQL Server uses various helper applications to assist in the replication process. These applications are called *replication agents* and they include:

- **Snapshot Agent (snapshot.exe)**   Creates snapshots of data. It includes schema and data, which are stored for distribution. The Snapshot Agent is also responsible for updating status information in the distribution database. The Snapshot Agent runs on the distributor. Each published database has its own Snapshot Agent that runs on the distributor and connects to the publisher. Snapshot Agents are used with all types of replication.

- **Distribution Agent (distrib.exe)**   Applies data from snapshot replication or transactions from transaction replication to subscribers. The Distribution Agent can run on the distributor or on subscribers. It runs on distributor for push subscriptions, and on subscriber for pull subscriptions. This agent is not used with merge replication.

- **Merge Agent (replmerg.exe)**   Synchronizes changes that occur after the initial snapshot is created. If any conflicts occur when the changes are being synchronized, the conflicts are resolved using the rules set with the conflict resolver. Depending on the configuration, Merge Agents run on the publisher or on subscribers. Merge Agents are used only with merge replication.

- **Log Reader Agent (logread.exe)**   Moves transactions marked for replication from the transaction log on the publisher to the distributor. Each database that is published using transactional replication has its own Log Reader Agent that runs on the distributor and connects to the publisher. Log Reader Agents are used only with transactional replication.

- **Queue Reader Agent (qrdrsvc.exe)**   Stores database changes in a queue where the updates can be asynchronously propagated to the publisher. This allows subscribers to modify published data and synchronize those changes without having an active network connection to the publisher. Queue Reader Agents are used only with transactional replication with the queued updating option.

SQL Server 2005 does not have a separate cleanup agent. Instead, the following replication maintenance jobs are used to perform cleanup tasks:

- **Agent History Clean Up:** *DistributionDBName*   Removes replication agent history from the distribution database. By default, this runs every ten minutes.
- **Distribution Clean Up:** *DistributionDBName*   Deactivates subscriptions that have not been synchronized within the maximum distribution retention period and removes replicated transactions from the distribution database. By default, this runs every ten minutes.
- **Expired Subscription Clean Up**   Removes expired subscriptions from publication databases. By default, this runs every day at 1:00 A.M.
- **Reinitialize Subscriptions Having Data Validation Failures**   Flags all subscriptions that have data validation failures. The next time the Merge Agent or Distribution Agent runs, a new snapshot is applied at the subscriber. By default, this job is not enabled.
- **Replication Agents Checkup**   Detects replication agents that are not actively logging history and writes an error to the Windows event logs if a job step fails. By default, this runs every ten minutes.
- **Replication Monitoring Refresher For** *DistributionDBName*   Refreshes cached queries used by the Replication Monitor. By default, this starts automatically when SQL Server Agent starts and runs continuously.

Replication Variants

SQL Server supports several different types of replication. These replication variants are as follows:

- **Snapshot replication**   Takes a snapshot of current data and replaces the entire copy of the data on one or more subscribers. With subsequent snapshots, the entire copy of the data is again distributed to subscribers. Although exact copies are a benefit of snapshot replication, this technique increases the amount of overhead and traffic on the network. Another disadvantage of snapshot replication is that it only runs periodically, which usually means that subscribers do not have the most current information. In SQL Server 2005, snapshot preparation has been enhanced to allow processing of multiple articles while scripting schema or bulk copying data. This technique, referred to as *parallel processing*, is used automatically when possible. SQL Server 2005 also features resumable snapshot delivery, which allows an interrupted snapshot delivery to be resumed automatically. When the delivery is resumed, only files that have not been transferred or are partially transferred are transferred—any snapshot files that have been completely transferred are not re-transferred.

- **Transactional replication** Uses transactions to distribute changes and primarily, in server-server environments. When replication starts, a snapshot of the data is sent to subscribers. After the snapshot is sent, selected transactions in the publisher's transaction log are marked for replication and then distributed to each subscriber separately. Snapshots are then taken periodically to ensure that the databases are synchronized. Distributed transactions are used to ensure that incremental changes are applied consistently. A benefit of transactional replication is that you replicate individual transactions rather than an entire data set. Transactional replication can also occur continuously or periodically, which makes the procedure more versatile than snapshot replication by itself. To allow for easier implementation of transactional replication of large databases, SQL Server 2005 allows you to initialize a transactional subscription from backup. Thus, rather than using a snapshot to initialize a subscription, you can restore any backup taken after the creation of the publication on a subscriber. SQL Server 2005 also creates concurrent snapshots whenever possible to reduce the amount of time that locks are held during snapshot generation. This limits the impact on users that are working with the database while the snapshot is being generated.

- **Merge replication** Allows subscribers to make changes to replicated data independently, and primarily in a server-client environment. Later, you can merge these changes into all of the related source and destination databases. The snapshots needed to initialize merge replication can be pre-generated for each subscriber, or you can specify that subscribers can initiate snapshot generation during the initial synchronization. Merge replication does not use distributed transactions and cannot guarantee transactional consistency. Instead, merge replication uses a conflict resolver to determine which changes are applied. By default, merge replication processes changes on a row-by-row basis. You can also group sets of related rows as a logical record. This ensures that related sets of records are always processed in their entirety at the same time on a subscriber. SQL Server 2005 provides article-level statistics during merge replication. This gives better tracking of the merge phase and also allows you to define the order of article processing during merge synchronization. This technique, referred to as *declarative ordering*, is useful if you use triggers or rely on triggers firing in a specific order.

In snapshot and transactional replication, subscribers normally do not change data. However, with transactional replication, you have several options for allowing subscribers to change data:

- **Immediate updating** Allows subscribers to make changes and then immediately update the publisher. The publisher then replicates these changes to other subscribers.

- **Queued updating** Allows subscribers to make changes and then store the changes in a queue until they can be applied to the publisher. The publisher then replicates the changes to other subscribers. Immediate and queued updating is only supported in snapshot and transactional publications.

Queued updating provides fault tolerance that may be needed when databases are geographically separated. Immediate updating requires an active connection to the publisher, but queued updating does not. By using queued updating, subscribers can asynchronously apply changes, which means that they can store changes when a link is inactive, and then when the link is active, they can submit the changes to the publisher.

You can also use immediate updating, with queued updating as a failover, when you expect publishers and subscribers to be connected but do not want to lose the ability to make updates if a link fails. Here, you configure both updating options, using immediate updating as the primary update mechanism and then switching to queued updating when needed. You can invoke failover at any time. However, you cannot fail back afterward until the subscriber and publisher are connected and the Queue Reader Agent has applied all pending updates in the queue.

Both immediate updating and queued updating use transactions and the standard two-phase commit process to apply updates to the publisher. Transactions ensure that the update can be committed if it is successfully applied or rolled back if there is a problem. The transactions are applied from a specific subscriber to the publisher. After changes are made to the publisher, the publisher replicates the changes to other subscribers.

Transactions are completed automatically through the update process and are managed by the Distributed Transaction Coordinator. Custom applications that modify subscriber data can be written as though they were updating a single database. In a standard (default) configuration, updates to the subscriber are applied only when they can be replicated through a transaction. If the update cannot be replicated through a transaction, the subscriber will not be able to modify the subscription data.

SQL Server detects subscriber changes that would conflict with changes on the publisher. If it detects a conflict, it rejects the transaction and does not allow the data changes. Usually, a rejection means that the subscriber needs to synchronize with the publisher before attempting to update the data locally.

When you include stored procedures as articles in a snapshot publication, SQL Server replicates the entire stored procedure from the publisher to the subscribers. Changes caused by the execution of the stored procedures are replicated with new snapshots. If you use transactional replication, however, you can replicate execution of the stored procedure instead of replicating the changes that the execution causes. By sending an execute command rather than data changes, you reduce the amount of data that needs to flow across the network and improve the performance of SQL applications that use replication.

If you replicate the execution of stored procedures, you have two configuration settings. You can use *standard* procedure execution, or you can use *serialized* procedure execution. With standard procedure execution, procedure execution is replicated to all subscribers, even if those procedures are executed in different transactions. Because multiple transactions may be executing at a particular time, subscribers' data cannot be guaranteed to be consistent with the publisher's data. With serialized stored procedures, procedures are executed in sequence if they are referenced within serialized transactions. If the procedures are executed outside of serialized transactions, changes to the data are replicated instead. This behavior guarantees that the subscribers' data is consistent with the publisher's data.

Planning for Replication

As you have learned, the architecture for the replication process is extensive. This ensures that the architecture is versatile enough to meet the needs of almost any replication situation. Unfortunately, this versatility also makes replication tricky to configure. To make the replication go smoothly, you should do a bit of planning, which involves selecting a specific replication model and performing any necessary preliminary tasks before you start configuring replication.

Replication Models

The main decision to make when you select a replication model involves the physical layout of the publisher, distributor, and subscriber databases. Replication models you may want to use include:

- **Peer-to-peer model**   Allows replication between identical participants in the topology. The advantage of this model is that it permits roles to move between replicated nodes dynamically for maintenance or failure management. The disadvantage is the additional administration overhead involved with moving roles.

- **Central publisher model**   Maintains the publisher and distributor databases on the same server, with one or more subscribers configured on other servers. The advantages of this model are manageability and ease of maintenance. The disadvantages include the extra workload and resource usage on the publication server.

Tip   The central publisher model is the most commonly used replication model. Unfortunately, you will often find that the extra load on the publication server slows down server performance. To reduce the server load, you should put the distributor on its own server. Be aware, however, that doing this will not entirely eliminate the workload on the publication server. The publisher and distributor still need to communicate, and they still need to pass data back and forth.

- **Central publisher with remote distributor model**   Maintains the publisher and distributor databases on different servers, with one or more subscribers configured on other servers. The advantage of this model is that the workload is more evenly distributed. The disadvantage is that you have to maintain an additional server.

- **Central subscriber model**   A single subscriber database that collects data from several publishers. For example, if you have ServerA, ServerB, and ServerC, ServerA and ServerB would act as central publishers, and ServerC would act as the central subscriber. In this configuration, when updates are distributed from ServerA and ServerB, they are collected on ServerC. A central subscriber could then republish the combined data to other servers. To use this model, all tables used in replication must have a unique primary key; otherwise, the replication model will not work properly.

- **Publishing subscriber model**   Relays the distribution of data to other subscribers; you can use this with any of the other models. For example, if you have two geographically separated sites, a publisher could replicate data to servers at site A and then have a publishing subscriber at site B that distributes the data to servers at site B.

Preliminary Replication Tasks

After selecting the replication type and model you want to use, you prepare for the replication by performing preliminary tasks. The following subsections describe the main tasks involved, according to replication type.

Preparing for Snapshot Replication

If you use snapshot replication, the data being replicated is copied in full to data files on the distributor. Normally these snapshot files are the same size as the data you are replicating, and they are stored in the SQL Server Repldata folder by default. You should make sure that the drive on which the replication data is stored has adequate free space. For example, if you are using snapshot replication to distribute publication A with 500 MB of data, publication B with 420 MB, and publication C with 900 MB, you should have at least 2 GB of free space. Some of the free space is needed for processing overhead; the rest is required for the actual data.

You can also store snapshot data in an alternate location where subscribers can retrieve it at a later time. If you use an alternate location, you have the option of compressing the snapshot file, which reduces the disk space requirements only for the files you are compressing. It does not change the overall space requirements, and it does not always reduce the initial and final space requirements. With compression, the Snapshot Agent generates the necessary data files and then uses the Microsoft CAB utility to compress the files. When the subscriber receives compressed snapshot files, the files are written to a temporary location, which is either the default client working directory or an alternate location specified in the subscription properties. The subscriber uses the CAB utility to decompress the files before reading them.

 Real World   When you create snapshot files in the default location and in an alternate location on different drives, the files are created separately. This means that the total disk space required typically is what you would expect, based on the size of the files. However, when you create snapshot files in the default location and in an alternate location on the same drive, both files are initially created in the default location and then the alternate location file is copied to its final destination. This means that the total disk space required in the default location is twice what you might expect. Compression does not help because the Snapshot Agent generates the necessary data files and then compresses them.

Replication timing is another important consideration in snapshot replication. When the Snapshot Agent creates a snapshot of a published table, the agent locks the entire table while it bulk copies the data from the publisher to the distributor. As a result, users cannot update any data in the table until the lock is released. To reduce the impact on operations, you should carefully schedule when replication occurs. Some actions that may help include:

- Identifying times when operations are at their lowest levels or users do not need write access to the tables you are replicating
- Identifying times when snapshots must be made and scheduling users to do work during that time that does not require write access to the tables you are replicating

SQL Server 2005 processes multiple articles while scripting schema or bulk copying data. This parallel processing can increase the speed and efficiency of the snapshot generation process. SQL Server 2005 also features resumable snapshot delivery, which allows an interrupted snapshot delivery to be automatically resumed. When the delivery is resumed, only files that have not been transferred yet or have been transferred partially are transferred—any snapshot files that have been completely transferred already are not retransferred.

Preparing for Transactional Replication

Because transactional replication builds on the snapshot replication model, you will want to prepare for both snapshot and transactional replication. When you use transactional replication, an initial snapshot is sent to the distributor, and this snapshot is then updated on a periodic basis, such as once a month. Between snapshots, transactions are used to update subscribers. These transactions are logged in the distributor's database and are cleared out only after a new snapshot is created.

Transaction logs for published databases are extremely important to successful replication. As long as replication is enabled, pending transactions cannot be cleared out of a published database until they have been passed to the distributor. Because of this, you may need to increase the size of a published database's transaction log. Furthermore, if the publisher cannot contact the distributor or if the Log Reader Agent is not running, transactions will continue to build up in the publisher's transaction logs.

With transactional replication, all published tables must have a declared primary key. You can add a primary key to an existing table using the ALTER TABLE statement (see Chapter 9, "Manipulating Schemas, Tables, Indexes, and Views"). Additionally, if a publication uses very large data types, you must make sure that you keep the following limitations in mind:

- When updating *varchar(max)*, *nvarchar(max)*, and *varbinary(max)* data types, you should use the .WRITE clause of the UPDATE statement to perform a partial or full update. If you are performing a partial update of a *varchar(max)* column, you might update the first 100 characters of a column. If you are performing a full update, you might modify all the data in a column. *@Offset* and *@Length* values for the .WRITE clause are specified in bytes for *varbinary(max)* and *varchar(max)* data types and in characters for the *nvarchar(max)* data type.

 Best Practices For best performance, you should insert or update data in multiples of 8,040 bytes, which ensures that the data is written using whole data pages. Any .WRITE updates that insert or append new data are minimally logged when the database recovery model is set to Simple or Bulk Logged. Minimal logging is not used when you update existing values.

- When modifying *text*, *ntext*, or *image* data types, UPDATE initializes the column, assigns a valid text pointer to it, and allocates at least one data page unless the column is being updated with NULL. To replace or modify large blocks of *text*, *ntext*, or *image* data, Microsoft recommends that you use WRITE-TEXT or UPDATETEXT instead of the UPDATE statement. However, support for WRITETEXT and UPDATETEXT is deprecated and may be removed in future versions of SQL Server.
- The SQL Server configuration option MAX TEXT REPL SIZE controls the maximum byte size of the text and image data that can be replicated. Operations that exceed this limit will fail. Set the maximum text replication size with the *sp_configure* system stored procedure.

The snapshot process can be modified for transactional replication in several important ways. To allow for easier implementation of transactional replication of large databases, SQL Server 2005 allows you to initialize a transactional subscription from backup. Thus, rather than using a snapshot to initialize a subscription, you can restore on a subscriber any backup taken after the creation of the publication. SQL Server 2005 also creates concurrent snapshots whenever possible to reduce the amount of time that locks are held during snapshot generation. This limits the impact on users that are working with the database while the snapshot is being generated.

Preparing for Merge Replication

For merge replication, all published tables must have primary keys. If a table contains foreign keys or is used in validation, you must include the reference table in the publication. Otherwise, update operations that add new rows will fail because SQL Server cannot find the required primary key. Additionally, merge replication affects time-stamp column usage. Time stamps are generated automatically and are guaranteed to be unique only in a specific database. Because of this, SQL Server replicates time-stamp columns but does not replicate the literal time-stamp values contained in the columns. These values are regenerated when the initial snapshot rows are applied at the subscriber.

Like transactional replication, merge replication has a few limitations when it comes to text and image columns. For example, you must explicitly update text and image columns with an UPDATE statement. When using merge replication, subscribers can make changes to replicated data independently, and these changes can be merged into all of the related source and destination databases. The Merge Agent watches for changes that conflict with other changes. If it detects a conflict, a conflict resolver is used to determine which change is applied and which change is rolled back. The Merge Agent can track changes at a column level or at a row level. In column-level tracking, a conflict exists when changes are made to the same column in a table in more than one copy. In row-level tracking, a conflict exists when changes are made to the same row in a table in more than one copy.

Normally, subscribers to merge publications only synchronize updates with the publisher. Subscribers can also synchronize with other servers, and they do this by designating alternate synchronization partners. It is useful to have an alternate synchronization partner when you want to ensure that updates can be made even if the primary publisher is offline or otherwise unavailable.

Note By default, merge replication processes changes on a row-by-row basis. You can group sets of related rows as a logical record. This ensures that related sets of records are always processed in their entirety at the same time on a subscriber. You can also use declarative ordering to define the order of article processing during merge synchronization.

Distributor Administration

As the name indicates, you use distributors to distribute replicated data. When you work with distributors, the core set of administration tasks you will perform includes setting up a new distributor, updating an existing distributor, and deleting distributors.

Setting Up a New Distributor

Setting up a new distributor is the first major step in configuring replication. Before you get started, you should prepare as follows:

- Select a replication type—either snapshot, transactional, or merge.
- Select a replication model, such as the central publisher model.
- Perform any necessary preliminary tasks. To meet certain limitations, you may need to update clients and applications that modify published databases directly.

When you are ready to proceed, configure the distributor by completing the following steps:

1. Start SQL Server Management Studio. In Object Explorer view, connect to the server you want to use, and then work your way down to the Replication folder.

Tip If you cannot successfully connect to a remote server, the server might not be configured to accept remote connections. As discussed in Chapter 3, "Managing the Surface Security, Access, and Network Configuration," you will need to use the SQL Server 2005 Surface Area Configuration tool to allow remote connections.

2. Right-click the Replication folder, and then select Configure Distribution. This starts the Configure Distribution Wizard.

3. Click Next to move past the Welcome screen. On the next page of the wizard, you can select a distributor, as shown in Figure 12-1.

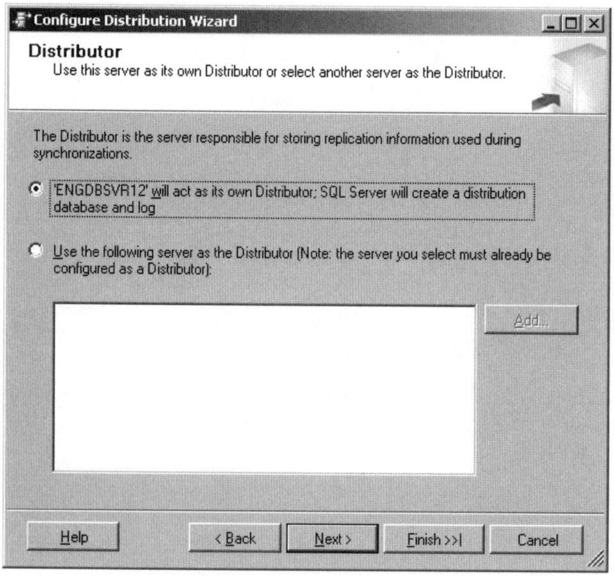

Configure Distribution Wizard

Distributor
Use this server as its own Distributor or select another server as the Distributor.

The Distributor is the server responsible for storing replication information used during synchronizations.

○ 'ENGDBSVR12' will act as its own Distributor; SQL Server will create a distribution database and log

○ Use the following server as the Distributor (Note: the server you select must already be configured as a Distributor):

Add...

Help   < Back   Next >   Finish >>| Cancel

Figure 12-1   The Configure Distribution Wizard

4. Because you want to set up a new distributor, accept the default to allow the current server to act as its own distributor, and then click Next.

5. If the SQL Server Agent is not already started and configured to start automatically, you will see the SQL Server Agent Start page. Select Yes, Configure The SQL Server Agent Service To Start Automatically, and then click Next.

6. On the Snapshot Folder page, set the location of the folder used to store snapshots, and then click Next. The default path is to the %ProgramFiles%\ Microsoft SQL Server\MSSQL.1\MSSQL\ReplData folder on the server designated as the distributor. To guarantee that Distribution and Merge Agents running on subscribers can access snapshots of their push and pull subscriptions, you should place the snapshot folder on a network share and specify the network path by typing it in the text box provided, such as **\\CorpSvr09\ ReplData**.

7. On the Distribution Database page, provide information for the distribution database using the dialog box shown in Figure 12-2. Enter a name for the distribution database, and then set folder locations for the corresponding data and log files. Click Next when you are ready to continue.

Tip You cannot use mapped network drives as folder locations for the data and log files.

Note Be sure to use a descriptive name for the database, such as EmployeeDistribution or EmpDistr.

![Configure Distribution Wizard dialog box]

Configure Distribution Wizard

Distribution Database
Select the name and location of the distribution database and log files.

The distribution database stores changes to transactional publications until Subscribers can be updated. It also stores historical information for snapshot and merge publications.

Distribution database name:

EmployeeDistribution

Folder for the distribution database file:

C:\Program Files\Microsoft SQL Server\MSSQL.1\MSSQL\Data

Folder for the distribution database log file:

C:\Program Files\Microsoft SQL Server\MSSQL.1\MSSQL\Data

The paths must refer to disks that are local to the Distributor and begin with a local drive letter and colon (for example, C:). Mapped drive letters and network paths are invalid.

| Help | < Back | Next > | Finish >>| | Cancel |

Figure 12-2 The Distribution Database page of the Configure Distribution Wizard

8. As shown in Figure 12-3, you need to enable publishers for this distribution database. Only registered servers in the current domain are shown. If you want to add a server so that it can use this distributor when it becomes a publisher, click Add, and then:

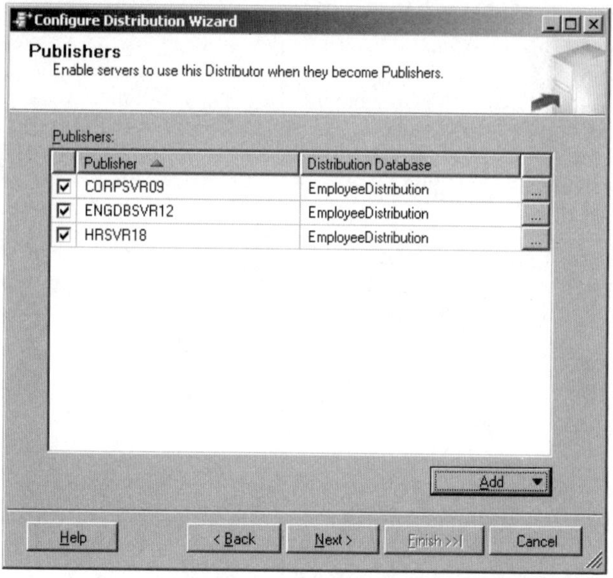

Figure 12-3   The Publishers page of the Configure Distribution Wizard

❑ Choose Add SQL Server Publisher to configure a connection to a SQL Server using the Connect To Server dialog box. Registered servers are listed in the Server Name drop-down list, and you can browse for others. The default authentication is Windows Authentication, which uses your current login and password. Click Connect.

❑ Choose Add Oracle Publisher to configure a connection to an Oracle server using the Connect To Server dialog box. Registered servers are listed in the Server Name drop-down list, and you can browse for others. The default authentication is Oracle Standard Authentication, which requires a user login and password. Click Connect.

9. To the right of registered publisher entries, you will see the Properties button (...). Click this button to open the Properties dialog box to set publisher options for the related server. As Figure 12-4 shows, the following options are available:

   ■ **Agent Connection Mode**   Distributors use SQL Server Agent to handle replication tasks. The SQL Server Agent must be configured to start automatically. By default, synchronization agents log in to the publishers using the SQL Server Agent account (determined by selecting the Impersonate The Agent Process Account option). If you want synchronization agents to use a specific login when connecting to publishers, select SQL Server Authentication from the drop-down list, and then enter the login and password to use.

   ■ **Default Snapshot Folder**   Sets the location of the folder used to store snapshots. The Snapshot folder is stored on the distribution database and can be in a different location for each publisher that uses the distribution database.

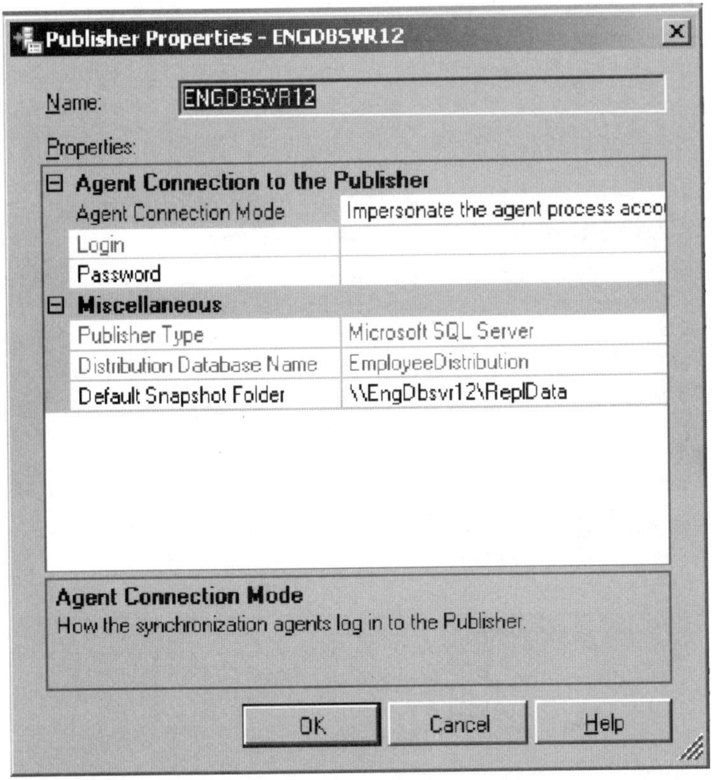

Figure 12-4 The Properties dialog box

10. Click Next. If you specified a remote server as a possible publisher, you next must specify and confirm the password that remote publishers will use to connect to the distributor. This password must be provided when a remote publisher connects to the distributor to perform replication administrative operations. The password must meet the Windows policy requirements for length and complexity. Click Next.

11. By default, the wizard will configure the distributor immediately when you click Finish. If you would rather have the wizard generate a script that you can run at a later time or can schedule to be run, select the Generate A Script File... option.

12. Click Next, and then click Finish. The wizard will configure the distributor or generate the script according to the option you specified. The success or failure of each step is shown in the related dialog box. If a step fails, click the link provided to display the error details. Click Close.

When you establish a server as a distributor, many areas of the server are updated. You may note that there is a new distribution database; additional jobs, alerts, and proxies for replication may now be listed; and other updates may be evident. The Replication Monitor tool also becomes available. To learn how to work with this SQL Server feature, see Chapter 13, "Profiling and Monitoring Microsoft SQL Server 2005."

Configure publications and subscriptions as explained in the subsections titled "Enabling and Updating Publishers," "Enabling Publication Databases," and "Creating Subscriptions" later in this chapter.

Updating Distributors

When you configure a new distributor, you can set up a new distribution database, as discussed in the subsection titled "Setting Up a New Distributor" earlier in this chapter. If you have already configured a distributor, you can update the distributor and create additional distribution databases by completing the following steps:

1. Start SQL Server Management Studio. In Object Explorer view, connect to the server you want to use, and then work your way down to the Replication folder.

2. Right-click the Replication folder, and then select Distributor Properties. This opens the dialog box shown in Figure 12-5.

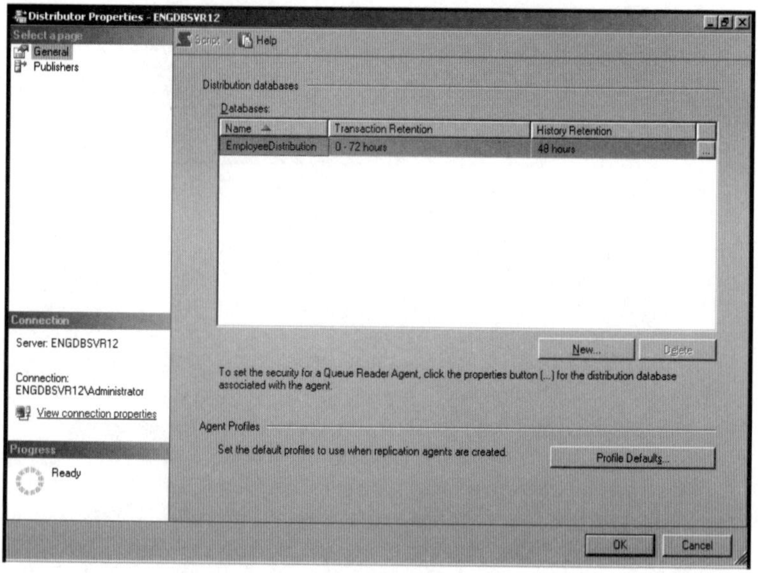

Figure 12-5 The Distributor Properties dialog box

3. You can use the options in the dialog box to change publisher and distributor data properties for the currently selected distributor. Use the dialog box pages as follows:

   - **General**   Configure distribution databases, agent profiles, and properties for retention and queuing.
   - **Publishers**   Enable and disable publishers for the distributor, set publisher properties, and configure passwords for administrative links.

4. On the General page, you will see a list of current distribution databases and their settings for transaction and history retention. By default, new distribution databases store transactions only as long as they are needed [determined by the retention setting of at least zero (0) hours] but not more than 72 hours, and they retain replication performance history data for at least 48 hours.

5. To view the current location of database and log files for a selected distribution database or change the retention settings, click the Properties button (...) in the third column to the right of the database name. This displays the Distribution Database Properties dialog box shown in Figure 12-6. Use the text boxes and option buttons provided to manage the retention settings as necessary. Click OK when you are finished to apply the changes.

6. On the Publishers page, you will see a list of current publishers for this distributor and the distribution databases they use. A check mark next to a publisher's name indicates that the publisher is enabled.

7. Click OK to close the dialog box and apply any changes.

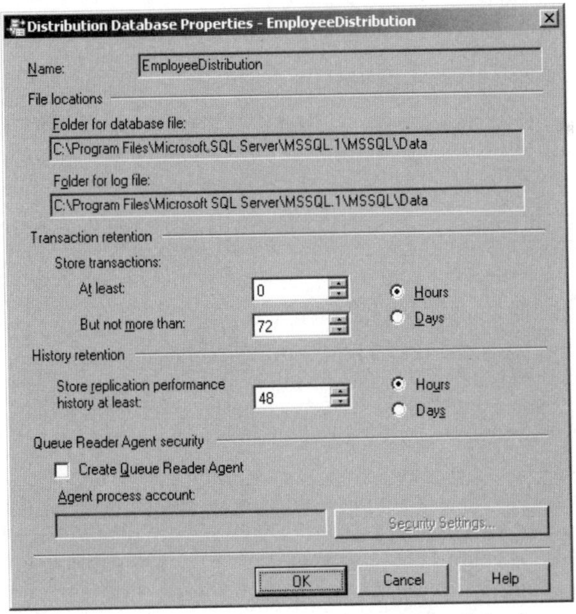

Figure 12-6   The Distributor Database Properties dialog box

Creating Distribution Databases

Distribution databases are used to store the information being distributed to subscribers. Each publisher that uses a distributor is assigned a distribution database to which it can connect. Publishers can share distribution databases, and you also can create additional databases as necessary. If you have already configured a distributor, you can create additional distribution databases by completing the following steps:

1. Start SQL Server Management Studio. In Object Explorer view, connect to the server you want to use, and then work your way down to the Replication folder.

2. Right-click the Replication folder, and then select Distributor Properties. This opens the dialog box shown previously in Figure 12-5.

3. On the General page, click New. You can now configure the distribution database.

4. Enter a name for the distribution database, and then set folder locations for the corresponding data and log files. You cannot use mapped network drives.

5. Use the options in the Transaction Retention and History Retention areas to determine how long transactions and performance history are retained for the distribution database.

6. Click OK twice to close the open dialog boxes and create the distribution database.

   You can assign the new distribution database to any new publishers you configure.

Enabling and Updating Publishers

Distributors can work only with servers and databases that are enabled for their use. You can enable publishers when you create a new distributor or by completing the following steps:

1. Start SQL Server Management Studio. In Object Explorer view, connect to the server you want to use, and then work your way down to the Replication folder.

2. Right-click the Replication folder, and then select Distributor Properties.

3. In the Distributor Properties dialog box, select the Publishers page. Use the check boxes provided to enable or disable publishers. Only registered publishers are shown. If you want to add a server so that it can use this distributor when it becomes a publisher, click Add, and then:

   ❑ Choose Add SQL Server Publisher to configure a connection to a SQL Server using the Connect To Server dialog box. Registered servers are listed in the Server Name drop-down list, and you can browse for others. The default authentication is Windows Authentication, which uses your current login and password. Click Connect. If there is more than one distribution database available, the Distribution Database box will have a drop-down list allowing you to choose the database to use.

❑ Choose Add Oracle Publisher to configure a connection to an Oracle server using the Connect To Server dialog box. Registered servers are listed in the Server Name drop-down list, and you can browse for others. The default authentication is Oracle Standard Authentication, which requires a user login and password. Click Connect. If there is more than one distribution database available, the Distribution Database box will have a drop-down list allowing you to choose the database to use.

4. To the right of registered publisher entries, you will see the Properties button (...). Click this button to set publisher options for the related server. The following options are available:

- **Agent Connection Mode** Distributors use SQL Server Agent to handle replication tasks. The SQL Server Agent must be configured to start automatically. By default, synchronization agents log in to the publishers using the SQL Server Agent account (determined by selecting the Impersonate The Agent Process Account option). If you want synchronization agents to use a specific login when connecting to publishers, select SQL Server Authentication in this box, and then enter the login and password to use. (This is the Administrative Link Password, which also can be set by selecting the publisher on the Publishers page and then using the boxes and options provided in the lower-right area of the dialog box.)

- **Default Snapshot Folder** Sets the location of the folder used to store snapshots. The Snapshot folder is stored on the distribution database and can be in a different location for each publisher that uses the distribution database.

Enabling Publication Databases

After you configure distributors and publishers, you can enable publication databases by completing the following steps:

1. Start SQL Server Management Studio. In Object Explorer view, connect to the server you want to use, and then work your way down to the Replication folder.

2. Right-click the Replication folder, and then select Publisher Properties. This opens the Publisher Properties dialog box.

3. To enable publication databases, select the Publication Databases page. Then select entries under the Transactional column to enable a database for snapshot or transactional replication, or select entries under the Merge column to enable a database for merge replication.

4. To enable a publication database for any type of replication, select both the corresponding Transactional and Merge check boxes.

Deleting Distribution Databases

Before you can delete a distribution database, you must remove all publications and disable all the publishers using the distribution database. Once you have done this, you can delete distribution databases by completing the following steps:

1. Start SQL Server Management Studio. In Object Explorer view, connect to the server you want to use, and then work your way down to the Replication folder.
2. Right-click the Replication folder, and then select Distributor Properties. This opens the Distributor Properties dialog box.
3. On the General page, select the distribution database you want to delete, and then click Delete.
4. Click OK to close the dialog box and perform the delete operation.

Disabling Publishing and Distribution

By using the Disable Publishing And Distribution Wizard in SQL Server Management Studio, you can disable publishing and distribution. When you disable publishing:

- All publications on the selected server are dropped.
- All subscriptions to the affected publications are dropped.
- The server is disabled as a distributor.

You can disable publishing and distribution by completing the following steps:

1. Start SQL Server Management Studio. In Object Explorer view, connect to the server you want to use, and then work your way down to the Replication folder.
2. Right-click the Replication folder, and then select Disable Publishing And Distribution. This starts the Disable Publishing And Distribution Wizard.
3. Click Next to skip the Welcome screen, and then choose Yes, Disable Publishing On This Server.
4. Click Next. Review the publishers that will be disabled.
5. Click Next twice, and then click Finish.

Creating and Managing Publications

After you have configured a distributor and enabled publishers, publication databases, and subscribers, you can create publications. You will manage the publications you create as you would any other SQL Server resource.

Creating Publications

The easiest way to create publications is by using SQL Server Management Studio. To do this, complete the following steps:

1. Start SQL Server Management Studio. In Object Explorer view, connect to the server you want to use, and then work your way down to the Replication folder.

2. Right-click the Local Publications folder, and then select New Publication. This starts the New Publication Wizard. Click Next to skip the Welcome screen.

Note If you want to create an Oracle publication, you would select New Oracle Publication. This starts the New Oracle Publication Wizard, which is similar to the New Publication Wizard.

3. Choose the database on the selected server that contains the data or objects you want to publish. You can select user databases only. Click Next.

4. Choose the type of replication you want to use for the publication. The options are:

   ■ **Snapshot publication** Creates a publication setup for snapshot replication.

   ■ **Transactional publication** Creates a publication setup for transactional replication.

   ■ **Transactional publication with updatable subscriptions** Creates a publication setup for transactional replication with subscriptions that can be updated.

   ■ **Merge publication** Creates a publication setup for merge replication.

5. If you are creating a snapshot or transactional publication, continue using the steps listed in the following subsection, "Snapshot and Transactional Publications."

6. If you are creating a merge publication, continue using the steps listed in the subsection titled "Merge Publications" later in this chapter.

Snapshot and Transactional Publications

Snapshot and transactional publications are the most commonly used types of publications. With snapshot publications, the publisher periodically replaces subscriber data with an updated snapshot. With transactional publications, the publisher updates data and changes are sent to subscribers through transactions.

After you have started a new publication, as discussed in the subsection titled "Creating Publications" earlier in this chapter, you can create a snapshot or transactional publication by completing the following steps:

1. Click Next to continue. On the Articles page, shown in Figure 12-7, select the objects for replication. The Objects To Publish pane shows the types of objects that are available for replication. Click the plus sign (+) next to the object to see a list of available objects of the specified type.

2. To select all the columns in a table or view, select the table or view name entry. Which objects are available depends on the types of objects in the database

and may include tables, stored procedures, user-defined functions, and views. Tables without primary keys cannot be published for transactional replication, and you will see a key surrounded by a red circle with a line through it in the Specify Articles dialog box. Additionally, tables referenced by views are required.

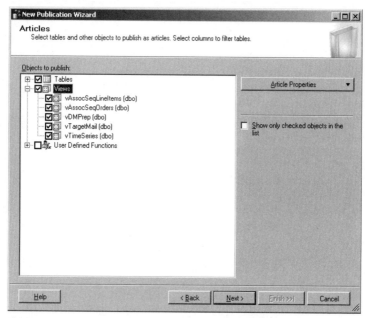

Figure 12-7   The Articles page of the New Publication Wizard

3. To select individual columns in a table or view, expand the table or view entry, and then select the appropriate entries for the columns to include. If you are using transactional replication and selecting individual columns, keep in mind that primary key columns are required and must be published. Primary key columns are indicated by a key with a green asterisk. By clearing a column check box, you exclude the related column from replication (which was previously referred to as vertically filtering a table).

4. Default properties are set for each selected object (article), including the destination object name and object owner, action to use if the object exists, and if user triggers and extended properties should be copied. You can manage these default properties by setting global defaults, by setting defaults for an individual article, or both:

   ❑ To set defaults for an individual article, select it under Objects To Publish, click Article Properties, and then select Set Properties Of Highlighted... Article. Refer to the subsection titled "Setting Publication Properties" later in this chapter for details.

❏ To set defaults for all articles of a particular type, select the object type under Objects To Publish, click Article Properties, and then select Set Properties Of All... Articles. Refer to the subsection titled "Setting Publication Properties" later in this chapter for details.

5. After you select objects to use in the publication, click Next. If there are any issues that require changes to the publication, you will see a prompt similar to the one shown in Figure 12-8. Read the description carefully to determine how to resolve the issue and make changes as necessary. Some important issues that may be described in a prompt include the following:

❏ Tables referenced by views are required and so are objects referenced by stored procedures. If you do not select referenced tables or objects, you must create them manually at the subscriber.

❏ SQL Server adds *uniqueidentifier* columns to any tables you have selected for replication. Adding a *uniqueidentifier* column will cause INSERT statements without column lists to fail and will increase the time needed to generate the first snapshot.

❏ IDENTITY columns require the NOT FOR REPLICATION option. If a published IDENTITY column does not use this option, INSERT commands may not replicate properly.

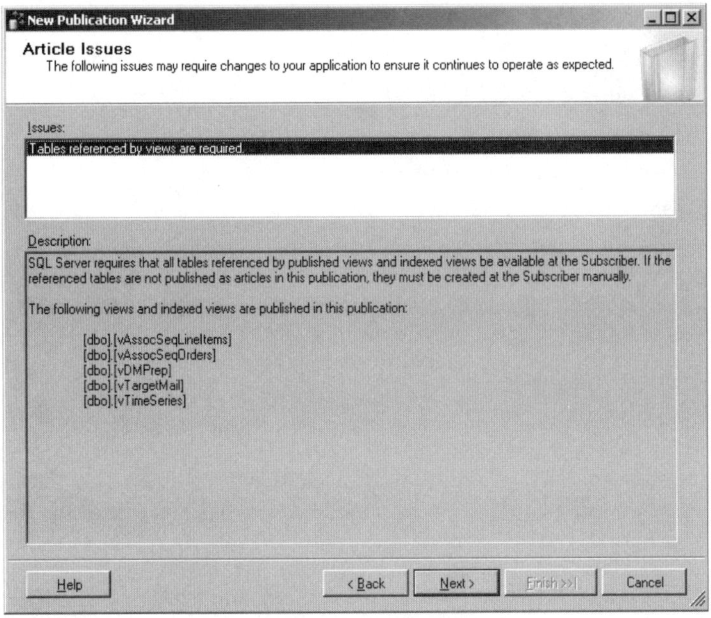

Figure 12-8   Article Issues dialog box

6. Click Next. Use the Filter Table Rows page to exclude unwanted rows from published tables. As you define filters, they are added to the Filtered Tables list. Selecting a filter shows the related WHERE clause in the Filter box. If you want to define a new filter, click Add to display the Add Filter dialog box shown in Figure 12-9. By default, all rows are published. To change this behavior, select a table to filter, and then create a filter statement that identifies which rows subscribers will receive. Enter a WHERE clause for the corresponding SELECT *published_columns* FROM *TableName* statement.

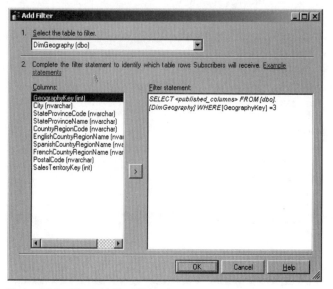

Figure 12-9 The Add Filter dialog box

7. Click Next. The Snapshot Agent initializes subscriptions by creating a snapshot of publication schema and data that can be pushed to subscribers or pulled by subscribers. You can create a snapshot immediately by selecting Create A Snapshot Immediately. If you want the Snapshot Agent to create snapshots periodically, select Schedule The Snapshot Agent To Run.... By default, snapshots are made once a day. To change this schedule, click Change, and then set a new schedule.

8. Click Next. Set a login for each agent used in replication, which can include the Snapshot, Log Reader, and Queue Reader Agents. To configure the login for the Snapshot Agent, click the related Security Settings button, and then:

   ❑ Specify the Windows account under which the agent runs at the Distributor. This account is referred to as the process account. The account must be a member of the db_owner fixed database role in the *distribution* database and must have write permissions on the snapshot share. Be sure to type domain account names in the form *domain\account*, such as **cpandl\sqlserver**. Then type and confirm the account password.

❏ Specify whether the agent should make connections to the publisher by impersonating the account specified in the Process Account text box or by using a SQL Server account. If you choose to use a SQL Server account, enter a SQL Server login and password. Typically, you will want to impersonate the Windows account rather than use a SQL Server account.

9. The Log Reader Agent is used with updatable and nonupdatable transactional publications. By default, the Log Reader Agent uses the same login as the Snapshot Agent. To specify separate security settings for the Log Reader Agent, clear the Use The Security Settings From The Snapshot Agent check box, and then click the related Security Settings button. You can then specify the process account and how connections to the publisher are made.

10. The Queue Reader Agent is used with updatable transactional publications. By default, the Queue Reader Agent has a separate security context from the other agents. To configure security, click the related Security Settings button, and then specify the process account.

11. Click Next. Choose the wizard action upon completion. By default, the wizard creates the publication. You can also generate a script file with the steps to create the publication. If you want to only generate a script, clear Create The Publication. Click Next.

12. On the Complete The Wizard page, type a name for the publication, and then click Finish. You will see a dialog box that shows the progress of the creation process. If errors occur, you must resolve any problems before you can continue, or else you must restart the publication definition process.

Merge Publications

Once you have started a new publication, as discussed in the subsection titled "Creating Publications" earlier in the chapter, you can create a merge publication by completing the following steps:

1. Click Next to continue. Select the types of subscribers that will subscribe to the publication. You can choose any or all of the following:

   ▪ **SQL Server 2005**   With this type of subscriber, snapshots are formatted using Native SQL Server format.

   ▪ **SQL Server 2005 Mobile Edition**   With this type of subscriber, snapshots are formatted using Character format.

   ▪ **SQL Server 2000**   With this type of subscriber, logical records, replication of DDL changes, and some filter optimizations are not supported.

   ▪ **SQL Server for Windows CE**   With this type of subscriber, snapshots are formatted using Character format. Additionally, logical records, replication of DDL changes, and some filter optimizations are not supported.

2. Click Next to continue. On the Articles page, shown previously in Figure 12-7, select the objects for replication. The Objects To Publish pane shows the types of objects that are available for replication. Click the plus sign (+) next to the object to see a list of available objects of the specified type.

3. To select all the columns in a table or view, select the table or view name entry. The objects available depend on the types of objects in the database; they can be tables, stored procedures, user-defined functions, and views. Tables referenced by views are required.

4. To select individual columns in a table or view, expand the table or view entry, and then select the appropriate entries for the columns to include. If you are selecting individual columns, keep in mind that both primary key and Rowguid columns are required and must be published. Primary key columns are indicated by a key and a green asterisk. Rowguid columns are indicated by a green asterisk. By clearing a column check box, you exclude the related column from replication (which was previously referred to as vertically filtering a table).

5. Default properties are set for each selected object (article), including the destination object name and object owner, action to use if the object exists, and if user triggers and extended properties should be copied. You can manage these default properties by setting global defaults, by setting defaults for an individual article, or both:

   ❑ To set defaults for an individual article, select it under Objects To Publish, click Article Properties, and then select Set Properties Of Highlighted... Article. Refer to the subsection titled "Setting Publication Properties" later in this chapter for details.

   ❑ To set defaults for all articles of a particular type, select the object type under Objects To Publish, click Article Properties, and then select Set Properties Of All... Articles. Refer to the subsection titled "Setting Publication Properties" later in this chapter for details.

6. After you select objects to use in the publication, click Next. If there are any issues that require changes to the publication, you will see a prompt, similar to the one previously shown in Figure 12-8, describing the issue or issues. Read the description carefully to determine how to resolve the problems indicated, and then make changes as necessary. Common issues include:

   ❑ Tables referenced by views are required and so are objects referenced by stored procedures. If you do not select referenced tables or objects, you must create them manually at the subscriber.

   ❑ SQL Server adds *uniqueidentifier* columns to any tables you have selected for replication. Adding the *uniqueidentifier* column will cause INSERT statements without column lists to fail and will increase the time needed to generate the first snapshot.

   ❑ IDENTITY columns require the NOT FOR REPLICATION option. If a published IDENTITY column does not use this option, INSERT commands may not replicate properly.

7. Click Next. Use the Filter Table Rows page to exclude unwanted rows from published tables. As you define filters, they are added to the Filtered Tables list. Selecting a filter shows the related WHERE clause in the Filter text box. You can define filters manually and then extend those filters to other tables, or you can attempt to automate the process.

8. If you want to define a new filter:

  ❑ Click Add, and then select Add Filter to display the Add Filter dialog box. By default, all rows are published. To change this behavior, select a table to filter, and then create a filter statement that identifies which rows subscribers will receive. Enter a WHERE clause for the corresponding SELECT *published_columns* FROM *TableName* statement.

  ❑ Specify how many subscribers will receive data from this table: one or many. Merge publications use static or parameterized filters. Static filters are evaluated when the publication is created, and all subscribers to the publication receive the same data. Parameterized filters are evaluated during replication synchronization, and different subscribers can receive different partitions of data based on the subscriber login or computer name.

9. After you define a filter, you can extend the filtering to a related table by defining a join. To do this, create a filter on a table as discussed in the previous step, then in the New Publication Wizard, select the filter, click Add, and then select Add Join To Extend The Selected Filter. This displays the Add Join dialog box shown in Figure 12-10. You must now:

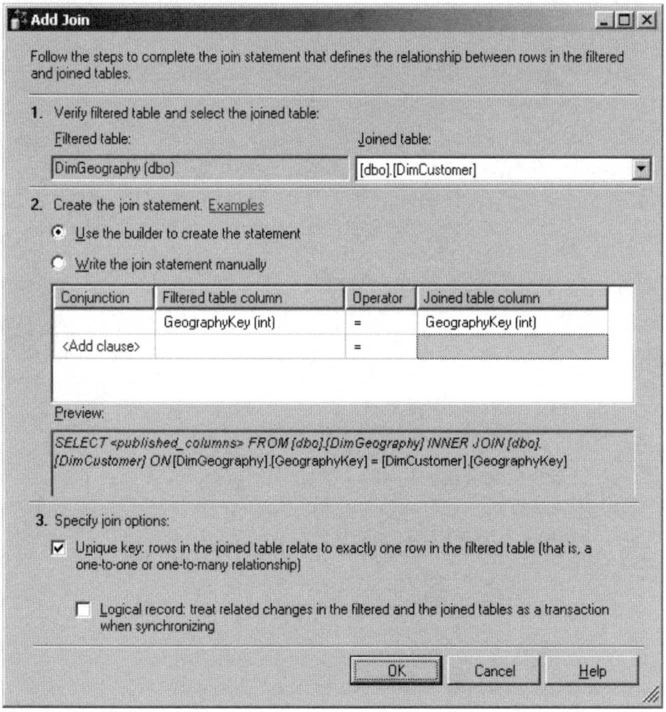

Figure 12-10   The Add Join dialog box

- ❑ Select the joined table from the list of published tables available in the Joined Table drop-down list, and then define the INNER JOIN clause using the builder or manually.

- ❑ Specify the join options. If there is a one-to-one or one-to-many relationship between rows in the joined table, select Unique Key. If rows in the joined table do not relate to exactly one row in the filtered table, clear Unique Key. Additionally, if related changes should be handled as a logical record and you are working with a unique key, select Logical Record.

10. An alternative to defining filters manually is to generate filters automatically. Click Add, and then select Automatically Generate Filters. In the Generate Filters dialog box, you must then define a new filter as explained previously. SQL Server will then use defined relationships to add joins that extend the filter to other tables.

11. Click Next. The Snapshot Agent initializes subscriptions by creating a snapshot of publication schema and data that can be pushed to subscribers or pulled by subscribers. You can create a snapshot immediately by selecting Create A Snapshot Immediately. If you want the Snapshot Agent to create a snapshot periodically, select Schedule The Snapshot Agent To Run.... By default, snapshots are made once every 14 days. To change this schedule, click Change, and then set a new schedule.

12. Click Next. Configure the login for the Snapshot Agent. Click the related Security Settings button.

13. Specify the Windows account under which the agent runs at the Distributor. This account is referred to as the process account. The account must be a member of the db_owner fixed database role in the *distribution* database and must have write permissions on the snapshot share. Be sure to type domain accounts names in the form *domain\account*, such as **cpandl\sqlserver**. Then type and confirm the account password.

14. Specify whether the agent should make connections to the publisher by impersonating the account specified in the Process Account text box or by using a SQL Server account. If you choose to use a SQL Server account, enter a SQL Server login and password. Typically, you will want to impersonate the Windows account rather than use a SQL Server account. Click OK.

15. Click Next. Choose the wizard action upon completion. By default, the wizard creates the publication. You can also generate a script file with the steps to create the publication. If you want to only generate a script, clear Create The Publication. Click Next.

16. On the Complete The Wizard page, type a name for the publication, and then click Finish. You will see a dialog box that shows the progress of the creation process. If errors occur, you must resolve any problems before you can continue or you must restart the publication definition process.

Viewing and Updating Publications

You can view or change the properties of publications at any time. To do so, complete the following steps:

1. Start SQL Server Management Studio. In Object Explorer view, connect to the server you want to use, and then work your way down to the Replication folder.

2. Click the Local Publications folder to see a list of publications for the replicated database. The icon associated with a publication tells you its type:

   - **Snapshot** Purple book icon with a blue circle
   - **Transactional** Blue book icon with a green arrow pointing right
   - **Merge** Yellow book icon with green arrows pointing left and right

3. Right-click the publication you want to change, and then select Properties to display the Properties dialog box.

4. Use the Properties dialog box to configure all of the publication options discussed in the subsection titled "Creating Publications" earlier in this chapter.

Setting Publication Properties

Publication properties control the behavior of replication. You can modify the properties at any time. To edit the properties of an existing publication, follow these steps:

1. Start SQL Server Management Studio. In Object Explorer view, connect to the server you want to use, and then work your way down to the Replication folder.

2. Click the Local Publications folder to see a list of publications for the replicated database.

3. Right-click the publication you want to edit, and then select Properties.

4. This displays the Publication Properties dialog box. The available publication properties depend on the replication type, and you may see one or more of the following pages:

   - **General** Allows you to configure basic options and is available for all replication types. You can view the article name, source database, and type. You can set the description and the subscription expiration. By default, subscriptions do not expire, but you can set an expiration interval in hours.

   - **Articles** Allows you to view and configure published articles.

   - **Filters Rows** Allows you to view and work with row filters.

   - **Snapshot** Sets options for snapshots, which are used with all replication types. You can set options that control the snapshot format, either Native SQL Server or Character. Native SQL Server can only be used when all subscribers are running SQL Server. Character format is required when a publisher or subscriber is not running SQL Server. You can also specify where to put snapshot files and additional scripts to run before or after applying a snapshot.

- **FTP Snapshot**   Allows subscribers to download snapshot files using FTP. If selected, snapshot files are placed in the FTP root folder by default, and anonymous login is used. You can specify an alternate path from the root folder and provide a login and password.

- **Subscription Options**   Provides options for allowing or disallowing anonymous subscriptions, attachable subscription databases, pull subscriptions, non-SQL Server subscribers, and replication of schema changes. By default, anonymous subscriptions, pull subscriptions, and replication of schema changes are allowed.

- **Publication Access List**   Controls who can access the publication. By default, only sa, local administrators, the database owner, the process accounts and distributor_admin have access to the publication data.

- **Agent Security**   Allows you to view or change the process account for agents used by the publication.

Setting Agent Security and Process Accounts

All publications use one or more replication agents, including the Snapshot, Log Reader, and Queue Reader Agents. The Snapshot Agent is used with all publication types. The Log Reader Agent is used with updatable and nonupdatable transactional publications. By default, the Log Reader Agent uses the same login as the Snapshot Agent. The Queue Reader Agent is used with updatable transactional publications. By default, the Queue Reader Agent has a security context that is separate from the other agents.

If agent security is not configured properly, replication will fail. You can configure security for these agents by completing the following steps:

1. Start SQL Server Management Studio. In Object Explorer view, connect to the server you want to use, and then work your way down to the Replication folder.

2. Click the Local Publications folder to see a list of publications for the replicated database.

3. Right-click the publication you want to configure, and then select Properties to display the Properties dialog box.

4. Select the Agent Security page.

5. To configure the login for the Snapshot Agent or Log Reader Agent, click the related Security Settings button, and then:

   ❏ Specify the Windows account under which the agent runs. This account is referred to as the process account. Be sure to type domain account names in the form *domain\account*, such as **cpandl\sqlserver**. Then type and confirm the account password.

❑ Specify whether the agent should make connections to the Publisher by impersonating the account specified in the Process Account text box or by using a SQL Server account. If you choose to use a SQL Server account, enter a SQL Server login and password. Typically, you will want to impersonate the Windows account rather than use a SQL Server account.

6. To configure security for the Queue Reader Agent, which is used for transaction replication with updating, click the related Security Settings button, and then specify the process account.

Controlling Subscription Access to a Publication

All publications have access control lists (ACLs). For publications, access control lists determine which logins can be used by pull and immediate updating subscribers to access the publication. By default, only sa, local administrators, the database owner, the process accounts, and distributor_admin have access to the publication data. To add or remove users, complete the following steps:

1. Start SQL Server Management Studio. In Object Explorer view, connect to the server you want to use, and then work your way down to the Replication folder.

2. Click the Local Publications folder to see a list of publications for the replicated database.

3. Right-click the publication you want to change, and then select Properties to display the Properties dialog box.

4. Select the Publication Access List page. Use the buttons provided to add or remove logins.

Creating a Script for a Publication

Scripts can help you manage publications. You can generate scripts to create the objects specified in a publication and enable the publication, or to drop the objects specified in a publication and disable the publication.

To create a script for a publication, complete the following steps:

1. Start SQL Server Management Studio. In Object Explorer view, connect to the server you want to use, and then work your way down to the Replication folder.

2. Click the Local Publications folder to see a list of publications for the replicated database.

3. Right-click the publication you want to edit, and then select Generate Scripts.

4. In the Generate SQL Script dialog box, specify the type of script to generate. Typically, you will want to create or enable the replicated objects rather than drop or disable them.

5. The script will call replication stored procedures to perform the necessary tasks, and it creates any necessary jobs when executing. To script the jobs and create a record of the jobs, select the Replication Jobs check box.

6. Click Script To File. Use the Script File Location dialog box to select the location where you want to save the script to a .sql file, and then click Save. By default, the file is saved as Unicode text. The file can be executed in Query view to recreate or drop the publication.

7. Click Close.

 Note   In Query view, you can access scripts by clicking the Open File button on the toolbar and then entering the location of the script file.

Deleting a Publication

When you are finished using a publication, you can delete it to release resources that it is using. But before you do this, you may want to create a script that allows you to recreate the publication automatically if you need it again. After creating the script, you can delete the publication by completing the following steps:

1. Start SQL Server Management Studio. In Object Explorer view, connect to the server you want to use, and then work your way down to the Replication folder.

2. Click the Local Publications folder to see a list of publications for the replicated database.

3. Right-click the publication you want to remove, and then select Delete.

4. When prompted to confirm the action, click Yes.

Subscribing to a Publication

The final step in the replication process is having servers subscribe to the publication. You can do this using *push* or *pull* subscriptions.

Subscription Essentials

With push subscriptions, the publisher is responsible for replicating all changes to subscribers without subscribers asking for the changes. You will usually use push subscriptions when you need to send changes to subscribers immediately or when you want to schedule updates periodically. Because the publisher initiates the replication, push subscriptions also offer more security than pull subscriptions. Making the publisher responsible for replicating changes, however, increases overhead on the publisher and may not be the ideal subscription model for a server with a heavy workload.

With pull subscriptions, subscribers request periodic updates of all changes from the publisher. You will usually use pull subscriptions when you have a large number of subscribers or when you need to reduce overhead on the publisher. You also may want to use pull subscriptions for independent mobile users. A single publication can support a mixture of push and pull subscriptions.

You can also use a special type of pull subscription called an *anonymous* subscription. With an anonymous subscription, the publisher and distributor do not maintain subscription information. Instead, the subscriber is responsible for maintaining and synchronizing the subscription, which increases the load on the subscriber, but reduces the load on the publisher and distributor. Accordingly, anonymous subscriptions are most useful when you have a large number of subscribers or when you allow subscriptions using the Internet.

> **Note**   You create anonymous subscriptions to publications in the same way you create pull subscriptions. You enable anonymous subscriptions using the Subscription Options page of the Publication Properties dialog box. Set the Allow Anonymous Subscriptions option to True to allow anonymous subscriptions. Set Allow Anonymous Subscriptions to False to prevent anonymous subscriptions.

The Distribution Agent and Merge Agent are responsible for synchronizing subscriptions and resetting their retention period. If these agents are not running, subscriptions become incompatible with their publications and are marked as deactivated. A deactivated subscription is a subscription that has exceeded the publication retention period. Deactivated subscriptions no longer receive updates during synchronization, and you must mark these subscriptions for reinitialization to enable them again. If you do not re-enable deactivated subscriptions before they expire, the Expired Subscription Clean Up job will delete them.

Creating Subscriptions

The main difference between push and pull subscriptions involves how they are initiated. The subscriber initiates pull subscriptions. The distributor initiates push subscriptions. You configure pull subscriptions by completing the following steps:

1. Start SQL Server Management Studio. In Object Explorer view, connect to the database server instance that will act as a subscriber or distributor, and then work your way down to the Replication folder.

2. Right-click the Local Subscriptions folder and select New Subscriptions. This starts the New Subscription Wizard.

3. Click Next. You use the Publication page, shown in Figure 12-11, to specify where you want to look for a publication. Select Find SQL Server Publisher, Find Oracle Publisher, or a registered server as appropriate.

4. After you select a server, you can browse available publications on that server. Select the publication to which you want to subscribe, and then click Next.

5. Choose where to run the Distribution Agent or agents used with this publication. If you want the agents to run on the distributor and therefore create a push subscription, select Run All Agents At The Distributor. If you want the agents to run on each subscriber and therefore create a pull subscription, select Run Each Agent At Its Subscriber.

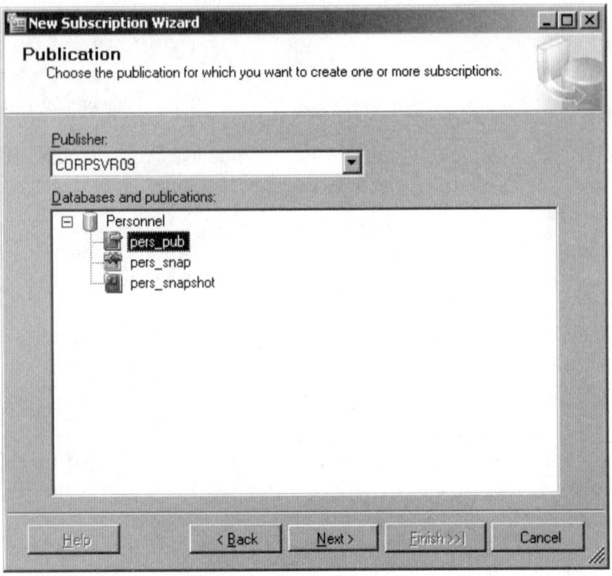

Figure 12-11 The Publication page of the New Subscription Wizard

6. Click Next. On the Subscribers page shown in Figure 12-12, choose one or more subscribers for the publication.

7. If you are using updatable transactional replication and a server you want to act as a subscriber is not listed, click Add SQL Server Subscriber, and then configure a connection to a SQL Server using the Connect To Server dialog box.

8. If you are using merge, snapshot, or nonupdatable transactional replication and a server you want to act as a subscriber is not listed, click Add Subscriber, and then:

   ❑ Choose Add SQL Server Subscriber to configure a connection to a SQL Server using the Connect To Server dialog box. Registered servers are listed in the Server Name drop-down list, and you can browse for others. The default authentication is Windows Authentication, which uses your current login and password. Click Connect. In the New Subscription Wizard page, specify the destination database in which to create the subscription or select New Database to create a new database for the subscription.

   ❑ Choose Add Non-SQL Subscriber to configure a connection to an Oracle or IBM DB2 server using the Add Non-SQL Server Subscriber dialog box. Enter the data source name that can be used to locate the database on the network. SQL Server generates a connection string for the database using the data source name, combined with the login, password, and any connection options you specify in the Distribution Agent Security page in this wizard. The data source name and connection string are not validated until the Distribution Agent attempts to initialize the subscription. Click OK. The subscription database is set as the default destination, which is the database you specified in the data source name.

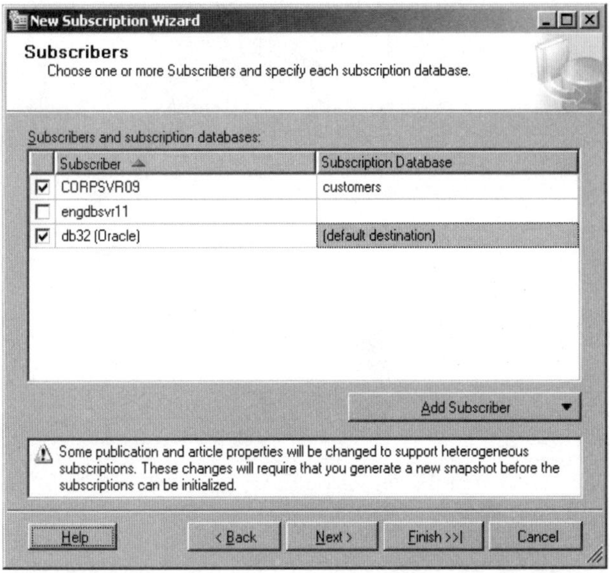

Figure 12-12   The Subscribers page of the New Subscription Wizard

9. Click Next. On the Distribution Agent Security page shown in Figure 12-13, set the process account and connection options for each subscriber (for pull subscriptions) or for the distributor (for push subscriptions) by clicking the related Properties button (...), and then:

❑ Specify the Windows account under which the Distribution Agent runs for the selected server (which is either a subscriber or a distributor). This account is referred to as the process account. Be sure to type domain account names in the form *domain\account*, such as **cpandl\sqlserver**. Then type and confirm the account password. The account must be a member of the Publication Access List. (To check or modify the access list, access the Local Publications folder in Object Explorer view, right-click the publication, and then select Properties. This displays the Publication Properties dialog box. Select the Publication Access List page.)

❑ Specify whether the agent should make connections to the distributor by impersonating the account specified in the Process Account text box or by using a SQL Server account. If you choose to use a SQL Server account, enter a SQL Server login and password. Typically, you will want to impersonate the Windows account rather than use a SQL Server account. The account must be a member of the Publication Access List.

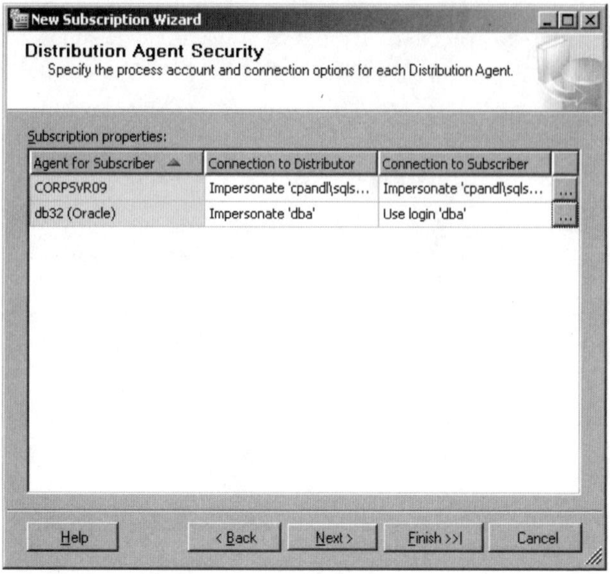

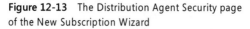

Figure 12-13   The Distribution Agent Security page
of the New Subscription Wizard

❑ Specify whether the agent should make connections to the Subscriber by
   impersonating the account specified in the Process Account text box or by
   using a SQL Server account. If you choose to use a SQL Server account,
   enter a SQL Server login and password. Typically, you will want to impersonate the Windows account rather than use a SQL Server account. The
   account must be a database owner of the *subscription* database.

10. Click OK to close the properties dialog box. Click Next. Set the synchronization
    schedule for Distribution or Merge Agents using one of the following options:

    ■ **Run Continuously**   Select this option to continuously check for updates
       on the publisher.

    ■ **Run On Demand Only**   Select this option if you want to update the sub-
       scription database manually.

    ■ **Define Schedule**   Select this option to set a periodic schedule, such as
       once an hour.

11. If you selected a publication that uses updatable transactions, the next wizard
    page will be titled Updatable Subscriptions. Specify if you want the subscrip-
    tion databases to be initialized.

    ❑ Clear the Replicate option check box for a subscriber if you do not want to
       create an updatable subscription at this time.

    ❑ Set the Commit At Publisher option to Simultaneously Commit Changes
       to enforce immediate updating. Changes are committed on both the

subscriber and the publisher at the same time, which requires a dedicated connection.

❑ Set the Commit At Publisher option to Queue Changes And Commit
When Possible to allow queuing of changes. Queued changes are committed on the subscriber immediately and on the publisher during the next
online synchronization.

12. If you choose to create an updatable subscription, the next dialog box allows
you to configure the technique that will be used by the subscriber to access the
publisher (see Figure 12-14). You can use an existing linked server or remote
server to establish the connection if you have already configured these options
as described in Chapter 11, "Linked Servers and Distributed Transactions." Or
you can use a SQL Server login and password, provided the login is listed on
the Publication Access List.

Tip   To check or modify the access list, access the Local Publications
folder in the Object Explorer view, right-click the publication, and then
select Properties. This displays the Publication Properties dialog box.
Select the Publication Access List page.

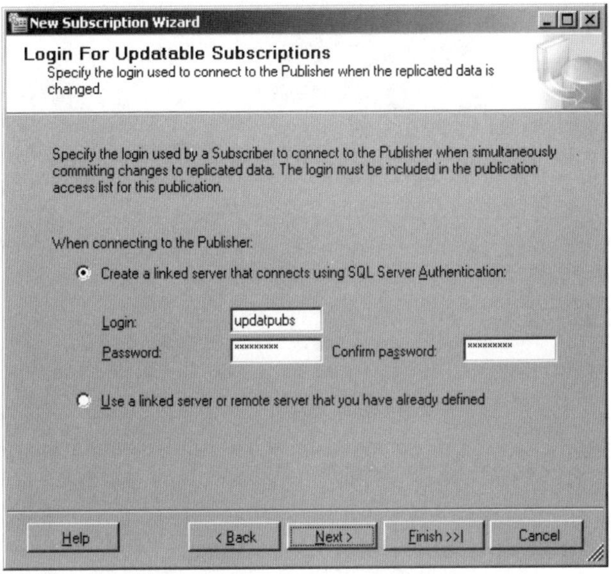

Figure 12-14   The Login For Updatable Subscriptions page
of the New Subscription Wizard

13. Use the Initialize Subscriptions page to determine whether or not the subscription databases should be initialized.

❑ Clear the Initialize option check box if you have already initialized the
subscription or will initialize a transactional subscription from backup.

❑ Set the Initialize When option to Immediately to initialize the subscription database with a snapshot of the publication data and schema as soon as possible after the Snapshot Agent generates the snapshot.

❑ Set the Initialize When option to At First Synchronization to initialize the subscription database with a snapshot of the publication data and schema the first time the subscription is synchronized.

 Note   Keep in mind that initialization is handled by the Snapshot and Distribution Agents. The Snapshot Agent creates the initial view of the schema and data, and then the Distribution Agent applies the snapshot either immediately or at first synchronization.

14. Click Next. Choose the wizard action upon completion. By default, the wizard creates the subscription(s). You can also generate a script file with the steps to create the subscription(s). If you want to only generate a script, clear Create The Subscription(s). Click Next.

15. Click Next. Check the setup and click Finish when you are ready to create the subscription(s). The Creating Subscription(s) dialog box shows you the status of the creation process. Click the message link provided for any errors to read the error text.

Viewing Subscription Properties

To view the configuration properties of a subscription, complete the following steps:

1. Start SQL Server Management Studio. In Object Explorer view, connect to the database server instance that will act as a subscriber or distributor, and then work your way down to the Replication folder.

2. Click the Local Publications folder to see a list of publications for the server instance. Click Refresh or press F5 if you do not see a list of publications.

3. Double-click a publication to show its current subscriptions.

4. To view the properties of a subscription, right-click the subscription name and choose Properties to display the Subscription Properties dialog box.

Updating, Maintaining, and Deleting Subscriptions

To update, maintain, or delete a subscription, complete the following steps:

1. Start SQL Server Management Studio. In Object Explorer view, connect to the database server instance that will act as a subscriber or distributor, and then work your way down to the Replication folder.

2. Click the Local Subscriptions folder to see a list of subscriptions for the server instance.

3. Right-click a subscription, and then choose one of the following options:

   - **View Synchronization Status**   Displays a status of the synchronization process for the selected subscription.

   - **Set Update Method**   For updatable subscriptions only, this option allows you to switch between immediate updating and queued updating.

   - **Delete**   Deletes the subscription. Confirm the action by clicking Yes when prompted.

4. You validate and reinitialize subscriptions through the associated publication. For more details, refer to the following two subsections, titled "Validating Subscriptions" and "Reinitializing Subscriptions."

Validating Subscriptions

You can validate subscriptions to verify that the subscribers have the same number of rows of replication data as the publisher. When you mark a subscription for validation, the validation occurs the next time the Distribution Agent runs, and the results are available in the Replication Monitor.

To validate one or more subscriptions, follow these steps:

1. Start SQL Server Management Studio. In Object Explorer view, connect to the database server instance that will act as a subscriber or distributor, and then work your way down to the Replication folder.

2. Click the Local Publications folder to see a list of publications for this server instance.

3. If you want to validate subscriptions for a transactional publication, right-click the transactional publication you want to use, and then choose Validate Subscriptions. This displays the Validate Subscriptions dialog box. You can validate all SQL Server subscriptions or the specified subscriptions on SQL Servers. Non-SQL Server subscriptions cannot be validated. Optionally, click Validation Options to configure how the Distribution Agent computes row counts, whether or not the agent compares checksums, and whether or not the Distribution Agent is stopped after the validation is completed.

4. If you want to validate all subscriptions for the selected merge publication, select Validate All SQL Server Subscriptions. This displays the Validate All Subscriptions dialog box. By default, the distributor validates only the row counts on the subscriber. If all subscribers are running SQL Server, you can also verify the data in rows by comparing checksum values.

5. Click OK. The validation occurs the next time the Distribution Agent runs, and the results are available in the Replication Monitor. More information about how to work with the Replication Monitor is provided in Chapter 13, "Profiling and Monitoring SQL Server 2005."

Reinitializing Subscriptions

You can reinitialize snapshots in a publication's subscription database by using the current snapshot or a new snapshot. To reinitialize all subscriptions, complete the following steps:

1. Start SQL Server Management Studio. In Object Explorer view, connect to the database server instance that will act as a subscriber or distributor, and then work your way down to the Replication folder.

2. Click the Local Publications folder to see a list of publications for this server instance.

3. Right-click the publication you want to work with, and then choose Reinitialize All Subscriptions. This displays the Reinitialize The Subscription(s) dialog box.

4. To use the current snapshot to reinitialize the subscriptions, select Use The Current Snapshot.

5. To generate a new snapshot to reinitialize the subscriptions, select Use A New Snapshot. If you want to generate the snapshot immediately, select Generate The New Snapshot Now.

6. Click Mark For Reinitialization.

To reinitialize a specific subscription, complete the following steps:

1. Start SQL Server Management Studio. In Object Explorer view, connect to the database server instance that will act as a subscriber or distributor, and then work your way down to the Replication folder.

2. Click the Local Publications folder to see a list of publications for this server instance.

3. Double-click the publication you want to use to show its current subscriptions.

4. Right-click the subscription you want to reinitialize, and then choose Reinitialize. This displays the Reinitialize The Subscription(s) dialog box.

5. Select Use The Current Snapshot or Use A New Snapshot as appropriate. If you want to generate a new snapshot immediately, select Generate The New Snapshot Now.

6. Click Mark For Reinitialization.

Part IV
Microsoft SQL Server 2005 Optimization and Maintenance

This part of the book explains the administration tools that you will use to enhance and maintain Microsoft SQL Server 2005. Chapter 13 provides the essentials for working with server logs, monitoring SQL Server performance, and solving performance problems. Chapter 14 begins by explaining how to create a backup and recovery plan, and then discusses common tasks associated with creating and restoring backups. Chapter 15 explores database automation. You will learn how to configure alerts, schedule jobs, and manage database operators. You will also learn how to create maintenance plans and resolve database consistency problems.

Chapter 13

Profiling and Monitoring Microsoft SQL Server 2005

Monitoring server performance, tracking user activity, and troubleshooting errors are essential parts of database administration, and Microsoft SQL Server has several tools that you can use to perform these tasks. Performance Monitor, the standard Microsoft Windows tool for monitoring servers, has updated counters for SQL Server. These counters allow you to track many different server resources and activities. SQL Server Profiler, an analysis and profiling tool, allows you to trace server events. Other tools and resources are available, such as stored procedures and the SQL Server logs.

Monitoring Server Performance and Activity

Monitoring SQL Server is not something you should do haphazardly. You need to have a plan—a set of goals that you hope to achieve. Let's look at some reasons you may want to monitor SQL Server and the tools you can use to do this.

Reasons to Monitor SQL Server

One of the main reasons you monitor SQL Server performance is to troubleshoot problems. For example, if users are having problems connecting to the server, you will want to monitor the server to find out more about what is causing these problems. Your goal is to track down the problem using the available monitoring resources and then solve the problem effectively.

Another common reason to monitor SQL Server is to improve server performance. To achieve optimal performance, you need to minimize the time it takes for users to see the results of queries and maximize the total number of queries that the server can handle simultaneously. You do this by using the following techniques:

- Resolve hardware issues that may be causing problems. For example, if disk read/write activity is slower than expected, work on improving disk input/output (I/O).

401

- Monitor memory and CPU usage and take appropriate steps to reduce the load on the server. For example, other processes running on the server may be using memory and CPU resources needed by SQL Server.

- Cut down the network traffic load on the server. With replication, for example, you can configure remote stored procedure execution rather than transmit large data changes individually.

Unfortunately, you often have to make tradeoffs in resource usage. For example, as the number of users accessing SQL Server grows, you may not be able to reduce the network traffic load, but you may be able to improve server performance by optimizing queries or indexing.

Getting Ready to Monitor

Before you start monitoring SQL Server, it is a good idea to establish baseline performance metrics for your server. To do this, you measure server performance at various times and under different load conditions. You can then compare the baseline performance with subsequent performance to determine how SQL Server is performing. Performance metrics that are well above the baseline measurements may indicate areas in which the server needs to be optimized or reconfigured.

After you establish the baseline metrics, prepare a monitoring plan. A comprehensive monitoring plan involves the following steps:

1. Determine which server events should be monitored to help you accomplish your goal.
2. Set filters to preferentially select the amount of information that is collected.
3. Configure monitors and alerts to watch the events.
4. Log the event data so that it can be analyzed.
5. Analyze the event data and replay the data to find a solution.

These procedures will be examined later in this chapter in the section entitled "Monitoring SQL Server Performance." Although you should develop a monitoring plan in most cases, sometimes you may not want to go through all these steps to monitor SQL Server. For example, if you only want to check current user activity levels, you may not want to use Performance Monitor and can run the stored procedure *sp_who* instead. Or you can examine this information in the Current Activity window in SQL Server Management Studio.

 Note   The stored procedure *sp_who* reports on current users and processes. When you execute *sp_who*, you can pass a login name as an argument. If you do not specify a login name, NULL is passed in this argument, so all logins are returned. If you use the keyword *active* as the login name, you will see only active processes; any processes waiting for the next command from a user will be excluded. Instead of a specific login name, such as sa, you can use the numeric value for a system process ID as well.

Monitoring Tools and Resources

The primary monitoring tools you will use are Windows Performance Monitor and SQL Server Profiler. Other resources for monitoring SQL Server include:

- **Activity Monitor**   This monitor provides information on current users, processes, and locks as discussed in the section titled "Managing Server Activity" in Chapter 5, "Managing the Enterprise."

- **Replication Monitor**   This monitor provides details on the status of SQL Server replication and allows you to configure replication alerts.

- **SQL Server logs**   The information in these event logs allows you to view informational, auditing, warning, and error messages that can help you troubleshoot SQL Server problems.

- **SQL Server Agent logs**   The information in these event logs allows you to view informational, auditing, warning, and error messages that can help you troubleshoot SQL Server Agent problems.

Note   SQL Server documentation refers to the SQL Server and SQL Server Agent logs as *error logs*. In their current implementation, however, the logs are more accurately called *event logs*, which is the terminology used in this chapter. Similar to event logs in Windows, these logs in SQL Server contain informational and security messages as well as error messages.

- **Event logs**   The information in the event logs allows you to troubleshoot system-wide problems, including SQL Server and SQL Server Agent problems.

- *sp_helpdb*   This stored procedure displays information about databases.

- *sp_helpindex*   This stored procedure reports information about indexes on a table.

- *sp_helpserver*   This stored procedure provides information in SQL Server instances configured for remote access or replication.

- *sp_lock*   This stored procedure shows information about object locks.

- *sp_monitor*   This stored procedure shows key SQL Server usage statistics, such as CPU idle time and CPU usage.

- *sp_spaceused*   This stored procedure shows an estimate of disk space used by a table or database.

- *sp_who*   This stored procedure shows a snapshot of current SQL Server users and processes.

- **DBCC statements**   This set of commands allows you to check SQL Server statistics, to trace activity, and to check database integrity.

In addition to log files and Transact-SQL statements, you will find a set of built-in functions that return system information. Table 13-1 provides a summary of key functions and their usages. The values returned by these functions are cumulative from the time SQL Server was last started.

Table 13-1   Built-In Functions for Monitoring SQL Server Performance
and Activity

Function	Description	Example
@@connections	Returns the number of connections or attempted connections.	SELECT @@connections AS 'Total Login Attempts'
@@cpu_busy	Returns CPU processing time in milliseconds for SQL Server activity.	SELECT @@cpu_busy AS ' CPU Busy', GETDATE() AS 'Since'
@@idle	Returns SQL Server idle time in milliseconds.	SELECT @@idle AS 'Idle Time', GETDATE() AS 'Since'
@@io_busy	Returns I/O processing time in milliseconds.	SELECT @@io_busy AS 'IO Time', GETDATE() AS 'Since' for SQL Server
@@pack_received	Returns the number of input packets read from the network by SQL Server.	SELECT @@pack_received AS 'Packets Received'
@@pack_sent	Returns the number of output packets written to the network by SQL Server.	SELECT @@pack_sent AS 'Packets Sent'
@@packet_errors	Returns the number of network packet errors for SQL Server connections.	SELECT @@packet_errors AS 'Packet Errors'
@@timeticks	Returns the number of milliseconds per CPU clock tick.	SELECT @@timeticks AS 'Clock Ticks'
@@total_errors	Returns the number of disk read/write errors encountered by SQL Server.	SELECT @@total_errors AS 'Total Errors', GETDATE() AS 'Since'
@@total_read	Returns the number of disk reads by SQL Server.	SELECT @@total_read AS 'Reads', GETDATE() AS 'Since'
@@total_write	Returns the number of disk writes by SQL Server.	SELECT @@total_write AS 'Writes', GETDATE() AS 'Since'

Working with Replication Monitor

When you have configured replication as discussed in Chapter 12, "Implementing Snapshot, Merge, and Transactional Replication," you will use the Replication Monitor to track the status of replication throughout the enterprise. By default, only the currently selected publisher is displayed in the Replication Monitor window, but you can add any publishers that you want to monitor and organize them into publisher groups as necessary.

Starting and Using the Replication Monitor

To start Replication Monitor, right-click the Replication folder in Object Explorer view, and then select Launch Replication Monitor. Replication Monitor uses icons to indicate the general status of replication. If any publication has an error status, the error status is indicated by a red circle around an X at all levels within Replication Monitor.

When you select a publisher in the left pane, the right pane shows the replication details for that publisher. By default, this information is refreshed every five seconds, and it can be refreshed immediately by pressing F5. As Figure 13-1 shows, the publisher view has three tabs:

- **Publications**   Has individual entries for each configured publication. An icon indicates the type and status of the publication:
  - ❑ A purple book icon with a blue circle in it for snapshot replication
  - ❑ A blue book icon with a right-facing green arrow in it for transactional replication
  - ❑ A yellow book icon with left- and right-facing green arrows in it for merge replication
  - ❑ A red circle around an X for error status

  At a glance, you can also see the number of subscriptions to the publication, the number of subscriptions being synchronized, the current average performance for subscribers, and the current worst performance for subscribers.

- **Subscription Watch List**   Shows the status of individual subscriptions by type. Use the first drop-down list to specify the type of subscriptions to display and the second drop-down list to specify whether to display all subscriptions of the specified type or some subset, such as the top 25 worst-performing subscriptions. Note the status, such as running, error, and so on; the performance level, such as excellent, good, poor, and so on; and the latency.

- **Common Jobs**   Shows the SQL Server Agent jobs common to all publications on the selected publisher. To determine if there are potential replication problems, note the status, last start time, and duration. There may be a problem with jobs that have a status of Never Started and with jobs that have been running for a long time.

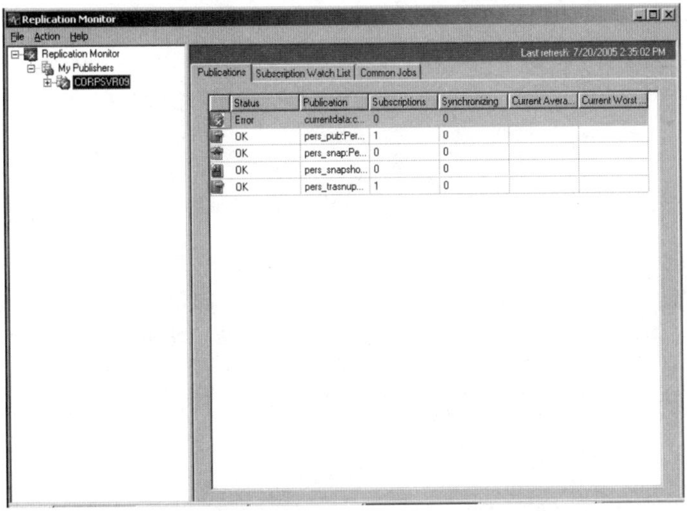

Figure 13-1   The Replication Monitor

Adding Publishers and Publisher Groups

When you first start Replication Monitor, only the currently selected publisher is displayed in Replication Monitor. You can add publishers that you want to monitor and organize them into publisher groups as necessary.

To start monitoring additional publishers and create publisher groups, follow these steps:

1. Start Replication Monitor. In the left pane, right-click the Replication Monitor node and select Add Publisher. This displays the Add Publisher dialog box, shown in Figure 13-2.

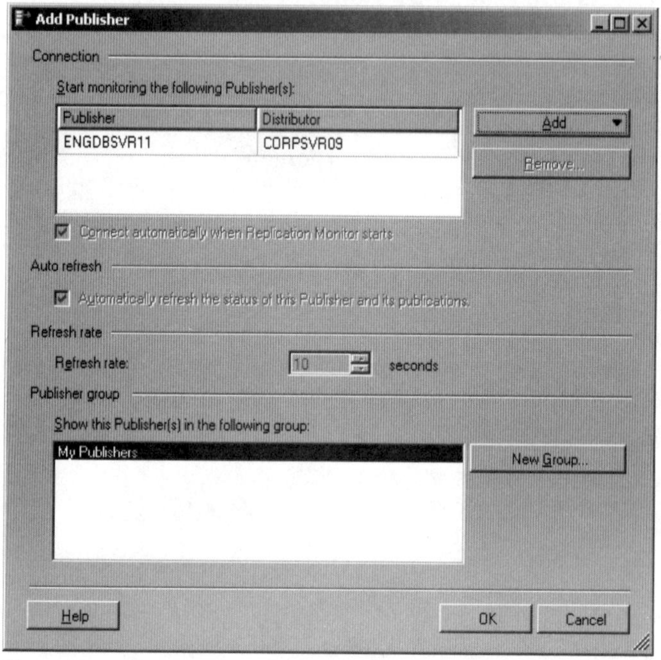

Figure 13-2   The Add Publisher dialog box

2. Click Add, and then:

    ❏ Choose Add SQL Server Publisher to configure a connection to a SQL Server using the Connect To Server dialog box. Registered servers are listed in the Server Name drop-down list, and you can browse for others. The default authentication is Windows Authentication, which uses your current login and password. Click Connect.

    ❏ Choose Specify A Distributor And Add Its Publishers to configure a connection to a distributor using the Connect To Server dialog box. Registered servers are listed in the Server Name drop-down list, and you can browse for others. The default authentication is Windows Authentication, which uses your current login and password. When you click Connect, Replication Monitor connects to the distributor, obtains a list of publishers for the distributor, and then connects to these publishers as well.

❑ Choose Add Oracle Publisher to configure a connection to an Oracle server using the Connect To Server dialog box. Registered servers are listed in the Server Name drop-down list, and you can browse for others. The default authentication is Oracle Standard Authentication, which requires a user login and password. Click Connect.

Note Before you can add an Oracle publisher, you must first configure a connection to the Oracle publisher's distributor by choosing Specify A Distributor And Add Its Publishers.

3. Publisher groups make it easier to manage monitoring in complex enterprise environments. Select the publisher group to which to add the publisher(s). If you want to create a new group, click New Group, specify the group name, and then click OK. Then select the new group under Show This Publisher(s) In The Following Group.

4. Click OK.

Working with the Event Logs

Event logs provide historical information that can help you track down problems with SQL Server. SQL Server writes events to the SQL Server event logs, the SQL Server Agent event logs, and the Windows application log. You can use all three logs to track messages related to SQL Server. However, there are some things you should know about these logs:

■ Only the application log provides additional information on all applications running on the server, and only the application log provides features for filtering events based on type. For example, you can filter events so that only error and warning messages are displayed.

■ If you start the MSSQLServer or MSSQL$*instancename* service from the command prompt, events are logged to the SQL Server event log and to standard output. No events are recorded in the Windows application log.

■ Windows has additional logs that can be helpful when tracking issues. If you are tracking security issues, start with the SQL Server event logs and also examine the Windows security log. If you are having trouble finding the source of a problem that is preventing proper operation of SQL Server, start with the SQL Server logs and also examine the Windows application and system logs.

SQL Server error messages can be cryptic and difficult to read if you do not understand the formatting. Error messages logged by SQL Server can have:

■ **An error number that uniquely identifies the error message** System error numbers have one to five digits. System errors are numbered from 1 to 50,000. User-defined errors start at 50,001.

■ **A severity level that indicates how critical the message is** Severity levels range from 1 to 25. Messages with a severity level of 0 to 10 are informational messages. Severity levels from 11 to 16 are generated by users and users can correct them. Severity levels from 17 to 25 indicate software or hardware errors that you should examine.

■ **An error state number that indicates the source of the error** Error state numbers have one to three digits and a maximum value of 127. Normally, error state numbers indicate the line number in the SQL Server code that generated the message.

■ **A message that provides a brief description of the error** Read the message to get more information about the error, which will help you in troubleshooting problems.

You may see ODBC (open database connectivity) and OLE (object linking and embedding) return errors from SQL Server that contain similar information as well. The *sysmessages* table in the *master* database contains a list of error messages and descriptions that can be returned by SQL Server. To see all error messages that can be returned by SQL Server, you can execute the following T-SQL statement:

```
USE master
GO
SELECT * FROM sysmessages
```

Examining the Application Log

The application log contains entries for all database server instances running on the computer as well as entries for other business applications. You access the application log by completing the following steps:

1. Click Start | Programs or All Programs | Administrative Tools, and then choose Event Viewer. This starts Event Viewer.

2. Event Viewer displays logs for the local computer by default. If you want to view logs on a remote computer, right-click the Event Viewer entry in the console tree (left pane), and then select Connect To Another Computer to display in the Select Computer dialog box. In the dialog box, enter the name of the computer you want to access, and then click OK.

3. In the console tree (left pane), click Application Log. You should see an application log similar to the one shown in Figure 13-3. Use the information in the Source column to determine which service or database server instance logged a particular event.

The entries in the main window of Event Viewer provide a quick overview of when, where, and how an event occurred. To obtain detailed information about an event, double-click its entry. A summary icon that tells you the event type precedes the date and time of the event. Event types include:

■ **Informational** An informational event that is generally related to a successful action

■ **Success audit** An event related to the successful execution of an action

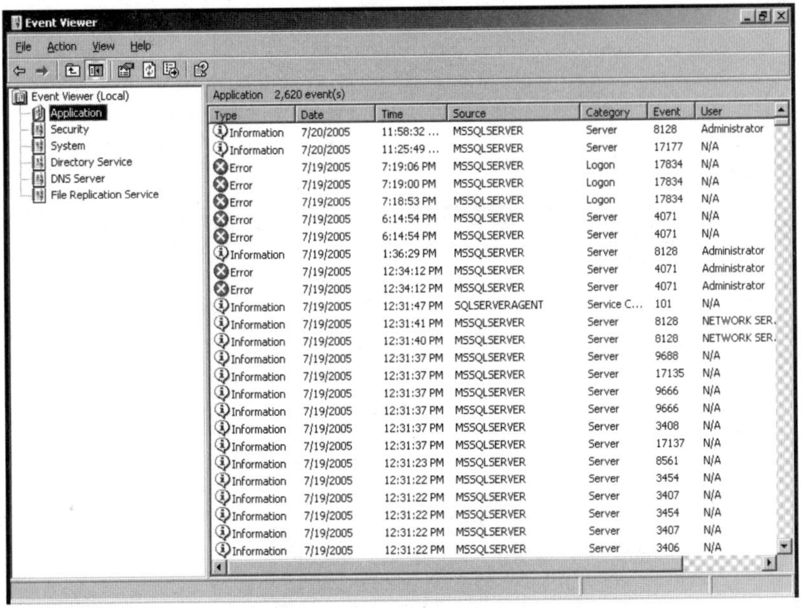

Figure 13-3 A Windows application log

- **Failure audit** An event related to the failed execution of an action
- **Warning** A noncritical error that provides a warning. Details for warnings are often useful in preventing future system problems.
- **Error** An error, such as the failure of a service to start

In addition to the date, time, and event type indicator, the summary and detailed event entries provide the following information:

- **Source** The application, service, or component that logged the event
- **Category** The category of the event, which is sometimes used to further describe the related action
- **Event_ID** An identifier for the specific event
- **User** The user account that was logged on when the event occurred
- **Computer** The computer name on which the event occurred
- **Description** A text description of the event, provided in detailed entries
- **Data** Any data or error code output by the event, provided in detailed entries

Warnings and errors are the two main types of events that you want to examine closely. Whenever one of these types of events occur and you are unsure of the cause, double-click the entry to view the detailed event description. If you want to see only warnings and errors, you can filter the log by completing the following steps:

1. From the View menu, choose the Filter option. This opens the dialog box shown in Figure 13-4.

2. Clear the following check boxes: Information, Success Audit, and Failure Audit.

3. Select the Warning and Error check boxes, if they are not already selected.

4. Click OK. You should now see a list of warning and error messages only. Remember that these messages are for all applications running on the server and not just for SQL Server.

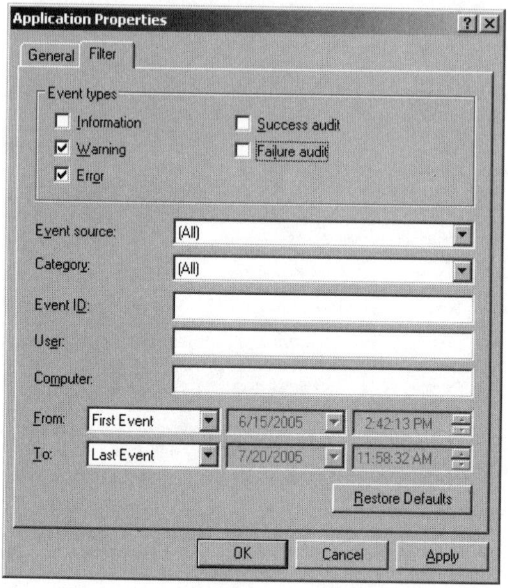

Figure 13-4   The Filter tab in the Application Log Properties dialog box

Examining the SQL Server Event Logs

The SQL Server logs record information, warnings, errors, and auditing messages pertaining to SQL Server activity. New logs are created when you start the SQL Server service or when you run the *sp_cycle_errorlog* stored procedure. When a new log is created, the current log is cycled to the archive. SQL Server maintains up to five archived logs (by default).

You can view the SQL Server event logs in SQL Server Management Studio or through a text editor. In SQL Server Management Studio, you access the event logs by completing the following steps:

1. Start SQL Server Management Studio. In Object Explorer view, connect to the database server of your choice, and then work your way down to the Management folder.

2. Expand the Management folder, and then double-click the SQL Server Logs entry. The current log is shown with the label *Current*. Archived logs are shown with descriptive labels such as *Archive #1*.

3. Double-click the log you want to view to open it in the Log File Viewer.

4. With the Log File Viewer open, you can add other logs to the log file summary by selecting their check boxes, as shown in Figure 13-5.

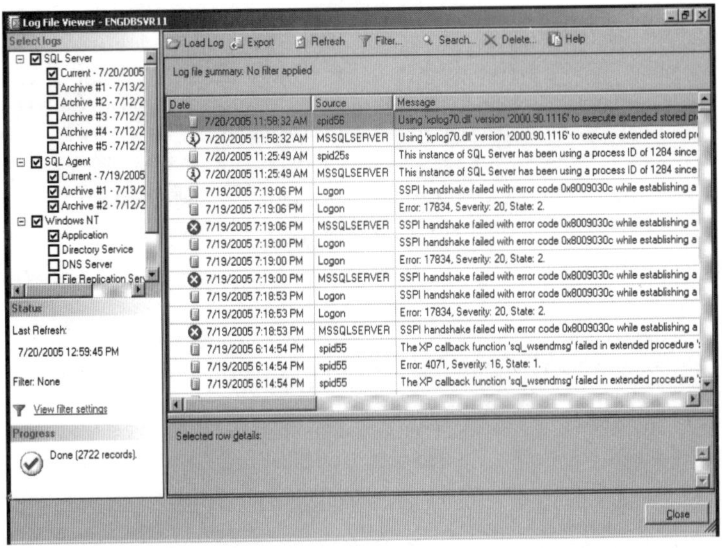

Figure 13-5   The Log File Viewer

To access the event logs in a text editor, complete the following steps:

1. Start a text editor, such as WordPad, and then use its Open dialog box to access the SQL Server Log folder, normally located in MSSQL.1\mssql\Log or MSSQL.1\mssql$*instancename*\Log.

2. Open the log you want to examine. The current log file is named ERRORLOG with no file extension. The most recent log backup has the extension .1, the second most recent has the extension .2, and so on.

To change the number of logs that SQL Server maintains, right-click the SQL Server Logs entry in Object Explorer view and select Configure. In the Configure SQL Server Error Logs dialog box, select Limit The Number Of Error Log Files..., and then set the maximum number of error log files to retain using the Maximum Number Of Error Log Files combo box. The default number of log files maintained is six: one current log and five archive logs. You can change the number of logs maintained to any value between 6 and 99.

Examining the SQL Server Agent Event Logs

The SQL Server Agent logs record information, warnings, and errors pertaining to SQL Server Agent activity. New logs are created only when you start the SQL Server Agent service. When a new log is created, the current log is cycled to the archive. SQL Server maintains up to five archived agent logs (by default).

In SQL Server Management Studio, you access the current SQL Server Agent log by completing the following steps:

1. Start SQL Server Management Studio. In Object Explorer view, connect to the database server of your choice, and then work your way down to the SQL Server Agent node.

2. Expand the SQL Server Agent node, and then double-click the SQL Server Agent Error Logs entry. The current log is shown with the label *Current*. Archived logs are labeled *Archive #1* and so on.

3. Double-click the log you want to view to open it in the Log File Viewer.

4. With the Log File Viewer open, you can add other logs to the log file summary by selecting their check boxes.

To access archived SQL Server Agent event logs in a text editor, complete the following steps:

1. Start the text editor, and then use its Open dialog box to access the SQL Server Log folder, which is normally located in mssql\Log or mssql$*instancename*\Log.

2. Open the log you want to examine. The current log file is named SQLAGENT.OUT. The most recent log backup has the extension .1, the second most recent has the extension .2, and so on.

You can manage the SQL Server Agent logs in several ways. You can force the SQL Server Agent to recycle the current log by right-clicking the SQL Server Agent Error Logs node in Object Explorer view and then selecting Recycle and clicking OK. When you do this, SQL Server closes out the current agent log, moves it to an archive log, and starts a new agent log. You can control the level of logging and set the log file location as well. To do this, complete the following steps:

1. Right-click the SQL Server Agent Error Logs node in Object Explorer view, and then select Configure.

2. Use the Error Log File box to set the folder path and file name of the agent log. The default path is %ProgramFiles% \Microsoft SQL Server\MSSQL.1\ MSSQL\LOG\SQLAGENT.OUT. New archive files will also be created in the folder specified as part of the path.

3. Use the Agent Log Level check boxes to control the level of logging for the SQL Server Agent. By default, only error and warning messages are logged. If you want to view informational messages in the logs, select the Informational check box as well.

4. Click OK.

Monitoring SQL Server Performance

Windows Performance Monitor is the tool of choice for monitoring SQL Server performance. Performance Monitor graphically displays statistics for the set of performance parameters you select. These performance parameters are referred to as *counters*.

When you install SQL Server on a system, Performance Monitor is updated with a set of counters for tracking SQL Server performance parameters. These counters also can be updated when you install services and add-ons for SQL Server. For example, when you configure replication on a server, the Replication Monitor is added and made available through SQL Server Management Studio, and Performance Monitor is again updated with a set of objects and counters for tracking replication performance.

Performance Monitor creates a graph depicting the various counters you are tracking. You can configure the update interval for this graph, but it is set to three seconds by default. As you will see when you work with Performance Monitor, the tracking information is most valuable when you record the information in a log file and when you configure alerts to send messages when certain events occur or when certain thresholds are reached, such as when a database log file gets close to running out of free space.

The following subsections examine the procedures you will use with Performance Monitor.

Choosing Counters to Monitor

Performance Monitor displays information only for counters you are tracking. More than one hundred SQL Server counters are available—and if you have configured replication, you can use even more counters. These counters are organized into object groupings. For example, all lock-related counters are associated with the *SQLServer:Locks* object.

To select which counters you want to monitor, complete the following steps:

1. Access the Performance console by clicking Start | Programs or All Programs | Administrative Tools | Performance.

2. Select the System Monitor entry in the left pane, as shown in Figure 13-6. Any default counters are shown in the lower portion of the Performance Monitor window. To delete a default counter, click its entry in the Performance Monitor window, and then press the Delete key.

3. Performance Monitor has several viewing modes. Make sure you are in View Current Activity and View Graph display mode by clicking the View Current Activity and View Graph buttons on the Performance Monitor toolbar. Alternatively, you can press Ctrl+T and then Ctrl+G.

4. To add counters, click the Add button on the toolbar, or press Ctrl+I. This displays the Add Counters dialog box shown in Figure 13-7. Use the options and boxes in the dialog box to configure the counters as follows:

   - **Use Local Computer Counters** Configures performance options for the local computer.

   - **Select Counters From Computer** Enters the UNC (Uniform Naming Convention) name of the SQL Server you want to work with, such as \\ZETA.

   - **Performance Object** Selects the type of object you want to work with, such as *SQLServer:Locks*.

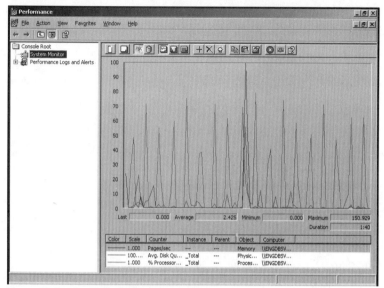

Figure 13-6   The Performance Monitor window

Tip   The easiest way to learn what you can track is by exploring the objects and counters available in the Add Counters dialog box. Select an object in the Performance Object list, click Explain, and scroll through the list of counters for the object.

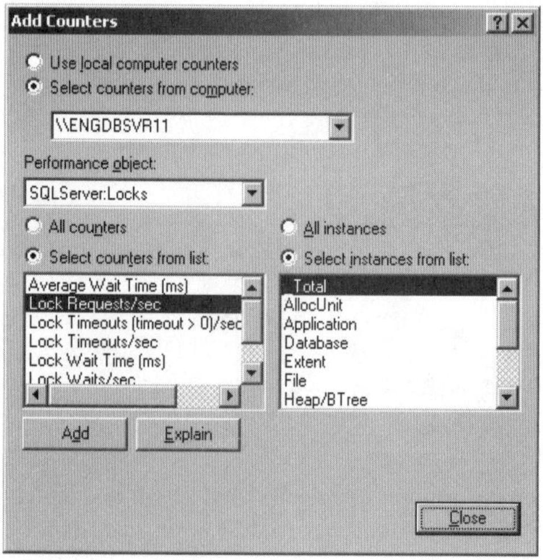

Figure 13-7   The Add Counters dialog box

- **All Counters**   Selects all counters for the current object.
- **Select Counters From List**   Selects one or more counters for the current object. For example, you could select Lock Requests/sec, Lock Timeouts/sec, and Number of Deadlocks/sec.
- **All Instances**   Selects all counter instances for monitoring.
- **Select Instances From List**   Selects one or more counter instances to monitor. For example, you could select instances of the Lock Requests/sec counter for Database, Extent, and Page.

Best Practices   Do not try to chart too many counters or counter instances at the same time, or the display will be difficult to read and you will use system resources—CPU time and memory—that may affect server responsiveness.

5. When you have selected all the necessary options, click Add to add the counters to the chart. Repeat this process to add other performance parameters.
6. Click Close when you are finished.

Creating and Managing Performance Monitor Logs

You can use performance logs to track the performance of SQL Server, and you can replay them at a later date. As you begin to work with logs, remember that the parameters you track in log files are recorded separately from the parameters you are charting in the Performance Monitor window. You can configure log files to update counter data automatically or manually. With automatic logging, a snapshot of key parameters is recorded at specific time intervals, such as every 10 seconds. With manual logging, you determine when snapshots are created. Two types of performance logs are available:

- **Counter Logs**   Record performance data on the selected counters when a predetermined update interval has elapsed.
- **Trace Logs**   Record performance data whenever related events occur.

Creating and Managing Performance Logging

To create and manage performance logging, complete the following steps:

1. Access the Performance console by clicking Start | Programs or All Programs | Administrative Tools | Performance.
2. Expand the Performance Logs And Alerts node. If you want to configure a counter log, select Counter Logs. Otherwise, select Trace Logs.
3. As shown in Figure 13-8, you will see a list of current logs (if any) in the right pane. A green log symbol next to the log name indicates that logging is active. A red log symbol indicates that logging is stopped.
4. You can create a new log by right-clicking in the right pane and choosing New Log Settings from the shortcut menu. A New Log Settings box appears. You

must provide a name to the new log settings. Type a descriptive name, and then click OK. You will then be able to configure logging using a properties dialog box.

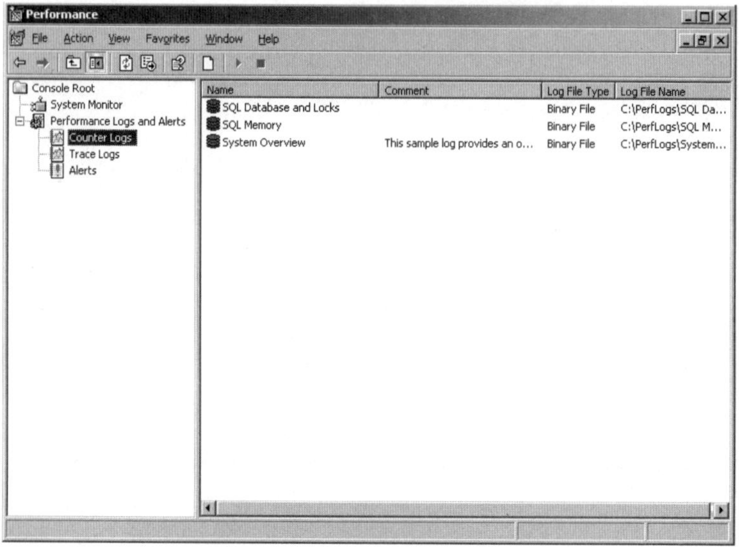

Figure 13-8   Current performance logs with summary information in the Performance Monitor

5. You can manage an existing log by right-clicking its entry in the right pane and then selecting one of the following options:
   - **Start**   To activate logging
   - **Stop**   To halt logging
   - **Delete**   To delete the log
   - **Properties**   To display the Log Properties dialog box

Creating Counter Logs

Counter logs record performance data on the selected counters at a specific sample interval. For example, you could sample performance data for the CPU every 15 minutes. To create a counter log, complete the following steps:

1. Select Counter Logs in the left pane of the Performance console, and then right-click in the right pane to display the shortcut menu. Choose New Log Settings.

2. In the New Log Settings dialog box, type a name for the log, such as **SQL Server Locks Monitor** or **SQL Server Memory Monitor**. Click OK. This opens a properties dialog box.

3. To add all counters for specific performance objects, click Add Objects, and then use the Add Object dialog box to select the objects you want to add. All counters for these objects will be logged.

4. To add specific counters for objects, click Add Counters, and then use the Add Counters dialog box to select the counters you want to add.

5. In the Sample Data Every box, type a sample interval value and select a time unit in seconds, minutes, hours, or days. The sample interval specifies when new data will be collected. For example, if you sample every 15 minutes, the log is updated every 15 minutes.

6. In the Run As text box, type the name of the account under which the counter log will run, and then click Set Password. After you type the password for the account and confirm the password, click OK to close the Set Password dialog box. To run the log under the default system account, Run As should be set to **<Default>**.

7. Click the Log Files tab to display the dialog box shown in Figure 13-9. By default, counter logs are saved as sequentially numbered binary files in the %SystemDrive%\PerfLogs directory. You can change the log file defaults using the following options:

   ❑ **Log File Type**   Changes the default log type. Text File (Comma Delimited) creates a log file with comma-separated entries. Text File (Tab Delimited) creates a log file with tab-separated entries. Binary File creates a binary file that Performance Monitor can read. Binary Circular File creates a binary file that overwrites old data with new data when the file reaches a specified size limit. SQL Database writes the performance data to a SQL database file.

Tip   If you plan to use Performance Monitor only to analyze or view the log, use one of the binary file formats.

   ❑ **End File Names With**   Sets an automatic suffix for each new file created when you run the counter log. Logs can have a numeric suffix or a suffix in a specific date format.

   ❑ **Start Numbering At**   Sets the first serial number for a log that uses an automatic numeric suffix.

   ❑ **Comment**   Sets an optional description of the log, which is displayed in the Comment column.

   ❑ **Overwrite Existing Log File**   Select this option to overwrite any existing log file with the same name.

8. After you set the log file type, click Configure to configure the log file location. If you selected SQL Database as the file type, use the Configure SQL Logs dialog box to select a previously configured system data source name (DSN). The DSN is used to establish a connection to a SQL-compliant database. If you selected another file type, you will be able to set the log file name

and folder location. Using either selection, you have the option of limiting the log file size to a specific value. Click OK, and if prompted to create the log folder, click Yes.

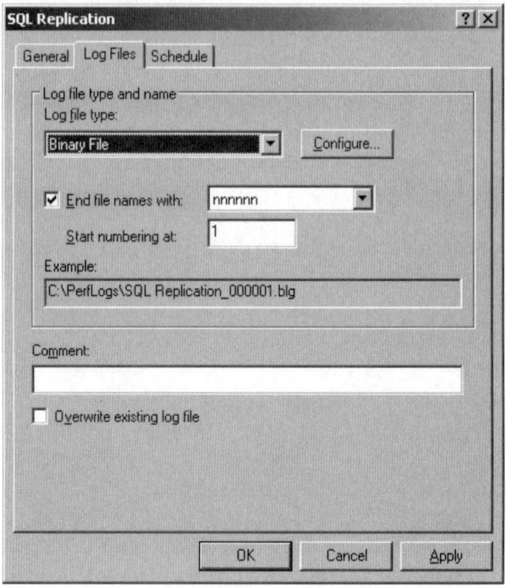

Figure 13-9   The Log Files tab

Tip   Log files can grow quickly. If you plan to log data for an extended period, be sure to place the log file on a drive with lots of free space. Remember, the more frequently you update the log file, the more the drive space will be used and the higher CPU resource usage will be on the system.

9. Click the Schedule tab, shown in Figure 13-10, and then specify when logging should start and stop. You can configure the logging to start manually or automatically at a specific date. Select the appropriate option and then specify a start date if necessary.

10. You can configure the log file to stop manually after a specified period of time, such as seven days; at a specific date and time; or when the log file is full (if you have set a specific file size limit). When a log file closes, you can start a new log file or run a command automatically.

11. Click OK when you have finished setting the logging schedule. Then the log will be created, and you can manage it as explained in the subsection titled "Creating and Managing Performance Logging" earlier in this chapter.

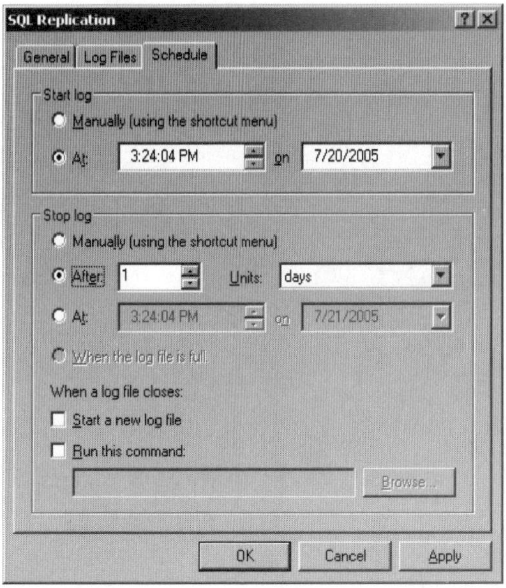

Figure 13-10   The Schedule tab

Creating Trace Logs

Trace logs record performance data whenever events related to their source providers occur. A source provider is an application or operating system service that has traceable events.

To create a trace log, complete the following steps:

1. Right-click Trace Logs in the left pane of the Performance console, and then choose New Log Settings.

2. In the New Log Settings dialog box, type a name for the log, such as **Database Locks Trace** or **SQL Server Trace**. Then click OK. This opens the SQL Trace dialog box shown in Figure 13-11.

3. If you want to trace operating system events, select the Events Logged By System Provider option button. As shown in Figure 13-11, you can now select system events to trace.

   Caution   Collecting page fault and file detail events puts a heavy load on the server and causes the log file to grow rapidly. Because of this, you should collect page faults and file details only for a limited amount of time.

4. If you want to trace another provider, select the Nonsystem Providers option button, and then click Add. This displays the Add Nonsystem Providers dialog box, which you use to select the provider to trace, such as MSSQLServer Trace.

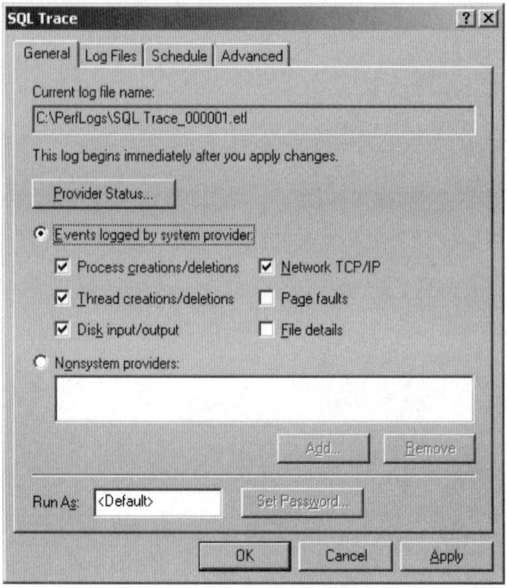

Figure 13-11   The SQL Trace dialog box

5. In the Run As text box, type the name of the account under which the counter log will run, and then click Set Password. After you type the password for the account and confirm the password, click OK to close the Set Password dialog box. To run the log under the default system account, Run As should be set to **<Default>**.

6. When you are finished selecting providers and events to trace, select the Log Files tab in the dialog box. You can now configure the trace file as explained in steps 7 and 8 in the subsection titled "Creating Counter Logs" earlier in this chapter. The only difference is in the log file available. There are two types of trace log types:

   ■ **Sequential Trace File**   Writes events to the trace log sequentially up to the maximum file size (if any).

   ■ **Circular Trace File**   Overwrites old data with new data when the file reaches a specified size limit.

7. Choose the Schedule tab, and then specify when tracing starts and stops, as discussed in the subsection titled "Creating Counter Logs" earlier in the chapter.

8. You can configure the logging to start manually or automatically at a specific date. Select the appropriate option, and then specify a start date, if necessary.

9. You can configure the log file to stop manually, after a specified period of time (such as seven days), at a specific date and time, or when the log file is full (if you have set a specific file size limit). When a log file closes, you can start a new log file or run a command automatically as well.

10. When you have finished setting the logging schedule, click OK. The log is then created, and you can manage it as explained in the subsection titled "Creating and Managing Performance Logging" earlier in this chapter.

Replaying Performance Logs

When you are troubleshooting problems, you will often want to log performance data over an extended period of time and analyze the data later. To do this, complete the following steps:

1. Configure automatic logging as described in the section titled "Creating and Managing Performance Monitor Logs" earlier in this chapter.

2. In Performance Monitor, select the System Monitor entry from the left pane, and then right-click the System Monitor details pane.

3. Select Properties from the shortcut menu to open the System Monitor Properties dialog box.

4. Click the Source tab. You can now configure the source:

   ❏ If you logged the data to a file, click Log Files, and then click Add to open the Select Log File dialog box. You can now select the log file you want to analyze.

   ❏ If you logged the data to a database, click Database and then select a previously configured system data source name (DSN). The DSN is used to connect to a specific database. Select the set of log records for the database selected.

5. Specify the time window that you want to analyze. Click Time Range, and then drag the Total Range bar to specify the appropriate starting and ending times. Drag the left edge to the right to move up the start time. Drag the right edge to the left to move down the end time.

6. Select the Data tab. You can now select counters to view. Click the Add button. This displays the Add Counter dialog box, which you can use to select the counters that you want to analyze.

Note   Only counters that you selected for logging are available. If you do not see a counter that you want to use, you will need to modify the log properties, restart the logging process, and then check the logs at a later date.

7. Click OK. Then in System Monitor, use the View Graph, View Histogram, and View Report buttons on the toolbar to display information based on the counters selected.

Configuring Alerts for Performance Counters

You can configure alerts to notify you when certain events occur or when certain performance thresholds are reached. You can send these alerts as network messages and as events that are logged in the application event log. You also can configure alerts to start applications and performance logs.

To add alerts in Performance Monitor, complete the following steps:

1. Right-click Alerts in the left pane of the Performance console, and then choose New Alert Settings.

2. In the New Alert Settings dialog box, type a name for the alert, such as **Database Alert** or **SQL Server Locks Alert**. Then click OK. This opens the dialog box shown in Figure 13-12.

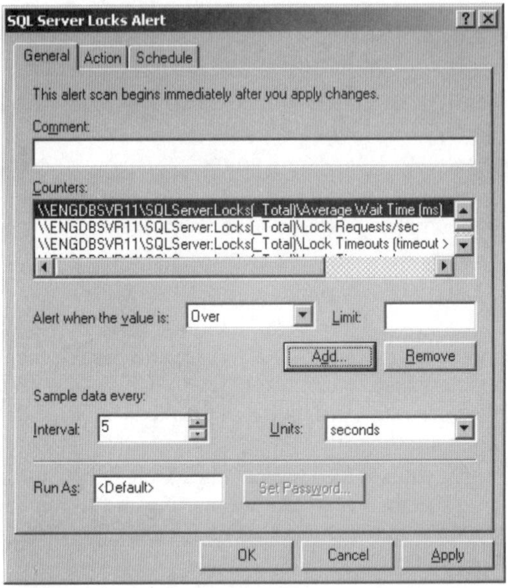

Figure 13-12   The SQL Server Locks Alert dialog box

3. In the General tab, type an optional description of the alert. Then click Add to display the Add Counters dialog box.

4. Use the Add Counters dialog box to add counters that trigger the alert. Click Close when you are finished.

5. In the Counters panel, select the first counter, and then use the Alert When Value Is box to set the occasion that will trigger an alert for this counter. Alerts can be triggered when the counter is over or under a specific value. Select Over or Under, and then set the trigger value. The unit of measurement is whatever makes sense for the currently selected counter(s). For example, to trigger an alert if processor time is over 95 percent, you would select Over, and then type **95** in the Limit text box. Repeat this process to configure other counters you have selected.

6. In the Sample Data Every text box, type in a sample interval and select a time unit in seconds, minutes, hours, or days. The sample interval specifies when

new data is collected. For example, if you sample every 10 minutes, the log is updated every 10 minutes.

Caution   Do not sample too frequently. Sampling uses system resources and might cause the server to seem unresponsive to user requests.

7. In the Run As text box, type the name of the account under which the counter log will run, and then click Set Password. After you type the password for the account and then confirm the password, click OK to close the Set Password dialog box. To run alert logging under the default system account, Run As should be set to **<Default>**.

8. Select the Action tab, shown in Figure 3-13. You can now specify any of the following actions to happen when an alert is triggered:

   - **Log An Entry In The Application Event Log**   Creates log entries for alerts.
   - **Send A Network Message To**   Sends a network message to the computer specified.
   - **Start Performance Data Log**   Sets a counter log to start when an alert occurs.
   - **Run This Program**   Sets the complete file path of a program or batch file script to run when the alert occurs.

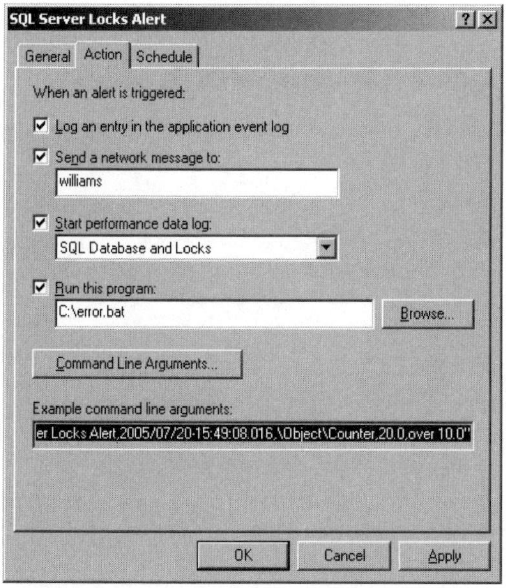

![SQL Server Locks Alert dialog box showing the Action tab with "When an alert is triggered:" options: Log an entry in the application event log (checked); Send a network message to: williams (checked); Start performance data log: SQL Database and Locks (checked); Run this program: C:\error.bat (checked) with Browse button; Command Line Arguments button; Example command line arguments: "er Locks Alert,2005/07/20-15:49:08.016,\Object\Counter,20.0,over 10.0"; OK, Cancel, Apply buttons]

Figure 13-13   The Action tab of the SQL Server Locks Alert dialog box

Tip Alerts can be configured to run executable programs with the .exe extension and batch files with the .bat or .cmd extension when an alert is triggered. Be sure to type the full path to the program or batch file you want to run. The Run This Program text box will accept only valid file paths. If you enter an invalid file path, you will see a warning indicating that the path is invalid when you click OK or try to access another tab. To pass arguments to an executable or batch file application, use the options in the Command Line Arguments panel. Normally, arguments are passed as individual strings. However, if you select Single Argument String, the arguments are passed in a comma-separated list within a single string. The Example Command Line Arguments drop-down list shows how the arguments would be passed.

9. Choose the Schedule tab, and then specify when alerting starts and stops. For example, you could configure the alerts to start on a Friday evening and stop on Monday morning. Then each time an alert occurs during this period, the specified action(s) are executed.

10. You can configure alerts to start manually or automatically at a specific date. Select the appropriate option, and then specify a start date, if necessary.

11. You can configure alerts to stop manually or automatically after a specified period of time, such as seven days, or at a specific date and time.

12. When you have finished setting the alert schedule, click OK to create the alert. Then you can manage the alert in much the same way that you manage counter and trace logs.

Solving Performance Problems with Profiler

Whether you are trying to track user activity, troubleshoot connection problems, or optimize SQL Server, SQL Server Profiler is one of the best utilities available. Profiler enables you to trace events that occur in SQL Server. Events you can track in Profiler are similar to counters you can monitor in Performance Monitor. They are organized into groups called *event classes*, and you can track one or more events for any of the available event classes. The strengths of Profiler are its advanced features and extensive customization capabilities.

You can record and replay Profiler traces when you want to analyze the data—and this is one area in which Profiler excels. You can:

- Use the information to find slow-running queries and then determine what is causing the queries to run slowly.
- Go through statements a step at a time to find the cause of a problem.
- Track a series of statements that cause a particular problem, and then replay the trace on a test server to determine the cause.
- Use trace information to determine the cause of deadlocks.
- Monitor user and application activity to determine actions that are using CPU time or queries that are taking a long time to process.

Let's look at how you can work with Profiler. Then I will examine how to create and manage traces.

Using Profiler

You can start Profiler in two ways. You can:

1. Click Start | Programs or All Programs | Microsoft SQL Server 2005 | Performance Tools, and then choose SQL Server Profiler.

2. In SQL Server Management Studio, select SQL Server Profiler from the Tools menu.

Figure 13-14 shows Profiler in the process of running a trace. The columns shown for the trace, such as Event Class, are completely configurable when you are setting up the trace, allowing you to select or clear columns as necessary. Two columns you will want to pay particular attention to are Duration and CPU. The Duration column shows how long a particular event has been running in milliseconds. The CPU column shows the amount of CPU processing time the event requires in milliseconds.

Stored procedures provide an alternative to Profiler. Using these stored procedures gives you some options that you do not have with SQL Server Profiler. You can:

- Store traces in the Windows application log.
- Autostart a trace when SQL Server starts.
- Forward event data to another computer running SQL Server (Windows only).

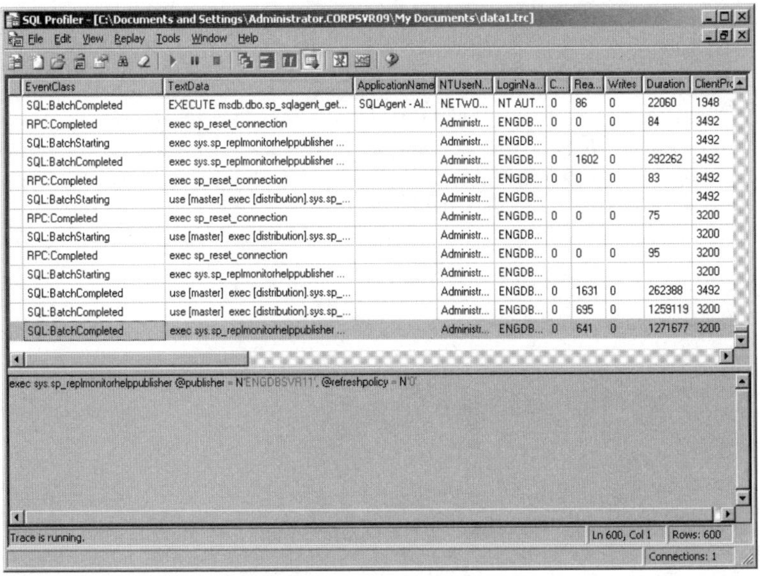

Figure 13-14   The SQL Server Profiler dialog box

To create traces with stored procedures, complete the following steps:

1. Create a trace definition using *sp_trace_create*.
2. Set events to capture using *sp_trace_setevent*.
3. Set event filters using *sp_trace_setfilter*.

Creating New Traces

You use traces to record events generated by local and remote SQL servers. You run traces in the Profiler window and store them for later analysis.

To start a new trace, complete the following steps:

1. Start SQL Server Profiler, and then click the New Trace button. Or select File | New Trace.
2. Use the Connect To Server dialog box to connect to the server you want to trace.
3. You will see the Trace Properties dialog box.
4. In the Trace Name text box, type a name for the trace, such as **Data Trace** or **Deadlock Trace For CustomerDB**.
5. You can store traces as they are being created by setting the Save To File or the Save To Table option, or both. Or you can store a running trace later by selecting File, then selecting Save As, and then choosing either the Trace File option or the Trace Table option.

Tip   There are advantages and disadvantages to using trace files and trace tables. You can use trace files to store traces quickly and efficiently using minimal system resources. Trace tables make it easy to store a trace directly in a table on another server, but you use much more of the system resources and usually have slower response times. Note also that storing a trace only saves the trace data. It does not save the trace definition. To reuse the trace definition, you will have to export the trace definition.

6. SQL Profiler templates are used to save trace definitions that contain the events, data columns, and filters used in a trace. Use the Template Name dropdown list to choose a template to use as the basis of the trace. Select the TSQL_Replay template if you want to replay the trace.

Tip   SQL Profiler templates end with the .tdf file extension.

7. Click the Events Selection tab, as shown in Figure 13-16. The currently selected template determines the events that are selected for tracking by default. The best way to learn the types of events you can trace is to select each event or event class and read its description at the bottom of the Events tab. Move the pointer to a specific column to see details about that data column.

8. Only a subset of the traceable events and event classes is displayed by default. To see all event classes available, select Show All Events. The event classes that can be traced include Broker, CLR, Cursors, Database, Deprecation, Errors And Warnings, Full Text, Locks, OLEDB, Objects, Performance, Progress Report, Query Notifications, Scans, Security Audit, Server, Sessions, Stored Procedures, TSQL, Transactions, and User Configurable.

9. Only a subset of the traceable data columns is displayed by default. To see all data columns, select Show All Columns.

10. Select event subclasses to add to the trace. If you select a subclass, all data columns for that class are tracked.

11. As necessary, select individual data columns for event subclasses to track specific data columns for an event subclass (versus all data columns for a subclass). At a minimum you must track:

   ❑ Cursors, CursorExecute
   ❑ Cursors, CursorOpen
   ❑ Cursors, CursorPrepare
   ❑ Sessions, ExistingConnection
   ❑ Stored Procedures, RPC:OutputParameter
   ❑ Stored Procedures, RPC:Starting
   ❑ TSQL, Exec Prepared SQL
   ❑ TSQL, Prepare SQL
   ❑ TSQL, SQL:BatchStarting

Tip   If you are tracking distributed queries, be sure to add the Host-Name column that corresponds to the ServerName in the display window. For transactions, be sure to add the TransactionID column. Also, if you plan to replay the trace for troubleshooting, refer to the subsection titled "Replaying a Trace" later in this chapter for specific event classes and data columns that you need to select.

12. To focus the trace on specific types of data, you may want to set criteria that exclude certain types of events. If so, select an event category you want to filter, click the Column Filters button to open the Edit Filter dialog box, and then set filter criteria. For each event category, you can use different filtering criteria. To use the criteria, you click on the related plus sign, and then enter the appropriate value in the text box provided. (When you are finished, click Close to close the Edit Filter dialog box.) You use the filter criteria as follows:

   ■ **Equals, Not Equal To, Greater Than Or Equal, or Less Than Or Equal**
   Use these criteria to set the values that trigger the event. Events with values outside the specified range are excluded. For example, with the CPU event category you can specify that only events using greater than or equal to 1000 milliseconds of CPU time are captured. If events use less CPU time than specified, they are excluded.

- **Like or Not Like**   Enter strings to include or exclude for this event category. Use the wildcard character (%) to match a series of characters. Use the semicolon (;) to separate multiple strings. For example, you can use the Application Name category to exclude all application names that start with MS and SQL Server by typing **MS%;SQL Server%**.

13. When you are finished configuring the trace, click Run to start the trace.

Working with Traces

Profiler displays information for multiple traces in separate windows that can be cascaded or tiled. Use the buttons on the Profiler toolbar to control work with traces. Create a new trace by clicking the New Trace button, and then use the options in the New Trace dialog box to configure the trace. Create a trace template by clicking New Template, setting trace properties, and then clicking Save. Once you have an active trace:

- Start the trace by clicking the Start Selected Trace button.

- Pause the trace by clicking the Pause Selected Trace button. You can then use the Start Selected Trace button to resume the trace at the point at which it was stopped.

- Stop the trace by clicking the Stop Selected Trace button. If you start the trace again with the Start Selected Trace button, the Profiler displays data again from the beginning of the trace process; new data is appended to the files or tables to which you are capturing data.

- Edit trace properties by clicking the Properties button.

Saving a Trace

When you create traces in Profiler, you create trace data and trace definitions. The Profiler window displays trace data, and you can also store it in a file or a table, or both. The trace data records a history of events that you are tracking, and you can use this history to replay the events for later analysis. The Trace Properties dialog box displays the trace definition. You can use the trace definition to create a new trace based on the existing trace.

To save trace data, complete the following steps:

1. Access the Profiler window that displays the trace you want to save.
2. Select File, point to Save As, and then select Trace File or Trace Table.
3. Use the Save As dialog box to select a folder location. Type a file name, and then click Save. Trace files end with the .trc extension.

To save a trace definition, complete the following steps:

1. Access the Profiler window that displays the trace with the definition you want to save.
2. Select File, point to Save As, and then select Trace Template.
3. Use the Select Template Name dialog box to select a folder location. Type a file name, and then click Save. Trace templates end with the .tdf extension.

Replaying a Trace

One of the main reasons you will want to create traces is to save them and replay them later. When replaying traces, Profiler can simulate user connections and authentication, which allows you to reproduce the activity recorded in the trace. You can replay traces in different ways to help you troubleshoot different kinds of problems:

- Execute traces step by step to closely monitor each step in the trace.
- Execute traces using the original timeline to simulate user loads.
- Execute traces with a high replay rate to stress test servers.

As you monitor the trace execution, you can look for problem areas. Then, when you identify the cause of problems you are trying to solve, you can correct them and rerun the original trace definition. If you are still having problems, you will need to reanalyze the trace data or look at other areas that may be causing problems. Keep in mind that you may need to specify different events to capture in the subsequent trace.

Requirements for Replaying Traces

Traces that you want to replay must contain a minimum set of events and data columns. If the trace does not contain the necessary elements, you will not be able to replay the trace. The required elements are in addition to any other elements that you want to monitor or display with traces. You must capture the following events in order to allow a trace to be replayed and analyzed correctly:

- Connect
- CursorExecute (required only when replaying server-side cursors)
- CursorOpen (required only when replaying server-side cursors)
- CursorPrepare (required only when replaying server-side cursors)
- Disconnect
- Exec Prepared SQL (required only when replaying server-side prepared SQL statements)
- ExistingConnection
- Prepare SQL (required only when replaying server-side prepared SQL statements)
- RPC:OutputParameter
- RPC:Starting
- SQL:BatchStarting

You must capture the following data columns to allow a trace to be replayed and analyzed correctly:

- Application Name
- Binary Data
- Connection ID or SPID
- Database ID
- Event Class

- Event SubClass
- Host Name
- Integer Data
- Server Name
- SQL User Name
- Start Time
- Text

Replaying Traces on a Different Server

You can replay a trace on a server other than the server originally traced. When you replay a trace on another server, this server is called the *target system*. To replay traces on the target, you should ensure that all logins contained in the trace:

- Are created on the target system and are in the same database as the source system.
- Have the same permissions they had originally.
- Have the same passwords they had originally.
- Are set to use a default database that matches the database on the source system.

If these settings are not the same, you will see errors, but the replay operation will continue. Also, database IDs on the target system must be the same as those on the source system. The easiest way to set up databases on the target is to complete the following steps:

1. Back up the *master* database on the source and any user databases used in the trace.

2. Restore the databases on the target as explained in the subsection titled "Restoring a Database to a Different Location" in Chapter 14, "Backing Up and Recovering SQL Server 2005."

Replaying and Analyzing a Trace

Replaying a trace allows you to analyze problems. To begin, start Profiler, and then select the Open Trace File or Open Trace Table button, as appropriate for the type of trace you want to replay. After you select the trace to replay, the trace is then loaded into the Profiler window. Events and commands recorded in the trace are summarized in the Profiler window, as shown in Figure 13-15. You can select an entry to see an expanded list of commands executed.

As Figure 13-15 also shows, the toolbar in the replay window differs from the standard toolbar. The buttons provide just about everything that you need to debug traces, including:

- **Start Replay** Starts executing the trace.
- **Pause Replay**   Pauses execution of the trace.
- **Stop Replay**   Stops execution of the trace.

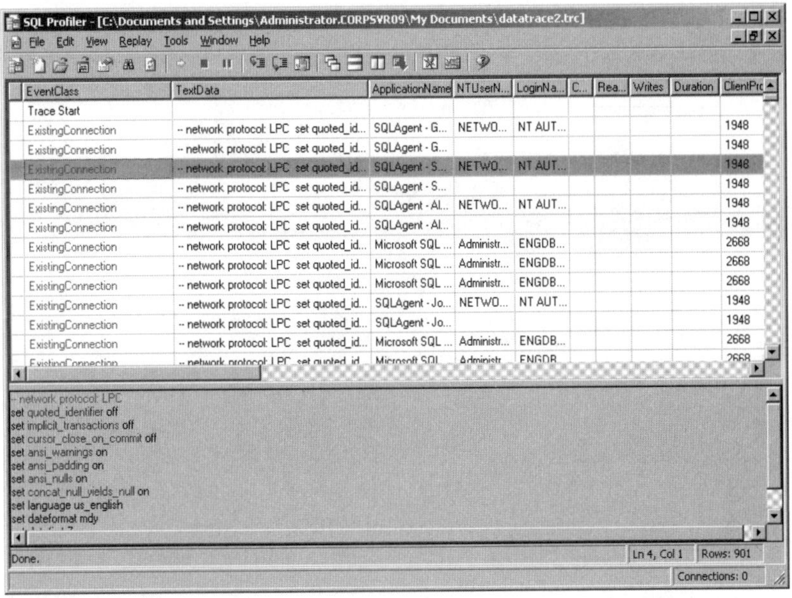

Figure 13-15 The Profiler window

- **Execute One Step** Allows you to move through the trace one step at a time.
- **Run To Cursor** Allows you to move through the trace using cursor sets.
- **Toggle Breakpoint** Allows you to set breakpoints for the trace execution.

When you start the replay, you will need to connect to the server, and then the initial dialog box displays to configure replay options (see Figure 13-16). You configure the options in the Replay Configuration dialog box to control where and how the playback takes place. Start by setting the destination server for the replay operation. By default, the replace server is set to the current (local) server. Click Change to use a different replay server, and then set replay options.

The replay options determine how closely the replay mirrors the original event execution. You can choose from the following options in the dialog box:

- **Replay Events In The Order They Were Traced** Events are started in the order in which they originally started. This enables debugging but it does not guarantee timing of event execution. Events may be executed sooner than their original start time or after their original start time, depending on current activity levels, the current speed of connections, and other factors.

- **Replay Events Using Multiple Threads** Events are replayed as quickly as they can be processed. No timing is maintained between events. When one event completes, the next event is started. This optimizes performance and disables debugging.

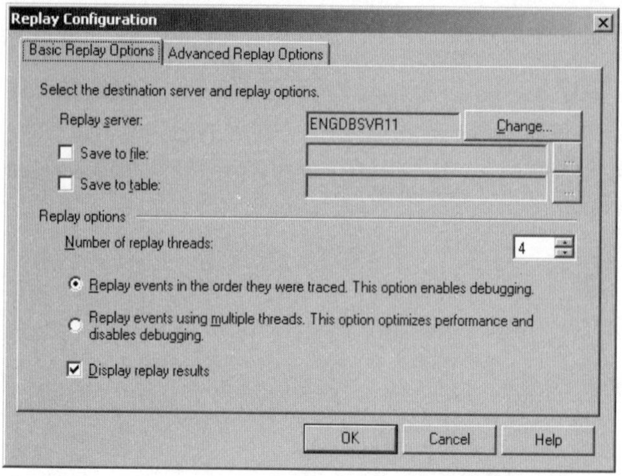

Figure 13-16   The Replay Configuration dialog box

The Display Replay Results check box controls whether or not the replay results are displayed in the Profiler window. To display results, select this option. Otherwise, clear this option.

You can also select an output file to save the result of the replay for later viewing. The output file allows you to review the replay just as you would any other trace file.

Chapter 14

Backing Up and Recovering SQL Server 2005

Information is the fuel that drives the enterprise, and the most critical information is often stored in databases. Databases are where you will find an organization's customer account information, partner directories, product knowledge base, and other important data. To protect an organization's data and to ensure the availability of its databases, you need a solid database backup and recovery plan.

Backing up databases can protect against accidental loss of data, database corruption, hardware failures, and even natural disasters. It is your job as a database administrator to perform backups and store the backups you create in a safe and secure location.

Creating a Backup and Recovery Plan

Creating and implementing a backup and recovery plan is one of your most important duties as a database administrator. Think of database backup as an insurance plan for the future–and for your job. Important data is deleted accidentally all the time. Mission-critical data can become corrupt. Natural disasters can leave your office in ruins. With a solid backup and recovery plan in place, you can recover from any of these situations. Without one, you are left with nothing after a disaster of any kind.

Initial Backup and Recovery Planning

Creating and implementing a backup and recovery plan takes time. You will need to figure out which databases need to be backed up, how often the databases should be backed up, and more. To help you create a plan, consider the following questions:

- **What type of databases are you backing up?** System and user databases often have different backup and recovery needs. For example, the *master* database is essential for all Microsoft SQL Server operations. If the *master* database fails or becomes corrupt, it takes the whole server down with it. But you do not need to back up *master* every hour, as you might need to do with a critical user database that handles real-time customer transactions. You need to back up *master* only after you create a database, change configuration values, configure SQL logons, or perform similar activities that make changes to databases on a server.

- **How important is the data in the database?** How you judge the data's importance can help determine *when* and *how* you should back it up. Although you may back up a development database weekly, you would probably back up a production database at least daily. The data's importance also drives your decision about the *type* of backup. To protect the data in that development database, you would probably want to make a full backup once a week. For an in-house customer order database that is updated throughout each weekday, you would probably want to perform full backups twice a week and supplement this with daily differential backups and hourly backups for the transaction logs. You may even want to set named log marks that allow recovery up to a specific point in the work.

- **How often are changes made to the database?** The frequency of change can drive your decision about how often the database should be backed up. Because a read-only database does not ordinarily change, it does not need to be backed up regularly. On the other hand, a database that is updated nightly should be backed up after the nightly changes are posted. A database that is updated around the clock should be backed up continually.

- **How quickly do you need to recover the data?** It is important to consider the amount of time it will take to recover lost data when you create a backup plan. For mission-critical databases, you may need to get the database back online swiftly; to do this, you may need to alter your backup plan. Instead of backing up to tape, for example, you might want to back up to disk drives or use multiple backup devices. Both options are much faster than restoring from a single tape device.

- **Do you have the equipment to perform backup?** You need backup hardware to perform backups. If you do not have the hardware, you cannot perform backups. To perform timely backups, you may need several backup devices and several sets of backup media. Backup hardware includes a tape drive, optical drives, removable disk drives, and plain old disk drives.

- **What is the best time to schedule backups?** You will want to schedule backups when database usage is as low as possible. This will speed the backup process. However, in the real world, you cannot always schedule backups for off-peak hours. So you will need to carefully plan when important databases are backed up.

- **Do you need to store backups off site?** Storing copies of backup tapes at an off-site location is essential to the recovery of your systems in the case of a natural disaster. In your off-site storage location, you should also include copies of the software required to restore operations on a new system.

Note Availability options, such as log shipping, are not a substitute for backups. Even if you use log shipping, mirroring, or clustering, you will still need to create backups.

Backing up a database differs from backing up a server or a workstation, primarily because you often need to combine all (or nearly all) of the available techniques to ensure that you can recover a database completely. The basic types of backups you can perform include:

- **Full database backups** Used to perform a full backup of the database, including all objects, system tables, and data. When the backup starts, SQL Server copies everything in the database and also includes portions of the transaction log that are needed while the backup is in progress. Because of this, you can use a full backup to recover the complete state of the data in the database at the time the backup operation finishes.

- **Differential backups** Designed to back up data that has changed since the last full backup. Because you store only the changes, this type of backup is faster and you can perform it more often. As with full backups, differential backups include portions of the transaction logs that are needed to restore the database to the time when the backup operation finishes.

Tip You can use differential backups only in conjunction with full backups, and you cannot perform differential backups on the *master* database. Do not confuse differential backups with incremental backups. Differential backups record all changes since the last full backup (which means the amount of data that is backed up grows over time). Incremental backups record changes since the most recent full or incremental backup (which means the size of the data backed up incrementally is usually much smaller than a full backup).

- **Transaction log backups** Transaction logs are serial records of all database modifications and are used during recovery operations to commit completed transactions and to roll back uncompleted transactions. When you back up a transaction log, the backup stores the changes that have occurred since the last transaction log backup, and then truncates the log, which clears out transactions that have been committed or aborted. Unlike full and differential backups, transaction log backups record the state of the transaction log at the time the backup operation starts (not when it ends).

- **File and filegroup backups** Allow you to back up database files and filegroups rather than the entire database. This is useful if you are dealing with large databases and you want to back up individual files rather than the entire database in order to save time. Many factors affect file and filegroup backups. When you use file and filegroup backups, you must back up the transaction log as well. Because of this dependency, you cannot use this backup technique if Truncate Log On Checkpoint is enabled. Furthermore, if objects in the database span multiple files or filegroups, you must back up all the related files and filegroups at the same time.

 Note Full-text catalogs are treated as a type of database file and are associated with a specific filegroup. You set the location of the catalog when you create the catalog. Whenever the associated filegroup is backed up or restored, the catalog will be backed up or restored as well.

SQL Server 2005 uses recovery models to help you plan backups. The types of databases you are backing up and the types of backups you perform drive the choices for recovery models. Three recovery models are available:

- **Simple** The simple recovery model is designed for databases that need to be recovered to the point of the last backup. The backup strategy with this model should consist of full and differential backups. You cannot perform transaction log backups when the simple recovery model is enabled. SQL Server 2005 turns on the Truncate Log On Checkpoint option, which clears out inactive entries in the transaction log on checkpoint. Because this model clears out transaction logs, it is ideal for most system databases.
- **Full** The full recovery model is designed for databases that need to be recovered to the point of failure or to a specific point in time. Using this model, all operations are logged, including bulk operations and bulk loading of data. The backup strategy with this model should include full, differential, and transaction log backups or full and transaction log backups only.
- **Bulk-logged** The bulk-logged recovery model reduces the log space usage yet retains most of the flexibility of the full recovery model. With this model, bulk operations and bulk loads are minimally logged and cannot be controlled on a per operation basis. You will need to manually redo bulk operations and bulk loads if the database fails before you perform a full or differential backup. The backup strategy with this model should include full, differential, and transaction log backups or full and transaction log backups only.

Each database can have a different recovery model. By default, *master*, *msdb*, and *tempdb* use the simple recovery model, and the *model* database uses the full recovery model. The *model* database is the template database for all new databases, so if you change the default setting, all new databases for the database server instance use the new default model. You set the recovery model by completing the following steps:

1. Start SQL Server Management Studio. In Object Explorer view, connect to the appropriate server.
2. If you plan to switch from bulk-logged recovery to simple recovery, perform a transaction log backup prior to making the change, and then change your backup strategy so that you no longer perform transaction log backups.

3. Expand the Databases folder. If you are configuring recovery for a system database, expand the System Databases folder as well.

4. Right-click the database you want to change and choose Properties. This displays the database's Properties dialog box.

5. Use the Recovery Model drop-down list on the Options page to change the recovery model, and then click OK.

6. If you switched from simple recovery to full or bulk-logged recovery, add transaction log backups to your backup strategy for the database.

SQL Server 2005 includes several features that allow you to create standby servers. The three general types of standby servers are:

■ **Hot standby server**   An automatically updated server that automatically comes online if a primary server/database fails.

■ **Warm standby server**   An automatically updated server that must be brought online manually if a primary server/database fails.

■ **Cold standby server**   A manually updated server that must be brought online manually if a primary server/database fails.

Database mirroring, log shipping, and database copies allow you to create standby servers. You use database mirroring to establish a hot standby server, called a *mirror server*, on which the database is continuously brought up to date and to which failover can occur automatically if the primary database fails. You use log shipping to establish a warm standby server, called a *secondary server*, on which the database is automatically updated from log backups, but which must be brought online manually if the primary database fails. You create a copy of a database to establish a cold standby server, on which the database is manually updated and which must be brought online manually if the primary database fails.

Planning for Mirroring and Mirrored Database Backups

Mirroring allows you to create hot standby servers. You can mirror any database except for *master, msdb, temp,* and *model*. You can configure and enable mirroring using the Mirroring page in the Database Properties dialog box. As discussed in the subsection titled "Ensuring Availability and Scalability" in Chapter 2, "Deploying Microsoft SQL Server 2005," mirroring requires up to three servers: a principal server, a mirror server, and a witness server.

Backups are not used with mirrored databases in the same way as they are with other databases. When mirroring is configured, backups of a principal database are used to initialize the mirror database on the mirror server. As part of the mirror creation process, you can back up and restore individual files and filegroups. However, you must restore all files and filegroups before you begin mirroring. If you only want to work with a subset of a database and its objects, use replication instead, as discussed in Chapter 12, "Implementing Snapshot, Merge, and Transactional Replication."

When mirroring databases, remember the following information:

- While database mirroring is active, you cannot back up or restore the mirror database.
- Although you can back up the principal database, you cannot use BACKUP LOG WITH NORECOVERY.
- You cannot restore the principal database (that is what mirroring is for). The mirror will correct itself after failover.

Planning for Backups of Replicated Databases

Databases that are replicated present a special problem for backup and restoration planning, primarily because the traditional database architecture is extended to include three server roles (which all have related databases):

- **Publisher** A server that makes data available for replication, tracks changes to data, and maintains other information about source databases. Each publisher has a *publication* database.
- **Distributor** A server that distributes replicated data and stores the *distribution* database. Each distributor has a *distribution* database.
- **Subscriber** A destination server for replication. The subscriber databases store the replicated data, receive updates, and in some cases can also make changes to data. Each subscriber has a *subscription* database.

As with other system databases, you should regularly back up the publication, distribution, and subscription databases. At the publisher, distributor, and all subscriber servers, you should back up both the *master* and *msdb* system databases at the same time as you back up the replication databases. When you restore the *publication* database, you should also restore the *master* and *msdb* databases at the publisher server. When you restore the *distribution* database, you should also restore the *master* and *msdb* databases at the distributor server. When you restore the *subscription* database, you should also restore the *master* and *msdb* databases at the subscriber server.

Subscription database backups should be no older than the shortest retention period of all publications to which the subscriber subscribes. If the shortest retention period is 10 days, the backup you plan to restore should be no older than 10 days. To ensure successful recovery of a *subscription* database, subscribers should synchronize with the publisher before the *subscription* database is backed up. They should also synchronize after the *subscription* database is restored. Synchronizing prior to backup helps ensure that if a subscriber is restored from backup, the subscription is still within the publication retention period.

You can restore replicated databases to the same server and database from which the backup was created or to another server or database. If you restore a backup of a replicated database to another server or database, replication settings are not preserved, and you will need to recreate all publications and subscriptions after backups are restored, except in the case of log shipping. If you use log shipping, you can restore a replicated database to a standby server and the replication settings are preserved.

With merge replication, any replication-related changes should be captured in the log backups. If you do not perform log backups, the *publication* database should be backed up whenever a setting relevant to replication is changed. After restoring the *publication* database from a backup, you should either synchronize the *publication* database with a *subscription* database or reinitialize all subscriptions to the publications in the *publication* database. You can synchronize the *publication* database or reinitialize subscriptions as discussed in the section titled "Subscribing to a Publication" in Chapter 12. Be sure to check the identity ranges in tables that contain IDENTITY columns after restoring a database.

> **Note**   In merge replication, the *distribution* database has a limited role. It does not store any data used in change tracking, and it does not provide temporary storage of merge replication changes to be forwarded to *subscription* databases (as it does in transactional replication).

With transactional replication, you set the Sync With Backup option on the *distribution* and *publication* databases. You should:

- Turn this option on for the *distribution* databases to ensure that transactions in the log of the *publication* database will not be truncated until they have been backed up at the *distribution* database. This allows the *distribution* database to be restored to the last backup, and any missing transactions then can be delivered from the *publication* database to the *distribution* database while replication continues unaffected. Although this has no effect on replication latency, it can delay the truncation of the log on the *publication* database until the corresponding transactions in the *distribution* database have been backed up.

- Turn this option on for the *publication* database if your application can tolerate additional latency to ensure that transactions are not delivered to the *distribution* database until they are backed up at the *publication* database. This allows you to restore the last *publication* database backup at the publisher without any possibility of the *distribution* database having transactions that the restored *publication* database does not have. Latency and throughput are affected because transactions cannot be delivered to the *distribution* database until they have been backed up at the Publisher.

Planning for Backups of Very Large Databases

If you must develop a plan to back up and restore very large databases, you may want to take advantage of parallel backup and restore. The parallel backup and restore process allows SQL Server to use multiple threads to read and write data. This means SQL Server can read data from, and write data to, multiple data sources. The backup and restore process uses parallel input/output (I/O) in different ways:

- Backup uses one thread per disk device to read data from the database when a database has files on several disk devices.

- Restore uses one thread per disk device as it initializes a database that it is creating for the restore process if the database is defined with files on several disks.

- Both backup and restore use one thread per backup device when a backup set is stored on multiple backup devices.

As you can see from this information, to take advantage of parallel I/O, you must implement your backup strategy so that databases use:

- Multiple disk drives for storing data.
- Multiple backup devices for backing up and restoring data.

After you determine the backup operations to use on each database and how often you want to back up each database, you can select backup devices and media that meet these requirements. The next section covers backup devices and media.

Selecting Backup Devices and Media

Many different solutions are available for backing up data. Some are fast and expensive. Others are slow but very reliable. The backup solution that is right for your organization depends on many factors, including the following:

- **Capacity**   This refers to the amount of data that you need to back up on a routine basis. Can the backup hardware support the required load given your time and resource constraints?

- **Reliability**   The reliability of the backup hardware and media determines how useful the backups you create will be when you need them to restore lost data. Can you afford to sacrifice reliability to meet budget or time needs?

- **Extensibility**   The extensibility of the backup solution refers to its ability to expand beyond its original capacity. Will this solution meet your needs as your organization grows?

- **Speed**   Consider the speed with which data can be backed up and recovered when selecting an appropriate solution. Can you afford to sacrifice speed to reduce costs?

- **Cost**   The cost of backup solution choices will affect your decision. Does the solution fit within your budget?

Capacity, reliability, extensibility, speed, and cost are the main issues that will influence your choice of a backup plan. If you determine the relative value of these issues to your organization, you will be able to select an appropriate backup solution for your situation. Some of the most commonly used backup solutions include the following hardware and media:

- **Tape drives**   Tape drives are the most common backup devices. Tape drives use magnetic tape cartridges to store data. Magnetic tapes are relatively inexpensive, but they are not highly reliable. Tapes can break or stretch. They can also lose information over time. The average capacity of tape cartridges ranges from 4 GB to 10 GB. Compared with other backup solutions, tape drives are fairly slow, but their biggest advantage is low cost.

- **Digital audio tape (DAT) drives**   DAT drives are quickly replacing standard tape drives as the preferred type of backup devices. Many DAT formats are available. The most commonly used format is Digital Linear Tape (DLT) or Super DLT. With DLT IV, tapes have a capacity of either 35 GB or 40 GB uncompressed (70 GB or 80 GB compressed). If yours is a large organization, you might want to look at Linear Tape Open (LTO) or Advanced Intelligent Tape (AIT) tape technologies. Typically, LTO tapes have a capacity of 100 GB uncompressed (200 GB compressed), and AIT-3 tapes also have a capacity of 100 GB uncompressed (260 GB compressed).

Tip   To perform faster backup and recovery operations, you can use multiple backup devices with SQL Server. For example, if it normally takes four hours to perform a full backup or restoration of the database, you can cut the backup and restoration time in half by using two backup devices; with four backup devices, you could fully back up or restore the database in an hour.

- **Autoloader tape systems**   Autoloader tape systems use a magazine of tapes to create extended backup volumes capable of meeting an enterprise's high-capacity needs. With an autoloader system, tapes within the magazine are automatically changed as needed during the backup or recovery process. Most autoloader tape systems use DAT tapes formatted for DLT, LTO, or AIT. Typical DLT drives can record up to 45 GB per hour, and you can improve that speed by purchasing a type library system with multiple drives. In this way, you can record on multiple tapes simultaneously. In contrast, most LTO and AIT drives record over 100 GB per hour, and by using multiple drives in a system, you can record hundreds of GB per hour.
- **Optical jukeboxes**   Optical jukeboxes are similar to autoloader tape systems. Jukeboxes use magnetic optical disks rather than DAT tapes to offer high-capacity solutions. These systems load and unload disks stored internally for backup and recovery operations. The main disadvantage of optical jukeboxes is their high cost.
- **Removable disks**   Removable disks, such as an Iomega Jaz disk with 1 GB or 2 GB capacity, are increasingly being used as backup devices. Removable disks offer good speed and ease of use for a single drive or single system backup. However, the disk drives and the removable disks tend to be more expensive than standard tape or DAT drive solutions.
- **Disk drives**   Disk drives provide the fastest way to back up and restore files. Using disk drives, you can often accomplish in minutes what takes a tape drive hours. So when business needs mandate a speedy recovery, nothing beats a disk drive. The cost of disk drives, however, may be higher compared to tape library systems.

Selecting a backup device is an important step in implementing a backup and recovery plan, but it is not the only step. You also need to purchase the tapes or the disks, or both, that will allow you to implement your backup and recovery plan. The number of tapes, disks, or drives you need depends on:

- How much data you will be backing up.
- How often you will be backing up the data.
- How long you need to keep additional data sets.

Typically, you implement backups by using a rotation schedule with two or more sets of tapes, disks, or files on a drive. Having more than one set of media allows you to increase media longevity by reducing media usage, and at the same time it reduces the number of actual tapes, disks, or files you need to ensure that you have data available when necessary.

 Best Practices For important databases, I recommend using four media sets. Use two sets in regular rotation. Use the third set for the first rotation cycle at the beginning of each month, and use the fourth set for the first rotation cycle of each quarter. This technique allows you to recover the database in a wide variety of situations.

Using Backup Strategies

Table 14-1 lists backup strategies you may want to use. As you can see, these backup strategies are based on the type of database as well as the type of data. When planning a backup strategy, remember the following:

- The *master* database stores important information about the structure of other databases, including the database size. Any time database information or structure changes, *master* may be updated without your knowing about it. For example, the size of most databases changes automatically, and when this happens *master* is updated. Because of this, often the best backup strategy for *master* is to schedule backups every other day and to rotate through several backup sets so that you can go back to several different versions of *master* if necessary.

- You can use transaction logs to recover databases up to the point of failure and up to a point of work. To recover a database to a point of work, you must insert named log marks into the transaction log using BEGIN TRANSACTION WITH MARK. You can then recover to a mark in the log using RESTORE LOG WITH STOPATMARK or RESTORE LOG WITH STOPBEFOREMARK.

Table 14-1   Backup Strategies for System and User Databases

Database Type	Details	Strategy
User	Recovery up to the minute	Run full backups twice a week, if possible. Use nightly differential backups and back up the recovery transaction log every 10 minutes during business hours. Do not use Truncate Log On Checkpoint, as this will make it impossible to recover some transactions. To improve backup restore speed, use multiple backup devices whenever possible.

Table 14-1 Backup Strategies for System and User Databases   *(continued)*

Database Type	Details	Strategy
	Recovery up to a point of work	Run full backups twice a week, if possible. Use nightly differential backups and back up the recovery transaction log every 10 minutes during business hours. Do not use Truncate Log On Checkpoint. Use named transactions to insert named marks into the transaction logs. To improve backup/restore speed, use multiple backup devices whenever possible.
	Recovery up to the hour	Run full backups twice a week, if possible. Use nightly differential backups and back up the recovery transaction log every 30 minutes during business hours. Do not use Truncate Log On Checkpoint. To improve backup/restore speed, use multiple backup devices whenever possible.
	Recovery of daily changes	Run full backups at least once a week. Use daily nightly differential backups and back up the changes transaction log every four hours during business hours. Do not use Truncate Log On Checkpoint.
	Read-only	Schedule a full backup of the database every 30 days and supplement this with an additional full backup whenever the database is modified.
System	*distribution*	Available when you configure replication and the server is acting as a distributor. Schedule full backups after snapshots. With transactional replication, schedule regular log backups.
	master	Run full backups immediately after creating or removing databases, changing the size of a database, adding or removing logins, or modifying server configuration settings. Do not forget to maintain several backup sets for *master*.
	msdb	If you schedule jobs through the SQL Server Agent, back up this database regularly because this is where the job schedule and history is maintained and backup history is stored.
	model	Treat like a read-only database.
	publication	Available when you configure replication and the server is acting as a distributor. If you do not perform log backups, the *publication* database should be backed up whenever a setting relevant to replication is changed.
	subscription	Available when you configure replication and the server is acting as a subscriber. *Subscription* database backups should be no older than the shortest retention period of all publications to which the subscriber subscribes.
	tempdb	Normally does not need to be backed up. This database is recreated each time you start SQL Server.

Creating a Backup Device

Early versions of SQL Server required you to configure backup devices before you could back up databases. With SQL Server 2005, you do not need to explicitly define backup devices. Nevertheless, backup devices do provide an easy way to ensure that you create backups that have the same file name and location time after time. By using consistent names and locations, you can more easily manage the backup and recovery process.

To create a backup device using SQL Server Management Studio, complete the following steps:

1. Start SQL Server Management Studio. In Object Explorer view, connect to the appropriate server.

2. Expand the server's Server Objects folder.

3. Right-click Backup Devices, and then choose New Backup Device to open the dialog box shown in Figure 14-1.

4. In the Device Name box, type the name of the logical backup device. Use a short but descriptive name, such as **Customer Device** or **Master Device**.

5. If you have installed a tape drive and want to back up to the tape drive, select the Tape option button, and then use the related drop-down list box to select the target drive.

6. If you are backing up to a file, select the File option button, and then type the full path to the backup file you want to associate with this device, such as **E:\MSSQL\BACKUP\PERSONNEL.BAK**.

7. Click OK. SQL Server will attempt to verify the backup file location. If there is a problem, you will see a prompt notifying you of any issues.

With Transact-SQL, you create backup devices using *sp_addumpdevice*. Sample 14-1 shows the syntax and usage for this command, which uses many different arguments, including *device_type, logical_name, physical_name, controller_type,* and *device_status*. The *device_type* is the type of device you are using—disk or tape. The *logical_name* is the name of the backup device. The *physical_name* is the full path to the backup file. The *controller_type* is 2 for a disk or 5 for a tape. The *device_status* is either *noskip,* to read ANSI tape headers, or *skip,* to skip ANSI tape headers.

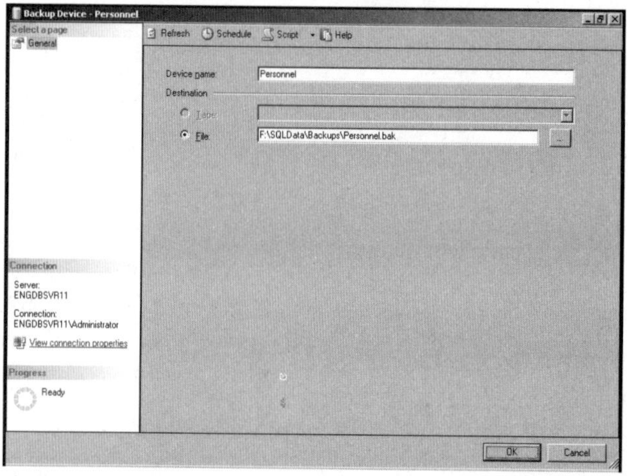

Figure 14-1 The Backup Device dialog box

Sample 14-1   *sp_addumpdevice* Syntax and Usage

Syntax

```
sp_addumpdevice [@devtype =]'device_type',

    [@logicalname =] 'logical_name',
    [@physicalname =] 'physical_name'
    [, {
            [@cntrltype =] controller_type |
            [@devstatus =] 'device_status'
    }
    ]
```

Usage

```
EXEC sp_addumpdevice 'disk', 'Customer',
    'c:\mssql\backup\cust.bak'

EXEC sp_addumpdevice 'disk', 'Customer on Backup Server',
    '\\omega\backups\cust.bak'
EXEC sp_addumpdevice 'tape', 'Customer on Tape',
'\\.\tape0'
```

Performing Backups

Backups are an essential part of database administration. They are so important that SQL Server provides multiple backup procedures and several ways to create backups—all designed to help you manage database backup and recovery easily and effectively. In this section, you will learn about standard backup procedures and the Transact-SQL backup process. The final component in a successful backup strategy involves database maintenance plans, which you will learn about in Chapter 15, "Database Automation and Maintenance."

Creating Backups in SQL Server Management Studio

In SQL Server Management Studio, you can start the backup process by right-clicking the database you want to back up, pointing to Tasks, and then selecting Back Up. I will focus on how you use the Backup Database dialog box to perform backups in these situations:

■ When you want to create a new backup set

■ When you want to add to an existing backup set

Creating a New Backup Set

Whenever you back up a database for the first time or start a new rotation on an existing backup set, follow these steps to create the backup:

1. Start SQL Server Management Studio. In Object Explorer view, connect to the appropriate server.
2. Expand the Databases folder. Right-click the database you want to back up, point to Tasks, and then select Back Up. This opens the Backup Database dialog box shown in Figure 14-2.

3. The database you want to back up should be selected in the Database drop-down list in the dialog box. The current recovery model for this database is also shown, but it is shaded because the recovery model cannot be changed. You cannot create transaction log backups when the recovery model is set to Simple.

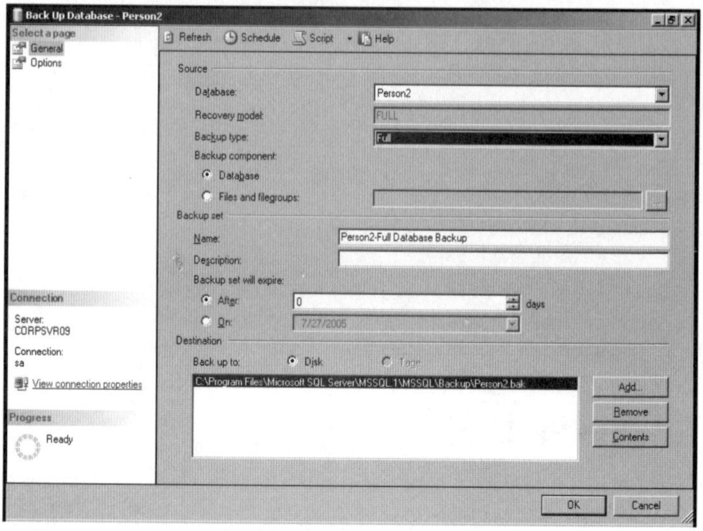

Figure 14-2 The Back Up dialog box

4. Since this is a new backup set, select the type of backup you want to perform. Typically, for a first backup, you will want to perform a full backup. Then you can add to the backup set later using other types of backups.

5. You can back up the entire database or a subset of its files and filegroups. By default, Backup Component is set to Database to create a database backup. If you want to create a file and filegroup backup, select the Files And Filegroups option button. The Select Files And Filegroups dialog box displays, and you can choose the files and filegroups you want to back up. Click OK after making your selections.

 Note The only available backup option for the *master* database is Full. That is because you can run only full backups on *master*.

6. In the Name text box in the Backup Set area, type a name for the backup set you are creating. This is an ordinary, nontechnical name that will help you tell at a glance what the backup contains. For example, name the first backup set for the *Customer* database **Customer Backup Set 1**. Then you can add the full, differential, and transaction log backups for this rotation to the set.

7. In the Description box, type a description of the backup, such as **Set 1 contains the weekly full, daily differential, and hourly transaction log backups. This is the full backup for the week.**

8. Use the Backup Set Will Expire options to set an expiration interval or date. This allows the backup to overwrite the media after a specified period or date.

9. If a backup set exists and is listed in the Destination area, select it and click Remove.

10. Click Add to display the Select Backup Destination dialog box shown in Figure 14-3. To use a new file as the backup destination, select the File Name option button and type the full path to the backup file, such as **E:\DATA\ BACKUPS\CUST.BAK** or **\\OMEGA\BACKUPS\CUST.BAK**. To use a backup device, select the Backup Device option button, and then choose the backup destination using the drop-down list box. Click OK when you are ready to continue.

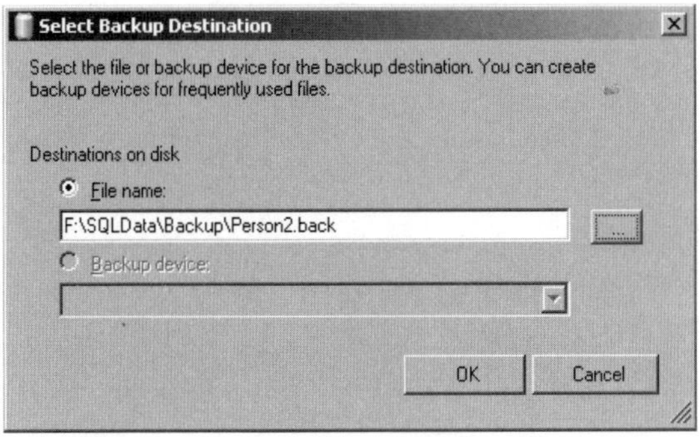

Figure 14-3 The Select Backup Destination dialog box

11. To schedule the backup, click Schedule, and then configure the backup schedule as discussed in Chapter 15.

12. To set additional options for the backup, select the Options page. You use the available options as follows:

   - **Back Up To The Existing Media Set** Select this option if you are using an existing media set. You can specify whether to append to the existing backup set or overwrite all existing backup sets.

   - **Check Media Set Name And Backup Set Expiration** Use this option to ensure that you are writing to the correct tape set and that the tape expiration date has not been reached. If you select this option, enter the media set name that should be verified.

   - **Back Up To A New Media Set, And Erase All Existing Backup Sets** Select this option if you want to create a new media set and erase all existing media sets. Then enter the media set name and an optional description.

   - **Verify Backup When Finished** Choose this option to verify the entire backup and check for errors. Generally, it is a very good idea to verify your backups.

   - **Perform Checksum Before Writing To Media** Use this option to check the data you are backing up prior to writing. This is the same as using the

CHECKSUM or NOCHECKSUM options with the BACKUP statement. If you perform a checksum, you can also specify to continue on checksum error.

- **Truncate The Transaction Log By Removing Inactive Entries** Select this option to clean out entries that are no longer needed after the backup. These entries are for transactions that have been committed or rolled back. (This option is set by default for transaction log backups.)

- **Back Up The Tail Of The Log...** Use this option to back up the active transaction log (those transactions that have not been completed and are at the tail of the log). When you use the full or bulk-logged recovery model, you must back up the active transaction log before you can restore the database using SQL Server Management Studio.

 Tip You will usually want to perform one last log backup before you try to restore a corrupt database. When you do, you will want to clear this option and perform the log backup without truncation. This option is the same as running BACKUP LOG NO_TRUNCATE.

- **Unload The Tape After Backup** Select this option to eject the tape after the backup (only valid with tape devices).

13. Click OK to start the backup or confirm that you want to schedule the backup. If you opted to verify the data, the verification process starts immediately after the backup ends.

Adding to an Existing Backup Set

When you want to add to an existing backup set, complete the following steps:

1. Start SQL Server Management Studio. In Object Explorer view, connect to the appropriate server.

2. Expand the Databases folder. Right-click the database you want to back up, point to Tasks, and then select Back Up to open the Backup Database dialog box (shown in Figure 14-2).

3. The database you want to back up should be selected in the Database drop-down list.

4. Select the type of backup you want to perform: Full, Differential, or Transaction Log. Typically, when you are adding to an existing set, you do so using a differential or transaction log backup. You cannot create transaction log backups when the recovery model is set to Simple.

5. You can back up the entire database or a subset of its files and filegroups. By default, Backup Component is set to Database to create a database backup. If you want to create a file and filegroup backup, select the Files And Filegroups option button. The Select Files And Filegroups dialog box is then displayed, allowing you to choose the files and filegroups to back up. Click OK after making your selections.

6. In the Backup Set panel's Name box, type a name for the backup you are creating. In the Description box, type a description of the backup, such as **Daily differential backup**.

7. Use the Backup Set Will Expire options to set an expiration interval or date. This allows the backup to overwrite the media after a specified period or date.

8. A backup set should be listed in the Destination area. If so, click Contents to see the current contents of this backup set. If a backup set is not listed, click Add to display the Select Backup Destination dialog box, and then enter the location of the existing backup. Click OK when you are ready to continue.

9. Select the Options page. Since you are adding additional data to the existing backup set, the options Backup To The Existing Media Set and Append To The Existing Backup Set should be selected.

Real World   Whether you back up data to a tape or disk drive, you should use the tape rotation technique. Create multiple sets, and then write to these sets on a rotating basis. With a disk drive, for example, you could create these backup files on different network drives and use them as follows:

❑ //omega/data1drive/backups/cust_set1.bak   Used in week 1, 3, 5, and so on for full and differential backups of the customer database.

❑ //omega/data2drive/backups/cust_set2.bak   Used in week 2, 4, 6, and so on for full and differential backups of the customer database.

❑ //omega/data3drive/backups/cust_set3.bak   Used in the first week of the month for full backups of the customer database.

❑ //omega/data4drive/backups/cust_set4.bak   Used in the first week of the quarter for full backups of the customer database.

Do not forget that each time you start a new rotation on a tape set, you should overwrite the existing media. For example, you would append all backups in week 1. Then, when starting the next rotation in week 3, you would overwrite the existing media for the first backup and then append the remaining backups for the week.

10. For transaction log backups, you usually will want to select the Truncate The Transaction Log By Removing Inactive Entries check box. This ensures that inactive entries are cleared out of the transaction log after a backup.

11. To schedule the backup, click Schedule, and then configure the backup schedule as discussed in Chapter 15.

12. Click OK to start the backup or to confirm that you want to schedule the backup. If you opted to verify the data, the verify process starts immediately after the backup ends.

Using Striped Backups with Multiple Devices

Through a process called *parallel striped backups*, SQL Server can perform backups to multiple backup devices simultaneously. As you can imagine, writing multiple backup files at the same time can dramatically speed backup operations. The key to this speed, however, is having physically separate devices, such as three different tape devices or three different drives that you are using for the backup. You cannot write parallel backups to a single tape device, and you cannot write parallel backups to the same drive.

Multiple devices used in a backup operation are referred to as a *media set*. SQL Server allows you to use from 2 to 32 devices to form the media set. These devices must be of the same type. For example, you cannot create a striped backup with one backup tape device and one backup drive device.

The two main operations involved in parallel striped backups are:

- Creating a new media set.
- Adding to an existing media set.

Creating a New Media Set

To create a new media set using multiple devices, complete the following steps:

1. Select the server you want to use, and then create each of the backup devices you need in the media set, as described in the section titled "Creating a Backup Device" earlier in this chapter.
2. Right-click the database you want to back up, point to Tasks, and then select Back Up to display the Backup Database dialog box.
3. Follow the steps outlined in the subsection titled "Creating a New Backup Set" earlier in this chapter. Repeat step 10 for each backup device you want to use in the media set.

Adding to an Existing Media Set

To add to an existing media set, complete the following steps:

1. Right-click the database you want to back up, point to Tasks, and then select Back Up to display the Backup Database dialog box.
2. Follow the steps outlined in the subsection titled "Adding to an Existing Backup Set" earlier in this chapter. The only difference is that in step 8 you should see a list of all the backup devices used in the media set. If you do not, you will need to add them one by one using the Add button and the related Select Backup Destination dialog box.

Using Transact-SQL Backup

An alternative to using the backup procedures in SQL Server Management Studio is to use the T-SQL BACKUP statement. You use BACKUP DATABASE to back up databases and BACKUP LOG to back up transaction logs.

Tip   If you back up databases using Transact-SQL, you lose one of the biggest benefits of SQL Server—the automated recovery process. With automated recovery, you do not have to worry about which backup to apply in which situation, which command flags to use, and so on. Furthermore, because you can schedule automated and unattended backups, you do not really need to run backups manually through SQL as often as in the past. I recommend using the SQL Server Management Studio backup and restore process whenever possible.

BACKUP DATABASE has dual syntax. Sample 14-2 shows the syntax and usage for full and differential backups. A full backup is the default operation.

Sample 14-2   BACKUP DATABASE Syntax and Usage for Full and Differential Backups

Syntax

```
BACKUP DATABASE { database_name | @database_name_var }
TO < backup_device > [ ,...n ]
[ [ MIRROR TO < backup_device > [ ,...n ] ] [ ...next-mirror ] ]
[ WITH
     [ BLOCKSIZE = { blocksize | @blocksize_variable } ]
     [ [ , ] { CHECKSUM | NO_CHECKSUM } ]
     [ [ , ] { STOP_ON_ERROR | CONTINUE_AFTER_ERROR } ]
     [ [ , ] DESCRIPTION = { 'text' | @text_variable } ]
     [ [ , ] DIFFERENTIAL ]
     [ [ , ] EXPIREDATE = { date | @date_var }
     | RETAINDAYS = { days | @days_var } ]
     [ [ , ] PASSWORD = { password | @password_variable } ]
     [ [ , ] { FORMAT | NOFORMAT } ]
     [ [ , ] { INIT | NOINIT } ]
     [ [ , ] { NOSKIP | SKIP } ]
     [ [ , ] MEDIADESCRIPTION = { 'text' | @text_variable } ]
     [ [ , ] MEDIANAME = { media_name | @media_name_variable } ]
     [ [ , ] MEDIAPASSWORD = { mediapassword | @mediapassword_variable } ]
     [ [ , ] NAME = { backup_set_name | @backup_set_name_var } ]
     [ [ , ] { NOREWIND | REWIND } ]
     [ [ , ] { NOUNLOAD | UNLOAD } ]
     [ [ , ] RESTART ]
     [ [ , ] STATS [ = percentage ] ]
     [ [ , ] COPY_ONLY ]
]
```

Usage

```
USE master
EXEC sp_addumpdevice 'disk', 'Customer Backup Set 1',
   'f:\data\backup\Cust2.dat'
BACKUP DATABASE 'Customer' TO 'Customer Backup Set 1'
```

Sample 14-3 shows the BACKUP DATABASE syntax for file and filegroup backups.

Listing 14-3 Sample 14-3 BACKUP DATABASE Syntax and Usage for File or Filegroup Backups

Syntax

```
BACKUP DATABASE { database_name | @database_name_var }
    <file_or_filegroup> [ ,...f ]
TO <backup_device> [ ,...n ]
[ [ MIRROR TO <backup_device> [ ,...n ] ] [ ...next-mirror ] ]
[ WITH
    [ BLOCKSIZE = { blocksize | @blocksize_variable } ]
    [ [ , ] { CHECKSUM | NO_CHECKSUM } ]
    [ [ , ] { STOP_ON_ERROR | CONTINUE_AFTER_ERROR } ]
    [ [ , ] DESCRIPTION = { 'text' | @text_variable } ]
    [ [ , ] DIFFERENTIAL ]
    [ [ , ] EXPIREDATE = { date | @date_var }
    | RETAINDAYS = { days | @days_var } ]
    [ [ , ] PASSWORD = { password | @password_variable } ]
    [ [ , ] { FORMAT | NOFORMAT } ]
    [ [ , ] { INIT | NOINIT } ]
    [ [ , ] { NOSKIP | SKIP } ]
    [ [ , ] MEDIADESCRIPTION = { 'text' | @text_variable } ]
    [ [ , ] MEDIANAME = { media_name | @media_name_variable } ]
    [ [ , ] MEDIAPASSWORD = { mediapassword | @mediapassword_variable } ]
    [ [ , ] NAME = { backup_set_name | @backup_set_name_var } ]
    [ [ , ] { NOREWIND | REWIND } ]
    [ [ , ] { NOUNLOAD | UNLOAD } ]
    [ [ , ] RESTART ]
    [ [ , ] STATS [ = percentage ] ]
    [ [ , ] COPY_ONLY ]
]
<file_or_filegroup> :: =
    { FILE = { logical_file_name | @logical_file_name_var }
    |
    FILEGROUP = { logical_filegroup_name | @logical_filegroup_name_var }
    | READ_WRITE_FILEGROUPS }
```

Usage

```
USE master
EXEC sp_addumpdevice 'disk', 'Customer Backup Set 1',
    'f:\data\backup\Cust2.dat'
BACKUP DATABASE Customer
    FILE = 'Customer_data',
    FILEGROUP = 'Primary',
    FILE = 'Customer_data2',
    FILEGROUP = 'Secondary'
    TO 'Customer Backup Set 1'
```

Sample 14-4 shows the syntax for BACKUP LOG. By default, this command truncates the log after the backup.

Sample 14-4   BACKUP LOG Syntax and Usage

Syntax for Backing Up the Log

```
BACKUP LOG { database_name | @database_name_var }
{
    TO <backup_device> [ ,...n ]
[ [ MIRROR TO <backup_device> [ ,...n ] ] [ ...next-mirror ] ]
    [ WITH
    [ BLOCKSIZE = { blocksize | @blocksize_variable } ]
    [ [ , ] { CHECKSUM | NO_CHECKSUM } ]
    [ [ , ] { STOP_ON_ERROR | CONTINUE_AFTER_ERROR } ]
    [ [ , ] DESCRIPTION = { 'text' | @text_variable } ]
    [ [ ,] EXPIREDATE = { date | @date_var }
    | RETAINDAYS = { days | @days_var } ]
    [ [ , ] PASSWORD = { password | @password_variable } ]
    [ [ , ] { FORMAT | NOFORMAT } ]
    [ [ , ] { INIT | NOINIT } ]
    [ [ , ] { NOSKIP | SKIP } ]
    [ [ , ] MEDIADESCRIPTION = { 'text' | @text_variable } ]
    [ [ , ] MEDIANAME = { media_name | @media_name_variable } ]
    [ [ , ] MEDIAPASSWORD = { mediapassword | @mediapassword_variable } ]
    [ [ , ] NAME = { backup_set_name | @backup_set_name_var } ]
    [ [ , ] NO_TRUNCATE ]
    [ [ , ] { NORECOVERY | STANDBY = undo_file_name } ]
    [ [ , ] { NOREWIND | REWIND } ]
    [ [ , ] { NOUNLOAD | UNLOAD } ]
    [ [ , ] RESTART ]
    [ [ , ] STATS [ = percentage ] ]
    [ [ , ] COPY_ONLY ]
    ]
}
<backup_device> ::=
    {
    { logical_backup_device_name | @logical_backup_device_name_var }
    |
    { DISK | TAPE } = { 'physical_backup_device_name' |
@physical_backup_device_name_var }
    }
```

Syntax for Truncating the Log

```
BACKUP LOG { database_name | @database_name_var }
{
    WITH
        { NO_LOG | TRUNCATE_ONLY } ]
}
```

Usage

```
USE master
EXEC sp_addumpdevice 'disk', 'Customer_log1',
   'f:\data\backup\Cust_log.dat'
BACKUP LOG Customer
   TO Customer_log1
```

Performing Transaction Log Backups

Transaction logs are essential to the timely recovery of SQL Server databases. Unlike database backups, which can be full or differential, transaction log backups are usually incremental. This means that each transaction log backup has a record of transactions only within a certain time frame. Transaction logs are always applied in sequence—with the completion time of the last full or differential backup marking the beginning of a transaction log sequence.

Consequently, to restore the database you must apply each transaction log in sequence up to the point of failure. For example, if you run a full backup at 1:00 P.M. and the database fails at 1:46 P.M., you would restore the last full backup and then apply each transaction log created after that time, such as the backups at 1:15 P.M., 1:30 P.M., and 1:45 P.M. As you can see, without the incremental transaction log backups, you would lose all the transactions that took place after the 1:00 P.M. full backup.

You can perform transaction log backups like any other backup. Still, there are a few details that you should know before beginning this kind of backup, and the following subsections cover these details.

Options and Commands That Invalidate Log Sequences

Although the normal backup process for transaction logs is fairly straightforward, SQL Server has some tricky features involving the option flags that you can set for the backup or the database, or both. The following database options prevent you from using a transaction log sequence to recover a database:

- **Truncate Log On Checkpoint** Clears out inactive entries in the transaction log on checkpoint, which means you cannot use the log for recovery.
- **Using Non-Logged Operations** Commands that bypass the log invalidate a log backup sequence.
- **ALTER DATABASE** Adding or deleting files with ALTER DATABASE invalidates a backup sequence.

 Tip As mentioned previously, the completion time of the last full or differential backup marks the beginning of a transaction log sequence. If you use any of the previous commands and invalidate a log sequence, perform a full or differential backup to start a new sequence.

Log Truncation Options

When you back up transaction logs, you have several options that determine how the backups are made. With SQL Server Backup in SQL Server Management Studio, you can use the Truncate The Transaction Log By Removing Inactive Entries option. Setting this option clears committed transactions out of the log after a log backup. The BACKUP LOG command normally clears out committed or aborted transactions after a log backup as well. However, you can override this behavior with these options:

- **TRUNCATE_ONLY** Removes inactive entries from the log without creating a backup. This invalidates the log sequence.
- **NO_LOG** Same as TRUNCATE_ONLY, but this option does not log the BACKUP LOG command in the transaction log. This option is designed for a situation in which the transaction log or its home drive is full, and you must truncate the log without writing to the log device.
- **NO_TRUNCATE** Writes all the transaction log entries from the last backup to the point of failure. Use this option when the database is corrupt and you are about to restore it.

> **Tip** After you use TRUNCATE_ONLY or NO_LOG, always perform a full or differential backup. This revalidates the log sequence. Additionally, because you can grow logs automatically, you should rarely encounter a situation in which you need to truncate the log without logging. The log can run out of space only if you set a maximum size or the drive(s) that the log uses runs out of space.

Backing Up Full-Text Search Catalogs

In SQL Server 2005, full-text catalogs are treated as files and are included in the database file set for the purposes of backup and restore. When you back up a database, the full-text catalogs are backed up automatically. When you back up the filegroup associated with one or more full-text catalogs, the catalogs are backed up as well. Changes to full-text catalogs are backed up with standard differential backups of a database or the associated filegroup.

You can back up a full-text catalog by itself using T-SQL. To do this, you specify the logical file name of the full-text catalog using the FILE clause of the BACKUP statement. Consider the following example:

```
USE master

EXEC sp_addumpdevice 'disk', 'Customer_Catalog',
'\\omega\backups\cust.bak'

BACKUP DATABASE Customer

FILE = 'customerdb_cat'

TO Customer_Catalog
```

In this example, you specify the backup device to use as Customer_Catalog. You then create a full backup of the full-text catalog named customerdb_cat. If you later wanted to save only the changes since the full backup of the catalog, you could create a differential backup of the catalog:

```
USE master

BACKUP DATABASE Customer

FILE = 'customerdb_cat'

TO Customer_Catalog

WITH DIFFERENTIAL
```

You can back up multiple full-text catalogs using filegroup backups. For example, if you have created a filegroup called Catalogs_Primary and associated multiple catalogs with it, you can perform a full backup of the filegroup using:

```
USE master

BACKUP DATABASE Customer

FILEGROUP = 'Catalogs_Primary'

TO Customer_Catalog
```

Restoring a Database

Occasional database corruption, hardware failure, and natural disasters do happen, and as a database administrator, you need to be able to restore the database if any of these events occur. Even if you are a pro at backup and restore, keep in mind that restoring a database is different from restoring an operating system or recovering other types of applications. The mix of full, differential, and transaction log backups ensures that you can get up-to-the-minute recovery of a database, but it complicates the recovery process.

In the following subsection, you will find tips and advice on troubleshooting database corruption. After that you will find step-by-step procedures for restoring a database in various situations, including:

- Restoring a database using backups created in SQL Server Management Studio.
- Restoring a file or filegroup.
- Restoring a database to a different location.
- Restoring a database using Transact-SQL.

Database Corruption and Problem Resolution

All the knowledge you have accumulated as a database administration is most important in one defining moment. That is the moment when you attempt to restore a database. The techniques you use to restore a database depend on the backup options you have used and the state of the database. As you know, the backup techniques available are full, differential, transaction log, and file/file-groups. What you may not know is how to restore a database by combining these techniques.

Table 14-2 lists some suggested recovery strategies for corrupted databases. These strategies show how to recover a database with various combinations of the available backup operations. If you use SQL Server Management Studio for backup and restore, these procedures are done for you automatically in most cases. The actual step-by-step process is covered later in this chapter.

Table 14-2 Recovery Strategies for Databases

Backup Type	Restore Process
Full backups only	Restore the database using the last full backup.
Full and differential backups	Restore the last full backup with NORECOVERY. Then restore the last differential backup with RECOVERY.
Full and transaction log backups	Back up the current transaction log with NO_TRUNCATE. Restore the last full backup with NORECOVERY. Apply log backups from that time forward in sequence, using NORECOVERY. Apply the last differential backup with the RECOVERY option.
Full, differential, and transaction log backups	Back up the current transaction log with NO_TRUNCATE. Restore the last full backup with NORECOVERY and transaction log backups and then the last differential backup with NORECOVERY. Apply log backups from that time forward in sequence, using NORECOVERY. Apply the last backup using the RECOVERY option.

Now you know how to restore a database in theory. But before you begin, you should make sure the database is really corrupt and cannot be recovered by other means. To troubleshoot database problems and potential corruption, complete the following steps:

1. Start with the SQL Server logs. See what types of error messages are in the logs, paying particular attention to errors that occur during database startup. Also take a look at user-related errors. If you find errors, you can look up the error numbers in the SQL Server Books Online or the Microsoft Online Support Web site (*http://search.support.microsoft.com*). You access the server logs through the Management folder in SQL Server Management Studio as discussed in Chapter 13, "Profiling and Monitoring Microsoft SQL Server 2005."

2. Check the state of the database. Every time you start SQL Server, it goes through a recovery process on each database. If the recovery process has problems, the mode or state of the database may be abnormal. To check mode or state, use these properties of the *databaseproperty* function:

   ■ **IsShutDown**   If set to 1, the database is shut down because of problems during startup.

- **IsEmergencyMode**   If set to 1, the database is in emergency mode, which allows a suspect database to be used.
- **IsSingleUser, IsDboOnly, IsReadOnly,** or **IsOffline**   If set to 1, the database is in a limited or no access mode and needs to be made operational so it can be accessed.
- **IsSuspect**   If set to 1, the database is suspect, which means it is possibly corrupted.
- **IsInLoad**   If set to 1, the database is going through the loading process.
- **IsInRecovery**   If set to 1, the database is going through the recovery process.
- **IsNotRecovered**   If set to 1, the database failed to recover and is in an unstable state.

3. If possible, try to use the DBCC command to further troubleshoot or repair the database. DBCC is covered in Chapter 15.
4. If these procedures indicate that you have a corrupt database that cannot be repaired, restore the database from backup.

You can use the *databaseproperty* function as shown in Sample 14-5.

Sample 14-5   The *databaseproperty* Function Syntax and Usage

Syntax
```
databaseproperty('database','property')
```

Usage
```
select databaseproperty('Customer','IsEmergencyMode')
```

Restoring a Database from a Normal Backup

SQL Server Management Studio tracks all the backups you create for each database; when you need to restore a database, SQL Server Management Studio automatically configures the restore. You can restore a database using these default settings or fine-tune the restore operation as necessary.

To restore a database, complete the following steps:

1. If you are using transaction logs and the database is still running, you should back up the current transaction log with NO_TRUNCATE. When you are using the SQL Server Backup dialog box, this means you should select Back Up The Tail Of The Log on the Options page of the Back Up Database dialog box when performing the transaction log backup.
2. In SQL Server Management Studio, connect to the appropriate server in Object Explorer view.

3. Expand the Databases folder. Right-click the database you want to restore. On the shortcut menu, point to Tasks, select Restore, and then select Database. This opens the Restore Database dialog box shown in Figure 14-4.

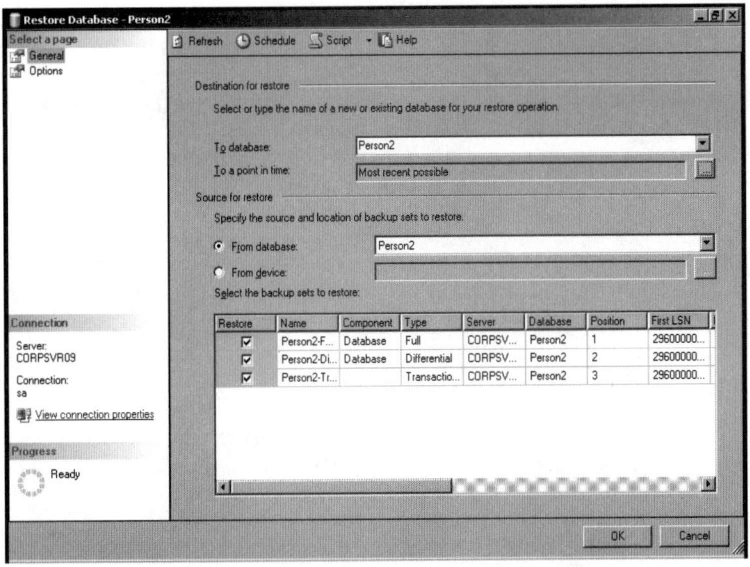

Figure 14-4   The Restore Database dialog box

4. The database currently selected is listed as the To Database in the Destination For Restore area at the top of the dialog box. If you are restoring the database to its original location, leave the database in the To Database box as it is. If you want to restore the database to an alternate location, select a different database to use as the destination or type the name of a new database for the restore operation.

Note   This option is provided to allow you to restore a database to a different location, as described in the subsection titled "Restoring a Database to a Different Location" later in this chapter. All databases on the server are included in the drop-down list as possible values except *master* and *tempdb*.

5. By default, the database is restored to the most recent possible point in time. If multiple backups are available, you may be able to select a point in time for the restore. For example, if you know that GOTEAM accidentally deleted the Accounts table at 12:16 P.M., you could restore the database to a point just prior to this transaction, such as 12:15 P.M. To use the point in time option, click the Properties (...) button to the right of the To A Point In Time text box.

This opens the Point In Time Restore dialog box. Choose A Specific Date And Time, select a date and time using the text boxes provided, and then click OK.

Note   Restoring a database from a tape device or other backup device differs from a normal backup. This is primarily because you have to work with backup media (tapes) that may contain multiple backups, as well as multiple backup media sets (tape sets). If you are restoring from a device, select From Device, and then click the related Properties (...) button. You can then use the Specify Backup dialog box to specify the backup media and its location for the restore operation. You can add multiple locations and view the contents of added backup sets as well.

6. The database currently selected is listed as the From Database under Source For Restore. If you are restoring a different database, choose this database instead. Only databases that have backup history in the *msdb* are listed.

7. Use the Select The Backup Sets To Restore option to select the backup set to restore. By default, the last full set (including the last full backup, differential backups since the last full backup, and transaction log backups since the last full backup) should be selected. The selected backups can also represent the most current backup set (according to a recovery plan) that meets the point in time recovery requirements.

Real World   Normally, you will want to start with the last complete backup set. However, if you know that the last backup set is bad or contains transactions that you do not want to apply, such as a massive table deletion, go back to a previous backup set by selecting a different full backup and its related differential and transaction log backups as the starting point.

8. The lower portion of the Restore Database dialog box provides a backup history for the selected database. You can use the information in the history as follows:

■ **Restore**   Allows you to select which backup sets to restore. Default selections are based on the first backup to restore and go forward in time through differential and transaction log backups. You should rarely change the default selections.

■ **Name**   Indicates the name of the backup set.

■ **Component**   Shows the backed-up component as Database, File, or a blank entry. A blank entry indicates a transaction log backup.

■ **Type**   Indicates the type of backup performed as Full, Differential, or Transaction Log.

■ **Server**   Shows the database engine instance that performed the backup.

■ **Database**   Displays the name of the database backed up.

- **Position**   Shows the position of the backup set in the volume.
- **First LSN**   For log backups, this is the log sequence number of the first transaction in the backup set, which helps with ordering transaction logs for the restore operation.
- **Last LSN**   For log backups, this is the log sequence number of the last transaction in the backup set, which helps with ordering transaction logs for the restore operation.
- **Checkpoint LSN**   For log backups, this is the log sequence number of the most recent checkpoint at the time the backup was created, which helps with ordering transaction logs for the restore operation.
- **Start Date**   Displays a date and time stamp that indicates when the backup operation started.
- **Finish Date**   Displays a date and time stamp that indicates when the backup operation finished.
- **Size**   Shows the size of the backup.
- **User Name**   Displays the name of the user who performed the backup operation.
- **Expiration**   Indicates the date and time the backup set expires.

9. Select the Options page to configure options for the restore operation. The Options page is shown in Figure 14-5. You use the available options as follows:

- **Overwrite The Existing Database**   Allows the restore operation to overwrite any existing databases and their related files. (This is the same as using RESTORE with the REPLACE option.)
- **Preserve The Replication Settings**   Ensures that any replication settings are preserved when restoring a published database to a server other than the server where the database was originally created. You must select Leave The Database Ready For Use By Rolling Back The Uncommitted Transactions option. (This is the same as using RESTORE with the PRESERVE_REPLICATION option.)
- **Prompt Before Restoring Each Backup**   Automatically prompts after completing a successful restore and before starting the next restore. The prompt includes a Cancel button, which is useful to cancel the restore operation after a particular backup is restored. This is a good option to use when you need to swap tapes for different media sets.
- **Restrict Access To The Restored Database**   Sets the database in restricted-user mode so only the dbo, dbcreator, and sysadmin can access it. (This is the same as using RESTORE with the RESTRICTED_USER option.)
- **Restore Database Files As**   Allows you to change the restore location for database files.

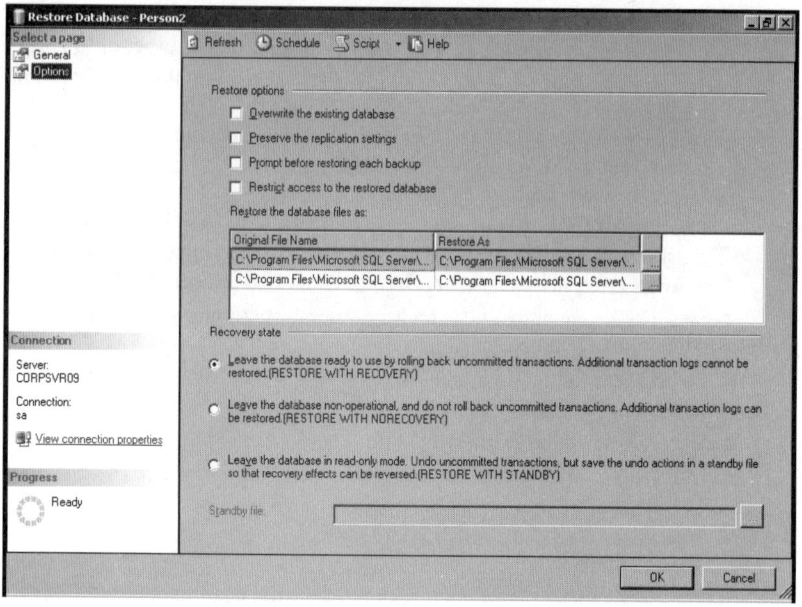

Figure 14-5 The Options page of the Restore Database dialog box

10. Set the recovery state using one of the following options:

- **Leave The Database Ready For Use** Completes the entire restore process and applies all the selected backups, which can include a full backup, a differential backup, and multiple transaction log backups. All completed transactions are applied, and any uncompleted transactions are rolled back. When the restore process is completed, the database is returned to ready status and you can use it for normal operations. (This is the same as using RESTORE WITH RECOVERY.)

- **Leave Database Non-Operational** This is essentially a manual restore that allows you to go step-by-step through the backups. SQL Server completes the entire restore process and applies all the selected backups, which can include a full backup, a differential backup, and multiple transaction log backups. When the restore is completed, the database is not returned to ready status, and you cannot use it for normal operations. All transactions have not been processed, and the database is waiting for you to apply additional transaction logs. Apply these transaction logs using this mode, and then for the last transaction log, set the mode to Leave Database Operational. All completed transactions are then applied, and any uncompleted transactions are rolled back. (This is the same as using RESTORE WITH NORECOVERY.)

- **Leave Database In Read-Only Mode** This is similar to the Leave Database Non-Operational option, with some exceptions. When the restore process ends, the database is in Read-Only mode, and it is ready for additional transaction logs to be applied. In Read-Only mode, you can check the data and test the database. If necessary, apply additional transaction logs. Then for the last transaction log, set the mode to Leave Database Operational. All completed transactions are then applied, and any uncompleted transactions are rolled back. (This is the same as using RESTORE WITH STANDBY.)

Real World   When you use the option Leave Database In Read-Only Mode, SQL Server also creates an Undo file, which you can use to undo the restore operation. To commit the restore operations and the final transactions without restoring another transaction log, you could use:

```
RESTORE DATABASE Customer

WITH RECOVERY
```

This commits final transactions (if possible), deletes the Undo file, and puts the database back in operations mode. Although you may want to use WITH RECOVERY at this stage, you probably do not want to use WITH NORECOVERY because you will undo all the changes from the restore and may end up with an empty database.

11. When you are ready to start the restore operation, click OK. Stop the restore at any time by clicking Stop Action Now. If an error occurs, you will see a prompt with an error message.

Restoring Files and Filegroups

You can restore files and filegroups from database backups or file backups either individually, in combination with each other, or all together. If any changes were made to the files or filegroups, you must also restore all transaction log backups that were created after the files or filegroups were backed up.

Although you can usually recover individual files or filegroups, there are exceptions. If tables and indexes are created that span multiple filegroups, all the related filegroups must be restored together. Do not worry, for SQL Server generates an error prior to starting the restore if a needed filegroup is missing. Further, if the entire database is corrupted, you must restore all files and filegroups in the database. In both cases, you must also apply transaction log backups created after the file or filegroup backups you are restoring.

To restore files or filegroups, complete the following steps:

1. If you are using transaction logs and the database is still running, you should back up the current transaction log with NO_TRUNCATE. When you are using the SQL Server Backup dialog box, this means you should select Back

Up The Tail Of The Log on the Options page of the Back Up Database dialog box when performing the transaction log backup.

2. In SQL Server Management Studio, connect to the appropriate server in Object Explorer view.

3. Expand the Databases folder. Right-click the database you want to restore. On the shortcut menu, point to Tasks, select Restore, and then select Files And Filegroup. This opens the Restore Files And Filegroups dialog box, shown in Figure 14-6.

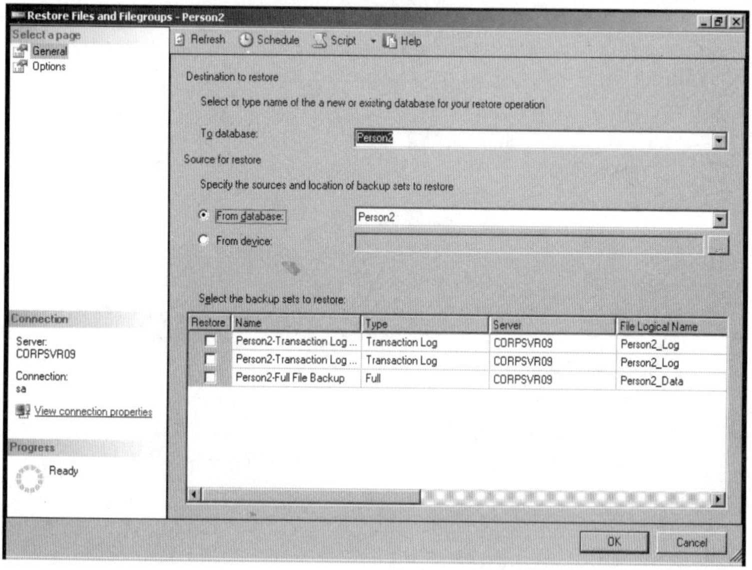

Figure 14-6 The Restore Files And Filegroups dialog box

4. The database currently selected is listed as the To Database under Destination To Restore. If you are restoring a file or filegroup to its original database, this is what you want to use. If you want to restore the file or filegroup to a different database, select the different database to use as the destination or type the name of a new database for the restore operation.

Note This option is provided to allow you to restore a database to a different location, as described in the subsection titled "Restoring a Database to a Different Location" later in this chapter. All databases on the server are listed as possible values except *master* and *tempdb*.

5. The database currently selected is listed as the From Database under Source For Restore. If you are restoring files and filegroups for a different database, choose this database instead. Only databases that have backup history in the *msdb* are listed.

6. The lower portion of the Restore Files And Filegroups dialog box provides a backup history for the files and filegroups in the selected database. You can use the information in the history as follows:

   - **Restore**   The backup files to restore

Note   No default selections are made in the Restore text box; you must choose the files manually.

   - **Name**   The name of the backup set
   - **Type**   The type of backup performed as Full, Differential, or Transaction Log
   - **Server**   The database engine instance that performed the backup
   - **File Logical Name**   The logical name of the file
   - **Database**   The name of the file that was backed up
   - **Start Date**   A date and time stamp indicating when the backup operation started
   - **Finish Date**   A date and time stamp indicating when the backup operation finished
   - **Size**   The size of the backup
   - **User Name**   The name of the user who performed the backup operation

7. Select the backup files you want to restore.
8. Select the Options page to configure options for the restore operation. The available options are the same as those discussed in the subsection titled "Restoring a Database from a Normal Backup" earlier in this chapter.
9. When you are ready to start the restore operation, click OK. You can stop the restore at any time by clicking Stop.

Restoring a Database to a Different Location

When you restore a database to a different location, you are essentially copying the database from backups. If you use this procedure to copy a database to a new location on the same computer, you create a copy of the database that can have separate files and a different database name. Restoring a database to a different location is similar to the process of restoring files and filegroups discussed previously. The main differences are as follows:

1. On the General page under Destination For Restore, type a new name for the database in the To Database box. For example, if you are restoring the *Customer* database to a new location, name the copy ***Customer 2*** or ***CustomerCopy***.
2. When you access the Options page, you must override the default destination paths and enter new destination paths for all of the files you are restoring. Simply click in the Restore As box, and then enter a new file path. Or you can click the related Properties (...) button to select a new Restore As location.

If you use this procedure to copy a database to a different computer, you can create a working copy of the database on another server. You do not need to create a new database or perform any preliminary work, with one exception—if you want to use backup devices on the destination server, you should set them up beforehand. Also, before you begin the restore, you should ensure that the destination computer is using the same code page, sort order, Unicode collation, and Unicode locale as the source server. If these configuration settings are not identical, you will not be able to run the database on the destination server.

Recovering Missing Data

If you suspect part of the database is missing or corrupted, you can perform a partial restore to a new location so that you can recover the missing or corrupted data. To do this, use the PARTIAL option with the RESTORE DATABASE statement as discussed in the subsection titled "Using Transact-SQL Restore Commands" later in this chapter. You can restore partial databases only at the filegroup level. The primary file and filegroup are always restored along with the files that you specify and their corresponding filegroups. Files and filegroups that are not restored are marked as offline and you cannot access them.

To carry out the restore and recovery process, complete the following steps:

1. Perform a partial database restore. Give the database a new name and location in the RESTORE DATABASE statement and use MOVE/TO to move the original database source files to new locations, such as:

```
RESTORE DATABASE new_custdb_partial

        FILEGROUP = 'Customers2'

        FROM DISK='g:\cust.dmp'

        WITH FILE=1,NORECOVERY,PARTIAL,

        MOVE 'cust' TO 'g:\cu2.pri',

        MOVE 'cust_log' TO 'g:\cu2.log',

        MOVE 'cust_data_2' TO 'g:\cu2.dat2'

    GO
```

2. Extract any needed data from the partial restore and insert it into the database from which it was deleted.

Creating Standby Servers

The notion of restoring a backup to a different computer can be extended to create a standby backup server that you can bring online if the primary server fails. When you create a standby server, you have two options:

- You can create a *cold* standby that you synchronize manually.
- Or you can create a *warm* standby that SQL Server synchronizes automatically.

Creating a Cold Standby

To create a standby that you synchronize manually, complete the following steps:

1. Install SQL Server on a new server system using an identical configuration. This means that the destination server should use the same code page, sort order, Unicode collation, and Unicode locale as the source server.
2. Copy all of the databases on the primary server to this new system by specifying a different restore location in the Restore Database dialog box.
3. Maintain the copies of the databases by periodically applying the transaction log backups from the primary to the standby server.
4. You may want to leave the standby server in Standby mode so that the database is read-only. This allows users to access the database but not make changes.

If one or more databases on the primary server fail for any reason, you can make the corresponding databases on the standby server available to users. However, before you do this, you should synchronize the primary and the standby servers by completing the following steps:

1. On the standby server, apply any transaction log backups created on the primary server that have not been applied yet. You must apply these backups in the proper time sequence.
2. Create a backup of the active transaction log on the primary server and apply this backup to the database on the standby server. This ensures up-to-the-minute synchronization. Be sure to recover the database or specify that the database should be put in operational mode after this backup is applied.

> **Tip** If you need to make the standby server appear to be the primary server, you may need to take the primary off the network and rename it. Then rename the standby so that it appears to be the primary.

3. After you restore the primary server to working condition, any changes to the standby's databases need to be restored to the primary server. Otherwise, those changes are lost when you start using the primary server again.

> **Note** Standby servers are not the same as a SQL Server failover cluster, which is created using the SQL Server Failover Cluster Wizard and Microsoft Cluster Service. Standby servers store a second copy of databases on their hard disk drives. Virtual servers use a single copy of databases that is accessed from a shared storage device.

Creating a Warm Standby

SQL Server 2005 Enterprise Edition includes a feature called *log shipping*. You can use log shipping to create a standby server that is automatically synchronized with the primary server. To do this, follow these steps:

1. Install SQL Server on a new server system using an identical configuration. This means that the destination server should use the same code page, sort order, Unicode collation, and Unicode locale as the source server.

2. Copy all of the databases on the primary server to this new system by specifying a different restore location in the Restore Database dialog box.

3. On the primary server, configure log shipping as described in the section titled "Configuring Log Shipping" in Chapter 15.

The primary server is referred to as the *source server*. The servers receiving the logs are referred to as *destination servers*. After configuring log shipping, you should check the status of log shipping on the source and destination servers periodically.

If one or more databases on the primary server fail for any reason, you can make the corresponding databases on the standby available to users. To do that, follow these steps:

1. Make sure that the most recent logs have been applied by checking the status of log shipping on the destination server.

2. Take the primary server off the network and rename it.

3. Rename the standby server so that it appears to be the primary server.

4. Check connections to the new primary server.

After you restore the primary server to working condition, any changes to the standby's databases need to be restored to the primary server. Otherwise, those changes are lost when you start using the primary server again.

Using Transact-SQL Restore Commands

You can also restore databases using Transact-SQL. The commands you will use are RESTORE DATABASE and RESTORE LOG. You can use RESTORE DATABASE to restore an entire database, specific files and filegroups, or part of a corrupted database. Sample 14-6 shows the syntax and usage for a complete restore. The option WITH RECOVERY is the default mode.

Sample 14-6   RESTORE DATABASE Syntax and Usage for a Complete Restore

Syntax

```
RESTORE DATABASE { database_name | @database_name_var }
[ FROM <backup_device> [ ,...n ] ]
[ WITH
    [ { CHECKSUM | NO_CHECKSUM } ]
    [ [ , ] { CONTINUE_AFTER_ERROR | STOP_ON_ERROR } ]
    [ [ , ] FILE = { file_number | @file_number } ]
    [ [ , ] KEEP_REPLICATION ]
    [ [ , ] MEDIANAME = { media_name | @media_name_variable } ]
    [ [ , ] MEDIAPASSWORD = { mediapassword |
                @mediapassword_variable } ]
    [ [ , ] MOVE 'logical_file_name' TO 'operating_system_file_name' ]
            [ ,...n ]
    [ [ , ] PASSWORD = { password | @password_variable } ]
```

```
    [ [ , ] { RECOVERY | NORECOVERY | STANDBY =
          {standby_file_name | @standby_file_name_var } }
    ]
    [ [ , ] REPLACE ]
    [ [ , ] RESTART ]
    [ [ , ] RESTRICTED_USER ]
    [ [ , ] { REWIND | NOREWIND } ]
    [ [ , ] STATS [ =percentage ] ]
       [ [ , ] STOPAT = { date_time | @date_time_var } |
       [ , ] STOPATMARK = { 'mark_name' | 'lsn:lsn_number' }
              [ AFTER datetime ] |
       [ , ] STOPBEFOREMARK = { 'mark_name' | 'lsn:lsn_number' }
              [ AFTER datetime ]
    ]
    [ [ , ] { UNLOAD | NOUNLOAD } ]
]
[;]
<backup_device> ::=
{ { 'logical_backup_device_name' |
           @logical_backup_device_name_var }
   | { DISK | TAPE } = { 'physical_backup_device_name' |
           @physical_backup_device_name_var } }
```

Usage

```
RESTORE DATABASE Customer
   FROM TAPE = '\\.\tape0'
```

Usage

```
RESTORE DATABASE Customer
   FROM Customer_1
   WITH NORECOVERY,
       MOVE 'CustomerData1' TO 'F:\mssql7\data\NewCust.mdf',
       MOVE 'CustomerLog1' TO 'F:\mssql7\data\NewCust.ldf'
RESTORE LOG Customer
   FROM CustomerLog1
   WITH RECOVERY
```

Using RESTORE DATABASE, you also can restore files and filegroups. Sample 14-7 shows the related syntax and usage.

Sample 14-7 RESTORE DATABASE Syntax and Usage for File and Filegroup Restore

Syntax

```
RESTORE DATABASE { database_name | @database_name_var }
      <file_or_filegroup_or_pages> [ ,...f ]
[ FROM <backup_device> [ ,...n ] ]
[ WITH
   [ { CHECKSUM | NO_CHECKSUM } ]
   [ [ , ] { CONTINUE_AFTER_ERROR | STOP_ON_ERROR } ]
   [ [ , ] FILE = { file_number | @file_number } ]
```

```
        [ [ , ] MEDIANAME = { media_name | @media_name_variable } ]
        [ [ , ] MEDIAPASSWORD = { mediapassword |
                              @mediapassword_variable } ]
        [ [ , ] MOVE 'logical_file_name' TO 'operating_system_file_name' ]
                    [ ,...n ]
        [ [ , ] PASSWORD = { password | @password_variable } ]
        [ [ , ] NORECOVERY ]
        [ [ , ] REPLACE ]
        [ [ , ] RESTART ]
        [ [ , ] RESTRICTED_USER ]
        [ [ , ] { REWIND | NOREWIND } ]
        [ [ , ] STATS [ =percentage ] ]
        [ [ , ] { UNLOAD | NOUNLOAD } ]
]
[;]
<backup_device> ::=
{ { logical_backup_device_name|
             @logical_backup_device_name_var }
    | { DISK | TAPE } = { 'physical_backup_device_name' |
                @physical_backup_device_name_var } }
<file_or_filegroup_or_pages> ::=
{  FILE = { logical_file_name | @logical_file_name_var }
    | FILEGROUP = { logical_filegroup_name | @logical_filegroup_name_var
}}
    | PAGE = 'file:page [ ,...p ]'  }
```

Usage

```
RESTORE DATABASE Customer
    FILE = 'Customerdata_1',
    FILE = 'Customerdata_2',
    FILEGROUP = 'Primary'
    FROM Customer_1
    WITH NORECOVERY
RESTORE LOG Customer
    FROM CustomerLog1
```

Sample 14-8 shows the syntax for performing a partial restore. This command creates a new database that is based on a partial copy of the backup data. When you use this procedure, the database_name represents the new name for the database, and the MOVE/TO command is used to move the original database source files to new locations.

Sample 14-8 RESTORE DATABASE Syntax and Usage for Partial Restore

Syntax

```
RESTORE DATABASE { database_name | @database_name_var }
      <files_or_filegroups>
[ FROM <backup_device> [ ,...n ] ]
[ WITH
     { PARTIAL }
```

```
   [ [ , ] { CHECKSUM | NO_CHECKSUM } ]
   [ [ , ] { CONTINUE_AFTER_ERROR | STOP_ON_ERROR } ]
   [ [ , ] FILE = { file_number | @file_number } ]
   [ [ , ] MEDIANAME = { media_name | @media_name_variable } ]
   [ [ , ] MEDIAPASSWORD = { mediapassword |
                    @mediapassword_variable } ]
  [ [ , ] MOVE 'logical_file_name' TO 'operating_system_file_name' ]
             [ ,...n ]
   [ [ , ] PASSWORD = { password | @password_variable } ]
   [ [ , ] NORECOVERY ]
   [ [ , ] REPLACE ]
   [ [ , ] RESTART ]
   [ [ , ] RESTRICTED_USER ]
   [ [ , ] { REWIND | NOREWIND } ]
   [ [ , ] STATS [=percentage ] ]
   [ [ , ] STOPAT = { date_time | @date_time_var } |
     [ , ] STOPATMARK = { 'mark_name' | 'lsn:lsn_number' }
             [ AFTER datetime ] |
             [ , ] STOPBEFOREMARK = { 'mark_name' | 'lsn:lsn_number' }
             [ AFTER datetime ]
    ]
   [ [ , ] { UNLOAD | NOUNLOAD } ]
]
[;]
<backup_device> ::=
{ { logical_backup_device_name |
            @logical_backup_device_name_var }
  | { DISK | TAPE } = { 'physical_backup_device_name' |
             @physical_backup_device_name_var } }

<files_or_filegroups> ::=
    { FILE = { logical_file_name | @logical_file_name_var }
    |
    FILEGROUP = { logical_filegroup_name | @logical_filegroup_name_var }}
  [ ,...f ]
```

Usage

```
RESTORE DATABASE cust_part
   FILEGROUP = 'Customers2'
   FROM DISK='g:\cust.dmp'
   WITH FILE=1,NORECOVERY,PARTIAL,
   MOVE 'cust' TO 'g:\cu2.pri',
   MOVE 'cust_log' TO 'g:\cu2.log',
   MOVE 'cust_data_2' TO 'g:\cu2.dat2'
GO
RESTORE LOG cust_part
   FROM DISK = 'g:\cust.dmp'
   WITH FILE = 2,RECOVERY
GO
```

Sample 14-9 shows how you can use RESTORE LOG.

Sample 14-9   RESTORE LOG Syntax and Usage

Syntax

```
RESTORE LOG { database_name | @database_name_var }
      <file_or_filegroup_or_pages> [ ,...f ]
[ FROM <backup_device> [ ,...n ] ]
[ WITH
    [ { CHECKSUM | NO_CHECKSUM } ]
    [ [ , ] { CONTINUE_AFTER_ERROR | STOP_ON_ERROR } ]
    [ [ , ] FILE = { file_number | @file_number } ]
    [ [ , ] KEEP_REPLICATION ]
    [ [ , ] MEDIANAME = { media_name | @media_name_variable } ]
    [ [ , ] MEDIAPASSWORD = { mediapassword | @mediapassword_variable }
]
    [ [ , ] MOVE 'logical_file_name' TO 'operating_system_file_name' ]
                [ ,...n ]
    [ [ , ] PASSWORD = { password | @password_variable } ]
    [ [ , ] { RECOVERY | NORECOVERY | STANDBY =
              {standby_file_name | @standby_file_name_var } }
      ]
    [ [ , ] REPLACE ]
    [ [ , ] RESTART ]
    [ [ , ] RESTRICTED_USER ]
    [ [ , ] { REWIND | NOREWIND } ]
    [ [ , ] STATS [=percentage ] ]
    [ [ , ] STOPAT = { date_time | @date_time_var } |
      [ , ] STOPATMARK = { 'mark_name' | 'lsn:lsn_number' }
              [ AFTER datetime ] |
      [ , ] STOPBEFOREMARK = { 'mark_name' | 'lsn:lsn_number' }
              [ AFTER datetime ]
      ]
    [ [ , ] { UNLOAD | NOUNLOAD } ]
]
[;]
<backup_device> ::=
{ { logical_backup_device_name |
            @logical_backup_device_name_var }
    | { DISK | TAPE } = { 'physical_backup_device_name' |
            @physical_backup_device_name_var } }
<file_or_filegroup_or_pages> ::=
{ FILE = { logical_file_name | @logical_file_name_var }
    | FILEGROUP = { logical_filegroup_name | @logical_filegroup_name_var }
}
    | PAGE = 'file:page [ ,...p ]' }
```

Usage

```
RESTORE DATABASE Customer
    FROM Customer_1, Customer_2
    WITH NORECOVERY
```

```
RESTORE LOG Customer
    FROM CustomerLog1
    WITH NORECOVERY
RESTORE LOG Customer
    FROM CustomerLog2
    WITH RECOVERY, STOPAT = 'Dec 11, 2006 3:30 PM'
```

Restoring Full-Text Catalogs

In SQL Server 2005, full-text catalogs are treated as files and are included in the database file set for the purposes of backup and restore. When you restore a database, the full-text catalogs are restored automatically. When you restore the filegroup associated with one or more full-text catalogs, the catalogs are restored as well. Changes to full-text catalogs are backed up with standard differential backups of a database or the associated filegroup. Although full-text catalogs are backed up and restored in association with database files, there are also ways to back up and restore only your full-text catalogs.

You can restore a full-text catalog by itself using T-SQL. To do this, you specify the logical file name of the full-text catalog using the FILE clause of the RESTORE statement. Consider the following example:

```
RESTORE DATABASE Customer

FILE = 'customerdb_cat'

FROM Customer_Catalog

WITH NORECOVERY

RESTORE DATABASE Customer

FILE = 'customerdb_cat'

FROM Customer_Catalog2
```

In this example, you specify the backup device to use for the restore as Customer_Catalog. You restore the last full backup of the full-text catalog named customerdb_cat. Next, you restore the differential backup of the full-text catalog. It is important to note that the first restore uses the NORECOVERY option to ensure that the database is offline, and the Full-Text Search service is stopped during the restore. After the second restore, however, the database is brought back online and the Full-Text Search service is started.

You can restore multiple catalogs as part of a filegroup as well. To do this, use the FILEGROUP option to specify the logical name of the filegroup to restore, such as:

```
RESTORE DATABASE Customer

FILEGROUP = 'Catalogs_Primary'

FROM Customer_Catalog
```

You can restore catalogs to an alternate location using the WITH MOVE option. This option lets you set the root folder location for catalogs being restored. Consider the following example:

```
RESTORE DATABASE Customer

FROM Customer_Catalog

WITH MOVE 'customerdb_cat' TO 'C:\Data\Catalogs'
```

Here, you specify the backup device to use for the restore as Customer_Catalog. You restore the last full backup of the full-text catalog named customerdb_cat to the C:\Data\Catalogs folders.

Restoring the *Master* Database

The *master* database is the most important database on SQL Server. This database stores information about all the databases on the server, server configuration, server logons, and other important information. If *master* gets corrupted, operations on the server may grind to a halt, and you will have to recover *master* using one of two techniques.

If you can start SQL Server, you can restore *master* from backup using a process similar to what you would use to restore any other database. To do this, complete the following steps:

1. You can only back up *master* using a full backup. As a result, no differential or transaction log backups will be available. This means you may not be able to restore *master* exactly as it was before the failure and that normally you should use the Recovery state of Leave Database Operational.

2. When you finish restoring the *master* database, you may need to apply any changes made since the last full backup manually.

3. After you check the server and verify that everything is okay, make a full backup of *master*.

If you cannot start SQL Server and you know *master* is the cause of the problem, you can restore *master* by completing the following steps:

1. Rebuild the *master* database by running Setup. Use Setup to rebuild, verify, and repair the SQL Server instance and its system databases.

2. Once you rebuild *master* and get SQL Server back online, you can restore the last backup of *master* in order to return the server to its most current state.

3. Because Rebuild Master rebuilds the *msdb* and *model* databases, you may need to restore these databases from backup as well.

4. Re-create any backup devices if necessary.

5. Re-enter logins and other security settings if necessary.

6. Restore replication databases if necessary.

7. Restore or attach user databases if necessary.

8. Restore other server configuration settings if necessary.

As you can see from this step-by-step procedure, restoring *master* can take a lot of time and work, which is why it is so important to back up *master* regularly. When you finish recovering the server, be sure to make a full backup of the *master* database.

Mirroring Databases

Mirroring allows you to create hot standby servers. SQL Server 2005 allows you to mirror any database except for *master*, *msdb*, *temp*, and *model*. You can configure and enable mirroring using the Mirroring page in the Database Properties dialog box. As discussed in Chapter 2 in the subsection titled "Ensuring Availability and Scalability," mirroring requires up to three servers: a principal server, a mirror server, and a witness server.

Configuring Mirroring

After you have installed SQL Server 2005 on the servers that will be used in mirroring, you must prepare for mirroring by doing the following:

1. Start SQL Server Management Studio. In Object Explorer view, connect to the server you want to act as the principal.

2. Right-click the database you want to work with and choose Properties. This displays the database's Properties dialog box. On the Options page, set the Recovery Model to Full. Click OK.

3. Right-click the server and choose Properties to display the Server Properties dialog box. On the General page, click Configure. This starts SQL Server Configuration Manager with the server selected for configuration.

4. Select the SQL Server 2005 Services node in the left pane. In the right pane, note the Log On As account for the SQL Server service on the instance that will act as the principal.

5. Perform a full backup of the principal database.

6. In Object Explorer view, connect to the server you want to act as the mirror.

7. Restore a full backup of the principal database on the mirror server instance with NORECOVERY.

8. Right-click the database you want to work with on the mirror and choose Properties to display the database's Properties dialog box. On the Options page, set the Recovery Model to Full. Click OK.

9. Right-click the server and choose Properties to display the Server Properties dialog box. On the General page, click Configure. This starts SQL Server Configuration Manager with the server selected for configuration.

10. Select the SQL Server 2005 Services node in the left pane. In the right pane, note the Log On As account for the SQL Server service on the instance that will act as the mirror.

11. In Object Explorer view, connect to the server you want to act as the witness (if any).

12. Right-click the server and choose Properties to display the Server Properties dialog box. On the General page, click Configure. This starts SQL Server Configuration Manager with the server selected for configuration.

13. Select the SQL Server 2005 Services node in the left pane. In the right pane, note the Log On As account for the SQL Server service on the instance that will act as the witness (if any).

After you prepare for mirroring, you then must configure the mirror endpoints and mirror security. To do this, complete the following steps:

1. Start SQL Server Management Studio. In Object Explorer view, connect to the server you want to act as the principal.

2. Expand the Databases folder. Right-click the database you want to work with and choose Properties to display the database's Properties dialog box.

3. On the Mirroring page, click Configure Security. When the wizard starts, click Next on the opening page.

4. If you are using a witness server to allow synchronous mode with automatic failure, accept the default answer of Yes in the next page of the wizard, and then click Next. Otherwise, click No to specify that you will not be using a witness server.

5. Typically, you will want to configure security on all the servers that are part of the mirror set, so accept the default (which has the appropriate server types selected) on the next page of the wizard and click Next.

6. The current server is selected by default as the principal. Set a listener port and endpoint name for this server as part of the mirror set. If the principal, mirror, and witness are instances on the same server, the related endpoints must use different listener ports. Otherwise, the endpoints can use the same listener ports. The default is TCP port 5022.

7. Next, use the Mirror Server Instance drop-down list to select the server that will act as the mirror. The principal and mirror cannot be the same server instance.

8. Set a listener port and endpoint name. The default endpoint name is Mirroring. If the principal, mirror, or witness are instances on the same server, the related endpoints must use different listener ports. Otherwise, the endpoints can use the same listener ports. The default is TCP port 5022.

 Note   If the server you want to work with is not listed, click Connect. Then use the Connect To Server dialog box to connect to the server you want to use.

9. Next, use the Witness Server Instance drop-down list to select the server that will act as the witness. The principal and witness cannot be the same server.

10. Set a listener port and endpoint name for the witness server. The default endpoint name is Mirroring. If the principal, mirror, or witness are instances on the same server, the related endpoints must use different listener ports.

Otherwise, the endpoints can use the same listener ports. The default is TCP port 5022.

11. If the server instances use different domain accounts for their SQL Server service accounts, enter the account names in the boxes provided. For domain accounts, be sure to enter the account name in DOMAIN\username format. If the service accounts are different, the wizard will grant CONNECT permissions on the endpoints for each account.

12. Click Next, and then click Finish. The wizard then configures security for mirroring.

13. Set the mirror operating mode you want to use, and then click OK. If you have configured a witness server, you can use Synchronous With Automatic Failover mode to ensure high availability.

14. To start mirroring, click Start Mirroring on the Options page in the Database Properties dialog box.

15. Click Yes to allow SQL Server to close all other connections to the database temporarily while configuring mirroring.

Managing Mirroring

You can view the current status of mirroring by completing the following steps:

1. Start SQL Server Management Studio. In Object Explorer view, connect to the server you want to act as the principal.

2. Expand the Databases folder. Right-click the database you want to work with and choose Properties to display the database's Properties dialog box.

3. Select the Mirroring page. The current mirroring status is displayed at the bottom of the page.

After you have configured and started mirroring, you can manage mirroring on the Mirroring page by using the following options:

- Click Pause to temporarily stop mirroring. When prompted to confirm, click Yes. Click Resume to resume mirroring.

- Click Stop Mirroring to stop mirroring. When prompted to confirm, click Yes. Click Start Mirroring to start mirroring again.

- If you are using a witness, failover occurs automatically. You can also force failover by clicking the Failover button.

Monitoring Mirroring Status and Performance

Mirroring details can be obtained using the following catalog views:

- *sys.database_mirroring*   This catalog view displays the database mirroring metadata for each mirrored database in a server instance.

- *sys.database_mirroring_endpoints*   This catalog view displays information about the database mirroring endpoint of the server instance.

- *sys.database_mirroring_witnesses*   This catalog view displays the database mirroring metadata for each of the sessions in which a server instance is the witness.

In Performance Monitor, you can use the SQL Server:Database Mirroring object to monitor mirroring performance:

- Use the Log Bytes Sent/sec counter to monitor the amount of log data sent per second.
- Use the Transaction Delay counter to determine if mirroring is impacting performance on the principal server.
- Use Redo Queue and Log Send Queue counters to determine if the mirror database is keeping up with the principal database.

Chapter 15
Database Automation and Maintenance

Automation and maintenance go hand in hand. You can automate many routine database administration tasks, most of which have to do with maintenance issues, such as backing up databases or running consistency checks. Automation allows you to increase productivity, complete tasks while away from your computer, and more. You can configure the server to monitor processes and user activities, to check for errors, and to alert you when related events occur. If you configure alerts properly, Microsoft SQL Server 2005 can monitor itself and you can focus on other areas of administration. You can also schedule jobs to automate routine administration tasks. You can configure these jobs to run once or on a recurring basis, such as once a week or the third Tuesday of every month.

Overview of Database Automation and Maintenance

SQL Server 2005 has four main database automation and maintenance components:

- **Database Mail** Enables e-mail alerts and notifications.

- **SQL Server Agent**   Enables self-monitoring using alerts, operator notifications, and scheduled jobs.
- **Database Maintenance Plans**   Enables automated maintenance.
- **Log Shipping**   Enables automatic synchronization with standby servers.

Typically, when you want to use these automation and maintenance features, you will select the following configurations:

1. Configure Database Mail for *msdb* and other databases. The *msdb* database is used by SQL Server Agent for scheduling alerts and jobs and to track operators. When you enable Database Mail, Database Mail objects are created in the *msdb* database. These objects allow *msdb* to act as a mail host database for sending alerts, notifications, and other types of messages.

2. Configure the SQL Server Agent service for your environment. Typically, you want to ensure that the service is automatically started with the operating system, that it uses the correct startup account, and that it has the correct mail profile so it can be used with Database Mail.

3. Configure SQL Server Agent alerts, jobs, and operators to enable automatic alerts and scheduled jobs. *Alerts* are automatically generated messages that bring an error or issue to the attention of an administrator or other user. *Jobs* are scheduled tasks that run automatically when triggered or at a specific interval. *Operators* are individuals to whom you want to send alerts and notifications.

4. Configure Database Maintenance Plans to automate routine database optimization and maintenance. Even though you can automate many routine tasks, you should regularly review report histories to track maintenance plan execution. Additionally, you may find that occasionally you need to perform some optimization and maintenance tasks manually, and you can do this with Database Maintenance Plans as well.

5. Optionally, configure log shipping to enable other SQL Servers to act as standby servers that can be brought online manually in case of primary server failure. Typically, log shipping is used as an alternative to database mirroring, which was discussed in Chapter 14, "Backing Up and Recovering SQL Server 2005." However, both features can be configured, enabled, and in use simultaneously on any given SQL Server instance.

Using Database Mail

Database Mail is an essential part of database automation. You must configure Database Mail so that alerts and other types of messages can be sent to administrators or other users. Database Mail provides SQL Server with the ability to generate and send e-mail messages as a mail client using the Simple Mail Transfer Protocol (SMTP). The Database Mail configuration process:

- Installs database messaging objects in the *msdb* database.

- Configures database mail accounts and profiles.
- Configures database mail security.

Database Mail is a full-featured replacement for SQL Mail. Database Mail acts as a mail client and sends its messages to designated SMTP servers. Any SMTP server including Microsoft Exchange can receive and deliver messages generated by Database Mail.

Performing the Initial Database Mail Configuration

Like most mail clients, Database Mail uses mail profiles and mail accounts to send e-mail messages. The profile defines the mail environment Database Mail will use and can be associated with one or more SMTP mail accounts. Because the mail accounts are used in priority order, you can configure multiple accounts on different mail servers as a safeguard against mail server failure or network problems that could prevent message delivery and then configure the Database Mail profile to use these separate accounts. If mail cannot be delivered to the first account listed in the profile, the second one is tried, and so on.

The mail profile can be public or private. A public profile is available to any user or application for any configured database mail host on the current server instance. A private profile is only available to explicitly defined users and applications. If you are configuring Database Mail for SQL Server Agent or a specific application, you will usually want to use a private profile. If you are configuring Database Mail for general use, you will usually want to use a public profile.

Before you configure Database Mail, you should create the SMTP accounts Database Mail will use or have your organization's mail administrator do this. If you are configuring Database Mail for SQL Server Agent, it is a good idea to have the e-mail address and account name to reflect this. For example, set the user name as SQL Agent and the e-mail address as sqlagent@yourcompany.com. To configure Database Mail, you need the account user name, e-mail address, and SMTP server name. If the SMTP server requires authentication, and most do, you will also need the logon user name and password for the account.

Real World   Some database maintenance tasks may require exclusive access to SQL Server. For example, if a database on the current server instance is in single-user mode and there is an active connection to the database, you may not be able to perform a maintenance task. You need to put the database back in multiuser mode before continuing. If you cannot get access to the database to put it back in multiuser mode, you can force the database mode change by following these steps:

1. Log on to the server and start a command prompt. Use the NET STOP command to stop the SQL Server instance you want to change. For example, if you wanted to stop the default SQL Server instance, you would type **net stop mssqlserver**.

2. Use the CD command to change to the Binn directory for the SQL Server instance. For example, type **cd "C:\Program Files\Microsoft SQL Server\MSSQL.1\MSSQL\Binn"** or cd C:\Progra~1\Micros~1\ MSSQL.1\MSSQL\Binn.

3. Put the database in single-user mode by typing **sqlservr –m**.

4. Start a second command prompt and open a dedicated administrator connection to SQL Server by typing **sqlcmd–A**. Be sure to provide a user name and password if necessary, using the –U and –P parameters.

5. Perform the necessary maintenance tasks using sqlcmd.

6. Set the database in single-user mode back to normal mode using *sp_dboption*. For example, if the database is named *cust*, you would type:

```
use master

exec sp_dboption 'cust', 'single user', 'FALSE';

go
```

7. At the first command prompt (where SQL Server is running), press Ctrl+C to stop SQL Server. When prompted to confirm, type **Y**.

8. Start the SQL Server instance you are working with by using NET START. For example, if you wanted to start the default SQL Server instance, you would type **net start mssqlserver**.

You can use SQL Server Management Studio to configure Database Mail for the first time by completing the following steps:

1. Start SQL Server Management Studio. In Object Explorer view, connect to the server instance of your choice, and then expand the server's Management folder.

2. Right-click Database Mail, and then select Configure Database Mail. This starts the Database Mail Configuration Wizard. Click Next.

3. To configure Database Mail for the first time, accept the default value of Setup Database Mail, and then click Next.

4. When prompted to enable the Database Mail feature, click Yes.

5. On the New Profile page, type the name and description of the mail profile that Database Mail will use, such as **Mail Profile For SQL Server Agent**. The profile is used to define the mail environment Database Mail will use.

6. To specify an SMTP account the profile will use to send e-mail messages, click Add. This displays the New Database Mail Account dialog box shown in Figure 15-1.

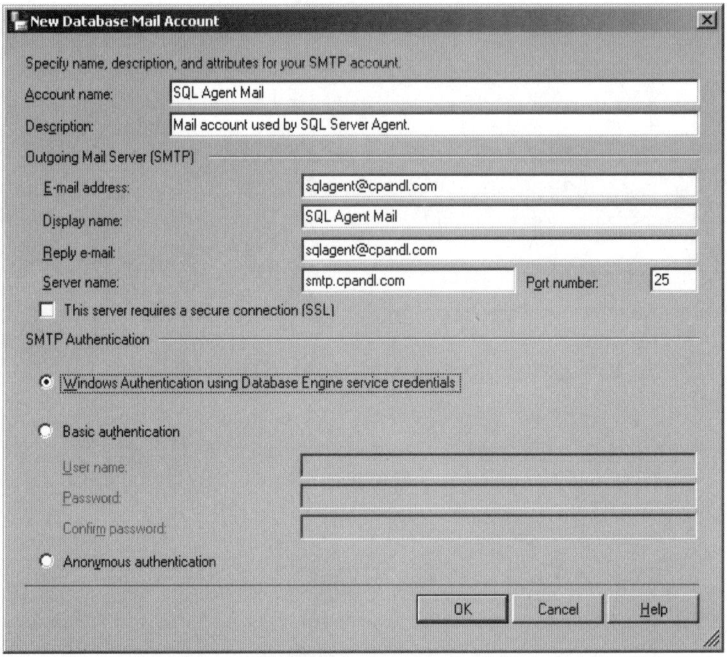

Figure 15-1 The New Database Mail Account dialog box

7. In the Account Name and Description text boxes, enter the name and description of the account you are configuring for use with Database Mail. This information is only used with Database Mail and is shown in SQL Server dialog boxes.

8. In the E-Mail Address box, type the e-mail address of the Database Mail account, such as **sqlagent@cpandl.com**.

9. In the Display Name box, type the name that will appear in the From field of outgoing messages.

10. In the Reply E-Mail box, type the e-mail address to which replies to Database Mail messages can be sent. For example, if you want administrators to send follow-up information to a lead administrator, you would put the administrator's e-mail address in the Reply E-Mail text box.

11. In the Server Name box, type the host name of the mail server, such as **smtp**. You can also type the fully qualified domain name of the mail server, such as **smtp.cpandl.com**. Using the full domain name ensures a successful connection when the mail server is in a different domain.

12. Database Mail will need to log in to the mail server to submit mail for delivery. Select the appropriate authentication option SMTP, based on your mail server configuration:

    ■ **Windows Authentication Using Database Engine Service Credentials**   SQL Mail logs in to the designated mail server using the credentials of the SQL Server service (MSSQLService) for the current Database Engine instance.

    ■ **Basic Authentication**   SQL Mail logs in to the designated mail server using the user name and password you have provided. Enter a user name for the account. Type and confirm the password for the account in the text boxes provided.

    ■ **Anonymous Authentication**   SQL Mail logs in to the designated mail server as an anonymous user. The mail server must be configured to allow anonymous log in (which is not a good security practice).

13. Click OK to close the New Database Mail Account dialog box.

14. Repeat steps 6 through 13 to specify other mail accounts to associate with the Database Mail profile. The account listed first is the account that Database Mail will try to use first. As necessary, use the Move Up and Move Down buttons to set the usage priority for multiple accounts. Click Next.

15. If you are creating a public profile, select the Public check box on the Public Profiles tab. To make the profile the default for all mail host databases and users, set Default Profile to Yes (see Figure 15-2).

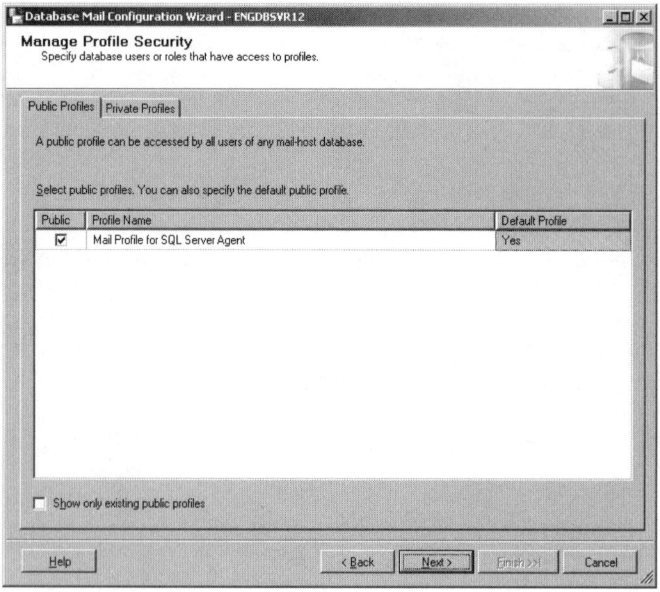

Figure 15-2   The Public Profiles tab

16. If you are creating a private profile, select the Private Profiles tab. Use the User Name drop-down list to select a user to which you will grant profile access. The default user is the SQL Server Agent service account. After you select a user on the drop-down list, select the Access check box to grant access to the profile, and then repeat as necessary to grant access to other users. To make the profile the default for the selected mail host database and user, set Default Profile to Yes.

17. System parameters are used by all database mail hosts configured for a SQL Server instance. Configure the default system parameters using the following options, and then click Next:

- **Account Retry Attempts**   Sets the number of times to retry sending the message. The default is 1. If you have configured multiple accounts, this may be sufficient because it provides for one retry. However, when you are configuring mail for SQL Server Agent, you usually want to set this to try three to five times to send a message.

- **Account Retry Delay**   Sets the delay (in seconds) between retry attempts. The default is 60 seconds, which is far too long if Database Mail is trying to deliver critical alerts. A retry delay of 30 to 60 seconds may be preferred when you are configuring mail for SQL Server Agent.

- **Maximum File Size**   Sets the maximum size (in bytes) for any generated message, including headers, message text, and included attachments. The default is 1,000,000 bytes (976 KB). When you are configuring mail for SQL Server Agent, this is usually sufficient. If applications generate messages which include graphics or multimedia, however, this may not be sufficient.

- **Prohibited Attachment File Extensions**   Sets the types of files that cannot be sent as attachments according to their file extension. To prevent abuse of Database Mail, a more inclusive list would include all file extensions designated as high risk by Attachment Manager in Group Policy, including: .ade, .adp, .app, .asp, .bas, .bat, .cer, .chm, .cmd, .com, .cpl, .crt, .csh, .exe, .fxp, .hlp, .hta, .inf, .ins, .isp, .its, .js, .jse, .ksh, .lnk, .mad, .maf, .mag, .mam, .maq, .mar, .mas, .mat, .mau, .mav, .maw, .mda, .mdb, .mde, .mdt, .mdw, .mdz, .msc, .msi, .msp, .mst, .ops, .pcd, .pif, .prf, .prg, .pst, .reg, .scf, .scr, .sct, .shb, .shs, .tmp, .url, .vb, .vbe, .vbs, .vsmacros, .vss, .vst, .vsw, .ws, .wsc, .wsf, and .wsh.

- **Database Mail Executable Minimum Lifetime**   Sets the minimum time for Database Mail to run while generating a message. The lifetime should be set to optimize usage of the Database Mail executable file. You do not want the server to create the related objects in memory and then remove them from memory over and over again. You do want the related objects to be cleared out when they are not needed. The default 600 seconds (10 minutes) is typically sufficient.

- **Logging Level**   Determines the level of logging with regard to Database Mail. The default value, Extended, configures Database Mail to perform extended logging of related events. To reduce logging, you can set the level to Normal so only important events, such as warnings and errors, are logged.

Note   The logging level also can be set to Verbose. However, this setting should be used only to troubleshoot Database Mail. When you are finished troubleshooting, reset the logging level to Extended or Normal.

18. Review the setup actions that will be performed, and then click Finish. The Configuring page shows the success or failure of each action. Click the link provided for any error message to see details about the error that occurred, and then take any necessary corrective action. Click Close.

Tip   If you are enabling Database Mail for use with SQL Server Agent service, you must ensure the service is running and configured for automatic startup. See the subsection titled "Configuring the SQL Server Agent Service" later in this chapter for details. You can check the status of SQL Server Agent in Object Explorer view in SQL Server Management Studio. If the service is not running, right-click the SQL Server Agent node, and then select Start.

Managing Database Mail Profiles and Accounts

Database Mail can be configured to use one or more mail profiles, and each of those mail profiles can have one or more mail accounts associated with it. Database Mail profiles can be:

- **Public**   Available to any user or application on the current server instance.
- **Private**   Available only to explicitly defined users and applications.

Database mail accounts are used in priority order and are a safeguard against mail server failure or network problems that could prevent message delivery. If mail cannot be delivered to the first account listed in the profile, the second one is tried, and so on.

To manage profiles and their accounts or add a profile, follow these steps:

1. Start SQL Server Management Studio. In Object Explorer view, connect to the server instance of your choice, and then expand the server's Management folder.
2. Right-click Database Mail, and then select Configure Database Mail to display the Database Mail Configuration Wizard. Click Next.
3. Select Manage Database Mail Accounts And Profiles, and then click Next.
4. If you have configured multiple database mail hosts on this server instance and want to define separate profiles for these database mail hosts, select Create A New Profile, click Next, and then follow steps 5 through 13 in the subsection

titled "Performing the Initial Database Mail Configuration" earlier in this chapter to define the new profile and the accounts associated with this profile.

5. If you want to modify an existing profile or add an account to an existing profile, select View, Change, Or Delete An Existing Profile, and then click Next. Use the Profile Name drop-down list to select the profile to manage. You can then add, remove, or prioritize accounts for this profile, as discussed in steps 6 through 13 in the subsection titled "Performing the Initial Database Mail Configuration" earlier in this chapter to define the new profile and the accounts associated with this profile.

6. Click Next, and then click Finish. The Configuring page shows the success or failure of each action. Click the link provided for any error message to see details about the error that occurred, and then take any necessary corrective action. Click Close.

To set a mail profile as public or private, follow these steps:

1. Start SQL Server Management Studio. In Object Explorer view, connect to the server instance of your choice, and then expand the server's Management folder.

2. Right-click Database Mail, and then select Configure Database Mail to display the Database Mail Configuration Wizard. Click Next.

3. Select Manage Profile Security, and then click Next.

4. The Public Profiles tab shows public profiles. Clear the Public check box if you want to make a profile private. To make a public profile the default for all mail host databases and users, set Default Profile to Yes.

5. The Private Profiles tab shows private profiles which are accessible only to a specific database and user. Use the drop-down lists to select the database and user for which you want to configure a private profile. After selecting a user on the drop-down list, select the Access check box to grant access to the profile and repeat as necessary to grant access to other users. To make a private profile the default for the selected mail host database and user, set Default Profile to Yes.

6. Click Next, and then click Finish. The Configuring page shows the success or failure of each action. Click the link provided for any error message to see details on the error that occurred, and then take any necessary corrective action. Click Close.

Viewing or Changing Database Mail System Parameters

Database Mail system parameters are set globally for each SQL Server instance. If you want to manage the global system parameters for Database Mail, follow these steps:

1. Start SQL Server Management Studio. In Object Explorer view, connect to the server instance of your choice, and then expand the server's Management folder.

2. Right-click Database Mail, and then select Configure Database Mail to display the Database Mail Configuration Wizard. Click Next.

3. Select View Or Change System Parameters. Click Next.

4. Make changes as appropriate to the system parameters. See the subsection titled "Performing the Initial Database Mail Configuration" earlier in this chapter for details on configuring individual parameters.

5. Click Next, and then click Finish. The Configuring page shows the success or failure of each action. Click the link provided for any error message to see details about the error that occurred, and then take any necessary corrective action. Click Close.

Using SQL Server Agent

SQL Server Agent is the driving force behind database automation. It is responsible for processing alerts and running scheduled jobs. When alerts are triggered and when scheduled jobs fail, succeed, or complete, you can notify SQL Server operators. Operator notifications are also processed through SQL Server Agent.

Accessing Alerts, Operators, and Jobs

You can use SQL Server Management Studio to access resources related to SQL Server Agent by completing the following steps:

1. Start SQL Server Management Studio. In Object Explorer view, connect to the server instance of your choice, and then expand the server's SQL Server Agent folder. (The SQL Server Agent must be running to expand the related node.)

2. You should see entries for Alerts, Operators, and Jobs. Select one of these entries in the left pane to display its properties in the right pane, as shown in Figure 15-3.

3. Any jobs or alerts that are shaded are configured but not enabled. Double-click an alert, operator, or job entry to access its associated Properties dialog box.

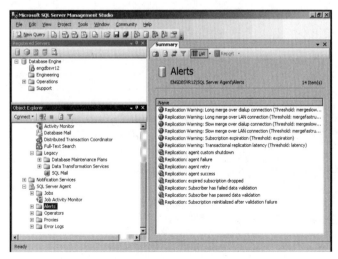

Figure 15-3   SQL Server Agent alerts listing

Note   If you have configured replication on the server, you will see
many alerts and jobs that you configure to make it easier to monitor
replication. To start these alerts or jobs, you need to enable them and
set the appropriate property settings.

Configuring the SQL Server Agent Service

SQL Server Agent service executes scheduled jobs, triggers alerts, and performs
other automated tasks. Each SQL Server Database Engine instance has its own SQL
Server Agent service. You can control the related service (SQLServerAgent or
SQLAgent$instancename) just as you do the SQL Server service. For SQL Server
Agent to work properly, you should configure the SQL Server Agent service to run
automatically. The startup account used by the SQL Server Agent service determines access permissions for SQL Server Agent. If the startup account does not
have appropriate permissions, SQL Server Agent will not run properly. In most
cases, you will want to use a Microsoft Windows domain account that is a member
of the sysadmin role. This ensures that SQL Server Agent can generate alerts, run
jobs, and restart services, as necessary.

To configure the SQL Server Agent service complete the following steps:

1. In SQL Server Configuration Manager, select the SQL Server 2005 Services
   node in the left pane to see the related SQL Server services in the right pane.

2. Right-click the SQL Server Agent service for the Database Engine instance you
   are configuring and select Properties.

3. SQL Server Agent can run using a built-in system account or a designated Windows account:

   ❑ Choose Built-in Account to use one of the built-in system accounts as the
   startup account. The drop-down menu gives you three options: Local System, Local Service, or Network Service. Local System grants access to the
   local system and certain system-wide privileges, such as Act As Part Of
   The Operating System. Local Service grants access to the local system as a
   regular service account. Network Service grants access to the local system
   and allows SQL Server Agent to access the network, such as would be necessary to connect to remote systems.

   ❑ Choose This Account to control permissions and privileges using a Windows account. Type the user name and password of a Windows domain
   account. You can also click Browse to search for an account using the
   Select User Or Group dialog box.

4. If you changed the service account, you must stop and then start the service.
   Do this by clicking Restart. If the service is stopped already, click Start instead.

5. On the Service tab, Start Mode should be set to Automatic. If it is not, click in
   the Start Mode drop-down list and select Automatic.

6. Click OK.

Setting the SQL Server Agent Mail Profile

The SQL Server Agent service sends alerts and notifications through e-mail messages. Two options are allowed. You can use Database Mail or SQL Mail (which has been deprecated). When you initially set Database Mail to send alerts and notifications, you configure one or more databases as mail hosts and define client settings so that users and applications, such as SQL Server Agent, can send SMTP e-mail messages through your organization's SMTP mail server. To use Database Mail for SQL Server Agent alerts and notifications, you must:

1. Configure *msdb* as a database mail host.
2. Designate a profile for this database.
3. Grant profile access to the SQL Server Agent service account.

SQL Mail configures SQL Server Agent as a mail client to send mail by using the Messaging Application Programming Interface (MAPI) through your organization's MAPI-compliant mail server. To use SQL Mail with SQL Server Agent, you must configure SQL Mail, create a MAPI profile on the system (such as an Outlook mail profile), and then modify the SQL Server Agent Properties so that the SQL Mail profile is enabled for the MAPI profile.

You designate the SQL Mail profile by completing the following steps:

1. Right-click the SQL Server Agent entry in the SQL Server Management Studio Management folder, and then select Properties.
2. On the Alert System page, select Enable Mail Profile.
3. Select SQL Mail as the Mail System, and then select the appropriate mail profile. If you want to test the configuration, click Test.
4. Click OK.

 Tip   If you are using Database Mail with SQL Server Agent, Enable Mail Profile should not be selected. The mail profile is configured through Database Mail.

Using SQL Server Agent to Restart Services Automatically

You can configure SQL Server Agent to restart the SQL Server and SQL Server Agent services automatically if they stop unexpectedly. Configuring automatic restart of these services is a good idea because it may keep you from getting paged if the server stops for some reason at 3:00 A.M. on a Tuesday morning.

To configure automatic service restart, complete the following steps:

1. Right-click the SQL Server Agent entry in the SQL Server Management Studio Management folder, and then select Properties.
2. Select Auto Restart SQL Server If It Stops Unexpectedly.
3. Click OK.

Managing Alerts

Using alerts, you can send e-mail, pager, or Net Send alerts when errors occur or when performance conditions are reached. For example, you can configure an alert to send a message when a Log File Is Full error occurs or when the number of deadlocks per second is more than five. You can also execute a job on an alert event.

Using Default Alerts

Default alerts are configured when you configure features such as replication. The names of alerts configured when you set up replication begin with Replication: and include the following:

- **Replication: Agent Success**   An alert that tells you that the replication agent was successful.
- **Replication: Agent Failure**   An alert that tells you that the replication agent failed.
- **Replication: Agent Retry**   An alert that tells you that the replication agent failed and is retrying.
- **Replication: Expired Subscription Dropped**   An alert that tells you that an expired subscription was dropped, which means the subscriber will not be updated anymore.
- **Replication: Subscriber Has Failed Data Validation**   An alert that tells you that data in the subscriber's subscription could not be validated.
- **Replication: Subscriber Has Passed Data Validation**   An alert that tells you that data in the subscriber's subscription was validated.
- **Replication: Subscriber Reinitialized After Validation Failure**   An alert that tells you that data in the subscriber's subscription was reinitialized with a new snapshot.

These replication alerts are disabled and do not have operators assigned either. So if you want to use these alerts, you will need to enable them and assign operators. Other default alerts for replication are used to issue warnings and are enabled in a standard configuration.

Creating Error Message Alerts

Error message alerts are triggered when SQL Server generates an error message. You can create an error message alert by completing the following steps:

1. In SQL Server Management Studio, access the Management folder on the server running SQL Server Agent.
2. Expand the SQL Server Agent entry in the left pane by double-clicking it.
3. Right-click Alerts, and then select New Alerts from the shortcut menu. This displays the New Alert Properties dialog box, shown in Figure 15-4.
4. Type a short but descriptive name for the alert in the Name text box. In Figure 15-4, the alert is named Database Consistency Error.

5. In the Type selection list, choose SQL Server Event Alert. You can now set alerts according to the number or severity level of error messages.

6. Use the Database Name selection list to choose the database in which the error must occur in order to trigger the alert. To specify all databases on the server, select the <All Databases> option.

7. To set alerts by error number, choose Error Number, and then type an error number in the related text box. To see all error messages that can be returned by SQL Server, you query master using SELECT * FROM SYSMESSAGES as discussed in Chapter 13, "Profiling and Monitoring Microsoft SQL Server 2005."

8. To set alerts by severity level, choose Severity, and then use the related selection list to choose a severity level that triggers the alert. You will usually want to configure alerts for severity levels 19 through 25 (which are the levels for fatal errors).

9. To restrict alerts to messages containing specific text strings, type the filter text in the Error Message Contains This Text box.

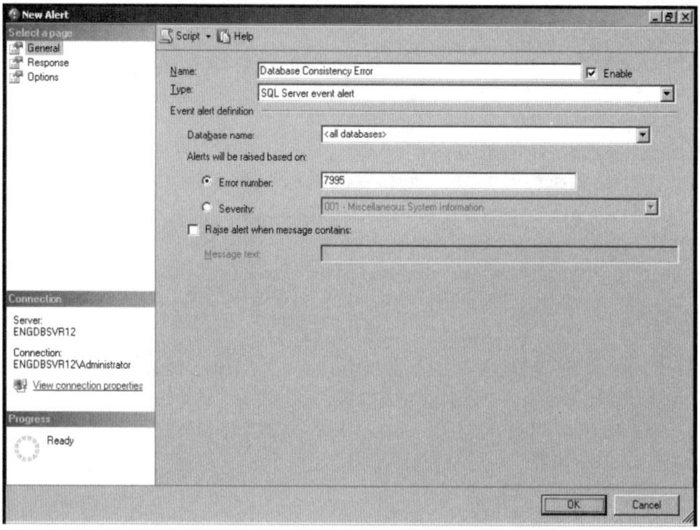

Figure 15-4   The New Alert Properties dialog box

10. Configure the alert response as explained in the next subsection, "Handling Alert Responses." Click OK to create the alert.

Handling Alert Responses

In response to an alert, you can execute SQL Server jobs or notify operators of the alert, or both. To configure the alert response, complete the following steps:

1. In SQL Server Management Studio, access the Management folder on the server running SQL Server Agent.

2. Expand the SQL Server Agent and Alerts folders.

3. Double-click the alert you want to configure. Then select the Response page, as shown in Figure 15-5.

4. To execute a job in response to the alert, select Execute Job.

5. If you want to execute an existing job, click the Properties (...) button to display the Locate Job dialog box. Enter the full or partial job name, and then click Check Names. If multiple possible matches are found, choose the job you want to run, and then click OK. Click OK to close the Locate Job dialog box. To be sure you have the right job, you can click View Job to view the job properties.

6. If you want to create a new job, click New Job, and then configure the job as discussed in the section titled "Scheduling Jobs" later in this chapter.

7. To notify designated operators of an alert rather than just logging the alert, select Notify Operators.

8. Operators configured to handle alerts and schedule jobs are shown in the Operators List area. The available notification methods depend on how the operator account is configured. You can select E-Mail, Pager, or Net Send notification, or all three. Click New Operator to configure a new operator or View Operator to view the properties of an operator currently selected in the Operator List.

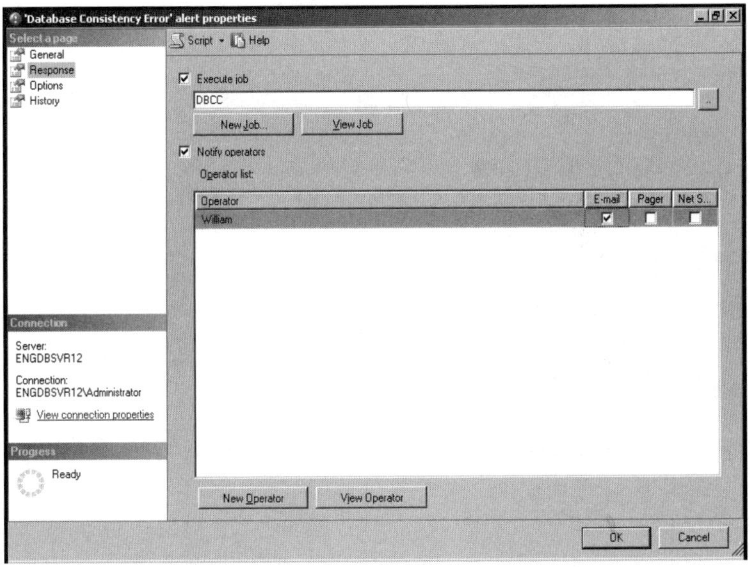

Figure 15-5   The Response page of the New Alert dialog box

9. Select the Options page.

10. Use the Include Alert Error Text In check boxes to specify if error text should be sent with the notification message. By default, error text is sent only with E-Mail and Net Send notifications.

11. Set an additional message to operators using the Additional Notification Message To Send text box.

12. Set the delay between responses for subsequent alert notifications using the Delay Between Responses boxes labeled Minutes and Seconds.

 Tip   To limit the number of alert responses triggered, you will probably want to set a delay response value of five minutes or more.

13. Click OK to complete the configuration.

Deleting, Enabling, and Disabling Alerts

Deleting an alert removes its entry from the alerts list. Because old alerts may be useful to you (or another database administrator) in the future, you may want to disable them instead of deleting them. When an alert is disabled, no alerts are triggered if the related event occurs.

To delete, enable, or disable an alert, complete the following steps:

1. In SQL Server Management Studio, access the Management folder on the server running SQL Server Agent.

2. Expand the SQL Server Agent and Alerts folders.

3. Any alerts that are shaded are configured but not enabled. To enable or disable an alert, right-click it, and then select Enable or Disable as appropriate. Click Close.

4. To delete an alert, click it, and then press Delete. In the Delete Object dialog box, click OK to confirm the deletion.

Managing Operators

Operators are special accounts that can be notified when alerts are triggered and when scheduled jobs fail, succeed, or complete. Before operators become available, you need to register them. After you register operators, you can enable or disable them for notifications.

Registering Operators

You register operators by completing the following steps:

1. In SQL Server Management Studio, access the Management folder on the server running SQL Server Agent.

2. Expand the SQL Server Agent folder.

3. Right-click the Operators entry in the left pane, and then choose New Operator to display the New Operator dialog box shown in Figure 15-6.

4. Type a name for the operator in the Name text box.

5. Specify E-Mail, Pager, or Net Send accounts (or all three) to notify.

> **Tip** If you specify a pager account for the operator, you can set a duty schedule for the pager using the Pager On Duty Schedule area's text boxes and check boxes. This option is helpful if you have operators who should be notified only during working hours. To set default configuration settings for pagers, access the Alert System page of the SQL Server Agent Properties dialog box.

6. Select the Notifications page to specify existing alerts that the operator should receive (if any). Existing alerts are listed in the Alert Name column. If you find an alert that the operator should receive, select the corresponding check boxes in the E-Mail, Pager, and Net Send columns as appropriate.

7. Click OK to register the operator.

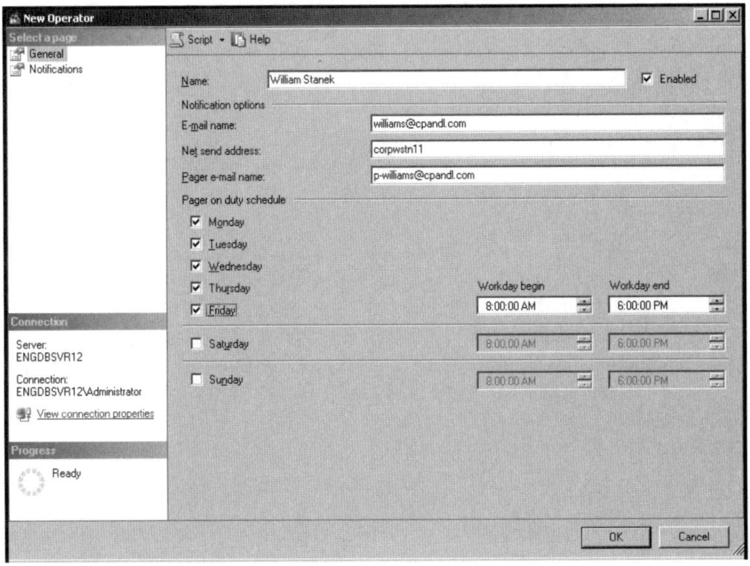

Figure 15-6   New Operator dialog box

Deleting and Disabling Notification for Operators

When database administrators leave the organization or go on vacation, you may want to delete or disable their associated operator accounts. To do this, complete the following steps:

1. In SQL Server Management Studio, access the Management folder on the server running SQL Server Agent.

2. Expand the SQL Server Agent and Operators folders.

3. To disable an operator, double-click the operator entry in the right pane to display the Operator Properties dialog box. Clear Enabled on the General page. Click OK.

4. To delete an operator, click its entry in the right pane, and then press Delete. The Delete Object dialog box is displayed.

5. If the operator has been selected to receive alert or job notifications, you will see a Reassign To option in the Delete Object dialog box. To reassign notification duty, select a different operator using the Reassign To drop-down list. You can view or change the properties of this operator by clicking Properties.

6. Click OK to delete the operator.

Configuring a Fail-Safe Operator

When things go wrong with notification, operators do not get notified and problems may not be corrected in a timely manner. To prevent this, you may want to designate a fail-safe operator. The fail-safe operator is notified when:

- SQL Server Agent cannot access system tables in the *msdb* database, which is where operator definitions and notification lists are stored.

- All pager notifications to designated operators have failed or the designated operators are off duty (as defined in the pager schedule).

 Note Using the fail-safe operator on pager notification failure may seem strange, but it is a good way to ensure that alerts are handled efficiently. E-mail and Net Send messages almost always reach their destination—but the people involved are not always watching their mail or sitting at their computer to receive Net Send messages, so the fail-safe operator is a way to guarantee notification.

To configure a fail-safe operator, complete the following steps:

1. Right-click the SQL Server Agent entry in the SQL Server Management Studio Management folder, and then select Properties.

2. In the SQL Server Agent Properties dialog box, select the Alert System page.

3. Select Enable Fail-Safe Operator to define a fail-safe operator.

4. Use the Operator drop-down list to choose an operator to designate as the fail-safe operator. You can reassign the fail-safe duty by selecting a different operator or disable the feature by clearing Enable Fail-Safe Operator.

5. Use the Notify Using check boxes to determine how the fail-safe operator is notified.

6. Click OK.

Scheduling Jobs

Job scheduling is a key part of database automation. You can configure SQL Server jobs to handle almost any database task.

Creating Jobs

You create jobs as a series of steps that contain actions in the sequence in which you want to execute them. When you schedule jobs in conjunction with other SQL Server facilities, such as database backups or data transformation, the necessary commands are configured for you. Normally these commands are set as step 1, and all you need to do is set a run schedule for the job. You can add extra steps to these jobs and thus perform other tasks. For example, after importing data, you may want to back up the related database. In the SQL Server Import And Export Wizard, you would schedule the import, and then you would edit the associated job in SQL Server Management Studio to add an additional step for backing up the database. By coordinating the two processes, you ensure that the import operation is completed before starting the backup.

Another reason for editing a job created by another SQL Server facility is to add notifications based on success, failure, and completion of the job. In this way, you can notify operators of certain conditions, and you do not have to search through logs to determine if the job executed properly.

When you schedule jobs to execute for alerts, you configure the entire job process from start to finish by performing the following tasks:

- Create a job definition.
- Set steps to execute.
- Configure a job schedule.
- Handle completion, success, and failure notification messages.

Assigning or Changing Job Definitions

Whether you are creating a new job or editing an existing job, the steps for working with job definitions are the same:

1. In SQL Server Management Studio, access the Management folder on the server running SQL Server Agent.
2. Expand the SQL Server Agent and Jobs folders.
3. Existing jobs are shown in the right pane. Double-click a job to access its related properties dialog box, which is essentially the same as the New Job dialog box shown in Figure 15-7.
4. To create a new job, right-click the Jobs entry and, from the shortcut menu, choose New Job to display the New Job dialog box shown in Figure 15-7.
5. In the Name text box, type a descriptive name for the job. The name can be up to 128 characters long. If you change the name of an existing job, the job is

displayed with the new name. Any references to the old job name in logs or history files remain the same and are not modified.

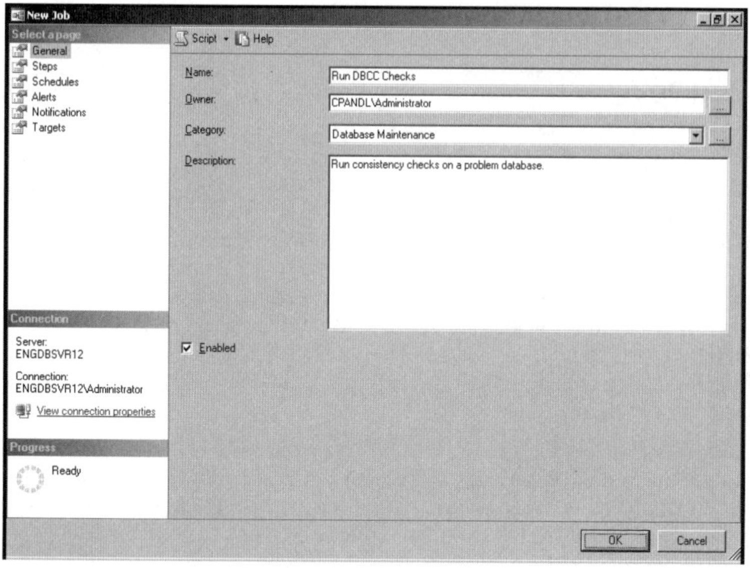

Figure 15-7   The General tab of the New Job dialog box

6. Job categories allow you to organize jobs so they can be easily searched and differentiated. The default category is Uncategorized (Local). Use the Category selection list to choose a different category for the job.

Note   Job categories are created and managed through a separate process. To create a new job category or update an existing category, use the techniques described in the subsection titled "Managing Job Categories" later in this chapter.

7. By default, the current user owns the job. Administrators can reassign jobs to other users. To do this, use the Owner selection list. You can use only predefined logons. If the logon you want to use is not available, you will need to create a logon for the account.

8. Type a description of the job in the Description text box. You can use up to 512 characters.

9. If job scheduling across multiple servers is configured, select the Targets page, and then designate the target server. The target server is the server on which the job runs. To run on the currently selected server, select Target Local Server.

To run on multiple servers, select Target Multiple Servers, and then choose the target servers.

10. Set Steps, Schedules, and Notifications as explained in the following subsections.

Setting Steps to Execute

Jobs can have one or more steps. SQL Server Agent always attempts to execute the Start step, but additional steps can be executed conditionally, such as only when the Start step succeeds or fails. You work with steps using the Steps page in the New Job dialog box, as shown in Figure 15-8. The page displays any existing steps for the job. You can use the boxes and buttons in this dialog box as follows:

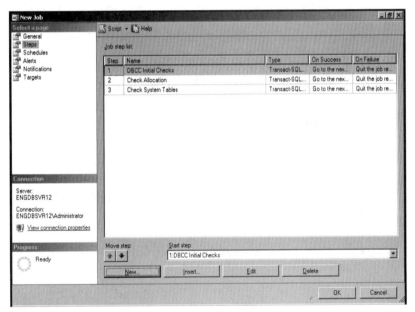

Figure 15-8 The Steps page of the New Job dialog box

- **New**   Creates a new step.
- **Insert**   Inserts a step before the currently selected step.
- **Edit**   Allows edits to the selected step.
- **Delete**   Deletes the selected step.
- **Move Step Up/Down**   Changes the order of the selected step.
- **Start Step**   Sets which step is executed first. The green flag icon highlights the start step in the step list.

When you create or edit a step, you see a dialog box similar to the one shown in Figure 15-9. To configure this dialog box, complete the following steps:

1. Type a short but descriptive name for the step in the Step Name text box.

2. Use the Type drop-down list to choose a step type from the following choices:

   - **Transact-SQL Commands**   Execute Transact-SQL commands. Type Transact-SQL commands in the Command area or load the statements from a Transact SQL script. To load commands from a script, click Open, and then select the Transact-SQL script you want to use. The entire contents of the script are then stored with this step.

   - **ActiveX Scripts**   Run ActiveX scripts. You can write ActiveX scripts in VBScript, JScript, or another active scripting language configured for use on the system. Enter script statements directly into the Command area or load the statements from a script file. Again, the entire contents of the script are then stored with this step, and later changes to the script file are not updated automatically.

   - **Operating System Commands**   Execute Operating System commands. Enter the operating system commands on a separate line, making sure that you specify the full path to commands and in command parameters. Commands can run batch scripts, Windows scripts, command-line utilities, or applications.

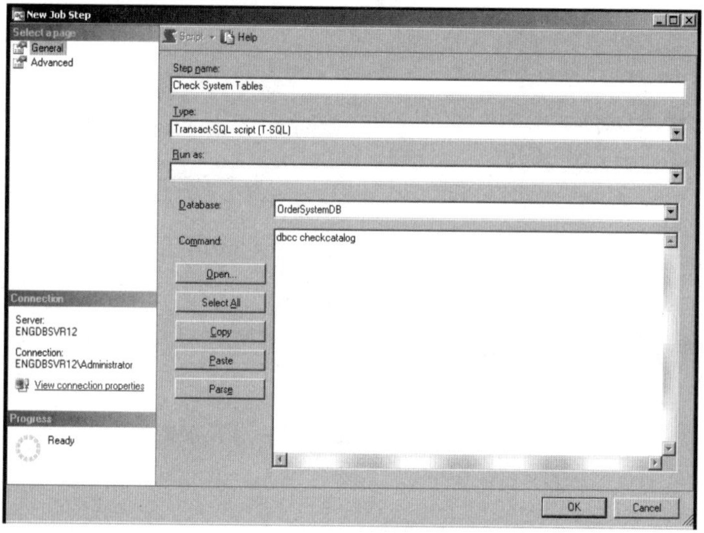

Figure 15-9   The New Job Step dialog box

   - **Replication [Agent Name]**   Pass Transact-SQL commands to designated replication agents. You can script the Distributor, Snapshot, Merge, Queue Reader, and Transaction–Log Reader agents with Transact-SQL commands. To see examples, refer to the existing jobs that are configured to handle replication, distribution, and subscription processes on the server (if available).

- **SQL Server Analysis Services Command/Query**   Pass commands or queries to SQL Server Analysis Services. Type commands and queries in the Command area or load the commands and queries from an Analysis Server file. To load from a file, click Open, and then select the Analysis Server Command (.xmla) or Analysis Server Query (.mdx) file to use. The entire contents of the file will be stored with this step.

- **SQL Server Integration Services Package**   Execute SQL Server Integration Services packages stored on a specific server.

Tip   Subsequent changes to scripts are not updated automatically. You will need to edit the step properties and reload the script file. Additionally, you should not edit existing replication jobs. Instead, modify the replication process as described in Chapter 12, "implementing Snapshot, Merge, and Transactional Replication."

3. When executing Transact-SQL commands or scripts, use the Database drop-down list to set the database on which the commands are executed.

4. Select the Advanced page as shown in Figure 15-10.

5. Use the On Success Action drop-down list to set the action to take when the step succeeds. You can:

   ❑ Go to the next step to continue sequential execution of the job.

   ❑ Go to a different step to continue execution of the job on a different step.

   ❑ Quit the job and report success or failure.

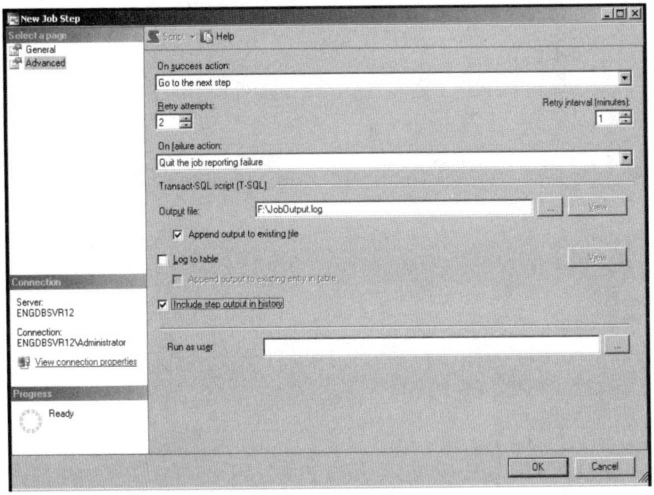

Figure 15-10   The Advanced page of the New Job Step dialog box

6. By default, Retry Attempts is set to zero and SQL Server Agent does not try to execute steps again. You can change this behavior by setting the number of retry attempts and a retry interval. You do this by using the Retry Attempts and Retry Interval (Minutes) boxes, respectively. The retry interval is the delay in minutes between retries.

7. If the job fails on all retry attempts (if any), the action set in the On Failure Action drop-down list is executed. The available options are the same as those for success.

8. If desired, configure a file for logging output from Transact-SQL and CmdExec commands. Type the file name and path in the Output File text box or use the find file button (...) to search for an existing file.

Tip   You may want to create a central log file for the output of all jobs or only all jobs in a particular category. If you do this, be sure to select the Append Output To Existing File option rather than allowing the file to be overwritten. This ensures that the output file does not get overwritten. An alternative is to include the step output in the job history.

9. Click the Run As User Properties (...) button to set the login to use when executing commands. By default, commands are run using the current login ID.

10. Choose OK to complete the step configuration.

Configuring Job Schedules

You track schedules on the Schedules page of the New Job dialog box, as shown in Figure 15-11. Jobs can have one or more schedules associated with them, and just as you can enable or disable jobs and their individual steps, you can enable or disable individual schedules. This makes the job scheduling process very flexible. For example, you could set one schedule to execute the job on weekdays at 2 A.M., another to execute the job every Sunday at 8 A.M., and another for execution at 10 P.M. only when needed.

Whether you are creating a new job or editing an existing job, you work with schedules on the Schedules page as follows:

- **Create a new schedule**   Click New to configure a new schedule.

- **Edit a schedule**   Select an existing schedule, and then click Edit to view or modify its properties.

- **Delete a schedule**   Select an existing schedule, and then click Delete to remove the schedule.

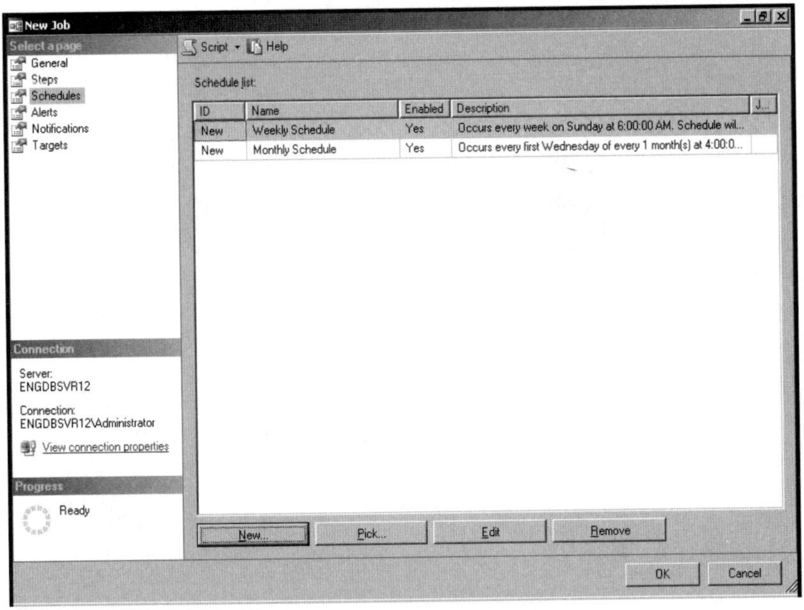

Figure 15-11   The Schedules page of the New Job dialog box

You create or edit schedules by completing the following steps:

1. Click New to open the New Job Schedule dialog box, or click Edit to open the Edit Job Schedule dialog box. These dialog boxes are essentially the same except for the title. Figure 15-12 shows the New Job Schedule dialog box.

2. Type a name for the schedule, and then select one of the following schedule types:

   ■ **Start Automatically When SQL Server Agent Starts**   Runs the job automatically whenever SQL Server Agent starts.

   ■ **Start Whenever The CPUs Become Idle**   Runs the job whenever the CPU is idle. CPU idle time is specified on the Advanced page of the SQL Server Agent Properties dialog box.

   ■ **One Time**   Runs the job once at the date and time specified in the Date and Time boxes.

   ■ **Recurring**   Runs the job according to the recurring schedule displayed.

3. Recurring jobs are the ones that need the most explanation. You can schedule recurring jobs to run on a daily, weekly, or monthly basis. To run the job on a daily basis, set Occurs to Daily. Then use the Recurs Every box to set the run interval. Daily recurring jobs can run every day, every other day, or every Nth day.

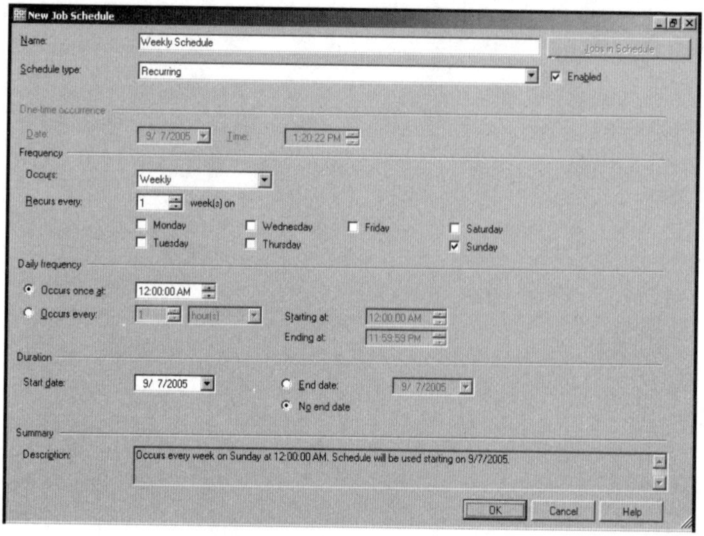

Figure 15-12   The New Job Schedule dialog box

4. To run the job on a weekly basis, set Occurs to Weekly. Then configure the job using these boxes:

- **Recurs Every Nth Week(s)**   Allows you to run the task every week, every other week, or every Nth week.
- **Day of Week**   Sets the day(s) of the week when the task runs, such as on Monday or on Monday, Wednesday, and Friday.

5. To run the job on a monthly basis, set Occurs to Monthly. Then configure the job using these boxes:

- **Day N of Every Nth Month**   Sets the day of the month and on which months the job runs. For example, if you select Day 15 of every second month, the job runs on the 15th day of alternating months.
- **The Nth Day of Every Nth Month**   Sets the job to run on the Nth occurrence of a day in a given month, such as the second Monday of every month or the third Sunday of every other month.

6. Set the Daily Frequency for the daily, weekly, or monthly job. You can configure jobs to run one or more times on their scheduled run date. To run the job once on a given date, select Occurs Once At, and then set a time. To run the job several times on a given date, select Occurs Every, and then set a time interval in hours or minutes. Afterward, set a start and end time, such as from 7:30 A.M. to 5:30 P.M.

7. By default, schedules begin on the current date and do not have a designated end date. To change this behavior, select the End Date option, and then use the Start Date and End Date boxes to set a new duration for the schedule.

8. Click OK again to complete the schedule process.

Handling Job Alerts

Alerts can be generated when jobs are run. You can define and manage job-specific alerts using the Alerts page of the New Job dialog box. To configure alerts, complete the following steps:

1. Access the Alerts page of the job you want to configure.
2. Any current alerts are listed by name and type. You can:
   - Edit an alert by selecting it and clicking Edit.
   - Add an alert by clicking Add to display the New Alert dialog box, and then using the dialog box features to define the alert as discussed previously.
   - Remove an alert by selecting it and clicking Remove.

Handling Notification Messages

Notification messages are generated when a job succeeds, fails, or completes. You can handle these messages in several ways. You can notify operators, log the related event, automatically delete the job, or do all three. To configure notification, complete the following steps:

1. Access the Notifications page of the job you want to configure. This page is shown in Figure 15-13.
2. You can notify operators by e-mail, pager, or Net Send message. Select the check box for the technique you want to use. Choose an operator to handle the notification. Then choose a notification type. Repeat this process to configure other notification methods.

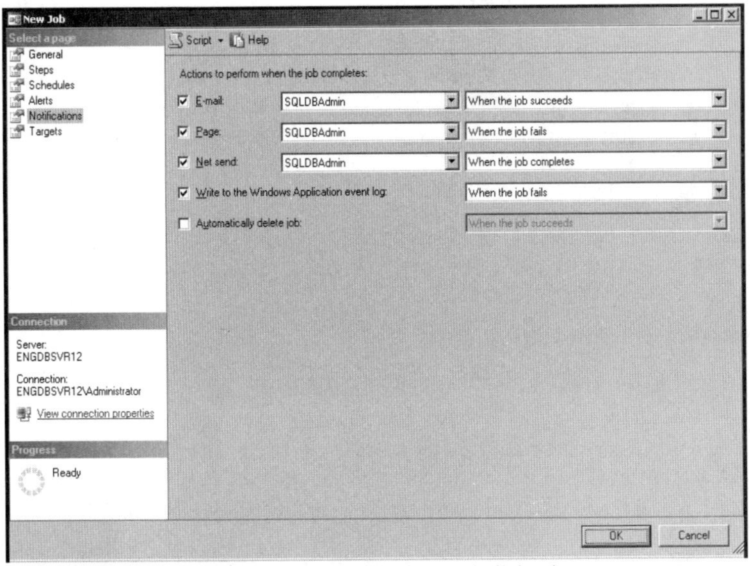

Figure 15-13   The Notifications page of the New Job dialog box

3. To log a particular type of notification message in the event log, select Write To The Windows Application Event Log, and then select the notification type to log. Usually, you will want to log failure, so select When The Job Fails.

4. To delete a job upon notification, select Automatically Delete Job, and then choose the notification type that triggers the deletion.

5. Click OK.

Managing Existing Jobs

In SQL Server Management Studio, you manage jobs with the SQL Server Agent. To do that, complete the following steps:

1. In SQL Server Management Studio, access the Management folder on the server running SQL Server Agent.

2. Expand the SQL Server Agent and Jobs folders.

3. You can now double-click a job entry to access its related properties dialog box or right-click a job entry to display a shortcut menu. The following commands are available on the shortcut menu:

- **Delete**   Deletes the job definition. Before deleting a complex job, you may want to create a script that can be used to recreate the job.
- **Disable**   Disables the job so it will not run.
- **Enable**   Enables the job so it will run.
- **Rename**   Allows you to rename the job. Type the new name, and then press Enter or Tab.
- **Script Job As**   Choose Create To, and then select File to generate a Transact-SQL script file that you can use to recreate the job.
- **Start Job**   Starts the selected job if it is not already running.
- **Stop Job**   Stops the selected job if it is running.
- **View History**   Displays the Log File Viewer dialog box. This dialog box enables you to view summary or detail information on the job execution.

Managing Job Categories

You use job categories to organize jobs into topical folders. When you install SQL Server, default job categories are created automatically. You can add new job categories and change the existing categories at any time.

Working with Job Categories

To create a new job category or update an existing category, complete the following steps:

1. In SQL Server Management Studio, access the Management folder on the server running SQL Server Agent.

2. Expand the SQL Server Agent. Right-click Jobs, and then choose Manage Job Categories. This displays the Manage Job Categories dialog box.

3. You can delete a category by selecting it and clicking Delete.

4. You can view the jobs associated with a category by selecting it and clicking View Jobs.

5. To add categories or to change the properties of a category, follow the steps outlined in the following subsections, "Creating Job Categories" or "Updating Job Categories," respectively.

Creating Job Categories

You can create a new job category by completing the following steps:

1. Access the Manage Job Categories dialog box as explained previously. Click Add to display a properties dialog box.

2. Type a name for the category in the Name text box, and then select Show All Jobs.

3. All jobs defined on the current server should now be listed. Add a job to the new category by selecting the corresponding check box in the Select column. Remove a job from the new category by clearing the corresponding check box in the Select column.

4. Click OK when you are finished.

Updating Job Categories

You can update an existing job category by completing the following steps:

1. Access the Manage Job Categories dialog box as explained previously. Click View Jobs to display a properties dialog box.

2. Select Show All Jobs. All jobs defined on the current server should now be listed.

3. Add a job to a new category by selecting the corresponding check box in the Select column. Remove a job from the category by clearing the corresponding check box in the Select column.

4. Click OK when you are finished.

Automating Routine Server-to-Server Administration Tasks

Anytime you deploy multiple SQL Servers or multiple instances of SQL Server within an organization, you will need a way to handle routine server-to-server administration tasks. For example, if you have a database on one server, you may need to copy users from one server to another. SQL Server 2005 allows you to automate routine server-to-server administration tasks using scripts. You can write the scripts to the Query Editor or save them to a file for later use.

The server-to-server administration tasks you can automate include:

- Copying users, tables, views, and other objects from one database to another.
- Copying alerts, jobs, and scheduled jobs from one server to another.

The subsections that follow explain how you can automate these administration tasks.

Copying Users, Tables, Views, and Other Objects from One Database to Another

Using the Script Wizard, you can generate T-SQL scripts that allow you to re-create the objects contained in a specified database. Scripts can be written to the Query Editor window so you can run them immediately, or they can be saved to files so you can run them later. By running the script against a database other than the one from which it was generated, you can create copies of objects in other databases.

You can create copies of objects by completing the following steps:

1. Start SQL Server Management Studio, and then access the server of your choice.

2. In Object Explorer view, right-click the Management folder, and then select Generate Scripts. This starts the Script Wizard. Click Next.

3. Select the database you want to script, and then click Next.

4. Set the script options summarized in Table 15-1 to determine how the copy operation works, and then click Next.

5. Select the objects you want to script, and then click Next. Objects you can script include database roles, schema, tables, user-defined functions, shared stored procedures, users, and views.

6. You will have one Choose ... page for each type of object you selected. Use this page to choose the individual objects to script. For example, if you are scripting tables and views, you will be able to choose the tables to script and then the views to script.

7. Choose an output option. You can create the script as a file, copy it to the Windows clipboard, or send it to the New Query Editor window. Click Next when you are ready to continue.

8. When you click Finish, the script is created and copied to your chosen destination. Click Close. You can then run the script as needed against a specified database. For example, if you are copying users from *Customer* to *Projects*, you would insert USE PROJECTS at the beginning of the script before running it on the server containing the *Projects* database.

Table 15-1   Script Options for the Script Wizard

Script Option	Default	When True...
Append To File	False	Appends to an existing file rather than overwriting.
Continue Scripting On Error	False	Continues writing the script if an error occurs.
Convert UDDTs To Base Types	False	Converts user-defined data types to base types.
Generate Script For Dependent Objects	True	Scripts dependent objects.

Table 15-1   Script Options for the Script Wizard   *(continued)*

Script Option	Default	When True...
Include Descriptive Headers	False	Includes descriptive header comments for each object scripted. (Does not affect how objects are created later, only sets comments.)
Include If NOT EXISTS	True	Scripts the objects so that they are only re-created if they do not already exist.
Script Behavior	Generate CREATE statements only	Script creates designated objects. (as opposed to dropping designated objects).
Script Check Constraints	True	Scripts check constraints for each table or view scripted.
Script Collation	False	Writes the collation settings of the object to the script.
Script Defaults	True	Scripts the default values for the object.
Script Extended Properties	True	Scripts the extended properties of objects.
Script for Server Version	SQL Server 2005	Creates the script to be compatible with the specified SQL Server version.
Script Foreign Keys	True	Scripts foreign keys for each table or view scripted.
Script Full-Text Indexes	False	Scripts full-text indexes for each table or view scripted.
Script Indexes	False	Scripts indexes for each table or view scripted.
Script Logins	False	Scripts all logins available on the server. Passwords are not scripted.
Script Object-Level Permissions	False	Scripts permissions for the object as per the original database.
Script Owner	True	Scripts the owner for the object.
Script Primary Keys	True	Scripts primary keys for each table or view scripted.
Script Statistics	Do not script statistics	Controls whether statistics for table or indexed view objects are scripted.
Script Triggers	True	Scripts triggers for each table or view scripted.
Script Unique Keys	True	Scripts unique keys for each table or view scripted.
Script Use Database	False	Sets a USE statement with the name of the original database at the top of the script.

Copying Alerts, Operators, and Scheduled Jobs from One Server to Another

You use alerts, operators, and scheduled jobs to automate routine administration tasks. If you have already created alerts, operators, and jobs on one server, you can reuse them on another server. To do this, you would create a script for the alert, operator, or job you want to copy, and then run the script against a target server. You would then need to edit the job properties to ensure that they make sense for the target server. For example, if you created a set of jobs to periodically check the *Support* database and then added custom steps to handle various database states, you could copy these jobs to another server and then edit the job properties to apply the tasks to the *Customer* database on the target server.

You can copy alerts, operators, or jobs from one server to another server by completing the following steps:

1. In SQL Server Management Studio, access the Management folder on the server running SQL Server Agent.

2. Expand the SQL Server Agent, and then expand the Alerts, Jobs, or Operators folder as appropriate for the type of object you are copying.

3. Right-click the alert, operator, or job, point to Script ... As, Create To, and then select File. In the Select A File dialog box, specify the save location and name for the T-SQL script file.

4. Connect to the server on which you want to create the new alert, operator, or job in Object Explorer view. Right-click the server in Object Explorer view, and then select New Query.

5. Click the Open File button or press Ctrl+O. Select the script file you previously created.

6. The script is set to use the *msdb* database because alert, job, and operator objects are stored in that database.

7. Click Execute or press F5 to run the script and create the object in the *msdb* database.

Multiserver Administration

Multiserver administration allows you use one server to manage alerts and job scheduling for other servers from a central location. You centrally manage alerts through event forwarding. You centrally manage job scheduling by designating master servers and target servers.

Event Forwarding

If you have multiple instances of SQL Server running on multiple systems throughout the network, event forwarding is a time and resource saver. With event forwarding, you can forward application log events to a central server and then process those events on this server. Thus, rather than having to configure alerts on 12 different server instances, you configure event forwarding on 11 servers and have one server handle all the incoming events. You could then use the application log's Computer field to determine the system on which the event occurred and take the appropriate corrective actions using scripts or remote procedure calls.

To configure event forwarding, complete the following steps:

1. In SQL Server Management Studio, access the Management folder on the server running SQL Server Agent.
2. Right-click the SQL Server Agent entry and select Properties.
3. Access the Advanced page of the SQL Server Agent Properties dialog box, as shown in Figure 15-14.
4. Select Forward Events To A Different Server.
5. Use the Server selection list to choose a registered server that will handle the events. If the server you want to use is not listed, you will need to register it. Then access the SQL Server Agent Properties dialog box again.
6. Set the type of events to forward by selecting Unhandled Events or All Events. An unhandled event is one that you have not configured alerts for on the current server.

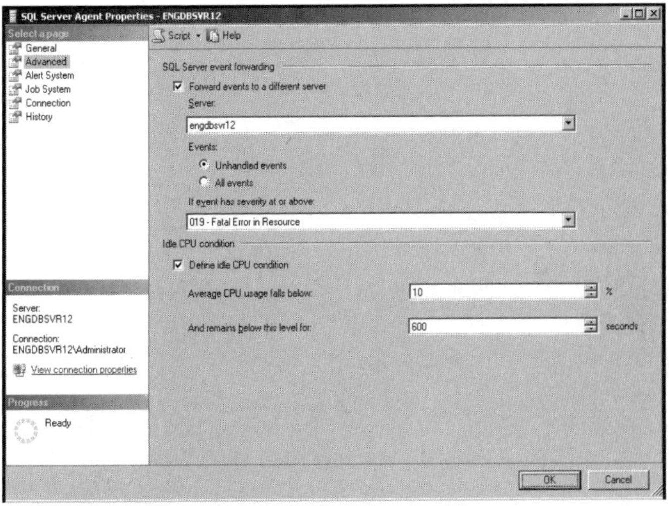

![SQL Server Agent Properties - ENGDBSVR12 dialog box. Select a page list shows: General, Advanced, Alert System, Job System, Connection, History. The Advanced page shows SQL Server event forwarding with "Forward events to a different server" checked, Server: engdbsvr12. Events: Unhandled events selected, All events option. If event has severity at or above: 019 - Fatal Error in Resource. Idle CPU condition with "Define idle CPU condition" checked, Average CPU usage falls below: 10 %, And remains below this level for: 600 seconds.]

Figure 15-14   The SQL Server Agent Properties dialog box

7. From the If Event Has Severity At Or Above drop-down list, select the severity threshold for events that are forwarded.

> **Tip**   To reduce network traffic caused by event forwarding, set the severity threshold to a fairly high value. Fatal errors have a severity level of 19 through 25.

8. Click OK.

Multiserver Job Scheduling

When you want to centrally manage job scheduling, you will need to create a master server and one or more target servers. The SQL Server Agent running on the master server can:

- Centrally manage jobs for the target servers. Then you create jobs on the master server that run on the targets. For details, see the subsection titled "Assigning or Changing Job Definitions" earlier in this chapter.

- Download jobs to a target. For details, see the subsection titled "Managing Existing Jobs" earlier in this chapter.

Multiserver Scheduling Requirements

For the master/target relationship to work correctly, you must:

- Make sure that the master server and all target servers are running SQL Server 2005.

- Use domain accounts, not local accounts, when configuring the master and target.

- Make sure that SQL Server Agent is running on the master server and all target servers.

Configuring Master Servers

To create a master server, complete the following steps:

1. In SQL Server Management Studio, access the Management folder on the server running SQL Server Agent.

2. Right-click the SQL Server Agent entry, point to Multi Server Administration, and then select Make This A Master. This starts the Master Server Wizard.

3. Read the welcome dialog box, and then click Next.

4. As shown in Figure 15-15, create a special operator to handle multiserver job notifications. This operator, called the Master Server Operator, is created on the master and on all target servers that use this master. Set an e-mail, pager, and Net Send address, as appropriate. You can change this information later by editing the Master Server Operator properties on the master server.

5. Select the target servers to associate with this master server. If a server is not registered, you can add a connection for it by clicking Add Connection. The process of associating target servers with a master is called *enlisting*. Later, you can remove the association by right-clicking SQL Server Agent in SQL Server Management Studio, selecting Multi Server Administration, and then selecting Manage Target Servers.

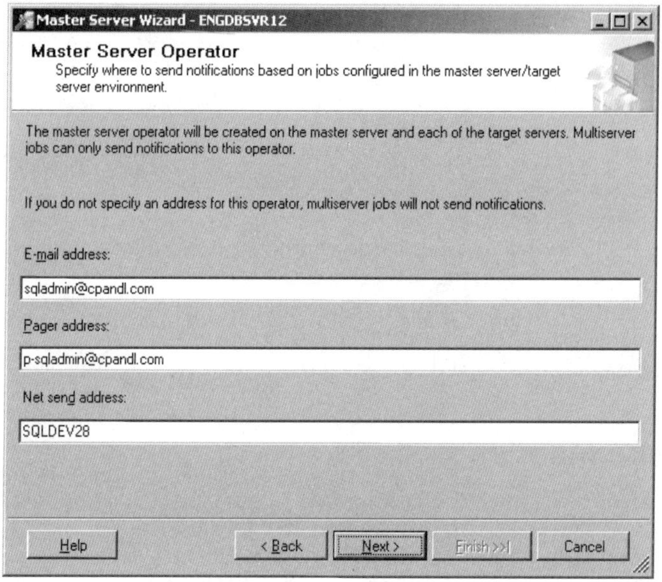

Figure 15-15   The Master Server Operator page of the Master Server Wizard

6. When you click Next, the wizard will check to make sure that the versions of SQL Server running on the master and target servers are compatible. If target servers are running different versions of SQL Server, note any compatibility issues listed. Click Close.

7. Specify the account that the target server will use to connect to the master server and download jobs. If Windows Authentication is allowed on the master server, the new login will be created automatically.

8. Click Next, and then click Finish. The wizard performs the necessary tasks and reports its progress. You will be notified of any errors.

9. Click Close when the configuration is finished.

Configuring Target Servers

You can configure one or more target servers for each master server. You create target servers by completing the following steps:

1. In SQL Server Management Studio, access the Management folder on the server running SQL Server Agent.

2. Right-click the SQL Server Agent entry, point to Multi Server Administration, and then select Make This A Target. This starts the Make TSX Wizard.

3. Read the welcome dialog box, and then click Next.

4. Click Pick Server to select a master server for this target server. Use the Connect To Server dialog box to connect to the master server. The master server is the source server from which SQL Server Agent jobs will be downloaded.

5. When you click Next, the wizard will check to make sure that the versions of SQL Server running on the master and target servers are compatible. If target servers are running different versions of SQL Server, note any compatibility issues listed. Click Close.

6. Specify the account that the target server will use to connect to the master server and download jobs. If Windows Authentication is allowed on the master server, the new login will be created automatically.

7. Click Next, and then click Finish. The wizard performs the necessary tasks and reports its progress. You will be notified of any errors.

8. Click Close when the configuration is finished.

Database Maintenance

Database maintenance involves different tasks. Because most of these tasks have been discussed in previous chapters, this section does not go into detail on tasks already covered. Instead, there is a checklist that you can use as a starting point for your maintenance efforts. The rest of the section explains how to set up maintenance plans and run database consistency checks.

Database Maintenance Checklist

The following checklists provide recommended daily, weekly, and monthly maintenance tasks.

Daily

- ✓ Monitor application, server, and agent logs.
- ✓ Configure alerts for important errors that are not configured for alert notification.
- ✓ Check for performance and error alert messages.
- ✓ Monitor job status, particularly jobs that back up databases and perform replication.
- ✓ Review the output from jobs in the job history or output file, or both.
- ✓ Back up databases and logs (as necessary, and if not configured as automatic jobs).

Weekly

- ✓ Monitor available disk space on drives.
- ✓ Monitor the status of linked, remote, master, and target servers.
- ✓ Check the maintenance plan reports and history to determine the status of maintenance plan operations.

✓ Generate an updated record of configuration information by executing
sp_configure.

Monthly

✓ Monitor server performance, tweaking performance parameters to improve
response time.

✓ Manage logins and server roles.

✓ Audit server, database, and object permissions to ensure that only authorized
users have access.

✓ Review alert, job, and operator configurations.

As Needed

✓ Back up the SQL Server Registry data.

✓ Update the Emergency Repair Disk.

✓ Run database integrity checks and update database statistics. (SQL Server
2005 handles this automatically in most cases.)

Using Maintenance Plans

Maintenance plans provide an automated way to perform essential maintenance
tasks. You can run a maintenance plan against a single database or multiple databases running on a designated target server. You can also generate report histories
for maintenance plan execution.

You create maintenance plans with the Maintenance Plan Wizard or with the Maintenance Plan Package Designer. Both techniques are similar:

■ With the wizard, the wizard pages guide you through the steps of choosing
servers, selecting maintenance tasks to perform, configuring execution history
logging, and setting an execution schedule. When you complete the wizard
steps, the wizard generates the package that will perform the designated maintenance tasks.

■ With the package designer, you specify servers, add tasks to perform from a
pre-defined list of maintenance tasks, and configure execution history logging
as necessary. After you configure connections to the server on which you want
to perform maintenance, you build the maintenance plan by dragging tasks
from the Maintenance Tasks toolbox to the design window. The order in which
you add tasks sets the order of execution. If a task requires additional input,
such as database or server names, double-clicking the task opens a properties
dialog box that lets you specify the needed information.

The set of maintenance tasks you can perform is similar whether you are working
with the wizard or the designer. These tasks are:

■ **Back Up Database**   Allows you to specify the source databases, destination
files or tapes, and overwrite options for a full, differential or transaction log
backup. In the wizard interface, there are separate task listings for each backup
type.

- **Check Database Integrity**   Performs internal consistency checks of the data and index pages with the designated databases.

- **Execute SQL Server Agent Job**   Allows you to select SQL Server Agent jobs to run as part of the maintenance plan.

- **Execute T-SQL Statement**   Allows you to run any T-SQL script as part of the maintenance plan. (Only available in the Maintenance Plan Package Designer.)

- **Cleanup History**   Deletes historical data about Backup and Restore, SQL Server Agent, and Maintenance Plan operations.

- **Maintenance Cleanup**   Deletes files created when executing maintenance plans. (Only available in the Maintenance Plan Package Designer.)

- **Notify Operator**   Sends an e-mail message to a designated SQL Server agent operator. (Only available in the Maintenance Plan Package Designer.)

- **Rebuild Index**   Rebuilds indexes to improve the performance of index scans and seeks. This task also optimizes the distribution of data and free space on the index pages, allowing for faster future growth.

- **Reorganize Index**   Defragments and compacts clustered and nonclustered indexes on tables and views to improve index-scanning performance.

- **Shrink Database**   Reduces the disk space used by the designated databases by removing empty data and log pages.

- **Update Statistics**   Updates the query optimizer statistics regarding the distribution of data values in the tables. This improves the query optimizer's ability to determine data access strategies, which can ultimately improve query performance.

When you first start working with maintenance plans, you will probably want to run the Maintenance Plan Wizard and let the wizard design the necessary package for you. After you have created a package, you modify it in Maintenance Plan Package Designer view.

Tip   For most installations, I recommend configuring separate maintenance plans for system and user databases. This gives you greater flexibility when determining how and when maintenance operations are performed. For large installations, you may want to have separate maintenance plans for each database so that you can work with different databases on different days or at different times of the day.

Creating Maintenance Plans

You can create a maintenance plan by completing the following steps:

1. In SQL Server Management Studio, access the Management folder on the server where you want to create the maintenance plan. This can be a different server from the one on which the maintenance plan will run.

2. Right-click Maintenance Plans, and then select Maintenance Plan Wizard. This starts the Maintenance Plan Wizard.

3. Read the welcome dialog box, and then click Next. Type a name and description for the maintenance plan, such as **Engineering DB Server Maintenance and Backup Plan**.

4. Use the Server list box to specify the server on which you want to perform the maintenance tasks. The currently selected server is listed by default. To select a different server, click the Properties (...) button and select an available SQL Server.

5. Choose the authentication mode for connecting to the server specified in step 4, and then click Next. If you choose Use Windows Authentication, the login account and password from the server's connection setting are used to determine the authentication method for connecting to the target server. If you choose Use SQL Server Authentication, you can specify the user name and password for a SQL Server login.

6. As shown in Figure 15-16, select the maintenance tasks you want to perform, and then click Next. The order in which tasks are listed on the Select Maintenance Task Order page determines the order in which the tasks are executed. Select a task and then click the Move Up or Move Down button as appropriate to change the task's order. When the tasks are in the desired run order, click Next.

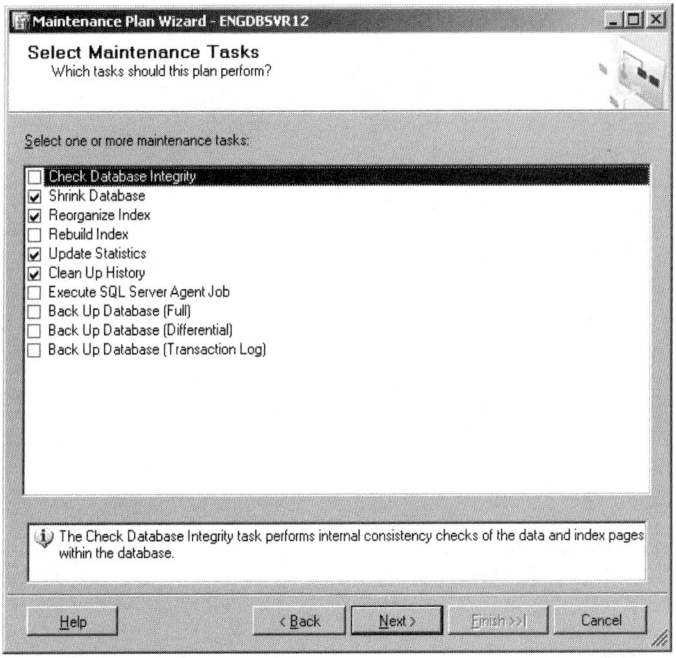

Figure 15-16   The Select Maintenance Tasks page of the Maintenance Plan Wizard

7. Next, for each task that can be applied to one or more databases, you will need to choose the database(s) on which the tasks will be performed. Typically, you

can perform a task on all databases, all system databases, all user databases, or a combination of one or more individual databases. You may also need to configure individual task parameters. When you are finished configuring tasks, click Next. Following are guidelines for each task:

■ **Back Up Database**   Select the databases for which you want to create a full, differential, or transaction log backup. You can back up to disk or tape, and either append or overwrite existing backup files. Typically, you will want to create a backup file for every selected database. With disk-based backups, you can set a specific backup directory and create subdirectories for each database being backed up. You can also set the file extension for the backups. The default extension is .bak. To verify the integrity of backups upon completion, select Verify Backup Integrity.

■ **Check Database Integrity**   Select the databases on which you want to perform internal consistency checks. By default, both data and index pages are checked. If you only want to check data pages, clear Include Indexes.

■ **Execute SQL Server Agent Job**   Select SQL Server Agent jobs to run as part of the maintenance plan. Any available jobs on the server are listed, and you can select the related check box to execute the job whenever the maintenance plan runs.

■ **Cleanup History**   Historical data about backup and restore, SQL Server Agent, and maintenance plan operations is stored in the *msdb* database. When the history cleanup task runs, any historical data older than four weeks is deleted on the target server by default. You can modify the type of historical data cleaned up and set the Older Than criteria to different values. For example, you might find that you need to maintain historical data for a full quarter. If so, you would set Remove Historical Data Older Than to 3 Months.

■ **Rebuild Index**   Select the databases on which you want to rebuild indexes. If you select specific databases, you can specify whether all table and view indexes are rebuilt or only a specific table or view index is rebuilt. For example, if you want to rebuild the *NWCustomer* view in the *Orders* database, you would click in the Databases drop-down list, select These Databases, choose the *Orders* database, and then click OK. Next, under Object, select View, and then click in the Selection drop-down list, select These Objects, choose *dbo.NWCustomers*, and click OK. The affected indexes are dropped and re-created with a new fill factor. You can chose Reorganize Pages With The Default Amount Of Free Space to re-create indexes with the original fill factor that was specified when the indexes were created. Or you can choose Change Free Space Per Page Percentage To if you want to specify a new fill factor. The higher the percentage, the more free space is reserved on the index pages and the larger the index grows. The default is 10 percent. Valid values are from 0 to 100.

Note   Fill factors are discussed in Chapter 6, "Configuring SQL Server with SQL Server Management Studio," in the subsection titled "Setting the Index Fill." Reorganizing pages changes table indexes and thus invalidates existing statistics. You cannot reorganize data and update statistics in the same plan, and you may want to create separate maintenance plans for handling each of these important tasks.

- **Reorganize Index**   Select the databases you want to defragment and compact. If you select specific databases, you can specify whether all tables and views are reorganized or only a specific table or view is reorganized. For example, if you want to reorganize the *Customer* table in the *Orders* database, you would click in the Databases drop-down list, select These Databases, choose the *Orders* database, and then click OK. Next, under Object, select Table, and then click in the Selection drop-down list, select These Objects, choose *dbo.Customers*, and click OK.

- **Shrink Database**   Select the databases on which you want to reduce the disk space by removing empty data and log pages. Use Shrink Database When It Grows Beyond to specify the database size that triggers this task. Free space in a database is removed only when the size of the database file exceeds this value. The default value is 50 MB, which means that if there is more than 50 MB of free space, SQL will shrink the database to the size specified. Use Amount Of Free Space To Remain After Shrink to set the amount of unused space that should remain after the database is reduced in size. The value is based on the percentage of the actual data in the database. The default value is 10 percent. Valid values are from 0 through 100. Free space can be returned to the operating system or retained for future use by the database.

- **Update Statistics**   Select the databases on which you want to update query optimizer statistics. If you select specific databases, you can specify whether statistics for all tables and views are updated or only a specific table or view is updated. By default, both column and index statistics are updated. You also can specify to only update column or index statistics.

8. When you are finished configuring tasks, you will see the Select Plan Properties page shown in Figure 15-17. By default, maintenance plans are configured to run manually when you run them (on demand). You can schedule the maintenance plan to run automatically by defining a run schedule. Click Change, and then set a schedule for the maintenance operations you have selected. Click OK to set the schedule, and then click Next.

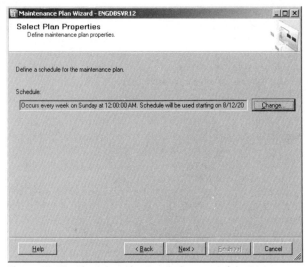

Figure 15-17   The Select Plan Properties page of the Maintenance Plan Wizard

9. Use the Select Report Options page, shown in Figure 15-18, to determine how maintenance plan reports are handled. By default, whenever a maintenance plan runs, a report is generated. The report can be written to a file in any designated folder location, can be sent by e-mail to a SQL Server Agent operator, or both. Click Next.

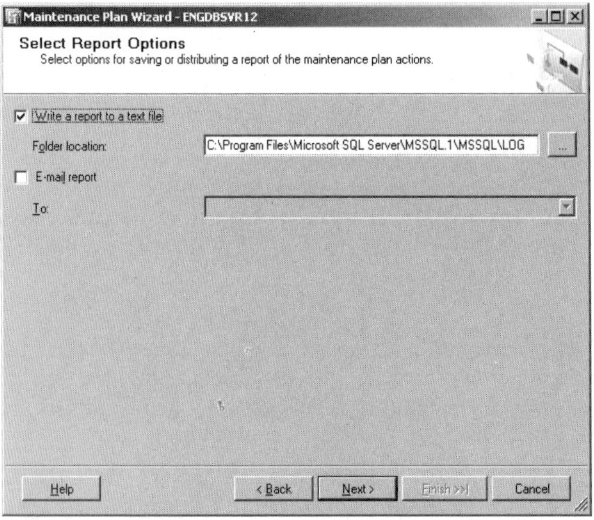

Figure 15-18   The Select Report Options page of the Maintenance Plan Wizard

10. Review the maintenance plan. Click Finish to complete the process and generate the SQL Server Agent job to handle the designated maintenance tasks. These jobs are labeled according to the name of the maintenance plan. Click Close.

Checking Maintenance Reports and History

Creating a maintenance plan is only the beginning. After you create the plan, you will need to check the maintenance reports and history periodically. Maintenance reports are stored as text files in a designated directory, are sent as e-mail to designated SQL Server Agent operators, or both. You can view file-based reports in a standard text editor or word processor. To access the maintenance history through SQL Server Management Studio, complete the following steps:

1. In SQL Server Management Studio, access the Management folder on the server of your choice.
2. Right-click Maintenance Plans, and then select View History. This displays the Log File Viewer as shown in Figure 15-19.

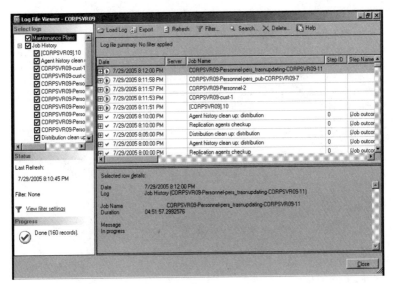

Figure 15-19   The Log File Viewer

3. Under Select Logs in the left pane, Maintenance Plans should be selected by default. There should also be a log entry for each maintenance plan configured on the server.
4. Choose the maintenance plan(s) for which you want to review a job history.
5. Use the summary in the right pane to review the job history. Click Close when you are finished.

Viewing, Editing, Running, and Deleting Maintenance Plans

You can view, edit, run, or delete maintenance plans by completing the following steps:

1. In SQL Server Management Studio, access the Management folder on the server of your choice.

2. Select Maintenance Plans in the left pane. You will see the existing maintenance plans in the right pane.

3. You can now:

   ❑ View or edit a maintenance plan by double-clicking the maintenance plan entry in the right pane. This opens the plan in the Maintenance Plan Package Designer.

   ❑ Delete a maintenance plan by selecting its entry and pressing Delete. In the Delete Object dialog box, click OK to confirm the deletion.

   ❑ Execute the maintenance plan by right-clicking it and selecting Execute.

Checking and Maintaining Database Integrity

You rarely have to perform database integrity checks with SQL Server 2005, and when you do, you can use maintenance plans to handle most of the work. On those rare occasions when you want to perform consistency checks manually, you will use the DBCC command. DBCC stands for *database consistency check*. There are many different DBCC commands, and the ones you will use most often to maintain a database are covered in the following sections.

Using DBCC CHECKDB

The DBCC CHECKDB command checks the consistency of the entire database and is the primary method used to check for database corruption. The command ensures that:

- Index and data pages are linked correctly.
- Indexes are up to date and sorted properly.
- Pointers are consistent.
- The data on each page is up to date.
- Page offsets are up to date.

Sample 15-1 shows the syntax and usage for the DBCC CHECKDB command. When you run the command without a repair option, errors are reported but not corrected. To correct errors, you need to put the database in single-user mode, and then set a repair option. After you repair the database, create a backup.

Sample 15-1 DBCC CHECKDB Syntax and Usage

Syntax

```
DBCC CHECKDB
(   'database_name' | database_id | 0
    [ , NOINDEX
    | { REPAIR_ALLOW_DATA_LOSS
    | REPAIR_FAST
    | REPAIR_REBUILD
    } ] )
    [ WITH        {
                [ ALL_ERRORMSGS ]
                [ , [ NO_INFOMSGS ] ]
                [ , [ TABLOCK ] ]
                [ , [ ESTIMATEONLY ] ]
                [ , [ PHYSICAL_ONLY ] ]
                [ , [ DATA_PURITY ] ] }
    ]
```

Usage

```
DBCC CHECKDB ('customer', NOINDEX)
DBCC CHECKDB ('customer', REPAIR_REBUILD)
```

The REPAIR_FAST option performs minor repairs that do not consume a lot of time and will not result in data loss. The REPAIR_REBUILD option performs comprehensive error checking and correction that requires more time to complete but does not result in data loss (but the database must be in single-user mode). The REPAIR_ALLOW_DATA_LOSS option performs all the actions of REPAIR_REBUILD and adds new tasks that may result in data loss. These tasks include allocating and deallocating rows to correct structural problems and page errors as well as deleting corrupt text objects.

> **Tip** When trying to fix database problems, start with REPAIR_FAST or REPAIR_REBUILD. If these options do not resolve the problem, use REPAIR_ALLOW_DATA_LOSS. Remember that running the REPAIR_ALLOW_DATA_LOSS option may result in unacceptable loss of important data. To ensure that you can recover the database in its original state, place the DBCC command in a transaction so that you can inspect the results and roll back the transaction, if necessary.

Using DBCC CHECKTABLE

To correct problems with individual tables, you can use the DBCC CHECKTABLE command. As shown in Sample 15-2, the syntax and usage for this command are almost the same as for DBCC CHECKDB. The database you want to work with must be selected for use.

Sample 15-2   DBCC CHECKTABLE Syntax and Usage

Syntax

```
DBCC CHECKTABLE
(    'table_name' | 'view_name'
     [ , NOINDEX
     | index_id
     | { REPAIR_ALLOW_DATA_LOSS
     | REPAIR_FAST
     | REPAIR_REBUILD }
     ] )
     [ WITH
         { [ ALL_ERRORMSGS | NO_INFOMSGS ]
           [ , [ TABLOCK ] ]
           [ , [ ESTIMATEONLY ] ]
           [ , [ PHYSICAL_ONLY ] ] }
     ]
```

Usage

```
DBCC CHECKTABLE ('receipts')
DBCC CHECKTABLE ('receipts', REPAIR_REBUILD)
```

Using DBCC CHECKALLOC

To check the consistency of database pages, you can use DBCC CHECKALLOC. Again, the syntax for this command is nearly identical to the previous DBCC commands. One item worth noting is that although Sample 15-3 shows a NOINDEX option, it is maintained only for backward compatibility with previous SQL Server versions. The command always checks the consistency of page indexes.

Sample 15-3   DBCC CHECKALLOC Syntax and Usage

Syntax

```
DBCC CHECKALLOC
(    [ 'database_name' | database_id | 0 ]
          [ , NOINDEX
     |
     { REPAIR_ALLOW_DATA_LOSS
     | REPAIR_FAST
     | REPAIR_REBUILD
     } ] )
     [ WITH { [ ALL_ERRORMSGS ]
              [ , NO_INFOMSGS ]
              [ , TABLOCK ]
              [ , ESTIMATEONLY ] }
     ]
```

Usage

```
DBCC CHECKALLOC ('customer')
DBCC CHECKALLOC ('customer', REPAIR_REBUILD)
```

Using DBCC CHECKCATALOG

Another useful DBCC command is CHECKCATALOG. You use this command to check the consistency of a database's systems tables. Sample 15-4 shows the syntax and usage of this command.

Sample 15-4   DBCC CHECKCATALOG Syntax and Usage

Syntax

```
DBCC CHECKCATALOG
[ ( 'database_name' | database_id | 0 ) ]
    [ WITH NO_INFOMSGS ]
```

Usage

```
DBCC CHECKCATALOG ('customer')
```

Using DBCC DBREINDEX

To rebuild one or more indexes on a database, you can use DBCC DBREINDEX. Sample 15-5 shows the syntax and usage of this command.

Sample 15-5   DBCC DBREINDEX Syntax and Usage

Syntax

```
DBCC DBREINDEX
    ( ['database.owner.table_name'
            [, index_name
            [, fillfactor ]
            ]
    ) [WITH NO_INFOMSGS]
```

Usage

```
DBCC DBREINDEX ('customer.dbo.customers', PK_cust, 75)
DBCC DBREINDEX (customers, '', 85)
```

Managing Log Shipping

Log shipping is used to establish one or more secondary databases that can be brought online manually if a primary database fails. Following is an overview of log shipping and then a discussion of how it is implemented.

Log Shipping: How It Works

Log shipping requires at least two separate SQL Server instances:

- A primary server instance on which you have configured a database to act as the primary for log shipping
- A secondary server instance on which you have configured a database to act as the secondary for log shipping

All administration of the log shipping configuration is performed on the primary server. You can extend log shipping in several ways:

- By configuring multiple secondary databases, you can establish multiple standbys that can be brought online in case the primary database fails. You can think of each secondary as a cold standby.

- By configuring an optional monitoring server, you can track the history and status of log shipping. The monitor server can also be configured to raise alerts if log shipping operations fail to occur as scheduled.

- By configuring secondary servers for query processing, you can reallocate query processing from a primary server to one or more secondary servers.

Log shipping uses a backup folder for logs. Because all log shipping servers must have access to this folder, this folder should be on a network or distributed share and the secondary server proxy accounts (which are by default the SQL Server Agent accounts used on the secondary servers) must have Read and Write permissions on this folder.

SQL Server Agent is the essential ingredient that enables log shipping. A SQL Server Agent job is scheduled to copy the primary server's transaction logs to the backup folder. This job is referred to as the backup job. Other SQL Server Agent jobs also are used to copy the transaction logs from the backup share to the secondary server and to restore the transaction logs on the secondary server. These jobs are referred to as copy and restore jobs. By default, the backup, copy, and restore jobs run every 15 minutes.

When you enable and configure log shipping, the related SQL Server Agent jobs are created automatically. There will always be only one of each job on a server, even if you have configured log shipping on multiple databases. You should never edit the job properties directly. Instead, edit the backup settings on the primary database for log shipping.

 Real World When a database is updated frequently, a short interval between backup, copy, and restore operations helps ensure that the secondaries are synchronized with the primary. In some situations, however, you might want to set a longer interval to reduce the workload and resource usage associated with the backup, copy, and restore operations. If the primary is overworked and has few resources available, you might want to set a longer interval for each of the jobs. If the primary database is updated infrequently, you might want to set a longer interval for each of the jobs as well.

When you configure log shipping, tables are created in the *msdb* database on the servers acting as primary, secondary, and monitoring servers. Stored procedures also are created to perform the necessary operations, cleanup, and monitoring. Related alerts are configured automatically to help you monitor log shipping.

Preparing for Log Shipping

Log shipping requires a very specific configuration to work properly. To prepare your servers for log shipping, follow these general steps:

1. Log shipping is set on a per database basis. Access the Database Properties dialog box for the primary database. On the Options page, ensure that the Recovery Model is set to Full or Bulk-Logged. Log shipping databases cannot use the Simple recovery model.

2. Create a shared resource to use as the backup folder for log shipping. Set permissions so that secondary server proxy accounts (which are by default the SQL Server Agent accounts used on the secondary servers) have Read and Write permissions on this folder.

> **Tip** A good resource for creating shared folders and setting shared folder permissions is *Microsoft Windows Server 2003 Administrator's Pocket Consultant, 2nd Edition* (Microsoft Press, 2006). See the sections titled "Creating Shared Folders" and "Managing Share Permissions" in Chapter 14 of this reference.

3. Enable log shipping on the primary database as discussed in "Enabling Log Shipping on the Primary Database" later in this chapter.

4. Specify the log shipping secondary databases as discussed in "Adding Log Shipping Secondaries" later in this chapter.

5. Optionally, add a monitoring server to track job history and alerts. The monitoring server runs an alert job that generates alerts when backup operations have not completed successfully in the predefined intervals.

Upgrading SQL Server 2000 Log Shipping to SQL Server 2005 Log Shipping

Unlike SQL Server 2000 log shipping, which is configured using maintenance plans, SQL Server 2005 log shipping is configured as part of the standard database properties. Because of this, you cannot directly update SQL Server 2000 log shipping to SQL Server 2005 log shipping. You can, however, migrate your SQL Server 2000 log shipping configuration to SQL Server 2005 log shipping.

To upgrade the log shipping configuration easily, complete the following steps:

1. Upgrade all secondary server instances to SQL Server 2005. When you upgrade the secondary server instances, any log shipping databases will remain SQL Server 2000 databases because they will be in an offline state.

2. Upgrade the primary server to SQL Server 2005. The primary database will be unavailable while the upgrade is in progress, and you will not be able to failover to a secondary server.

3. Enable the primary database for log shipping. To ensure that backup logs are applied properly, use the same backup share that you used with your SQL Server 2000 log shipping configuration.

4. Specify the secondary servers. In the Secondary Database Settings dialog box, you must select the option No, The Secondary Database Is Initialized during the configuration. The secondary database is upgraded automatically to a SQL Server 2005 database when you start shipping logs.

SQL Server 2005 does not use any of the log shipping tables used by SQL Server 2000. After the migration, you can remove the following SQL Server 2000 log shipping tables:

- *log_shipping_databases*
- *log_shipping_monitor*
- *log_shipping_plan_databases*
- *log_shipping_plan_history*
- *log_shipping_plans*
- *log_shipping_primaries*
- *log_shipping_secondaries*

You can also delete any log shipping SQL Server Agent jobs created by SQL Server 2000.

Enabling Log Shipping on the Primary Database

You can enable log shipping by completing the following steps:

1. In SQL Server Management Studio, access the primary server in Object Explorer view.
2. Right-click the database you want to be the primary database and select Properties.
3. On the Transaction Log Shipping page, select Enable This As A Primary Database In A Log Shipping Configuration, as shown in Figure 15-20.

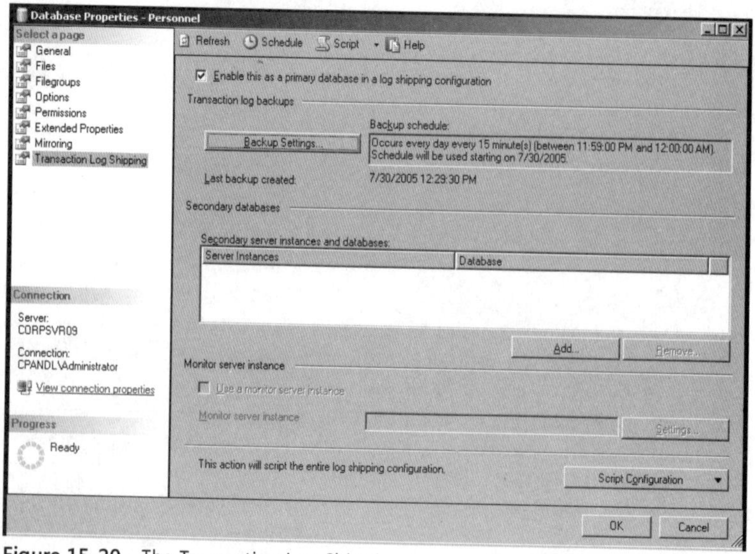

Figure 15-20 The Transaction Log Shipping page on the Database Properties dialog box

4. Click Backup Settings to display the Transaction Log Backup Settings dialog box shown in Figure 15-21.

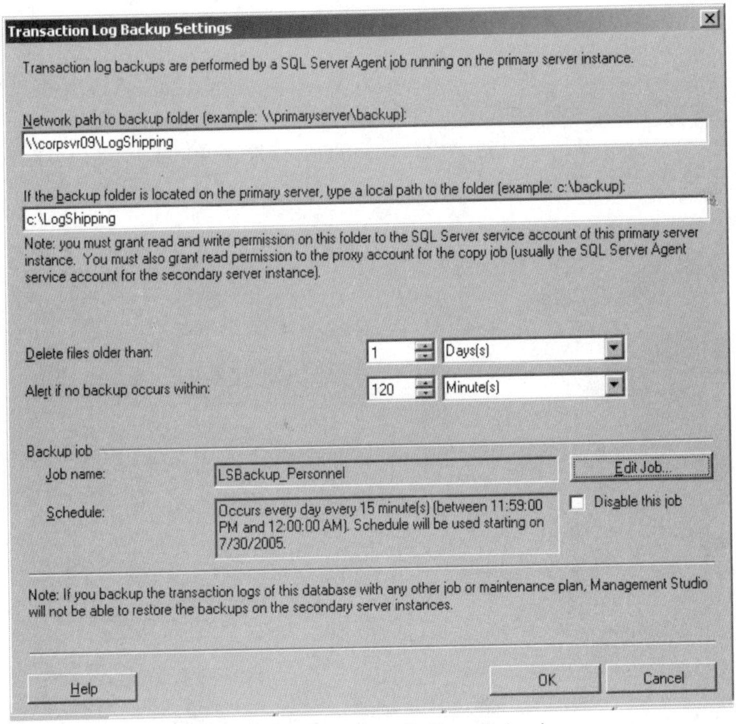

Transaction Log Backup Settings

Transaction log backups are performed by a SQL Server Agent job running on the primary server instance.

Network path to backup folder (example: \\primaryserver\backup):

`\\corpsvr09\LogShipping`

If the backup folder is located on the primary server, type a local path to the folder (example: c:\backup):

`c:\LogShipping`

Note: you must grant read and write permission on this folder to the SQL Server service account of this primary server instance. You must also grant read permission to the proxy account for the copy job (usually the SQL Server Agent service account for the secondary server instance).

Delete files older than: `1` ⏶⏷ `Days(s)` ▼

Alert if no backup occurs within: `120` ⏶⏷ `Minute(s)` ▼

Backup job

Job name: `LSBackup_Personnel`   [Edit Job...]

Schedule: `Occurs every day every 15 minute(s) (between 11:59:00 PM and 12:00:00 AM). Schedule will be used starting on 7/30/2005.`   ☐ Disable this job

Note: If you backup the transaction logs of this database with any other job or maintenance plan, Management Studio will not be able to restore the backups on the secondary server instances.

[Help]   [OK]   [Cancel]

Figure 15-21 The Transaction Log Backup Settings dialog box

5. Type the UNC path for the network share where the transaction logs are created on the primary server, such as **\\ENGSQL\Data\Logs**.

6. If the network share location is an actual folder on the local server, you can set the local path for the primary server to use. Otherwise, leave the related box blank.

7. Use the Delete Files Older Than boxes to configure how long old transaction logs copied to the backup folder will be retained.

8. By default, the backup job runs every 15 minutes. If no backup occurs within a specified time, you can configure log shipping to generate an alert. Set Alert If No Backup Occurs Within to the time to wait before generating an alert for failed copy operations.

9. Click OK to complete the backup configuration. Click OK to close the database properties dialog box.

Adding Log Shipping Secondaries

After you enable log shipping, you can add a log shipping secondary by completing the following steps:

1. In SQL Server Management Studio, access the primary server in Object Explorer.

2. Right-click the database you want to be the primary database and select Properties.

3. On the Transaction Log Shipping page, click Add under Secondary Databases. This displays the Secondary Database Settings dialog box shown in Figure 15-22.

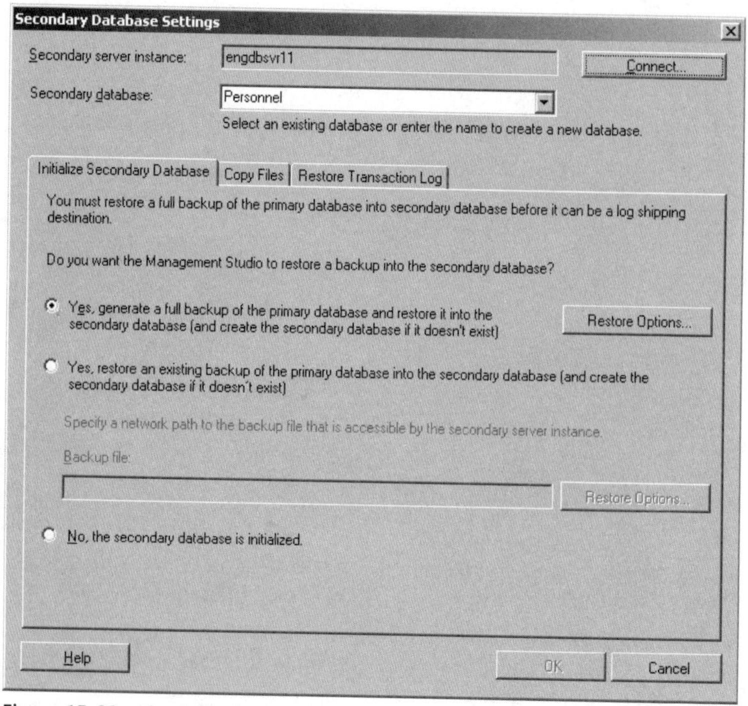

Figure 15-22   The Secondary Database Settings dialog box

4. Click Connect. Use the Connect To Server dialog box to connect to the secondary server.

5. To initialize the secondary, you must restore a full backup of the primary database on the secondary WITH NORECOVERY. This initializes the secondary. If you have already done this, select the option No, The Secondary Database Is Initialized. Otherwise, select one of the following options to initialize the secondary:

- **Yes, Generate A Full Backup...** Creates a full backup of the primary and restores it WITH NORECOVERY on the secondary. Click Restore Options to set the folder paths for data and log files.
- **Yes, Restore An Existing Backup...** Uses the full backup of the primary specified in the Backup File box. Click Restore Options to set the folder paths for data and log files.

Note The Restore operation will fail if a database with the same name as the primary database exists on the secondary server.

6. On the Copy Files tab, specify the local folder to use as the destination folder for transaction log copy operations. A SQL Server Agent job running on the secondary server handles this copy task, and the SQL Server Agent service account must have access to the specified folder.

7. Use the Delete Copied Files After boxes to configure how long transaction log copies are retained. Typically, you will want to retain copies for at least 24 hours.

8. By default, the copy job runs every 15 minutes. Click Schedule to change the run schedule.

9. On the Restore Transaction Log tab, specify the database state when restoring backups as either No Recovery Mode or Standby Mode. With No Recovery Mode, the transaction logs are applied WITH NORECOVERY, and the database is left in a nonoperational state. With Standby Mode, the database is in an operational standby state.

10. By default, backups are restored whenever the restore job runs. If you want to delay restoring backups, you can set a specific delay in minutes, hours, or days. The delay should never be longer than the Delete Copied Files After setting (and be sure to account for the restore job run interval).

11. Set Alert If No Restore Occurs Within to the time to wait before generating an alert for failed restore operations.

12. Click OK to start the secondary configuration. The progress of the configuration is displayed. If an error occurs, click the related link to read the error message and take corrective action as necessary.

13. Click Close when the configuration is complete. Click OK to close the database properties dialog box.

Changing the Transaction Log Backup Interval

By default, transaction log backups are created every 15 minutes. To change the frequency of backup creation, follow these steps:

1. In SQL Server Management Studio, access the primary server in Object Explorer view.

2. Right-click the database you want to be the primary database and select Properties.

3. On the Transaction Log Shipping page, select Backup Settings. This displays the Transaction Log Backup Settings dialog box.

4. Note the Job Name under Backup Job. Click Edit Job to display the Job Properties dialog box.

5. Click the Schedule button to display the Job Schedules Properties dialog box, and then select the schedule item for the current database you are configuring.

6. Set the run frequency for the backup job.

7. Click OK three times to close all open dialog boxes and apply the settings.

Changing the Copy and Restore Intervals

By default, transaction logs copied from backup and restore are performed every 15 minutes. To change the frequency of the copy and restore operations, follow these steps:

1. In SQL Server Management Studio, access the primary server in Object Explorer view.

2. Right-click the database you want to be the primary database and select Properties.

3. On the Transaction Log Shipping page, secondary servers and databases are listed by server instance and database name. Select the secondary you want to modify, and then click the related Properties (...) button. This displays the Secondary Database Settings dialog box.

4. On the Copy Files tab, click Schedule to display the Job Properties dialog box. Set the run frequency for the copy job, and then click OK.

5. On the Restore Transaction Log tab, click Schedule to display the Job Properties dialog box. Set the run frequency for the restore job, and then click OK.

Failing Over to a Secondary Database

In most cases, when you manually fail over from a primary database to a secondary database, the two databases will not be fully synchronized. This can occur because some transaction log backups created on the primary server may not yet have been copied or applied to the secondary server because changes to the databases on the primary server may have occurred since the last transaction log backup, or both. Because of this, before using a secondary database, you should synchronize the primary database with the secondary database and then bring the second server online. To do this, follow these steps:

1. Copy any remaining transaction log backup files from the backup share location to the copy destination folder on the secondary server. You can do this manually or by starting the copy job on each secondary server.

2. Apply any unapplied transaction log backups. You can do this manually or by running the restore job on the secondary server.

3. If possible, back up the active transaction log on the primary server with NO_TRUNCATE. When you are using the SQL Server Backup dialog box, this

means you should select Back Up The Tail Of The Log on the Options page of the Back Up Database dialog box when performing the transaction log backup.

4. If you are able to back up the active transaction log, apply the log backup to the secondary server. This ensures that the secondary server has the most up-to-date version of the data. Regardless, uncommitted transactions from the primary are lost.

5. Make the secondary database available for use by recovering the database on the secondary server. Execute the RESTORE DATABASE statement using the WITH RECOVERY clause, such as:

```
RESTORE DATABASE Customer

WITH RECOVERY

GO
```

After you have failed over to the secondary server, you can configure the secondary database to act as the primary database. Then, you will be able to swap primary and secondary databases as needed. The steps required for the initial role change are different from those required on subsequent role changes.

The first time you want to fail over to the secondary database and make it your new primary database, you must:

1. Manually fail over from the primary database to a secondary database, as discussed previously.

2. Disable the log shipping backup job on the original primary server and the copy and restore jobs on the original secondary server.

3. Configure log shipping on the secondary database, which is now acting as the primary database. You must use the same backup share as the original primary server, add the original primary as a secondary in the log shipping configuration, and choose No, The Secondary Database Is Initialized.

After you have completed the steps for an initial role change, you can perform subsequent role changes by completing these steps:

1. Perform the manual failover steps and bring the secondary database online. When you are backing up the active transaction log on the primary server, you must use WITH NORECOVERY.

2. Disable the log shipping backup job on the original primary server and the copy and restore jobs on the original secondary server.

3. Enable the log shipping backup job on the secondary server, which is now acting as the primary server, and enable the copy and restore jobs on the primary server, which is now acting as the secondary server.

Using Mirroring and Log Shipping

Mirroring and log shipping are two different options that you can use to improve availability. The principal database used in database mirroring can act as the primary database in log shipping as well. You might want to do this is in a situation in which you have a critical database and you want to have multiple standby servers available. For example, you might use:

- Mirroring to establish a single standby that will come online if the primary fails. With a fully synchronous mirroring configuration, automatic failover occurs if the principal database is lost, as long as the mirror server and witness can communicate with each other. Automatic failover causes the mirror server to assume the principal role and bring its database online as the principal database. When the former primary comes back online, it comes online as the mirror.

- Log shipping to establish one or more standbys, which can be manually brought online in case the primary and mirror both fail. Transaction logs are shipped from a primary database to a central backup folder. Secondary servers access the backup folder and restore the transaction logs in their secondary databases to keep the servers synchronized. If the primary database fails, any secondary database can be brought online manually as the new primary database.

If you want to use both mirroring and log shipping, you will usually configure mirroring first, and then log shipping, by following these general steps:

1. Restore backups of the principal database with NORECOVERY onto the server that will act as the mirror.

2. Set up database mirroring by configuring the primary and mirror servers, and as necessary, the witness server (required for synchronous mirroring and automatic failover).

3. Restore backups of the principal database to servers that will act as log shipping secondary (destination) databases.

4. Create a shared resource to use as the backup folder for log shipping.

5. Configure the principal database as the log shipping primary for one or more secondary (destination) databases.

6. Configure the mirror server as a log shipping primary with the same log shipping configuration as the primary server. This allows log shipping to continue after database mirroring fails over.

7. If mirroring fails over, the former mirror server comes on line as the primary server. If the backup folder is not available to both the primary and mirror, log shipping backup jobs will fail when the mirror takes over as the primary. To prevent this, create the backup folder on a shared network resource.

Index